AIA

Professional 1 Level

BUSINESS LAW FOR ACCOUNTANTS

LEARNING & PRACTICE WORKBOOK

In this 2025 edition
- A **user-friendly format** for easy navigation
- **Exam-centred topic coverage**, directly linked to AIA's syllabus
- **Exam focus points** showing you what the examiner will want you to do
- Regular **fast forward** summaries emphasising the key points in each chapter
- **Questions** and **quick quizzes** to test your understanding
- **Practice question bank** containing exam-standard questions with answers
- **Exam question bank** containing recent exam questions with answers
- **Mock exam** for real practice
- **A full index**

FOR EXAMS FROM MAY 2025

Second edition August 2024
ISBN 9781 0355 2575 1
eISBN 9781 0355 2603 1

British Library Cataloguing-in-Publication Data
A catalogue record for this book
is available from the British Library

Published by
BPP Learning Media Ltd
BPP House, Aldine Place
142-144 Uxbridge Road
London W12 8AA

learningmedia.bpp.com

Printed in the United Kingdom

Your learning materials, published by BPP Learning Media Ltd, are printed on paper obtained from traceable sustainable sources.

All rights reserved. No part of this publication may be reproduced, stored in a retrieval system or transmitted in any form or by any means, electronic, mechanical, photocopying, recording or otherwise, without the prior written permission of BPP Learning Media.

Contains public sector information licensed under the Open Government Licence v3.0.

The contents of this book are intended as a guide and not professional advice. Although every effort has been made to ensure that the contents of this book are correct at the time of going to press, BPP Learning Media makes no warranty that the information in this book is accurate or complete and accept no liability for any loss or damage suffered by any person acting or refraining from acting as a result of the material in this book.

We are grateful to the Association of International Accountants for permission to reproduce past examination questions. The suggested solutions in the exam answer bank have been prepared by BPP Learning Media Ltd.

©
BPP Learning Media Ltd
2024

A note about copyright

Dear Customer

What does the little © mean and why does it matter?

Your market-leading BPP books, course materials and e-learning materials do not write and update themselves. People write them: on their own behalf or as employees of an organisation that invests in this activity. Copyright law protects their livelihoods. It does so by creating rights over the use of the content.

Breach of copyright is a form of theft – as well as being a criminal offence in some jurisdictions, it is potentially a serious breach of professional ethics.

With current technology, things might seem a bit hazy but, basically, without the express permission of BPP Learning Media:

- Photocopying our materials is a breach of copyright
- Scanning, ripcasting or conversion of our digital materials into different file formats, uploading them to facebook or emailing them to your friends is a breach of copyright

You can, of course, sell your books, in the form in which you have bought them – once you have finished with them. (Is this fair to your fellow students? We update for a reason.) But the e-products are sold on a single user license basis: we do not supply 'unlock' codes to people who have bought them second hand.

And what about outside the UK? BPP Learning Media strives to make our materials available at prices students can afford by local printing arrangements, pricing policies and partnerships which are clearly listed on our website. A tiny minority ignore this and indulge in criminal activity by illegally photocopying our material or supporting organisations that do. If they act illegally and unethically in one area, can you really trust them?

NO AI TRAINING. Unless otherwise agreed in writing, the use of BPP material for the purpose of AI training is not permitted. Any use of this material to "train" generative artificial intelligence (AI) technologies is prohibited, as is providing archived or cached data sets containing such material to another person or entity.

Contents

Page

Introduction

> The introductory pages contain lots of valuable advice and information. They include tips on studying for and passing the exam, also the content of the syllabus and what has been examined.

How the BPP Learning Media Learning & Practice Workbook can help you pass – Help yourself study for your AIA exams – Syllabus – Command words and learning outcomes – The exam paper

1 An introduction to the English legal system 1

Part A Principles of contract law
2 Formation and the content of contracts 13
3 Discharge of contract 57
4 Vitiating factors in contract 79

Part B Tort law in the business and professional context
5 The law of torts 103

Part C The agency relationship
6 The agency relationship 143

Part D The partnership relationship
7 The partnership relationship 157

Part E The employment relationship and social security law: the relationship with the state
8 The employment relationship 173
9 Ending the employment relationship 193

Part F Choice of business medium
10 Companies, sole traders and partnerships 219

Part G The formation of the company and its consequences
11 Company formation 237

Part H Capitalisation of the company
12 Share capital 259
13 Borrowing and loan capital 279
14 Capital maintenance and dividends 295

Part I The administration and control of the company
15 Meetings and resolutions 317
16 Company directors and other company officers 335
17 Majority control and minority protection 367
18 Accounts and audit 379
19 Criminal law 393

	Page

Part J Company rescue and action short of winding up
20 Company rescue and other actions ... 415

Part K Winding up of the company
21 Company winding up ... 431

Answers to end of chapter questions ... 453
Practice question bank ... 475
Practice answer bank ... 485
New Section - Exam question bank ... 511
New Section - Exam answer bank ... 525
Mock exam ... 559
Bibliography ... 571
Index ... 575

How the BPP Learning Media Learning & Practice Workbook can help you pass

> It provides you with the knowledge and understanding, skills and application techniques that you need to be successful in your exams

This Learning & Practice Workbook has been targeted at the **Business Law for Accountants** syllabus.

- It is **comprehensive**. It covers the syllabus content. No more, no less.
- It is written at the **right level**. Each Chapter is written with AIA's syllabus in mind.
- It is aimed at the **exam**. We have taken account of recent exams, guidance the examiner has given and the assessment methodology.

> It allows you to study in the way that best suits your learning style and the time you have available, by following your personal Study Plan (see page vii)

You may be studying at home on your own or you may be attending a course. You may like to read every word, or you may prefer to do a fast read through and learn through doing practice questions the rest of the time. However, you study, you will find the BPP Learning Media Learning & Practice Workbook meets your needs in designing and following your personal Study Plan.

Help yourself study for your AIA exams

Exams for professional bodies such as AIA are very different from those you have taken at college or university. You will be under **greater time pressure before** the exam – as you may be combining your study with work. Here are some hints and tips.

The right approach

1 **Develop the right attitude**

Believe in yourself	Yes, there is a lot to learn. But thousands have succeeded before and you can too.
Remember why you're doing it	You are studying for a good reason: to advance your career.

2 **Focus on the exam**

Read through the Syllabus	This tells you what you are expected to know and is supplemented by **Exam focus points** in the text.
Study the Exam paper section	Past papers are likely to be good guides to what you should expect in the exam.

3 **The right method**

See the whole picture	Keeping in mind how all the detail you need to know fits into the whole picture will help you understand it better. <ul><li>The **Introduction** of each Chapter puts the material in context.</li><li>The **Syllabus content** and **Exam focus points** show you what you need to **grasp**.</li></ul>
Use your own words	To absorb the information (and to practise your written communication skills), you need to **put it into your own words**. <ul><li>Take **notes**.</li><li>Answer the **questions** in each Chapter.</li><li>Draw **mind maps**.</li><li>Try **'teaching'** **a subject** to a colleague or friend.</li></ul>
Give yourself cues to jog your memory	The Learning & Practice Workbook uses **bold** to **highlight key points**. <ul><li>Try **colour coding** with a highlighter pen.</li><li>Write **key points** on cards.</li></ul>

4 **The right recap**

Review, review, review	Regularly reviewing a topic in summary form can **fix it in your memory**. The Learning & Practice Workbook helps you review in many ways. <ul><li>**Chapter roundups** summarise the 'Fast forward' key points in each Chapter. Use them to recap each study session.</li><li>The **Quick quiz** actively tests your grasp of the essentials.</li><li>Go through the **Examples** in each Chapter a second or third time.</li></ul>

Developing your personal Study Plan

BPP recommends that you follow a study plan. Planning and sticking to the plan are key elements of learning successfully.

Step 1   **How do you learn?**

What types of intelligence do you display when learning? You might be advised to brush up on certain study skills before launching into this Learning & Practice Workbook but refer to the 'tackling your studies' section below which will help.

Step 2   **What do you prefer to do first?**

If you prefer to get to grips with a theory before seeing how it is applied, we suggest you concentrate first on the explanations we give in each Chapter before looking at the examples and case studies. If you prefer to see first how things work in practice, read through the detail in each Chapter, and concentrate on the examples and case studies, before supplementing your understanding by reading the detail.

Step 3   **How much time do you have?**

Work out the time you have available per week, given the following:

- The standard you have set yourself
- The other exam(s) you are sitting
- Practical matters such as work, travel, exercise, sleep and social life

		Hours
Note your time available in box A.	A	

Step 4   **Allocate your time**

- Take the time you have available per week for this Learning & Practice Workbook shown in box A, multiply it by the number of weeks available and insert the result in box B.   B ☐

- Divide the figure in box B by the number of Chapters in this text and insert the result in box C.   C ☐

Remember that this is only a rough guide. Some of the Chapters in this book are longer and more complicated than others, and you will find some subjects easier to understand than others.

Step 5   **Implement**

Set about studying each Chapter in the time shown in box C, following the key study steps in the order suggested by your particular learning style.

This is your personal **Study Plan**. You should try to combine it with the study sequence outlined below. You may want to modify the sequence to adapt it to your **personal style**.

INTRODUCTION

Tackling your studies

The best way to approach this Learning & Practice Workbook is to tackle the chapters in order. Taking into account your individual learning style, you could follow this sequence for each chapter.

Key study steps	Activity
Step 1 **Topic list**	This topic list helps you navigate each chapter; each numbered topic is a numbered section in the chapter.
Step 2 **Introduction**	This sets your objectives for study by giving you the big picture in terms of the context of the chapter. The content is referenced to the syllabus, and Exam guidance shows how the topic is likely to be examined. The Introduction tells you **why** the topics covered in the chapter need to be studied.
Step 3 **Fast forward**	Fast forward boxes give you a quick summary of the content of each of the main chapter sections. They are listed together in the roundup at the end of each chapter to help you review each chapter quickly.
Step 4 **Explanations**	Proceed methodically through each chapter, particularly focusing on areas highlighted as significant in the chapter introduction, or areas that are frequently examined.
Step 5 **Key terms and Exam focus points**	• Key terms are definitions of important concepts that you really need to know and understand before the exam. • Exam focus points highlight areas or topics that may be examined.
Step 6 **Note taking**	Take brief notes, if you wish. Don't copy out too much. Remember that being able to record something yourself is a sign of being able to understand it. Your notes can be in whatever format you find most helpful; lists, diagrams, mind maps.
Step 7 **Examples**	Work through the examples very carefully as they illustrate key knowledge and techniques.
Step 8 **Case studies**	Study each one and try to add flesh to them from your own experience. They are designed to show how the topics you are studying come alive in the real world.
Step 9 **Questions**	Attempt each one, as they will illustrate how well you've understood what you've read.
Step 10 **Answers**	Check yours against ours, and make sure you understand any discrepancies.
Step 11 **Chapter roundup**	Review it carefully, to make sure you have grasped the significance of all the important points in the chapter.
Step 12 **Quick quiz**	Use the Quick quiz to check how much you have remembered of the topics covered and to practise questions in a variety of formats.
Step 13 **Question practice**	Attempt the quick quiz and end of chapter question suggested at the very end of each chapter. These are designed for you to confirm some of the key concepts set out in each chapter. Some of these questions are designed to cover more than one topic area to develop your ability to apply syllabus learning. You can then attempt the questions related to this chapter which are contained in the question bank at the end of this Learning & Practice Workbook.

AIA Achieve

AIA provides an interactive course of study AIA Achieve, which offers students the tools, resources and learning environment to study for the exams. The study tools include a course of study e-book, marked practice questions, marked mock exam paper and feedback and technical advice via an e-Tutor. Contact the Study Support team at: Achieve@aiaworldwide.com

Moving on...

When you are ready to start revising, you should still refer back to this Learning & Practice Workbook.

- As a source of **reference** (you should find the index particularly helpful for this)
- As a way to review (the Fast forwards, Exam focus points, Chapter roundups and Quick quizzes help you here)

PQ Qualification Syllabus

The assessment requirements in the AIA exams at the Foundation, Professional 1 and 2 stages reflect a progression of cognitive levels which successful students are expected to demonstrate in satisfying each stage of the qualification. The levels progress from an emphasis on 'knowledge and comprehension' at the Foundation stage, to a predominance of 'application and analysis' at the subsequent Professional 1 and 2 stages and incorporate 'synthesis and evaluation' at the Professional 2 stage.

Indicative weightings for the cognitive levels at each stage of the qualification are defined in the following table.

Stage of qualification	Cognitive levels of learning*			Associated learning outcomes
	Knowledge and comprehension	Application and Analysis	Synthesis and evaluation	
Foundation Level	90%	10%	0%	Outcomes consistent with the International Education Standards Board (IAESB) standards
Professional 1 Level	50%	50%	0%	
Professional 2 Level	10%	70%	20%	

*The cognitive levels of learning are associated with the following:

'Knowledge and comprehension' refer to

The acquisition of concepts, ideas, terms, facts, practices and techniques in accounting and related disciplines and understanding of how they relate to the conduct, management, reporting and assessment of the activities of business and other organisations.

'Application and analysis' refer to

The ability to apply knowledge and comprehension to actual circumstances and situations and to identify constituent components involved (concepts, ideas, terms, facts, practices, and techniques) and the relationship between these elements.

'Synthesis and evaluation' refer to

The ability to bring together a variety of components in order to form a coherent whole, and to form judgements about the application of and value of those components in a particular context or for a particular purpose.

Professional 1 Level Syllabus

Business Law for Accountants

An accountant must possess, and be able to demonstrate, both knowledge of the fundamental legal principles and rules encountered in professional practice, and an ability to apply those principles and rules to the real-world scenarios experienced in professional life.

The paper tests whether students possess, and are able to demonstrate, this knowledge, as well as the ability to apply it as described. The paper covers relevant aspects of law of contract and tort, legal relationships, including agency, partnership and employment relationships, company law and insolvency.

The coverage of the paper is consistent with the learning outcomes included in IES 2 Intermediate Standard for Business Law and Regulations.

In designing the syllabus and the related examination papers AIA has employed 'intended learning outcomes' as the means to communicate expectations to potential students and stakeholders and to inform the specification requirements to be tested in the assessment of students.

The use of learning outcomes:

- Is consistent with what is commonly acknowledged as good practice in the higher education sector; and
- Is consistent with the approach embodied in International Accounting Education Standards

At the Professional 1 Levels students are expected to demonstrate that they are able to achieve the following:

Intended Learning Outcomes[1] – Description of expectations	
Professional 1 level	At the Professional 1 level students are expected to demonstrate that they: • Understand basic principles and concepts underpinning accounting and related practices in organisations and can discuss the conceptual rationale that provides the basis for those practices. • Understand the role of accounting and related practices within the financial and governance context of organisations. • Are able to apply relevant regulations and standards in accounting, auditing, law and taxation. • Know and can execute basic recording and measurement techniques relevant to accounting, management and assurance • Are able to analyse financial information and interpret it for the purpose of supporting decision making

---

[1] The description of the levels of proficiency supports the IAESBs use of learning outcomes in its International Education Standards (IESs) 2, 3, and 4.

Relationship to Qualification Structure

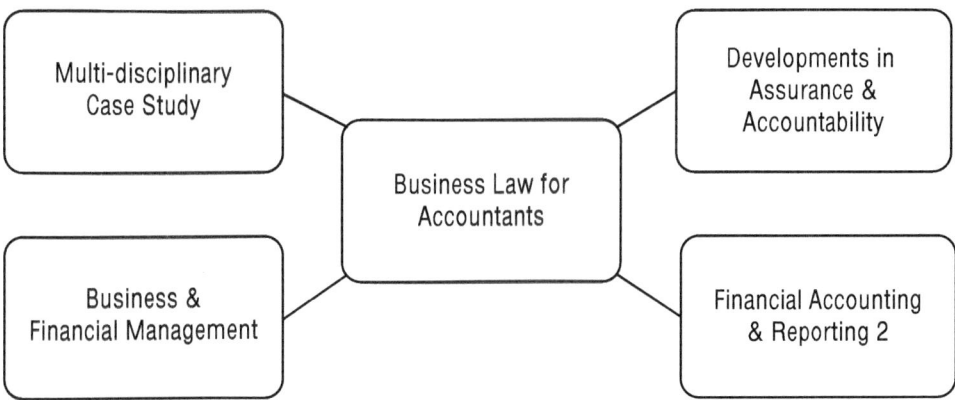

Aims

The aim of this paper is to develop and examine the candidate's:

- Knowledge and understanding of the legal principles and rules, relevant to situations which an accountant is most likely to be concerned with in professional practice
- Ability to apply those legal principles and rules to practical situations exemplifying professional practice

Business Law for Accountants Learning Outcomes

In order to successfully complete this paper, candidates will demonstrate that they are able to:

1. Explain and discuss the law regulating contracts, actions in tort, and the key relationships which impact on those engaged in business and demonstrate the ability to apply that knowledge to practical scenarios
2. Explain and discuss the law regulating companies, including relevant insolvency procedures, and demonstrate the ability to apply that knowledge to practical scenarios

Structure of the Paper

Assessment is by a three-hour 15 minute examination (including 15 minutes reading time) consisting of five compulsory questions. Candidates must answer all questions.

The allocation of marks to parts of a question will be disclosed in the examination paper.

Candidates are expected to support answers with references to statute and case law where appropriate.

Relationship to Qualification Structure

Legal considerations affect many of an accountant's activities, including their own professional relationships. Some, foundational, areas of legal knowledge, will already have been acquired by candidates, in the Foundation Level Unit.

This paper builds upon that Unit, encompassing the principal areas of law of greatest relevance to the accountant. Some of these areas of law will also be addressed, and in greater detail, in other papers.

Candidates sitting in non-UK jurisdictions can select a different version of the Business Law for Accountants paper.

Ethics

'Ethics', as such, is not currently included within the law paper.

Recommended reading

This reading list is recommended and not essential for your studies.

You can purchase any of the books listed quickly and easily on the AIA website
www.aiaworldwide.com/books

AIA Magazine - International Accountant
ISSN: 1465 - 5144

AIA Learning & Practice Workbook
Business Law for Accountants
Publisher: BPP
ISBN: 9781 5097 3210 4

The e-Book is available at: membership@aiaworldwide.com.
Contact AIA for information on purchasing a hard copy of the text book at: membership@aiaworldwide.com.

Business Law (9th Edition)
Authors: MacIntyre, E
Publisher: Pearson Education Limited
ISBN: 9781292219950

Law for Business Students premium pack (12th Edition)
Author: Adams, A
Publisher: Pearson Education Limited
ISBN: 9781292440484

Introduction to Business Law (5th Edition)
Author: Jones, L.
Publisher: Oxford University Press
ISBN: 9780198824886

Company Law (12th Edition)
Author: Dignam, A, Lowry, L
Publisher: Oxford University Press
ISBN: 9780192865359

Command words

The following list contains active command words appropriate for use at the Professional 1 Level of the AIA qualification. Reference to the command words is essential to understanding how the assessment is applied in AIA exams.

Cognitive Levels of Learning	Command Words	Definitions
Professional 1 Application and Analysis 50% Knowledge and Comprehension 50%	Advise	To inform or notify
	Analyse	Examine in detail in order to interpret its meaning or essential features
	Apply	To use information or a technique in a particular situation
	Calculate Compute	Select the appropriate method and techniques and apply your knowledge and understandings to work out and show how figures were arrived at
	Demonstrate	To show or prove by reasoning or evidence
	Determine	Find out or establish
	Perform	Carry out into effect
	Prepare	To make or get ready for use
	Record	Document the information
	Estimate	Make an approximate judgement/calculation
	Journalise	Produce a double entry of events

Please note:

1   The word 'Calculate' may be used at all levels of the syllabus

2   The word 'Advise' may be used at all levels of the syllabus

An introduction to the English legal system

Topic list	Syllabus reference
1 Types of law in the English legal system	N/A
2 The system of courts in the English legal system	N/A
3 English law and sustainability	N/A

Introduction

Welcome to your study of **Law**. In this introductory chapter we set the scene by introducing the framework of the English legal system.

We start by considering the **different types of law** and their **sources**, before looking at the system of **criminal and civil courts**. We will also briefly consider how English law is increasingly promoting **sustainability principles**.

Whilst you will not be examined directly on the material in this chapter, your studies in the following chapters require you to have a good understanding of the English legal system, so it is important to study this material carefully.

1 Types of law in the English legal system

FAST FORWARD

The **English legal system** distinguishes several different types of law.

- Common law and equity
- Statute law
- Public and private law
- Criminal law and civil law
- Soft law

1.1 Common law and equity

Common law is the oldest element of the English legal system. It is the system of rules that were initially laid down by **royal courts** following the Norman conquest. Application of these laws was by **judges** who effectively made new laws by **amalgamating** local customary laws into one 'law of the land'. In modern times, the common law refers to laws created as cases are decided by judges. **Remedies** under common law are **monetary**, and are known as **damages**.

However, there are times when money is not a **suitable remedy**. For example, you have agreed to buy a unique painting from an art dealer. Should the dealer at the last minute sell the painting to someone else, damages are unlikely to be acceptable, after all you wanted **that** painting.

Equity was developed two or three hundred years after common law, as a system to resolve disputes where damages are not a suitable remedy and to introduce **fairness** into the legal system. Equity offers a number of remedies that are not related to damages.

1.1.1 Doctrine of judicial precedent

The common law is based on the system of judicial precedent. A **precedent** is a previous court decision which another court is bound to follow by deciding a subsequent case in the same way.

The doctrine of **judicial precedent** means that a judge is bound to apply a decision from an earlier case to the facts of the case before them, provided, among other conditions, that there is no material difference between the cases and the previous case created a 'binding' precedent.

A judgement will start with a description of the facts of the case and probably a review of earlier precedents. The judge will then make **statements of law applicable to the legal problems** raised by the material facts. If these **statements are used as the basis for the decision**, they are **known as the ratio decidendi** of the case. This is the **vital element that binds future judges**.

Obiter dicta are other statements made by the judge which are not used as the basis for the decision.

1.2 Statute law (legislation)

Whilst the judiciary is responsible for the creation of common law, **Parliament** is responsible for **statute law** (or legislation). Statute law is usually made in areas so **complicated** or **unique** that suitable common law alternatives are unlikely, or would take an unacceptable length of time, to develop – company law is one example of this.

Legislation is used by Parliament to make new laws and altering existing ones. Parliament may also make existing laws clearer by passing a **codifying** statute putting case law on a statutory basis. It may also pass **consolidating** statutes that incorporate an original statute and its successive amendments into a single piece of legislation.

To save time in Parliament, statutes usually contain a section by which power is given to a minister, or public body such as a local authority, to make **subordinate** or **delegated legislation**.

Examples of delegated legislation include statutory instruments, that enable government ministers to exercise their powers and local authority bye laws.

1.3 Private law and public law

Most of the law that you will be studying is **private law**. That is law which deals with **relationships** and **interactions** between businesses, and **private individuals**, **groups** or **organisations**. Here, the **state** provides a **framework** for dealing with **disputes** and for **enforcing decisions**, but it is for individuals to handle matters between themselves.

Public law is mainly concerned with **government** and the **operation** and **functions** of **public organisations** such as councils and local authorities. It will not be of great interest to you in your studies of corporate law, however examples of public law can be found in **planning rules** that must be adhered to when building or expanding offices.

1.4 Criminal and civil law

The **distinction** between criminal and civil liability is central to the English legal system and to the way the court system is structured.

1.4.1 Criminal law

FAST FORWARD

In criminal cases, the **state** prosecutes the wrongdoer.

Key term

A **crime** is conduct prohibited by the law.

In criminal proceedings the State is the prosecutor because it is the community as a whole which suffers as a result of the law being broken and an **offence** taking place. There are two parties: the State bringing the claim (the **prosecution**) and the person accused of the crime (the **accused**). Persons **guilty** (or **convicted**) of crime may be **punished** by **fines** payable to the State, **imprisonment**, or a **community-based punishment**.

In a criminal trial, the **burden of proof** to convict the **accused** rests with the **prosecution**, which must prove its case **beyond reasonable doubt**.

The names of criminal cases are reported as *R v Jones* or *Rex v Jones*. This indicates that the State takes action on behalf of the Crown (*Rex* is Latin for King).

A person who has been **convicted** of a criminal offence is usually entitled to **appeal** against the decision and the punishment, in the hope of getting the conviction and punishment **overturned**. Even if the conviction stands, it may also be possible to get the punishment **reduced.**

1.4.2 Civil law

FAST FORWARD

Civil law exists to regulate disputes over the rights and obligations of persons dealing with each other and seeks to compensate injured parties.

Civil law is a form of **private law**. There are two parties: the person bringing the claim (the **claimant**) and the person defending the claim (the **defendant**). In civil proceedings, the case must be proved on the **balance of probability**. The **claimant** must convince the court that it is more probable than not that their assertions are true.

There is no concept of **punishment**, and **compensation** is paid to the wronged person. Both parties may choose to **settle** the dispute **out of court** should they wish.

Terminology in civil cases is different to that of criminal cases. Since a **claimant** sues a **defendant** a civil case is therefore referred to as, for example, *Smith v Metacarpi plc.*

A party to civil proceedings is usually entitled to **appeal** against the decision, in the hope of getting the decision and any other order of the court **overturned**. Even if the decision stands, it may also be possible to get the court order for compensation for instance **reduced.**

1.4.3 Distinction between criminal and civil cases

It is not an act or event which creates the distinction, but the **legal consequences**. A single event might give rise to criminal and civil proceedings.

Illustration

A broken leg caused to a pedestrian by a drunken driver is a single event which may give rise to:

- **Criminal case** (prosecution by the State for the offence of driving with excess alcohol), and
- **Civil case** (the pedestrian sues the driver for compensation for pain and suffering).

1.5 Soft law

Soft law is a term used to describe rules and regulations that organisations are expected to follow, but which are **not enforceable through the courts**. Examples of soft law include voluntary codes of conduct, as well as recommendations, principles and guidelines that are created by some international bodies such as the UN and EU.

2 The system of courts in the English legal system

FAST FORWARD

The **courts** have to be organised to facilitate the working of the legal system.

There are four main functional aspects of the court system which underlie its structure:

(a) **Civil and criminal law** differ so much in substance and procedure that they are best administered in separate courts.

(b) **Local courts** allow the vast bulk of small legal proceedings to be decentralised. But important civil cases begin in the High Court in London.

(c) Although the courts form a single system and many courts have a general civil jurisdiction, there is some **specialisation** both within the High Court and in other courts with separate functions.

(d) There is a system of review by **appeals** to higher courts.

Key terms

A **court of first instance** is the court where the case is originally heard in full. The **appeal court** is the court to which an appeal is made against the ruling or the sentence.

If the appeal court finds in favour of the appellant then the original decision is **reversed**, ie the result is changed, but the law is not. This is different from an **overruling** which happens when a higher court finds a lower court's decision to be wrong in law, and in future the law is changed.

1: AN INTRODUCTION TO THE ENGLISH LEGAL SYSTEM

2.1 The civil court structure

FAST FORWARD

The **civil court structure** comprises the following.

- **Magistrates' Courts** mostly deal with small domestic matters.
- **County Courts** hear claims in contract and tort, equitable matters and land and probate disputes among others.
- The **Crown Court** hears appeals from Magistrates' Courts.
- The **High Court** is divided into three specialist divisions: King's Bench, Family and Chancery.
- The **Court of Appeal** hears appeals against decisions by the County Court, the High Court, the Restrictive Practices Court, and the Employment Appeal Tribunal.
- The **Supreme Court** hears appeals against decisions by the Court of Appeal and the High Court.

The diagram below sets out the English **civil** court structure. **County Courts** deal with almost every kind of civil case that is **small** or which is deemed to be a simple case. **Complicated** or high value cases start at the **High Court**.

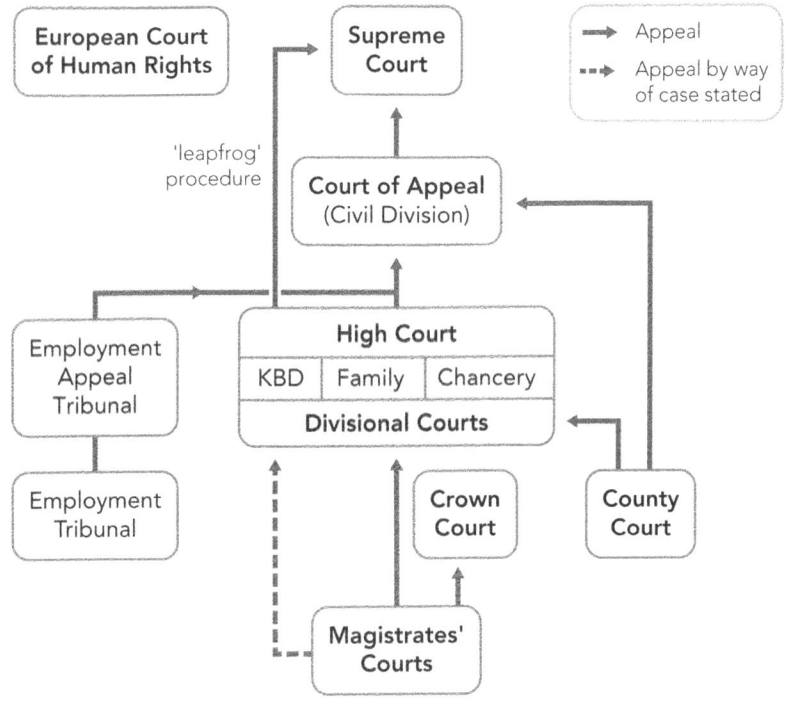

2.2 The criminal court structure

FAST FORWARD

The **criminal court structure** comprises the following.

- **Magistrates' Courts** hear summary offences and committal proceedings for indictable offences.
- The **Crown Court** tries serious criminal (indictable) offences and hears appeals from Magistrates' Courts.
- The **Divisional Court of KBD** hears appeals on points of law from Magistrates' Courts and the Crown Court.
- The **Court of Appeal** hears appeals against decisions by the Crown Court.
- The **Supreme Court** hears appeals from the Court of Appeal or a Divisional Court of KBD.

The diagram below sets out the English **criminal** court structure.

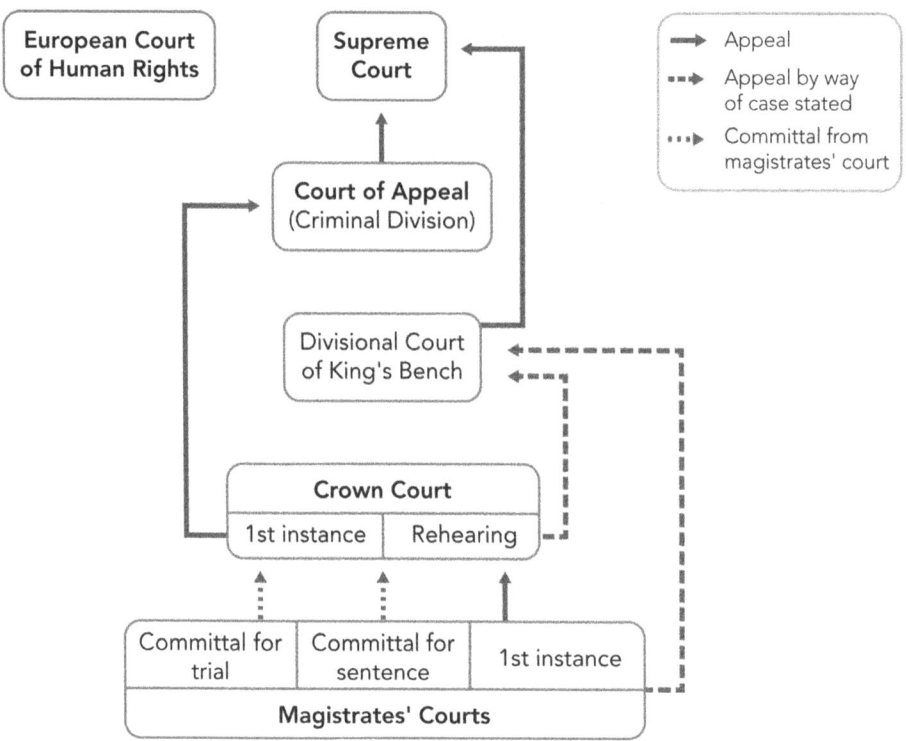

2.3 The final appeal courts

At the pinnacle of the UK's civil and criminal court systems is the **Supreme Court**. The role of the Supreme Court is to act as the **final appeal court**, hearing appeals on points of law that have **public** or **constitutional importance**. Cases are typically heard by panels of **five**, **seven** or **nine Justices** who give their verdicts collectively rather than as individual decisions. This is to **encourage discussion** among those at the top of the legal profession, which should result in **robust, clear decisions** that the rest of the judicial system can rely.

At the time of writing, and in appropriate cases, it is possible to refer a case to either the **European Court of Human Rights** or the **European Court of Justice**, although they are not strictly within the English court structure.

3 English law and sustainability

FAST FORWARD

English law is increasingly promoting **sustainability principles**.

English law is increasingly supporting **Environmental**, **Social** and **Governance** (ESG) principles of sustainability. For example:

(a) **Environmental principle**: The Environment Act 2021 gives the government powers to set targets in relation to environmental factors such as air and water quality.

(b) **Social principle**: The Equality Act 2010 makes it illegal to discriminate against people on the basis of a number of factors such as age, gender and religion.

(c) **Governance principle**: The Data Protection Act 2018 controls how organisations may collect, process and use data collected about individuals.

In **Chapter 16**, we shall also see how the law is impacting on how companies report environmental information about their activities in their strategic reports under The Companies (Strategic Report) (Climate Financial disclosures) Regulations 2022, how the Companies Act 2006 requires directors to consider the impact of their company on the local community and the environment, and other legislation relating to ESG.

Chapter Roundup

- The **English legal system** distinguishes several different types of law.
    - Common law and equity
    - Statute law
    - Public and private law
    - Criminal law and civil law
    - Soft law
- In criminal cases, the **state** prosecutes the wrongdoer.
- **Civil law** exists to regulate disputes over the rights and obligations of persons dealing with each other and seeks to compensate injured parties.
- The courts have to be organised to facilitate the working of the legal system.
- The **civil court structure** comprises the following.
    - **Magistrates' Courts** mostly deal with small domestic matters.
    - **County Courts** hear claims in contract and tort, equitable matters and land and probate disputes among others.
    - The **Crown Court** hears appeals from Magistrates' Courts.
    - The **High Court** is divided into three specialist divisions: King's Bench, Family and Chancery.
    - The **Court of Appeal** hears appeals from the County Court, the High Court, the Restrictive Practices Court, and the Employment Appeal Tribunal.
    - The **Supreme Court** hears appeals from the Court of Appeal and the High Court.
- The **criminal court structure** comprises the following.
    - **Magistrates' Courts** hear summary offences and committal proceedings for indictable offences.
    - The **Crown Court** tries serious criminal (indictable) offences and hears appeals from Magistrates' Courts.
    - The **Divisional Court of KBD** hears appeals on points of law from Magistrates' Courts and the Crown Court.
    - The **Court of Appeal** hears appeals against decisions by the Crown Court.
    - The **Supreme Court** hears appeals from the Court of Appeal or a Divisional Court of KBD.
- English law is increasingly promoting **sustainability principles**.

1: AN INTRODUCTION TO THE ENGLISH LEGAL SYSTEM

Quick Quiz

1 What is the standard of proof in civil proceedings?

2 All the following statements relate to criminal and civil law. Which one of the statements is correct?

   A A criminal case may subsequently give rise to a civil case, but a civil case cannot subsequently give rise to a criminal case.

   B The main purpose of civil law is to compensate the injured party and to punish the injuring party.

   C A custodial sentence can be passed on the defendant in a civil case, providing the defendant is a natural person and not an incorporated body.

   D The main purpose of civil law is to enforce the claimant's rights rather than to punish the defendant.

3 **Fill in the blanks** in the statements below, using the words in the box.

   In order that (1) .... provides (2) .... in the law, a precedent must be carefully examined before it can be applied to a particular (3) .... It must be a statement of (4) .... The (5) .... must be identified. The (6) .... must be the same.

   The (7) .... of the court which set the precedent must be such as to (8) .... the present court.

• bind	• judicial precedent
• case	• status
• ratio decidendi	• law
• material facts	• consistency

4 Which of these decisions bind the Crown Court?

   Decisions of the County Court ☐
   Decisions of the High Court ☐
   Decisions of the Court of Appeal ☐
   Decisions of the Supreme Court ☐

5 In 2017, Mr Justice Jeffries, a High Court judge sitting alone, is deciding a case which has similar material facts to one decided by the Court of Appeal in 1917. He can decline to be bound by this decision by showing that

   A The status of the previous court cannot bind them
   B The decision was taken too long ago to be of any relevance
   C The decision does not accord with the rules of a statute passed in 1975
   D The obiter dicta are obscure

Answers to Quick Quiz

1. The case must be proved on the balance of probability

2. D. Punishment is not an objective of civil law. A civil case may subsequently give rise to a criminal case.

3. (1) judicial precedent (2) consistency (3) case (4) law (5) ratio decidendi (6) material facts (7) status (8) bind

4. Decisions of the High Court, Court of Appeal and Supreme Court.

5. C. A High Court judge is bound by decisions of the Court of Appeal. However, he can decline to be bound because the 1975 statute has effectively overruled the previous decision.

End of chapter question

Introductory question: Legal system and courts

(a) In relation to the English legal system distinguish between the following:
   (i) Criminal law
   (ii) Civil law

(b) Explain the jurisdiction of the courts dealing with criminal and civil law.

Principles of contract law

Formation and the content of contracts

Topic list	Syllabus reference
1 Making an agreement	1.1
2 Essential elements of a contract	1.1
3 Offer	1.1
4 Termination of offer	1.1
5 Acceptance	1.1
6 Communication of acceptance	1.1
7 Consideration	1.1
8 Adequacy and sufficiency of consideration	1.1
9 Intention to create legal relations	1.1
10 Privity of contract	1.1
11 Contract terms	1.1
12 The Unfair Contract Terms Act 1977	1.1
13 The Consumer Rights Act 2015	1.1

Introduction

Having studied the framework of the English legal system in the previous chapter, we now begin our study of **business law** by looking at how businesses and individuals form legally binding agreements, known as **contracts**.

Contracts play an important role in **everyday life**. Individuals and businesses form contracts all the time, such as when a customer buys something from a shop, or when a business agrees to supply another with goods or services.

Contracts set out exactly what was **agreed between the parties** and are therefore important documents to refer to if there is a dispute, such as if the wrong or poor quality goods are supplied.

However, if contracts are to be **legally enforceable** they must be correctly formed. We shall see that a contract must contain several important factors (such as offer, acceptance, intention and consideration) in order to be **valid**.

We shall also look at the various **terms** used to form contracts and how some terms (such as exclusion clauses) are governed by legislation.

1 Making an agreement

The law seeks to protect the idea of 'freedom of contract', although **contractual terms** may be regulated by **statute**, particularly where the parties are of unequal bargaining strength.

A **valid contract is a legally binding agreement**, formed through negotiation and by the mutual consent of two parties who are free to come to any agreement that they wish to. In an ideal world each party will be equal in terms of power and influence, however this is not always the case and therefore it is important to give weaker parties a degree of protection to prevent them being taken advantage of.

Key term

> A **contract** may be defined as an **agreement which legally binds the parties.** The underlying theory is that a contract is the outcome of 'consenting minds'. However, parties are judged by what they have said, written or done, rather then by what they were actually thinking.

Exam focus point

> Almost every sitting will have at least one scenario-based contract law question requiring you to provide legal advice.

1.1 Inequality of bargaining power

When two parties are negotiating an agreement, they invariably have differing levels of **bargaining power**. Many contracts are made between experts and ordinary consumers. The law will intervene only where the former takes unfair advantage of their position and not simply because one party was in an inferior bargaining position. **Freedom of contract** is a term sometimes used and can be defined as follows.

> 'The principle that parties are completely unrestricted in deciding whether or not to enter into an agreement and, if they do so, upon the terms governing that relationship. In practice, this is not always the case because one may be in a much stronger economic position, and legislation has been introduced in order to redress the balance.'

1.2 The standard form contract

Mass production and consumerism have led to the **standard form contract**. The main effect of standard form contracts is that there is almost no room for negotiation. Either the other party accepts the terms or there is no agreement.

Key term

> The **standard form contract** is a document prepared by many large organisations setting out the terms on which they contract with their customers. The individual must usually take it or leave it. For example, a customer has to accept the supply of electricity on the electricity board's terms – they are not likely to succeed in negotiating special terms, unless they represent a large consumer such as a factory.

1.3 Consumer protection

The development of a **mass market** for complex goods in the last century meant that the consumer can no longer rely on their own judgement when buying sophisticated goods or services. **Consumer interests** are now served by two main areas.

(a) **Consumer protection agencies**, which include trading standards departments and independent bodies (the Consumers' Association).

(b) **Legislation**.

Public policy sometimes requires that the freedom of contract should be modified. For example, the **Consumer Credit Act 1974** regulates the extent to which contracts can contain certain terms relating to credit given to consumers.

1.4 The electronic contract

English law has been concerned with formulating the rules for oral and written contracts for centuries, and cases decided in the 1800s continue to be valid today. As you will see, there are a number of **important rules** which deal with the timing of the sending and receipt of letters by post. With the advent of **telex** and **fax machines**, the law had to be applied to new situations. Now the development of the internet for commercial purposes has brought new challenges as new ways of doing business come into being.

2 Essential elements of a contract

> **FAST FORWARD**
>
> The **three essential elements** of a contract are **offer and acceptance, consideration** and **intention to enter into legal relations**.
>
> As a general rule, **a contract may be made in any form**.

For an agreement to become a legally binding contract, it must contain **three essential elements**.

- There must be an **agreement** usually made by **offer and acceptance**.
- There must be a bargain by which the obligations assumed by one party are supported by **consideration** (value) given by the other.
- The parties must have an **intention to create legal relations** between themselves.

2.1 Capacity and other validity factors

Even if these **essential elements** can be shown, a contract may not necessarily be valid or may only be partially valid. The validity of a contract may also be affected by any of the following factors.

(a) **Capacity**. Some persons have restricted capacity to enter into contracts.

Minors (individuals under 18 years of age) cannot enter into contracts for goods other than necessities, nor do they have the capacity to contract for loans or other credit agreements.

Those who lack **mental capacity** or who were **intoxicated** can avoid contracts if they can show they did not understand the nature of their actions and the other party ought to have known about their disability. They still must pay a reasonable price for the goods received.

Certain artificial bodies such as **companies** and **local authorities** can only make contracts in areas they are authorised to do so. Contracts outside of the authorised areas are deemed *ultra vires* and are void (though there are detailed provisions in relation to companies which mean the effect of this is very limited).

(b) **Form**. Some contracts must be made in a particular form.

(c) **Content**. In general the parties may enter into a contract on whatever terms they choose. Some terms which the parties do not express may be **implied**, and some terms which the parties do express are **overridden** by statutory rules.

(d) **Genuine consent**. A mistake or misrepresentation made by one party may affect the validity of a contract. Parties may be induced to enter into a contract by **undue influence** or **duress**.

(e) **Legality**. The courts will not enforce a contract which is deemed to be illegal or contrary to public policy.

A contract which does not satisfy the relevant tests may be either **void, voidable** or **unenforceable**.

> **Key terms**
>
> A **void contract** is not a contract at all. The parties are not bound by it and if they transfer property under it they can sometimes recover their goods even from a third party.
>
> A **voidable contract** is a contract which one party may set aside. Property transferred before avoidance is usually irrecoverable from a third party.
>
> An **unenforceable contract** is a valid contract and property transferred under it cannot be recovered even from the other party to the contract. But if either party refuses to perform or to complete their part of the performance of the contract, the other party cannot compel them to do so. A contract is usually unenforceable when the required evidence of its terms, for example, written evidence of a contract relating to land, is not available.

2.2 Form of a contract

Contracts do not usually have to be in writing except in the following circumstances.

- Some contracts must be by **deed**.
- Some contracts must be in **writing**.
- Some contracts must be **evidenced in writing**.

2.3 Contracts by deed

A deed is a special type of legal document often used when transferring property such as a house. For a contract by formed by a deed must be in **writing** and it must be **signed**. Delivery must take place. Delivery is conduct indicating that the person executing the deed intends to be bound by it.

These contracts **must** be by deed.

- **Leases** for three years or more
- A **conveyance** or transfer of a legal estate in land (including a mortgage)
- A promise **not** supported by **consideration** (such as a **covenant** for example a promise to pay a regular sum to a charity)

> **Key terms**
>
> A **contract by deed** is sometimes referred to as a specialty contract. Any other type of contract may be referred to as a **simple contract**.

2.4 Contracts which must be in writing

The following contracts must be in **writing and signed** by at least one of the parties.

- A **transfer of shares** in a limited company
- The sale or disposition of an **interest in land**
- **Bills of exchange** and **cheques**
- **Consumer credit** contracts

In the case of **consumer credit transactions**, the effect of failure to make the agreement in the prescribed form is to make the agreement unenforceable against the debtor unless the creditor obtains a court order.

2.5 Contracts which must be evidenced in writing

Certain contracts may be made orally, but are not enforceable in a court of law unless there is written **evidence** of their terms. The most important contract of this type is the **contract of guarantee**.

3 Offer

FAST FORWARD The first essential element in the formation of a binding contract is **agreement**. This is usually evidenced by **offer and acceptance**. An offer is a definite promise to be bound on specific terms, and must be distinguished from the mere **supply of information** and from an **invitation to treat**.

Key term

An **offer** is a **definite promise to be bound on specific terms** and may be defined as follows.

'An express or implied statement of the terms on which the maker is prepared to be contractually bound if it is accepted unconditionally. The offer may be made to one person, to a class of persons or to the world at large, and only the person or one of the persons to whom it is made may accept it.'

A **definite offer does not have to be made to a particular person**. It may be made to a class of persons or to the world at large. However, it must be distinguished from a statement which constitutes a supply of information, from a statement of intention and from an invitation to treat.

Carlill v Carbolic Smoke Ball Co 1893

The facts: The manufacturers of a patent medicine published an advertisement by which they undertook to pay '£100 reward... to any person who contracts... influenza... after having used the smoke ball three times daily for two weeks'. The advertisement added that £1,000 had been deposited at a bank 'showing our sincerity in this matter'. The claimant read the advertisement, purchased the smoke ball and used it as directed. She contracted influenza and claimed her £100 reward. In their defence the manufacturers argued against this.

(a) The offer was so vague that it could not form the basis of a contract, as no time limit was specified.

(b) It was not an offer which could be accepted since it was offered to the whole world.

Decision: The court disagreed.

(a) The smoke ball must protect the user during the period of use – the offer was not vague.
(b) Such an offer was possible, as it could be compared to reward cases.

You should note that **Carlill is an unusual case** in that advertisements are not usually regarded as offers. **A statement which is vague** cannot be an offer, but an apparently vague offer can be made certain by reference to previous dealing or customs.

Gunthing v Lynn 1831

The facts: The offeror offered to pay a further sum for a horse if it was 'lucky'.

Decision: The offer was too vague and no contract could be formed.

Hillas & Co Ltd v Arcos Ltd 1932

The facts: The claimants agreed to purchase from the defendants '22,000 standards of softwood goods of fair specification over the season 1930'. The agreement contained an option to buy a further 100,000 standards in 1931, without terms as to the kind or size of timber being specified. The 1930 transaction took place, but the sellers refused to supply any wood in 1931, saying that the agreement was too vague.

Decision: The missing terms of the agreement could be ascertained by reference to the previous transactions.

3.1 Supply of information

Only an offer in the proper sense may be accepted so as to form a binding contract. A statement which sets out **possible terms** of a contract is not an offer unless this is clearly indicated.

> *Harvey v Facey 1893*
>
> *The facts:* The claimant telegraphed to the defendant 'Will you sell us Bumper Hall Pen? Telegraph lowest cash price'. The defendant telegraphed in reply 'Lowest price for Bumper Hall Pen, £900'. The claimant telegraphed to accept what he regarded as an offer; the defendant made no further reply.
>
> *Decision:* The defendant's telegram was merely a statement of his minimum price if a sale were to be agreed. It was not an offer which the claimant could accept.

If in the course of **negotiations for a sale**, the vendor states the price at which they will sell, that statement may be an offer which can be accepted.

> *Bigg v Boyd Gibbons 1971*
>
> *The facts:* In the course of correspondence the defendant rejected an offer of £20,000 by the claimant and added 'for a quick sale I would accept £26,000... if you are not interested in this price would you please let me know immediately'. The claimant accepted this price of £26,000 and the defendant acknowledged his acceptance.
>
> *Decision:* In this context the defendant must be treated as making an offer which the claimant had accepted.

Reference to a more **detailed document** will not necessarily prevent a statement from being an offer.

> *Bowerman and Another v Association of British Travel Agents Ltd 1996*
>
> *The facts*: The case arose out of the insolvency in 1991 of a tour operator through whom a school party had booked a holiday. The party claimed a full refund under the ABTA scheme of protection. The ABTA scheme did not extend to one item, namely the holiday insurance premium and this was explained in ABTA's detailed handbook. The claimant argued that the 'ABTA promise' (to refund holiday expenses, widely advertised in the press) constituted an offer to the public at large, and that offer was accepted when the holiday was booked with the relevant tour operator.
>
> *Decision*: The public had been encouraged by ABTA to read the written 'ABTA promise' as creating a legally binding obligation to reimburse all the expenses of the holiday.

3.2 A statement of intention

Advertising that an event such as an auction will take place is not an offer to sell. Potential buyers may not sue the auctioneer if the auction does not take place: *Harris v Nickerson 1873*. This is an example of a **statement of intention** which is not actionable.

3.3 An invitation to treat

Where a party is initiating negotiations they are said to have made an invitation to treat. An **invitation to treat** cannot be accepted to form a binding contract. Examples of invitations to treat include:

- **Auction** sales
- **Advertisements** (for example, price lists or newspaper advertisements)
- **Exhibition** of goods for sale
- An **invitation** for tenders

Key term

> An **invitation to treat** can be defined as follows.
>
> 'An indication that a person is prepared to receive offers with a view to entering into a binding contract, for example, an advertisement of goods for sale or a company prospectus inviting offers for shares. It must be distinguished from an offer which requires only acceptance to conclude the contract.'
>
> (Note that on the facts of a particular case, advertisements etc may be construed as an offer: the Carlill case is an example. However, in most exam questions, advertisements are invitations to treat: read the facts of the question carefully.)

3.3.1 Auction sales

The **bid itself is the offer**, which the auctioneer is free to accept or reject: *Payne v Cave 1789*. An auction is defined as a contract for the sale of property under which offers are made by bidders stating the price at which they are prepared to buy and **acceptance takes place by the fall of the auctioneer's hammer**. Where an auction is stated to be 'without reserve' the auctioneer is offering goods for sale and the bid is the acceptance *Barry v Davies 2000*. A reserve is a specified minimum price.

3.3.2 Advertisements

An **advertisement** of goods for sale is usually an **attempt to induce offers**.

> *Partridge v Crittenden 1968*
>
> *The facts:* Mr Partridge placed an advertisement for 'Bramblefinch cocks, bramblefinch hens, 25s each'. The RSPCA brought a prosecution against him for offering for sale a brambling in contravention of the Protection of Birds Act 1954. The justices convicted Partridge and he appealed.
>
> *Decision:* The conviction was quashed. Although there had been a sale in contravention of the Act, the prosecution could not rely on the offence of 'offering for sale', as the advertisement only constituted an invitation to treat.

The **circulation of a price list** is also an invitation to treat: *Grainger v Gough 1896*, where it was noted:

'The transmission of such a price-list does not amount to an offer... If it were so, the merchant might find themselves involved in any number of contractual obligations to supply wine of a particular description which he would be quite unable to carry out, his stock of wine of that description being necessarily limited.'

3.3.3 Exhibition of goods for sale

Displaying goods in a shop window, or on the open shelves of a self-service shop, or advertising goods for sale, are normally invitations to treat.

> *Fisher v Bell 1961*
>
> *The facts:* A shopkeeper was prosecuted for offering for sale an offensive weapon by exhibiting a flick knife in his shop window.
>
> *Decision:* The display of an article with a price on it in a shop window is merely an invitation to treat.

> *Pharmaceutical Society of Great Britain v Boots Cash Chemists (Southern) 1952*
>
> *The facts:* Certain drugs could only be sold under the supervision of a registered pharmacist. The claimant claimed this rule had been broken by Boots who displayed these drugs in a self-service shop. Boots contended that there was no sale until a customer brought the goods to the cash desk and offered to buy them. A registered pharmacist was stationed at this point.
>
> *Decision:* The court found for Boots and commented that if it were true that a customer accepted an offer to sell by removing goods from the shelf, he could not then change his mind and put them back as this would constitute breach of contract.

3.3.4 Invitation for tenders

A **tender** is an estimate submitted in response to a prior request. When a person tenders for a contract they are making an offer to the person who has advertised a contract as being available. An invitation for tenders does not generally amount to an offer to contract with the person quoting the lowest price, except where the person inviting tenders actually makes it clear that they are making an offer.

Question — Offer

Bindi goes into a shop and sees a price label on a T-shirt for £5. She takes the T-shirt to the checkout, but the checkout operator tells her that the label is misprinted and should read £15. Bindi maintains that she only has to pay £5. How would you describe the price on the price label in terms of contract law?

Answer

Display of goods for sale with a price label is an invitation to treat (*Fisher v Bell 1961*), that is an invitation to the customer to make an offer which the shop can either accept or reject.

Once a valid offer has been made it is capable of being accepted, which will create an **agreement**. However, it is also possible for an offer to end without acceptance and therefore no agreement will be formed.

4 Termination of offer

FAST FORWARD

An offer may only be accepted while it is still open. In the absence of an acceptance, an offer may be **terminated** in any of the following ways.
- Rejection
- Counter-offer
- Lapse of time
- Revocation by the offeror
- Failure of a condition to which the offer was subject
- Death of one of the parties

4.1 Rejection

As noted earlier, **outright rejection terminates an offer**. A counter-offer, when the person to whom the offer was made proposes new or amended terms, also terminates the original offer.

Hyde v Wrench 1840

The facts: The defendant offered to sell property to the claimant for £1,000 on 6 June. Two days later, the claimant made a counter-offer of £950 which the defendant rejected on 27 June. The claimant then informed the defendant on 29 June that he accepted the original offer of £1,000.

Decision: The original offer of £1,000 had been terminated by the counter-offer of £950.

4.2 Counter-offer

Acceptance must be **unqualified agreement to the terms of the offer**. A purported acceptance which introduces any new terms is a counter-offer, which has the effect of terminating the original offer.

Key term

A **counter-offer** is a final rejection of the original offer. If a counter-offer is made, the original offeror may accept it, but if they reject it, then their original offer is no longer available for acceptance.

A **counter-offer** may of course be accepted by the original offeror.

Butler Machine Tool Co v Ex-cell-O Corp (England) 1979

The facts: The claimant offered to sell tools to the defendant. Their quotation included details of their standard terms. The defendant 'accepted' the offer, enclosing their own standard terms. The claimant acknowledged acceptance by returning a tear-off slip from the order form.

Decision: The defendant's order was really a counter-offer. The claimant had accepted this by returning the tear-off slip.

4.2.1 Request for information

It is possible to respond to an offer by making a **request for information**. Such a request may be a request as to whether or not other terms would be acceptable – it is not a counter-offer.

Stevenson v McLean 1880

The facts: The defendant offered to sell iron at '40s net cash per ton, open till Monday'. The claimant enquired whether he would agree to delivery spread over two months. The defendant did not reply and (within the stated time limit), the claimant accepted the original offer. Meanwhile the defendant had sold the iron to a third party.

Decision: There was a contract since the claimant had merely enquired as to a variation of terms.

4.3 Lapse of time

An offer may be expressed to last for a **specified time**. If, however, there is no express time limit set, it expires after a **reasonable time**.

Ramsgate Victoria Hotel Co v Montefiore 1866

The facts: The defendant applied to the company in June for shares and paid a deposit. At the end of November the company sent him an acceptance by issue of a letter of allotment and requested payment of the balance due. The defendant contended that his offer had expired and could no longer be accepted.

Decision: The offer was valid for a reasonable time only and five months was too long.

4.4 Revocation of an offer

The offeror may **revoke** their offer at any time before acceptance: *Payne v Cave 1789*. If they undertake that their offer shall remain open for acceptance for a specified time they may still revoke it within that time, unless by a separate contract they have bound themselves to keep it open. This is known as an **option contract**.

> *Routledge v Grant 1828*
>
> *The facts:* The defendant offered to buy the claimant's house for a fixed sum, requiring acceptance within six weeks. Within the six weeks specified, he withdrew his offer.
>
> *Decision:* The defendant could revoke his offer at any time before acceptance, even though the time limit had not expired.

Revocation may be an **express statement** or may be an **act** of the offeror. their revocation does not take effect until the revocation is communicated to the offeree. This raises two important points.

(a) The first point is that **posting** a letter of revocation is not a sufficient act of revocation.

> *Byrne v Van Tienhoven 1880*
>
> *The facts:* The defendants were in Cardiff; the claimants in New York. The sequence of events was as follows.
>
> | | |
> |---|---|
> | 1 October | Letter posted in Cardiff, offering to sell 1,000 boxes of tinplates. |
> | 8 October | Letter of revocation of offer posted in Cardiff. |
> | 11 October | Letter of offer received in New York and telegram of acceptance sent. |
> | 15 October | Letter confirming acceptance posted in New York. |
> | 20 October | Letter of revocation received in New York. The offeree had meanwhile resold the contract goods. |
>
> *Decision:* The letter of revocation could not take effect until received (20 October); it could not revoke the contract made by the telegram acceptance of the offer on 11 October.

(b) The second point is that **revocation of offer may be communicated by any third party who is a sufficiently reliable informant**.

> *Dickinson v Dodds 1876*
>
> *The facts:* The defendant, on 10 June, wrote to the claimant to offer property for sale at £800, adding 'this offer to be left open until Friday 12 June, 9.00 am.' On 11 June the defendant sold the property to another buyer, A. B, who had been an intermediary between Dickinson and Dodds, informed Dickinson that the defendant had sold to someone else. On Friday 12 June, before 9.00 am, the claimant handed to the defendant a formal letter of acceptance.
>
> *Decision:* The defendant was free to revoke his offer and had done so by sale to a third party; the claimant could not accept the offer after he had learnt from a reliable informant of the revocation of the offer to him.

However, this case should be treated with **caution** and it may be that only an agent can revoke an offer.

4.5 Failure of a condition

An **offer may be conditional** in that it is dependent on some event occurring or there being a change of circumstances. If the condition is not satisfied, the offer is not capable of acceptance.

> *Financings Ltd v Stimson 1962*
>
> *The facts:* The defendant wished to purchase a car, and on 16 March signed a hire-purchase form. The form, issued by the claimants, stated that the agreement would be binding only upon signature by them. On 20 March the defendant, not satisfied with the car, returned it. On 24 March the car was stolen from the premises of the dealer, and was recovered badly damaged. On 25 March the claimants signed the form. They sued the defendant for breach of contract.
>
> *Decision:* The defendant was not bound to take the car. His signing of the agreement was actually an offer to contract with the claimant. There was an implied condition in this offer that the car would be in a reasonable condition.

4.6 Termination by death

The **death** of the offeree terminates the offer. The offeror's death terminates the offer, unless the offeree accepts the offer in ignorance of the death, and the offer is not of a personal nature.

> *Bradbury v Morgan 1862*
>
> *The facts:* X offered to guarantee payment by Y in respect of goods to be supplied by the claimant. X died and the claimant, in ignorance of his death, continued to supply goods to Y. The claimant then sued X's executors on the guarantee.
>
> *Decision:* X's offer was a continuing commercial offer which the claimant had accepted by supply of goods after X's death. The guarantee stood.

Offers which are not terminated are capable of being accepted. However, there are a number of rules which govern what **valid acceptance** is. If a response to an offer is not a valid acceptance, then an agreement will not be formed.

5 Acceptance

FAST FORWARD

> **Acceptance** must be an unqualified agreement to all the terms of the offer. **Acceptance** is generally not effective until **communicated** to the offeror, except where the **'postal rule'** applies. In which case acceptance is complete and effective as soon as it is posted.

Key term

> **Acceptance** may be defined as follows.
>
> 'A positive act by a person to whom an offer has been made which, if unconditional, brings a binding contract into effect.'

The contract comes into **effect** once the offeree has **accepted** the terms presented to them. This is the point of no return; after acceptance, the offeror **cannot withdraw** their offer and both parties will be **bound** by the terms that they have agreed.

Acceptance may be by **express words**, by **action** or **inferred from conduct**.

> **Brogden v Metropolitan Railway Co 1877**
>
> *The facts:* For many years the claimant supplied coal to the defendant. He suggested that they should enter into a written agreement and the defendant's agent sent a draft to him for consideration. The parties applied to their dealings the terms of the draft agreement, but they never signed a final version. The claimant later denied that there was any agreement between him and the defendant.
>
> *Decision:* The conduct of the parties was only explicable on the assumption that they both agreed to the terms of the draft.

5.1 Silence

There must be some **act** on the part of the offeree to indicate their acceptance.

> **Felthouse v Bindley 1862**
>
> *The facts:* The claimant wrote to his nephew offering to buy the nephew's horse, adding 'If I hear no more about him, I consider the horse mine'. The nephew intended to accept his uncle's offer but did not reply. He instructed the defendant, an auctioneer, not to sell the horse. Owing to a misunderstanding the horse was sold to someone else. The uncle sued the auctioneer.
>
> *Decision:* The action failed. The claimant had no title to the horse.

Goods which are sent or services which are rendered to a person who did not request them are not 'accepted' merely because they do not return them to the sender: **Unsolicited Goods and Services Act 1971 (HMSO, 1978)**. The recipient may treat them as an unsolicited gift.

5.2 Acceptance 'subject to contract'

Acceptance **'subject to contract'** means that the offeree is agreeable to the terms of the offer but proposes that the parties should negotiate a formal contract. Neither party is bound until the formal contract is signed. Agreements for the sale of land in England are usually made 'subject to contract'.

Acceptance 'subject to contract' must be distinguished from outright acceptance made on the understanding that the parties wish to replace the **preliminary contract** with another at a later stage. Even if the immediate contract is described as 'provisional', it takes effect at once.

> **Branca v Cobarro 1947**
>
> *The facts:* A vendor agreed to sell a mushroom farm under a contract which was declared to be 'a provisional agreement until a fully legalised agreement is signed'.
>
> *Decision:* By the use of the word 'provisional', the parties had intended their agreement to be binding until, by mutual agreement, they made another to replace it.

5.3 Letters of intent

Key term

> **Letters of intent** are an indication by one party to another that they may place a contract with them.

Thus a building contractor tendering for a large **construction contract** may need to sub-contract certain (specialist) aspects of the work. The sub-contractor will be asked to provide an estimate so that the main contractor can finalise their own tender.

Usually, a **letter of intent** is worded so as not to create any legal obligation. However, in some cases it may be phrased so that it includes an invitation to commence preliminary work. In such circumstances, it creates an obligation to pay for that work.

> *British Steel Corpn v Cleveland Bridge and Engineering Co Ltd 1984*
>
> *The facts:* The defendants asked the claimants to supply nodes for a complex steel lattice-work frame, and sent the claimants a letter of intent, stating their intention to place an order on their standard terms. The claimants stated that they were unwilling to contract on such terms, but started work, and eventually completed and delivered all the nodes. They sued for the value of the nodes and the defendants counter-claimed for damages for late delivery.
>
> *Decision:* Since the parties had not reached agreement over such matters as late delivery, there was no contract, and so there could be no question of damages for late delivery. However, since the claimants had undertaken work at the request of the defendants and the defendants had accepted this work, the claimants were entitled to a reasonable remuneration for services rendered.

5.4 Acceptance of a tender

An **invitation for tenders** is an invitation to treat. There are two distinct types of tender.

(a) A **tender to perform one task**, such as building a new hospital, is an offer which can be accepted.

(b) A **tender to supply or perform a series of things**, such as the supply of vegetables daily to a restaurant, is not accepted until an order is placed. It is a standing offer. Each order placed by the offeree is an individual act of acceptance creating a separate contract. Until orders are placed there is no contract and the tenderer can terminate his standing offer.

> *Great Northern Railways v Witham 1873*
>
> *The facts:* The defendant tendered successfully for the supply of stores to the claimant over a period of one year. In his tender he undertook 'to supply... such quantities as the company may order from time to time'. After making some deliveries he refused to fulfil an order which the claimant had given.
>
> *Decision:* He was in breach of contract in refusing to fulfil the order given but might revoke his tender and need not then fulfil any future orders within the remainder of the 12-month period.

5.5 Counter-offers and requests for information

A **counter-offer does not constitute acceptance**; it is the making of a new offer which may in turn be accepted or rejected. Nor is a request for further information an acceptance.

In *Neale v Merrett 1930* an offer to sell land at £280 was accepted, but payment consisted of £80 and an undertaking to pay the balance by instalments. The 'acceptance' amounted to a counter offer since it varied the method of payment.

Question — Offer and acceptance

In January Elle offered to buy Jin's boat for £3,000. Jin immediately wrote a letter to Elle saying 'For a quick sale I would accept £3,500. If you are not interested please let me know as soon as possible.' Elle did not see the letter until March when she returned from a business trip but then replied. 'I accept your offer. I trust that if I pay £3,000 now, you can wait until June for the remaining £500.' On receiving the letter, Jin attached a 'sold' sign to the boat but forgot to reply to Elle. Is there a contract between Elle and Jin? If so, what are its terms?

Answer

Elle's offer of £3,000 is an **offer**. Many offers are in fact made by prospective purchasers rather than by vendors. Jin's letter forms a **counter-offer**, which has the effect of terminating Elle's offer: *Hyde v Wrench 1840*. Elle may now accept or reject this counter-offer.

There is nothing to indicate that Jin's (counter) offer is not still open in March. An offer may be expressed to last for a **specified time**. It then expires at the end of that time. If, however, there is no express time limit set, it expires after a **reasonable time**.

Elle's reply, using the words 'I accept your offer' **appear conclusive. However they are not**. The enquiry as to variation of terms does not constitute acceptance or rejection: *Stevenson v McLean 1880*. The effect of Elle's reply is probably best analysed as being a **new counter-offer** including terms as to deferred payment, which **Jin purports to accept by affixing a 'sold' sign**. The court would need to decide whether, in all the circumstances, acceptance can be deemed to have been communicated.

Following *Butler Machine Tool Co v Ex-Cell-O Corp (England) 1979*, the **counter-offer introduces new terms**, that is, price. The price is therefore £3,500. As to **date of payment**, it would appear that the attachment of a 'sold' sign to the boat is confirmation that the revised terms proposed by Jin are acceptable.

As well as acceptance being an unqualified agreement to the terms of the offer, it must also be **communicated** in some way to the offeror to be valid (for example verbally or by email or in writing). However, there are exceptions to this rule which we shall now look at.

6 Communication of acceptance

FAST FORWARD

The general rule is that acceptance **must be communicated** to the offeror and that it is not effective (and hence there is no contract) until this has been done. However this rule does not apply in all cases.

6.1 Waiver of communication

The offeror may **dispense** with the need for communication of acceptance. Such a waiver may be express or may be inferred from the circumstances. In *Carlill v Carbolic Smoke Ball Co 1893*, it was held that it was sufficient for the claimant to act on the offer without notifying her acceptance of it. This was an example of a **unilateral contract**, where the offer takes the form of a promise to pay money in return for an act.

6.2 Prescribed mode of communication

The offeror may call for communication of acceptance by **specified means**. Communication of acceptance by some other means **equally expeditious** generally constitutes a valid acceptance unless specified otherwise: *Tinn v Hoffmann 1873*. This would probably apply also to acceptance by fax machine or email. The offeror would have to use very precise wording if a specified means of communication is to be treated as mandatory.

> *Yates Building Co v R J Pulleyn & Sons (York) 1975*
>
> *The facts:* The offer called for acceptance by registered or recorded delivery letter. The offeree sent an ordinary letter which arrived without delay.
>
> *Decision:* The offeror had suffered no disadvantage and had not stipulated that acceptance must be made in this way only. The acceptance was valid.

6.3 No mode of communication prescribed

The offeree can use any method but must ensure that their **acceptance is understood** if they choose an **instantaneous method of communication**.

> *Entores v Miles Far Eastern Corporation 1955*
>
> *The facts:* The claimants sent an offer by telex to the defendants' agent in Amsterdam and the latter sent an acceptance by telex. The claimants alleged breach of contract and wished to serve a writ.
>
> *Decision:* The acceptance took effect (and the contract was made) when the telex message was printed out on the claimants' terminal in London. A writ could therefore be issued. This position was confirmed in *Brinkibon Investments v Stahag Stahl 1983*, where the judge stated whilst no universal rule could cover all such scenarios, they would be judged by reference to the intention of the parties, sound business practice and a judgment of where the risks should lie.

6.4 The postal rule

The offeror may **expressly** or by **implication** indicate that they expect acceptance by means of a letter sent through the post.

Key term

> The **postal rule** states that, where the use of the post is within the contemplation of both the parties, the acceptance is complete and effective as soon as a letter is posted, even though it may be delayed or even lost altogether in the post.

> *Adams v Lindsell 1818*
>
> *The facts:* The defendants made an offer by letter to the claimant on 2 September 1817 requiring an answer 'in course of post'. It reached the claimants on 5 September; they immediately posted a letter of acceptance, which reached the defendants on 9 September. The defendants could have expected a reply by 7 September, and they assumed that the absence of a reply within the expected period indicated non-acceptance and sold the goods to another buyer on 8 September.
>
> *Decision:* The acceptance was made 'in course of post' (no time limit was imposed) and was effective when posted on 5 September.

The **intention** to use the post for communication of acceptance may be deduced from the **circumstances**.

> *Household Fire and Carriage Accident Insurance Co v Grant 1879*
>
> *The facts:* The defendant handed a letter of application for shares to the claimant company's agent in Swansea for posting to the company in London. The company posted an acceptance which never arrived. The defendant was called upon to pay the amount outstanding on his shares.
>
> *Decision:* The defendant had to pay. The contract had been formed when the acceptance was posted, regardless of the fact that it was lost.

Under the postal rule, the **offeror may be unaware** that a contract has been made. If that possibility is clearly inconsistent with the nature of the transaction the letter of acceptance takes effect only when received. In particular, if the offer stipulates a particular mode of communication, the postal rule may not apply.

> **Holwell Securities v Hughes 1974**
>
> *The facts:* Hughes granted to the claimant an option to purchase land to be exercised 'by notice in writing'. A letter giving notice of the exercise of the option was lost in the post.
>
> *Decision:* The words 'notice in writing' must mean notice actually received by the vendor; hence notice had not been given to accept the offer.

Acceptance of an offer may **only** be made **by a person authorised** to do so. This will usually be the offeree or their authorised agents.

> **Powell v Lee 1908**
>
> *The facts:* The claimant was appointed to a post as a headmaster. Without authorisation, he was informed of the appointment by one of the managers. Later, it was decided to give the post to someone else. The claimant sued for breach of contract.
>
> *Decision:* Since communication of acceptance was unauthorised, there was no valid agreement and hence no contract.

Exam focus point

> Offer and acceptance are key areas of contract law. You must be able to both identify and explain any relevant legal rules and principles, these will allow you to present a reasoned answer.

Question — Formation of contract

Frank writes to Xiao-Xiao on 1 July offering to sell him his sailing dinghy for £1,200. On 8 July, having received no reply, he decides to withdraw this offer and sends a second letter. On 10 July, Xiao-Xiao receives the original offer letter and immediately telephones his acceptance to Frank's wife. He follows this up with a letter posted the same day. Frank's second letter arrives on 14 July and Xiao-Xiao learns that Mel has bought the boat the previous day. What is the legal situation?

Answer

The revocation takes effect when received on 14 July (*Byrne v Van Tienhoven 1850*). The acceptance by Xiao-Xiao takes effect when posted on 10 July (*Adams v Lindsell 1818*). Therefore a contract is formed on 10 July and Frank's sale of the dinghy to Mel is in breach of his contract with Xiao-Xiao.

6.5 Cross-offers

If two offers, identical in terms, **cross in the post**, there is no contract: *Tinn v Hoffmann 1873*.

For example, if A offers to sell their car to B for £1,000 and B offers to buy A's car for £1,000, there is no contract, as there is no acceptance.

6.6 Unilateral contracts

The question arises as to whether contractual obligations arise if a party, in ignorance of an offer, performs an act which fulfils the terms of the offer. If A offers a **reward** to anyone who finds and returns their lost property and B, in ignorance of the offer, does in fact return it to them, is B entitled to the promised reward? There is agreement by conduct, but B is not accepting A's offer since she is unaware of it.

> *R v Clarke 1927*
>
> *The facts:* A reward was offered for information leading to the arrest and conviction of a murderer. If the information was provided by an accomplice, he would receive a free pardon. C claimed the reward, admitting that he had acted to save his own skin and that all thought of the reward had passed out his mind.
>
> *Decision:* There could not be acceptance without knowledge of the offer.

However, acceptance may still be **valid** even if the offer was not the sole reason for the action.

> *Williams v Carwardine 1833*
>
> *The facts:* A reward was offered to bring criminals to book. The claimant, an accomplice in the crime, supplied the information, with knowledge of the reward.
>
> *Decision:* As the information was given with knowledge, the acceptance was related to the offer.

Question — Communication of acceptance

John offers to sell his car to Ahmed for £2,000 on 1 July saying that the offer will stay open for a week. Ahmed tells his brother that he would like to accept the offer. Unknown to Ahmed, his brother informs John of this on 4 July. On 5 July John, with his girlfriend present, sells the car to Gina. John's girlfriend tells Ahmed about this later that day. The next day, Ahmed delivers a letter of acceptance to John. Is John in breach of contract?

Answer

Communication of acceptance may only be made by a person authorised to do so (*Powell v Lee 1908*), therefore Ahmed's brother's purported acceptance is not valid. Revocation of an offer may be communicated by a reliable informant (*Dickinson v Dodds 1876*), so Ahmed is made aware of the revocation on 5 July. His attempted acceptance on 6 July is therefore not valid.

As there was no consideration to support any separate agreement to keep the offer open for a week, John is free to sell the car to Gina.

The case of *Carlill v Carbolic Smoke Ball Company 1893* includes one example of a **unilateral contract**. Here the defendants advertised that they would pay £100 to anyone who caught influenza while using their product. This was held to be an offer to the world at large capable of being accepted by anyone fulfilling the necessary conditions. However, it was not necessary that anyone fulfilled the conditions, but as soon as Carlill began to **use** the product, the defendants were bound by their offer.

An ordinary offer can be revoked at any time before complete acceptance and, once revoked, can no longer be accepted (*Routledge v Grant 1828*). However, in the case of a **unilateral contract**, the courts have held that an **offer cannot be revoked once the offeree has begun to perform** whatever act is necessary (*Errington v Errington 1953*).

We've now seen all of the elements required to create a valid agreement and will now turn our attention to two things that both parties to an agreement need to bring with them for that agreement to be legally binding. They must bring something of value (**consideration**) and they must bring an **intention to be legally bound**. If one or other of these elements are not present, then an agreement will have been formed, but neither party can enforce it through the courts.

7 Consideration

FAST FORWARD

Consideration is an **essential** part of most contracts. It is what each party brings to the contract.

Key term

Consideration has been defined as:

'A valuable consideration in the sense of the law may consist either in some right, interest, profit or benefit accruing to one party, or some forbearance, detriment, loss or responsibility given, suffered or undertaken by the other.' From *Currie v Misa 1875*

Using the language of purchase and sale, it could be said that one party must know that they have bought the other party's **promises** either by performing some act of their own or by offering a promise of their own.

7.1 Valid consideration

FAST FORWARD

Consideration may be **executed** (an act in return for a promise) or **executory** (a promise in return for a promise). It may not be **past**, unless one of three recognised exceptions applies.

There are two broad types of valid consideration – **executed** and **executory**. If consideration is **past** then it is not enforceable.

Executed consideration **is an act in return for a promise**. The consideration for the promise is a performed, or executed, act.

Key term

Executed consideration can be defined as follows.

'That which takes place at the present time. Thus in a contract for the sale of goods, the consideration is executed if the price is paid at the same time that the goods are delivered.'

Executory consideration is a promise given for a promise. The consideration in support of each promise is the other promise, not a performed act.

 Illustration

If a customer orders goods which a shopkeeper undertakes to obtain from the manufacturer, the shopkeeper promises to supply the goods and the customer promises to accept and pay for them. Neither has yet done anything but each has given a promise to obtain the promise of the other. It would be breach of contract if either withdrew without the consent of the other.

Key term

> **Executory consideration** can be defined as follows.
>
> 'That which is to take place at some future time. The consideration for the delivery of goods would be executory if it is a promise to pay at a future date.'

7.1.1 Additional rules for valid consideration

As well as being either executed or executory, there are **additional** rules that must be met for consideration to be valid:

- **Performance must be legal**, the courts will not enforce payment for illegal acts
- **Performance must be possible,** agreeing to perform the impossible is not a basis for a binding contract
- **Consideration must pass from the promisee**
- **Consideration must be sufficient but not necessarily adequate**

7.2 Past consideration

Key term

> **Past consideration** can be defined as follows.
>
> '… something which has already been done at the time the promise is made. An example would be a promise to pay for work already carried out, unless there was an implied promise to pay a reasonable sum before the work began.'

Anything which has already been done before a promise in return is given is past consideration which, as a general rule, is not sufficient to make the promise binding. The following is the key case in this area:

> *Re McArdle 1951*
>
> *The facts:* Under a will the testator's children were entitled to a house after their mother's death. In the mother's lifetime one of the children and his wife lived in the house with the mother. The wife made improvements to the house. The children later agreed in writing to repay the wife 'in consideration of your carrying out certain alterations and improvements'. But at the mother's death they refused to do so.
>
> *Decision:* The work on the house had all been completed before the documents were signed. At the time of the promise the improvements were past consideration and so the promise was not binding.

If there is an **existing contract** and one party makes a further promise, no contract will arise. Even if the promise is directly related to the **previous bargain**, it has been made upon past consideration.

> *Roscorla v Thomas 1842*
>
> *The facts:* The claimant agreed to buy a horse from the defendant at a given price. When negotiations were over and the contract was formed, the defendant told the claimant that the horse was 'sound and free from vice'. The horse turned out to be vicious and the claimant brought an action on the warranty.
>
> *Decision:* The express promise was made after the sale was over and was unsupported by fresh consideration.

PART A PRINCIPLES OF CONTRACT LAW

In three instances **past consideration** for a promise is sufficient to make the promise binding.

(a) Past consideration is sufficient to create liability on a **bill of exchange** (such as a cheque). Most cheques are issued to pay existing debts.

(b) After six (or in some cases 12) years the right to sue for recovery of a debt becomes **statute barred** by the Limitation Act 1980 (HMSO, 1980). If, after that period, the debtor makes written acknowledgement of the creditor's claim, the claim is again enforceable at law.

(c) When a request is made for a **service** this request may imply a promise to pay for it. If, after the service has been rendered, the person who made the request promises a specific reward, this is treated as fixing the amount to be paid.

Key term

A bill of exchange can be defined as:

'A negotiable instrument, drawn by one party on another, for example by a supplier of goods on a customer, who by accepting (signing) the bill, acknowledges the debt, which may be payable immediately (a sight draft) or at some future date (a time draft). The holder of the bill can thereafter use an accepted time draft to pay a debt to a third party or discount it to raise cash.'

Lampleigh v Braithwaite 1615

The facts: The defendant had killed a man and had asked the claimant to obtain for him a royal pardon. The claimant did so at his own expense. The defendant then promised to pay him £100. He failed to pay it and was sued.

Decision: The defendant's request was regarded as containing an implied promise to pay, and the subsequent promise merely fixed the amount.

Both parties must have **assumed** during their negotiations that the services were ultimately to be paid for.

Re Casey's Patents 1892

The facts: A and B, joint owners of patent rights, asked their employee, C, as an extra task to find licensees to work the patents. After C had done so, A and B agreed to reward him for his past services with one third of the patent rights. A died and his executors denied that the promise was binding.

Decision: The promise to C was binding since it merely fixed the 'reasonable remuneration' which A and B by implication promised to pay before the service was given.

Question
Consideration

Esra, a law student, is in her car, waiting for the traffic lights to change at a busy intersection. Roger steps off the pavement with a bucket and cloth and proceeds to clean the windscreen of her car. Afterwards, Esra tells him that she will pay him £5. She then drives away. Advise Roger.

Answer

Esra is not bound to pay the £5, because at the time the promise was made, Roger's actions were past consideration.

We've seen that consideration can be executed or executory, but is it important for each party's consideration to be of **equal value**? As we shall see below, consideration need not be 'adequate' but it must be 'sufficient'.

8 Adequacy and sufficiency of consideration

FAST FORWARD The long-established rule is that consideration need **not be adequate** but it **must be sufficient**.

The court will also seek to ensure that a **particular act** or **promise** can actually be deemed to be consideration. Learn these rules:

(a) **Consideration need not be adequate** (that is, equal in value to the consideration received in return). There is no remedy at law for someone who simply makes a poor bargain.

(b) **Consideration must be sufficient**. It must be capable in law of being regarded as consideration by the courts.

8.1 Adequacy

It is presumed that each party is capable of serving their **own interests**, and the courts will not seek to weigh up the comparative value of the promises or acts exchanged.

Thomas v Thomas 1842

The facts: By his will the claimant's husband expressed the wish that his widow should have the use of his house during her life. The defendants, his executors, allowed the widow to occupy the house (a) in accordance with her husband's wishes and (b) in return for her undertaking to pay a rent of £1 per annum. They later said that their promise to let her occupy the house was not supported by consideration.

Decision: Compliance with the husband's wishes was not valuable consideration (no economic value attached to it), but the nominal rent was sufficient consideration.

8.2 Sufficiency

Consideration is sufficient if it has some **identifiable value**. The law only requires an element of bargain, not necessarily that it should be a good bargain.

Chappell & Co v Nestle Co 1960

The facts: As a sales promotion scheme, the defendant offered to supply a record to anyone who sent in a postal order for £1 and 6c and three wrappers from 6c bars of chocolate made by them. The claimants owned the copyright of the tune. They sued for infringement of copyright. In the ensuing dispute over royalties the issue was whether the wrappers, which were thrown away when received, were part of the consideration for the promise to supply the record. The defendants offered to pay a royalty based on the price of £1 and 6c per record, but the claimants rejected this, claiming that the wrappers also represented part of the consideration.

Decision: The wrappers were part of the consideration as they had commercial value to the defendants.

As stated earlier, forbearance or the promise of it may be **sufficient** consideration if it has some value, or amounts to giving up something of value.

> *Horton v Horton 1961*
>
> *The facts:* Under a separation agreement, the defendant agreed to pay his wife (the claimant) £30 per month. Under the deed this amount was a net payment after deduction of income tax; for nine months the husband paid it without any deduction so that the wife had to make the deductions herself. He then signed a document agreeing to pay such amount as 'after the deduction of income tax should amount to the clear sum of £30'. He paid this for three years, then stopped, pleading that the later agreement was not supported by consideration.
>
> *Decision:* The later agreement was supported by consideration: the wife could have sued to have the original agreement rectified, but did not.

8.2.1 Performance of existing contractual duties

Performance of an **existing obligation imposed by statute** is no consideration for a promise of reward.

> *Collins v Godefroy 1831*
>
> *The facts:* The claimant had been subpoenaed to give evidence on behalf of the defendant in another case. He alleged that the defendant had promised to pay him six guineas for appearing.
>
> *Decision:* There was no consideration for this promise.

But if some **extra service** is given that is sufficient consideration.

> *Glasbrook Bros v Glamorgan CC 1925*
>
> *The facts:* At a time of industrial unrest, colliery owners, rejecting the view of the police that a mobile force was enough, agreed to pay for a special guard on the mine. Later they repudiated liability saying that the police had done no more than perform their public duty of maintaining order, and that no consideration was given.
>
> *Decision:* The police had done more than perform their general duties. The extra services given, beyond what the police in their discretion deemed necessary, were consideration for the promise to pay.

In the *Glasbrook* case the threat to law and order was not caused by either of the parties. Where one party's actions lead to the need for heightened police presence, and the police deem this presence **necessary**, they may also be entitled to payment.

> *Harris v Sheffield United FC Ltd 1988*
>
> *The facts:* The defendants argued that they did not have to pay for a large police presence at their home matches.
>
> *Decision:* They had voluntarily decided to hold matches on Saturday afternoons when large attendances were likely, increasing the risk of disorder.

8.2.2 Promise of additional reward

If there is already a contract between A and B, and B promises **additional reward** to A if they (A) will perform their existing duties, there is no consideration from A to make that promise binding.

Stilk v Myrick 1809

The facts: Two members of the crew of a ship deserted in a foreign port. The master was unable to recruit substitutes and promised the rest of the crew that they would share the wages of the deserters if they would complete the voyage home short-handed. The shipowners however repudiated the promise.

Decision: In performing their existing contractual duties the crew gave no consideration for the promise of extra pay and the promise was not binding.

If a claimant does **more than perform an existing contractual duty**, this may amount to consideration.

Hartley v Ponsonby 1857

The facts: 17 men out of a crew of 36 deserted. The remainder were promised an extra £40 each to work the ship to Bombay. The claimant, one of the remaining crew-members, sued to recover this amount.

Decision: The large number of desertions made the voyage exceptionally hazardous, and this had the effect of discharging the original contract. The claimant's promise to complete the voyage formed consideration for the promise to pay an additional £40.

If the party promising the additional reward has received a 'practical' benefit, that may be treated as consideration even if, in law, they have received no more that they was already entitled to under the contract.

Williams v Roffey Bros & Nicholls (Contractors) Ltd 1990

The facts: The claimants agreed to do carpentry work for the defendants, who were engaged as contractors to refurbish a block of flats, at a fixed price of £20,000. The work ran late and so the defendants, concerned that the job might not be finished on time and that they would have to pay money under a penalty clause, agreed to pay the claimants an extra £10,300 to ensure the work was completed on time. They later refused to pay the extra amount.

Decision: The fact that there was no apparent consideration for the promise to pay the extra was not held to be important, as in the court's view both parties derived a practical benefit from the promise. The telling point was that the defendants' promise had not been extracted by duress or fraud: it was therefore binding. The defendant had avoided the possible penalty.

Exam focus point

Williams v Roffey Bros is important because it is a newer case than the bulk of contract cases, most of which were decided in the nineteenth century.

Re Selectmove 1994

The facts: A company which was the subject of a winding up order offered to settle its outstanding debts by instalment. An Inland Revenue inspector agreed to the proposal. The company tried to enforce it.

Decision: Despite the verdict in *Williams v Roffey Brothers* the court held that an agreement to pay in instalments is unenforceable. Even though the creditor may obtain some practical benefit this is not adequate consideration to render the agreement legally binding in respect of part payment of debts.

8.2.3 Performance of existing contractual duty to a third party

If A promises B a reward if B will perform their **existing contract** with C, there is consideration for A's promise since they obtain a benefit to which they previously had no right, and B assumes new obligations.

Shadwell v Shadwell 1860

The facts: The claimant, a barrister, was engaged to marry E. His uncle promised the claimant that if he (the nephew) married E (as he did), the uncle would during their joint lives pay to his nephew £150 pa until such time as the nephew was earning £600 pa at the bar (which never transpired). The uncle died after eighteen years owing six annual payments. The claimant claimed the arrears from his uncle's executors, who denied that there was consideration for the promise.

Decision: Sufficient consideration was provided by the claimant.

8.2.4 Waiver of existing rights

Illustration

If X owes Y £100 but Y agrees to accept a lesser sum, say £80, in full settlement of Y's claim, there is a promise by Y to waive their entitlement to the balance of £20. The promise, like any other, should be supported by consideration.

Foakes v Beer 1884

The facts: The defendant had obtained judgement against the claimant. Judgement debts bear interest from the date of the judgement. By a written agreement the defendant agreed to accept payment by instalments, no mention being made of the interest. Once the claimant had paid the amount of the debt in full, the defendant claimed interest, claiming that the agreement was not supported by consideration.

Decision: She was entitled to the debt with interest. No consideration had been given by the claimant for waiver of any part of her rights against him.

There are, however, **exceptions** to the rule that the debtor (denoted by 'X' in the following paragraphs) must give consideration if the waiver is to be binding.

	Exceptions
Alternative consideration *Anon 1495* *Pinnel's Case 1602*	If X offers and Y accepts anything to which Y is not already entitled, the extra thing is sufficient consideration for the waiver. • Goods instead of cash • Early payment
Bargain between the creditors *Woods v Robarts 1818*	If X arranges with creditors that they will each accept part payment in full entitlement, that is bargain between the creditors. X has given no consideration but he can hold the creditors individually to the agreed terms.
Third party part payment *Welby v Drake 1825*	If a third party (Z) offers part payment and Y agrees to release X from Y's claim to the balance, Y has received consideration from Z against whom he had no previous claim.

We've seen almost all of the essential elements required to form a contract, but will now look at the last one. It is important for both parties to have **intended** for their agreement to be legally binding. If one party can establish that they did not intend to be bound by the agreement then it will not be enforceable, even if all of the other elements of a contract are in place.

9 Intention to create legal relations

FAST FORWARD

> Various cases give us a set of rules to apply when determining whether the **parties** to a contract intended to be **legally bound** by it.

Where there is no express statement as to whether or not legal relations are intended, the courts apply one of two **rebuttable presumptions** to a case.

- **Social, domestic and family arrangements** are not usually intended to be binding.
- **Commercial agreements** are usually intended by the parties involved to be legally binding.

The word **'presumption'** means that it is assumed that something is the case, for example it is presumed that social arrangements are not deemed to be legally binding. **'Rebuttable'** means that the presumption can in some cases be refuted; the burden of proof for rebutting the presumption is on the party seeking to escape liability.

Key term

Intention to create legal relations can be defined as follows.

'An agreement will only become a legally binding contract if the parties intend this to be so. This will be strongly presumed in the case of business agreements but not presumed if the agreement is of a friendly, social or domestic nature.'

9.1 Domestic arrangements

9.1.1 Marriage and civil partnerships

The fact that the parties are married or in a civil partnership does not mean that they cannot enter into a **binding contract** with one another. Contrast the following two cases.

Balfour v Balfour 1919

The facts: The defendant was employed in Ceylon. He and his wife returned to the UK on leave but it was agreed that for health reasons she would not return to Ceylon with him. He promised to pay her £30 a month as maintenance. Later the marriage ended in divorce and the wife sued for the monthly allowance which the husband no longer paid.

Decision: An informal agreement of indefinite duration made between husband and wife whose marriage had not at the time broken up was not intended to be legally binding.

Merritt v Merritt 1970

The facts: The husband had left the matrimonial home, which was owned in the joint names of husband and wife, to live with another woman. The spouses met and held a discussion, in the course of which he agreed to pay her £40 a month out of which she agreed to keep up the mortgage payments. The wife made the husband sign a note of these terms and an undertaking to transfer the house into her name when the mortgage had been paid off. The wife paid off the mortgage but the husband refused to transfer the house to her.

Decision: In the circumstances, an intention to create legal relations was to be inferred and the wife could sue for breach of contract.

Where agreements between married couples, civil partners or other relatives relate to **property matters** the courts are very ready to impute an intention to create legal relations.

9.1.2 Relatives

Agreements between other **family members** may also be examined by the courts.

Jones v Padavatton 1969

The facts: The claimant wanted her daughter to move to England to train as a barrister, and offered to pay her a monthly allowance. The daughter did so in 1962. In 1964 the claimant bought a house in London; part of the house was occupied by the daughter and the other part let to tenants whose rent was collected by the daughter for herself. In 1967 the claimant and her daughter quarrelled and the claimant issued a summons claiming possession of the house. The daughter sued for her allowance.

Decision: There were two agreements to consider: the daughter's agreement to read for the bar in exchange for a monthly allowance, and the agreement by which the daughter lived in her mother's house and collected the rent from tenants. Neither agreement was intended to create legal relations.

9.1.3 Other domestic arrangements

Domestic arrangements extend to those between people who are not related but who have a **close relationship** of some form. The nature of the agreement itself may lead to the conclusion that legal relations were intended.

Simpkins v Pays 1955

The facts: The defendant, her granddaughter and the claimant, a paying boarder, took part together each week in a competition organised by a Sunday newspaper. The arrangements over postage and other expenses were informal and the entries were made in the grandmother's name. One week they won £750; the paying boarder claimed a third share, but the defendant refused to pay on the grounds that there was no intention to create legal relations.

Decision: There was a 'mutuality in the arrangements between the parties', amounting to a contract.

9.1.4 Social arrangements

Arrangements undertaken between friends in a social setting may be assumed not to have behind them the intention to create legal relations. This presumption can be rebutted by showing that the parties did, despite the context, intend to be bound (*Parker v Clark 1960*), as where the parties are connected by business as well as by friendship ie the relationship is not purely social: *Sadler v Reynolds 2005*.

Exam focus point

Scenario questions can often be argued either way. The examiner will give you credit for valid arguments that you make.

9.2 Commercial agreements

When business people enter into commercial agreements it is presumed that there is an intention to enter into legal relations (*Esso Petroleum v Commissioners of Customs 1976*) unless this is **expressly disclaimed** or the **circumstances indicate otherwise**.

> *Rose and Frank v Crompton 1923*
>
> *The facts:* A commercial agreement by which the defendants appointed the claimant to be its distributor in the USA contained a clause described as 'the Honourable Pledge Clause' which expressly stated that the arrangement was 'not subject to legal jurisdiction' in either country. The defendants terminated the agreement without giving notice as required, and refused to deliver goods ordered by the claimants although they had accepted these orders when placed.
>
> *Decision:* The general agreement was not legally binding as there was no obligation to stand by any clause in it. However the orders for goods were separate and binding contracts. The claim for damages for breach of the agreement failed, but the claim for damages for non-delivery of goods ordered succeeded.

The words relied on by a party to a commercial agreement to show that legal relations are not intended are not always clear. In such cases, the **burden of proof** is **on the party seeking to escape liability**.

> *Edwards v Skyways Ltd 1964*
>
> *The facts:* In negotiations over the terms for making the claimant redundant, the defendants gave him the choice either of withdrawing his total contributions from their contributory pension fund or of receiving a paid-up pension. It was agreed that if he chose the first option, the defendants would make an ex gratia payment to him. He chose the first option; his contributions were refunded but the ex gratia payment was not made. He sued for breach of contract.
>
> *Decision:* Although the defendants argued that the use of the phrase ex gratia showed no intention to create legal relations, this was a commercial arrangement and the burden of rebutting the presumption of legal relations had not been discharged by the defendants.

9.3 Statutory provisions

Procedural agreements between **employers and trade** unions for the settlement of disputes are not intended to give rise to legal relations in spite of their elaborate content: s 179 **Trade Union and Labour Relations (Consolidation) Act 1992** (HMSO, 1992).

9.4 Letters of comfort

For many years, holding companies have given **'letters of comfort'** to creditors of subsidiaries which purport to give some comfort as to the ability of the subsidiary to pay its debts. Such letters have always been presumed not to be legally binding.

> *Kleinwort Benson Ltd v Malaysia Mining Corpn Bhd 1989*
>
> *The facts:* The claimants lent money to the defendant's subsidiary, having received a letter from the defendant stating 'it is our policy to ensure that the business is at all times in a position to meet its liabilities to you.' The subsidiary went into liquidation, and the bank claimed against the holding company for the outstanding indebtedness.
>
> *Decision:* The letter of comfort was a statement of existing policy and not a promise that the policy would continue in the future. Because both parties were well aware that in business a 'letter of comfort' imposed moral and not legal responsibilities, it was held not to have been given with the intention of creating legal relations.

9.5 Transactions binding in honour only

If the parties state that an agreement is **'binding in honour only'**, this amounts to an express denial of intention to create legal relations.

> *Jones v Vernons Pools 1938*
>
> *The facts:* The claimant argued that he had sent to the defendant a football pools coupon on which his predictions entitled him to a dividend. The defendants denied having received the coupon. A clause on the coupon stated that the transaction should not 'give rise to any legal relationship… but… be binding in honour only'.
>
> *Decision:* This clause was a bar to an action in court.

We've now studied all of the elements required to create a valid and enforceable contract, but who has the power to **enforce** a **contract**? Can someone who is not a party enforce rights given under it? The subject of who can force a contract is covered by the next section.

10 Privity of contract

FAST FORWARD

> As a general rule, only a person who is a party to a contract has enforceable rights or obligations under it. This is the doctrine of **privity of contract**. The Contracts (Rights of Third Parties) Act 1999 had a fundamental effect on the doctrine.

There is a maxim in contract law which states that **consideration must move from the promisee**. As consideration is the price of a promise, the price must be paid by the person who seeks to enforce the promise.

Illustration

A promises B that (for a consideration provided by B) A will confer a benefit on C. Therefore, C cannot as a general rule enforce A's promise since C has given no consideration for it.

> *Tweddle v Atkinson 1861*
>
> *The facts:* The claimant married the daughter of G. On the occasion of the marriage, the claimant's father and G exchanged promises that they would each pay a sum of money to the claimant. G died without making the promised payment and the claimant sued G's executor for the specified amount.
>
> *Decision:* The claimant had provided no consideration for G's promise.

In *Tweddle's* case each father could have sued the other but the claimant could not sue. The rule that consideration must move from the promisee overlaps with the rule that **only a party to a contract can enforce it**. No-one may be entitled to or bound by the terms of a contract to which they are not an original party: *Price v Easton 1833*.

Key term

> **Privity of contract** can be defined as follows.
>
> As a general rule, only a person who is a party to a contract has enforceable rights or obligations under it. Third parties have no right of action save in certain exceptional instances.

The following is the **leading case** on privity of contract.

> *Dunlop v Selfridge 1915*
>
> *The facts:* The claimant supplied tyres to Dew & Co, a distributor, on terms that they would not re-sell the tyres at less than the prescribed retail price. If Dew & Co sold the tyres wholesale to trade customers, they must impose a similar condition on those buyers to observe minimum retail prices. Dew & Co resold tyres on these conditions to the defendant. Under the terms of the contract between Dew & Co and Selfridge, Selfridge was to pay to the claimant a sum of £5 per tyre if it sold tyres to customers below the minimum retail price. They sold tyres to two customers at less than the minimum price. The claimant sued to recover £5 per tyre as liquidated damages.
>
> *Decision:* The claimant could not recover damages under a contract (between Dew & Co and Selfridge) to which it was not a party.

The **party** to the contract who **imposes the condition** or obtains a promise of a benefit for a third party can usually **enforce it**, but damages cannot be recovered on the third party's behalf, since a claimant can only recover damages for a loss they have suffered. Other remedies may be sought however.

Where the contract is one which provides something for the **enjoyment** of both the contracting party and third parties – such as a family holiday – the contracting party may be entitled to recover damages for their loss of the benefit: *Jackson v Horizon Holidays Ltd 1975*.

10.1 Exceptions

There are a number of **exceptions** to the rule of privity of contract.

	Exceptions
The third party can sue in another capacity	*Beswick v Beswick 1968* The facts: X transferred his business to the defendant, his nephew, in consideration for a pension of £6.10s per week and, after his death, a weekly annuity to X's widow. Only one such annuity payment was made. The widow brought an action against the nephew, asking for an order of specific performance. She sued both as administratrix of her husband's estate and in her personal capacity as recipient. *Decision:* As her husband's representative, the widow was successful in enforcing the contract for a third party's (her own) benefit. In her personal capacity she had no right of action.
Collateral contracts	*Shanklin Pier Ltd v Detel Products Ltd 1951* *The facts:* Shanklin Pier contracted with painters to have the pier repainted using products from Detel. Detel had already communicated their paint's suitability to the claimants. The paint was not suitable and Shanklin took action against Detel Products even though their contract was with the painters. *Decision:* It was held that a collateral contract existed between Shanklin and Detel. Detel had confirmed the paint's suitability in return for Shanklin requiring the painters to use it.
Valid assignment	Benefit from a contract can be re-assigned from the original beneficiary to a third party if it is in writing, it transfers the same or no more benefits to the new beneficiary and has the consent of the other party.

PART A PRINCIPLES OF CONTRACT LAW

	Exceptions
Foreseeable loss to the third party	*Linden Gardens Trust Ltd v Lenesta Sludge Disposals Ltd 1994* *The facts:* Linden Gardens contracted with the defendants for work to be done on their property. The defendants knew there was the likelihood that the property would be transferred to a third party soon after. After the transfer it became apparent that the workmanship amounted to breach of contract. As the third party had no action against the defendants due to the rules on privity, Linden Gardens took action in their place. *Decision:* As the transfer was in the contemplation of both parties the original beneficiary could claim full damages on behalf of the third party.
Implied trusts	Equity may hold that an implied trust has been created *Gregory and Parker v Willimans 1817* *The facts:* P owed money to G and W. He agreed with W to transfer his property to W if W would pay his (P's) debt to G. The property was transferred, but W refused to pay G. G could not sue on the contract between P and W. *Decision:* P could be regarded as a trustee for G, and G would therefore bring an action jointly with P.
Statutory exceptions	Road Traffic Act 1972 (HMSO, 1972): A person injured in a road accident may claim against the motorist's insurers. Married Women's Property Act 1882 (HMSO, 1882): Permits husband and wife to insure his or her own life for the benefit of the other under a trust which the beneficiary can enforce. Contracts (Rights of Third Parties) Act 1999: see below.
Agency	In normal circumstances the agent discloses to a third party with whom they contracts that they are acting for a principal. The contract, when made, is between the principal and the third party. The agent has no liability under the contact and no right to enforce it.
Covenants	A restrictive covenant may run with land *Tulk v Moxhay 1848* *The facts:* The claimant owned several plots of land in Leicester Square. He sold one to X, who agreed not to build on it, but to preserve it in its existing condition. It was sold on, eventually being purchased by the defendant, who, although he was aware of the restriction, proposed to build on it. The claimant sought an injunction. *Decision:* The injunction was granted.

10.2 Contracts (Rights of Third Parties) Act 1999 (TSO, 1999)

This Act has a fundamental effect on the rule of **privity of contract** by setting out the circumstances in which a third party has a right to enforce a contract term or have it varied or rescinded, and a right to all the remedies that are available for breach of contract. It brings the law in England, Wales and Northern Ireland into line with Scotland, most of the EU and the US.

There is a **two-limbed test** for the circumstances in which a third party may enforce a contract term.

- Whether the **contract itself expressly so provides**.
- Where the **term confers a benefit on the third party**, unless it appears that the contracting parties did not intend them to have the right to enforce it.

The **third party** must be **expressly identified** in the contract by name, class or description, but need not be in existence when the contract is made (for example, an unborn child or a future spouse). The Act enables a third party to take advantage of exclusion clauses as well as to enforce 'positive' rights.

Section 2 of the Act **protects third parties** from the original parties varying contract terms without their consent.

Under section 5, the **promisor is protected from double liability**. Damages awarded to the third party will be reduced by the amount of damages already awarded to the original promisee.

The Act does not confer third party rights in relation to a **company's constitution**, or **employment contracts**. So, for example, a customer of an employer cannot use this Act to enforce a term of a contract of employment against an employee.

Having studied the essential elements of a contract and who has the power to enforce a contract, we are now going to look inside the **contents of a contract**. The nuts and bolts of a contract are its **terms**. Terms are simply statements that set out what each party has agreed. They are often what the parties have expressly said themselves, but we shall see that terms can also be implied into contracts from other sources as well.

The importance of terms becomes apparent when one party believes that the other **has breached the terms of the contract** and wishes to seek a remedy. Courts will look at the terms of a contract to determine whether or not the contract was actually breached.

11 Contract terms

FAST FORWARD

> Statements made by the parties may be classified as **terms or representations**. Different **remedies** attach to breach of a term and to misrepresentation respectively.

In addition to the final contract, many statements may be made during the process of negotiation. It is important to be able to establish whether what has been written or said actually amounts to a contract term or whether it is simply a representation. **Statements may be classified as terms or as representations**.

Key term

> A **representation** is something which induces the formation of a contract but which does not become a **term** of the contract. The importance of the distinction is that different remedies are available depending on whether a term is broken or a representation turns out to be untrue.

If something said in negotiations proves to be untrue, the party misled can claim for **breach of contract** if the statement became a **term** of the contract. If the pre-contract statement was merely a **representation** then the party misled can claim misrepresentation, resulting in a lesser remedy than for breach of contract. If the statement is made by a person with **special knowledge** it is more likely to be treated as a contract term.

11.1 Express terms

Key term

> An **express term** is a term expressly agreed by the parties to a contract to be a term of that contract. In examining a contract, the courts will look first at the terms expressly agreed by the parties.

An apparently binding legal agreement must be **complete in its terms** to be a valid contract. However, it is possible for the parties to leave an essential term to be **settled by other means**, for example by an independent third party.

> **Illustration**
>
> It may be agreed to sell at the open market price on the day of delivery, or to invite an arbitrator to determine a fair price. The price may be determined by the course of dealing between the parties.

11.2 Implied terms

There are occasions where certain terms are not **expressly** adopted by the parties. Additional terms of a contract may be **implied** by law: through custom, statute or the courts to bring efficacy to the contract. Implied terms may override express terms in certain circumstances such as where they are implied by statute.

Key term

> An **Implied term** can be defined as follows.
>
> 'A term deemed to form part of a contract even though not expressly mentioned. Some such terms may be implied by the courts as necessary to give effect to the presumed intentions of the parties. Other terms may be implied by statute, for example, the Sale of Goods Act.'

11.2.1 Terms implied by custom

The parties may enter into a contract subject to **customs** of their trade. Any express term overrides a term which might be implied by custom.

11.2.2 Terms implied by statute

Terms may be implied by statute. In some cases the statute may permit the parties to contract out of the **statutory terms**. In other cases the statutory terms are obligatory, for example the protection given by the Sale of Goods Act 1979 to a party who buys goods cannot be taken away from them .

11.2.3 Terms implied by the courts

Terms may be **implied** if the court concludes that the **parties intended those terms** to apply to the contract. A term of a contract which is left to be implied and is not expressed is often **something that goes without saying**; so that, if while the parties were making their bargain an officious bystander were to suggest some express provision for it, they would say 'why should we put that in? That's obvious': This was put forward in *Shirlaw v Southern Foundries 1940*. The terms are required to give **efficacy** to the contract, that is, to make it work in practice.

11.3 Conditions and warranties

The terms of the contract are usually classified by their relative importance as **conditions** or **warranties**.

(a) **A condition is a vital term**, going to the root of the contract, breach of which entitles the injured party to decide to treat the contract as **discharged** and to claim damages.

(b) **A warranty is a term subsidiary to the main purpose of the contract**, breach of which only entitles the injured party to claim damages.

> *Poussard v Spiers 1876*
>
> *The facts:* Mme Poussard agreed to sing in an opera throughout a series of performances. Owing to illness she was unable to appear on the opening night and the next few days. The producer engaged a substitute who insisted that she should be engaged for the whole run. When Mme Poussard recovered, the producer declined to accept her services for the remaining performances.
>
> *Decision:* Failure to sing on the opening night was a breach of condition which entitled the producer to treat the contract for the remaining performances as discharged.

Bettini v Gye 1876

The facts: An opera singer was engaged for a series of performances under a contract by which he had to be in London for rehearsals six days before the opening performance. Owing to illness he did not arrive until the third day before the opening. The defendant refused to accept his services, treating the contract as discharged.

Decision: The rehearsal clause was subsidiary to the main purpose of the contract.

Classification may depend on the following issues.

(a) **Statute** often identifies implied terms specifically as conditions or warranties.

(b) **Case law** may also define particular types of clauses as conditions, for example a clause as to the date of 'expected readiness' of a ship let to a charterer: *The Mihalis Angelos 1971.*

(c) The court may construe what was the **intention of the parties** at the time the contract was made as to whether a broken term was to be a condition or a warranty: *Bunge Corporation v Tradax SA 1981.*

It is important to remember that if the injured party merely wants damages, there is **no** need to consider whether the term broken is a condition or a warranty, since either type of breach entitles the injured party to damages.

Question — Conditions and warranties

Norma, a professional singer, enters into a contract to sing throughout a series of concerts. A term in the contract states that she must attend five rehearsals before the opening night. Norma falls ill and misses the last two rehearsals and the opening night. Is she in breach of contract? Give reasons.

Answer

Norma is in breach of contract as she has failed to fulfil the condition that she would sing on the opening night (*Poussard v Spiers 1876*). Had she just failed to attend the two rehearsals, this would have amounted to breach of warranty (*Bettini v Gye 1876*).

11.4 Innominate terms

Traditionally, terms were either classified as conditions or warranties and the injured party could choose to end the contract only for breach of condition. Sometimes a warranty was broken with catastrophic results, yet the court could not permit the injured party to end the contract because the term broken was not a condition. More recently the courts have held that where the breach deprives the injured party of **substantially the whole benefit** of the contract the term broken can be called '**innominate**' and the injured party can choose to end the contract even if it could not be regarded as a condition.

If the **nature and effect of the breach** is such as to deprive the injured party of most of their benefit from the contract then it will be treated as if the guilty party had breached a condition.

Question — Breach

Busola agrees with Professional Cars plc that they are to provide a white Rolls Royce for his daughter's wedding. On the day the driver arrives in a black Ford Scorpio. Busola sends him away. What is the consequence?

Answer

Busola can sue Professional Cars plc for breach of contract. The company has not agreed to supply 'a car' but 'a white Rolls Royce'. Its failure to fulfil this term allows Busola to sue for breach if he wishes to claim damages, eg the cost of hiring another car. It does not matter if the term broken is a condition or a warranty.

Question — Consequences of breach

To what is the injured party to a contract entitled in the event of breach of:

(a) A condition by the other party?
(b) A warranty by the other party?

Answer

(a) They may choose to treat the contract as discharged and repudiate or terminate the contract, or alternatively they may go on with it and sue for damages.
(b) They may claim damages only.

11.5 Exclusion clauses

An **exclusion** clause may attempt to restrict one party's liability for breach of contract or for negligence. To be enforceable, **a term must be validly incorporated into a contract**. Because most disputes about whether a term has been incorporated arise in the context of exclusion clauses, much of the relevant case law surrounds exclusion clauses – and in particular:

(a) Whether an exclusion clause (as a contract term) has been **validly incorporated** into the contract; and
(b) If so, how the exclusion clause should be **interpreted.** Courts will generally interpret exclusion clauses strictly which may actually prevent the clause being applied in practice.

For many years the courts demonstrated the hostility of the common law to exclusion clauses by developing various rules of case law designed to restrain their effect. To these must also be added the considerable statutory safeguards provided by the **Unfair Contract Terms Act 1977** (HMSO, 1977) (UCTA) and the **Consumer Rights Act 2015** (TSO, 2015).

11.5.1 Incorporation of exclusion clauses

The law seeks to protect parties (usually the weaker party to the contract) from the full force of exclusion clauses. They do this by applying the '**letter of the law**' to see if such clauses have been incorporated correctly. Where there is uncertainty the clauses may be excluded from the contract.

Such **uncertainty** can arise in several circumstances.

- The document containing notice of the clause must be an **integral part** of the contract.
- If the document is an integral part of the contract, a term may not usually be disputed if it is included in a document which a party has **signed.**

- The term must be put forward **before** the contract is made.
- If the contact is not signed, an exclusion clause is not a binding term unless the party whose rights it restricts was made **sufficiently aware** of it at the time of agreeing to it.
- **Onerous terms** must be sufficiently highlighted (it is doubtful whether this applies to signed contracts).

11.5.2 Contractual documents

Where the exclusion clause is contained in an **unsigned document** it must be shown that this document is an integral part of the contract and is one which could be expected to contain terms.

11.5.3 Signed contracts

If a party **signs** a document containing a term, they are held to have agreed to the term even if they have not read the document. But this is not so if the party who puts forward the document for signature gives a misleading explanation of the term's legal effect.

11.5.4 Unsigned contracts and notices

Each party must be aware of the contract's terms before or **at the time of entering into the agreement** if they are to be binding.

Olley v Marlborough Court 1949

The facts: A husband and wife arrived at a hotel and paid for a room in advance. On reaching their bedroom they saw a notice on the wall by which the hotel disclaimed liability for loss of valuables unless handed to the management for safe keeping. The wife locked the room and handed the key in at the reception desk. A thief obtained the key and stole the wife's furs from the bedroom.

Decision: The hotel could not rely on the notice disclaiming liability since the contract had been made previously and the disclaimer was too late.

Complications can arise when it is difficult to determine at exactly **what point in time** the contract is formed so as to determine whether or not a term is validly included.

Thornton v Shoe Lane Parking Ltd 1971

The facts: The claimant wished to park his car in the defendant's automatic car park. He had seen a sign saying 'All cars parked at owner's risk' outside the car park and when he received his ticket he saw that it contained words which he did not read. In fact these made the contract subject to conditions displayed obscurely on the premises. These not only disclaimed liability for damage but also excluded liability for injury. When he returned to collect his car there was an accident in which he was badly injured.

Decision: The reference on the ticket to conditions was received too late for the conditions to be included as contractual terms. At any rate, it was unreasonable for a term disclaiming liability for personal injury to be presented so obscurely. Note that now under statute (the Unfair Contracts Terms Act 1977 and the Consumer Rights Act 2015) the personal injury clause would be unenforceable anyway.

An exception to the rule that there should be prior notice of the terms is where the parties have had **consistent dealings** with each other in the past, and the documents used then contained similar terms.

> *J Spurling Ltd v Bradshaw 1956*
>
> *The facts:* Having dealt with a company of warehousemen for many years, the defendant gave it eight barrels of orange juice for storage. A document he received a few days later acknowledged receipt and contained a clause excluding liability for damage caused by negligence. When he collected the barrels they were empty and he refused to pay.
>
> *Decision:* It was a valid clause as it had also been present in the course of previous dealings, even though he had never read it.

If the parties have had previous dealings (but not on a consistent basis), then the person to be bound by the term must be **sufficiently aware** of it at the time of making the latest contract.

> *Hollier v Rambler Motors 1972*
>
> *The facts:* On three or four occasions over a period of five years the claimant had had repairs done at a garage. On each occasion he had signed a form by which the garage disclaimed liability for damage caused by fire to customers' cars. The car was damaged by fire caused by negligence of garage employees. The garage contended that the disclaimer had by course of dealing become an established term of any contract made between them and the claimant.
>
> *Decision:* The garage was liable. There was no evidence to show that the claimant knew of and agreed to the condition as a continuing term of his contracts with the garage.

11.5.5 Onerous terms

Where a term is **particularly unusual** and **onerous** it should be **highlighted** (although it is doubtful whether this applies to signed contracts). Failure to do so may mean that it does not become incorporated into the contract.

Question — Exclusion clause

Latifa hires a car from a car rental company. On arrival at their office she is given a form, which includes terms and conditions in small print on the back, and asked to sign it. She does so and pays the hire charge. When she gets into the car, she happens to look in the glove compartment and sees a document headed 'Limitation of Liability'. This states that the hire company will not be liable for any injury caused by a defect in the car unless this is as a result of the company's negligence. While Latifa is driving on the motorway, the airbag inflates and causes her to crash. She is badly injured. Assuming that negligence is not claimed, what is the status of the exclusion clause?

Answer

There must be prior notice of the presence of an exclusion clause. The answer here will depend on whether this exclusion was included in the original terms and conditions (and therefore merely reinforced by the later document) or not. The hire company's only other possible defence will be to show a consistent course of dealings with Latifa.

11.6 Interpretation of exclusion clauses

In deciding what an exclusion clause means, the courts interpret any ambiguity against the party who relies on the exclusion. This is known as the **contra proferentem rule**. Liability can only be excluded or restricted by clear words.

11.6.1 The 'main purpose' rule

When construing an exclusion clause the court will also consider the **main purpose rule**. By this, the court presumes that the clause was not intended to prevent the main purpose of the contract.

11.6.2 Fundamental breach

There is no doubt that at common law a **properly drafted** exclusion clause can cover any breach of contract.

As we saw at the start of the chapter, the law has protection in place to **protect parties** who are often in a weaker negotiating position. The Unfair Contract Terms Act 1977 and the Consumer Rights Act 2015 are two key examples and provide protection against unfair exclusion clauses and other unfair terms. The Unfair Contract Terms Act governs business to business contracts, and the Consumer Rights Act covers contracts involving consumers.

12 The Unfair Contract Terms Act 1977

> **FAST FORWARD**
>
> The **Unfair Contract Terms Act 1977 (HMSO, 1977)** (UCTA) aims to **protect businesses** when they enter contracts with each other by stating that some exclusion clauses are **void**, and considering whether others are **reasonable**.

When considering the **validity** of exclusion clauses the courts have had to strike a balance between:

- The principle that parties should have complete **freedom to contract** on whatever terms they wish; and
- The need to **protect parties** from unfair exclusion clauses.

Exclusion clauses do have a proper place in business. They can be used to **allocate contractual risk**, and thus to determine in advance who is to insure against that risk. Between businesses with similar bargaining power, exclusion clauses are a legitimate device.

Before we consider the specific terms of UCTA, it is necessary to describe how its **scope is restricted**.

(a) In general, UCTA only applies to **business-to-business contracts.** Business-to-consumer contracts are covered by the Consumer Rights Act 2015, and generally private individuals in consumer-to-consumer contracts may contract on any terms that they wish.

(b) UCTA **does not apply to some contracts**, for example contracts of insurance or contracts relating to the transfer of an interest in land.

(c) Specifically, UCTA **applies to**:
   (i) Clauses that attempt to limit liability for **negligence**;
   (ii) Clauses that attempt to limit liability for **breach of contract**.

UCTA uses two techniques for controlling exclusion clauses – some types of clauses are **void**, whereas others are subject to a **test of reasonableness**.

12.1 Clauses which are void

A clause is void in the following circumstances.

- A clause which purports to exclude or limit liability for **death or personal injury** resulting from negligence. This is the key circumstance to remember.
- In a contract for the sale or hire purchase of goods, a clause that purports to exclude the condition that the seller has a **right to sell** the goods.

12.2 Clauses which are subject to a test of reasonableness

If a clause is not automatically void, it is subject to a **statutory test of reasonableness**.

12.3 The statutory test of reasonableness

The term must be **fair and reasonable** having regard to all the circumstances which were, or which ought to have been, known to the parties when the contract was made. The burden of proving reasonableness lies on the person seeking to rely on the clause. Statutory guidelines are included in UCTA to assist the determination of reasonableness. For instance, the court will consider the following.

- The relative **strength** of the parties' bargaining positions
- Whether any **inducement** (for example, a reduced price) was offered to the customer to persuade them to accept limitation of their rights
- Whether the customer **knew or ought to have known** of the existence and extent of the clause
- If **failure to comply with a condition** (for example, failure to give notice of a defect within a short period) excludes or restricts the customer's rights, whether it was reasonable to expect when the contract was made that compliance with the condition would be practicable
- Whether the goods were made, processed or adapted to the **special order** of the customer

---

St Albans City and District Council v International Computers Ltd 1994

The facts: The defendants had been hired to assess population figures on which to base community charges (local government taxation). Their standard contract contained a clause restricting liability to £100,000. The database which they supplied to the claimants was seriously inaccurate and the latter sustained a loss of £1.3 million.

Decision: The clause was unreasonable. The defendants could not justify this limitation, which was very low in relation to the potential loss. In addition, they had aggregate insurance of £50 million. The defendants had to pay full damages.

---

13 The Consumer Rights Act 2015

The **Consumer Rights Act 2015 (TSO, 2015)** provides protection for consumers in contracts with businesses.

The **Consumer Rights Act 2015** (CRA) provides statutory protection in respect of **consumer contracts** and **consumer notices** (such as signs in car parks). It provides that terms in contracts between a business and a consumer will only be binding on the consumer if they are **'fair'**. However, the consumer may still rely on a term (and therefore enforce a contract) which is deemed 'unfair'.

13.1 Fairness

When considering whether a term is **'fair'**, a number of factors should be considered, such as whether it puts the **consumer at a disadvantage**, and whether there were any **relevant circumstances** when the contract was signed, as well as the **nature of the contract** itself. In addition, CRA requires that terms are set out in **plain, intelligible language** with any **relevant terms** made **prominent**.

CRA also provides an **indicative list of terms which may be regarded as unfair**. The **terms** on the list include:

- Excluding liability for death or personal injury
- Restriction of the consumer's legal rights
- Payment of disproportionate compensation by the consumer if they fail to perform their obligations
- Binding the consumer to terms that they had no real opportunity to read before the contract was concluded
- Allowing the business to unilaterally alter the terms of the contract with no valid reason
- Allowing the business to determine the price payable after the consumer has been bound by the contract
- Forcing the consumer to perform their obligations when the business does not perform theirs

13.2 Businesses acting as consumers

Where a business engages in an activity which is merely **incidental to the business**, the activity will only be in the course of the business if it is an integral part of the business and carried on with a degree of regularity. It will therefore be acting as a consumer and CRA may apply to it. However, the business must prove that it was acting as a consumer. The following case indicates how the law is likely to be applied in this area.

> *R & B Customs Brokers Ltd v United Dominions Trust Ltd 1988*
>
> *The facts:* The claimants, a company owned by Mr and Mrs Bell and operating as a shipping broker, bought a second-hand Colt Shogun car. The car was to be used partly for business and partly for private use.
>
> *Decision:* This was a consumer sale, since the company was not in the business of buying cars.

We've now seen how a valid contract is formed and how its contents are subject to statutory protection. In the next chapter we look at what happens at the end of a contract's life – known as **discharge of contract**.

Chapter Roundup

- The **three essential elements** of a contract are **offer and acceptance**, **consideration** and **intention to enter into legal relations**.

  As a general rule, **a contract may be made in any form**.

- The first essential element in the formation of a binding contract is **agreement**. This is usually evidenced by **offer and acceptance**. An offer is a definite promise to be bound on specific terms, and must be distinguished from the mere **supply of information** and from an **invitation to treat**.

- An offer may only be accepted while it is still open. In the absence of an acceptance, an offer may be **terminated** in any of the following ways.
  - Rejection
  - Counter-offer
  - Lapse of time
  - Revocation by the offeror
  - Failure of a condition to which the offer was subject
  - Death of one of the parties

- **Acceptance** must be an unqualified agreement to all the terms of the offer. **Acceptance** is generally not effective until **communicated** to the offeror, except where the **'postal rule'** applies. In which case acceptance is complete and effective as soon as it is posted.

- The general rule is that acceptance **must be communicated** to the offeror and that it is not effective (and hence there is no contract) until this has been done. However this rule does not apply in all cases.

- **Consideration** is an **essential** part of most contracts. It is what each party brings to the contract.

- Consideration may be **executed** (an act in return for a promise) or **executory** (a promise in return for a promise). It may not be **past**, unless one of three recognised exceptions applies.

- The long-established rule is that consideration need **not be adequate** but it **must be sufficient**.

- Various cases give us a set of rules to apply when determining whether the **parties** to a contract intended to be **legally bound** by it.

- As a general rule, only a person who is a party to a contract has enforceable rights or obligations under it. This is the doctrine of **privity of contract**. The Contracts (Rights of Third Parties) Act 1999 has had a fundamental effect on the doctrine.

- Statements made by the parties may be classified as **terms or representations**. Different **remedies** attach to breach of a term and to misrepresentation respectively.

- The **Unfair Contract Terms Act 1977 (HMSO, 1977)** (UCTA) aims to **protect businesses** when they enter contracts with each other by stating that some exclusion clauses are **void**, and considering whether others are **reasonable**.

- The **Consumer Rights Act 2015 (TSO, 2015)** provides protection for consumers in contracts with businesses.

Quick Quiz

1. How is the circulation of a price list categorised in the law of contract?

offer	tender
invitation to treat	auction

2. **Fill in the blanks** in the statements below, using the words in the box.

   As a general rule, acceptance must be (1) ……………….. to the (2) ……………….. and is not effective until this has been done.

   An (3) ……………….. is a definite promise to be bound on specific terms, and must be distinguished from a supply of (4) ……………….. and from an (5) ………………..

   A counter-offer counts as (6) ……………….. of the original offer.

• information	• offer	• invitation to treat
• rejection	• communicated	• offeror

3. As a general rule, silence cannot constitute acceptance.

   True ☐
   False ☐

4. Define the postal rule.

5. Give four instances when an offer is terminated.

6. Distinguish between executed and executory consideration.

7. **Fill in the blanks** in the statement below.

   Consideration need not be (1) ……………….. but it must be (2) ……………….. .

8. **Fill in the blanks** in the statement below.

   If Alice promises Ben that (for a consideration provided by Ben) Alice will confer a benefit on Charlotte, then (1)……………….. cannot at common law enforce Alice's promise. This is the doctrine of (2)……………….. .

9. A promise of additional reward for the performance of existing duties is not generally binding.

   True ☐
   False ☐

10. **Fill in the blanks** in the statements below, using the words in the box.

    A (1) ……………….. is a vital term, going to the root of the contract, breach of which entitles the injured party to treat the contract as (2) ……………….. and claim (3) ……………….. .

    A (4) ……………….. is a term (5) ……………….. to the main purpose of the contract.

    The consequence of a term being classified as innominate is that the court must decide what is the actual effect of its (6) ……………….. .

• breach	• condition	• subsidiary
• warranty	• damages	• discharged

PART A PRINCIPLES OF CONTRACT LAW

11 Terms implied by custom cannot be overridden.

   True ☐
   False ☐

12 A business is classed as a consumer if it does not make the contract in the course of its business.

   True ☐
   False ☐

13 Match the laws to their applications under the law of contract.

   A   Common law   (1) Does not apply to business-to-consumer contracts
   B   UCTA 1977   (2) Applies only to business-to-consumer contracts
   C   CRA 2015   (3) Applies to all contracts

14 What is the 'contra proferentem' rule?

Answers to Quick Quiz

1. Invitation to treat. *Grainger v Gough (1896)*

2. (1) communicated (2) offeror (3) offer (4) information (5) invitation to treat (6) rejection

3. True. Generally, silence cannot constitute acceptance.

4. The postal rule states that, where the use of the post is within the contemplation of both the parties, the acceptance is complete and effective as soon as a letter is posted, even though it may be delayed or even lost altogether in the post.

5. Any four of the following:

    Rejection
    Counter-offer
    Lapse of time
    Revocation by the offeror
    Failure of a condition to which the offer was subject
    Death of one of the parties

6. Executed consideration is an act in return for a promise such as paying for goods when the shopkeeper hands them over. Executory consideration is a promise given for a promise, such as promising to pay for goods that the shopkeeper puts on order for you.

7. (1) adequate, (2) sufficient

8. (1) Charlotte, (2) Privity of contract

9. True (as in *Stilk v Myrick*)

10. (1) condition (2) discharged (3) damages (4) warranty (5) subsidiary (6) breach

11. False. Such terms can be overridden.

12. True. Businesses are classed as consumers if it can prove the contract was not made in the ordinary course of its business.

13. A   (3)
    B   (1)
    C   (2)

14. In deciding what an exclusion clause means, the courts interpret any ambiguity against the person at fault who relies on the exclusion.

PART A   PRINCIPLES OF CONTRACT LAW

End of chapter question

Offer or invitation to treat?

After completing the construction of an office building, New Build Ltd has a surplus of 100 reinforced steel bars. These are advertised on www.buildingtrade.com, a website dedicated to the supply of materials for the construction industry. Bids are sought in the following terms:

'100 reinforced steel bars (available for inspection at the premises of New Build Ltd) for sale as a single lot to the highest bidder. Potential buyers must contact New Build Ltd with their bids by 5pm on 10 May.'

Having inspected the bars, Workman Ltd email New Build Ltd placing a £5,000 bid at 4pm on 10 May. This bid is not read by the employees of New Build Ltd until after 5pm.

Required

(a) Does New Build Ltd's advertisement constitute an offer or an invitation to treat? **(8 marks)**

(b) Assuming that the advertisement is found to constitute an offer, Workman Ltd argue that their acceptance is governed by the postal rule. Explain the operation of this rule and when the agreement would be concluded if it applied in this case. **(6 marks)**

(c) Assuming that the advertisement is found to constitute an offer, New Build Ltd counter that the ordinary principles of offer and acceptance govern this situation. Would this mean that acceptance does not take place within the time limit set out in the advertisement? **(6 marks)**

(Total = 20 marks)

Discharge of contract

Topic list	Syllabus reference
1 Discharge of contract	1.1
2 Agreement	1.1
3 Frustration	1.1
4 Breach of contract	1.1
5 Damages	1.1
6 Remoteness of damage	1.1
7 Measure of damages	1.1
8 Liquidated damages and penalty clauses	1.1
9 Other common law remedies	1.1
10 Equitable remedies	1.1

Introduction

We saw in the previous chapter how **contracts are created** and the **types of term** contained within them. Most contracts end with the intended result – with each party performing what they agreed to do; however some contracts end with one party breaching the **terms** of the deal.

This chapter examines what **breach of contract** is, and what the remedies are for the innocent party.

Damages are **monetary compensation** for a loss. However, there are rules concerning what damages can be claimed for and how much should be awarded.

Liquidated damages and **penalty clauses** are contractual terms that state how damages will be calculated so both parties agree to them in advance. You should be able to explain when these will and will not be enforced by the court.

There are also **equitable remedies**, which can be claimed if damages are not suitable. You should be able to explain all of them.

PART A PRINCIPLES OF CONTRACT LAW

1 Discharge of contract

> **FAST FORWARD** Contracts can be discharged through **agreement**, **frustration**, **performance** and **breach**.

A valid contract can be **discharged** in four ways. The most common method of discharge is **performance**. This is where each party's contractual obligations are exactly or substantially met (all contract terms are performed). However, there are **three** instances where the contract terms are not substantially performed.

These are:

- **Agreement**. Where both parties agree to end the agreement and this is supported by consideration.
- **Frustration**. Where performance of an obligation is impossible due to specific circumstances occurring after formation of the contract.
- **Breach**. Where one party fails to meet its contractual obligations.

We shall now look at each in more detail.

2 Agreement

> **FAST FORWARD** The obligations of the parties may also be discharged by **agreement**.

Instead of performing the contract, **the parties may agree to cancel the contract before it has been completely performed** on both sides.

If there are unperformed obligations of the original contract on both sides, each party provides consideration for their own release by agreeing to release the other (**bilateral discharge**). Each party surrenders something of value.

But if one party has completely performed their obligations, their agreement to release the other from their obligations (**unilateral discharge**) requires consideration, such as payment of a cancellation fee (this is called **accord and satisfaction**.

If the parties enter into a **new contract** to replace the unperformed contract, the new contract provides any necessary consideration. This is called **novation** of the old contract – it is replaced by a new one.

A contract may include provision for its own discharge by imposing a **condition precedent**, which prevents the contract from coming into operation unless the condition is satisfied.

Alternatively, it may impose a **condition subsequent** by which the contract is discharged on the later happening of an event. A simple example of this is provision for termination by notice given by one party to the other. Effectively these are contracts whereby discharge may arise through agreement.

3 Frustration

> **FAST FORWARD** If the parties to the contract assumed, at the time of the agreement, that certain underlying conditions would continue, the contract is discharged by **frustration** if these assumptions prove to be false. This is because the contract is fundamentally different in nature from the original agreement.

If it is **impossible** to perform the contract when it is made, there is usually no contract at all. In addition, the parties are free to negotiate escape clauses or *force majeure* clauses covering impossibility which arises after the contract has been made. If they fail to do so, they are, as a general rule, in **breach** of contract if they find themselves unable to do what they have agreed to do.

The rigour of this principle is modified by the doctrine that in certain circumstances a contract may be discharged by **frustration**. If it appears that the parties assumed that certain underlying conditions would continue, the contract may be frustrated if their assumption proves to be false.

Key term

> 'The term **frustration** refers to the discharge of a contract by some outside event for which neither party is responsible which makes further performance impossible. It must be some fundamental change in circumstances such as the accidental destruction of the subject-matter upon which the contract depends. The contract is thereby brought to an end and the rights and obligations of the parties will, in many cases, be adjusted by the application of the Law Reform (Frustrated Contracts) Act 1943.'

We shall now look at some examples of how a contract might be **frustrated**.

3.1 Destruction of the subject matter

In the case which gave rise to the doctrine of frustration, the **subject matter** of the contract was destroyed before performance fell due.

Taylor v Caldwell 1863

The facts: A hall was let to the claimant for a series of concerts on specified dates. Before the date of the first concert the hall was accidentally destroyed by fire. The claimant sued the owner of the hall for damages for failure to let him have the use of the hall as agreed.

Decision: Destruction of the subject matter rendered the contract impossible to perform and discharged the defendant from his obligations under the contract.

3.2 Personal incapacity to perform a contract of personal service

The principle that a physical thing must be available applies equally to a person, if that person's presence is a **fundamental requirement**. Not every illness will discharge a contract of personal service – personal incapacity must be established.

Condor v Barron Knights 1966

The facts: The claimant, aged 16, contracted to perform as drummer in a pop group. His duties, when the group had work, were to play on every night of the week. He fell ill and his doctor advised that he should restrict his performances to four nights per week. The group terminated his contract.

Decision: A contract of personal service is based on the assumption that the employee's health will permit him to perform his duties. If that is not so the contract is discharged by frustration.

3.3 Government intervention

Government intervention is a common cause of frustration, particularly in time of **war**. If maintenance of the contract would impose upon the parties a contract fundamentally different from that which they made, the contract is discharged.

Metropolitan Water Board v Dick, Kerr & Co 1918

The facts: The defendants contracted in July 1914 to build a reservoir for the claimants within six years, subject to a proviso that the time should be extended if delays were caused by difficulties, impediments or obstructions. In February 1916 the Minister of Munitions ordered the defendants to cease work and sell all their plant.

Decision: The proviso in the contract did not cover such a substantial interference with the contract. The interruption was likely to cause the contract, if resumed, to be radically different from that contemplated by the parties. The contract was discharged.

3.4 Supervening illegality

In many cases of government intervention, further performance of the contract becomes **illegal** – for example the outbreak of war.

Avery v Bowden 1855

The facts: The defendant entered into a contract to charter a ship from the claimant to load grain at Odessa within a period of 45 days. The ship arrived at Odessa and the charterer told the claimant that he did not propose to load a cargo. The master remained at Odessa hoping the charterer would change his mind. Before the 45 days (for loading cargo) had expired, the outbreak of the Crimean war discharged the contract by frustration.

Decision: The contract was discharged by frustration (the outbreak of war) without liability for either party.

3.5 Non-occurrence of an event if it is the sole purpose of the contract

Two contrasting examples of application of this doctrine are given by the so-called **coronation cases**.

Krell v Henry 1903

The facts: A room belonging to the claimant and overlooking the route of the coronation procession of Edward VII was let for the day of the coronation for the purpose of viewing the procession. The coronation was postponed owing to the illness of the King. The owner of the rooms sued for the agreed fee, which was payable on the day of the coronation.

Decision: The contract was made for the sole purpose of viewing the procession. As that event did not occur the contract was frustrated.

Herne Bay Steamboat Co v Hutton 1903

The facts: A steamboat was hired for two days to carry passengers, for the purpose of viewing a naval review and for a day's cruise round the fleet. The review had been arranged as part of the coronation celebrations. The naval review was cancelled owing to the King's illness but the steamboat could have taken passengers for a trip round the assembled fleet.

Decision: The royal review of the fleet was not the sole occasion of the contract, and the contract was not discharged. The owner of the steamboat was entitled to the agreed hire charge less what he had earned from the normal use of the vessel over the two day period.

3.6 Exceptions

A contract is not discharged by frustration in the following circumstances.

(a) If an **alternative mode of performance** is possible.

> *Tsakiroglou & Co v Noblee and Thorl GmbH 1962*
>
> *The facts:* In October 1956 the sellers contracted to sell 300 tons of Sudanese groundnuts and transport them to Hamburg. The normal and intended method of shipment from Port Sudan (on the Red Sea coast) was by a ship routed through the Suez Canal to Hamburg. Before departure, the Suez Canal was closed. The sellers refused to ship the cargo arguing that it was an implied term that shipment should be via Suez or alternatively that shipment via the Cape of Good Hope would make the contract 'commercially and fundamentally' different, so that it was discharged by frustration.
>
> *Decision:* Both arguments failed. There was no evidence to support the implied term argument nor was the use of a different (although more expensive) route an alteration of the fundamental nature of the contract sufficient to discharge it by frustration.

(b) If performance becomes suddenly more **expensive**.
(c) If one party **has accepted the risk** that they will be unable to perform.
(d) If one party **has induced frustration** by their own choice between alternatives.

Having seen how a contract might be frustrated, we shall now look at what happens to **each party's obligations** once frustration has occurred.

3.7 The Law Reform (Frustrated Contracts) Act 1943

FAST FORWARD

The common law consequences of frustration are modified by the **Law Reform (Frustrated Contracts) Act 1943 (HMSO, 1943)**, which regulates the rights and obligations of the parties to a contract discharged by frustration.

Where a contract is frustrated, the **common law** provides that the occurrence of the frustrating event brings the contract automatically to an end. The consequences of this can be harsh.

> *Chandler v Webster 1904*
>
> *The facts:* The defendant agreed to let the claimant have a room for £141.15s for the purpose of viewing the coronation procession of Edward VII. The contract provided that the money was payable immediately. The coronation was postponed owing to the illness of the King. The claimant sued for the return of his £100 and the defendant counterclaimed for the unpaid amount of £41.15s.
>
> *Decision:* The obligation to pay rent had fallen due before the frustrating event. The claimant's action failed.

This case contrasts with *Krell v Henry 1903*, where the payment was due on the day of the procession.

> *Fibrosa v Fairbairn 1942*
>
> *The facts:* The claimant placed an order for machinery to be delivered in Poland. He paid £1,000 of the contract price of £4,800 with his order. Shortly afterwards the outbreak of the Second World War frustrated the contract since the German army occupied Poland. The claimant sued to recover the £1,000 which had been paid.
>
> *Decision:* The deposit was repayable since the claimant had received absolutely nothing for it – there had been a total failure of consideration.

PART A PRINCIPLES OF CONTRACT LAW

Exam focus point

Do not overlook the importance of statute law in the area of frustration.

In most cases now the **rights and liabilities of parties to a contract discharged by frustration** are regulated by the Law Reform (Frustrated Contracts) Act 1943 as follows.

(a) Any money paid under the contract by one party to the other is to be repaid. Any sums due for payment under the contract then or later cease to be payable.

(b) If a person has to repay money under (a), or if they must forego payment earned, they may be able (at the court's discretion) to recover or set off expenses incurred up to the time the contract was frustrated.

(c) If either party has obtained a valuable benefit (other than payment of money) under the contract before it is discharged, the court may in its discretion order them to pay to the other party all or part of that value.

Having seen how a contract may be discharged through agreement of the parties, or through a frustrating event, we shall now look at what happens when a party fails to perform their obligations. This is known as **breach of contract** and is the cause of many contractual disputes.

4 Breach of contract

FAST FORWARD

A party is said to be in breach of contract where, without **lawful excuse**, they do not perform their contractual obligations precisely.

A person sometimes has a **lawful excuse** not to perform contractual obligations, if:

- Performance is **impossible**, perhaps because of some unforeseeable event.
- They have tendered performance but this has been **rejected.**
- The **other party** has made it **impossible** for them to perform.
- The contract has been discharged through **frustration**.
- The parties have by **agreement** permitted **non-performance.**

Breach of contract gives rise to a secondary **obligation to pay damages** to the other party. However, the primary obligation to perform the contract's terms remains, unless the party in default has **repudiated** the contract. This may be before performance is due, or before it has been completed, and repudiation has been accepted by the injured party.

Key term

Repudiation can be defined as a breach of contract which entitles the injured party to end the contract if they so choose.

4.1 Repudiatory breach

FAST FORWARD

Breach of a **condition** in a contract or other repudiatory breach allows the injured party to **terminate** the contract unless the injured party elects to treat the contract as continuing and merely claim **damages** for their loss.

Key term

A **repudiatory breach** occurs where a party indicates, either by words or by conduct, that they do not intend to honour their contractual obligations or commits a breach of condition or commits a breach which has very serious consequences for the injured party. It usually occurs when performance is due.

It does not **automatically** discharge the contract – indeed the injured party has a choice.

- They can elect to treat the contract as repudiated by the other, **recover damages** and treat themselves as being discharged from their primary obligations under the contract.
- They can elect to **affirm** the contract.

4.1.1 Types of repudiatory breach

Repudiatory breach arises in the following circumstances.

(a) **Refusal to perform (renunciation).** One party renounces their contractual obligations by showing that they haves no intention to perform them: *Hochster v De la Tour 1853*.

(b) **Failure to perform an entire obligation.** An entire obligation is said to be one where complete and precise performance of it is a precondition of the other party's performance.

(c) **Incapacitation.** Where a party prevents themselves from performing their contractual obligations they are treated as if they refused to perform them. For instance, where A sells a thing to C even though they promised to sell it to B, they are in repudiatory breach of their contract with B.

(d) **Breach of condition** (a fundamental term of the contract).

(e) **Breach of an innominate term** (a term of the contract, the effect of which cannot be determined until the contract is breached) which has the effect of depriving the injured party of substantially the whole benefit of the contract.

4.1.2 Anticipatory breach

> **FAST FORWARD**
>
> If there is **anticipatory breach** (one party declares in advance that they will not perform their side of the bargain when the time for performance arrives) the other party may treat the contract as discharged forthwith, or continue with their obligations until actual breach occurs. Their claim for damages will then depend upon what they have actually lost.

Repudiation may be **explicit** or **implicit**. A party may break a condition of the contract merely by declaring in advance that they will not perform it, or by some other action which makes future performance impossible. The other party may treat this as **anticipatory breach**.

- Treat the contract as **discharged** forthwith
- At their option may **allow the contract to continue** until there is an actual breach

---

Hochster v De La Tour 1853

The facts: The defendant engaged the claimant as a courier to accompany him on a European tour commencing on 1 June. On 11 May he wrote to the claimant to say that he no longer required his services. On 22 May the claimant commenced legal proceedings for anticipatory breach of contract. The defendant objected that there was no actionable breach until 1 June.

Decision: The claimant was entitled to sue as soon as the anticipatory breach occurred on 11 May.

Where the injured party allows the contract to continue, it may happen that the parties are discharged from their obligations **without** liability by some other cause which occurs later.

If the innocent party elects to treat the contract as still in force, the former may continue with their preparations for performance and **recover the agreed price** for their services. Any claim for damages will be assessed on the basis of what the claimant has really lost.

> **White & Carter (Councils) v McGregor 1961**
>
> *The facts:* The claimants supplied litter bins to local councils, and were paid not by the councils but by traders who hired advertising space on the bins. The defendant contracted with them for advertising of his business. He then wrote to cancel the contract but the claimants elected to advertise as agreed, even though they had at the time of cancellation taken no steps to perform the contract. They performed the contract and claimed the agreed payment.
>
> *Decision:* The contract continued in force and they were entitled to recover the agreed price for their services. Repudiation does not, of itself, bring the contract to an end. It gives the innocent party the choice of affirmation or rejection.

> **The Mihalis Angelos 1971**
>
> *The facts:* The parties entered into an agreement for the charter of a ship to be 'ready to load at Haiphong' (in Vietnam) on 1 July 1965. The charterers had the option to cancel if the ship was not ready to load by 20 July. On 17 July the charterers repudiated the contract believing (wrongly) that they were entitled to do so. The shipowners accepted the repudiation and claimed damages. On 17 July the ship was still in Hong Kong and could not have reached Haiphong by 20 July.
>
> *Decision:* The shipowners were entitled only to nominal damages since they would have been unable to perform the contract and the charterers could have cancelled it without liability on 20 July.

4.1.3 Termination for repudiatory breach

To terminate for repudiatory breach the innocent party must **notify** the other of their decision. This may be by way of refusal to accept defects in performance, refusal to accept further performance, or refusal to perform their own obligations.

- They are not bound by their **future** or **continuing contractual obligations**, and cannot be sued on them.
- They need not **accept** nor pay for further performance.
- They can **refuse to pay** for partial or defective performance already received, unless the contract is severable.
- They can **reclaim money** paid to a defaulter if they can and do reject defective performance.
- They are **not discharged** from the contractual obligations which were due at the time of termination.

The innocent party can also claim **damages** from the defaulter. An innocent party who began to perform their contractual obligations but who was prevented from completing them by the defaulter can claim **reasonable** remuneration on a *quantum meruit* basis.

4.1.4 Affirmation after repudiatory breach

If a person is aware of the other party's repudiatory breach and of their own right to terminate the contract as a result but still decides to treat the contract as being in existence they are said to have **affirmed the contract**. The contract remains fully in force.

Point to note

> Anticipatory breach occurs before the time that performance is due. Repudiatory breach usually occurs at the time of performance.

3: DISCHARGE OF CONTRACT

If the terms of a contract are breached then the innocent party will look for a **remedy** to compensate them. As we shall see in the next few sections, **damages** is the main remedy under common law and is **monetary compensation**. There are rules concerning the circumstances where damages can be payable (**remoteness of damage**) and on the amount of damages payable (**measure of damages**). Parties may also include a term into the contract which determines how damages should be calculated and this is known as **liquidated damages**, however if the term can be viewed as a **penalty** then it will not be valid.

5 Damages

> **FAST FORWARD**
>
> **Damages** are a common law remedy intended to restore the party who has suffered loss to the position they would have been in if the contract had been performed. The two tests applied to a claim for damages relate to **remoteness of damage** and **measure of damages**.

Key term

> **Damages** are a common law remedy intended to restore the party who has suffered loss to the same position they would have been in if the contract had been performed. The two tests applied to a claim for damages relate to **remoteness of damage** and **measure of damages**.

Damages form the **main remedy** in actions for breach of contract, but there are others: injunctions and specific performance are the most important.

In a claim for damages the first issue is **remoteness of damage**. Here the courts consider how far down the sequence of cause and effect the consequences of breach should be traced before they should be ignored. Secondly, the court must decide how much money to award in respect of the breach and its relevant consequences. This is the **measure of damages**.

6 Remoteness of damage

> **FAST FORWARD**
>
> **Remoteness of damage** is tested by the **two limbs** of the rule in **Hadley v Baxendale 1854**.
> - The first part of the rule states that the **loss must arise either naturally from the breach** or in a manner which the parties may reasonably be supposed to have contemplated when making the contract.
> - The second part of the rule provides that a **loss outside the usual course of events** will only be compensated if the exceptional circumstances which caused it were within the defendant's **actual or constructive knowledge** when they made the contract.

Under the rule in *Hadley v Baxendale* damages may only be awarded in respect of loss as follows.

(a) (i) **The loss must arise naturally** from the breach.

    (ii) The loss must arise **in a manner which the parties may reasonably be supposed to have contemplated**, in making the contract, as the probable result of the breach of it.

(b) A loss outside the **natural course** of events will only be compensated if the exceptional circumstances are within the defendant's knowledge when they made the contract.

> **Hadley v Baxendale 1854**
>
> *The facts:* The claimants owned a mill at Gloucester whose main crank shaft had broken. They made a contract with the defendant for the transport of the broken shaft to Greenwich to serve as a pattern for making a new shaft. Owing to neglect by the defendant, delivery was delayed and the mill was out of action for a longer period. The defendant did not know that the mill would be idle during this interval. He was merely aware that he had to transport a broken mill shaft. The claimants claimed for loss of profits of the mill during the period of delay.
>
> *Decision:* Although the failure of the carrier to perform the contract promptly was the direct cause of the stoppage of the mill for an unnecessarily long time, the claim must fail since the defendant did not know that the mill would be idle until the new shaft was delivered. Moreover it was not a natural consequence of delay in transport of a broken shaft that the mill would be out of action. The miller might have a spare.

The defendant is liable only if they knew of the **special circumstances** from which the abnormal consequence of breach could arise.

> **Victoria Laundry (Windsor) v Newman Industries 1949**
>
> *The facts:* The defendants contracted to sell a large boiler to the claimants 'for immediate use' in their business of launderers and dyers. Owing to an accident in dismantling the boiler at its previous site delivery was delayed. The defendants were aware of the nature of the claimants' business and had been informed that the claimants were most anxious to put the boiler into use in the shortest possible space of time. The claimants claimed damages for normal loss of profits for the period of delay and for loss of abnormal profits from losing 'highly lucrative' dyeing contracts to be undertaken if the boiler had been delivered on time.
>
> *Decision:* Damages for loss of normal profits were recoverable since in the circumstances failure to deliver major industrial equipment ordered for immediate use would be expected to prevent operation of the plant. The claim for loss of special profits failed because the defendants had no knowledge of the dyeing contracts.

Contrast this ruling with the case below.

> **The Heron II 1969**
>
> *The facts:* K entered into a contract with C for the shipment of a cargo of sugar belonging to C to Basra. He was aware that C were sugar merchants but he did not know that C intended to sell the cargo as soon as it reached Basra. The ship arrived nine days late and in that time the price of sugar on the market in Basra had fallen. C claimed damages for the loss due to the fall in market value.
>
> *Decision:* The claim succeeded. It is common knowledge that market values of commodities fluctuate so that delay might cause loss.

If the type of loss caused is not **too remote** the defendant may be liable for serious consequences.

> **H Parsons (Livestock) v Uttley Ingham 1978**
>
> *The facts:* There was a contract for the supply and installation of a large storage hopper to hold pig foods. Owing to negligence of the defendant supplier the ventilation cowl was left closed. The pig food went mouldy. Young pigs contracted a rare intestinal disease, from which 254 died. The pig farmer claimed damages for the value of the dead pigs and loss of profits from selling the pigs when mature.
>
> *Decision:* Some degree of illness of the pigs was to be expected as a natural consequence. Since illness was to be expected, death from illness was not too remote.

Question — Remoteness of damage

What is the two-limbed rule set out in Hadley v Baxendale?

Answer

1 The loss must arise naturally from the breach.
2 The loss must arise in a manner which the parties may reasonably be supposed to have contemplated when making the contract was made.

7 Measure of damages

FAST FORWARD

The **measure of damages** is that which will **compensate for the loss incurred**. It is not intended that the injured party should profit from a claim. Damages may be awarded for financial and non-financial loss.

As a general rule, the amount awarded as damages is what is needed to put the claimant in the position they would have achieved if the contract had been performed. This is sometimes referred to as protecting the **expectation interest** of the claimant.

A claimant may alternatively seek to have their **reliance interest** protected; this refers to the position they would have been in had they not relied on the contract. This compensates for wasted expenditure.

The onus is on the defendant to show that the expenditure would **not** have been recovered if the contract had been performed.

C & P Haulage v Middleton 1983

The facts: The claimants granted to the defendant a 6-month renewable licence to occupy premises as an engineering workshop. He incurred expenditure in doing up the premises, although the contract provided that he could not remove any fixtures he installed. He was ejected in breach of the licence agreement 10 weeks before the end of a 6-month term. He sued for damages.

Decision: The defendant could only recover nominal damages. He could not recover the cost of equipping the premises (as reliance loss) as he would not have been able to do so if the contract had been lawfully terminated.

If a contract is **speculative**, it may be unclear what profit might result.

Anglia Television Ltd v Reed 1972

The facts: The claimants engaged an actor to appear in a film they were making for television. He pulled out at the last moment and the project was abandoned. The claimants claimed the preparatory expenditure, such as hiring other actors and researching suitable locations.

Decision: Damages were awarded as claimed. It is impossible to tell whether an unmade film will be a success or a failure and, had the claimants claimed for loss of profits, they would not have succeeded.

The general principle is to compensate for **actual financial loss**.

PART A   PRINCIPLES OF CONTRACT LAW

> *Thompson Ltd v Robinson (Gunmakers) Ltd 1955*
>
> *The facts:* The defendants contracted to buy a Vanguard car from the claimants. They refused to take delivery and the claimants sued for loss of profit on the transaction. There was at the time a considerable excess of supply of such cars over demand for them and the claimants were unable to sell the car.
>
> *Decision:* The market price rule, which the defendants argued should be applied, was inappropriate in the current market as demand for such cars was so low as to effectively mean that no market for them existed. The seller had lost a sale and was entitled to the profit.

> *Charter v Sullivan 1957*
>
> *The facts:* The facts were the same as in the previous case, except that the sellers were able to sell every car obtained from the manufacturers.
>
> *Decision:* Only nominal damages were payable.

7.1 Market price rule

The measure of damages for breaches of contract for the sale of goods is usually made in relation to the **market price** of the goods. Where a seller fails to sell the goods, the buyer can go into the market and purchase **equivalent goods** instead. The seller would have to compensate the buyer for any additional cost the buyer incurred over the contract cost. The situation is reversed when the buyer fails to purchase the goods. The seller can sell the goods on the **open market** and recover any **loss of income** they incurred by having to sell the goods at a lower price than that they contracted to.

7.2 Non-financial loss

In some cases, damages have been recovered for **mental distress** where that is the main result of the breach. It is uncertain how far the courts will develop this concept. Contrast the cases below.

> *Jarvis v Swan Tours 1973*
>
> *The facts:* The claimant entered into a contract for holiday accommodation at a winter sports centre. What was provided was much inferior to the description given in the defendant's brochure. Damages on the basis of financial loss only were assessed at £32.
>
> *Decision:* The damages should be increased to £125 to compensate for disappointment and distress because the principle purpose of the contract was the giving of pleasure.

> *Alexander v Rolls Royce Motor Cars Ltd 1995*
>
> *The facts:* The claimant sued for breach of contract to repair his Rolls Royce motor car and claimed damages for distress and inconvenience or loss of enjoyment of the car.
>
> *Decision:* Breach of contract to repair a car did not give rise to any liability for damages for distress, inconvenience or loss of enjoyment.

7.3 Cost of cure

Where there has been a breach and the claimant is seeking to be put in the position they would have been in if the contract had been performed, by seeking a sum of money to 'cure' the defect which constituted the breach, they may be denied the cost of cure if it is **wholly disproportionate** to the breach.

Ruxley Electronics and Construction Ltd v Forsyth 1995

The facts: A householder discovered that the swimming pool he had ordered to be built was shallower than specified. He sued the builder for damages, including the cost of demolition of the pool and construction of a new one. Despite its shortcomings, the pool as built was perfectly serviceable and safe to dive into.

Decision: The expenditure involved in rectifying the breach was out of all proportion to the benefit of such rectification. The claimant was awarded a small sum to cover loss of amenity.

7.4 Mitigation of loss

In assessing the amount of damages it is assumed that the claimant will take any reasonable steps to reduce or **mitigate** their loss. The burden of proof is on the defendant to show that the claimant failed to take a reasonable opportunity of mitigation.

Payzu Ltd v Saunders 1919

The facts: The parties had entered into a contract for the supply of goods to be delivered and paid for by instalments. The claimants failed to pay for the first instalment when due, one month after delivery. The defendants declined to make further deliveries unless the claimants paid cash in advance with their orders. The claimants refused to accept delivery on those terms. The price of the goods rose, and they sued for breach of contract.

Decision: The seller had no right to repudiate the original contract. But the claimants should have mitigated their loss by accepting the seller's offer of delivery against cash payment. Damages were limited to the amount of their assumed loss if they had paid in advance, which was interest over the period of pre-payment.

The injured party is not required to take **discreditable** or **risky measures** to reduce their loss since these are not 'reasonable'.

Pilkington v Wood 1953

The facts: The claimant bought a house in Hampshire, having been advised by his solicitor that title was good. The following year, he decided to sell it. A purchaser was found but it was discovered that the house was not saleable at the agreed price, as the title was not good. The defendant was negligent in his investigation of title and was liable to pay damages of £2,000, being the difference between the market value of the house with good title and its market value with defective title. The defendant argued that the claimant should have mitigated his loss by taking action against the previous vendor for conveying a defective title.

Decision: This would have involved complicated litigation and it was not clear that he would have succeeded. The claimant was under no duty to embark on such a hazardous venture 'to protect his solicitor from the consequences of his own carelessness'.

Question — Measure of damages

Chana agrees to buy a car from Mike's Motors for £6,000. Mike paid £5,500 for the car. On the agreed day, Chana arrives at the dealers but refuses to accept or pay for the car. In the meantime, the car's market value has risen to £7,000. The following week Mike sells the car for £7,500. Mike claims against Chana for damages. How much is he likely to be awarded?

> **Answer**
>
> He is likely to be awarded nominal damages only, as he has incurred no loss.

8 Liquidated damages and penalty clauses

FAST FORWARD
> To avoid later complicated calculations of loss, or disputes over damages payable, the parties may include up-front in their contract a formula (**liquidated damages**) for determining the damages payable for breach.

Key term
> **Liquidated damages** can be defined as 'a fixed or ascertainable sum agreed by the parties at the time of contracting, payable in the event of a breach, for example, an amount payable per day for failure to complete a building. If they are a genuine attempt to pre-estimate the likely loss the court will enforce payment.'

> *Dunlop Pneumatic Tyre Co Ltd v New Garage & Motor Co Ltd 1915*
>
> *The facts:* The contract (for the sale of tyres to a garage) imposed a minimum retail price. The contract provided that £5 per tyre should be paid by the buyer if he resold at less than the prescribed retail price or in four other possible cases of breach of contract. He did sell at a lower price and argued that £5 per tyre was a 'penalty' and not a genuine pre-estimate of loss.
>
> *Decision:* As a general rule when a fixed amount is to be paid as damages for breaches of different kinds, some more serious in their consequences than others, that is not a genuine pre-estimate of loss and so it is void as a 'penalty'. In this case the formula was an honest attempt to agree on liquidated damages and would be upheld.

> *Ford Motor Co (England) Ltd v Armstrong 1915*
>
> *The facts:* The defendant had undertaken not to sell the claimant's cars below list price, not to sell Ford cars to other dealers and not to exhibit any Ford cars without permission. A £250 penalty was payable for each breach as being the agreed damage which the claimant would sustain.
>
> *Decision:* Since the same sum was payable for different kinds of loss it was not a genuine pre-estimate of loss and was in the nature of a penalty. Unlike the *Dunlop* case the figure set was held to be excessive.

A contractual term designed as a **penalty clause** to discourage breach is void and not enforceable. Relief from penalty clauses is an example of the influence of equity in the law of contract, and has most frequently been seen in consumer credit cases.

Key term
> A **penalty clause** can be defined as 'a clause in a contract providing for a specified sum of money to be payable in the event of a subsequent breach. If its purpose is merely to deter a potential difficulty, it will be held void and the court will proceed to assess unliquidated damages.'

> *Bridge v Campbell Discount Co 1962*
>
> *The facts:* A clause in a hire purchase contract required the debtor to pay on termination both arrears of payments due before termination and an amount which, together with payments made and due before termination, amounted to two thirds of the HP price, and additionally to return the goods.
>
> *Decision:* This was a penalty clause and void since, in almost all circumstances, the creditor would receive on termination more than 100% of the value of the goods.

We have seen that if a clause for liquidated damages is included in the contract it should be highlighted as an **onerous term.** In *Interfoto Picture Library Ltd v Stiletto Visual Programmes Ltd 1988* the defendants did not plead that the clause in question was a penalty clause and hence void, but it is probable that they could have done.

Having seen the rules on damages, we shall now look at a number of **other common law remedies** that are available to an innocent party in the event of a breach of contract.

9 Other common law remedies

9.1 Action for the price

FAST FORWARD

> A simple **action for the price** to recover the agreed sum should be brought if breach of contract is failure to pay the price. But property must have passed from seller to buyer, and complications arise where there is anticipatory breach.

If the breach of contract arises out of one party's **failure to pay the contractually agreed price** due under the contract, the creditor should bring a personal action against the debtor to recover that sum. This is a fairly straightforward procedure but is subject to two specific limitations.

The first is that the property must have passed to the buyer, unless the price has been agreed to be payable on a specific date.

Secondly, whilst the injured party may recover an **agreed sum** due at the time of an anticipatory breach, sums which become due after the anticipatory breach may not be recovered unless they affirm the contract.

Question — Action for the price

What are the two limitations on a creditor's right to bring an action for the price?

Answer

1. An action for the price may only be brought if property has passed (or price is payable on a specified date).
2. Sums which become due after an anticipatory breach may not be recovered unless the creditor has affirmed the contract.

PART A PRINCIPLES OF CONTRACT LAW

9.2 Quantum meruit

> **FAST FORWARD** A **quantum meruit** is a claim which is an alternative to damages. The injured party in a breach of a contract may claim the value of their work. The aim of such an award is to restore the claimant to the position they would have been in had the contract never been made. It is a **restitutory award**.

In particular situations, a claim may be made on a quantum meruit basis as an **alternative** to an action for damages for breach of contract.

Key term

> The phrase **quantum meruit** literally means **'how much it is worth'**. It is a measure of the value of contractual work which has been performed. The aim of such an award is to restore the claimant to the position they would have been in if the contract had never been made, and is therefore known as a **restitutory award**.

Quantum meruit is likely to be sought where **one party has already performed part of their obligations** and the other party then repudiates the contract.

> *De Barnardy v Harding 1853*
>
> *The facts:* The claimant agreed to advertise and sell tickets for the defendant, who was erecting stands for spectators to view the funeral of the Duke of Wellington. The defendant cancelled the arrangement without justification.
>
> *Decision:* The claimant might recover the value of services rendered.

In most cases, a quantum meruit claim is needed because the other party has unjustifiably prevented performance: *Planché v Colburn 1831*.

Because it is **restitutory**, a quantum meruit award is usually for a **smaller amount** than an award of damages. However where only **nominal damages** would be awarded (say because the claimant would not have been able to perform the contract anyway) a quantum meruit claim would still be available and would yield a **higher amount**.

As we saw in Chapter 1, the **law of equity** makes available a number of **other remedies** to an innocent party if remedies under common law are not adequate. Under equity, remedies are only available under the **discretion of the court** where damages are not deemed suitable.

10 Equitable remedies

10.1 Specific performance

> **FAST FORWARD** An order for **specific performance** is an equitable remedy. The party in breach is ordered to perform their side of the contract. Such an order is only made where damages are inadequate compensation, such as in a sale of land, and where actual consideration has passed.

The court may at its **discretion** give an equitable remedy by ordering the defendant to perform their part of the contract instead of letting them 'buy themselves out of it' by paying damages for breach.

Key term

> **Specific performance** can be defined as 'an order of the court directing a person to perform an obligation. It is an equitable remedy awarded at the discretion of the court when damages would not be an adequate remedy. Its principal use is in contracts for the sale of land but may also be used to compel a sale of shares or debentures. It will never be used in the case of employment or other contracts involving personal services.'

An order will be made for specific performance of a contract for the **sale of land** since the claimant may need the land for a particular purpose and would not be adequately compensated by damages for the loss of their bargain.

The order will **not** be made if it would require performance over a period of time and the court could not ensure that the defendant did comply fully with the order. Therefore specific performance is not ordered for contracts of **employment** or **personal service** nor usually for building contracts.

10.2 Injunction

> **FAST FORWARD**
>
> An **injunction** is a discretionary court order and an equitable remedy, requiring the defendant to observe a negative condition of a contract.

An injunction may be made to **enforce** a contract of **personal service** for which an order of specific performance would be refused.

Warner Bros Pictures Inc v Nelson 1937

The facts: The defendant (the film star Bette Davis) agreed to work for a year for the claimants and not during the year to work for any other producer nor 'to engage in any other occupation' without the consent of the claimants. She came to England during the year to work for a British film producer. The claimants sued for an injunction to restrain her from this work and she resisted arguing that if the restriction were enforced she must either work for them or abandon her livelihood.

Decision: The court would not make an injunction if it would have the result suggested by the defendant. But the claimants merely asked for an injunction to restrain her from working for a British film producer. This was one part of the restriction accepted by her under her contract and it was fair to hold her to it to that extent.

An injunction is limited to **enforcement** of **contract terms** which are in substance negative restraints.

Metropolitan Electric Supply Co v Ginder 1901

The facts: The defendant contracted to take all the electricity which he required from the claimants. They sued for an injunction to restrain him from obtaining electricity from another supplier.

Decision: The contract term (electricity only from the one supplier) implied a negative restriction (no supplies from any other source) and to that extent it could be enforced by injunction.

An injunction would **not** be made merely to **restrain** the defendant from acts inconsistent with their positive obligations.

Whitwood Chemical Co v Hardman 1891

The facts: The defendant agreed to give the whole of his time to his employers, the claimants. In fact he occasionally worked for others. The employers sued for an injunction to restrain him.

Decision: By his contract he merely stated what he would do. This did not imply an undertaking to abstain from doing other things.

10.2.1 Mareva or 'freezing' injunctions

The Mareva injunction is named from the case of *Mareva Compania Naviera SA v International Bulkcarriers SA 1975*, but it actually has **statutory effect**. If the claimant can convince the court that they have a good case and that there is a danger of the defendant's assets being exported or dissipated, they may be awarded an injunction which restricts the defendant's dealing with the assets.

10.3 Rescission

Strictly speaking the equitable right to **rescind** an agreement is not a remedy for breach of contract – it is a right which exists in certain circumstances, such as where a contract is **voidable**.

Rescinding a contract means that it is cancelled or rejected and the parties are restored to **their pre-contract condition**. Four conditions must be met.

- It **must be possible** for each party to be returned to the pre-contract condition *(restitutio in integrum)*.
- An **innocent third party** who has acquired rights in the subject matter of the contract will prevent the original transaction being rescinded.
- The right to rescission must be exercised within a **reasonable time** of it arising.
- Where a person **affirms** a contract expressly or by conduct it **may not then be rescinded**.

Exam focus point

> You may be asked for a general discussion of remedies for breach of contract. Alternatively, you may be asked whether a particular remedy, say specific performance, is appropriate in any given situation.

Chapter Roundup

- Contracts can be discharged through **agreement**, **frustration**, **performance** and **breach**.
- The obligations of the parties may also be discharged by **agreement**.
- If the parties to the contract assumed, at the time of the agreement, that certain underlying conditions would continue, the contract is discharged by **frustration** if these assumptions prove to be false. This is because the contract is fundamentally different in nature from the original agreement.
- The common law consequences of frustration are modified by the **Law Reform (Frustrated Contracts) Act 1943 (HMSO, 1943)**, which regulates the rights and obligations of the parties to a contract discharged by frustration.
- A party is said to be in breach of contract where, without **lawful excuse**, they do not perform their contractual obligations precisely.
- **Breach** of a **condition** in a contract or other repudiatory breach allows the injured party to **terminate** the contract unless the injured party elects to treat the contract as continuing and merely claim **damages** for their loss.
- If there is **anticipatory breach** (one party declares in advance that they will not perform their side of the bargain when the time for performance arrives) the other party may treat the contract as discharged forthwith, or continue with their obligations until actual breach occurs. Their claim for damages will then depend upon what they have actually lost.
- **Damages** are a common law remedy intended to restore the party who has suffered loss to the position they would have been in had the contract been performed. The two tests applied to a claim for damages relate to **remoteness of damage** and **measure of damages**.
- **Remoteness of damage** is tested by the **two limbs** of the rule in **Hadley v Baxendale 1854**.
  - The first part of the rule states that the **loss must arise either naturally from the breach** or in a manner which the parties may reasonably be supposed to have contemplated when making the contract.
  - The second part of the rule provides that a **loss outside the usual course of events** will only be compensated if the exceptional circumstances which caused it were within the defendant's **actual or constructive knowledge** when they made the contract.
- The **measure of damages** is that which will **compensate for the loss incurred**. It is not intended that the injured party should profit from a claim. Damages may be awarded for financial and non-financial loss.
- To avoid later complicated calculations of loss, or disputes over damages payable, the parties may include up-front in their contract a formula (**liquidated damages**) for determining the damages payable for breach.
- A simple **action for the price** to recover the agreed sum should be brought if breach of contract is failure to pay the price. But property must have passed from seller to buyer, and complications arise where there is anticipatory breach.
- A **quantum meruit** is a claim which is an alternative to damages. The injured party in a breach of a contract may claim the value of their work. The aim of such an award is to restore the claimant to the position they would have been in had the contract never been made. It is a **restitutory** award.
- An order for **specific performance** is an equitable remedy. The party in breach is ordered to perform their side of the contract. Such an order is only made where damages are inadequate compensation, such as in a sale of land, and where actual consideration has passed.
- An **injunction** is a discretionary court order and an equitable remedy, requiring the defendant to observe a negative conditions of a contract.

PART A   PRINCIPLES OF CONTRACT LAW

Quick Quiz

1   **Fill in the blanks** in the statements below, using the words in the box.

    (1) .... are a (2) .... remedy designed to restore the injured party to the position they would have been in had the contract been (3) ....

    A loss outside the natural course of events will only be compensated if the (4) .... circumstances are within the (5) ....'s knowledge at the time of making the contract.

    In assessing the amount of damage it is assumed that the (6) .... will (7) .... their loss.

    A contractual term designed as a (8) .... is (9) ....

• mitigate	• performed	• claimant
• penalty clause	• exceptional	• damages
• common law	• void	• defendant

2   **Fill in the blanks** in the statements below.

    When anticipatory breach occurs, the injured party has two options. These are

    (1) ....

    (2) ....

3   The amount awarded as damages is what is needed to put the claimant in the position they would have achieved if the contract had been performed. What interest is being protected here?

expectation
reliance

4   A court will never enforce a liquidated damages clause, as any attempt to discourage breach is void.

    True ☐
    False ☐

5   Are each of the following remedies based on (i) equity or (ii) common law?

    A   Quantum meruit
    B   Injunction
    C   Action for the price
    D   Rescission
    E   Specific performance

6   What four conditions must be met for rescission to be possible?

Answers to Quick Quiz

1. (1) damages (2) common law (3) performed
   (4) exceptional (5) defendant (6) claimant
   (7) mitigate (8) penalty clause (9) void

2. (1) Treat the contract as discharged forthwith
   (2) Allow the contract to continue until there is an actual breach

3. Expectation

4. False. Courts will enforce liquidated damages clauses if they are genuine.

5. A Common law
   B Equity
   C Common law
   D Equity
   E Equity

6. 1 It must be possible for each party to be returned to the pre-contract condition *(restitutio in integrum)*.
   2 An innocent third party who has acquired rights in the subject matter of the contract will prevent the original transaction being rescinded.
   3 The right to rescission must be exercised within a reasonable time of it arising.
   4 Where a person affirms a contract expressly or by conduct it may not then be rescinded.

PART A   PRINCIPLES OF CONTRACT LAW

End of chapter question

Frustration of contract

Eastham City Council organises a 'Victory Parade' to celebrate the expected success of the City's football team (Eastham FC) in the league this season. Fun Fairs Ltd is hired (at a cost of £5,000) to provide an open-top bus (decorated in Eastham FC's colours) for the team to ride through the streets on as part of the event.

Eastham FC win the league, but the day before the parade the train in which the team was travelling back from a match crashed and the majority of the players require several days of hospital treatment. Eastham City Council cancels the Victory Parade. Fun Fairs Ltd have delivered the open-top bus but the Council has not yet paid for it. The Leader of the Council seeks your advice on whether or not the Council can rely on the concept of frustration in relation to its contractual obligation to Fun Fairs Ltd.

Required

(a)   Explain what is meant by the concept of 'frustration of contract' and the different circumstances in which this concept can arise.   **(8 marks)**

(b)   Advise Eastham City Council as to whether the concept of frustration applies to its contract with Fun Fairs Ltd and the consequences that flow from this.   **(12 marks)**

(Total = 20 marks)

Vitiating factors in contract

Topic list	Syllabus reference
1 Misrepresentation	1.1
2 Mistake	1.1
3 Duress	1.1
4 Undue influence	1.1
5 Illegality	1.1

Introduction

We saw in Chapter 2 that even when the essential elements of a contract (agreement, intention and consideration) can be shown, the contract may not necessarily be valid (it may be '**vitiated**').

In this chapter we shall see that validity may also be affected by one of a number of **vitiating factors** which render the contract **void** or **voidable**. In such cases a variety of **remedies** may be available.

Misrepresentation (such as **fraud**) occurs at the point when a contract has not yet been formed, such as during the pre-contract negotiations.

We shall then look at **operative mistake** and its effect on a purported contract, before looking at the consequences of there having been **duress** or **undue influence** on one party by the other. Finally, we shall consider certain types of **illegal contract**.

PART A PRINCIPLES OF CONTRACT LAW

1 Misrepresentation

FAST FORWARD

A misrepresentation is a statement of fact, given **before the contract is made**, which is **untrue** and is made by one party to the other in order to **induce** the latter to enter into the agreement. A contract entered into following a **misrepresentation** is **voidable** by the person to whom the misrepresentation was made.

1.1 Consent

Exam focus point

You may be asked for a general discussion of remedies for breach of contract. Alternatively, you may be asked whether a particular remedy, say specific performance, is appropriate in any given situation.

A contract will not be valid if either of the two parties did not genuinely consent to the contract. This may occur, for example, where one party makes a **misrepresentation** to the other in the course of negotiations.

Key terms

A **misrepresentation** is:

- A representation of **fact** which is **untrue**
- Made by one party to the other **before the contract is made**
- Which is an **inducement** to the party misled actually to enter into the contract

1.1.1 Representation of fact

In order to analyse whether a statement may be a **misrepresentation**, it is first of all necessary to decide whether it could have been a representation at all.

- A statement of **fact** is a representation.
- A statement of law, intention, opinion or mere 'sales talk' is not a representation.
- Silence does not usually constitute a representation.

Bisset v Wilkinson 1927

The facts: A vendor of land which both parties knew had not previously been grazed by sheep stated that it would support about 2,000 sheep. This proved to be untrue.

Decision: In the circumstances this was an honest statement of opinion as to the capacity of the farm, not a statement of fact.

Smith v Land and House Property Corporation 1884

The facts: A vendor of property described it as 'let to Mr Frederick Fleck (a most desirable tenant) at a rental of £400 per annum for 27½ years, thus offering a first-class investment'. In fact F had only paid part of the rent due in the previous six months by instalments after the due date and he had failed altogether to pay the most recent quarter's rent.

Decision: The description of F as a 'desirable tenant' was not a mere opinion but an implied assertion that nothing had occurred which could make F an undesirable tenant. As a statement of fact this was untrue.

A **statement of intention**, or a statement as to **future conduct**, is not actionable. If a person enters into a contract or takes steps relying on a representation, the fact that the representation is false entitles them to remedies at law. If they sue on a statement of intention they must show that the promise forms part of a valid contract if they are to gain any remedy.

1.1.2 Silence

As a general rule neither party is under any duty to disclose what they know, however:

(a) What is said must be **complete enough** to **avoid** giving a **misleading impression**.

(b) There is a **duty to correct an earlier statement** which was true when made but **which becomes untrue** before the contract is completed.

> *With v O'Flanagan 1936*
>
> *The facts:* At the start of negotiations in January a doctor, who wished to sell his practice, stated that it was worth £2,000 per year. Shortly afterwards he fell ill and as a result the practice was almost worthless by the time the sale was completed in May.
>
> *Decision:* The defendant's illness and inability to sustain the practice's value falsified the January representation. His silence when he should have corrected the earlier impression constituted misrepresentation. The sale was set aside.

(c) In contracts of **extreme good faith** (*uberrimae fidei*) there is a duty to disclose the material facts which one knows. Non-disclosure can lead to the contract being voidable for misrepresentation. For example:

- Contracts of **insurance**
- Contracts preliminary to **family arrangements**
- Contracts in relation to **sale of land** (in regard to defects in title)
- Contracts where there is a **fiduciary relationship**, such as between solicitor and client
- **Prospectuses inviting a subscription for shares** (in regard to statutory matters)

The person to whom a representation is made is entitled to rely on it without investigation, even if they are invited to make enquiries.

> *Redgrave v Hurd 1881*
>
> R told H that the income of his business was £300 per annum and produced to H papers which disclosed an income of £200 per annum. H queried the figure of £300 and R produced additional papers which R stated showed how the additional £100 per annum was obtained. H did not examine these papers which in fact showed only a very small amount of additional income. H entered into the contract but later discovered the true facts and he refused to complete the contract.
>
> *Decision:* H relied on R's statement and not on his own investigation. H had no duty to investigate the accuracy of R's statement and might rescind the contract.

1.1.3 Statement made by one party to another

Although, in general, a misrepresentation must have been made by the misrepresentor to the misrepresentee there are two exceptions to the rule.

- A misrepresentation can be made to the **public in general**, as where an advertisement contains a misleading representation.
- It is sufficient that the misrepresentor knows that the misrepresentation would be **passed on** to the relevant person.

1.1.4 Inducement to enter into the contract

A representation must have induced the person to enter into the contract.

- They knew of its existence.
- They allowed it to affect their judgement.
- They were unaware of its untruth.

If the claimant was not aware of the misrepresentation, their action will fail.

> *Horsfall v Thomas 1862*
>
> H made a gun to be sold to T and, in making it, concealed a defect in the breech by inserting a metal plug. T bought the gun without inspecting it. The gun exploded and T claimed that he had been misled into purchasing it by a misrepresentation (the metal plug) that it was sound.
>
> *Decision:* T had not inspected the gun at the time of purchase. Therefore the metal plug could not have been a misleading inducement because he was unaware of it, and did not rely on it when he entered into the contract.

Since to be actionable a representation must have induced the person to enter into the contract, it follows that they must have known of its existence, allowed it to affect their judgement and been unaware of its untruth.

The representation must have been one of the factors which influenced the other party in their decision to enter into the contract (*Redgrave v Hurd 1881*), but it need not have been the only inducement (*Edgington v Fitzmaurice 1885*).

In *Peekay Intermark Ltd v Australia and New Zealand Banking Group Ltd 2005,* during a telephone call a regular customer was given information that was a misrepresentation. The court held they could claim for this even though they subsequently signed a contract with different terms, which they did not read.

1.2 Fraud and other types of misrepresentation

FAST FORWARD

Fraudulent misrepresentation is a statement made knowing it to be untrue, not believing it to be true or careless whether it be true or false. **Negligent misrepresentation** is a statement made in the belief that it is true but without reasonable grounds for that belief. **Innocent misrepresentation**, the residual category, is any statement made in the belief that it is true and with reasonable grounds for that belief.

Misrepresentation is classified for the purpose of determining what remedies are available as follows.

- **Fraud** or **fraudulent misrepresentation** – a statement made with knowledge that it is untrue, or without believing it to be true or careless whether it is true or false.

- **Negligent** – a statement made in the belief that it is true but without reasonable grounds for that belief.

- **Innocent** – a statement made in the belief that it is true and with reasonable grounds for that belief. It is a misrepresentation made without fault.

The **Misrepresentation Act 1967 (HMSO 1967)** provides the same remedy (damages) for a victim of non-fraudulent (ie negligent or innocent) representation as for a victim of fraudulent misrepresentation. The representor will escape liability if they can prove that they have reasonable grounds to believe that the facts represented were true.

> *Howard Marine and Dredging Co Ltd v A Ogden & Sons (Excavations) Ltd 1978*
>
> *The facts:* The defendants required two barges for use in an excavation contract. During negotiations with the claimants, the claimant's marine manager stated that the payload of two suitable barges was 1,600 tonnes. This was based on figures given by Lloyds Register, which turned out to be in error. The payload was only 1,055 tonnes. The defendants stopped paying the hire charges and were sued. They counterclaimed for damages at common law and under the Misrepresentation Act 1967.
>
> *Decision:* The court was unable to decide on whether there was a duty of care (in the common law action), but the claimants had not discharged the burden of proof under the Act, as shipping documents in their possession disclosed the real capacity.

Misrepresentation can give rise to **criminal liability** if it comes under the scope of the Trades Description Act 1968.

1.3 Remedies for misrepresentation

There is a fundamental principle that the effect of a misrepresentation is to make a contract **voidable** and not void. The contract remains valid unless set aside by the representee. This means that the representee may choose either to **affirm** the contract (incorporating the misrepresented terms into the contract) or to **rescind** it.

Key term

> **Rescission** can be defined as the act of repudiating or avoiding a contract which, for example, has been induced by misrepresentation or undue influence. It is not available if there has been undue delay, if the innocent party has affirmed the contract, or if the parties cannot be restored to their original positions.
>
> Rescission entails setting the contract aside as if it had never been made. It is an equitable remedy that courts may not apply it if would be unfair.

1.3.1 Rescission

A contract is rescinded if the misrepresentee makes it clear that they refuse to be bound by its provisions – it is then terminated from the beginning (*'ab initio'*). The misrepresentee must rescind the contract **reasonably promptly** after they discovered (or should have discovered) the misrepresentation.

The misrepresenteee must **communicate their decision to rescind** to the misrepresentor, but there are two exceptions to this.

- If property has been delivered to the misrepresentor as a result of the misrepresentation, it is enough simply to take the property back again.
- If the misrepresentor disappears, the representee may announce their intention to rescind by some act that is reasonable in the circumstances.

The misrepresentee may alternatively **affirm** the contract.

- Declare their intention to proceed with it
- Perform some act from which such an intention may reasonably be inferred

> *Car & Universal Finance Co Ltd v Caldwell 1965*
>
> *The facts:* A car was purchased from the defendant by a rogue with a fraudulent cheque. The seller was unable to communicate with the rogue, but informed the police and the AA of the fraud. The rogue had resold the car. (The rogue had fraudulently misrepresented that the cheque would be honoured.)
>
> *Decision:* The seller had rescinded the contract by taking all reasonable steps and the rogue did not transfer good title to the claimants in a subsequent sale.

Question: Rescission

In many cases, rescission is simply effected when the misrepresentee makes it clear that they refuse to be bound by the contract. When may it be advantageous to bring legal proceedings for an order of rescission?

Answer

Legal action may be desirable if the fraudulent party ignores the cancellation of the contract and fails to return what they have obtained under it. It may be necessary for a formal document, such as a lease, to be set aside by court order. There might also be a possibility that innocent third parties may act on the assumption that the contract still exists.

1.3.2 Damages

In some instances, there may be a right to **damages**, either instead of, or in addition to, the remedy of **rescission**. The available remedies vary depending on the type of misrepresentation.

The right to damages depends on showing that the statement made by the representor is either **fraudulent** or **negligent**.

In a case of **fraudulent misrepresentation** the party misled may, in addition to, or instead of, rescinding the contract, recover damages for any loss by a common law action for the **tort of deceit**.

Under the **Misrepresentation Act 1967 (HMSO, 1967)** the court may, in the case of negligent or innocent misrepresentation, award damages instead of rescission as follows.

(a) **Negligent misrepresentation**

An injured party may claim damages for **loss** caused by negligent misrepresentation. It is then up to the party who made the statement to prove that they had **reasonable grounds** for making it and that it was not negligent.

(b) **Innocent misrepresentation**

In the case of **innocent misrepresentation** the remedy of damages is discretionary. An indemnity may be awarded, indemnifying the misrepresentee against any obligations created by the contract. The misrepresentee may of course choose instead to rescind the contract and refuse to perform their obligations.

Having looked at misrepresentation, we shall now turn to the other vitiating factors, beginning with mistake.

2 Mistake

FAST FORWARD

The general rule is that a party to a contract is not discharged from their obligations because they are mistaken as to the terms of the contract or the relevant circumstances. Exceptional circumstances of 'operative mistake' may render the contract void, being common, mutual and unilateral mistake.

There are three types of **mistake** in contract law, and it is important that you understand each of them as they have different effects on the validity of the contract.

2.1 Operative mistake

Key terms

Operative mistake is usually classified as follows.

- **Common mistake** – there is complete agreement between the parties but both are equally mistaken as to some fundamental point.
- **Mutual mistake** – each believes that the other agrees with them and does not realise that there is a misunderstanding.
- **Unilateral mistake** – one party is mistaken and the other (who may have induced the mistake) is aware of it.

The basic principles of operative mistake are rules of common law. A key point is that the mistake, to be recognised at law, must exist at the time that the contract is formed.

Amalgamated Investments and Property Co Ltd v John Walker & Sons Ltd 1976

The facts: The claimants were buying a property from the defendants. In response to pre-contract enquiries, the defendants replied on 14 August that the property was not designated as a building of special historical interest. Neither party was aware that the Department of the Environment was planning to list the building. On 25 September a contract was signed. On 26 September the defendants were informed that the building was to be listed; this took effect from 27 September. The result was that the building was worth £210,000 instead of the contract price of £1.71 million. The claimants sought rescission of the contract on the grounds of common mistake.

Decision: The critical date was the date of the contract. At that date there was no mistake.

2.2 Common mistake

2.2.1 Res extincta

If the parties make a contract relating to subject matter which, unknown to them both, does not exist, or which has ceased to exist, there is no contract between them.

Couturier v Hastie 1852

The facts: A contract was made in London for the sale of a cargo of corn thought to have been shipped from Salonika. Unknown to the parties the cargo had already been sold by the master of the ship at Tunis since it had begun to rot. The London purchaser repudiated the contract and the agent who had sold the corn to him was sued.

Decision: The claim against the agent failed. The corn was not in existence when the contract was made.

2.2.2 Res sua

The rule on non-existent subject matter (res extincta) has been extended to the infrequent cases where a person buys what already belongs to them (res sua).

Cochrane v Willis 1865

The facts: Under a family settlement A would inherit property on the death of his brother B. B had become bankrupt in Calcutta and, to save the property from sale to a third party, A agreed with B's trustee in bankruptcy in England, to purchase the property from B's bankrupt estate. Unknown to A and B's trustee, B had already died in Calcutta and so the property had passed to A by inheritance before they bought it.

Decision: The contract was void and A was not liable to pay the agreed contract price.

The leading case on both parties being equally mistaken on some fundamental point left open the question as to whether common mistake could be extended any further.

> *Bell v Lever Bros 1932*
>
> *The facts:* L, the controlling shareholder of a Nigerian company, appointed B to be the managing director. Before five years had elapsed, B became redundant owing to a merger and L negotiated with B for the cancellation of his service agreement on payment to B of £30,000. Later L discovered that while serving as managing director, B had used inside information to trade in cocoa on his own account. This was serious misconduct for which B might have been summarily dismissed. B was said to have forgotten the
>
> significance of his past conduct in negotiating the cancellation of his service agreement and it was treated as a case of common mistake. L's claim to recover £30,000 from B was that the service agreement for which L had paid £30,000 was in fact valueless to B, since he could have been dismissed without compensation.
>
> *Decision:* L's claim may have been correct in its theoretical basis but there was not a sufficiently fundamental mistake as to the 'quality' of the subject matter.

Common mistake resulting in a contract being void from the beginning was upheld in the following case.

> *Associated Japanese Bank (International) v Credit du Nord SA 1988*
>
> *The facts:* A rogue entered into a sale and leaseback agreement with the claimant to fund the purchase of four machines. The defendant guaranteed the transaction as a leasing agreement. The claimant advanced £1m to the rogue, who made one quarterly repayment before being arrested for fraud, and adjudged bankrupt. The machines did not exist, and so the claimant sued to enforce the guarantee. The defendant claimed the contract was void for common or mutual mistake since the non-existence of the machines made the subject of the contract essentially different.
>
> *Decision:* The non-existence of the machines in the principal contract (the lease) on which the secondary contract (the guarantee) relied was so fundamental as to render the subject-matter essentially different. Hence there was common mistake – the guarantee was void and could not be enforced.

2.3 Mutual mistake

If the parties are at cross-purposes without either realising it, the terms of the contract usually resolve the misunderstanding in favour of one or the other.

> *Tamplin v James 1880*
>
> *The facts:* J went to an auction to bid for a public house. J believed that the property for sale included a field which had been occupied by the publican. The sale particulars, which J did not inspect, made it clear that the field was not included. J was the successful bidder but when he realised his mistake refused to proceed with the purchase.
>
> *Decision:* J was bound to pay the price which he had bid for the property described in the particulars of sale. The contract was quite clear and his mistake did not invalidate it.

The parties may have failed to reach any agreement at all if the terms of the contract fail to identify the subject matter. Such a mistake renders the contract void.

Raffles v Wichelhaus 1864

The facts: A and B agreed in London on the sale from A to B of a cargo of cotton to arrive 'Ex Peerless from Bombay'. There were in fact two ships named Peerless with a cargo of cotton from Bombay; one sailed in October and the other in December. B intended the contract to refer to the October sailing and A to the December one.

Decision: As a preliminary point B could show that there was an ambiguity and that he intended to refer to the October shipment. If the case had gone further the contract would have been void.

If each party is unaware that the other intends subject matter of a different quality they may perform their side of the contract according to their intention.

Smith v Hughes 1871

The facts: Oats were bought by sample. The buyer believed that they were old oats. The seller (who was unaware of the buyer's impression) was selling new oats which are less valuable. On discovering that they were new oats the buyer refused to complete the sale.

Decision: The contract was for the sale of 'oats' and the buyer's mistake as to a quality did not render the contract void. The seller was entitled to deliver and to receive payment for his oats.

Scriven Bros v Hindley & Co 1913

The facts: At an auction a buyer bid for two lots believing both to be hemp. In fact one lot was a mixed batch of hemp and tow. It was not normal practice to sell hemp and tow together and the sale particulars were confusing.

Decision: In the circumstances there was no agreement by which the buyer was bound to accept the mixed hemp and tow. The contract was therefore not binding.

2.4 Unilateral mistake

A unilateral mistake is usually the result of misrepresentation by one party. The party misled is entitled to rescind the contract for misrepresentation but it may then be too late to recover the goods. If, on the other hand, the contract is void for mistake at the outset, no title passes to the dishonest party and it may be possible for the party misled to recover their goods.

Most of the case law on this type of mistake is concerned with mistake of identity. A contract is only void for mistake by the seller about the buyer's identity if the seller intended to sell to someone different from the actual buyer.

The parties may negotiate the contract by correspondence without meeting face to face. If the buyer fraudulently adopts the identity of another person known to the seller the sale to the actual buyer is void.

Cundy v Lindsay 1878

The facts: Blenkarn wrote to C to order goods and signed the letter so that his name appeared to be 'Blenkiron & Co', a respectable firm known to C. The goods were consigned to Blenkiron & Co and Blenkarn re-sold the goods to L. C sued L for conversion to recover the value of the goods.

Decision: C intended to sell only to B & Co, and no title passed to Blenkarn. L was liable to C for the value of the goods.

But if the buyer fraudulently adopts the alias of a non-existent person who could not have been known to the seller, the contract is only voidable for misrepresentation.

> *King's Norton Metal Co v Edridge Merrett & Co 1897*
>
> *The facts:* The claimants received an order for goods from 'Hallam & Co', an alias assumed by a rogue called Wallis. The claimants had not heard of H & Co. On receiving the goods (consigned to H & Co), W re-sold them to the defendants and the claimants sued the defendants for the value of the goods.
>
> *Decision:* The claimants intended to sell to the writer of the letter, who was W trading as H & Co. There was a mistake as to the quality of creditworthiness, not as to identity. W acquired title to the goods and the defendants in turn acquired title before the contract between the claimants and W was rescinded by the claimants. The defendants were not accountable for the value of the goods.

2.4.1 Unilateral mistake: face-to-face transactions

When the parties meet face to face it is generally inferred that the seller intends to sell to the person whom they meet.

> *Phillips v Brooks 1919*
>
> *The facts:* A rogue entered a jeweller's shop, selected various items and proposed to pay by cheque. The jeweller replied that delivery must be delayed until the cheque had been cleared. The rogue then said that he was Sir George Bullough and the jeweller checked that the real Sir G. B. lived at the address given by the rogue. The rogue then asked to take a ring away with him and the jeweller accepted his cheque and allowed him to have it. The rogue pledged the ring to a pawnbroker, who was sued by the jeweller.
>
> *Decision:* The action must fail. The jeweller had intended to contract with the person in the shop. There was no mistake of identity which made the contract void but only a mistake as to the creditworthiness of the buyer. Good title had passed to the rogue until the contract was avoided.

> *Lewis v Averay 1972*
>
> *The facts:* Lewis agreed to sell his car to a rogue who gave the impression that he was the actor Richard Greene. The rogue paid with a bad cheque signed in the name R A Green and was allowed to take the car and documents when he produced a pass for Pinewood Studios with an official stamp.
>
> *Decision:* Lewis had contracted to sell the car to a rogue. The contract might be voidable for fraud but it was not void for mistake. Perusal of a pass was insufficient to demonstrate that he only wished to contract with the actor.

2.4.2 Mistakes over documents – non est factum

The law recognises the problems of a blind or illiterate person who signs a document which they cannot read. If it is not what they suppose, they may be able to repudiate it as not their deed (non est factum). The relief will not ordinarily be given to a person who merely failed to read what it was within their capacity to read and understand.

In the *Saunders* case described below the following conditions were laid down which must be satisfied in repudiating a signed document as non est factum:

- There must be a fundamental difference between the legal effect of the document signed and that which the person who signed it believed it to have and
- The mistake must have been made without carelessness on the part of the person who signs.

Saunders v Anglia Building Society 1971 (also known as Gallie v Lee)

The facts: Mrs Gallie agreed to help her nephew, Parkin, to raise money on the security of her house provided that she might continue to live in it until her death. Parkin arranged that Lee, a solicitor's clerk, should prepare the mortgage. Lee produced a document which was in fact a transfer of the house on sale to Lee. However, Lee told Mrs Gallie that the document was a deed of gift to Parkin and she signed it at a time when her spectacles were broken and she could not read. Lee paid nothing to Mrs Gallie or to Parkin. Mrs Gallie sought to repudiate the document as non est factum.

Decision: Mrs Gallie knew that she was transferring her house and her act in signing the document during a temporary inability to read amounted to carelessness. The claim to repudiate the transfer failed.

Foster v Mackinnon 1869

The facts: An elderly man of feeble sight was asked to sign a guarantee. He had done so before. The document put before him to sign was in fact a bill of exchange which he signed as acceptor. He repudiated it as non est factum.

Decision: The document signed was so different from what it was believed to be that a defence of non est factum could be available.

Lloyds Bank plc v Waterhouse 1990

The facts: The bank obtained a guarantee from a father as security for a loan to his son to buy a farm. It also took a charge over the farm. The father did not read the guarantee because he was illiterate (which he did not tell the bank) but he did enquire of the bank about the guarantee's terms. As a result he believed that he was guaranteeing only the loan for the farm. In fact he signed a guarantee securing all the son's indebtedness to the bank. The son defaulted and the bank called on the father's guarantee for that amount of the son's debts which was not repaid following the farm's sale.

Decision: The father had made adequate attempts to discover his liability by questioning the bank's employees. They had caused him to believe he was signing something other than he believed. This was a case of both non est factum and negligent misrepresentation.

2.5 Equitable reliefs for mistakes

2.5.1 Rescission

As you have seen, this is an equitable remedy which is available when a contract is voidable. A different type of relief – rectification – may be claimed when the document does not correctly express the common intention of the parties.

Joscelyne v Nissen 1970

The facts: J lived in the same house with his married daughter N. J agreed to transfer his car hire business to N and N undertook as part of the bargain to pay all the household expenses including the electricity, gas and coal bills due in respect of the part of the house occupied by J. The bargain, not amounting at that stage to a contract, was then expressed in a written agreement which made no reference to N's liability to pay the household bills.

Decision: J was entitled to have the written agreement rectified.

Key term

> **Rectification** can be defined as an equitable remedy whereby a court may correct a written document, which, by mistake, does not represent the real intentions of the parties.

2.6 Non-operative mistakes

Unless it is unfair, a party who has made a non-operative mistake must abide by their contract. Equity will sometimes impose a compromise on the parties:

> *Solle v Butcher 1950*
>
> *The facts:* Extensive improvements were made to what had been a rent-controlled flat. Both landlord and tenant believed that the flat had therefore ceased to be subject to rent control. It was let at a rent of £250 per annum. It was discovered that the flat was still subject to rent control. The tenant sought to recover the excess rent and the landlord to rescind the lease.
>
> *Decision:* The tenant should have the choice between a surrender of the lease and accepting a new lease at a controlled rent increased to make allowance for the landlord's improvements.

If A was aware of B's mistake but did not bring it about by misrepresentation, the court may refuse an order for specific performance since A is seeking to take unfair advantage of a mistake of the other party.

> *Webster v Cecil 1861*
>
> *The facts:* A was negotiating the purchase of property from B. A knew that B had refused an offer of £2,000. B however, wrote a letter to A offering to sell the property for £1,250. The court concluded that A knew that B wished to offer it at a price of £2,250. A sued for specific performance of the contract to purchase the land.
>
> *Decision:* The order for specific performance would not be made (for the reasons indicated above).

The next vitiating factor we shall consider is **duress**. This means that one party was effectively pressured into agreeing to the contract.

3 Duress

FAST FORWARD

> Duress (physical or economic) is fundamentally a threat. A person who has been induced to enter into a contract by duress is entitled to avoid it at common law. The contract is voidable at their option, because they have not given their genuine consent to its terms.

A person who has been induced to enter into a contract by duress is entitled to avoid it at common law – the contract is voidable at their option, because they have not given their genuine consent to its terms.

Key terms

> **Duress** is fundamentally a threat. This may be:
> - **Physical duress** – of physical violence, imprisonment or damage to people or to goods or business, or
> - **Economic duress** – when one party threatens to breach a contract if the other party does not submit.

The threat may be translated to actual violence etc, but duress may still be implied merely from the threat.

> *Cumming v Ince 1847*
>
> *The facts:* An elderly lady was induced to make a settlement of her property in favour of a relative by a threat of unlawful imprisonment in a mental home.
>
> *Decision:* The settlement would be set aside on account of duress. (Note that the principles of duress and undue influence are applied to gifts (as in this case) as well as to contracts).

Duress has been widened to include the concept of 'economic duress' in cases where, as a result of economic pressure, one party is forced into making a contract in such a way as to indicate that they do not consent to it.

> *North Ocean Shipping v Hyundai, The Atlantic Baron 1979*
>
> *The facts:* The parties had reached agreement on the purchase price of a ship. There was then a currency devaluation and the vendor claimed a 10% increase in price. The purchaser refused to pay. The vendor then stated that if the extra was not paid he would terminate the contract and amicable business relations would not continue. The purchaser then agreed to pay the increased price.
>
> *Decision:* The threat to terminate the contract and discontinue amicable business relations amounted to economic duress. The contract was therefore voidable.

> *Atlas Express Ltd v Kafco (Exporters and Distributors) Ltd 1989*
>
> *The facts:* K had a big order to fulfil with W for a supply of baskets. K negotiated with A that deliveries should be made at £7.50 each. This was confirmed by telex. Later A decided that £7.50 was not enough and drew up an updated 'agreement'. A's driver arrived at K's depot with the update and said that he would not collect goods unless K signed the update. K protested but was unable to speak to someone in charge at A. Being bound to supply to W, K signed under protest and continued to pay only the original agreed amount.
>
> *Decision:* A could not enforce the higher payment since consent had been obtained by economic duress – K would have suffered dire consequences if it had been unable to supply W.

Such threats can be termed 'illegitimate pressure'. Whether it is or not depends on the circumstances, but much depends on whether the person's will has been overcome to such an extent as to invalidate their consent. Obviously the doctrine does not prevent businessmen from taking a negotiating position – the courts must distinguish between usual commercial behaviour and unacceptable duress. The elements required for a court to establish economic duress, as opposed to acceptable negotiation of a contract, has taken place were set out by Lord Scarman in *Pau On v Lau Yiu Long 1980*. At issue is whether the person being coerced:

- Protested
- Could feasibly follow an alternate course of action
- Was independently advised to enter the agreement; and
- Quickly took steps to lawfully terminate the contract having entered into it.

The courts have shown themselves unwilling to introduce a concept of 'lawful act duress'.

> *CTN Cash and Carry Ltd v Gallaher Ltd 1994*
>
> *The facts:* The claimants purchased cigarettes wholesale from the defendants. The defendants made a delivery to the wrong warehouse (although this belonged to the claimants). They agreed to collect the consignment and re-deliver it, but the goods were stolen before this was possible. Each purchase constituted a separate sale under a separate credit contract. The defendants had a contractual right to withdraw the credit facilities, which they provided, at any time and for any reason. When the goods were stolen, they threatened to withdraw all credit facilities unless the claimants made full payment for the goods. The claimants paid, but later reclaimed the money arguing that they had paid under duress.
>
> *Decision:* Although the method of obtaining payment was questionable and 'unattractive', it did not amount to duress. The court was unwilling to introduce a concept of 'lawful act duress'.

Duress cases often arise where two parties have a contractual relationship and one of them obtains a promise of an additional payment of money from the other. The validity of this promise is determined according to whether or not duress was present, not according to whether consideration passed: *Williams v Roffey Bros & Nicholls (Contractors) Ltd 1990*.

Having seen how a party may be pressured into a contract through **duress**, we shall now look at the opposite situation. Where a party entered into a contract because they were **unfairly influenced** when making the agreement. Undue influence occurs where one party is in a **position of power** over the other who they persuade to enter into the contract against their own free will.

4 Undue influence

FAST FORWARD

> Undue influence may arise either where a relationship of trust and confidence exists (which gives rise to presumed undue influence) and one party exerts influence on the other party to a contract to the disadvantage of the weaker party or where there is actual wider influence. The contract is voidable at the option of the weaker party.

A contract (or a gift) is voidable if the party who made the contract or gift did so under the undue influence of another person (usually the other party to the transaction).

Key term

> **Undue influence** occurs where the free will to bargain is not possible.

To succeed in a claim for undue influence, the following must be shown.

- A relationship of trust and confidence existed (in some cases this is assumed).
- The weaker party did not exercise free judgement in making the contract.
- The resulting contract is to the manifest disadvantage of the weaker party and the obvious benefit of the stronger.
- The weaker party has sought to avoid the contract as soon as the undue influence ceased to affect them.

4.1 Presumed undue influence

When the parties stand in certain relationships the law presumes that one has undue influence over the other.

These relationships include the following in which the stronger party is mentioned first (this is not an exhaustive list).

- Parent and minor child (sometimes even if the child is an adult)
- Guardian and ward
- Trustee and beneficiary under the trust
- Religious adviser and disciple
- Doctor and patient
- Solicitor and client

Note that the following relationships are not presumed to be ones in which undue influence is exerted – although this assumption may of course be rebutted.

- Bank and customer
- Married couples/civil partners
- Brother and sister
- Employer and employee

Undue influence may be presumed where one party can show as a matter of fact that they maintained a relationship of great trust and confidence with the other, as has been established in cases where wives have been able to show the trust they placed in their husbands to deal with financial matters (*RBS v Etridge (No. 2) 2001*).

It is possible to argue that any other relationship in which one person places trust and confidence in another has given the latter the opportunity for undue influence. The courts will look at all the facts in ascertaining whether in a particular case undue influence has in fact been exercised.

Hodgson v Marks 1970

The facts: An elderly lady transferred her house to her lodger and allowed him to manage her affairs. He later sold the house.

Decision: Undue influence was to be inferred from the relationship and the benefits obtained by the lodger.

Williams v Bayley 1866

The facts: A bank official told an elderly man that the bank might prosecute his son for forgery and to avoid such action the father mortgaged property to the bank.

Decision: There is no presumption of undue influence in the relation of the bank and customer but it could be proved to exist (as it did in this case) by the relevant facts.

It is perfectly possible for a relationship to exist where one person places trust and confidence in another without a resulting contract being voidable for undue influence. It is only where the stronger person steps outside a fair and businesslike relationship and obtains a benefit from the abuse of trust that undue influence arises: *National Westminster Bank v Morgan 1985*.

4.2 Actual undue influence

An innocent party may also seek to have a contract set aside for undue influence where there is no presumption at all of undue influence, but there is evidence that power was unbalanced at the time the contract was formed.

4.3 Free judgement

If it appears that there is undue influence, the party who is deemed to have the influence may resist the attempt to set aside the contract by showing that the weaker party did in fact exercise a free judgement in making the contract. A person who has undue influence is presumed to have used it but this is rebuttable. In rebuttal it is usually necessary to show that the person, otherwise subject to undue influence, was advised by an independent adviser to whom the material facts were fully disclosed and that adequate consideration was given: *Inche Noriah v Shaik Ali bin Omar 1929*.

> *Lloyds Bank v Bundy 1975*
>
> *The facts:* On facts very like those of *Williams v Bayley* above (except that the son was in financial difficulty and the bank required additional security for its loan to him) a customer gave the bank a charge over his house.
>
> *Decision:* The bank could not itself give independent financial advice to a customer on a matter in which the bank was interested as a creditor. Since the bank had not arranged for the customer to have independent advice the charge in favour of the bank would be set aside.

However, there may be undue influence even where the defendant tries to rebut the presumption by showing that the claimant has refused independent advice.

> *Goldsworthy v Brickell 1987*
>
> *The facts:* G, an 85-year old man entered into an agreement to give tenancy of a farm to B, who had been helping him run it. The terms were highly favourable to B, but G had rejected opportunities to consult a solicitor. G sought for the agreement to be rescinded.
>
> *Decision:* Although there had been no domination (see *Morgan*'s case below), the fact that the agreement's terms were clearly unfair and that G placed trust in B meant that the presumption could not be rebutted by showing that free exercise of judgement was allowed. G could rescind.

4.4 Manifest disadvantage

A transaction will not be set aside on the ground of undue influence unless it can be shown that the transaction is to the manifest disadvantage of the person subjected to undue influence. The case below also demonstrates that a presumption of undue influence will not arise merely because a confidential relationship exists, provided that the person in whom confidence is placed keeps within the boundaries of a normal business relationship.

> *National Westminster Bank v Morgan 1985*
>
> *The facts:* A wife (W) signed a re-mortgage of the family home (owned jointly with her husband H) in favour of the bank, to prevent the original mortgagee from continuing with proceedings to repossess the home. The bank manager told her in good faith, but incorrectly, that the mortgage only secured liabilities in respect of the home. In fact, it covered all H's debts to the bank. W signed the mortgage at home, in the presence of the manager, and without taking independent advice. H and W fell into arrears with the payments and soon afterwards H died. At the time of his death, nothing was owed to the bank in respect of H's business liabilities. The bank sought possession, but W contended that she had only signed the mortgage because of undue influence from the bank and, therefore, it should be set aside.
>
> *Decision:* The House of Lords, reversing the Court of Appeal's decision, held that the manager had not crossed the line between explaining an ordinary business transaction and entering into a relationship in which he had a dominant influence. Furthermore, the transaction was not unfair to W. Therefore, the bank was not under a duty to ensure that W took independent advice. The order for possession was granted.

Despite the words 'dominant influence' in Lord Scarman's judgement in the *Morgan* case, the Court of Appeal stated subsequently in *Goldsworthy v Brickell 1987* (see above), in an apparent move away from the House of Lords position, that an influence stopping short of a dominant one may be sufficient to allow the court to set the contract aside on the basis of undue influence. Once trust has been shown to have existed, it is then necessary to demonstrate manifest disadvantage rather than that the position of trust has been abused and exercised as a dominating influence: *Woodstead Finance Ltd v Petrou 1986*.

The case below identifies what is and is not manifest disadvantage.

Bank of Credit and Commerce International v Aboody 1988

The facts: Mrs A purchased the family home in 1949 and it was registered in her sole name. Mr A ran a business in which his wife took no interest but in 1959 she became a director of his company on the understanding that she would have to do nothing. Between 1976 and 1980 she signed three guarantees and three mortgages over her house. Mr A deliberately concealed matters from his wife. The company collapsed due to Mr A's fraud and the bank sought to enforce the guarantees against Mr and Mrs A.

Decision: There had been actual undue influence over his wife by Mr A but Mrs A had suffered no manifest disadvantage since, at the time she signed the documents, her husband's business was comfortably supporting her and there was no indication that it would not continue to do so. She had benefited from the business which she secured and could not be said to have suffered manifest disadvantage in that sense.

4.5 Losing the right to rescission for undue influence

The right to rescind the contract (or gift) for undue influence is lost if there is delay in taking action after the influence has ceased to have effect.

Allcard v Skinner 1887

The facts: Under the influence of a clergyman, A entered a Protestant convent and in compliance with a vow of poverty transferred property worth about £7,000 to the order. After ten years A left the order and became a Roman Catholic. Six years later she demanded the return of the unexpended balance of her gift.

Decision: It was a clear case of undue influence since, among other things, the rules of the order forbade its members to seek advice from any outsider. But A's delay of six years (after leaving the order) in making her claim, debarred her from setting aside the gift and recovering her property. (This is an example of the equitable doctrine of 'laches' or delay).

The right to rescission is also lost if the party affirms the contract by performing obligations without protest, or if an innocent third party has acquired rights.

Having studied the first four vitiating factors, we shall now look at the final one. We shall see that some contracts can be **rendered unenforceable** because they are deemed **unlawful** or against **public policy**.

5 Illegality

FAST FORWARD

Certain categories of contract cannot be enforced in a court of law because they are unlawful in themselves or disapproved as contrary to public policy. All such contracts are void; some are also illegal.

Some types of contract, while validly formed, cannot be enforced in a court of law because they are **unlawful** in themselves or disapproved as **contrary to public policy**.

The following categories may be distinguished.

- Contracts which are **void at common law on the grounds of public policy**.
- Contracts which are **void at common law and illegal as contrary to public morals or the interests of the state**, including agreements to commit a crime or tort (such as assault or defrauding HM Revenue and Customs), contracts to promote sexual immorality or contracts to promote corruption in public life.
- Contracts **void by statute**, including restrictive trading agreements and resale price maintenance agreements.
- Contracts which are **void, illegal and prohibited by statute**, such as cartel agreements.

Since all such contracts are void, neither party can enforce them by legal action. In general, money paid or property transferred under a contract which is merely void may be recovered. If the void part can be separated from the other terms without rendering the agreement meaningless, then the remainder may be valid. But if the contract is also illegal the courts will not (subject to some exceptions) assist a party to recover their money or property. The rules on the consequences of illegal contracts are very involved and what follows is an outline only.

5.1 Effects of an illegal contract

If the contract is obviously illegal in its inception or if the contract appears to be legal but both parties intend to accomplish an illegal purpose by it, neither has an enforceable right at law against the other.

Pearce v Brooks 1866

The facts: The plaintiffs, who were coachbuilders, let a carriage described as 'of a somewhat intriguing nature' to a prostitute. They knew that she was a prostitute and the jury found (although they denied it) that they also knew that she intended to parade along the streets in the carriage as a means of soliciting clients and would pay for the carriage out of her immoral earnings. She failed to pay the agreed amount and they sued to recover it.

Decision: Although the letting of a carriage is not obviously unlawful, to do so to facilitate known immoral purposes is an illegal contract which will not be enforced.

If the contract is legal at its inception and one party later performs their side of it for illegal purposes, the other innocent party may recover money paid or property transferred or payment for services rendered (while in ignorance of the illegality).

Clay v Yates 1856

The facts: A printer agreed with an author to print copies of the author's book. The printer was unaware that the book contained libellous material. He discovered the libel after he had printed part of the book and refused to do any more. He claimed the value of work done (quantum meruit), but the author refused to pay for incomplete performance.

Decision: The printer was justified in ceasing work on the book and might recover payment for work done.

Chapter Roundup

- A misrepresentation is a statement of fact, given **before the contract is made**, which is **untrue** and is made by one party to the other in order to **induce** the latter to enter into the agreement. A contract entered into following a **misrepresentation** is **voidable** by the person to whom the misrepresentation was made.

- **Fraudulent misrepresentation** is a statement made knowing it to be untrue, not believing it to be true or careless whether it be true or false. **Negligent misrepresentation** is a statement made in the belief that it is true but without reasonable grounds for that belief. **Innocent misrepresentation**, the residual category, is any statement made in the belief that it is true and with reasonable grounds for that belief.

- The general rule is that a party to a contract is not discharged from their obligations because they are mistaken as to the terms of the contract or the relevant circumstances. Exceptional circumstances of 'operative mistake' may render the contract void, being common, mutual and unilateral mistake.

- Duress (physical or economic) is fundamentally a threat. A person who has been induced to enter into a contract by duress is entitled to avoid it at common law. The contract is voidable at their option, because they have not given their genuine consent to its terms.

- Undue influence may arise either where a relationship of trust and confidence exists (which gives rise to presumed undue influence) and one party exerts influence on the other party to a contract to the disadvantage of the weaker party or where there is actual wider influence. The contract is voidable at the option of the weaker party.

- Certain categories of contract cannot be enforced in a court of law because they are unlawful in themselves or disapproved as contrary to public policy. All such contracts are void; some are also illegal.

PART A   PRINCIPLES OF CONTRACT LAW

Quick Quiz

1. What is res sua?
2. What is the effect of a mistake concerning the qualities of the subject matter of a contract?
3. **Fill in the blanks** in the definition of misrepresentation below, using the words in the box.

    'A false (1) .... of fact made by one party to the other, (2) .... the contract is made, inducing the party misled to (3) .... the contract.'

• assertion	• before	• enter
• statement	• after	• terminate

4. What are the two categories of non-fraudulent misrepresentation?
5. How may the representee affirm a contract following a misrepresentation?
6. List four situations in which the right to rescind is lost.
7. What actions may constitute duress?
8. What four conditions must be demonstrated for a claim for undue influence to succeed?
9. Give three examples of relationships where a relationship of trust and confidence is assumed to exist.

Answers to Quick Quiz

1. When a person unwittingly buys something which already belongs to them.

2. The contract would remain valid.

3. (1) statement (2) before (3) enter

4. Negligent (ie reckless) and innocent (ie without fault).

5. By continuing to act under the contract after they are aware of the misrepresentation.

6.
    1. Party misled affirms the contract
    2. Pre-contractual position cannot be restored
    3. Rights of third parties prejudiced
    4. Lapse of time

7. A threat of physical violence, imprisonment, damage to goods or a business or intention of breach of contract.

8.
    1. A relationship of trust and confidence existed
    2. The weaker party did not exercise free judgement in making the contract
    3. The resulting contract is to the manifest disadvantage of the weaker party
    4. The weaker party sought to avoid the contract as soon as they were free of the undue influence.

9. Any 3 from:

    Parent and minor child

    Guardian and ward

    Trustee and beneficiary

    Religious advisor and follower

    Doctor and patient

    Solicitor and client

PART A PRINCIPLES OF CONTRACT LAW

End of chapter question

Misrepresentation

T.V. Diners Ltd owns a chain of restaurants. It wishes to buy out an existing restaurant in Oldbury in order to expand the business into this town. The company enters into negotiation with Bella, the owner of Ramshackle Restaurant, to purchase this property from her with a view to turning it into an outlet in the T.V. Diners chain.

During negotiations, Bella tells the representative from T.V. Diners Ltd, that 'Ramshackle Restaurant is licensed to sell alcohol and the local authority will allow this licence to pass to a new owner'. Whilst this was an accurate statement of local authority policy when Bella made it, she learnt prior to the completion of the sale that the policy had been changed and that the licence would not pass to a new owner. She did not inform T.V. Diners Ltd of this change in policy.

Bella's comments are not included in the provisions of the contract. After the sale of Ramshackle Restaurant was completed, T.V. Diners Ltd discovered the inaccuracy of this statement. T.V. Diners Ltd initially informs Bella that it remains happy with the purchase. However, two weeks later, and worried about annual profits, T.V. Diners Ltd seeks your advice on its legal position.

Required

(a) Advise T.V. Diners Ltd as to whether Bella's comments amount to an actionable misrepresentation under contract law. **(10 marks)**

(b) Advise T.V. Diners Ltd of the remedies available if Bella's comments are found to constitute an actionable misrepresentation. **(10 marks)**

(Total = 20 marks)

Tort law in the business and professional context

The law of torts

Topic list	Syllabus reference
1 The meaning of tort	1.2
2 Vicarious liability in tort	1.2
3 Strict liability in tort	1.2
4 Types of tort	1.2
5 Trespass	1.2
6 Nuisance	1.2
7 Defamation	1.2
8 Breach of statutory duty	1.2
9 The tort of negligence	1.2
10 Duty of care	1.2
11 Breach of duty of care	1.2
12 Causality and remoteness of damage	1.2
13 Defences to negligence	1.2
14 Negligent misstatement	1.2
15 Remedies in tort	1.2

Introduction

In the previous three chapters we saw how individuals and businesses can create **obligations** to each other through the use of **contracts**, and can have a **liability** to provide remedies to the other party if they fail to meet them.

In this chapter we introduce another source of liabilities, the law of torts. Torts are **wrongful acts** against an **individual**, a **company** or their **property** that gives rise to a **civil liability** against the person who committed them. In other words, one party can have a liability to another without any form of contractual agreement being in place. The source of the liability is an action by one party that had a negative impact on someone else.

There are a number of types of tort, including negligence, trespass, defamation, nuisance and breach of statutory duty. As an accountant, **negligence** is a key concern because a liability may be created if professional advice or work done is found to have been provided negligently, therefore this will be the main focus of the chapter.

Your syllabus requires you to understand the **nature** of torts and to explain the **factors** that must be present for claims to succeed. By focussing on the rules and their related **cases** you will be able to apply them to any case given to you in an exam question.

1 The meaning of tort

> **FAST FORWARD**
> The law gives various rights to persons. When such a right is infringed the wrongdoer is liable in **tort**.

We shall begin our study by looking at the meaning of tort. A tort is **distinguished** from other legal wrongs.

(a) It is **not** a **breach of contract**, where the obligation which is alleged to have been breached arose under an agreement between two parties.

(b) It is **not** a **crime**, where the object of proceedings is to punish the offender rather than compensate the victim.

Key terms

> A **tort** is a civil wrong and the person wronged sues in a **civil court** for compensation or an injunction. The claimant's claim generally is that they have suffered a loss such as personal injury at the hands of the defendant (the wrongdoer or tortfeasor) and that person should make remedy (normally by paying damages).
>
> **Tortfeasor**: a person who commits a tort.

In tort no previous transaction or contractual relationship need exist: the parties may be complete strangers, as when a motorist knocks down a pedestrian in the street. The claim in tort is based on the general law of duties and rights.

Several different kinds of tort exist, each dealing with different types of wrong. During the course of the last century the law of tort became centred on the tort of negligence, with claims in other torts being less common.

In this chapter we shall firstly consider **types of liability** that parties may be liable for. The two types of liability we shall look at are **vicarious liability** and **strict liability**. Once we understand how a party can be liable for a tort we shall move on to look at the various different types of tort.

2 Vicarious liability in tort

> **FAST FORWARD**
> An employer is liable for torts committed by their employees in the course of their employment. Vicarious liability may also arise for the torts of independent contractors in certain circumstances.

A tortfeasor (a party who has committed a tort) is always liable for their wrong, but others may be jointly and severally liable with them under the principle of **vicarious liability**. If, for example, a partner in a firm commits a tort either with the authority of the other partners or in the ordinary course of the firm's business, the other partners are liable with them.

Key term

> **Joint and several liability.** Where one person commits a tort, another person may be liable jointly with the tortfeasor, or even separately on their own if the tortfeasor has disappeared.

2.1 Vicarious liability and employment

The most important application of the principle of vicarious liability is to the **relationship of employer and employee**. It is often not worthwhile to sue the individual employee for damages since they are unable to pay them. The employer however has greater resources and may also have insurance cover.

To make the employer liable for a tort of the employee it is necessary that:

(a) There is the relationship between them of **employer and employee**; and
(b) The employee's tort is **committed in the course of their employment**.

The employee remains liable as a **joint tortfeasor** with the employer, and has an obligation to indemnify their employer where the latter has to pay damages. The employer's liability is 'strict', ie does not depend on proof of fault on the employer's part.

2.1.1 Torts committed in the course of employment

The employer is only liable for the employee's torts committed **in the course of employment**. Otherwise you could have the silly situation of an employer being liable for an employee's motorcycle accident while riding a private bike on holiday.

The law relating to whether an employee was acting in the course of their employment has recently been revised considerably by the following case:

Lister and ors v Hesley Hall Ltd 2001

The facts: The warden of a boarding school was found guilty of sexually abusing children resident there.

Decision: The school was vicariously liable. The nature of the warden's work created a sufficient connection between the acts of abuse which he had committed and the work which he was employed to do.

Obviously in this case the school did not employ the warden for the purposes of abusing the children. In that sense, he was not acting in the course of his employment when he carried out the abuse. However, the then House of Lords concluded that the acts that he carried out were so closely connected with the nature of his work, that it was fair and just to hold employer liable. In other words, he was employed to look after the children and the torts committed were in his work time, in the place where he was employed and while he was carrying out his employed duty to care for the children.

Even where the act complained of is committed while the employee is 'off-duty', the employer may still be held vicariously liable.

Ministry of Defence v Radcliffe 2009

The facts: Two soldiers asked an Army Captain whether they could jump off a bridge. The Captain gave them permission. The soldiers jumped and one was seriously injured.

Decision: Even though all three men were off-duty, the Captain could have ordered the soldiers not to jump. Military discipline and rank remained important even in an off-duty situation. The soldiers' reliance on the Captain's granting of permission made it fair and reasonable to impose a duty of care. The Ministry of Defence, as the Captain's employer, was vicariously liable.

Whether a 'close connection' between the employee's tort and their employment exists must be decided by the court on the facts of each case. Two further cases in which the test has been applied since the *Lister* case are:

Dubai Aluminium Co Ltd v Salaam and ors 2002

The facts: A, a solicitor, drafted bogus agreements.

Decision: The drafting of agreements of this nature (but for a proper purpose) would be within the ordinary course of business for a solicitor. Therefore the dishonest acts were sufficiently closely connected to the course of his business for his employers to be vicariously liable for those acts.

> *Attorney General v Hartwell 2004*
>
> *The facts:* A police constable in the British Virgin Islands was on duty when he went to a restaurant where his partner worked as a waitress. He fired several shots at his partner and her male companion. One shot hit a British tourist, who sustained serious injuries.
>
> *Decision:* The Privy Council found that the Attorney General (as the representative of the Government of the British Virgin Isles) was not vicariously liable for the personal injury sustained by the British tourist. The acts of the policeman were not closely connected to his employment, and in fact had nothing to do with his police duties. He was pursuing a personal vendetta.

2.2 Vicarious liability and agency

A principal is vicariously liable for a tort committed by an agent acting within the limits of their authority and carrying out the acts for which they were appointed as agent.

> *Ormrod v Crossville Motor Services 1953*
>
> *The facts:* A car owner asked a friend to drive his car to Monte Carlo where the owner was going to take part in a rally and then they were going to holiday together after the rally. The friend's negligent driving caused damage to the claimant's bus.
>
> *Decision:* The owner was vicariously liable for his friend's negligence. It was irrelevant that the friend was driving to Monte Carlo partly for his own purposes.

2.3 Vicarious liability and independent contractors

If someone works for someone else and is not an employee, they are likely to be described as an **independent contractor**. Normally the person who engages an independent contractor is not liable for the latter's tortious acts. Generally, independent contractors are liable for their own torts. For example a builder may engage casual workers, such as electricians and plumbers, to work on specific projects. Such individuals are likely to be liable for their own wrongful acts.

However, a person who has work done not by their employee but by an independent contractor, such as a freelance plumber used by a builder, is vicariously liable for torts of the contractor in the following circumstances.

(a) The operation creates a hazard for users of the highway, as in repair of a structure adjoining or overhanging a pavement or road.

(b) The operation is exceptionally risky.

> *Honeywill & Stein v Larkin Bros 1934*
>
> *The facts:* Decorators who had redecorated the interior of a cinema brought in a photographer to take pictures of their work. The photographer's magnesium flare set fire to the cinema.
>
> *Decision:* In commissioning an inherently risky operation through a contractor the decorators were liable for his negligence in causing the fire.

(c) The duty is personal. For example, an employer has a common law duty to their employees to take reasonable care in providing safe plant and a safe working system. If they employ a contractor they remain liable for any negligence of the latter in their work.

(d) There is negligence in selecting a contractor who is not competent to do the work entrusted to them.

(e) The operation is one for which there is strict liability (see below).

3 Strict liability in tort

FAST FORWARD The rule in *Rylands v Fletcher* defines a tort of strict liability, in which reasonable care is no defence. It covers the escape of anything brought onto the defendant's land and likely to do mischief if it escapes, but it does not cover things naturally on the land.

In many torts the defendant is liable because they acted intentionally or at least negligently. They may escape liability if they show that they acted with reasonable care. That is essentially the position in the tort of negligence itself, as we shall see later. But there are also torts which result from **breach of an absolute duty: the defendant is liable even though they took reasonable care**.

A significant example of a tort of strict liability is the rule in *Rylands v Fletcher*.

'Where a person who, for his own purposes, brings and keeps on land in his occupation anything likely to do mischief if it escapes, he must keep it in at his peril, and if he fails to do so he is liable for all damage naturally accruing from the escape.'

Rylands v Fletcher 1868

The facts: F employed competent contractors to construct a reservoir to store water for his mill. In their work the contractors uncovered old mine workings which appeared to be blocked with earth. They did no more to seal them off and it was accepted at the trial that there was no want of reasonable care on their part. When the reservoir was filled, the water burst through the workings and flooded the mine of R on adjoining land.

Decision: F was liable for the damage suffered by R, and the principle quoted above was laid down.

Many industrial processes entail the artificial ('non-natural') accumulation of water, gas or other materials which may cause damage if they escape. In such cases the occupier of the land is liable even if the escape occurs without negligence or want of care on their part. It has, however, been held in a more modern case (*British Celanese v Hunt 1969*) that not every escape of industrial materials gives rise to this strict liability. Industrial activities, as distinct from the accumulation of materials, can be a natural use of the land and so be outside the rule.

Polluters may be strictly liable for the tort of nuisance as we shall see shortly. However foreseeability of damage is required for there to be liability for nuisance.

Cambridge Water Co v Eastern Counties Leather plc 1994

The facts: The defendant, a firm involved in the tanning industry, stored organochlorines on its premises. The only foreseeable damage at the time was that someone working there might become overcome by fumes. The chemical seeped into the ground and a nearby public water supply borehole, over a mile away, became polluted. The claimant, who had to spend nearly £1 million developing a new source of supply to meet an EC directive on the quality of water, made claims in nuisance and based on the rule in *Rylands v Fletcher*.

Decision: the defendants were not liable. The claimants had a right to extract water from beneath their land and liability for interference with this right was strict. However, the then House of Lords decided unanimously that there could be no liability for unforeseeable damage.

It was argued in this case that the liability in *Rylands v Fletcher* is not intended to be any more strict than liability in nuisance. In *The Wagon Mound,* it was held that foreseeability of damage was essential for liability in nuisance. In addition, the language used in *Rylands v Fletcher* itself implies that damage must be foreseeable: 'anything likely to do mischief'. In giving judgement in the *Cambridge Water Co* case, the House of Lords made it clear that *Rylands v Fletcher* was broadly an extension of the principles of nuisance to cases of isolated escape from land. Thus the decision in *The Wagon Mound* should extend to determining whether there is liability in cases such as the *Cambridge Water Co* case.

The decision in the *Cambridge Water Co* case reduces the significance of *Rylands v Fletcher* and suggests that liability will in future be very close to 'ordinary' negligence liability, with foreseeability being a requirement.

Breach of statutory duty is also a strict liability tort.

4 Types of tort

> **FAST FORWARD** There are **five types of tort** that you need to be aware of.

Having seen what tort means and the types of liability we are now going to consider some examples of specific torts that might be committed. These are:

- Trespass
- Nuisance
- Defamation
- Breach of statutory duty
- Negligence

5 Trespass

> **FAST FORWARD** Trespass to land is the most common form of trespass. Claimants may seek damages, an injunction, or both.

Trespass is one of oldest torts and is committed when one party interferes with another's property or their person. It can therefore take the following forms.

(a) Trespass to land: unlawful interference with the possession of someone's land

(b) Trespass to goods: wrongful interference with a person's possession of goods, eg destroying or stealing them

(c) Trespass to the person: battery, assault and false imprisonment

5.1 Trespass to land

Trespass to land is one of the oldest actions known to the common law, and involves direct interference. No damage need be proved, as the interference itself is enough to establish liability. Being a wrong to possession rather than ownership, the claimant need not be the owner of the land. Thus a landlord cannot sue for trespass while a lease subsists. Deliberate entry to the land is sufficient, and it does not matter that the defendant did not know they were on the claimant's land, or believed the entry was authorised.

Actions in trespass and nuisance differ because nuisance normally requires proof of damage, and is concerned with consequential harm. (Nuisance is described below.) To take an example, it is trespass to throw stones onto somebody's land, but nuisance to allow a fence to become so dilapidated that it collapses on to land (*Mann v Saulnier 1959*). In *Southport Corporation v Esso Petroleum Co Ltd 1954* there was a question as to whether discharging oil into the sea, which was then carried to shore, amounted to trespass.

Trespass to land may take the following forms:

- Entering onto land
- Remaining on the land for longer than entitled
- Placing objects or rubbish on the land: *Westripp v Baldock 1938* (ladder against a wall)

- Abusing permission to be on the land: *Hickman v Maisey 1900* (racing tout watching racehorses in training)
- Driving animals on to land

Rights to possession of land extend to the subsoil beneath and the airspace above.

- Trespass in subsoil is limited to 300 metres by s 43 Infrastructure Act 2015 (TSO, 2015). This means that fracking for petroleum and geothermal energy can take place at a depth of more than 300m beneath any landowner's property without the landowner having any right to claim for trespass to their land.
- Trespass in airspace is limited to the height at which intrusion limits full use of the land *(Kelsen v Imperial Tobacco Co Ltd 1957)*. So it is not trespass to fly an aircraft over land at a reasonable height; Civil Aviation Act 1982 (HMSO, 1982).

5.1.1 Justification of trespass

Trespass to land may be justified in the following circumstances.

- After the granting of a licence to enter the land (eg to view a sporting event)
- Right of entry conferred by the owner
- Public right of way
- Statutory powers of entry (eg police powers)
- Necessity

5.1.2 Trespass ab initio

This is a special rule that applies where the defendant entered land under the authority of the law, but subsequently abuses that authority (eg police entering and seizing documents unlawfully: *Elias v Pasmore 1934*).

The rule is that the authority to enter, having been abused by the subsequent wrongful act, is cancelled retrospectively so that the exercise of the authority becomes actionable as a trespass. The claimant may recover damages for the entire trespass, and not merely the wrongful portion of it.

There are limits to the rule:

(a) It only applies to acts done in pursuance of an entry done under authority of the law.

(b) It only applies when the abuse amounts to a positive wrongful act, not an omission. In the *Six Carpenters' Case 1610*, where the carpenters refused to pay for bread and wine they had consumed at an inn, it was held that they were not trespassers ab initio.

(c) A lawful entry does not become a trespass ab initio unless the abuse takes away the entire grounds for the entry. Any independent grounds for entry which is unaffected by the abuse will protect it from the rule: *Chic Fashions (West Wales) Ltd v Jones 1968*.

5.1.3 Remedies to an action for trespass

The claimant may seek damages or an injunction or both. In the case of trivial trespass, damages are likely to be nominal, but where the trespass has caused physical damage, then damages are measured by diminution in value of the land.

A person who has been dispossessed may bring an action for ejection, or take it upon themselves to effect re-entry. They are entitled to use reasonable force to expel a trespasser if they have first asked them to leave.

5.2 Trespass to goods

Trespass to goods is a form of wrongful interference with goods (the other form being conversion). The law is covered by the Torts (Interference with Goods) Act 1977 (HMSO, 1977).

Key term

> **Trespass to goods** is the immediate and direct unauthorised interference with another individuals goods. This includes using, removing, touching or destroying another's goods, such as running a key along an individual's car and scratching the paintwork.

To prove trespass there must be intention on the part of the defendant to deliberately interfere with another's goods.

5.2.1 Remedies to an action for trespass to goods

If the defendant has committed wrongful interference with goods the following remedies are available to the claimant:

- Order for delivery of the goods and consequential damages
- Order for delivery of the goods where the defendant has the option of paying damages for the value of the goods

The most likely remedy to an individual whom has suffered a trespass to their goods would be damages, but where the goods have been detained following the claim the court may order delivery up of the goods.

5.2.2 Defences

There are two defences which can be used against a claim of wrongful interference with goods. They are as follows:

- **Consent**: if for example a car driver trespasses onto private land with their car and subsequently has their wheel clamped by the owner of the land, they cannot claim for wrongful interference with their vehicle. By trespassing on the land they are seen as consenting to the interference, that is the clamping.
- **Distress damage feasant**: in the case of a trespasser onto another's land, the owner of the land is entitled to seize and detain any property which the trespasser brought onto the land with them until the trespasser leaves or, if damage has been caused, until the trespasser pays for the damage caused.

5.3 Trespass to the person

Key term

> **Trespass to the person** is a wrong done to an individual, and can exist even if the victim suffers no physical harm. It consists of three separate trespasses to the person: assault, battery and false imprisonment.

All three are intentional torts that cannot be committed by accident, and while they are easily confused with crimes nevertheless they are civil wrongs actionable by one person against another in court (though the acts often result in a criminal action against the defendant as well). A person who is liable in tort for assault, battery or false imprisonment will not be punished but will instead be ordered to pay damages to the claimant.

5.3.1 Assault

Assault occurs when a person apprehends immediate and unlawful physical contact, that is being put in fear of physical attack whether or not the attack actually happens (though it must be capable of happening). Words may not be enough to create a liability unless they are accompanied by menacing or

threatening actions. For example, telling someone you will shoot them may not be classed as assault unless you are pointing a gun at them as well. The claimant does not have to prove the defendant intended to make physical contact, it is sufficient to prove that the claimant was in reasonable fear of it. Therefore pointing an unloaded gun constitutes assault even though there is no intention to cause injury.

5.3.2 Battery

Battery occurs when the physical contact that is apprehended in an assault actually takes place or is intended to take place, whether or not any injury or permanent damage is done.

The tortfeasor does not have to touch the claimant themself; throwing stones for instance is still battery. It can include non-violent acts such as the application of 'tone rinse' to a scalp – *Nash v Sheen 1953*. For liability to be created it is just the act that must be intentional – not the injury.

5.3.3 False imprisonment

False imprisonment occurs when there is unlawful restraint of a person which restricts that person's freedom of movement, whether by physical restraint or intimidation.

5.3.4 Defences

There are four defences which can be used against a claim of trespass to the person:

- **Consent**: If a person consents to being physically contacted, expressly or by implication from conduct, then no tort of battery exists. Thus patients are asked to sign a consent form before undergoing an operation, to protect the surgeon from a claim for battery.

- **Necessity**: A tortfeasor may be able to show it was necessary to act in the way they did, as where a doctor performs life-saving emergency surgery on an unconscious patient, who naturally cannot consent.

- **Self-defence**: This will only succeed if the force used was not excessive, being reasonable and necessary in the circumstances to prevent personal injury.

- **Defence of others**: A tortfeasor may argue that their actions were justified in order to assist a third party whom they reasonably believed was in immediate danger of being attacked, as where a parent or guardian is protecting a child.

In addition, in a claim for false imprisonment the tortfeasor may be able to claim that the claimant was restrained under legal authority or justification, or in the course of the tortfeasor exercising their legal rights or duties.

6 Nuisance

> **FAST FORWARD**
>
> Nuisance may be of two types – public and private. In private nuisance the central idea is that of continuous interference with the claimant's enjoyment of their property. Public nuisance does not require any 'invasion' of private land, rather the annoyance of the general public.

Nuisance is committed when one party interferes with another's enjoyment of their property. It can take one of two forms – public and private.

- In **private nuisance** the central idea is that of interference with the claimant's enjoyment of their property.

- **Public nuisance** does not require any 'invasion' of private land, rather the annoyance of the general public.

6.1 Private nuisance

Key term

> **Private nuisance** is unlawful interference with the claimant's use of their property or with their health and comfort or convenience.

Private nuisance often takes the form of emitting noise, smell or vibration – it is essentially an indirect form of interference. If A throws garden rubbish over the fence into B's garden that is trespass; if A burns their rubbish by a series of smoky bonfires which causes real discomfort to B, that may be private nuisance. Generally speaking, the interference must be continuous over a period of time.

6.1.1 What constitutes private nuisance?

It is important to note that private nuisance is **unlawful** interference. Many of the actions which constitute private nuisance are themselves lawful. It is only when they cause interference to such a degree as to be unreasonable that they become unlawful. Examples of interference which has been held to be unlawful are set out below.

(a) Physical damage to the claimant's land by flooding: *Sedleigh-Denfield v O'Callaghan 1940*.
(b) Encroachment onto the claimant's land by tree roots: *Davey v Harrow Corporation 1958*.
(c) Interference with the comfort of the claimant through smell: *Bone v Seal 1975*.

In private nuisance cases it is often necessary to strike a balance between the convenience and interests of two parties which conflict. The following factors may enter into the decision.

(a) If the activity causes significant physical damage to property it will generally be restrained as private nuisance. If it merely causes personal discomfort the advantages and disadvantages may be balanced to determine whether the activity complained of is so unreasonable as to amount to nuisance.

(b) Causing intentional discomfort to a neighbour is very likely to be restrained as unreasonable.

Christie v Davey 1893

The facts: C and D occupied adjoining semi-detached houses with a common party wall. D objected to the sounds of C's activities as a music teacher, so he made very loud noises, shouting and banging metal trays.

Decision: C's music lessons were a reasonable use of her house. D's deliberate racket, made purely to annoy, was unreasonable. D was restrained from this conduct by means of an injunction.

Where the claimant can establish actual physical damage to land or property, they are not normally required to show an additional element of interference.

St Helens Smelting Co v Tipping 1865

The facts: Fumes from a copper smelting works damaged shrubs belonging to the claimant, who lived on an estate in a manufacturing area.

Decision: Although locality was an important consideration where nuisance takes the form of interference with the occupier's comfort and enjoyment (one should not expect to breathe the clean air of the Lake District in an industrial town such as St Helens), the nature of the locality is irrelevant where the nuisance causes physical damage to property. An occupier is entitled to protection from physical damage wherever they live.

Where there is no element of physical damage, and the alleged nuisance consists of interference with the occupier's comfort and convenience, it is for the courts to balance the conflicting interests of claimant and defendant. The test has been stated to be whether the interference is an 'inconvenience materially interfering with the ordinary comfort physically of human existence, not merely according to elegant or dainty modes and habits of living, but according to plain and sober and simple notions among the English people': *Walter v Selfe 1851*.

Halsey v Esso Petroleum Co Ltd 1961

The facts: The defendant operated an oil depot. The claimant lived nearby. Acid damaged clothing hanging out to dry in his garden and the paintwork of his car parked on the highway. Noise from the depot's boilers and from oil tankers arriving and departing during the night interfered with his sleep.

Decision: The defendants were liable for private nuisance for the damage to clothes and the noise from the depot. (They were also liable for public nuisance for the damage to the motor vehicle and the noise of the oil tankers.)

By contrast in *Hunter and Others v Canary Wharf Ltd 1997* it was held that a landlord was generally entitled to build on their land as they wished and, accordingly, would not be liable in nuisance because a large building they had erected had interfered with television reception.

If the claimant or the claimant's property has some abnormal sensitivity, they will be unable to restrain an interference from which a person of normal sensitivity would not require protection.

Robinson v Kilvert 1889

The facts: The claimant manufactured brown paper on his premises, which were situated directly above the defendant's premises. Heat from the defendant's manufacturing process damaged the brown paper, which was sensitive to heat. Ordinary paper would not have been affected.

Decision: The defendant was not liable, because his action was lawful and the claimant was carrying on an exceptionally delicate operation.

As noted above (*Christie v Davey 1893*) actions motivated by malice may constitute nuisance although it is not a prerequisite, rather a factor in considering reasonableness. Even in the case of the claimant's abnormal sensitivity, malice may tip the balance towards the defendant's conduct being unreasonable.

Hollywood Silver Fox Farm Ltd v Emmett 1936

The facts: The claimants bred silver foxes, which become very nervous during their breeding season and may, if disturbed, devour their own young. The defendant discharged guns on his own land in order to interfere with the foxes' breeding.

Decision: The defendant was liable – he had been motivated by the malicious intention of causing damage. His argument that the noise was no more than a reasonable landowner might create during the course of shooting failed.

6.2 Public nuisance

Key term

Public nuisance 'Any nuisance which materially affects the reasonable comfort and convenience of life of a class of Her Majesty's subjects. The sphere of the nuisance may be described generally as the neighbourhood; but the question whether the local community within that sphere comprises a sufficient number of persons to constitute a class of the public is a question of fact in each case': *Attorney-General v PYA Quarries 1957*.

An action for public nuisance is conceptually different from an action for private nuisance, even though the two may arise from the same conduct: *Halsey v Esso Petroleum Co Ltd 1961*.

Public nuisance is essentially a criminal act for which the person at fault may be prosecuted on behalf of the public. A claimant who wishes to commence an action in *tort* for public nuisance must show that they have suffered 'particular damage' beyond the damage sustained by the general public.

Various types of public nuisance are now governed by legislation and have lost their significance in the law of tort. Legislation includes the Public Health Acts 1936, 1961 and 2006, the Clean Air Acts 1956 and 1968, the Environmental Protection Act 1990 and the EU Privacy and Electronic Communication Regulation 2003 (covering nuisance calls and spam).

Most cases of public nuisance in modern times concern obstruction of the highway or danger to the highway.

6.2.1 Obstruction of the highway

The public has a right of passage along the highway. Interference with this right by means of obstruction constitutes public nuisance. The test is one of whether the defendant's action is unreasonable.

> *Dymond v Pearce 1972*
>
> *The facts*: The defendant parked his lorry overnight on a dual-carriageway. The vehicle was parked under a street lamp and its lights were left on. The claimant, a pillion passenger on a motor cycle, was involved in a collision with the lorry.
>
> *Decision*: This was an unreasonable action as it had been done solely for the defendant's convenience. (The claimant's action failed because the cause of the accident was the motor cyclist's failure to look where he was going, not the parking of the lorry.)

The courts will consider whether the obstruction could have been avoided.

> *Silservice v Supreme Bread 1949*
>
> *The facts*: The defendant sold fresh bread. Queues formed each day to buy the bread and spilled onto the road.
>
> *Decision*: There was no other way in which the defendant could conduct his business. There was no public nuisance.

> *Lyons v Gulliver 1914*
>
> *The facts*: The defendant owned a theatre. Queues formed which obstructed access to the claimant's premises.
>
> *Decision*: The accumulation of people could have been avoided if the defendant had opened his doors earlier. He was liable. Even though he had not intended the crowd to gather, this was the probable consequence of his actions.

6.2.2 Danger to the highway

This may take the form of an obstruction which is dangerous, for example an unlit spiked barrier: *Clark v Chambers 1878*. It may also take the form of danger from buildings or premises adjoining the highway. 'If owing to want of repair, premises on a highway become dangerous and therefore a nuisance, and a passer by or neighbouring owner suffers damage by their collapse, the occupier, or the owner if they have

undertaken the duty of repair, is answerable whether they knew or ought to have known of the danger or not': *Wringe v Cohen 1940*.

> *Tarry v Ashton 1876*
>
> *The facts*: A lamp projecting over the highway fell on a passer-by.
>
> *Decision*: This was public nuisance.

7 Defamation

FAST FORWARD

The essence of a **defamatory statement** is that it causes serious harm to the reputation of the person defamed.

The purpose of the **law of defamation** is to protect reputations from statements made about a person or organisation which are damaging. However, as we shall see, not all damaging statements are defamatory and therefore protected against.

The essence of a defamatory statement is that it **damages the reputation** of the person defamed, ie it:

- Lowers their standing in society
- Causes them to be shunned or avoided
- Makes imputations which are damaging to them in their profession, business or occupation

Mere insults or 'abuse', spoken in the heat of a quarrel, are not necessarily defamatory, though the distinction is not always easy to make. To say to someone 'You devil!' might not be defamatory, but to say of them that 'They are a born criminal' probably would be. The law against defamation serves to protect 'interests in reputation', reputation being the estimation other people have of you. Injury to one's own self-respect, pride or dignity without further publication is not defamation.

Defamation involves the publishing of a statement which has the effect of causing 'right-minded persons' to think less of the person or to avoid them, causing the person serious harm. If a person makes a statement – written or spoken – which is 'defamatory', they may be liable to the person they have defamed, unless one of a number of recognised defences is available. If a High Court judge allows, it is possible to bring a criminal prosecution for a particularly offensive statement. In general, however, the remedy for defamation is a **civil action** to recover damages. Less often an injunction, which is a prohibition against the repetition of a defamatory statement, may be obtained.

7.1 Libel and slander

A statement is defamatory if its publication has caused or is likely to cause serious harm to the reputation of the claimant: s1 Defamation Act 2013 (TSO, 2013). In the case of a business, 'serious harm' only means serious financial loss. Before the 2013 Act the threshold of harm was lower; the aim of the Act was to avoid trivial claims for statements which do not truly damage a claimant's reputation.

There are two distinct forms of defamatory statement.

(a) A **libel** is typically made in writing, but it includes other statements made in a form which is likely to be disseminated widely or continuously, such as a film made for public exhibition (both sound and visual effects may be libellous), a programme broadcast by radio or television, a play; s 4 Theatres Act 1968 (HMSO, 1968) and effigies (*Monson v Tussauds Ltd 1894*).

> **Yousoupoff v MGM Pictures Ltd 1934**
>
> *The facts:* A film was produced in England depicting the rape of a lady by Rasputin, and his subsequent murder. The lady had been romantically linked with one of his murderers. The claimant, who was married to one of Rasputin's murderers, alleged that people thought she was the lady who had been raped.
>
> *Decision:* A talking film, even where the defamation is only in pictures, is libellous. Hence the claimant did not have to show special damage to obtain her damages.

(b)   A **slander** is typically spoken, or in some other transitory form, such as a gesture.

The distinction between these forms is important, since slander cannot be a criminal offence, whereas libel may be. In addition, some actions for slander will only produce a remedy if 'special damage' is proved by the claimant, whereas libel is actionable *per se*.

A person may sue for slander without proof of special damage if allegations are made that they have committed a criminal offence punishable by imprisonment *(Gray v Jones 1939)*. (Before 2013 this was also true of allegations of unchastity in a woman or girl, or that a person suffers from a contagious or infectious disease.)

'Special damage' must be proved in any other case of alleged slander to gain a remedy. This may be easier for a business to prove because it means financial loss. Telling a supplier that their customer is a crook may lead to the latter losing a contract and so incur special expense in loss of profit or in finding another supplier. But mental suffering and social ostracism leading to loss of habitual hospitality have been seen as special losses for individuals.

You should note that **each occasion on which a statement is made can be a separate case of defamation** – there may be liability for a defamatory statement each time it is made, by whomever it is made. The defence of 'privilege' is sometimes available to a person who repeats what was said by someone else (eg a newspaper reporter), but in principle it is no defence to assert that the statement is only a repetition and not an original statement.

Defamation cases are tried without a jury unless a court orders otherwise: s 11 Defamation Act 2013.

7.1.1 Defence of truth

A key defence to an action for defamation is that the imputation conveyed by the statement of fact complained of is substantially true: s 2 Defamation Act 2013. Previously this was the defence of 'justification'.

With one minor exception **a true statement is not defamatory** since a person is not entitled to protect their reputation against the truth, even if the statement is made with malice. There is an absolute defence to a defamation action where the statement was substantially accurate: *Alexander v North East Railway* 1865.

The exception arises where a statement is made about a criminal conviction where the person has been 'rehabilitated' under the Rehabilitation of Offenders Act 1974 (HMSO, 1974). The defence of justification will not succeed if such a statement is prompted by malice.

7.1.2 Defence of honest opinion

A second defence is that the statement was the defendant's honest opinion, not a statement of fact: s 3 Defamation Act 2013. Previously this was the defence of 'fair comment'. For the defence of honest opinion to be effective:

- The statement must be a statement of opinion which indicated, in general or specific terms, the basis of the defendant's opinion; and
- An honest person could have held the opinion on the basis of any fact which existed at the time the statement complained of was published.

If the claimant shows that the defendant did not in fact hold the opinion expressed, then the defence fails.

7.1.3 Defence of 'matter of public interest'

Whether the statement is one of fact or opinion, the defendant is not liable if they can show that the statement was on a matter of public interest, and the defendant reasonably believed publication was in the public interest: s 4 Defamation Act 2013. If the defendant was motivated by malice or self-interest, for instance, this defence is not available.

7.2 Who may bring an action for defamation?

Normally an action for defamation is brought by an **individual** to protect their reputation. Previously it was held that a local authority, being a corporate body, had a **corporate reputation** – for conduct or performance – and might sue if it is defamed in that respect: *Bognor Regis UDC v Campion 1972*. However, in *Derbyshire County Council v Times Newspapers plc 1993* the House of Lords held that the public interest in free speech gives priority to the critic of the elected local authority. A company may sue for defamation where its trading reputation in England or Wales is damaged or likely to be damaged, without having to prove actual damage, although if no financial loss is shown damages are likely to be modest *(Jameel & Others v Wall Street Journal Europe (No 2) 2006, House of Lords)*.

As an unincorporated body, such as a trade union, is merely an association of its individual members and officers, it has no corporate reputation to protect. A trade union may only sue for defamation if it is a 'special register' body within the meaning of s 10 Trade Union and Labour Relations (Consolidation) Act 1992: *Electrical Electronic Telecommunications and Plumbing Union (EETPU) v Times Newspapers Ltd 1980*.

7.3 Success in an action for defamation

To succeed in an action for defamation, the claimant must show three elements.

- The statement complained of was **defamatory**
- That it was **understood** to refer to them (the claimant)
- It was **published** so that third parties became aware of its contents

7.4 What is defamatory?

It is the **sense of the statement, as reasonably understood by those to whom it was communicated**, which determines whether it is defamatory. In other words, it does **not** have to be shown that the defendant intended to damage the claimant's reputation or even that they were aware of its defamatory nature.

This means that a statement may be defamatory by reason of facts which are unknown to the person who makes the statement. This is a risk to which newspapers are often exposed in reporting statements by others. The Press are given certain other defences, but mere innocence of intent to defame (or ignorance that a statement is defamatory) is not of itself a defence.

The statement must be both **false** and **capable of being construed in a defamatory way**. It is up to the judge to decide whether a statement **can** be defamatory (question of law). The jury – if there is one – decides whether it was defamatory (question of fact). This presents a number of problems.

7.4.1 Natural and ordinary meaning of words

This is deemed to be what an ordinary person would infer presuming they had no special information. But while some words – such as 'dishonest' or 'promiscuous' – can imply only one thing, many others – such as a popular euphemism, 'fun-loving' – may have different inferences for different persons depending on their dispositions. The judge therefore attempts to draw the most 'ordinary' inference, which is the one that most right-minded people would draw. It is not necessarily the literal meaning, nor will the judge set out to read something into a statement which is not reasonably there: *Sim v Stretch 1936*.

7.4.2 Fact and opinion

A statement of fact which proves to be false and which may be construed in a defamatory way – such as 'X is a thief' – can clearly lead to a claim for defamation. However, a statement of opinion – 'I believe that X will be struck off as a dentist for adultery with a patient' – is also defamatory.

7.4.3 Innuendo

A statement which on the face of it cannot have a defamatory meaning inferred may still qualify if the claimant can prove all of the following:

(a) That the statement contains a wider meaning

(b) That reasonable people with special knowledge could and would infer such a meaning from the words or from facts which are represented in the words

(c) That certain particular people with special knowledge did so infer

(d) That those persons knew of the special facts before or at the time of publication.

Tolley v Fry 1931

The facts: Fry, a chocolate manufacturer, published an advertisement which was a drawing of Tolley, a famous amateur golfer, making a shot with a verse which said in effect that both Fry's chocolate and Tolley's golf were excellent. Tolley objected to the advertisement, which had been published without reference to him, on the grounds that those who saw it would conclude that Tolley had accepted a fee from Fry for his permission, thus compromising his amateur status.

Decision: The advertisement did indeed convey the innuendo of which Tolley complained. It was therefore defamatory, since it tended to lower his reputation.

7.5 Did the statement refer to the claimant?

On this issue also, the deciding factor is not what was **intended** by the person who makes the statement, but what was *understood* by the persons to whom the statement was made: *Bourke v Warren 1826*.

Hulton v Jones 1910

The facts: A newspaper published a humorous article describing the peccadilloes, while on holiday in France, of a churchwarden from Peckham, giving the fictitious name (it was thought) of Artemus Jones. However there was a real Artemus Jones (a barrister who did not live in Peckham and who was not a churchwarden). He sued the newspaper, producing evidence from some of his acquaintances that they had understood the rather distinctive name to refer to him. The newspaper's defence was that it did not even know of the claimant's existence.

Decision: The article must be taken to refer to the claimant since it had been understood in that sense. It was defamatory because it alleged sexual misconduct.

In a similar later case (*Newstead v London Express Newspaper 1931*) the paper made an unsuccessful defence that its report (on bigamy) was a true story about another man called Newstead. However, evidence was produced that some readers who knew the claimant took the article to refer to him.

An individual may sometimes sue for a defamatory statement which was **made with reference to a class of which they are a member**. There must be evidence that the statement was reasonably understood to **refer to the claimant as an individual**. Remember that an unincorporated body, such as a trade union, cannot sue for defamation on its own behalf, having no corporate reputation, nor as representative of its individual members, unless they were referred to as individuals.

> *Orme v Associated Newspaper Group Ltd 1981*
>
> *The facts*: The claimant was the leader in England of a religious sect ('the Moonies') and sued for damage to his own reputation arising from statements published in the newspaper about the sect in general.
>
> *Decision*: On the facts, the statements could be reasonably understood to refer to the claimant himself (among others). However, the court went on to find that the statements were true, and therefore not defamatory.

If reference to the individual cannot be shown, the court need not decide whether or not the statement is defamatory in nature, because the action has already failed.

> *Knupffer v London Express Newspaper Ltd 1944*
>
> *The facts*: The claimant was the head in the UK of a Russian refugee organisation, which had only 24 members in England, though it was also active in France and in the USA. The newspaper described as 'fascist' this 'minute body established in France and in the USA'. There was no mention of the English branch.
>
> *Decision*: The action must be dismissed, since there was no reference to the claimant. It was therefore unnecessary to decide whether the term 'fascist' was defamatory.

Certain other defamatory statements may not be actionable because of their object.

(a) A dead person cannot be defamed.

(b) Inanimate objects, such as goods or chattels, may not be defamed – though if the statement extends from a businessman's products to their person then it may be defamatory.

7.6 Was the statement published?

For a statement to be defamatory, it must have been **published**. This means that some person other than the claimant, the defendant and the defendant's spouse must have knowledge of its contents. There is no case for defamation if the only way in which the statement is published is the action of the claimant themself, in showing a third party a defamatory letter which was addressed to them alone.

A person will be liable for any publication which was intended or which they could reasonably have anticipated. Case law sheds some interesting light on aspects of publication, including the following.

7.6.1 Letters

A letter addressed to a particular person is presumed to be published to the addressee, but the sender should anticipate in some cases that it may be read by someone else.

(a) If a sealed letter is addressed to someone at their **home address**, it will usually be accepted that the defendant expected it to be opened by the addressee and no one else. If someone else opens it without authorisation – such as a butler in *Huth v Huth 1915* – that is not publication. However, this depends on the facts of the case.

> *Theaker v Richardson 1962*
>
> *The facts:* A defamatory letter was addressed to a married woman who was a member of the local council, along with the letter's author. It was sent in a style to suggest it was an election address. The woman's husband opened it believing this to be so.
>
> *Held:* It was a natural and probable consequence that the husband would open it and hence the statement had been published.

(b) A letter sent to someone at **work** may well be opened by a secretary: the sender/defendant will be assumed to have intended publication to a third party, unless it was marked 'private and confidential' or 'personal'.

7.6.2 Postcards

If a defamatory postcard has been sent through the post to the claimant, the law will assume that a post office employee, or some other third party, has read it.

7.6.3 'Mechanical distributors'

There is a distinction between the originators of defamatory material and those who merely disseminate it. Booksellers, libraries, newsagents etc are not generally liable for innocently spreading abroad a publication which they do not know to be defamatory. To escape liability, these 'mechanical distributors' must prove that they did not know of the libel and that there was no reason why they ought to have known of it. If the publisher asks the distributors to return all copies of a book which has been discovered to be defamatory, any distributor who ignores the request and continues to sell copies (by oversight) may be sued: *Vizetelly v Mudie's Select Library 1900*.

7.6.4 Email

The increasing popularity of email has created an entirely new method of communication and publication of a defamatory statement on the internet may be libellous. In *Godfrey v Demon Internet Ltd 2001*, an internet service provider was held to be liable for defamation after failing to remove defamatory material when it was put on notice that the material existed.

This can also be applied to internal company email systems. In *Eggleton v Asda 1995*, a police officer brought an action for defamation against the supermarket, alleging that a defamatory message about them was on their email system.

7.6.5 Social media

Before the Defamation Act 2013 it was possible for a person on social media to hide behind the operator of the website on which they posted their defamatory statements. Now a website operator is not liable for defamatory comments posted on its website if they comply with certain requirements regarding the claimant's complaint: s 5 Defamation Act 2013. This provision, and the regulations that are made under it, means that a person who has been defamed on social media has a greater chance of getting a remedy.

8 Breach of statutory duty

FAST FORWARD

Breach of statutory duty causing harm to a person is a **strict liability tort** that does not require the claimant to prove negligence.

Where one person fails to comply with a legal duty imposed by legislation, and another person suffers harm as a result, the breach may in some cases give rise to an action in tort for breach of statutory duty.

Not every breach of legislation which causes harm to an individual will give rise to a cause of action. For example it was held in *X v Bedfordshire County Council 1995* that legislation requiring councils to provide protection to children did not give rise to an action for breach of statutory duty if a council failed to provide protection.

Some legislation expressly provides for civil liability (eg some regulations under the Health and Safety at Work Act 1974 (HMSO, 1974)) while others expressly exclude it (eg the Health and Safety at Work Act 1974 itself). If the legislation is silent on civil liability the courts have to determine the intention of Parliament.

In relation to accidents occurring at work, however, from October 2013 civil liability only arises from a breach of statutory duty if the relevant regulation expressly provides for it. This change was made by s69 of the Enterprise and Regulatory Reform Act 2013 (TSO, 2013).

To bring a successful action for breach of statutory duty the claimant must show that:

- Legislation (a statute or delegated legislation) imposes a duty on the defendant
- Parliament intended the legislation to give rise to civil liability
- The harm suffered by the claimant was within the scope of what the legislation sought to address. A breach of the Contagious Diseases (Animals) Act 1869 (HMSO, 1869), for instance, did not give rise to liability where the damage caused was loss of stock overboard in *Gorris v Scott 1874*.

The advantage to the claimant of bringing an action for breach of statutory duty as opposed to a negligence action is that there is strict liability for breach of statutory duty. If, for example, the Factories Act 1961 (HMSO, 1961) imposes a duty to take a particular action and the defendant fails to take that action, a claimant who was injured as a result of that failure does not have to prove negligence.

Having considered the torts of trespass, nuisance, defamation and breach of statutory duty, we shall now consider perhaps the most important tort from the perspective of **professional accountants** (and other professions) – the tort of negligence.

9 The tort of negligence

> **FAST FORWARD**
>
> **Negligence** is the most important modern tort. To succeed in an action for negligence the claimant must prove that:
>
> - The defendant had **a duty of care** to avoid causing injury, damage or loss
> - There was **a breach of that duty** by the defendant
> - In consequence the claimant suffered **injury, damage or loss**

9.1 Definition

The **tort of negligence** is committed where there is a failure to take reasonable care when there is a duty to do so and another party suffers a loss. This is the most important and far-reaching modern tort.

> **FAST FORWARD**
>
> The term negligence is used to describe **carelessly** carrying out an **act** and breaking a **legal duty of care** owed to another causing them **loss or damage.**

We shall now look at each of the three areas that must be proved in order for a party to be liable for negligence – that a **duty of care** existed, that **duty of care was breached** and as a consequence **loss or damage was suffered**. Once we have considered the general tort of negligence itself, we shall look at its application to the professions as **negligent misstatement**.

10 Duty of care

> **FAST FORWARD**
>
> In the landmark case of *Donoghue v Stevenson 1932* the House of Lords ruled that a person might **owe a duty of care to another with whom they had no contractual relationship** at all. The doctrine has been refined in subsequent rulings, but the principle is unchanged.

10.1 The basic rule

The question of whether or not a duty of care exists in any situation is generally decided by the courts on a **case by case basis**, with each new case setting a precedent based on its own particular facts.

In the case described below, the House of Lords was attempting to establish a **general duty** that could be applied to all subsequent cases and situations.

> *Donoghue v Stevenson 1932*
>
> *The facts*: A purchased a bottle of ginger beer for consumption by B. B drank part of the contents, which contained the remains of a decomposed snail, and became ill. The manufacturer argued that as there was no contract between himself and B he owed her no duty of care and so was not liable.
>
> *Decision*: The House of Lords laid down the general principle that every person owes a duty of care to his 'neighbour', to 'persons so closely and directly affected by my act that I ought reasonably to have them in contemplation as being so affected'.

10.2 Development of the doctrine

This narrow doctrine has been much refined over the years since the snail made its celebrated appearance. For any duty of care to exist, it was stated in *Anns v Merton London Borough Council 1977* that two stages must be tested:

- Is there sufficient **proximity** between the parties, such that the harm suffered was **reasonably foreseeable**?
- Should the duty be **restricted** or **limited** for reasons of economic, social or public policy?

The latest stage in the doctrine's development came in *Caparo Industries plc v Dickman 1990*. We shall come back to this case when we study the duty of care of accountants and auditors, however it established a three-stage test for establishing a duty of care that still stands:

- Was the harm **reasonably foreseeable**?
- Was there a relationship of **proximity** between the parties?
- Considering the circumstances, is it **fair, just and reasonable** to impose a duty of care?

11 Breach of duty of care

FAST FORWARD

The second element that must be proven by a claimant in an action for negligence is that there was a **breach of the duty** of care by the defendant.

11.1 The basic rule

Breach of duty of care is the second issue to be considered in a negligence claim. The standard of reasonable care requires that the person concerned should do what a **reasonable man** would do, and should not do what a reasonable man would not do: *Blyth v Birmingham Water Works 1856*. This will also mean the reasonable **employer**, or the reasonable **adviser**.

The following factors should be considered when deciding if a duty of care has been breached:

(a) **Probability of injury**

It is presumed that a reasonable man takes **greater precautions** when the risk of injury is high: *Bolton v Stone 1951*. Therefore when the risk is higher the defendant must do more to meet their duty. In *Glasgow Corporation v Taylor 1992* a local authority was held to be negligent when children ate poisonous berries in a park. A warning notice was not considered to be sufficient to protect children.

(b) **Seriousness** of the risk

The young, old or disabled may be prone to more serious injury than a fit able-bodied person. The **'eggshell skull'** rule means that you must take your victim as they are. Where the risk to the vulnerable is high, the level of care required is raised.

> *Paris v Stepney Borough Council 1951*
>
> *The facts:* P was employed by K on vehicle maintenance. P had already lost the sight of one eye. It was not the normal practice to issue protective goggles since the risk of eye injury was small. A chip of metal flew into P's good eye and blinded him.
>
> *Decision:* There was a higher standard of care owed to P because an injury to his remaining good eye would blind him.

(c) Issues of **practicality and cost**

It is not always reasonable to ensure all possible precautions are taken. Where the **cost** or **disruption** caused to eliminate the danger far **exceeds the risk** of it occurring it is likely that defendants will be found not to have breached their duty if they do not implement them.

> *Latimer v AEC Ltd 1952*
>
> *The facts:* The defendants owned a factory that become flooded after a period of heavy rain. The water mixed with oil on the factory floor causing it to become very slippery. Sawdust was applied to the majority of the areas affected, but the claimant slipped on one of the few areas that was not treated.
>
> *Decision:* The defendant did all that was necessary to reduce the risk to its employees and was not held liable. The only other option was to close the factory, however no evidence could be provided that would indicate a reasonable employer would have taken that course of action. Closing the factory would have outweighed the risk to the employees.

(d) **Common practice**

Where an individual can prove their actions were in line with **common practice** or **custom** it is likely that they would have met their duty of care. This is unless the common practice itself is found to be negligent.

(e) **Social benefit**

Where an action is of **some benefit** to society, defendants may be **protected** from liability even if their actions create risk. For example, a fire engine that speeds to a major disaster provides a social benefit that may outweigh the greater risk to the public.

(f) **Professions and skill**

Persons who hold themselves out to possess a particular skill should be judged on what a **reasonable person possessing the same skill** would do in the situation rather than that of a reasonable man. Professions are able to set their own **standards of care** for their members to meet and therefore members should be judged against these standards rather than those laid down by the courts.

11.2 Res ipsa loquitur

In some circumstances the claimant may argue that the **facts speak for themselves** (*res ipsa loquitur*) – want of care being the only possible explanation for what happened, negligence on the part of the defendant must be presumed.

Key term

> **Res ipsa loquitur** can be defined as: 'The thing speaks for itself'. If an accident occurs which appears to be most likely caused by negligence, the court may apply this maxim and infer negligence from mere proof of the facts. The burden of proof is reversed and the defendant must prove that they were not negligent.

The **claimant must demonstrate** the following to rely on this principle:

(a) The thing which caused the injury was under the **management and control** of the defendant.

(b) The accident was such as would not occur if those in control used **proper care**. Therefore in *Richley v Fould 1965* the fact that a car skidded to the wrong side of the road was enough to indicate careless driving.

In *Mahon v Osborne 1939* a surgeon was required to prove that leaving a swab inside a patient after an operation was not negligent.

12 Causality and remoteness of damage

FAST FORWARD

> Finally the claimant must demonstrate that they suffered injury or loss as a **result** of the breach.

12.1 Damage or loss

This is the third element of a negligence claim. A claim for compensation for negligence will not succeed if **damage** or **loss** is not proved. A person will only be compensated if they have suffered actual loss, injury, damage or harm **as a consequence** of another's actions. Examples of such loss may include:

- Personal injury
- Damage to property
- Financial loss which is directly connected to personal injury, for example, loss of earnings
- Pure financial loss is rarely recoverable

12.2 The 'But for' test

To satisfy the requirement that harm must be caused by another's actions, the **'But for' test** is applied. The claimant must prove that if it was not 'but for' the other's actions they would not have suffered damage. Therefore claimants are **unable** to claim for any harm that would have happened to them **anyway** irrespective of the defendant's actions.

> *Barnett v Chelsea and Kensington HMC 1969*
>
> *The facts:* A casualty doctor sent a patient home without treatment, referring him to his own doctor. The patient died of arsenic poisoning.
>
> *Decision:* Whilst the doctor was held negligent, the negligence did not cause the patient's death as they would have died anyway.

12.2.1 Multiple causes

The courts often have difficulty in determining **causation** where there are a number of possible causes of injury including the negligent act. The courts must decide on the **facts** if the negligent act was the one that most likely caused the injury.

> *Wilsher v Essex AHA 1988*
>
> *The facts:* A premature baby suffered blindness after birth. It was claimed that a doctor failed to notice that the baby received high doses of oxygen and this caused the blindness.
>
> *Decision:* Evidence was provided that there was six possible causes of the blindness including the one claimed. However, the court could not ascertain which of the six actually occurred and therefore could not create a direct causal link.

The case below indicates the court's flexibility when applying legal principles in **exceptional** cases.

> *Fairchild v Glenhaven Funeral Services Ltd & Others 2002*
>
> *The facts:* The claimants all contracted a disease caused by contact with asbestos over extended periods of time with several different employers. The defence claimed that the disease could be contracted by exposure to one asbestos fibre and as the claimants were employed by a number of employers it could not be established at which employer they contracted the disease.
>
> *Decision:* The House of Lords held that all the employers (who had failed to take reasonable care), contributed to the cause and were all liable.

12.2.2 Novus actus intervieniens

Courts will only impart liability where there is a cause of events that are a **probable** result of the defendant's actions. Defendant's will not be liable for damage when the chain of events is broken. There are **three types** of intervening act that will break the chain of causation.

12.2.3 Act of the claimant

The actions of the claimant themselves may **break** the chain of causation. The rule is that where the act is **reasonable** and in the **ordinary course of things** an act by the claimant will not break the chain.

> *McKew v Holland, Hannen and Cubbitts (Scotland) Ltd 1969*
>
> *The facts:* The claimant had a leg injury which was prone to causing his leg to give way from time to time. Whilst at work he failed to ask for assistance when negotiating a flight of stairs. He fell and was injured as a result.
>
> *Decision:* The fact that the claimant failed to seek assistance was unreasonable and was sufficient to break the chain of causality.

12.2.4 Act of a third party

Where a **third party** intervenes in the course of events the defendant will normally only be liable for damage **until** the intervention. For example, in *Knightley v Johns 1982* the defendant caused a road traffic accident. A police inspector negligently handled traffic control following the accident. This negligence led to the claimant, a police officer, being killed. The defendant who caused the accident successfully argued that the negligent handling by the police inspector broke the chain of causation between their negligence and the death of the officer.

> *Lamb v Camden LBC 1981*
>
> *The facts:* The defendant negligently caused a house to be damaged, and as a result it had to be vacated until it could be repaired. During the vacant period, squatters took up residence and the property suffered further damage.
>
> *Decision:* Intrusion by squatters was a possibility that the defendant should have considered, but it was not held to be a likely event. Therefore the defendant should not be liable for the additional damage caused by the intervening actions of the squatters.

12.2.5 Natural events

The chain of causality is **not automatically** broken due to an intervening natural event. In situations where the breach puts the claimant at risk of **additional** damage caused by a natural event the chain will not be broken. However, where the natural event is **unforeseeable**, the chain will be broken.

> *Carslogie Steamship Co Ltd v Royal Norwegian Government 1952*
>
> *The facts:* A ship owned by the claimants was damaged as a result of the defendant's negligence and required repair. During the trip to the repair site the ship was caught in severe weather conditions that resulted in additional damage being caused and therefore a longer repair time was required. The claimants claimed loss of charter revenue for the period the ship was out of action for repairs caused by the original incident.
>
> *Decision:* The House of Lords held that the defendants were liable for loss of profit suffered as result of the defendants' wrongful act only. Whilst undergoing repairs, the ship ceased to be a profit-earning machine as the weather damage had rendered her unseaworthy. The weather conditions created an intervening act and the claimants had sustained no loss of profit due to the ship being out of action as it would have been unavailable for hire anyway due to the weather damage.

12.3 Remoteness of damage

Even where causation is proved, a negligence claim can still fail if the damage caused is '**too remote**'. The test of **reasonable foresight** developed out of *The Wagon Mound 1961*. Liability is limited to damage that a **reasonable man** could have foreseen. This does not mean the exact event must be foreseeable in detail, just that the eventual outcome is foreseeable.

> *The Wagon Mound 1961*
>
> *The facts:* A ship was taking on oil in Sydney harbour. Oil was spilled onto the water and it drifted to a wharf 200 yards away where welding equipment was in use. The owner of the wharf carried on working because he was advised that the sparks were unlikely to set fire to furnace oil. Safety precautions were taken. A spark fell onto a piece of cotton waste floating in the oil, thereby starting a fire which damaged the wharf. The owner of the wharf sued the charterers of the Wagon Mound.
>
> *Decision:* The claim must fail. Pollution was the foreseeable risk: fire was not.

The House of Lords decided in the case of *Jolley v London Borough of Sutton 2000* that the remoteness test can be passed if **some** harm is foreseeable even if the exact nature of the injuries could not be.

> *Jolley v London Borough of Sutton 2000*
>
> *The facts:* The defendants should have removed a boat which had been dumped two years previously. A teenage boy was injured while attempting to repair it.
>
> *Decision:* Even though the precise incident was not foreseeable, the authority should have foreseen that some harm could be caused since they knew children regularly played on the abandoned boat.

We have seen how the breach of a duty of care that caused loss or damage can create a liability in negligence, however this is not the end of the story. As we shall see now, a party may have a partial or complete defence against their negligence.

5: THE LAW OF TORTS

13 Defences to negligence

FAST FORWARD

The amount of damages awarded to the claimant can be reduced if it is shown that they **contributed** to their injury. The defendant can be **exonerated** from paying damages if it can be proved that the claimant **expressly** or **impliedly** consented to the risk.

13.1 Contributory negligence

A court may **reduce** the amount of damages paid to the claimant if the defendant establishes that they **contributed** to their own **injury** or **loss**, this is known as **contributory negligence**.

> *Sayers v Harlow UDC 1958*
>
> *The facts:* The claimant was injured whilst trying to climb out of a public toilet cubicle that had a defective lock.
>
> *Decision:* The court held that the claimant had contributed to her injuries by the method by which she had tried to climb out.

If the defendant proves that the claimant was at least **partially** at fault, courts will reduce the damages awarded to them by a **percentage** that is **just** and **reasonable**. This percentage is calculated according to what is established as the **claimant's share of the blame**. This is typically in the range of 10% to 75%, however it is possible to reduce the claim by up to 100% *Jayes v IMI (Kynoch) Ltd 1985*.

In *Fitzgerald v Lane & Patel 1989* the claimant crossed the road whilst the lights were at red for pedestrians. The first defendant driver collided with them and the claimant was thrown from the bonnet of that car into the road, where they were run over by a car driven by the second defendant. The claimant suffered severe spinal injuries that led to partial paralysis, but it could not be proven which impact caused the paralysis. In awarding damages the then House of Lords attributed blame in the proportion of 50% against the claimant and 25% each against the two speeding drivers. Damages were thus awarded in those relative proportions.

13.2 Volenti non fit injuria

Where a defendant's actions carry the risk of a tort being committed they will have a defence if it can be proved that the claimant consented to the risk. *Volenti non fit injuria* literally means the **voluntary acceptance** of the **risk of injury**.

This defence is available to the defendant where both parties have **expressly** consented to the risk (such as waiver forms signed by those taking part in dangerous sports), or it may be **implied** by the **conduct** of the claimant.

> *ICI v Shatwell 1965*
>
> *The facts:* The claimant and his brother disregarded safety precautions whilst using detonators, resulting in injury to the claimant.
>
> *Decision:* The court upheld the defence of *volenti non fit injuria*. The claimant disregarded his employer's statutory safety rules and consented to the reckless act willingly.

An **awareness** of the risk **is not sufficient to establish consent**. For this defence to be successful the defendant must **prove** that the claimant was **fully informed** of the **risks** and that they consented to them.

This point was made in *Dann v Hamilton 1939* where a girl passenger in a car driven by a drunk driver was injured. The defendant established that she was aware of the risk but could offer no evidence that she consented to it. As a result of this case the defence of *volenti* is unlikely to succeed in cases where consent is **implied**.

Question: Volenti non fit injuria

Briefly describe the defence of volenti non fit injuria.

Answer

Volenti non fit injuria is a valid defence to a negligence claim where the claimant expressly or impliedly consented to the risk.

We shall now turn our attention to how the law relating to **negligent professional advice** has been developed through the operation of precedent, being refined and explained with each successive case that comes to court. It illustrates the often step-by-step development of English law, which has gradually refined the principles laid down in *Donoghue v Stevenson* and *Anns v Merton London Borough Council* to cover **negligent misstatements which cause financial loss**.

14 Negligent misstatement

> **FAST FORWARD**
>
> Professional individuals and organisations have a special relationship with their clients and those who rely on their work. This is because they act in an **expert capacity**. The law of negligence has been refined in the case of professional advisers to form the tort of **negligent misstatement**.

14.1 The special relationship

Before 1963, it was held that any liability for careless statements was limited in scope and depended upon the existence of a **contractual** or **fiduciary relationship** between the parties. Lord Denning's tests of a further (later termed 'special') relationship were laid down in the Court of Appeal in his dissenting judgement on *Candler v Crane, Christmas & Co 1951*.

> **FAST FORWARD**
>
> According to Lord Denning, to establish a **special relationship** the person who made the statement must have done so in some professional or expert capacity which made it likely that others would rely on what they said. This is the position of an adviser such as an accountant, banker, engineer, solicitor or surveyor.

It follows that a duty could not be owed to complete strangers, but Lord Denning also stated at the time: 'Accountants owe a duty of care not only to their own clients, but also to **all those whom they know will rely on their accounts** in the transactions for which those accounts are prepared.' This was to prove a significant consideration in later cases.

However, Lord Denning's view was a dissenting voice in 1951 in the *Candler* case, where the Court of Appeal held that the defendants were **not** liable (for a bad investment based upon a set of negligently prepared accounts) because there was no direct contractual or fiduciary relationship with the claimant investor.

It was 12 years later that the **special relationship** was accepted as a valid test. Our starting point is a **leading case** (*Hedley*) on negligent misstatement which was the start of a **new judicial approach** to cases involving negligent misstatement. You must make sure that you are familiar with it.

Hedley Byrne & Co Ltd v Heller and Partners Ltd 1963

The facts: HB were advertising agents acting for a new client, Easipower Ltd. HB requested information from Easipower's bank (HP) on its financial position. HP returned non-committal replies, which expressly disclaimed legal responsibility, and which were held to be a negligent misstatement of Easipower's financial resources.

Decision: While HP were able to avoid liability by virtue of their disclaimer, the House of Lords went on to consider whether there ever could be a duty of care to avoid causing financial loss by negligent misstatement where there was no contractual or fiduciary relationship. It decided (as obiter dicta) that HP were guilty of negligence having breached the duty of care, because a special relationship did exist. Had it not been for the disclaimer, a claim for negligence would have succeeded.

In reaching the decision in *Hedley Byrne*, Lord Morris said the following:

> 'If someone possessed of a special skill undertakes... to apply that skill for the assistance of another person who **relies** on that skill, a duty of care will arise... If, in a sphere in which a person is so placed that others could reasonably rely on his skill... a person takes it on himself to give information or advice to... another person who, as he **knows or should know**, will place reliance on it, then a duty of care will arise.'

Point to note

As you know, *obiter dicta* such as those made in 1963 do not form part of the *ratio decidendi*, and are not binding on future cases. They will, however, be **persuasive**. Indeed the approach taken in *Hedley Byrne* was approved in a quite recent case, *Commissioners of Customs v Barclays Bank 2006*.

Note that at the time liability did not extend to those whom the advisor might merely **foresee as a possible user** of the statement.

However in a subsequent case, the courts extended potential liability, and started to take account of third parties not known to the adviser. The following case echoed the principles laid down in *Anns* and addressed the question of **reasonable foresight** being present to create a duty of care.

JEB Fasteners Ltd v Marks, Bloom & Co 1982

The facts: The defendants, a firm of accountants, prepared an audited set of accounts showing overvalued stock and hence inflated profit. The auditors knew there were liquidity problems and that the company was seeking outside finance. The claimants were shown the accounts; they took over the company for a nominal amount, since by that means they could obtain the services of the company's two directors. At no time did MB tell JEB that the stock value was inflated. With the investment's failure, JEB sued MB, with the following claims.

(a) The accounts had been prepared negligently.

(b) They had relied on those accounts.

(c) They would not have invested had they been aware of the company's true position.

(d) MB owed a duty of care to all persons whom they could reasonably foresee would rely on the accounts.

Decision: Even though JEB had relied on the accounts (b), they would not have acted differently if the true position had been known (c), since they had really wanted the directors and not the company. Hence the accountants were not the cause of the consequential harm and were not liable. Significantly (although this did not affect the decision as to liability) it was the judge's view that MB did indeed owe a duty of care through foresight (d) and had been negligent in preparing the accounts (a).

Decisions since *JEB Fasteners* have, however, shied away from the foresight test and gone back to looking at whether the adviser has **knowledge of the user** and the **use to which the statement will be put**.

14.2 The Caparo decision

FAST FORWARD

> The **Caparo case** is fundamental to understanding professional negligence. It was decided that **auditors do not owe a general duty of care to the public at large** or to **shareholders increasing their stakes in the company in question**.

This important and controversial case made considerable changes to the tort of negligence as a whole, and the negligence of **professionals** in particular. It set a precedent which forms the basis for courts when considering the liability of professional advisers.

> *Caparo Industries plc v Dickman and Others 1990*
>
> *The facts:* Caparo, which already held shares in Fidelity plc, bought more shares and later made a takeover bid, after seeing accounts prepared by the defendants that showed a profit of £1.3m. Caparo claimed against the directors (the brothers Dickman) and the auditors for the fact that the accounts should have shown a loss of £400,000. The claimants argued that the auditors owed a duty of care to investors and potential investors in respect of the audit. They should have been aware that a press release stating that profits would fall significantly had made Fidelity vulnerable to a takeover bid and that bidders might well rely upon the accounts.
>
> *Decision:* The auditor's duty did not extend to potential investors nor to existing shareholders increasing their stakes. It was a duty owed to the body of shareholders as whole.

In the *Caparo* case the House of Lords decided that there were **two** very different situations facing a person giving professional advice.

(a) Preparing information in the knowledge that a **particular person** was contemplating a transaction and would rely on the information in deciding whether or not to proceed with the transaction (the 'special relationship').

(b) Preparing a statement for **general circulation**, which could foreseeably be relied upon by persons unknown to the professional for a variety of different purposes.

It was held therefore that a public company's auditors owe **no general duty of care to the public at large** who rely on an audit report when deciding to invest – and, in purchasing additional shares, an existing shareholder is in no different position to the public at large.

In *MacNaughton (James) Papers Group Ltd v Hicks Anderson & Co 1991*, it was stated that it was necessary to examine each case in the light of the following.

- Foreseeability
- Proximity
- Fairness

This is because there could be **no single overriding principle** that could be applied to all individual cases. Lord Justice Neill set out the matters to be taken into account in considering this.

- The purpose for which the statement was **made**
- The purpose for which the statement was **communicated**
- The **relationship** between the maker of the statement, the recipient and any third party
- The **size** of any class to which the recipient belonged
- The **state of knowledge** of the maker
- Any **reliance** by the recipient

14.3 Non-audit role

The duty of care of accountants is held to be higher when advising on matters such as takeovers than when auditing. The directors and financial advisors of the target company in a contested takeover bid owe a duty of care to a **known** takeover bidder in respect of express representations made about financial statements prepared for the purpose of contesting the bid on which they knew the bidder would rely: *Morgan Crucible Co plc v Hill Samuel Bank Ltd and others 1991*.

14.4 The law since *Caparo*

The case below highlighted the need for a cautious approach and careful evaluation of the circumstances when giving **financial advice**, possibly with the need to issue a disclaimer.

ADT Ltd v BDO Binder Hamlyn 1995

The facts: Binder Hamlyn was the joint auditor of BSG. In October 1989, BSG's audited accounts for the year to 30 June 1989 were published. Binder Hamlyn signed off the audit as showing a true and fair view of BSG's position. ADT was thinking of buying BSG and, as a potential buyer, sought Binder Hamlyn's confirmation of the audited results. In January 1990, the Binder Hamlyn audit partner attended a meeting with a director of ADT. This meeting was described by the judge as the 'final hurdle' before ADT finalised its bid for BSG. At the meeting, the audit partner specifically confirmed that he 'stood by' the audit of October 1989. ADT proceeded to purchase BSG for £105m. It was subsequently alleged that BSG's true value was only £40m. ADT therefore sued Binder Hamlyn for the difference, £65m plus interest.

Decision: Binder Hamlyn assumed a responsibility for the statement that the audited accounts showed a true and fair view of BSG which ADT relied on to its detriment. Since the underlying audit work had been carried out negligently, Binder Hamlyn was held liable for £65m. The courts expect a higher standard of care from accountants when giving advice on company acquisitions since the losses can be so much greater.

This situation was different from *Caparo* since the court was specifically concerned with the **purpose of the statement made at the meeting**. Did Binder Hamlyn **assume any responsibility** as a result of the partner's comments? The court decided that it did. The court did not need to consider the question of duty to individual shareholders, because *Caparo* had already decided that there was none.

Following the *ADT* case, another case tested the court's interpretation.

NRG v Bacon and Woodrow and Ernst & Young 1996

The facts: NRG alleged that the defendants had failed to suggest the possibility that certain companies it was targeting might suffer huge reinsurance losses. They had also failed to assess properly whether these losses could be protected against, because defective actuarial methods had been used. As a result, it overpaid for these companies by £255m.

Decision: The judge observed that accountants owe a higher standard of care when advising on company purchases, because the potential losses are so much greater, following *ADT*. However, applying this higher standard of care to the facts, it was decided that NRG had received the advice that any competent professional would have given, because the complex nature of the losses that the companies were exposed to were not fully understood at the time. In addition, the use of defective actuarial methods had not led directly to the losses, because NRG would have bought the companies anyway.

There have been some other **important clarifications** of the law affecting accountants' liability in the area of responsibility towards non-clients. The following two cases both concern auditors' liability to group companies.

> **Barings plc v Coopers & Lybrand 1997**
>
> *The facts:* Barings collapsed in 1995 after loss-making trading by the general manager of its Singapore subsidiary, BFS. BFS was audited by the defendant's Singapore firm, which provided Barings directors with consolidation schedules and a copy of the BFS audit report. The defendant tried to argue that there was no duty of care owed to Barings, only to BFS.
>
> *Decision:* A duty of care was owed to Barings, as the defendants must have known that their audit report and consolidation schedules would be relied upon at group level.

> **BCCI (Overseas) Ltd v Ernst & Whinney 1997**
>
> *The facts:* In this case, the defendants audited the group holding company's accounts, but not those of the claimant subsidiary. The claimant tried to claim that the defendants had a duty of care to them.
>
> *Decision:* No duty of care was owed to the subsidiary because no specific information is normally channelled down by a holding company's auditor to its subsidiaries.

14.5 Extension of liability to third parties

Although the *Caparo* case states that **no general duty** is owed by auditors to third parties, a number of cases have found that an **auditor can owe a duty** in **limited circumstances**.

In *Law Society v KPMG Peat Marwick 2000* it was held that an accountant who reported on a solicitor's client accounts owed a duty to the solicitor's regulator as well as to the solicitor. This is because a solicitor is legally and professionally required to obtain an accountant's report on their client accounts by their regulator (then the Law Society, now the Solicitors Regulation Authority), and the regulator may be liable to pay compensation to clients of a solicitor who has mismanaged their accounts.

In *Royal Bank of Scotland v Bannerman Johnstone Maclay 2005* it was held that a third party can be owed a duty of care where auditors know their identity, the use to which the information would be put and that the third party intends to rely on it.

In this case, the banker and major financier to a company was entitled to the monthly management accounts and audited financial statements as part of its lending agreement. Over a number of years, the bank acquired a majority shareholding in the business but the accounts on which they relied were misstated and the business collapsed with debts of £13 million owed to the bank. The duty of care was owed as a consequence of the auditors being aware that the accounts would be sent to the bank as part of the lending agreement and would therefore be relied upon. The auditors could have disclaimed responsibility to the bank if they wanted to avoid liability.

The Bannerman case was upheld in the decision of *Barclays Bank plc v Grant Thornton UK LLP 2015*. In this case, the auditors disclaimed liability on the face of its audit reports which were relied upon by the lender of a hotel chain that went into administration. The court struck out the case brought by the bankers who claimed that the disclaimer was not valid in law. The court held that it is not unreasonable for auditors to include a disclaimer stating that they do not accept responsibility to anyone other than the addressees of the audit report.

To counter the risk of liability to clients and third parties, UK accountancy firms have been investigating ways of **limiting liability** in the face of increasing litigation.

In 2000, the **Limited Liability Partnerships Act 2000** was passed, and limited liability partnerships have been permitted under law since 2001.

This **protects the partners** of accountancy firms from the financial consequences of **negligent actions** as their liability to third parties (previously unlimited) can now be limited.

Having considered liability in tort as well as a range of torts, in the final section below we shall see the two main **remedies** available to those affected by a tort – damages and injunctions.

15 Remedies in tort

15.1 Damages in tort

FAST FORWARD

Damages will only be awarded for loss which is not too remote from the actions of the defendant. Chains of causation may be broken by the actions of others, or may become too tenuous when the consequences go beyond what could reasonably have been foreseen. However, the thin skull principle may allow damages to be awarded for unexpected damage.

Damages may only compensate for loss which is not too remote.

15.1.1 Remoteness of damage

When there is a sequence of physical cause and effect without human intervention, the ultimate loss is too remote (so that damages cannot be recovered for it) unless it could have been reasonably foreseen that some loss of that kind might occur as a consequence of the wrong.

Hughes v Lord Advocate 1963

The facts: Workmen left lighted paraffin lamps as a warning sign of an open manhole in the street. Two small boys took one of the lamps as a light and went down the manhole. As they clambered out the lamp fell into the hole and caused an explosion in which the boys were injured. Evidence was given that a fire might have been foreseen but an explosion was improbable.

Decision: The defendants were liable for negligence in leaving the lamps where they did. A risk of fire was foreseeable and the explosion must be regarded as 'an unexpected manifestation of the apprehended physical dangers'. It was not (as it was in the Wagon Mound case) damage of an entirely different kind.

Doughty v Turner Manufacturing Co 1964

The facts: An asbestos cement lid accidentally fell into a cauldron of sodium cyanide at a temperature of 800 degrees Centigrade. The intense heat caused a chemical change in the asbestos lid as a result of which there was an explosion. The claimant was injured by the eruption of molten liquid. The chemical reaction leading to the explosion was previously unknown to science.

Decision: A splash of sodium cyanide was foreseeable but a violent explosion was not. The result was unforeseeable as no one knew it could happen and therefore too remote.

The then House of Lords decided in the case below that the remoteness test can be passed if **some** harm is foreseeable even if the exact nature of the injuries could not be.

Jolley v London Borough of Sutton 2000

The facts: The defendants should have removed a boat which had been dumped two years previously. A teenage boy was injured while attempting to repair it.

Decision: Even though the precise incident was not foreseeable, the authority should have foreseen that some harm could be caused since they knew children regularly played on the abandoned boat.

In cases of physical injury which is more serious than would normally be expected because the plaintiff proves to be abnormally vulnerable, the defendant is liable for the full amount of injury done. This is the thin skull (or 'eggshell skull') principle: if A taps B on the head and cracks B's skull because it is abnormally thin, A is liable for the fracture.

> *Smith v Leech Braine & Co 1962*
>
> *The facts*: A workman was near a tank of molten zinc in which metal articles were dipped to galvanise them. One article was allowed to slip and the workman was burnt on the lip by a drop of molten zinc. The burn activated latent cancer from which he died three years later. His widow sued for damages.
>
> *Decision*: Damages for a fatal accident would be awarded. Some physical injury (the burn on the lip) was a foreseeable consequence. The defendants must accept liability for the much more serious physical injury (cancer) caused by their negligence.

If the claimant suffers avoidable loss because their lack of resources prevents them from taking costly measures to reduce their loss, they may still recover damages for it: *Martindale v Duncan 1973*.

15.1.2 Amount of damages

> **FAST FORWARD**
>
> The amount of damages is based on the principle of compensating the claimant for their financial loss and not of punishing the defendant for their wrong. Aggravated or exemplary damages may be awarded in limited circumstances.

The amount of damages is generally based on the principle of compensating the claimant for their financial loss and not of punishing the defendant for their wrong. There are several categories of damages related to the circumstances.

- **Ordinary damages** are assessed by the court as compensation for losses which cannot be positively proved or ascertained, and depend on the court's view of the nature of the claimant's injury.
- **Special damages** are those which can be positively proved, such as damage to clothing, cars etc.
- **Exemplary or aggravated damages** are intended to punish the defendant for their act, and to deter them and others from a similar course of action in the future. These damages are only rarely awarded, eg where in a defamation case the defendant raises the defence of justification but loses. In *Rookes v Barnard 1964* the then House of Lords set down that exemplary damages could only be awarded for torts where the defendant calculated to make more money from the tort than they would have to pay in damages (as is sometimes the situation in newspaper libel cases), where a government official acts oppressively, arbitrarily or unconstitutionally, or where statute permits.
- **Nominal damages** are given where the claimant has suffered injury, but has suffered no real damage (eg trespass to land without damage to that land).

15.1.3 Economic loss for negligent misstatement

Key terms

> **Economic loss** is a financial detriment that is reflected in the decrease in value of an asset rather than in physical loss of an asset. There are two forms.
>
> **Consequential economic loss** arises directly from some physical damage, for instance an individual's loss of earnings following an accident at work.
>
> **Pure economic loss** is the residual category of economic loss, such as the loss of income for a family when the chief breadwinner is killed at work, the loss in value of a poorly built home and the loss in profit suffered by a business whose production is interrupted by power shortages: *Spartan Steel and Alloys v Martin 1973*.

Historically there was a fear that potentially claims for pure economic loss could be unlimited and the risks could be unknowable (so they are impossible to insure). How far pure economic loss arising from negligence and in particular negligent misstatement could be recovered was therefore limited until *Hedley Byrne*.

Question
Damages in tort

What are the categories of damages in tort?

Answer

In tort, the categories of damages are: ordinary, special, exemplary and nominal.

15.2 Injunction

This is an order by the court which requires an individual to refrain from doing a certain act ('**prohibitory injunction**'), or orders them to do a certain act ('**mandatory injunction**'). Injunctions may be granted at various stages of proceedings:

(a) **Interim injunctions**: these are awarded before the hearing of an action so as to preserve the status quo, and are effective until trial. Here, the claimant enters into an undertaking to pay the defendant for any loss arising out of the granting of the injunction.

(b) **Perpetual injunctions**: these are granted after the full hearing and continue until revoked by the court. (*'Final injunctions'* may also be granted at trial and are effective for a specified period.)

Failure to comply with an injunction is a **contempt of court**, which then empowers the court to fine the person in default or imprison them until their contempt is purged, when they apologise and promise not to breach the court order again in the future.

Question
Injunctions

In a single sentence, explain the purpose of an injunction.

Answer

The purpose of an injunction is to either prevent an individual from doing something, or ordering them to do something.

Chapter Roundup

- The law gives various rights to persons. When such a right is infringed the wrongdoer is liable in **tort**.

- An employer is liable for torts committed by their employees in the course of their employment. Vicarious liability may also arise for the torts of independent contractors in certain circumstances.

- The rule in *Rylands v Fletcher* defines a tort of strict liability, in which reasonable care is no defence. It covers the escape of anything brought onto the defendant's land and likely to do mischief if it escapes, but it does not cover things naturally on the land.

- There are **five types of tort** that you need to be aware of.

- Trespass to land is the most common form of trespass. Claimants may seek damages, an injunction, or both.

- Nuisance may be of two types – public and private. In private nuisance the central idea is that of continuous interference with the claimant's enjoyment of their property. Public nuisance does not require any 'invasion' of private land, rather the annoyance of the general public

- The essence of a **defamatory statement** is that it causes serious harm to the reputation of the person defamed.

- Breach of statutory duty causing harm to a person is a **strict liability tort** that does not require the claimant to prove negligence.

- **Negligence** is the most important modern tort. To succeed in an action for negligence the claimant must prove that:

    - The defendant had **a duty of care** to avoid causing injury, damage or loss
    - There was **a breach of that duty** by the defendant
    - In consequence the claimant suffered **injury, damage or loss**

- The term negligence is used to describe **carelessly** carrying out an **act** and breaking a **legal duty of care** owed to another causing them **loss or damage.**

- In the landmark case of *Donoghue v Stevenson 1932* the House of Lords ruled that a person might **owe a duty of care to another with whom they had no contractual relationship** at all. The doctrine has been refined in subsequent rulings, but the principle is unchanged.

- The second element that must be proven by a claimant in an action for negligence is that there was a **breach of the duty** of care by the defendant.

- Finally the claimant must demonstrate that they suffered injury or loss as a **result** of the breach.

- The amount of damages awarded to the claimant can be reduced if it is shown that they **contributed** to their injury. The defendant can be **exonerated** from paying damages if it can be proved that the claimant **expressly** or **impliedly** consented to the risk.

- Professional individuals and organisations have a special relationship with their clients and those who rely on their work. This is because they act in an **expert capacity**. The law of negligence has been refined in the case of professional advisers to form the tort of **negligent misstatement.**

- According to Lord Denning, to establish a **special relationship** the person who made the statement must have done so in some professional or expert capacity which made it likely that others would rely on what they said. This is the position of an adviser such as an accountant, banker, solicitor or surveyor.

- The **Caparo case** is fundamental to understanding professional negligence. It was decided that **auditors do not owe a general duty of care to the public at large** or to **shareholders increasing their stakes in the company in question**.

- Damages will only be awarded for loss which is not too remote from the actions of the defendant. Chains of causation may be broken by the actions of others, or may become too tenuous when the consequences go beyond what could reasonably have been foreseen. However, the thin skull principle may allow damages to be awarded for unexpected damage.

- The amount of damages is based on the principle of compensating the claimant for their financial loss and not of punishing the defendant for their wrong. Aggravated or exemplary damages may be awarded in limited circumstances.

Quick Quiz

1. In tort no previous transaction or contractual relationship need exist.

   True ☐
   False ☐

2. The 'neighbour' principle was established by the landmark case

   A   Caparo v Dickman 1990
   B   Anns v Merton London Borough Council 1977
   C   Donoghue v Stevenson 1932
   D   The Wagon Mound 1961

3. When the court applies the maxim *res ipsa loquitur*, it is held that the facts speak for themselves and the defendant does not have to prove anything, since the burden of proof is on the claimant.

   True ☐
   False ☐

4. **Fill in the blanks** in the statements below.

   Which three things must a claimant prove to succeed in an action for negligence?

   The defendant owed the claimant a (1)……………. ……… …………..

   These was a (2)……. of the (3)……….. by the defendant

   In (4)…………………….. the claimant suffered (5)………….., (6)…………. or (7)………….

5. Which of the following would prevent a claim for negligence from being successful?

   A   The claimant acted unreasonably.
   B   The defendant caused the harm to the claimant.
   C   A third party is the actual cause of harm.
   D   The parties were proximate and the harm suffered was reasonably foreseeable.
   E   An intervening act broke the 'chain of causation'.
   F   The duty of care was restricted by public policy.

6. Under which circumstance will a court reduce the award of damages to a claimant?

   A   The claimant intervened in the chain of causality
   B   A natural event occurred which caused additional damage
   C   The claimant contributed to the loss they suffered
   D   The defendant acknowledged they were to blame

7. The duty of care owed by accountants is greater when advising on takeovers than when auditing.

   True ☐
   False ☐

8. How may remoteness of damage affect a claim in tort?

Answers to Quick Quiz

1. True. No transaction or relationship is needed.
2. C. Donoghue v Stevenson 1932
3. False. The burden of proof under *res ipsa loquitur* is reversed, the defendant must prove that they were not negligent.
4. (1) duty of care
   (2) breach
   (3) duty
   (4) consequence
   (5) injury
   (6) loss
   (7) damage
5. A, C, E, F
6. C. The correct answer describes contributory negligence. Options A and B are intervening acts that break the chain of causality.
7. True. This was the decision in *Morgan Crucible Co plc v Hill Samuel Bank Ltd and others 1990*
8. Damages are not recoverable where the loss suffered is too remote.

End of chapter question

Negligence

Peter is a warehouse employee with Power House Ltd, a company which sells compact discs over the internet and dispatches them to the buyers. Last month Peter needed to retrieve particular compact discs for an order from a particularly high and unstable stack (such stacks were a common occurrence in the warehouse). The stack collapsed, knocking Peter off the ladder on which he was standing. Peter fell, breaking his leg. Although Peter had not been responsible for the stacking, the way in which he positioned his ladder meant that he had to climb higher than was necessary to reach the compact discs, increasing the distance he fell and the injuries resultant from the fall.

Required

(a) Advise Peter on the possibility of bringing an action in negligence. **(14 marks)**

(b) Advise Peter on whether his own actions will impact upon any remedy he might receive.

(6 marks)

(Total = 20 marks)

PART B TORT LAW IN THE BUSINESS AND PROFESSIONAL CONTEXT

The agency relationship

The agency relationship

Topic list	Syllabus reference
1 Role of agency and agency relationships	2.1
2 Formation of agency	2.1
3 Authority of the agent	2.1
4 Relations between agents and third parties	2.1

Introduction

Having looked at the framework of the **English legal system** and **the law of contract** and **tort** in previous chapters, in this chapter we begin our study of the laws which affect business organisations directly.

In this and the next three chapters we shall look at the **key relationships** organisations have, before, in later chapters, looking in detail at the rules which govern how business organisations are run.

So, in this chapter we shall look at the first type of relationship that affects businesses – the **agency relationship**. Agency is the foundation of most business relationships where more than one person engages in commerce together (for example **partnerships** and **companies**).

We shall see how this relationship arises, what an **agent** is and how an **agent's authority** is acquired and defined.

PART C THE AGENCY RELATIONSHIP

1 Role of agency and agency relationships

FAST FORWARD

Agency is a relationship which exists between two legal persons (the **principal** and the **agent**) in which the function of the agent is to form a **contract between their principal and a third party**. Partners, company directors, factors, brokers and commercial agents are all acting as agents.

Agency is a very important feature of **modern commercial life**. It can be represented diagrammatically as follows:

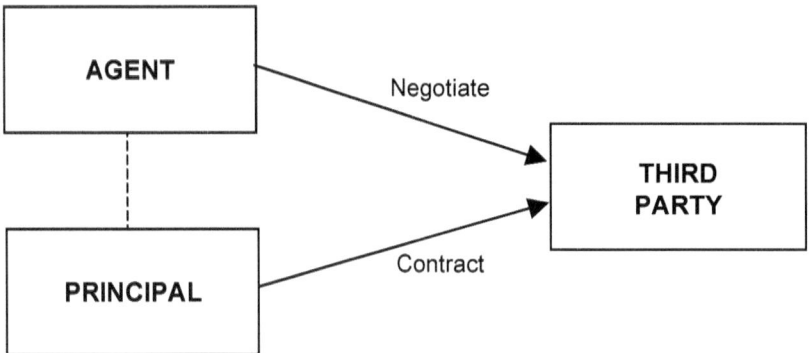

For instance Pendo may ask Alan to take Pendo's shoes to be repaired. Pendo and Alan expressly agree that Alan is to do this on Pendo's behalf. In other words, Alan becomes her agent in making a contract between Pendo and Thierry, the shoe repairer, for her shoes to be mended.

1.1 Types of agent

In practice, there are many **examples of agency relationships**, to which you are probably aware of in everyday life, although you might not know that they illustrate the law of agency. For your studies, the most important agency relationships are those of partners and company directors.

Types of agent	
Partners	This is a particularly important example of agents in your syllabus as accountants who own and run an accountancy practice together are partners, and are therefore agents of each other.
Company directors	Company directors act as agents of their company when running the business and entering the organisation into contracts.
Promoters	A promoter is someone (except professionals acting in their professional capacity) who undertakes to form a company.
Factors	A factor, sometimes called a mercantile agent, is a person whose job is to sell or buy goods on behalf of another person. For example, motor dealers are often factors.
Brokers	A broker may operate in many trades. The are essentially an intermediary who arranges contracts in return for commission. An example is an insurance broker who acts as intermediary between the insurer and the insured.
Auctioneers	Auctioneers are agents authorised to sell property at auction on behalf of the seller. When an auctioneer accepts a bid from a buyer, they become the agent of the buyer for the purpose of making a record of the sale.
Commercial agents	A commercial agent is an independent agent who has continuing authority in connection with the sale or purchase of goods.

Having seen the role of an agent and some examples of the types of agent, we shall no look at how an agency relationship is formed.

2 Formation of agency

> **FAST FORWARD**
>
> The relationship of principal and agent is created by **mutual consent** in the vast majority of cases. This **agreement does not have to be formal or written**.
>
> The mutual consent comes about usually by **express agreement**, even if it is informal. However, it may also be **implied agreement**, due to the **relationship** or **conduct** of the parties.

2.1 Express agreement

Agency by **express agreement** is where the agent is **expressly appointed** by the principal. This may be orally, or in writing. In most commercial situations, the appointment would be made in writing to ensure that everything was clear. An agent expressly appointed by the principal has **actual authority** of the principal to act on their behalf.

2.2 Implied agreement

An agency relationship between two people may also be implied by their **relationship** or by their **conduct**.

For example if an employee's duties include making contracts for their employer, say by ordering goods on their account, then they are, by implied agreement, the agent of the employer for this purpose. An agent authorised in this way is said to have implied authority.

2.3 Ratification of an agent's act: retrospective agreement

> **FAST FORWARD**
>
> A principal may subsequently **ratify** an act of an agent retrospectively.

An agency relationship may be created **retrospectively**, by the 'principal' **ratifying** the act of the 'agent'. Therefore it is created after the 'agent' has formed a contract on behalf of the 'principal'. If the principal agrees to the acts of the agent after the event, they may approve the acts of the agent and make it as if they had been principal and agent at the time of the contract.

The **conditions for ratification** are:

- The principal must have **existed** at the time of the contract made by the agent
- The principal must have had **legal capacity** at the time the contract was made
- The ratification must take place **within reasonable time**
- They ratify the contract in its **entirety**
- They **communicates** their ratification to the third party sufficiently clearly

Once a contract has been ratified by the principal, the effect is that it is as if the agency relationship had been **expressly formed before** the contract made by the agent took place.

2.4 Formation of agency agreement without consent

> **FAST FORWARD**
>
> An agency may be created, or an agent's authority may be extended, without express consent. This happens **by estoppel**, when the principal **'holds out'** a person to be their agent, and when there is an **agent of necessity**.

2.4.1 Implied agreement

In some cases, an agency created by implied agreement might result in the agent having **more implied authority** than the principal might have consented to.

2.4.2 Agent by estoppel

An agency relationship may be formed by implication when the **principal holds out to third parties** that a person is their agent, even if the principal and the 'agent' do not agree to form such a relationship. In such a case, the principal is estopped from denying the agent's apparent/ostensible authority, hence the name **'agent by estoppel'**. An agency relationship is not so formed if it is the 'agent' who creates the impression that they are in an agency relationship with a 'principal'.

2.4.3 Agent by necessity

In some rare situations, it may be necessary for a person to take action in respect of someone else's goods in an **emergency situation**. That person can become an **agent of necessity** of the owner of the goods, as they take steps in respect of the goods.

Question — Agency by necessity

Can you think of an example of a situation of agency by necessity?

Answer

A seller is shipping frozen goods to a buyer in another country. While the ship is docked, the freezers in the ship break down and the relevant part required to fix them cannot be obtained. If the ship's captain cannot make contact with the owner of the goods, they might, of necessity, sell the goods while they are still frozen, rather than allow them to spoil by defrosting.

This principle is a historic part of English shipping and merchant law and you should be aware that it might be possible, but do not worry about the other details of the doctrine.

Having seen how an agency relationship can be formed, we shall now consider an important aspect of the relationship – **authority**. This is what a principal has permitted their agent to do on their behalf.

3 Authority of the agent

FAST FORWARD

If an agent acts within the limits of their authority, any contract they make on the principal's behalf is **binding** on both principal and third party. The extent of the agent's authority may be **express, implied** or **ostensible**. Express and implied authority are both forms of **actual authority**.

A principal does not give the agent unlimited authority to act on their behalf. A **contract** made by the agent is **binding** on the principal and the other party **only if** the **agent was acting within the limits of their authority** from their principal.

In analysing the **limits of an agent's authority**, three distinct sources of authority can be identified:

- Express authority
- Implied authority
- Ostensible authority

3.1 Express authority

Express authority is a matter between principal and agent. This is authority explicitly given by the principal to the agent to perform particular tasks, along with the powers necessary to perform those tasks.

The extent of the agent's express authority will depend on the **construction of the words used on their appointment**. If the appointment is in **writing**, then the document will need to be examined. If it is oral, then the scope of the agent's authority will be a matter of evidence. If the agent contracts outside the scope of their express (actual) authority, they may be **liable** to the principal and the third party for **breach of warrant of authority**.

Illustration

A board of directors may give an individual director express authority to enter the company into a specific contract. The company would be bound to this contract, but not to one made by the individual director outside the express authority.

3.2 Implied authority

Where there is no express authority, authority may be **implied** from the **nature** of the agent's activities or from what is **usual** or **customary** in the **circumstances**. Between principal and agent the latter's express authority is paramount. The agent cannot contravene the principal's express instructions by claiming that they had implied authority for acting in the way they did. As far as **third parties** are concerned, they are entitled to assume that the agent has implied usual authority unless they know to the contrary.

> *Watteau v Fenwick 1893*
>
> *The facts:* The owner of a hotel (F) employed the previous owner (H) to manage it. F forbade H to buy cigars on credit but H did buy cigars from W. W sued F for payment but F argued that he was not bound by the contract, since H had no actual authority to make it, and that W believed that H still owned the hotel.
>
> *Decision:* It was within the usual authority of a manager of a hotel to buy cigars on credit and F was bound by the contract (although W did not even know that H was the agent of F) since his restriction of usual authority had not been communicated.

> *Hely-Hutchinson v Brayhead Ltd 1968*
>
> *The facts:* The chair and chief executive of a company acted as its *de facto* managing director, but he had never been formally appointed to that position. Nevertheless, he purported to bind the company to a particular transaction. When the other party to the agreement sought to enforce it, the company claimed that the chair had no authority to bind it.
>
> *Decision:* Although the director derived no authority from his position as chair of the board, he did acquire authority from his position as chief executive. Therefore the company was bound by the contract as it was within the implied authority of a person holding such a position.

Illustration

A principal employs a stockbroker to sell shares. It is an implied term of the arrangement between them that the broker shall have **actual authority** to do what is usual in practice for a broker selling shares for a client. Any person dealing with the broker is entitled to assume (unless informed to the contrary) that the broker has the usual authority of a broker acting for a client.

3.3 Actual authority

Express and implied authority are sometimes referred to together as **actual authority**. This distinguishes them from **ostensible** or **apparent authority**.

Key term

> **Actual authority** is a legal relationship between principal and agent created by a consensual agreement between them.

3.4 Apparent/ostensible authority

FAST FORWARD

> An agent's **apparent** or **ostensible authority** may be greater than their express or implied authority. This occurs where a **principal** holds it out to be so to a third party, who relied on the representation and altered their position as a result. It may be **more extensive** than what is usual or incidental.

The **ostensible** (or **apparent**) authority of an agent is what a principal **represents** to other persons that they have given to the agent (authority by '**holding out**'). As a result, an agent with **express** or **implied** authority which are limited can be held in practice to have a more extensive authority.

Apparent/ostensible authority usually **arises** either

(a) Where the **principal** has **represented** the agent as having authority even though they have not actually been appointed; or

(b) Where the **principal** has **revoked** the agent's **authority** but the **third party** has **not had notice** of this: *Willis Faber & Co Ltd v Joyce 1911*.

3.4.1 The extent of ostensible authority

Ostensible authority is not restricted to what is usual and incidental. The principal may expressly or by inference from their conduct **confer on the agent any amount of ostensible authority**.

3.4.2 Example: partnership

A **partner** has considerable but **limited implied authority** by virtue of being a partner. If, however, the other partners allow them to exercise greater authority than is implied, they have represented that they have wider authority. They will be bound by the contracts which they make within the limits of this **ostensible authority**.

3.4.3 Example: companies

> *Freeman & Lockyer v Buckhurst Park Properties (Mangal) Ltd 1964*
>
> *The facts:* K and H carried on business as property developers through a company which they owned in equal shares. Each appointed another director, making four in all. H lived abroad and the business of the company was left entirely under the control of K. As a director K had no actual or apparent authority to enter into contracts as agent of the company, but he did make contracts as if he were a managing director without authority to do so. The other directors were aware of these activities but had not authorised them. The claimants sued the company for work done on K's instructions.
>
> *Decision:* There had been a representation by the company through its board of directors that K was the authorised agent of the company. The board had authority to make such contracts and also had power to delegate authority to K by appointing him to be Managing Director. Although there had been no actual delegation to K, the company had by its acquiescence led the claimants to believe that K was an authorised agent and the claimants had relied on it. The company was bound by the contract made by K under the principle of 'holding out' (or estoppel). The company was estopped from denying (that is, not permitted to deny) that K was its agent although K had no actual authority from the company.

It can be seen that it is the **conduct** of the '**principal**' which **creates ostensible authority**. It does not matter whether there is a pre-existing agency relationship or not.

> **Exam focus point**
>
> This is important – ostensible authority arises in two distinct ways. It may arise where a **person makes a representation to third parties** that a particular person has the authority to act as their agent without actually appointing them as their agent. Alternatively, it may arise where a **principal has previously represented to a third party** that an agent has authority to act on their behalf.

3.4.4 Representations creating ostensible authority

The **representation must be made by the principal or an agent acting on their behalf.** It cannot be made by the agent who is claiming ostensible authority: *Armagas Ltd v Mundogas SA, The Ocean Frost 1986*.

It must be a **representation of fact, not law**, and must be **made to the third party**. This distinguishes ostensible authority from actual authority, where the third party need know nothing of the agent's authority.

3.4.5 Reliance on representations

It must be shown that the **third party relied on the representation**. If there is no causal link between the third party's loss and the representation, the third party will not be able to hold the principal as liable.

Illustration

If the third party did not believe that the agent had authority, or if they positively knew they did not, then ostensible authority cannot be claimed. This is true even if the agent appeared to have authority.

3.4.6 Alteration of position following a representation

It is enough that the third party **alters their position as a result of reliance on the representation**. They do not have to suffer any detriment as a result, but damages would in such an event be minimal.

3.5 Revocation of authority

Where a principal has represented to a third party that an agent has authority to act, and has subsequently **revoked the agent's authority**, this may be **insufficient to escape liability**. The principal should inform third parties who have previously dealt with the agent of the change in circumstances. This is particularly relevant to partnerships and the position when a partner leaves a partnership.

3.6 Termination of agency

> **FAST FORWARD**
>
> Agency is terminated by **agreement** or by **operation of law** (death, insanity, insolvency).

Agency is terminated when the **parties agree** that the relationship should end.

It may also be terminated by **operation of law** in the following situations:

- Principal or agent dies
- Principal or agent becomes insane
- Principal becomes bankrupt, or agent becomes bankrupt and this interferes with their position as agent

4 Relations between agents and third parties

FAST FORWARD

An agent usually has **no liability** for a contract entered into as an agent, nor any **right to enforce it**. Exceptions to this: when an agent is **intended** to have liability; where it is **usual business practice** to have liability; when the agent is actually acting on their own behalf; where agent and principal have joint liability.

A third party to a contract entered into with an agent acting outside their ostensible authority can sue for breach of **warranty of authority**.

4.1 Liability of the agent for contracts formed

An agent contracting for their principal within their actual and/or apparent authority generally **has no liability** on the contract and **is not entitled to enforce it**. However, there are **circumstances** when the **agent will be personally liable** and can enforce it.

(a) When they **intended to undertake personal liability** – for example where they sign a contract as party to it without signifying that they are an agent.

(b) Where it is **usual business practice or trade custom** for an agent to be liable and entitled.

(c) Where the agent **is acting on their own behalf** even though they purport to act for a principal.

Where an agent enters into a **collateral contract** with the third party with whom they have contracted on the principal's behalf, there is separate liability and entitlement to enforcement on that collateral contract.

It can happen that there is **joint liability** of agent and principal. This is usually the case where an agent did not disclose that they acted for a principal.

4.2 Breach of warranty of authority

An agent who **exceeds their ostensible authority** will generally have **no liability to their principal**, since the latter will not be bound by the unauthorised contract made for them. But the agent **will be liable** in such a case **to the third party** for breach of warranty of authority.

Chapter Roundup

- **Agency** is a relationship which exists between two legal persons (the **principal** and the **agent**) in which the function of the agent is to form a **contract between their principal and a third party**. Partners, company directors, factors, brokers and commercial agents are all acting as agents.

- The relationship of principal and agent is created by **mutual consent** in the vast majority of cases. This **agreement does not have to be formal or written**.

    The mutual consent comes about usually by **express agreement**, even if it is informal. However, it may also be **implied agreement**, due to the **relationship** or **conduct** of the parties.

- A principal many later **ratify** an act of an agent retrospectively.

- An agency may be created, or an agent's authority may be extended, without express consent. This happens **by estoppel**, when the principal **'holds out'** a person to be their agent, and when there is an **agent of necessity**.

- If an agent acts within the limits of their authority, any contract they make on the principal's behalf is **binding** on both principal and third party. The extent of the agent's authority may be **express, implied** or **ostensible**. Express and implied authority are both forms of **actual authority**.

- An agent's **apparent** or **ostensible authority** may be greater than their express or implied authority. This occurs where a **principal** holds it out to be so to a third party, who relied on the representation and altered their position as a result. It may be **more extensive** than what is usual or incidental.

- Agency is terminated by **agreement** or by **operation of law** (death, insanity, insolvency).

- An agent usually has **no liability** for a contract entered into as an agent, nor any **right to enforce it**. Exceptions to this: when an agent is **intended** to have liability; where it is **usual business practice** to have liability; when the agent is actually acting on their own behalf; where agent and principal have joint liability.

    A third party to a contract entered into with an agent acting outside their ostensible authority can sue for breach of **warranty of authority**.

PART C THE AGENCY RELATIONSHIP

Quick Quiz

1 **Fill in the blanks** in the statements, using the words in the boxes below.

Agency is the (1)..................... which exists between two (2)..................... persons. They are the (3)............... and the agent, in which the function of the agent is to form a (4)............... between their (5)............... and a (6)...............

• relationship	• contract	• legal
• third party	• principal	• principal

2 A principal may, in certain circumstances, ratify the acts of the agent which has retrospective effect.

True ☐

False ☐

3 What is the best definition of ostensible authority?

A   The authority which the principal represents to other persons that they have given to the agent.
B   The authority implied to other persons by the agent's actions.

4 What point of law is explained in the case of *Freeman & Lockyer v Buckhurst Park Properties (Mangal) Ltd 1964*?

5 Which of the following are circumstances where an agent may enforce a contract?

1   Where the agent is intended to take personal liability
2   Where it is usual business practice to allow enforcement
3   Where the agent acts on their own behalf even if they purport to act for a principle

A   1, 2
B   2, 3
C   1, 3
D   1, 2, 3

Answers to Quick Quiz

1. (1) relationship (2) legal (3) principal
   (4) contract (5) principal (6) third party

2. True. Principals may ratify retrospectively.

3. A. The key word is represents.

4. A director may have ostensible authority to contract if although they does not have their express permission, the other directors are aware that contracts are being made and do nothing to prevent it.

5. D. They are all valid circumstances.

End of chapter question

Agency

Doug owns a number of different businesses and is heavily involved in the acquisition of a new petrol station. As a result of his involvement in this deal, he appoints a trusted friend, Larry, to temporarily oversee the running of a supermarket. Doug verbally informs Larry that he can deal as he chooses with existing suppliers but that he must not make contracts with any new suppliers.

Bill represents a meat wholesaler which has supplied meat to Doug's supermarket for several years. He makes a contract with Larry for the supply of meat for the supermarket for the next year which includes a clause stating that the wholesaler will be the exclusive supplier of fresh meat to the supermarket.

Fred is a local farmer who produces organic vegetables. He contacts Doug just before Larry takes over the running of the supermarket to attempt to agree a contract to supply vegetables. Doug informs him that Larry will negotiate the contract when he takes his position in the supermarket.

Required

Advise Doug on the following issues:

(a) Does the concept of agency apply to the relationship between Doug and Larry? **(8 marks)**

(b) Is Doug bound by the two contracts made by Larry? **(12 marks)**

(Total = 20 marks)

PART C THE AGENCY RELATIONSHIP

The partnership relationship

The partnership relationship

Topic list	Syllabus reference
1 Partnerships	2.2
2 Limited liability partnerships	2.2
3 Rights and duties of partners	2.2

Introduction

In this chapter we look at the second type of relationship in business, the **partnership relationship**. This relationship is based on the rules of **agency** that we saw in the previous chapter, and is used to describe how organisations that are formed as partnerships operate.

Partnerships are a common form of business organisation and are often used for **small businesses** and some **professional businesses**, for example accountants. This type of organisation is the product of are a group of individuals who have an **agency relationship** with each other coming together.

We shall look at how partnerships are **formed** and later **terminated**, then at how **relationships** with other partners and with third parties work, including how partnerships can **limit the liability of partners**.

We will then look at the various **rights** and **duties** that partners in a partnership have.

PART D THE PARTNERSHIP RELATIONSHIP

1 Partnerships

> **FAST FORWARD**
>
> **Partnership** is defined as 'the relation which subsists between persons carrying on a business in common with a view of profit'. A partnership is **not** a separate legal person distinct from its members, it is merely a 'relation' between persons. Each partner (there must be at least two) is **personally liable** for all the debts of the firm.

Partnership is a common form of business association. It is **flexible**, because it can either be a **formal** or **informal** arrangement, so can be used for large organisations or a small operations such as those run by a family.

Partnership is normal practice in the **professions** as most professions prohibit their members from carrying on practice through limited companies, though some professions permit their members to trade as limited liability partnerships which have many of the characteristics of companies. Business people are not so restricted and generally prefer to trade through a limited company for the advantages this can bring.

1.1 Definition of partnership

Key term

> '**Partnership** is the relation which subsists between persons carrying on a business in common with a view of profit.' S1 Partnership Act 1890 (HMSO, 1890).

We shall look at some points raised by this definition now.

1.1.1 The relation which subsists between persons

'**Person**' includes a corporation such as a **registered company** as well as an **individual** living person.

There must be at least **two** partners. If, therefore, two people are in partnership, one dies and the survivor carries on the business, that person becomes a 'sole trader'. There is no longer a partnership and there is no legal distinction between that individual and their business.

1.1.2 Carrying on a business

Business can include **every trade**, **occupation** or **profession**. But three points should be noted.

(a) A business is a **form of activity**. If two or more persons are merely the passive joint owners of revenue-producing property, such as rented houses, that fact does not make them partners.

(b) A business can consist of a **single transaction**. These situations are often described as 'joint ventures'.

(c) Carrying on a business must have a **beginning and an end**. A partnership begins when the partners agree to conduct their **business activity** together. This can be before the business actually begins to trade, such as when premises are leased and a bank account opened: *Khan v Miah 2001*.

1.1.3 In common

Broadly this phrase means that the partners must be associated in the business as **joint proprietors**. The evidence that this is so is found in their taking a share of the profits, especially **net profit**.

1.1.4 A view of profit

If persons enter into a partnership with a **view of making profits** but they actually suffer losses, it is still a partnership. The test to be applied is one of **intention**. If the intention of trading together is just to gain experience, for example, there is no partnership: *Davies v Newman 2000*.

1.2 Consequences of the definition

In most cases there is no doubt about the existence of a partnership. The partners declare their intention by such steps as signing a **written partnership agreement** and adopting a **firm name**. These outward and visible signs of the existence of a partnership are not essential however – a partnership can exist without them.

1.2.1 Terminology

The word 'firm' is correctly used to denote a partnership. It is **not** correct to apply it to a registered company (though the newspapers often do so).

The word 'company' may form part of the name of a partnership, for example, 'Smith and Company'. But 'limited company' or 'registered company' is **only** applied to a properly registered company.

1.3 Liability of the partners

We shall see later that every partner is liable **without limit** for the debts of the partnership. It is possible to register a limited partnership in which one or more individual partners have limited liability, but the limited partners may not take part in the management of the business: Limited Partnerships Act 1907 (HMSO, 1907).

The **limited partnership** is useful where one partner wishes to invest in the activities of the partnership without being involved in its day-to-day operation. Such partners are entitled to inspect the accounts of the partnership.

Under the **Limited Liability Partnership Act 2000 (TSO, 2000)** it is possible to register a partnership with limited liability (an LLP). These are discussed in detail later in this chapter.

1.4 Forming a partnership

> **FAST FORWARD**
>
> Partnerships can be **formed** very informally, but there may be complex formalities to ensure clarity.

A partnership can be a very **informal arrangement**. This is reflected in the procedure to form a partnership.

A partnership is **formed when two or more people agree to run a business together**. Partnerships can be formed in any trade or occupation or profession.

In order to be a partnership, the business must be **'carried on in common'**, meaning that all parties must have **responsibility** for the business. In other words, there is **more than one proprietor**.

A couple who run a shop together are partners, but a shop owner and their employee are not.

In law then, the formation of a partnership is essentially straightforward. People **make an agreement** together to run a business, and **carry that agreement out**.

1.4.1 Common formation formalities

In practice, the formalities of setting up a partnership may be more **complex** than simple agreement. Many professional people use partnerships. These business associations can be vast organisations with substantial revenue and expenditure, such as the larger accountancy firms and many law firms.

Such organisations have so many partners that the relationships between them has to be **regulated**. Thus forming some partnerships can involve creating **detailed partnership agreements** which lay out terms and conditions of partnership.

1.4.2 The partnership agreement

A written **partnership agreement** is **not** legally required. In practice there are advantages in setting down in writing the terms of their association.

(a) It **fills** in the **details** which the law would not imply – the nature of the firm's business, its name, and the bank at which the firm will maintain its account for instance.

(b) A written agreement serves to **override terms** otherwise implied by the Partnership Act 1890 which are inappropriate to the partnership. The Act for example implies that partners share profits equally, which will not suit all partnerships.

(c) Additional clauses can be developed. **Expulsion clauses** are an example and they provide a mechanism to expel a partner where there would be no ability to do so otherwise.

1.5 Termination of partnership

FAST FORWARD

Partnerships may be **terminated** by passing of time, termination of the underlying venture, death or bankruptcy of a partner, illegality, notice, agreement or by order of the court.

Termination is when the partnership comes to an end. In this context, 'partnership' means the existing partners.

Question — Termination of partnership 1

Ali, Ben, Cheng and Dimitri are in an ordinary (not limited or limited liability) partnership as accountants. Cheng decides to change career and become an interior designer. In his place, Ali, Ben and Dimitri invite Emily to join the partnership.

As far as third parties are concerned, what do you think happens to the partnership? What is the legal position?

Answer

As far as third parties are concerned, a partnership offering accountancy services still exists. In fact, however, the legal position is that the old partnership (ABCD) has been dissolved, and a new partnership (ABDE) has replaced it.

1.5.1 Events causing termination

The **Partnership Act 1890 (HMSO, 1890)** states that partnership is terminated in the following instances.

- **Passing of time**, if the partnership was entered into for a fixed term
- **Termination of the venture**, if entered into for a single venture
- The **death or bankruptcy** of a partner (partnership agreement may vary this)
- **Subsequent illegality**
- **Notice** given by a partner if it is a partnership of indefinite duration
- **Order of the court** granted to a partner
- **Agreement** between the partners

In the event of the **termination** of a partnership, the partnership's **assets are realised** and the proceeds applied in this order.

- Paying off **external debts**
- Repaying to the **partners** any **loans** or **advances**
- Repaying the partners' **capital contribution**
- Anything left over is then **repaid** to the **partners** in the **profit sharing ratio**

The partnership agreement can exclude some of these provisions and can **avoid dissolution** in the following circumstances.

- Death of a partner
- Bankruptcy of a partner

It is wise to make such provisions to give **stability** to the partnership.

1.6 Authority of partners

> The **authority** of partners to bind each other in contract is based on the principles of agency.

In simple terms, a partner is the **agent of the partnership and their co-partners**. This means that some of their acts bind the other partners, either because they have, or because they appear to have, authority. The **Partnership Act 1890 defines** the **authority** of a partner to make contracts as follows.

Authority of a partner

Every partner is an **agent** of the firm and their other partners for the purpose of the business of the partnership, and the acts of every partner who do any act for carrying on the **usual way** of business if the kind carried on by the firm of which they are a member **bind the firm** and their partners, **unless** the partner so acting has **in fact no authority** to act for the firm in the particular matter, **and the person with whom they are dealing** either **knows that they have no authority**, or **does not know or believe them to be a partner.**

Where a partner pledges the credit of the firm for a **purpose apparently not connected** with the firm's ordinary course of business, the **firm is not bound, unless** they are in fact **specially authorised** by the other partners; but this section does not affect any personal liability incurred by an individual.

If it has been **agreed between the partners** that any **restriction** shall be placed on the power of any one or more of them to bind the firm, **no act** done in contravention of the agreement is **binding** on the firm with respect to **persons having notice of the agreement.**

The key point to note about authority of partners is that, other than when the partner has actual authority, the authority often **depends on the perception of the third party**. If the third party genuinely believes that the partner has authority, the partner is likely to bind the firm.

Partners are also **jointly liable** for **crimes** and **torts** committed by one of their number in the course of business.

1.7 Liability of partners in an unlimited liability partnership

> Partners are **jointly liable** for all partnership debts that result from contracts that the partners have made which bind the firm.

Partners are **jointly liable** for all partnership debts that result from contracts made by other partners which bind the firm. The **Civil Liability Act 1978 (HMSO, 1978)** provides that judgement against one partner does not prevent subsequent actions against other partners.

The link between authority and liability can be seen in the following diagram.

```
                    The firm (that is, all the individual partners) is liable under the contract
                    ▲           ▲           ▲           ▲           ▲
                   YES         YES         YES          NO         YES
                Did the      Did the    Would a partner  Did the other   Did the
                partner have transaction in such a firm  party know, or  other party
                actual       relate to the usually have  have reason     know or
                authority?   business     authority to   to know, that   believe that
                             carried on by do this?      the partner     the 'partner'
                             the firm?                   had no          was a partner?
                                                         authority?
                   NO          NO          NO           YES          NO
                                    ▼
                         The individual partner only is liable
```

There are particular rules on liability for new and retiring partners.

Partner	Partner liability
New partners	A new partner admitted to an existing firm is liable for **debts incurred** only **after** they become a partner. They are not liable for debts incurred before they were a partner unless they agree to become liable.
Retiring partners	A partner who retires is still **liable** for any **outstanding debts** incurred while they were a partner, unless the creditor has agreed to release them from liability. They are also **liable** for debts of the firm **incurred after their retirement** if the creditor knew them to be a partner (before retirement) and has not had **notice** of their retirement. Therefore, it is **vital** on retirement that a partner **gives notice** to all the creditors of the firm. The retiring partner may have an indemnity from the remaining partners with respect to this issue.

1.8 Supervision and regulation

There is **no formal statutory supervision** or **regulation** of partnerships. Their accounts need not be in prescribed form nor is an audit necessary. The public has no means or legal right of inspection of the firm's accounts or other information such as companies must provide.

If, however, the partners carry on business under a firm name which is not the surnames of them all, say, 'Smith, Jones & Co', they are required to disclose the **names** of the **partners** on their letterheads and at their places of business. They are required to make a **return** of their **profits** for income tax and **usually** to **register** for VAT.

1.9 Property

Partnerships **can** grant a **mortgage** or **fixed charge** over property, but **cannot** grant **floating changes**.

2 Limited liability partnerships

FAST FORWARD

A **limited liability partnership** formed under the 2000 Act combines the features of a traditional partnership with the limited liability and creation of legal personality more usually associated with limited companies.

We saw in the previous section that partners are generally jointly liable for contracts that the partnership has entered into. They are also liable for any torts committed by the firm, such as professional negligence. In this section we shall look at two types of partnership where the **liability of the partners is reduced**.

The first form of limited partnership we shall consider is used particularly by professional partnerships, is known as the **limited liability partnership (LLP)**. This type of business association was created by the Limited Liability Partnership Act 2000 (TSO, 2000).

LLPs are similar to limited companies (which will be covered in Chapter 10), in that they have a separate legal identity and unlimited liability for debts. The liability of the individual partners (or members) is **limited to the amount of their capital contribution**.

LLPs have requirements for governance and accountability that are similar to those of limited companies. They are generally set up by firms of professionals such as accountants and lawyers, who wish to operate as partnerships but who seek to have the protection of limited liability.

Key term

A **limited liability partnership (LLP)** is a corporate body which has separate legal personality from its members and therefore some of the advantages and disadvantages of a company.

The **main advantage of an LLP** over a traditional partnership is that the LLP will be liable for its own debts rather than the partners. All contracts with third parties will be with the LLP. This means that the partners are exposed to much less risk than they would be in a normal partnership.

2.1 Formation

A limited liability partnership may be formed by persons associating to carry on lawful business with a view to profit, but it **must be incorporated** to be recognised. LLPs can have an unlimited number of partners. To be incorporated, the subscribers must send an **incorporation document** and a **statement of compliance** to the **Registrar of Companies** at Companies House.

The **document must be signed** and **state** the following:

- The **name** of the LLP
- The **location** of its **registered office** (England and Wales/Wales/Scotland)
- The **address** of the registered office
- The name and address of all the **members** of the LLP
- Which of the members are to be **designated members**

A **registration fee** is also payable to Companies House.

2.2 Internal regulation

LLPs are more **flexible** than companies as they provide **similar protection** for the owners, but **with less statutory rules** on areas such as meetings and management. No board of directors is needed. As can be seen in the incorporation procedures, LLPs come under the supervision of the **Registrar of Companies** (the Registrar).

The members of the LLP are those who **subscribe** to the original incorporation document, and those admitted afterwards in accordance with the terms of the partnership agreement.

The **rights and duties** of the **partners** will usually be set out in a **partnership agreement**. In the absence of a partnership agreement, the rights and duties are set out in regulations under the Act.

LLPs must have **two designated members**, who take responsibility for the publicity requirements of the LLP. With regard to **publicity**, the LLP's designated members must:

- **File** certain notices with the Registrar, such as when a member leaves
- Sign and file **accounts**
- Appoint **auditors** if appropriate

The Registrar will maintain a file containing the **publicised documents** of the LLP at Companies House.

2.3 External relationships

Every member is an **agent** of the LLP. As such, where the member has authority, the LLP will be bound by the acts of the member. The **LLP will not be bound by the acts of the member where:**

- They have no authority and the third party is aware of that fact
- They have ceased to be a member, and the third party is aware of that fact

2.4 Dissolution

An LLP **does not dissolve when a member leaves** in the same way that a traditional partnership does. Where a member has died or (for a corporate member) been wound up, that member ceases to be a member, but the LLP continues in existence. An **LLP must therefore be wound up** when the time has come for it to be dissolved. This is achieved under provisions **similar to company winding up** provisions.

Question — Termination of partnership 2

Ali, Ben, Cheng and Dimitri are in a limited liability partnership as accountants. Cheng decides to change career and become an interior designer. In his place, Ali, Ben and Dimitri invite Emily to join the partnership.

As far as third parties are concerned, what do you think happens to the partnership? What is the legal position?

Answer

As with the previous question, as far as third parties are concerned, a partnership offering accountancy services still exists. In this case however, the legal position is that the same partnership is still in existence because LLPs do not terminate when a member leaves.

2.5 Limited partnership

A second type of limited liability partnership available in the UK (although rarely used) is simply called the **limited partnership**. Under the Limited Partnership Act 1907 (HMSO, 1907), a partnership may be formed in which at least one partner (the general partner) must have **full, unlimited liability**. The other partners have **limited liability** for the debts of the partnership beyond the extent of the capital they have contributed. The rules are as follows:

- Limited partners may not withdraw their capital
- Limited partners may not take part in the management of the partnership

- Limited partners cannot bind the partnership in a contract with a third party without losing the benefit of limited liability
- The partnership must be registered with Companies House

Exam focus point

Partnership questions in scenarios are a regular occurrence and often revolve around a partner's authority to enter into contracts and the liability of all the partners when debts are incurred.

3 Rights and duties of partners

FAST FORWARD

Partners in a partnership have certain **rights**, however, they also owe a number of **duties** as well.

Partners in a partnership have both certain rights that they can enforce, together with number of duties that they owe to the other partners.

3.1 Rights of partners

The main rights of partners in a partnership include:

Right	Description
Right to share profit	Partners have a right to claim their share of the profit. Either in relation to the size of the capital they invested, or as agreed in a written partnership agreement.
Right to inspect accounts and accounting records	Partners have a right of timely access to the financial statements and trial balance as well as the accounting records.
Right to be indemnified	Partners have a right to be repaid for expenses they personally incur when running the partnership.
Right to manage the business	Partners have a right to have an equal say in how the business is run, such as in planning, decision making and control activities.
Right to use business property	Partners have a right to use any business property for the purpose of running the business. There is no right to use business property for personal reasons.
Right to joint ownership of business property	Partners have an equal right to business property, and partners cannot sell business property without the agreement of the other partners.

3.1 Duties of partners

The main duties of partners in a partnership include:

Duty	Description
Duty of mutual confidence, understanding and trust	A partnership is based on agreement between the partners who have a duty to honour the confidence, understanding and trust that is the basis of it.
Duty to indemnify the business	Partners have a duty to repay any losses to the business that result from their negligence.

Duty	Description
Duty to share losses	Whilst partners have a right to share profit, they also have a duty to share losses in the same way.
Duty to act within their authority	Partners have a duty not to act outside of any authority given to them.
Duty not to run a competitive business	Partners have a duty not to set up a business that competes with the partnership.
Duty not to demand remuneration	Partners share in the profits and losses of the business. They cannot demand remuneration unless it is provided for in a written partnership agreement.

Question — Rights of partners

Briefly explain the right of partners to manage the business.

Answer

Partners have a right to an equal say in how the business is run. This right extends to all areas of running the business, such as in planning, decision making and control activities.

Chapter Roundup

- **Partnership** is defined as 'the relation which subsists between persons carrying on a business in common with a view of profit'. A partnership is **not** a separate legal person distinct from its members, it is merely a 'relation' between persons. Each partner (there must be at least two) is **personally liable** for all the debts of the firm.

- Partnerships can be **formed** very informally, but there may be complex formalities to ensure clarity.

- Partnerships may be **terminated** by passing of time, termination of the underlying venture, death or bankruptcy of a partner, illegality, notice, agreement or by order of the court.

- The **authority** of partners to bind each other in contract is based on the principles of agency.

- Partners are **jointly liable** for all partnership debts that result from contracts that the partners have made which bind the firm.

- **A limited liability partnership** formed under the 2000 Act combines the features of a traditional partnership with the limited liability and creation of a legal personality more usually associated with limited companies.

- Partners in a partnership have certain **rights**, however, the also owe a number of **duties** as well.

Quick Quiz

1. Which one of the following statements about traditional (unlimited) partnerships is **incorrect**?

    A In England a partnership has no existence distinct from the partners.
    B A partnership must have a written partnership agreement.
    C A partnership is subject to the Partnership Act.
    D Each partner is an agent of the firm.

2. An LLP dissolves when a member leaves.

    True ☐
    False ☐

3. Which of the following statements is an inaccurate description of a partnership?

    A A partnership is a relationship which subsists between parties carrying on a business in common with a view of profit.
    B A partnership business may be any trade, occupation or profession but must be more than a single transaction.
    C Every partner is liable without limit for the debts of the partnership (except in the case of a registered limited partnership).
    D A written partnership agreement is not a legal requirement.

4. In a partnership, all partners share profits and losses equally.

    True ☐
    False ☐

5. In a partnership, partners only have a right to use business assets if it is for a business reason.

    True ☐
    False ☐

Answers to Quick Quiz

1. B. A written agreement is not needed.
2. False. LLPs are only dissolved when they cease to trade.
3. B. A partnership can consist of a single transaction (such businesses are often described as joint ventures).
4. False. In a partnership, profits and losses are shared based on the amount of capital each partner invested or as otherwise set out in a written partnership agreement.
5. True. Partners have no right to use business assets other than for business reasons.

End of chapter question

Partnerships

Ben, Will and Diane want to enter into business together to run a bakery and café. They have all been good friends since they attended university together. Ben recently inherited a large sum of money from his grandmother which he wishes to invest in the business. Diane has a degree in marketing and a large number of contacts throughout the UK that would be helpful to the new business.

Will is a very talented patisserie chef. However, he admits he is 'not good with money' and currently has many debts. Ben and Diane are worried that his personal debts will affect them if they go into business with him, and that he will make irresponsible financial decisions in relation to the new business. They cannot however start the bakery without him. They have little knowledge of the different forms of businesses available, but a friend has advised them that a partnership would suit them best.

Required

Explain to Ben and Diane what a partnership is, and whether it would provide a suitable legal vehicle for running their proposed business. If they decide to form a partnership, would you advise them to have a written partnership agreement, and why? **(20 marks)**

PART D THE PARTNERSHIP RELATIONSHIP

PART E

The employment relationship and social security law: the relationship with the state

The employment relationship

Topic list	Syllabus reference
1 What is an employee?	2.3
2 Why does it matter?	2.3
3 The employment contract	2.3
4 Varying the terms of an employment contract	2.3
5 Common law duties	2.3
6 Statutory duties	2.3

Introduction

In this chapter we begin our study of the third type of relationship in business – the **relationship between employees and employers**.

This relationship is governed by **employment law** and we begin by looking at the **distinction** between the **employment** and **self-employment**. This distinction is very important as it has implications for employee **rights** and **liabilities**.

The chapter continues by examining a key element of an employment relationship - an **employment contract**. Like any other contract it may include **express** and **implied terms**, and you should be able to explain how these terms are included.

As part of the relationship, employers and employees owe certain **duties** to one another; breach of these duties may result in legal action against the party who breached their duty. Learn these duties and the supporting case law as they are an important part of your syllabus.

From this chapter onward you will start to see references to relevant legislation. These references can be used for further reading if you wish to do so, but it is not a requirement for your exam.

Statutory references in this chapter are to the Employment Rights Act 1996 (TSO, 1996) (ERA 1996) and Small Business, Enterprise and Employment Act 2015 (TSO, 2015) unless otherwise noted.

1 What is an employee?

FAST FORWARD

It is important to distinguish between a **contract of service** (employment) and a **contract for services** (independent contractor). Each type of contract has different rules for taxation, health and safety provisions, protection of contract and vicarious liability in tort and contract.

A contract of service is **distinguished** from a contract for services usually because the parties **express** the agreement to be one of service. This does not always mean that an employee will not be treated as an independent contractor by the court, however; much depends on the three tests.

- Control test
- Integration test
- Economic reality test

A general rule is that an employee is someone who is employed under a **contract of service**, as distinguished from an independent contractor, who is someone who works under a **contract for services**.

However, it is important to note that some **statutory provisions** (such as minimum wage rates and amounts of paid leave) apply to '**workers**' and this term is wider than '**employees**' and includes those personally performing work or services unless they are truly self-employed.

In *Uber BV and others (Appellants) v Aslam and others (Respondents) 2021* it was decided that people employed in the **gig economy** (in this case working for Uber) could be treated as workers rather than as independent contractors. This was because Uber had a degree of control over factors such as assigning jobs to Uber drivers and determining how much they are paid. Uber could also discipline them if it was not happy with feedback from customers.

Key terms

An **employee** is 'an individual who has entered into, or works under a contract of employment': Employment Rights Act 1996 (ERA).

A **contract of employment** is 'a contract of service or apprenticeship, whether express or implied, and (if it is express) whether it is oral or in writing.'

In practice this distinction depends on **many factors** and it can be very important to know whether an individual is an employee or an independent contractor. The courts will apply a series of **tests**.

Primarily, the court will look at the **reality of the situation**. This may be in spite of the form of the arrangement.

Ferguson v John Dawson & Partners 1976

The facts: A builder's labourer was paid his wages without deduction of income tax or National Insurance contributions and worked as a self-employed contractor providing services. His 'employer' could dismiss him, decide on which site he would work and direct him as to the work he should do. It also provided the tools which he used. He was injured in an accident and sued his employers on the basis that they owed him legal duties as his employer.

Decision: On the facts taken as a whole, he was an employee working under a contract of employment.

Where there is some **doubt** as to the nature of the relationship the courts will then look at any **agreement between the parties**.

> *Massey v Crown Life Assurance 1978*
>
> *The facts*: The claimant was originally employed by an insurance company as a departmental manager; he also earned commission on business which he introduced. At his own request he changed to a self-employed basis. Tax and other payments were no longer deducted by the employers but he continued to perform the same duties. The employers terminated these arrangements and the claimant claimed compensation for unfair dismissal.
>
> *Decision*: As he had opted to become self-employed and his status in the organisation was consistent with that situation, his claim to be a dismissed employee failed.

It can still be unclear whether a person is an employee or an independent contractor. Historically, the tests of **control, integration** into the employer's organisation, and **economic reality** (or the multiple test) have been applied in such cases.

The fundamental prerequisite of a contract of employment is that there must be **mutual obligations** on the employer to provide, and the employee to perform, work.

1.1 The control test

The court will consider whether the employer has **control** over the way in which the employee performs their duties.

> *Mersey Docks & Harbour Board v Coggins & Griffiths (Liverpool) 1947*
>
> *The facts:* Stevedores (dockworkers) hired a crane with its driver from the harbour board under a contract which provided that the driver (appointed and paid by the harbour board) should be the employee of the stevedores. Owing to the driver's negligence a checker was injured. The case was concerned with whether the stevedores or the harbour board were vicariously liable as employers.
>
> *Decision:* It was decided that the issue must be settled on the facts and not on the terms of the contract. The stevedores could only be treated as employers of the driver if they could control in detail how he did his work. But although they could instruct him what to do, they could not control him in how he operated the crane. The harbour board (as 'general employer') was therefore still the driver's employer.

Another example of this test is in *Walker v Crystal Palace FC 1910* where it was held that a **professional footballer** was employed because he was subject to the control of his club in the form of training, discipline and method of pay.

1.2 The integration test

The courts consider whether the employee is so skilled that they cannot be controlled in the performance of their duties. Lack of control indicates that an employee is **not integrated** into the employer's organisation, and therefore not employed.

> *Cassidy v Ministry of Health 1951*
>
> *The facts:* The full-time assistant medical officer at a hospital carried out a surgical operation in a negligent fashion. The patient sued the Ministry of Health as employer. The Ministry resisted the claim arguing that it had no control over the doctor in his medical work.
>
> *Decision:* In such circumstances the proper test was whether the employer appointed the employee, selected him for his task and so integrated him into the organisation. If the patient had chosen the doctor the Ministry would not have been liable as employer. But here the Ministry (the hospital management) made the choice and so it was liable.

The control and integration tests are important, but **no longer decisive** in determining whether a person is an employee.

1.3 The multiple (economic reality) test

Courts also consider whether the employee was **working on their own account** and require numerous factors to be taken into account.

> *Ready Mixed Concrete (South East) v Ministry of Pensions & National Insurance 1968*
>
> *The facts*: The driver of a special vehicle worked for one company only in the delivery of liquid concrete to building sites. He provided his own vehicle (obtained on hire purchase from the company) and was responsible for its maintenance and repair. He was free to provide a substitute driver. The vehicle was painted in the company's colours and the driver wore its uniform. He was paid gross amounts (no tax etc deducted) on the basis of mileage and quantity delivered as a self-employed contractor. The Ministry of Pensions claimed that he was in fact an employee for whom the company should make the employer's insurance contributions.
>
> *Decision*: In such cases the most important test is whether the worker is working on his own account. On these facts the driver was a self-employed transport contractor and not an employee.

In the above case, the judge held that a contract of service existed where:

- There is **agreement** from the worker that they will provide work for their master in exchange for remuneration.
- The worker agrees either expressly or impliedly that their master can exercise **control** over their performance.
- There are other **factors** included in the contract that make it **consistent** with a contract of service.

The fact that the drivers could appoint a **replacement** for themselves was a major factor in the decision that found them as contractors rather than employees.

1.4 Agency workers

The status of agency workers has been the subject of numerous cases in recent years as the numbers employed under such contracts have increased. Two key cases have considered **length of service** of agency workers and **control** that the client of the agency has over the worker.

(a) **Length of service**

In *Franks v Reuters Ltd 2003*, the agency worker had been providing services to the client for some **six years,** engaged in a variety of jobs, and was effectively so thoroughly integrated with the employer's organisation as to be **indistinguishable** from the employer's staff.

Mummery LJ, said that an 'implied contract of employment did not arise simply by virtue of the length of the employment, but it could well be a factor in applying the overall tests appropriate to establish (or otherwise) an employment status'.

The case was remitted to the tribunal for further consideration, but the length of an assignment of an agency worker clearly has implications for the development of other indications of an employment relationship, with those utilising the services of the worker forgetting the true nature of the relationship and behaving towards the work as if they were an employee. It may be that at this point the relevant approach also starts to involve the 'integration test'.

(b) **Control over the worker**

Where the client of the agency has **sufficient control** over the employee provided by the agency, it could be held that they are in fact the true employer.

> *Motorola v Davidson and Melville Craig 2001*
>
> *The facts:* Davidson was contracted with the Melville Craig agency and was assigned to work for Motorola. Both the agency and Motorola had agreed that Davidson could be sent back to the agency if his work was unacceptable. Following a disciplinary hearing Davidson was found unacceptable and returned to the agency. Davidson took Motorola to an employment tribunal for unfair dismissal.
>
> *Decision:* Motorola had sufficient control over Davidson to make them the employer. It was held that the court should look beyond the pure legal situation and look at the practical control aspects in such cases as well.

1.5 Relevant factors

Significant factors that you should consider when deciding whether or not a person is employed or self-employed are as follows.

- Does the employee use their **own tools and equipment** or does the employer provide them?
- Does the alleged employer have the power to **select or appoint** its employees, and may it dismiss them?
- **Payment of salary** is a fair indication of there being a contract of employment.
- **Working for a number of different people** is not necessarily a sign of self-employment. A number of assignments may be construed as 'a series of employments'.

In difficult cases, courts will consider whether the employee can **delegate** all their obligations, whether there is restriction as to place of work, whether there is a **mutual obligation** and whether holidays and hours of work are agreed.

> *O'Kelly v Trusthouse Forte Plc 1983*
>
> *The facts:* The employee was a 'regular casual' working when required as a waiter. There was an understanding that he would accept work when offered and that the employer would give him preference over other casual employees. The employment tribunal held that there was no contract of employment because the employer had no obligation to provide work and the employee had no obligation to accept work when offered.
>
> *Decision:* The Court of Appeal agreed with this finding. Whether there is a contract of employment is a question of law but it depends entirely on the facts of each case; here there was no 'mutuality of obligations' and hence no contract.

The decision whether to classify an individual as an employee or not is also influenced by **policy considerations**. For example, an employment tribunal might regard a person as an employee for the purpose of unfair dismissal despite the fact that the tax authorities treated them as self-employed.

> *Airfix Footwear Ltd v Cope 1978*
>
> *The facts:* The case concerned a classic outworking arrangement under which the applicant (having been given training and thereafter supplied with the necessary tools and materials) generally worked five days a week making heels for shoes manufactured by the respondent company. She was paid on a piece work basis without deduction of income tax or NIC.
>
> *Decision:* Working for some seven years, generally for five days a week, resulted in the arrangement being properly classified as employment under a contract of employment.

PART E THE EMPLOYMENT RELATIONSHIP AND SOCIAL SECURITY LAW: THE RELATIONSHIP WITH THE STATE

Question — Court tests

Which tests are applied by the courts when answering the following questions?

(1) Has the employer control over the way in which the employee performs their duties?
(2) Is the skilled employee part of the employer's organisation?
(3) Is the employee working on their own account?

Answer

(1) Control test
(2) Integration test
(3) Multiple (economic reality) test

Having studied the difference between employment and self-employment, as well as the tests used to determine whether someone is employed or self-employed, we shall now look at why it is important to distinguish between the two. As you will see, a key reason is because employees have certain rights of protection in employment law that the self-employed do not enjoy.

2 Why does it matter?

FAST FORWARD

The distinction between **employed** and **self-employed** is important as to whether certain **rights** are available to an individual and how they are treated for **tax purposes**.

The first thing that it is important to note is that much of the legislation which gives protection to employees **extends further than employees**. Much of it is drafted to cover 'workers', a term which has a wide definition to cover most people providing services to others outside of the course of (their own) business.

This has reduced the importance of the **distinction** between employee and independent contractor in this area.

However, there are several other **practical reasons** why the distinction between a contract of service and a contract for services is important.

SIGNIFICANCE OF THE DISTINCTION		
	Employed	**Self-employed**
Social security	Employers must pay secondary Class 1 National Insurance contributions on behalf of employees Employees make primary Class 1 National Insurance contributions There are also differences in statutory sick pay and levies for industrial training purposes	Independent contractors pay Class 2 and 4 contributions
Taxation	Deductions must be made for income tax by an employer under PAYE from salary paid to employee	The self-employed are taxed under self-assessment for income tax and are directly responsible to HM Revenue and Customs for tax due

8: THE EMPLOYMENT RELATIONSHIP

SIGNIFICANCE OF THE DISTINCTION		
	Employed	**Self-employed**
Employment protection	There is legislation which confers protection and benefits upon employees under a contract of service, including • Minimum periods of notice • Remedies for unfair dismissal	Employment protection is not available for contractors
Tortious acts	Employers are generally vicariously liable for tortious acts of employees, committed in the course of employment	Liability of the person hiring an independent contractor for the contractor's acts is severely limited unless there is strict liability
Implied terms	There are rights and duties implied by statute for employers and employees This will affect things such as copyrights and patents	These implied rights and duties do not apply to such an extent to a contract for services
VAT	Employees do not have to register for or charge VAT	An independent contractor may have to register for, and charge, VAT
Insolvency	In an employer's liquidation, an employee has preferential rights as a creditor for payment of outstanding salary and redundancy payments, up to a statutory limit	Contractors are treated as non-preferential creditors if their employer is wound up
Health and safety	There is significant common law and legislation governing employers' duties to employees with regards to health and safety	The common law provisions and much of the legislation relating to employees also relates to independent contractors

Question — Employed v self-employed

List five reasons why the distinction between employed and self-employed workers is important.

Answer

Five reasons include:

1. Social security
2. Taxation
3. Employment protection
4. Tortious acts
5. Health and safety

(Also implied terms, VAT, rights in bankruptcy)

We have now seen the difference between the employed and self-employed and why the difference is important. We shall now focus our studies on the relationship between employee and employer by considering the key document in the relationship, the employment contract. As with any contract, an employment contract formalises how the parties expect the relationship to operate.

3 The employment contract

> **FAST FORWARD**
>
> There are no particular legal rules relating to the commencement of employment – it is really **just like any other contract** in requiring offer and acceptance, consideration and intention to create legal relations.

An employment contract is a contract of service which may be **express** or **implied**. If express, it can be either **oral** or **written**. This means that employment contracts can be simple, straightforward agreements. The contact must, of course, comply with the usual rules relating to the formation of a valid contract.

As with any other contract, agreements for employment require offer, acceptance, consideration and the intention to create legal relations:

- Generally the offer comes from the employer and acceptance from the employee, who may write a letter or simply turn up for work at an agreed time.
- Consideration comprises the promises each party gives to the other – a promise to work for a promise to pay. If there is no consideration, a deed must be executed for there to be a contract of employment.
- The intention to create legal relations is imputed from the fact that essentially employment is a commercial transaction.

At the one extreme, an employment contract may be a **document** drawn up by solicitors and signed by both parties; at the other extreme it may consist of a **handshake** and a 'See you on Monday'. In such cases the court has to clarify the agreement by determining what the parties must be taken to have agreed.

Senior personnel may sign a contract specially drafted to include terms on **confidentiality** and **restraint of trade**. Other employees may sign a standard form contract, exchange letters with the new employer or simply agree terms orally at interview.

Each of these situations will form a valid contract of employment, subject to the requirements regarding written particulars, as long as there is **agreement** on **essential terms** such as hours and wages. Nor should it be forgotten that even prior to employment commencing the potential employer has legal obligations, for example not to discriminate in recruitment.

3.1 Implied terms

Implied terms usually arise out of **custom** and **practice** within a profession or industry. In *Henry v London General Transport Services Ltd 2001* it was held that four requirements should be met before such terms can be read into a contract.

- The terms must be **reasonable, certain** and **notorious**
- They must represent the **wishes** of both parties
- **Proof** of the custom or practice must be provided by the party seeking to rely on the term
- A **distinction** must be made between implying terms that make minor, and terms that make **fundamental** changes to the contract

3.2 Requirement for written particulars

On or before the first day of employment, the employer must give to an employee a written **statement of prescribed particulars** of their employment: s 1.

The statement should identify the following.

- The names of **employer** and **employee**
- The **date** on which employment began
- Whether any service with a previous employer forms part of the employee's **continuous period** of employment

- **Pay** – scale or rate and intervals at which paid
- **Hours** of work (including any specified 'normal working hours')
- The **title** of the job which the employee is employed to do (or a brief job description)
- Any **holiday** and **holiday pay** entitlement (for a person working five days per week. The statutory holiday entitlement is 5.6 weeks or 28 days, which may include bank and public holidays depending on the contract of employment)
- **Sick leave** and **sick pay** entitlement
- **Pensions** and pension **schemes**
- Length of **notice** of termination to be given on either side
- Details of **disciplinary procedures** (or reference to where they can be found)

The last four of the particulars may be given by way of separate documents. If the employee has a **written contract of employment** covering these points and has been given a copy it is not necessary to provide them with separate written particulars.

If the employer fails to comply with these requirements the employee may apply to an **employment tribunal** for a declaration of what the terms should be: s 11. S38 Employment Act 2002 allows a tribunal to award compensation to an employee claiming unfair dismissal if the particulars are incomplete.

Having considered the contents of employment contracts, it is important to realise that they are not set in stone forever. Because they deal with a **relationship** which might change over time there must be flexibility to allow the contract to be **amended** as and when required. For example, an employee who becomes a parent may wish to reduce their working hours to allow them time to look after the child. How an employment contract can be altered (or varied) is the subject of the following section.

4 Varying the terms of an employment contract

FAST FORWARD

A contract of employment can only be **varied** if the contract **expressly** gives that right, or if all parties consent to the variation.

It should be clear, from your earlier studies of general contract law, that a change in contract terms **can only be made with the consent of both parties** to the contract.

4.1 Varying terms without changing the contract

There may be circumstances in which an employer can vary the terms of an employment contract without actually needing to vary the contract itself. For example, there may be an **express term** in the contract which itself gives rights of variation, for example to allow a change in area of work.

Alternatively, an **implied term** may act to vary the contract.

(a) A sales representative may be required to take responsibility for such area as their employer considers necessary in order to meet changing market conditions

(b) Terms may also be implied by custom, for example, where a steel erector is required at the request of their employer to change sites: *Stevenson v Teeside Bridge & Engineering Co Ltd 1971*

4.2 Changing the existing contract

The existing contract can be changed by **consent**. Consent might be demonstrated by **oral agreement** to new terms, by the **signing** of a new statement of terms and conditions or by the employee showing acceptance by **working** under the new terms. If an employee's contract is varied without consent, the employee may have a claim for **constructive dismissal**.

4.3 Signing a new contract

The third option open to the employer is to give contractual notice to the employee and then offer a new contract on the new terms. This opens the employer to a **potential claim** for unfair dismissal. It is generally best for the employer to obtain consent to vary the terms of an existing contract.

The employment contract is an important document in the **employment relationship**, however there are two other sources of rules that govern the relationship. These come in the form of duties that employers and employees are expected to honour. These duties come from both common law and statutory sources.

5 Common law duties

> **FAST FORWARD**
>
> The **employer** has an implied **duty at common law** to take **reasonable care** of their employees; they must select proper staff, materials and provide a safe system of working.
>
> The **employee** has a duty of **faithful service** and to exercise **care and skill** in performance of their duties.

5.1 Employee's duties

The employee has a **fundamental duty of faithful service** to their employer. All other duties are features of this general duty.

Hivac Ltd v Park Royal Scientific Instruments Ltd 1946

The facts: In their spare time certain of the claimant's employees worked for the defendant company, which directly competed with the claimant.

Decision: Even though the employees had not passed on any confidential information, they were still in breach of their duty of fidelity to the claimants.

This duty also extends after the employment where **trade secrets** are concerned. Employees will be in breach of their duty if they disclose such secrets to their new employer. The **facts of the case** and the **nature of employment** should be considered when making a decision, for example customer lists of a chicken selling business was not considered a trade secret when a sales manager set up their own competing organisation *(Faccenda Chicken Ltd v Fowler 1986)*.

The **implied** duties of the employee include the following.

(a) **Reasonable competence** to do their job.

(b) **Obedience** to the employer's instructions unless they require them to do an unlawful act or to expose themselves to personal danger (not inherent in their work) or are instructions outside the employee's contract.

Pepper v Webb 1969

The facts: The defendant, a gardener refused to obey instructions from his employer regarding planting in the garden. He also swore at him.

Decision: The gardener was in breach of his implied duty to obey as the instructions were lawful and reasonable.

(c) **Duty to account for all money and property** received during the course of their employment except what is customary to be received or is trivial.

> *Boston Deep Sea Fishing and Ice Co v Ansell 1888*
>
> *The facts:* The defendant, who was managing director of the claimant company, accepted personal commissions from suppliers on orders which he placed with them for goods supplied to the company. He was dismissed and the company sued to recover from him the commissions.
>
> *Decision:* The company was justified in dismissing the claimant and he must account to it for the commissions.

(d) **Reasonable care and skill** in the performance of their work: *Lister v Romford Ice and Cold Storage Co 1957*. What is reasonable depends on the degree of skill and experience which the employee professes to have.

(e) **Personal service** – the contract of employment is a personal one and so the employee may not delegate their duties without the employer's express or implied consent.

5.2 Employer's duties

There is an overriding **duty of mutual trust and confidence** between the employer and the employee. Examples of where this duty have been breached include:

- A director calling his secretary 'an intolerable bitch on a Monday morning' – *Isle of Wight Tourist Board v Coombes 1976*
- Failure to investigate a sexual harassment claim – *Bracebridge Engineering v Darby 1990*

The employer usually also has the following duties at common law:

(a) To **pay remuneration** to employees. If there is no rate fixed by the parties, this duty is to pay **reasonable** remuneration.

(b) To **indemnify the employee** against expenses and losses incurred in the course of employment.

(c) To take care of the employees' **health and safety** at work. This is also provided for in statute.

(d) To **provide work**, where:

- The employee is an apprentice
- The employee is paid with reference to work done
- The opportunity to work is the essence of the contract (for example, for actors)
- There is work available to be done (subject to contractual terms to the contrary) **and** the relevant employee is a skilled worker who needs work to preserve their skills – *William Hill Organisation v Tucker 1998*

There is no breach of duty if there is **no work** available and the employer continues to pay its employees. However, if an employee was appointed to a **particular role** and no work was provided there may be a breach of duty to provide work if it denies the employee the opportunity to maintain their skills – *Collier v Sunday Referee Publishing Co Ltd 1940*.

There is no duty to provide a **reference** when employees leave service. Employers may be liable under negligence for not taking reasonable care over accuracy and fairness if they do provide one: *Cox v Sun Alliance Life 2001*.

The **importance** of these common law implied duties on both parties is that:

- **Breach of a legal duty**, if it is important enough, may entitle the injured party to treat the contract as **discharged** and to claim damages for breach of contract at common law; and

- In an employee's claim for compensation for unfair dismissal, the employee may argue that it was a case of **constructive dismissal** by the employer, or the employer may seek to justify their express dismissal of the employee by reference to their conduct.

Question — Fundamental duty

What is an employee's fundamental duty to their employer?

Answer

An employee's fundamental duty to their employer is of faithful service.

6 Statutory duties

FAST FORWARD

Statute implies terms into employment contracts, which may not usually be overridden, regarding pay and equality, maternity leave and work/life balance generally, time off, health and safety and working time.

Various matters are implied into contracts of employment by statute. Some of them build upon the **basic matters** covered by the common law. Most of the employment statutes in this area implement European Directives on employment law issues. An **employer** has **statutory duties** in the following areas:

- Pay and equality
- Time off work
- Maternity rights and the 'work/life balance'
- Health and safety
- Working time

6.1 Pay and equality

There are two key pieces of legislation in relation to pay. These are the **National Minimum Wage Act 1998 (TSO, 1998)** and the **Equality Act 2010 (TSO, 2010)**.

6.1.1 National Minimum Wage Act 1998

A **national minimum hourly wage** was introduced in the UK in 1999 and the rate is reviewed annually. A company will be penalised financially if it does not pay all or some of its employees the statutory minimum. The penalty is calculated on a per worker basis.

Since April 2016 workers over 25 have been entitled to the **National Living Wage**. This is paid at a higher rate than the national minimum wage, which applies to workers under 25.

6.1.2 Equality Act 2010

The **Equality Act 2010** seeks to ensure **equal treatment** in **employment** and **access to employment** for employees, applicants for employment and contract workers, and therefore to **outlaw direct discrimination** (including associative and perceived discrimination), **indirect discrimination**, **harassment** (including harassment by a third party) and **victimisation**.

Under this Act, discrimination in the workplace is illegal. The Act covers terms such as pay, sick pay, holiday pay, benefits and working hours, and it applies to all forms of full-time and part-time work.

The Act is applied on the basis of **'protected characteristics'**, namely:

- Age
- Disability
- Gender
- Sexual orientation
- Gender re-assignment
- Race (that is colour, nationality and ethnic or racial origins)
- Religion or belief
- Marriage or civil partnership
- Being pregnant or having a child

Discrimination judgements are viewed in light of a single **'objective justification' test**: employers must prove their actions were a **'proportionate means of meeting a legitimate aim'**.

The **'objective justification' test** is based on **the Employment Statutory Code of Practice** which identifies that the meaning of the terms **'proportionate'** and **'legitimate aims' derive from EU law**.

Proportionate means:

- The discriminatory effect should be significantly outweighed by the benefits of achieving the aim.
- There is no reasonable alternative. If the aim can be achieved with less discrimination, that option should be followed.

The law generally views treatment as proportionate if it is an 'appropriate and necessary' means of achieving a legitimate aim. But 'necessary' does not mean that the provision, criterion or practice is the only possible way of achieving the legitimate aim; it is sufficient that the same aim could not be achieved by less discriminatory means.

Legitimate aims include:

- Business needs and efficiency
- Health and safety reasons
- Particular training requirements of the job

The **Employment Statutory Code of Practice** states that the aim of the provision, criterion or practice should be legal, should not be discriminatory in itself, and must represent a real, objective consideration. The health, welfare and safety of individuals may qualify as legitimate aims provided that risks are clearly specified and supported by evidence. Although reasonable business needs and economic efficiency may be legitimate aims, an employer solely aiming to reduce costs cannot expect to satisfy the test. For example, the employer cannot simply argue that to discriminate is cheaper than avoiding discrimination.

6.1.3 Pay statements

Under the Employment Rights Act 1996 (TSO, 1996), employers are obliged to provide an itemised pay statement.

6.2 Time off work

In addition to the rights relating to maternity, paternity, adoption and parental leave (see below), statute lists several occasions when an employee has a right to time off work.

(a) **Trade union officials** are entitled to time off on full pay at the employer's expense to enable them to carry out **trade union duties**.

(b) An employee who has been given notice of dismissal for **redundancy** may have time off to look for work or to arrange training for other work.

(c) A member of a recognised independent **trade union** may have time off work (without statutory right to pay) for **trade union activities**, for example, attending a branch meeting.

(d) Employers also have a duty to allow an employee to have reasonable time off to carry out certain **public duties**, for example performing their duties as a magistrate. There is **no statutory provision** entitling an employee to time off for jury service, but prevention of a person from attending as a juror is contempt of court.

6.3 Maternity rights and the 'work/life balance'

Employees who are pregnant are given **substantial rights** under statute, including:

- The right to **time off work** for ante-natal care
- The right to **ordinary maternity leave**
- The right to **additional maternity leave**
- The right to **maternity pay**
- The right to **return to work** after maternity leave
- If dismissed, a claim for **unfair dismissal**

Much recent employment legislation has been concerned with the introduction of **family-friendly** employment policies and the '**work/life balance**'. The law has developed as a result in the areas of maternity leave and pay, paternity leave, rights of adoptive parents and a right to request flexible working.

6.3.1 Ante-natal care

An employee has a right not to be **unreasonably refused time** off for ante-natal care during working hours.

6.3.2 Maternity leave and pay

Employees who are pregnant are entitled to **statutory maternity leave** of up to **52 weeks** if they give 15 weeks' notice of their due date to their employer. **Statutory maternity pay** is paid for **39 weeks** during statutory maternity leave but is only paid if the employee has at least 26 weeks' service at the time of giving their notice and earns more than a statutory minimum. The amount of maternity pay received is based on the employee's salary and is subject to a **statutory maximum**. The employee must take a minimum of two weeks' leave after the birth of their baby but has the option to share the balance of their maternity leave and pay allowance with their partner if they wish. This is known as **shared parental leave** and **statutory shared parental pay**.

6.3.3 Paternity leave and pay

To qualify for paternity leave a partner must qualify as an employee and must generally have been with the employer for at least 26 weeks before the 15th week before the baby is due. On giving the required notice, eligible employees are entitled to take either **one week** or **two consecutive weeks** paid paternity leave. The leave must be completed within 56 days of the actual birth of the child and, like maternity pay, paternity pay is based on salary and is subject to a statutory maximum.

6.3.4 Adoption leave and pay

Parents who adopt their child have a right to **statutory adoption leave** (SAL) and **statutory adoption pay** (SAP). The rules for qualifying for this, and the amounts of leave and pay, are the same as for statutory maternity leave and pay.

6.3.5 Flexible working

All employees who have worked continuously for the same employer for at least 26 weeks have the **right** to make a 'statutory application' for a change in terms and conditions of employment in respect of hours, time and place of work and not to be unreasonably refused. For instance they may apply to job share, or work from home.

The employer must consider the statutory application for flexible working within three months (or longer, if the employee agrees), and must deal with such requests 'in a reasonable manner'.

The employer may **reasonably refuse** a request on the grounds of:

- The burden of additional cost
- A detrimental effect on ability to meet customer demand
- An inability to re-organise the work amongst existing staff or to recruit additional staff
- A detrimental impact on quality or performance
- Insufficiency of work during the periods the employee proposes to work
- Planned structural changes to the workforce

6.3.6 Unpaid parental leave

Any employee with a year's continuous service who has parental responsibility is entitled to **unpaid parental leave** of up to 18 weeks to care for each child up to the child's eighteenth birthday. The maximum that can be taken in any one year is four weeks per child, unless the employer agrees to more. This is different from, and should not be confused with, the shared parental leave that we saw earlier in relation to the birth of a child.

6.4 Health and safety

The key legislation under which an employer has a duty to their employees with regard to **health and safety** is the Health and Safety at Work Act 1974 (HMSO, 1974), which has been augmented by subsequent regulations, notably the Health and Safety at Work Regulations 1999 (TSO, 1999).

This **duty** includes the following issues:

- Provide and maintain plant and systems of work which are safe and without risk
- Make arrangements to ensure safe use, handling, storage and transport of articles/substances
- Provide adequate information, instruction, training and supervision
- Maintain safe places of work and ensure that there is adequate access in and out
- Provide a safe and healthy working environment

Under the **Enterprise and Regulatory Reform Act 2013 (TSO, 2013)**, employers are only liable to pay compensation to employees injured at work if the employer is found to have acted negligently. Employees are not entitled to compensation if their employer has taken all reasonable steps to prevent injury.

6.4.1 Employment rights

The contract of employment contains an **implied right not to be subjected to detriment** by the employer on grounds of health and safety. Specifically, the employee has a right not to be subjected to detriment on the ground that they intended to, or did:

- Carry out activities designated to them in connection with preventing/reducing health and safety risks at work
- Perform duties as a representative of workers on issues of health and safety
- Take part in consultation with the employer under the Health and Safety (Consultation with Employees) Regulations 1996 (TSO, 1996)
- Leave their place of work or refused to work in circumstances which they reasonably believed to be serious or imminent and they could not reasonably be expected to avert
- Take appropriate steps to protect themselves or others from circumstances of danger which they believed to be serious and imminent

6.5 Working time

The Working Time Regulations 1998 (TSO, 1998) provide broadly that a worker's **average working time in a 17-week period,** including overtime, shall **not exceed 48 hours for each seven-day period**, unless the worker has agreed in writing that this limit shall not apply.

6.6 Continuous employment and transfer of undertakings

> **FAST FORWARD**
>
> Many rights given to employees under the **Employment Rights Act 1996** are only available if an employee has a specified period of **continuous employment**.

You may have noticed references to '**continuous employment**' previously. Most of the employment protection which is available is only given to employees who have continuous service of a particular duration.

There are provisions in statute for how the period of continuous service should be calculated, and what counts as service and what does not. **The basic rule is that a year is 12 calendar months.**

Certain weeks might not be taken into account in calculating continuous service, but they do not break the period of continuous service. This might be the case if the employee takes part in a strike, or is absent due to service in the armed forces.

Another factor that impacts on continuous service is when a business or undertaking is transferred by one person to another. Where the business is **transferred**, so that an employee works for a new employer, this change represents **no break in the continuous service of the employee**.

Chapter Roundup

- It is important to distinguish between a **contract of service** (employment) and a **contract for services** (independent contractor). Each type of contract has different rules for taxation, health and safety provisions, protection of contract and vicarious liability in tort and contract.

  A contract of service is **distinguished** from a contract for services usually because the parties **express** the agreement to be one of service. This does not always mean that an employee will not be treated as an independent contractor by the court, however; much depends on the three tests.
  - Control test
  - Integration test
  - Economic reality test

- The distinction between **employed** and **self-employed** is important as to whether certain **rights** are available to an individual and how they are treated for **tax purposes.**

- There are no particular legal rules relating to the commencement of employment – it is really **just like any other contract** in requiring offer and acceptance, consideration and intention to create legal relations.

- A contract of employment can only be **varied** if the contract **expressly** gives that right, or if all parties consent to the variation.

- The **employer** has an implied **duty at common law** to take **reasonable care** of their employees; they must select proper staff, materials and provide a safe system of working.

  The **employee** has a duty of **faithful service** and to exercise **care and skill** in performance of their duties.

- **Statute** implies terms into employment contracts, which may not usually be overridden, regarding pay and equality, maternity leave and work-life balance generally, time off, health and safety and working time.

- Many rights given to employees under the **Employment Rights Act 1996** are only available if an employee has a specified period of **continuous employment**.

Quick Quiz

1. The statutory rules on minimum notice periods and unfair dismissal apply equally to both employees and contractors.

   True ☐
   False ☐

2. Working for a number of different people is an automatic sign of self employment.

   True ☐
   False ☐

3. Which of the following statements regarding a written statement of particulars is correct?

   A It must be provided within two weeks of the commencement of employment
   B It must be provided on the day employment commences
   C It must be provided before or on the day employment commences
   D It must be provided to all employees within a reasonable period of the employment commencing

4. How can an employee show acceptance when the terms of their employment contract have changed?

   (i)   Signing a wholly new contract
   (ii) Working under the new terms
   (iii) Agreeing verbally

   A (iii) only
   B (i) and (ii) only
   C (ii) and (iii) only
   D (i), (ii) and (iii)

5. Employees have a right to ask for flexible working, but employers may reasonably refuse the request.

   True ☐
   False ☐

Answers to Quick Quiz

1 False. Contractors do not have this statutory protection.

2 False. Other facts will be considered.

3 C. A written statement of particulars must be provided before or on the day employment commences. It does not have to be provided to employees whose employment contracts include them.

4 D. All the options are acceptable methods of showing agreement to the new terms.

5 True. Although employees have a right to request flexible working, employers may reasonably refuse it.

End of chapter question

Employers' duties

What terms may be included in a contract of employment? Where might they be found? **(20 marks)**

PART E THE EMPLOYMENT RELATIONSHIP AND SOCIAL SECURITY LAW: THE RELATIONSHIP WITH THE STATE

Ending the employment relationship

Topic list	Syllabus reference
1 Termination by notice	2.3
2 Termination of employment by breach of contract	2.3
3 Wrongful dismissal	2.3
4 Remedies for wrongful dismissal	2.3
5 Unfair dismissal	2.3
6 Unfair dismissal – justification of dismissal	2.3
7 Remedies for unfair dismissal	2.3
8 Redundancy	2.3
9 Social security law: The relationship with the state	2.4

Introduction

In the previous chapter we saw what an **employment relationship** is and how the relationship is governed. In this chapter we shall look at what happens at when an **employment relationship ends** (or is **terminated**). This can be caused by the employee choosing to work elsewhere or to retire, by the employer terminating the employment contract due to a disciplinary issue, or having to make employees redundant.

Ending an employment contract can be a **traumatic time** for all involved and it can result in legal action. Both employees and employers must know their rights and obligations to minimise the risk of such action.

We shall look at the various **types of dismissal**, together with the protections and **remedies** available to those who may be dismissed. Finally, we shall look at **social security**, and how the state provides support to those who are out of work or cannot work.

Statutory references in this chapter are to the Employment Rights Act 1996 (TSO, 1996) and the Small Business, Enterprise and Employment Act 2015 (TSO 2015) unless otherwise noted.

1 Termination by notice

FAST FORWARD > When an employment contract is terminated by notice there is **no** breach of contract unless the **contents** of the notice (such as notice period) are themselves in breach.

A contract of employment may be terminated by the employee or employer giving **notice**. This means to formally tell the other party that they wish to end the relationship. Notice is the time between asking to end the relationship and the actual end date. The particular time period required will be set out in the employment contract which is subject to a statutory minimum.

Where notice is given the following rules apply.

(a) The period of notice given must **not be less than the statutory minimum,** whatever the contract may specify.

(b) It **may be given without specific reason** for so doing, unless the contract requires otherwise.

(c) If the contract states that notice may **only be given in specific circumstances** then generally it may **not** be given for any other reason.

> *McClelland v Northern Ireland General Health Services Board 1957*
>
> *The facts:* The claimant's contract gave the employer a right to terminate his employment for misconduct or inefficiency.
>
> *Decision:* There was no contractual right of termination for redundancy – it was a breach of contract to do so.

Although there is no breach of contract, **termination by notice** or **non-renewal** qualifies as 'dismissal' under the statutory code. This means that the employee may be entitled to compensation for unfair dismissal.

Statute imposes a **minimum period of notice** of termination to be given on either side.

1.1 Minimum period of notice

FAST FORWARD > Where employment is **terminated by notice** the period given must **not be less** than the **statutory minimum**.

If an **employer terminates the contract** of employment by giving notice, the **minimum period of notice** to be given is determined by the employee's length of continuous service for the employer as follows: s 86.

(a) An employee who has been continuously employed for **one month or more** but less than two years is entitled to not less than **one week's** notice.

(b) An employee who has been continuously employed for **two years or more** but less than 12 years is entitled to **one week's notice for each year of continuous employment.**

(c) Any employee who has been employed for **12 years** or more is entitled to not less than **12 weeks** notice.

If the **employee** gives notice, the minimum period required is **one week** if they have been employed for at least one month.

The notice must specify the **date of its expiry**. Either party may waive their entitlement to notice or accept a sum in lieu of notice.

The statutory rules on length of notice merely prescribe a **minimum**. If the contract provides for a longer period, notice must be given in accordance with the contract.

During the period of notice an employee is entitled to pay at a rate not less than the **average** of their **earnings** over the **previous 12 weeks**.

If the employee is **dismissed** in any way they may request their employer gives them a **written statement of the reasons** for their dismissal and **the employer must provide it** within 14 days. The statement must contain at the least a simple summary of the reasons for dismissal and can be used as **admissible evidence** before an employment tribunal: s 92.

Dismissal is the word used to describe **termination of an employment contract by the employer**. Here are a few definitions relating to dismissal.

Key terms

Summary dismissal is where the employer dismisses the employee without notice. They may do this if the employee has committed a serious breach of contract.

Constructive dismissal is where the employer commits a breach of contract, thereby causing the employee to resign. By implication, this is also dismissal without notice.

Wrongful dismissal is a common law concept arising in specific circumstances. It gives the employee an action for breach of contract.

Unfair dismissal is a statutory concept introduced by employment protection legislation. As a rule, every employee has the right not to be unfairly dismissed: s 54.

Correspondingly, **fair dismissal** is a statutory concept where a person has been dismissed as a result of a fair reason under legislation.

Exam focus point

Note that the distinction between wrongful and unfair dismissal depends not so much upon the nature of the dismissal, as on the **remedies available**.

Question
Notice period

How much notice is an employee with five years of continuous service entitled to?

Answer

An employee with five years of continuous service is entitled to five weeks of notice (one week for each year's continuous service).

2 Termination of employment by breach of contract

FAST FORWARD

Breach of the employment contract occurs where there is **summary dismissal**, **constructive dismissal**, **inability** on the employer's side to **continue employment**, or **repudiation** of the contract by the employee.

As well as ending the relationship by giving notice, an employment contract can be terminated by **breach of contract**. This occurs **in the following circumstances**.

- Summary dismissal
- Constructive dismissal
- Inability on the employer's behalf to continue
- Repudiation of the contract by the employee

The concepts of **summary dismissal** and **constructive dismissal** are both examples of **dismissal without proper notice**. A dismissal with proper notice is generally held to be lawful, unless it is shown to be wrongful or unfair.

However, under the ERA 1996, the **reason for dismissal** has to be determined in relation to both when the notice is given and when the employment is terminated.

2.1 Summary dismissal

Summary dismissal occurs where the employer dismisses the employee without notice. They may do this if the employee has committed a serious breach of contract and, if so, the employer incurs no liability.

If, however, they have **no sufficient justification** the employer is liable for **breach of contract** and the employee may claim a remedy for wrongful dismissal. Whether the employee's conduct justifies summary dismissal will vary according to the circumstances of the case.

> *Wilson v Racher 1974*
>
> *The facts:* A gardener swore at his employer using extreme obscenities.
>
> *Decision:* His action for wrongful dismissal succeeded, as the employer's own conduct had provoked the outburst. This was a solitary outburst following a history of diligence and competence.

Contrast this with *Pepper v Webb 1969*. The decision in this case favoured the employer as the incident also included a **refusal to obey a reasonable** and **lawful instruction** by the employee.

2.2 Constructive dismissal

Constructive dismissal occurs where the employer, although willing to continue the employment, repudiates some **essential term** of the contract, for example by the imposition of a complete change in the employee's duties, and the employee resigns. The employer is liable for breach of contract.

2.2.1 Establishing constructive dismissal

To establish constructive dismissal, an **employee** must show that:

- Their employer has committed a serious breach of contract (a repudiatory breach).
- They left because of the breach.
- They have not 'waived' the breach, thereby affirming the contract.

Examples of breaches of contract which have lead to claims of **constructive dismissal** include the following.

- A reduction in pay: *Industrial Rubber Products v Gillon 1977*
- A complete change in the nature of the job: *Ford v Milthorn Toleman Ltd 1980*
- A failure to follow the prescribed disciplinary procedure: *Post Office v Strange 1981*
- A failure to provide a suitable working environment: *Waltons and Morse v Dorrington 1997*
- A failure to implement a proper procedure: *WA Goold (Pearmak) Ltd v McConnell & Another 1995*

The breach must be a **serious** one.

> *Western Excavating (ECC) Ltd v Sharp 1978*
>
> *The facts:* The defendant was suspended without pay for misconduct. This caused him financial difficulties, and so he applied for an advance against holiday pay but was refused. He then left and claimed for constructive dismissal.
>
> *Decision:* The employers had not repudiated the contract and so there had been no dismissal.

2.3 Employer's inability to continue employment

If a personal employer dies, an employing firm of partners is dissolved, an employing company is **compulsorily wound up**, a receiver is appointed or the employee's place of employment is permanently closed, the employer may become unable to continue to employ the employee.

2.4 Repudiation of the contract by the employee

Resignation, striking or failing to perform the contract and to observe its conditions, is **breach of contract** by the employee. The employer may dismiss them or treat the contract as discharged by the employee's breach.

2.5 Employment tribunals

Employment tribunals have jurisdiction to deal with all manner of employment-related disputes, such as wrongful and unfair dismissal and redundancy, which formerly had to be heard in the civil courts. The Employment Tribunals (Constitution and Rules of Procedure) Regulations 2013 (TSO, 2013) apply to them.

The objective of an employment tribunal is to resolve **employment disputes**. A hearing is normally convened with an Employment Judge and two other individuals. Each side makes its case and a decision is made. In some cases, the parties will be encouraged to settle their dispute informally through **mediation**.

The first stage of a tribunal is where the claimant submits a **claim form** that sets out their case. The other party submits a **response form** that sets out their case. The second, **'sift' stage** involves an Employment Judge reviewing all the documentation and deciding whether the case should go to a hearing. A case may be rejected if there is no case for the respondent to answer or if the matter is outside the scope of a tribunal. A **preliminary hearing** is set where any case management or other issues are heard and this may be converted into a **final hearing** if no party is materially prejudiced. Otherwise, a final hearing date is set, when the case is heard before the tribunal panel and a decision is reached.

There are processes in place under the **Small Business, Enterprise and Employment Act 2015 (TSO, 2015)** that aim to **manage the tribunal process efficiently** by minimising the postponement of hearings. Also, where a tribunal settlement is not paid on time or in full, the employer will face a financial penalty.

2.6 Settlement agreements and early conciliation

The **Enterprise and Regulatory Reform Act 2013 (TSO, 2013)** aims to reduce the number of employment disputes that go to tribunal, to save the cost and time involved in them. The Act allows employers and employees to use settlement agreements to part company on agreed terms.

The Act also requires employees to contact **ACAS** (the government-sponsored organisation that aims to prevent and resolve employment disputes) before filing a claim at an employment tribunal. This allows the parties to resolve the situation before incurring the expense of going to tribunal.

Question | Summary dismissal

Is summary dismissal ever justified, and if so, in what circumstances?

Answer

Yes, summary dismissal is justified in cases of serious breach of contract by the employee.

Having seen how an employment contract can be terminated by giving notice or through breach of contract, we shall now focus on the **remedies** available to the employee if their employment contract is terminated by their employer. In some cases, where the employee is found to be **wrongfully** or **unfairly dismissed**, compensation or other remedies may be available to them. A redundancy payment may also be payable to employees who are made **redundant** through no fault of their own. The reason that these remedies are in place is to **protect employees** from being treated unfairly and to provide a degree of compensation to help them cope financially until they find new employment.

However, remedies are not given payable without good reason. To be eligible for a remedy for wrongful or unfair dismissal or redundancy, the dismissal must meet certain criteria. In the next few sections we shall look at what those are and what specific remedies are available.

3 Wrongful dismissal

FAST FORWARD

> Where the employer has **summarily dismissed** an employee without notice (as where the employer becomes insolvent), there may be a claim for **damages** at common law for **wrongful dismissal**.

Wrongful dismissal is simply a dismissal that is in **breach of the employment contract**. An action for wrongful dismissal, since it derives from the employee's **common law** rights in contract, must be brought in the County Court or the High Court. Claimants must show that they were **dismissed in breach of contract**, for example with less than the statutory minimum period of notice and that they have **as a result suffered loss**.

As the action is taken for a breach of contract, the courts will usually only **award damages** for the **loss of notice period**. This was confirmed in *Johnson v Unisys Ltd 2001*, in which the claimant was refused damages for breach of implied contractual terms that they said damaged their mental health.

A dismissal will not be wrongful if it is **justified**.

3.1 Justification of dismissal

The following have been taken as **justifiable circumstances**.

(a) **Wilful disobedience of a lawful order** suffices if it amounts to wilful and serious defiance of authority.

(b) **Misconduct**, in connection with the business or outside it if it is sufficiently grave. For example, acceptance of a secret commission, disclosure of confidential information, assault on a fellow employee or even financial embarrassment of an employee in a position of trust (*Pearce v Foster 1886* – stockbroker's clerk who incurred heavy gambling losses).

(c) **Dishonesty**, where the employee is in a position of particular trust.

(d) **Incompetence or neglect**, insofar as the employee lacks or fails to use skill which they profess to have.

(e) **Gross negligence**, depending on the nature of the job.

(f) **Immorality**, only if it is likely to affect performance of duties or the reputation of the business.

(g) **Drunkenness**, only if it occurs in aggravated circumstances such as when driving a vehicle or a train, or is repeated: *Williams v Royal Institute of Chartered Surveyors 1997*.

4 Remedies for wrongful dismissal

FAST FORWARD

Generally, the **only effective remedy** available to a **wrongfully dismissed** employee is a claim for **damages** based on the **loss of earnings**. The measure of damages is usually the sum that would have been earned if **proper notice** had been given.

As with any other case of compensation, the wronged party is expected to **mitigate** their loss by, say, seeking other employment.

Where breach of contract leaves the **employer as the injured party**, they may dismiss the employee and withhold wages. The employer may recover confidential papers, or apply for an injunction to enforce a valid restrictive covenant: *Thomas Marshall (Exporters) v Guinle 1978*.

Employment tribunals have jurisdiction to deal with wrongful dismissal cases, which formerly had to be heard in the civil courts.

5 Unfair dismissal

FAST FORWARD

Certain employees have a right not to be **unfairly dismissed**. Breach of that right allows an employee to claim compensation from a tribunal. To claim for unfair dismissal, the employee must satisfy certain criteria.

Unfair dismissal is an extremely important element of employment protection legislation. To be eligible for a remedy for unfair dismissal an employee must prove that the dismissal meets certain **statutory criteria**. The employer can counter this claim by proving the dismissal was for one of a number of fair reasons.

The remedies available following a successful action for **wrongful dismissal** are **limited to damages** compensating for the sum which would have been earned **if proper notice had been given.**

Legislation seeks to **widen the scope of protection** and **increase the range of remedies** available to an employee who has been unfairly dismissed. Under the terms of the Employment Rights Act 1996 a statutory maximum **compensatory award** is set every year which a tribunal may award to an employee who is unfairly dismissed.

5.1 Scope

Every **included employee who qualifies** under the criteria (a) and (b) below has a statutory right not to be unfairly dismissed: s 94. Certain categories of employee are **excluded** from the statutory unfair dismissal code.

- Persons employed to work **outside the UK**
- Employees dismissed while taking **unofficial strike** or other industrial action
- Other categories, including members of the police

In order to **obtain compensation** or **other remedies** for **unfair dismissal** the employee must satisfy several criteria.

(a) Have been **continuously employed for two years,** whether full-time or part-time.

(b) Have been **dismissed.** This may have to be determined by the tribunal, for example if the employee resigned claiming constructive dismissal.

(c) Have been **unfairly** dismissed. Dismissal may be unfair even though it is not a breach of contract by the employer.

There are some **exceptions** to the two years continuous service qualification. These are:

- Where the matter concerns a **safety representative** being penalised for carrying out legitimate health and safety activities
- Where an employee is being **denied a statutory** right (for example an unlawful deduction from wages)
- Where the employee is **pregnant**

The **effective date** of **dismissal** is reckoned as follows.

- Where there is termination by notice, the date on which the notice expires
- Where there is termination without notice, the date on which the termination takes effect
- Where an employee's fixed term contract is not renewed, the date on which that term expires

5.2 Making a claim

There are four steps to making a claim for **compensation** for unfair dismissal.

Step 1 The **employee** must **apply to a tribunal** within **three months** of dismissal.

Step 2 The **employee** must **show** that they are a **qualifying employee** and that they have in fact been **dismissed**.

Step 3 Then the **employer** must **demonstrate**:

(a) What was the alleged **only or principal reason** for dismissal

(b) That it was one of the statutory fair reasons for dismissal or was otherwise a '**substantial reason** of a kind such as to be capable of justifying the dismissal of an employee' in this position

Step 4 Then the tribunal must decide if the **principal reason** did in fact **justify the dismissal** and whether the employer acted reasonably in treating the reason as sufficient.

If the employer cannot show that the principal reason allegedly justifying the dismissal was one of the **fair reasons** given in statute, the dismissal is unfair.

Dismissal may be **identified** in three separate circumstances.

(a) **Actual dismissal** can usually be clearly recognised from the words used by an employer.

(b) **Constructive dismissal**, as described earlier, involves a fundamental breach of the employment contract by the employer.

(c) **Expiry of a fixed-term contract** without renewal amounts to a dismissal.

The employee must show that they have in fact been dismissed. The courts often have to debate whether or not the use of **abusive language** by employers constitutes mere abuse or indicates dismissal.

5.3 The reason for dismissal

As noted above, if the principal reason for dismissal was not one of the statutory fair reasons, then dismissal will be unfair. However, even if the employer shows that they dismissed the employee for a reason which is recognised as capable of being sufficient, **a tribunal may still decide that the dismissal was unfair**. It may do this if it considers that on the basis of **equity and the merits** of the case, **the employer acted unreasonably** in dismissing the employee: s 98.

5.3.1 Reasonableness of employer

The **employment tribunal** is required to review the circumstances and to decide whether dismissing the employee was a reasonable response (*Iceland Frozen Foods v Jones 1983*).

Determining whether the **employer has acted reasonably** requires the tribunal to ask:

- Has the correct **procedure** been applied?
- Did the employer take all **circumstances** into consideration?
- What would any **reasonable employer** have done?

The employer does not act reasonably unless they **take account of the relevant circumstances**. If an inexperienced employee is struggling to do their work, the employer is expected to help by advice or supervision in the hope that they may improve.

The emphasis placed on giving **one or more warnings** before dismissing is partly so that the employee may heed the warning and amend their conduct or their performance.

5.3.2 Disciplinary procedure

Under the Trade Union and Labour Relations (Consolidation) Act 1992 (HMSO, 1992) and the **Employment Act 2008 (TSO, 2008)**, employers are required to follow ACAS's statutory Code of Practice on Disciplinary and Grievance Procedures. This provides basic practical guidance to employers, employees and their representatives, and sets out principles for handling disciplinary and grievance situations in the workplace.

A **failure to follow the Code** does not, in itself, make a person or organisation liable to proceedings. However, employment tribunals take the Code into account when considering relevant cases, and they are also able to adjust any awards made in relevant cases by up to 25% for unreasonable failure to comply with any provision of the Code. Thus if the tribunal feels that an employer has unreasonably failed to follow the Code it can increase any award it has made by up to 25%. Conversely, it can reduce an award by up to 25% if it feels an employee has unreasonably failed to follow the Code.

The **code** aims to ensure fairness in any **disciplinary procedure**, and this includes the following elements:

Stage 1   The **employer investigates the matter** to establish the facts of the case

Stage 2   The **employee is informed** of the problem

Stage 3   A **meeting is held** between the parties to discuss the problem (the **employee** has the right to be **accompanied**)

Stage 4   A **decision is made** and appropriate **action taken**

Stage 5   The **employee** has an **opportunity to appeal** the decision

A similar process applies to a **grievance process** instituted by the employee. During either process **both parties should act promptly** and without causing undue delay in the procedure and **be consistent** in their actions.

5.3.3 Warnings

Except in severe cases it is **not reasonable for an employer to dismiss an employee without first warning them** that if they continue or repeat their behaviour they are likely to be dismissed.

> *Newman v T H White Motors 1972*
>
> *The facts:* An employee used foul language to a trainee. The employer asked him not to do so. When he persisted the employer dismissed him.
>
> *Decision:* This was an unreasonable and therefore unfair dismissal. The employer must make it clear to the employee that he risks dismissal if he persists.

5.3.4 Concluding on reasonableness

In reaching its conclusion on the issue of reasonableness, **the tribunal should not substitute what it would have done if placed in the employer's situation**. It is necessary to set the rights and interests of the employee against the interests of the employer's business and then decide whether **any reasonable employer could have come to a different conclusion**.

Unreasonableness and breach of contract by the employer must be distinguished. Some unreasonable conduct by the employer may be serious enough to repudiate the contract, and if the employee leaves they can claim for constructive dismissal by the employer.

If the employer acts **unreasonably** but in a manner which does not amount to repudiation of the contract, any resigning employee cannot claim constructive dismissal: *Western Excavating (ECC) Ltd v Sharp 1978*.

6 Unfair dismissal – justification of dismissal

FAST FORWARD

Dismissal must be **justified** if it is related to the employee's capability or qualifications, the employee's conduct, redundancy, legal prohibition or restriction on the employee's continued employment or some other substantial reason.

Dismissal is **automatically unfair** if it is on certain specified grounds.

6.1 Potentially fair reasons for dismissal

To justify dismissal as fair dismissal, employers must show their **principal reason** relates to either:

(a) The **capability or qualifications** of the employee for performing work of the kind which they were employed to do

(b) The **conduct** of the employee

(c) **Redundancy**

(d) **Legal prohibition** or restriction that prevents the employee from lawfully working in the position which they held. For example, if a doctor is struck off the relevant professional register, or an employee loses their driving licence which they need to be able to do their job

(e) **Some other substantial reason** which justifies dismissal

6.1.1 Capability/qualifications

If the employer dismisses for want of **capability** on the part of the employee, the employer has to establish that fault.

- What does the contract require?
- What is the general standard of performance of their employees in this trade?
- What is the previous standard of performance of the dismissed employee themselves?

If the employee is **incompetent** it must be of such a nature and quality as to justify dismissal. For example a shop manager who left their shop dirty and untidy and who failed to maintain cash registers: *Lewis Shops Group Ltd v Wiggins 1973*.

'**Capability**' is to be assessed by reference to skills, aptitude, health or any other physical or mental quality. '**Qualification**' means any academic or technical qualifications relevant to the position that the employee holds': s 98(3).

'**Reasonableness**' on the part of the employer is required, for example:

- **Consultation** with the employee to determine areas of difficulty
- Allowing a **reasonable time** for improvement
- Providing **training** if necessary
- Considering **all alternatives** to dismissal

If the employer relies on **ill health** as the grounds of incapability there must be **proper medical evidence**. The employer is entitled to consider their own business needs. A reasonable procedure involves cautions, confrontation with records and the granting of a period for improvement.

International Sports Ltd v Thomson 1980

The facts: The employee had been away from work for around 25% of the time, suffering from a number of complaints all of which were certified by medical certificates. She received a number of warnings. Prior to dismissal the company consulted their medical adviser. As the illnesses were unrelated and unverifiable, he did not consider an examination worthwhile. She was dismissed.

Decision: The dismissal was fair.

6.1.2 Misconduct

It is usual to apply the common law distinction between **gross misconduct**, which justifies summary dismissal on the first occasion and **ordinary misconduct**, which is not usually sufficient grounds for dismissal unless it is persistent.

Assault on a fellow employee, conduct exposing others to danger (for example, smoking in an area prohibited for safety reasons), unpleasant behaviour towards customers and persistent absences from work have been treated as sufficient misconduct to justify dismissal.

6.1.3 Redundancy

If an employee is dismissed mainly or only on the ground of **redundancy**, they may claim remedies for unfair dismissal if they can show one of the following.

(a) There were other employees in similar positions who might have been made redundant and that **selection for redundancy was in breach of a customary arrangement or agreed procedure**.

(b) They were selected for a reason connected with **trade union membership**.

A redundancy selection procedure should be in conformity with **good industrial relations practice** which requires consultation and objective criteria of selection. The criteria set out by the EAT in *Williams v Compair Maxam Ltd 1982* have been accepted as standards of behaviour.

(a) The employer should give as much **warning** as possible of impending redundancies.

(b) The employer should **consult with the trade union** as to the best means of achieving the desired management result. In *Mugford v Midland Bank plc 1997* it was held that even when an employer consults a trade union over the selection criteria for redundancy, the employer must still consult the individuals to be made redundant before a final decision is taken.

(c) It should be possible to check **criteria** for selection against such things as attendance records, efficiency at the job and length of service.

(d) The employer should ensure that the selection is made **fairly**.

(e) The employer should consider whether an **offer of alternative employment** can be made.

6.1.4 Other substantial reason

The category of **other substantial reason** permits the employer to rely on some factor which is unusual and likely to affect them adversely.

An employer has justified dismissal on specific grounds.

(a) The employee was married to one of their competitors.

(b) The employee refused to accept a reorganisation. For example, a change of shift working made in the interests of the business and with the agreement of a large majority of other employees.

6.1.5 Automatically fair reasons for dismissal

Other reasons are designated as being **automatically fair** by legislation.

- Taking part in **unofficial industrial action**
- Being a **threat to national security** (to be certified by the government)

An employee who strikes or refuses to work normally may be fairly dismissed unless the industrial action has been **lawfully organised** under the protection conferred by the Employment Relations Act 1999 (TSO, 1999). Where dismissal results from a lock-out or a strike, the tribunal cannot deal with it as a case of alleged unfair dismissal unless victimisation is established.

6.1.6 Automatically unfair reasons for dismissal

Some reasons are automatically unfair (known as **'inadmissible reasons'**). Examples include:

- Discrimination on the grounds of a protected characteristic
- Pregnancy or other maternity-related grounds
- A spent conviction under the Rehabilitation of Offenders Act 1974
- Trade union membership or activities
- Dismissal on transfer of an undertaking (unless there are 'economic, technical or organisational reasons' justifying the dismissal)
- Taking steps to avert danger to health and safety at work
- Seeking to enforce rights relating to the national minimum wage or national living wage
- Exercising rights under the Working Time Regulations 1998
- Refusing or opting out of Sunday working (in the retail sector)
- Making a protected disclosure order under the Public Interest Disclosure Act 1998 (TSO, 1998) (whistleblowing)

6.2 Proving what was the reason for dismissal

The employer may be required to give to the employee a **written statement** of the **reason for dismissal**: s 92.

If an employee is dismissed for trying to **enforce their employment rights**, by for example asking for a written statement of particulars or an itemised pay statement, they may claim unfair dismissal **regardless of the length of service** and hours worked.

> **Question** — Automatically fair reasons for dismissal

State two automatically fair reasons for dismissal.

> **Answer**

Being a threat to national security and taking part in unofficial industrial action.

7 Remedies for unfair dismissal

FAST FORWARD

Remedies for **unfair dismissal** include:

- **Reinstatement**
- **Re-engagement**
- **Compensation**

An employee who alleges unfair dismissal must present their complaint to an **employment tribunal** within three months of the effective date of termination. The dispute is referred to a Conciliation Officer and only comes before the tribunal if their efforts to promote a settlement fail.

7.1 Reinstatement

If unfair dismissal is established, the tribunal first considers the possibility of ordering reinstatement.

Key term

> **Reinstatement** is return to the same job without any break of continuity: s 114.

7.2 Re-engagement

The tribunal may alternatively order **re-engagement**. The new employment must be comparable with the old or otherwise suitable.

Key term

> **Re-engagement** means that the employee is given new employment with the employer (or their successor or associate) on terms specified in the order.

In deciding whether to exercise these powers, the tribunal must take into account whether the complainant wishes to be reinstated and, whether it is practicable and just for the employer to comply. **Such orders are in fact very infrequent**.

The **Employment Appeal Tribunal** has ruled that an order for re-engagement should not be made if there has been a breakdown in confidence between the parties: *Wood Group Heavy Industrial Turbines Ltd v Crossan 1998*. In this case the employee was dismissed following allegations of drug dealing on company premises and time-keeping offences.

7.3 Compensation

If the tribunal does not order reinstatement or re-engagement the tribunal may award **compensation**, which may be made in three stages, as follows.

(a) A **basic award** calculated as follows. Those aged 41 and over receive one-and-a-half weeks' pay (up to a statutory maximum per week) for each year of service up to a maximum of 20 years. In other age groups the same provisions apply, except that the 22–40 age group receive one week's pay per year and the 21-and-under age group receive half a week's pay.

(b) A **compensatory award** for any additional loss of earnings, expenses and benefits, on common law principles of damages for breach of contract. This is to compensate the employee for financial loss suffered as a result of unfair dismissal insofar as that loss is attributable to action taken by the employer. This is limited to a statutory maximum and may be awarded in cases where reinstatement or re-engagement are deemed inappropriate by the tribunal.

(c) If the employer does not comply with an order for reinstatement or re-engagement, and does not show that it was impracticable to do so, a punitive **additional award** is made of between 26 and 52 weeks' pay (again subject to a statutory weekly maximum).

The tribunal may **reduce the amount** of the award in any of the following circumstances.

- If the employee **contributed** in some way to their own dismissal
- If they have **unreasonably refused** an offer of reinstatement
- If it is **just and equitable** to reduce the basic award by reason of some matter which occurred before dismissal

Exam focus point

Unfair dismissal is a popular topic in exam questions.

8 Redundancy

FAST FORWARD

Dismissal is caused by **redundancy** when the employer has ceased to carry on the business in which the employee has been employed or the business no longer needs employees to carry on that work. In these circumstances, dismissal is **presumed** by the courts to be by redundancy unless otherwise demonstrated.

The final type of dismissal we shall look at is redundancy. An employee may claim a **redundancy payment** where they are:

- Dismissed by their employer by reason of redundancy
- Laid off or kept on short time

8.1 What is redundancy?

Key term

A dismissal is treated as caused by **redundancy** if the only or main reason is that:

- The employer has ceased, or intends to cease, to carry on the business (or the local establishment of the business) in which the employee has been employed
- The requirements of that business for employees to carry on the work done by the employee have ceased or diminished (or are expected to): s 139 (1)

If the employee's contract has a **mobility clause** (a clause that allows the employer to change the place of work) there is no redundancy if the employee is relocated. However, in some cases it might be classed as constructive dismissal.

A key test for determining whether or not an employee is redundant is to see whether there has been a reduction of the employers' requirements for employees to work **at the place where the person concerned is employed**.

> *High Table Ltd v Horst and Others 1997*
>
> *The facts*: High Table Ltd, contract caterers, employed waitresses who had worked for several years at one company. The client company told High Table that the waitresses were no longer required, so they were dismissed by High Table on the grounds of redundancy. The waitresses, who had mobility clauses in their contracts, alleged unfair dismissal since High Table had not tried to re-employ them somewhere else.
>
> *Decision*: The Court of Appeal ruled against them, saying that the place of work was at the client company premises and the dismissals were for genuine redundancy.

In considering whether the requirements of the business for staff have diminished, it is the **overall** position which must be considered. If for example A's job is abolished and A is moved into B's job and B is dismissed, that is a case of redundancy although B's job continues.

In *British Broadcasting Corporation v Farnworth 1998* a radio producer's fixed term contract was not renewed and the employer advertised for a radio producer with more experience. It was held by the EAT that the less experienced radio producer was indeed redundant as the **requirement for their level of services had diminished**.

If the employer **reorganises their business** or alters their methods so that the same work has to be done by different means which are beyond the capacity of the employee, that is not redundancy.

> *North Riding Garages v Butterwick 1967*
>
> *The facts*: A garage reorganised its working arrangements so that the workshop manager's duties included more administrative work. He was dismissed when it was found he could not perform these duties.
>
> *Decision*: His claim for redundancy pay must fail since it was not a case of redundancy.

> *Vaux and Associated Breweries v Ward 1969*
>
> *The facts*: The owners of a public house renovated their premises and as part of the new image they dismissed the middle-aged barmaid and replaced her with a younger employee.
>
> *Decision*: The claim for redundancy pay must fail since the same job still existed: she was not redundant. This case was decided before legislation came in outlawing age discrimination.

Exam focus point

> Like unfair dismissal, redundancy is a popular topic in exam questions. Link your studies on redundancy and unfair dismissal to the material on remedies.

8.2 Calculation of redundancy pay

Redundancy pay is calculated on the same basis as the **basic compensation for unfair dismissal.**

8.3 Exceptions to the right to redundancy payment

A person is **excluded** from having a right to redundancy payment where

- They do not fit the **definition** of 'employee' given in statute
- They have not been **continuously employed** for **two** years
- They have been or could be dismissed for **misconduct**
- An offer to **renew the contract** is unreasonably **refused**
- The claim is made **out of time** (after six months)
- The **employee leaves** before being made redundant having been notified of the possibility of redundancies

8.3.1 Misconduct of the employee

An employee who is dismissed for **misconduct** is **not entitled to redundancy pay** even though they may become redundant.

> *Sanders v Neale 1974*
>
> *The facts*: In the course of a dispute employees refused to work normally. The employer dismissed them and closed down his business. The employees claimed redundancy pay.
>
> *Decision*: The claim must be dismissed since the employees had repudiated the contract before the employer's decision to close down made them redundant.

An employee can be dismissed for misconduct but still claim redundancy pay in the event of a **strike**.

- After receiving notice of termination of the contract from the employer
- After the employee has given notice claiming redundancy pay on account of lay-off or short time

8.3.2 Offer of further employment

The employer may offer a redundant employee alternative employment for the future. If the employee then unreasonably refuses the offer, they lose their entitlement to redundancy pay: s 141.

The offer must be of alternative employment **in the same capacity**, at the same place and on the same terms and conditions as the previous employment. It should not be perceived as being lower in status: *Cambridge District Co-operative Society v Ruse 1993*.

When there is a difference between the terms and conditions of a new contract and the previous contract, the employee is entitled to a **four week trial** period in the new employment. If either party terminates the new contract during the trial period, it is treated as a case of dismissal for redundancy at the expiry date of the previous employment. The employee can also still bring claims for unfair dismissal: *Trafalgar House Services Ltd v Carder 1997*.

8.4 Lay-off and short time

An employee's exact remuneration may depend on the employer providing work. They are 'laid off' in any week in which they earn nothing by reason of lack of work or they are '**kept on short time**', which is any week in which they earn less than half a normal week's pay: s 86.

When an employee is **laid off** or **kept on short time** for four or more consecutive weeks, or six weeks in a period of thirteen weeks they **may claim redundancy** pay by giving notice to the employer of their intention to claim.

In addition to their **notice of claim** the employee must also give notice to the employer to terminate the contract of employment: s 150(1).

8.5 Strike action

Employees involved in **strike action after** redundancy notice is served **will** be entitled to redundancy payments. However, if they are **on strike** when the notice is served they will **not** be eligible for the payment.

We have seen the various protections and remedies available for employees as part of the employment relationship, but we shall now look at a **final relationship** that the employee has, the **relationship with the state**.

In the UK there is a **social security system** whose purpose is to provide support to people in financial or other need. As we shall see, much of this system is funded through taxation and by contributions individuals make whilst they are employed.

9 Social security law: The relationship with the state

> **FAST FORWARD**
>
> The purpose of UK's **social security system** is to provide **monetary assistance** to those who do not have an adequate income to live on. There are many types of **benefits** that individuals can claim which are funded out of **national insurance contributions** and **taxation**.

9.1 The purpose of the social security system

The overall purpose of UK's **social security system** is to provide **monetary assistance** to those who do not have an adequate income to live on, for example due to illness, disability and loss of employment. In the UK the state also supports those who work but who have low levels of income, for example if they work part-time or irregular hours. Support is also given to **parents of children** to help with the costs of raising them. The **social** aspect of the system is that this assistance is provided by society; **security** refers to the sense of protection that the system offers to individuals.

The system consists of a number of specific payments (or **benefits**) that are paid to individuals based on their personal circumstances. Individuals can receive more than one benefit depending on their situation. However, the **overall amount** that can be paid from certain benefits is **capped** (currently at £25,320 per year for couples or single parents with children in London and £22,020 for those outside of London. The cap is lower for individuals without children) (gov.uk, 2024).

Access to benefits is not automatic. Those wishing to claim must be **eligible** for them, and are responsible for making a claim. Eligibility will depend on the particular benefit in question, but in general terms it is based on factors such as:

- Contributions made to the national insurance system (see later) whilst working.
- Having a low income (for income-based benefits).
- Meeting the criteria of the specific benefit being applied for.

9.2 Benefits payable under the system

The table below summarises some of the benefits currently available in the UK. However, numerous other benefits are available too.

Benefit	Description
Universal credit (UC)	A means tested allowance that replaces six of the benefits in the table below (jobseeker's allowance (income-based), employment and support allowance (income based), income support, working tax credit, child tax credit and housing benefit).
	The purpose of this benefit is to simplify the benefits system by rolling the most commonly claimed benefits into a single payment.
	The total amount of the benefit paid reduces when employment income exceeds a certain amount. At this point, for every £1 earned, the benefit is reduced by 63p.

PART E   THE EMPLOYMENT RELATIONSHIP AND SOCIAL SECURITY LAW: THE RELATIONSHIP WITH THE STATE

Benefit	Description
Job seeker's allowance (JSA)	A payment to individuals who are capable of work and are actively seeking it. Individuals can work up to 16 hours per week and still be entitled to claim it. There are two types of JSA, income-based and contributions-based. Income-based is means tested and takes into account of any income or capital an individual and their partner have. Contribution-based ignores capital and income for 6 months but eligibility depends on national insurance contributions made.
Employment and support allowance (ESA)	This benefit works in a similar way to JSA, and is also income- and contribution-based. However, it is paid to those who have a limited capacity for work due to illness or disability.
Income support (IS)	A means-tested payment made to carers and pregnant or a lone parents of a child under 5 years old.
Housing benefit (HB)	A means-tested payment made to help pay rental costs for those on low incomes.
Child tax credit (CTC)	A payment made to those on low incomes to help support bringing up a child. Eligibility depends on issues such as the number of children, their ages and whether any have a disability.
Working tax credit (WTC)	A payment made to those on low incomes but who are working. Eligibility depends on hours worked and whether or not the person has a disability or has children or pays for childcare.
Personal independence payment (PIP)	A non-means tested benefit paid to those between 16 and 64 who have additional care needs due to illness or disability. It consists of two parts, a daily living component and a mobility component. PIP replaced DLA (below) for new claims in 2013.
Disability living allowance (DLA)	A non-means tested payment made for children under 16 who have additional care needs. It consists of a personal care component and a mobility component.
Attendance allowance (AA)	A non-means tested benefit paid to those over 64 who have a physical or mental disability who require assistance or supervision in regards their personal care.
Carer's allowance (CA)	A payment made to those who provide 35 hours or more care per week to a person who has an illness or disability. To claim this benefit, the person being cared for must be themselves in receipt of AA, PIP or DLA.
Maternity allowance (MA)	A payment to pregnant women who are not entitled to statutory sick pay.
Bereavement allowance (BA)	A payment to an individual whose husband, wife or civil partner has died.

Benefit	Description
State pension (SP)	A payment to individuals who are over the state pension age. Depending on when the pensioner was born, they will be paid either the basic state pension and/or an additional state pension. A new state pension scheme that replaces these has also been established.
Pension credit (PC)	A means-tested benefit paid to pensioners who are on a low income, which tops up their income to a minimum level.

9.3 Funding the social security system

The **social security system** was forecast to cost the UK £315.8 billion (Gov.uk, 2024) in the year 2024 to 2025. The UK government funds the costs of the social security system from **national insurance contributions** and **general taxation**.

9.3.1 National insurance contributions

When an individual reaches 16 years of age, they are issued with a **national insurance number**. On starting work they must provide this number to their employer who uses it to make payments out of the employee's salary to their **national insurance record**. Employers are also required to make their own employer's contributions for their employees. If an individual is self-employed then they supply their national insurance number when they submit their tax return, and make a regular contributions throughout the year.

Over time, each individual builds up **'contributions'** on their national insurance record and it is these contributions that make them eligible for some of the benefits we have seen. For example, to be entitled to the full state pension after April 2016, an individual must have 35 full years of national insurance contributions. However, the state recognises that sometimes individuals are not able to make contributions (for example if they are out of work or raising children), and will therefore **'credit'** their national insurance record when they claim certain benefits to ensure that they do not lose out.

The following **benefits** are funded out of national insurance contributions:

- Basic state pension
- Additional state pension
- New state pension
- Jobseeker's allowance (contribution-based)
- Employment and support allowance (contribution-based)
- Maternity allowance
- Bereavement allowance

Employees and **employers** pay what are known as **class 1** national insurance contributions. They can also make **class 3 voluntary contributions** to their national insurance record at any time (for example to fill gaps in their contributions).

The **self-employed** make **class 4 contributions** once their profit exceeds a certain amount. They can also choose to make **voluntary class 2 contributions** if they wish, where their profit is less than this amount. The different classes are simply the way the system groups the types of payment made.

9.3.2 Taxation

The other benefits we have seen are payable regardless of whether an individual has made national insurance contributions. They are made because as society, the UK believes that it is important to **support those on low incomes** or have **illnesses and disabilities**, as well as those **raising children** to help support the child. The objective is to ensure that all have a basic level of income to enable them to live and to support their families.

These benefits are funded through the UK's **taxation system**. Taxes are payable for many things, such as an individual's income from work or self-employment, profits made by companies or where profits are made on the sale of assets or on a person's estate when they die. All of these taxes are collected by government, which then decides how best to use the money raised, including making benefit payments.

Question — National insurance contributions

Briefly explain who is responsible for making class 1 national insurance contributions and whether they can also make voluntary contributions to the social security system.

Answer

Employees and their employers are required to make class 1 national insurance contributions. Employees (not employers) may choose to make class 3 voluntary contributions should they wish to. The purpose of the voluntary contributions is to ensure that an individual's national insurance record has sufficient contributions for them to be eligible for certain benefits (such as the state pension).

Chapter Roundup

- When an employment contract is terminated by notice there is **no** breach of contract unless the **contents** of the notice (such as notice period) are themselves in breach.
- Where employment is **terminated by notice** the period given must **not be less** than the **statutory minimum**.
- **Breach of the employment contract** occurs where there is **summary dismissal**, **constructive dismissal**, **inability** on the employer's side to **continue employment**, or **repudiation** of the contract by the employee.
- Where the employer has **summarily dismissed** an employee without notice (as where the employer becomes insolvent), there may be a claim for **damages** at common law for **wrongful dismissal**.
- Generally, the only **effective remedy** available to a **wrongfully dismissed** employee is a claim for **damages** based on the **loss of earnings**. The measure of damages is usually the sum that would have been earned if **proper notice** had been given.
- Certain employees have a right not to be **unfairly dismissed**. Breach of that right allows an employee to claim compensation from a tribunal. To claim for unfair dismissal, the employee must satisfy certain criteria.
- Dismissal must be **justified** if it is related to the employee's capability or qualifications, the employee's conduct, redundancy, legal prohibition or restriction on the employee's continued employment or some other substantial reason.
- Dismissal is **automatically unfair** if it is on certain specified grounds.
- Remedies for **unfair dismissal** include:
    - Reinstatement
    - Re-engagement
    - Compensation
- Dismissal is caused by **redundancy** when the employer has ceased to carry on the business in which the employee has been employed or the business no longer needs employees to carry on that work. In these circumstances, dismissal is **presumed** by the courts to be by redundancy unless otherwise demonstrated.
- The purpose of UK's **social security system** is to provide **monetary assistance** to those who do not have an adequate income to live on. There are many types of **benefits** that individuals can claim which are funded out of **national insurance contributions** and **taxation**

Quick Quiz

1. If an employer cannot continue with the employment contract because the company has gone into liquidation, does that constitute breach of contract?

   Yes ☐
   No ☐

2. **Fill in the blanks** below, using the words in the box.

   To claim (1) .... for unfair dismissal, three issues have to be considered.

   The employee must show that they are a (2) .... employee and that they have been (3) ....

   The (4) .... must show what the (5) .... was for dismissal.

   Application has to be made to the (6) .... within (7) .... months of the dismissal.

• qualifying	• dismissed	• employer
• reason	• three	• compensation
• employment tribunal		

3. Expiry of a fixed term contract without renewal amounts to a dismissal.

   True ☐
   False ☐

4. Which one of the following is **not** a question that a tribunal, when considering an employer's reasonableness in an unfair dismissal claim, will want to answer?

   A   What would a reasonable employer have done?
   B   Has the correct procedure been applied?
   C   Has any employee been dismissed in this way before?
   D   Did the employer take all circumstances into consideration?

5. Which is the most common remedy awarded for unfair dismissal?

compensation
re-engagement
re-instalment

6. An employee is not entitled to redundancy pay if they resign voluntarily before being made redundant even if they were aware of the possibility of redundancy.

   True ☐
   False ☐

7. Universal credit is a means tested allowance that replaces six other social security benefits that individuals may be entitled to.

   State the six benefits that universal credit replaced.

Answers to Quick Quiz

1 Yes. The contract is effectively repudiated.

2 (1) compensation (2) qualifying (3) dismissed (4) employer (5) reason (6) employment tribunal (7) three

3 True. Non-renewal constitutes dismissal.

4 C. The question is irrelevant to the employee's situation.

5 Compensation, as in most cases the working relationship would have been irrevocably damaged.

6 True, as they are not being made redundant.

7 Universal credit replaced jobseeker's allowance (income-based), employment and support allowance (income based), income support, working tax credit, child tax credit and housing benefit.

End of chapter question

Unfair dismissal

Derek is a 34-year-old advertising assistant who has been working for the advertising agency Multi Media Ltd for the last four years. One evening Derek is entertaining some of the clients of Multi Media Ltd. The events of this evening are paid for using the company's hospitality budget.

Eager to make a good impression with these clients, Derek offered to drive them back to their hotel despite his having drunk several glasses of wine. In the course of this journey he is stopped by the police and is subsequently convicted of driving whilst under the influence of alcohol. As a result of this conviction, Derek receives a phone call from his manager informing him that he has lost his job with Multi Media Ltd.

Required

(a) Explain to Derek the legal requirements that individuals must fulfil in order to bring unfair dismissal claims, and whether his own claim conforms to these requirements. **(8 marks)**

(b) Assuming that these requirements are met in the instant case, explain whether these facts disclose a fair reason for Multi Media Ltd's decision to dismiss Derek. **(8 marks)**

(c) What internal procedures must a company follow to effect a lawful dismissal, and have these requirements been adhered to in the instant case? **(4 marks)**

(Total = 20 marks)

PART E THE EMPLOYMENT RELATIONSHIP AND SOCIAL SECURITY LAW: THE RELATIONSHIP WITH THE STATE

Choice of business medium

Companies, sole traders and partnerships

Topic list	Syllabus reference
1 Sole traders	3.1
2 Companies	3.1
3 Limited liability of members	3.1
4 Types of company	3.1
5 Additional classifications	3.1
6 Comparison of companies, sole traders and partnerships	3.1

Introduction

In this chapter we begin our study of the laws which govern a particular type of business organisation – a **company**.

We shall begin this chapter by considering what companies are before moving onto more specific rules that govern how they are run. In future chapters we shall look at how they are **formed**, **funded** and **managed** before seeing how the law interacts with them through the rules on **accounts** and **audit**, **criminal activity** and **insolvency**.

For now, we will introduce companies as **business vehicles** that are distinct from both **sole traders** and **partnerships** (that we saw in a previous chapter). The key difference between them is the concept of **separate legal personality** (which we shall come back to in the next chapter).

We shall also look at the **different types of company** that can be used to carry out business.

The **Companies Act 2006**, (TSO, 2006) and the **Small Business, Enterprise and Employment Act 2015**, (TSO, 2015) apply to this and all chapters unless otherwise stated.

PART F CHOICE OF BUSINESS MEDIUM

1 Sole traders

FAST FORWARD

In a **sole tradership**, there is no legal distinction between the individual and the business.

1.1 Introduction

We shall begin this chapter by considering sole traders. A **sole trader owns** and **runs a business**. They contribute capital to start the enterprise, run it with or without employees, and earn the profits or stand the losses of the venture.

Sole traders are found mainly in the **retail trades** (local newsagents), **small scale service industries** (plumbers), and **small manufacturing** and **craft industries**. An accountant may operate as a sole trader.

1.2 Legal status of the sole trader

Whilst the business is a separate accounting entity the business is **not legally distinct** from the person who owns it. In law, the person and the business are viewed as the same entity.

The **advantages** of being a sole trader are as follows.

(a) **No formal procedures** are required to set up in business. However, for certain classes of business a licence may be required (eg retailing wines and spirits), and VAT registration is often necessary.

(b) **Independence** and **self-accountability**. A sole trader need consult nobody about business decisions and is not required to reveal the state of the business to anyone (other than the tax authorities each year).

(c) **Personal supervision** of the business by the sole trader should ensure its effective operation. Personal contact with customers may enhance commercial flexibility.

(d) **All** the **profits** of the business **accrue** to the sole trader. This can be a powerful motivator, and satisfying to the individual whose ability/energy results in reward.

The **disadvantages** of being a sole trader include the following.

(a) If the business gets into debt, a sole trader's **personal wealth** (for example, private house) might be lost if the debts are called in, as they are the same legal entity.

(b) Expansion of the business is usually only possible by **ploughing back** the **profits** of the business as further capital, although loans or overdraft finance may be available.

(c) The business has a **high dependence** on the **individual** which can mean long working hours and difficulties during sickness or holidays.

(d) The **death** of the proprietor may make it **necessary** to **sell** the **business** in order to pay the resulting tax liabilities, or family members may not wish to continue the business anyway.

(e) The **individual** may **only have one skill**. A sole trader may be, say, a good technical engineer or craftsman but may lack the skills to market effectively or to maintain accounting records to control the business effectively.

(f) Other **disadvantages** include lack of diversification, absence of economies of scale and problems of raising finance.

Having seen what a sole trader is, we shall now move on to look at companies and how the corporate form addresses some of the disadvantages of operating the business as a sole trader.

2 Companies

FAST FORWARD

By its nature, a **company** is more formal than **a partnership** or a **sole trader**. There is often substantially more **legislation** on the formation and procedures of companies than any other business association. In particular, a great deal of information about individual companies is available in the public domain because there is a Registrar of Companies who maintains information on **public registers** about each one.

A company is the most popular form of business association. The key reason for this is that the **liability of its members to contribute to the debts of the entity is significantly limited**. For many people, this benefit outweighs the disadvantage of the formality and publicity surrounding companies, and encourages them not to trade as sole traders or (unlimited) partnerships.

2.1 Definition of a company

Key terms

For the purposes of this Workbook, a **company** is an entity registered as such under the Companies Act 2006.

The key feature of a company is that it has a **legal personality** (existence) distinct from its members and directors.

2.2 Legal personality

A person possesses legal rights and is subject to legal obligations. In law, the term 'person' is used to denote two categories of legal person.

- An individual human being is a **natural person**. A sole trader is a natural person, and there is legally no distinction between the individual and the business entity in sole tradership

- The law also recognises **artificial persons** in the form of companies and limited partnerships. Unlimited partnerships are not artificial persons.

Key term

Corporate personality is a common law principle that grants a company a legal identity, separate from the members who comprise it. It follows that the property of a company belongs to that company, debts of the company must be satisfied from the assets of that company, and the company has perpetual succession until wound up.

A corporation is a **legal entity separate** from the natural persons connected with it, for example as members or directors. We shall come back to this principle in the next chapter. In the next section we shall look at one of the impacts of separate legal personality – the limited liability of members.

3 Limited liability of members

FAST FORWARD

The fact that a company's members – not the company itself – have **limited liability** for its debts **protects** the **members** from the company's creditors and ultimately from the full risk of business failure.

A key consequence of the fact that the company is distinct from its members is that its members have **limited liability**.

Key term

Limited liability is a protection offered to members of certain types of company. In the event of business failure, the members will only be asked to contribute identifiable amounts to the assets of the business.

3.1 Protection for members against creditors

The **company** itself is **liable without limit for its own debts.** If the company buys plastic from another company, for example, it owes the other company money.

Limited liability is a benefit to members. They own the business, so might be the people whom the creditors logically asked to pay the debts of the company if the company is unable to pay them itself.

Limited liability prevents this by stipulating the **creditors** of a limited company **cannot demand payment of the company's debts** from members of the company.

3.2 Protection from business failure

As the company is liable for all its own debts, limited liability only becomes an issue in the event of a business failure when the **company is unable to pay its own debts**.

This will result in the **winding up** of the company which will enable the creditors to be paid from the proceeds of any assets remaining in the company. It is at winding up that limited liability becomes most relevant.

3.3 Members asked to contribute identifiable amounts

Although the creditors of the company cannot ask the members of the company to pay the debts of the company, there are some amounts that **members are required to pay, in the event of a winding up**.

Type of company	Amount owed by member at winding up
Company limited by shares	Any **outstanding amount** from when they originally purchased their shares from the company.
	If the member's shares are fully paid, they **do not have to contribute anything in the event of a winding up**.
Company limited by guarantee	The **amount they guaranteed** to pay in the event of a winding up.

Question
Limitations of liability

Anvi and two friends wish to set up a small business. Anvi is concerned that, following her initial investment, she will have no access to additional funds, and is worried what might happen if anything goes wrong. Advise her on the relative merits of a company and an unlimited partnership.

Answer

The question of liability appears to be important to Anvi. As a member of a limited company, her liability would be limited – as a member at least – to any outstanding amount payable for her shares. If the three friends decide to form an unlimited partnership, they should be advised that they will have **unlimited** liability for the debts of the partnership. (An unlimited partnership does **not** have a legal personality distinct from the partners.)

Having seen what a company is and the impact of separate legal personality, we shall now look at the various types of company that a business might be incorporated into.

4 Types of company

FAST FORWARD

Most companies are those **incorporated** under the **Companies Act**. However there are other types of company such as **corporations sole**, **chartered corporations**, **statutory corporations** and **community interest companies**.

Corporations are classified in one of the following categories.

Categories	Description
Corporations sole	A corporation sole is an **official position** which is filled by one person who is replaced from time to time. The Public Trustee and the Treasury Solicitor are corporations sole.
Chartered corporations	These are usually **charities** or bodies such as the Association of Chartered Certified Accountants, formed by Royal Charter.
Statutory corporations	Statutory corporations are formed by special Acts of Parliament. This method is little used now, as it is slow and expensive. It was used in the nineteenth century to form railway and canal companies.
Registered companies	Registration under the Companies Act is the normal method of incorporating a commercial concern. Any body of this type is properly called a company.
Community Interest Companies (CICs)	A special form of company for use by 'social' enterprises pursuing purposes that are beneficial to the community, rather than the maximisation of profit for the benefit of owners, created by the Companies (Audit, Investigation and Community Enterprise) Act 2004 (TSO, 2004).

4.1 Limited companies

The meaning of limited liability has already been explained. It is the **member**, not the company, whose liability for the company's debts may be limited.

4.1.1 Liability limited by shares

Liability is usually **limited by shares.** This is the position when a company which has share capital states in its constitution that 'the liability of members is limited'.

4.1.2 Liability limited by guarantee

Alternatively a company may be **limited by guarantee.** Its constitution states the amount which each member **undertakes** to **contribute** in a winding up (also known as a liquidation). A creditor has no direct claim against a member under their guarantee, nor can the company require a member to pay up under their guarantee until the company goes into liquidation.

Companies limited by guarantee are appropriate to **non-commercial activities**, such as a charity or a trade association which is non-profit making but wish to have a form of reserve capital if it becomes insolvent. They do not have **share capital**.

4.2 Unlimited liability companies

Key term

An **unlimited liability company** is a company in which members do not have limited liability. In the event of business failure, the liquidator can require members to contribute as much as may be required to pay the company's debts in full.

An unlimited company **can only be a private company** as, by definition, a **public company is always limited**.

An unlimited company need not **file** a copy of its **annual accounts** and reports with the Registrar, unless during the relevant accounting reference period:

(a) It is (to its knowledge) a **subsidiary** of a limited company.

(b) **Two** or more **limited companies** have **exercised rights** over the **company**, which (had they been exercised by only one of them) would have **made** the **company** a **subsidiary** of that one company.

(c) It is the **parent company** of a limited liability company.

The unlimited company certainly has its uses. It provides a **corporate body** (a separate legal entity) which can conveniently hold assets to which liabilities do not attach.

Question — Limited liability

Explain the liability of members of companies limited by guarantee.

Answer

Members of companies limited by guarantee are required to pay the amount they guaranteed if required when the company is wound up.

4.3 Public and private companies

FAST FORWARD — A company may be **private** or **public**. Only the latter may offer its share to the public.

Key terms

A **public company** is a company whose constitution states that it is public and that it has complied with the registration procedures for such a company.

A **private company** is a company which has not been registered as a public company under the Companies Act. The major practical distinction between a private and public company is that the former may not offer its securities to the public.

A **public** company is a company registered as such under the Companies Act 2006 (TSO, 2006) with the Registrar. **Any company not registered as public is a private company**.

A public company may be one which was **originally incorporated** as a public company or one which re-registered as a public company having been previously a private company.

4.4 Conditions for being a public company

FAST FORWARD — To trade, a public company must hold a **Registrar's trading certificate** having met the requirements, including **minimum capital** of **£50,000**.

4.4.1 Registrar's trading certificate

Before it can trade a company originally incorporated as a public company must have a trading certificate issued by the Registrar. The conditions for this are:

- The **name** of the company identifies it as a public company by ending with the words 'public limited company' or 'plc' or their Welsh equivalents, 'ccc', for a Welsh company.
- The **constitution** of the company states that 'the company is a public company' or words to that effect.
- The **allotted share capital** of the company is not less than the authorised minimum which is currently £50,000.
- It is a **company** limited by shares.

With regard to the minimum share capital of £50,000:

- A company originally incorporated as a public company will not be permitted to trade until its **allotted** share capital is at least £50,000.
- A private company which re-registers as a public company will not be permitted to trade until it has **allotted** share capital of at least £50,000; this needs only be paid up to one quarter of its nominal value (plus the whole of any premium).

- A private company which has share capital of £50,000 or more may of course continue as a private company; it is always **optional** to become a public company.

A company limited by guarantee which has no share capital, and an unlimited company, **cannot** be public companies.

4.4.2 Minimum membership and directors

A public company must have a minimum of **one member**. This is the same as a private company. However, unlike a private company it must have at least **two directors**. A private company may have just one director. All companies must have at least one director who is **a 'natural person'** (that is a person as opposed to a company). Directors do not usually have liability for the company's debts.

4.5 Private companies

A private company is the residual category and so does not need to satisfy any special conditions. Private companies are generally small to medium-sized enterprises in which some if not all shareholders are also directors and *vice versa*. Ownership and management are combined in the same individuals. Therefore, it is unnecessary to impose on the directors complicated restrictions to safeguard the interests of members, and so the number of rules that apply to public companies are reduced for private companies.

4.6 Differences between private and public companies

FAST FORWARD

The main differences between public and private companies relate to: **capital**, **dealings in shares**, **accounts**, **commencement of business**, **general meetings**, **names**, **identification**, and **disclosure requirements**.

Some differences between public and private companies imposed by law relate to the following factors.

4.6.1 Capital

The main differences are:

(a) There is a minimum amount of **£50,000** for a **public** company, but **no minimum** for a **private** company.

(b) A public company may **raise capital** by **offering** its **shares** or debentures to the public; a **private** company is **prohibited** from doing so.

(c) Both **public** and **private companies** must generally **offer** to existing **members first** any ordinary shares to be allotted for cash. However a **private** company **may permanently disapply** this pre-emption rule.

4.6.2 Dealings in shares

Only a **public company** can obtain a listing for its shares on the **Stock Exchange** or other investment exchange. To obtain the advantages of listing the company must agree to elaborate conditions contained in particulars in a **listing agreement** with The London Stock Exchange. However, by no means all public companies are listed.

4.6.3 Accounts

(a) A **public** company has **six** months from the end of its accounting reference period in which to produce its statutory audited accounts. The period for a **private** company is **nine** months.

(b) A **private** company, if qualified by its size, may have **partial exemption** from various **accounting provisions** (discussed later in this text). These exemptions are not available to a public company or to its subsidiaries (even if they are private companies).

(c) A **listed public company** must publish its full accounts and reports on its **website**.

(d) Public companies must lay their **accounts** and reports before a general meeting of shareholders annually. Private companies have no such requirement.

4.6.4 Commencement of business

A **private** company can commence business **as soon** as it is **incorporated**. A **public** company, if incorporated as such, must first **obtain a trading certificate from the Registrar**.

4.6.5 General meetings

Private companies are not required to hold annual general meetings (AGMs). **Public companies** must hold one within six months of their financial year end.

4.6.6 Names and identification

The rules on identification as public or private are as follows.

- The word **'limited'** or **'Ltd'** (or the Welsh equivalent) in the name denotes a private company; **'public limited company'** or **'plc'** (or the Welsh equivalent) must appear at the end of the name of a public company.

- The **constitution** of a **public** company must state that it is a public company. A **private company** should be identified as private.

4.6.7 Disclosure requirements

There are **special disclosure and publicity requirements** for public companies.

The main advantage of carrying on business through a public rather than a private company is that a public company, by the issue of listing particulars, may obtain a **listing** on The London Stock Exchange and so access capital from the investing public generally.

Attention!

> There is an important distinction between public companies and **listed public companies**. Listed (or quoted) companies are those which trade their shares (and other securities) on stock exchanges. Not all public companies sell their shares on stock exchanges (although, in law, they are entitled to sell their shares to the public). **Private** companies are not entitled to sell shares to the public in this way.
>
> In practice, only public companies meeting certain criteria are allowed to obtain a listing on the Main Market of the London Stock Exchange.

Private companies may be broadly classified into two groups: independent (also called **free-standing**) private companies and **subsidiaries** of other companies.

As well as the various types of companies that we have just seen, there are other sub-sets of companies that we need to consider too. These **additional classifications** are covered in the next section.

5 Additional classifications

There are a number of other ways in which companies can be **classified**.

5.1 Parent (holding) and subsidiary companies

The Companies Act 2006 (TSO, 2006) draws a distinction between an 'accounting' definition and a 'legal' definition in s 1162.

A company will be the **parent** (or **holding**) **company** of another company, its **subsidiary company**, if it meets the following criteria.

10: COMPANIES, SOLE TRADERS AND PARTNERSHIPS

Key term

Parent company

(a) It holds a **majority of the voting rights** in the subsidiary.

(b) It **is a member of the subsidiary and has the right to appoint or remove a majority of its board of directors.**

(c) **It has the right to exercise a dominant influence over the subsidiary**:

    (i) By virtue of provisions contained in the subsidiary's articles.
    (ii) By virtue of a control contract.

(d) **It is a member of the subsidiary and controls alone**, under an agreement with other members, **a majority of the voting rights in the company**.

(e) **A company is also a parent if:**

    (i) It has the power to exercise, or actually exercises, a dominant influence or control over the subsidiary.
    (ii) It and the subsidiary are managed on a unified basis.

(f) **A company is also treated as the parent of the subsidiaries of its subsidiaries.**

A company (A Ltd) is a **wholly owned subsidiary** of another company (B Ltd) if it has no other members except B Ltd and its wholly owned subsidiaries, or persons acting on B Ltd's or its subsidiaries' behalf.

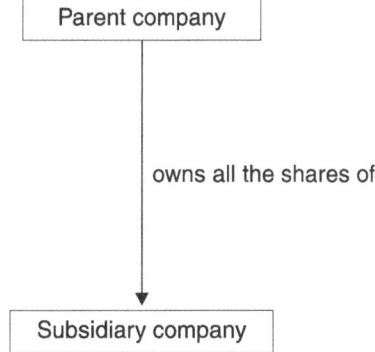

The diagram illustrates a **simple group**. In practice, such groups might be much larger and much more complex.

The importance of the parent and subsidiary company relationship is recognised in company law in a number of rules.

(a) A parent company must generally prepare **group accounts** in which the financial situation of parent and subsidiary companies is consolidated as if they were one person.

(b) A subsidiary may **not ordinarily be a member** of its parent company.

(c) Since directors of a parent company can **control** its **subsidiary**, some rules designed to regulate the dealings of companies with directors also apply to its subsidiaries, particularly loans to directors.

5.2 Quoted companies

As we have seen public companies may seek a listing on a public exchange. This option is not open to private companies, who are not allowed to offer their shares for sale to the public. Listed companies are sometimes referred to as quoted companies (because the price of their shares are quoted publicly).

5.3 Medium-sized companies

Medium-sized companies are permitted to take advantage of more **relaxed accounting rules** and **disclosure requirements** as compared to larger companies. For example, the format of the profit and loss account is simpler and there are reduced reporting requirements in respect of their business review or strategic report.

A company is classed as **'medium-sized'** if it meets at least **two** of the following **conditions**:

- Annual turnover must be not more than £36 million
- The balance sheet total must be not more than £18 million
- The average number of employees must be not more than 250.

5.4 Small companies

Small companies benefit from the **small companies regime's** reduced legal requirements in terms of accounting rules, abridged accounts filing and exemption from obtaining an audit.

In **accounting terms**, a company is small if it meets **two** of the following applicable **criteria**:

(a) Balance sheet total of not more than £5.1 million.
(b) Turnover of not more than £10.2 million.
(c) 50 employees or fewer on average.

5.5 Micro-entities

A **micro-entity** has to option to take advantage of **accounting** exemptions that are not available to small companies.

An **entity** is classed as **'micro'** if it meets at least **two** of the following **conditions**:

(a) Annual turnover must be not more than £632,000.
(b) The balance sheet total must be not more than £316,000.
(c) The average number of employees must be not more than 10.

Attention!

> The turnover and balance sheet thresholds for micro, small and medium size companies have been proposed to increase from October 2024. At the time of publication, this has not yet been confirmed.
>
> The proposed new thresholds are:
>
> Micro-companies: Turnover <£1million, balance sheet <£500,000
> Small companies: Turnover <£15m, balance sheet <£7.5 million
> Medium companies: Turnover <£54 million, balance sheet <£27 million
>
> The thresholds for average number of employees are proposed to remain the same.
>
> The same set of proposals also set out changes to the reporting requirements of the different types of company.
>
> Unless you are notified otherwise, you should treat the current thresholds and reporting requirements as still valid.

5.6 Multinational companies

Key term

> The vast majority of companies will simply operate in one country. However, some of the larger companies in the world will operate in more than one country. Such companies are **multinational**. A **multinational company** is a company that produces and markets its products in more than one country.

Some examples of multinational companies include:

- Wal-mart Stores Inc
- Royal Dutch Shell plc
- Exxon Mobil Corporation

Such companies sell their shares on stock exchanges around the world.

Question

Small companies

State the criteria that a company must meet to be classified as small.

Answer

A small company must meet two of the following criteria:

- Its balance sheet total must not exceed £5.1 million.
- Turnover must be no more than £10.2 million.
- It must employ fewer than 50 employees.

We've now seen what a company is and a large number of types of company that might be incorporated. The next section contains a useful comparison between companies, sole traders and partnerships. It is important to study this section carefully as exam questions could test your knowledge of the various differences.

6 Comparison of companies, sole traders and partnerships

FAST FORWARD

Since it is a separate legal entity, a company has a number of features which are different from a sole trader or partnership. The most important of these is that a company has a **separate legal personality** from its members, while a sole tradership or traditional partnership does not.

6.1 The differences

The separate legal personality of a company gives rise to a number of characteristics which mark it out from a sole tradership or traditional partnership. These are outlined below. The other key differences relate to the **formality** of a company and the **regulations** it has to adhere to.

Factor	Company	Sole tradership/traditional partnership
Entity	Is a legal entity separate from its members	Has no existence apart from the owner or partners
Liability	Members' liability can be limited	Owner/partner liability is usually unlimited
Size	May have any number of members (at least one)	Partnerships must have a minimum of two partners. Sole traders have just the owner.
Succession	Perpetual succession – change in ownership does not affect existence	The business is dissolved when the owner, or any of the partners leaves it
Owners' interests	Members own transferable shares	Owners of a sole tradership can transfer the business to another party. Partners cannot assign their interest in the partnership.
Assets	Company owns the assets	Sole traders own the business assets. Partners own business assets jointly.
Management	Company must have at least one director (two for a public company)	The sole trader makes their own business decisions. All partners can participate in the management of a partnership.
Constitution	Company must have a written constitution.	Sole traders do not need a constitution. A partnership may have a written partnership agreement, but also may not.

Factor	Company	Sole tradership/traditional partnership
Accounts	A company must usually deliver accounts to the Registrar.	Sole traders or partners do not have to send their accounts to the Registrar.
Security	A company may offer a floating charge over its assets.	A sole tradership or partnership may not usually give a floating charge on assets.
Withdrawal of capital	Strict rules concerning repayment of subscribed capital.	No rules on how sole traders and partners may withdraw capital.
Taxation	Company pays tax on its profit. Directors are taxed through PAYE system. Shareholders receive dividends which are taxed 10 months after the tax year.	Partners extract 'drawings' weekly or monthly. No tax is deducted. Income tax is payable on their share of the final profit for the year. Sole traders pay income tax on business profits.
Management	Members elect directors to manage the company.	Sole traders manage the business themselves. All partners have a right to be involved in the management of the partnership.

Chapter Roundup

- In a **sole tradership**, there is no legal distinction between the individual and the business.

- By its nature, a **company** is more formal than **a partnership** or a **sole trader**. There is often substantially more **legislation** on the formation and procedures of companies than any other business association. In particular, a great deal of information about individual companies is available in the public domain because there is a Registrar of Companies who maintains information on **public registers** about each one.

- The fact that a company's members – not the company itself – have **limited liability** for its debts **protects** the **members** from the company's creditors and ultimately from the full risk of business failure.

- Most companies are those **incorporated** under the **Companies Act**. However there are other types of company such as **corporations sole**, **chartered corporations**, **statutory corporations** and **community interest companies**.

- A company may be **private** or **public**. Only the latter may offer its shares to the public.

- To trade, a public company must hold a **Registrar's trading certificate** having met the requirements, including **minimum capital** of £50,000.

- The main differences between public and private companies relate to: **capital**; **dealings** in **shares**; **accounts**; **commencement of business**; **general meetings**; **names**; **identification**; and **disclosure requirements**.

- There are a number of other ways in which companies can be **classified**.

- Since it is a separate legal entity, a company has a number of features which are different from a sole trader or partnership. The most important of these is that a company has a **separate legal personality** from its members, while a sole tradership or traditional partnership does not.

PART F CHOICE OF BUSINESS MEDIUM

Quick Quiz

1   Businesses in the form of sole traders are legally distinct from their owners.

    True ☐

    False ☐

2   Which of the following types of company can be incorporated under the Companies Act 2006?

    A   A private limited company
    B   A public limited company
    C   A company limited by guarantee with a share capital
    D   A company limited by guarantee with no share capital
    E   A private unlimited company
    F   A public unlimited company

3   Which TWO of the following statements are true? A private company:

    A   Is defined as any company that is not a public company
    B   Sells its shares on the junior stock market known as the Alternative Investment Market and on the Stock Exchange
    C   Must have at least one director with unlimited liability
    D   Is a significant form of business organisation in areas of the economy that do not require large amounts of capital

4   Under which circumstance would a member of a limited company have to contribute funds on winding up?

    A   Where there is not enough cash to pay the creditors
    B   Where they have an outstanding amount from when they originally purchased their shares
    C   To allow the company to repurchase debentures it issued
    D   Where the company is a community interest company and the funds are required to complete a community project

5   The minimum allotted and paid up share capital of a company incorporated as a public limited company is

    A   £12,500
    B   £50,000
    C   £100,000
    D   £500,000

6   **Fill in the blanks** in the statement below using the figures in the box.

    A micro company must meet two of the following criteria.

    Its balance sheet total must be less than £ (1) ... ,000,000 and its turnover must be less than £ (2) ... ,000,000. The number of employees must be less than (3) ... people.

• 10	• 632
• 316	• 50

7   Which TWO of the following are correct? A public company or plc:

    A   Is defined as any company which is not a private company
    B   Has a legal personality that is separate from its members or owners
    C   Must have at least one director with unlimited liability
    D   Can own property and make contracts in its own name

8   State the main advantage of forming an unlimited company.

Answers to Quick Quiz

1. False. Sole trader businesses are not legally distinct from their owners.

2. A, B, D and E are correct. It is not possible to incorporate a company limited by guarantee with a share capital, so C is incorrect. A public limited company is by definition limited, so F is wrong.

3. A and D are correct. A private company cannot sell its shares to the public on any stock market, so B is incorrect. Directors need not have unlimited liability, so C is incorrect.

4. B. Members only have a liability for any outstanding amounts of share capital partly paid for.

5. B. £50,000. Where the company was incorporated as a private one but subsequently re-registered as a public one, only a quarter of the minimum must be paid up (£12,500).

6. (1) 316 (2) 632 (3) 10

7. B and D are correct. A public company has to be defined as such in its constitution so A is incorrect. No directors **need** have unlimited liability, so C is incorrect.

8. An unlimited company need not usually file annual accounts.

End of chapter question

Partnerships and companies

John and Sarah have been equal partners in a plumbing business for the past 15 years. They wish to expand their activities into house building generally but need more capital in order to do so. Joe has offered to invest £50,000 cash and additionally to provide them with equipment worth a further £50,000, 'in return for a stake in the new business and a share of the profits'. Joe is not interested in any managerial role in the new business. The value of John and Sarah's plumbing business (prior to Joe's investment) is £200,000.

Required

(a) Outline for the three parties whether a partnership would be a suitable legal structure for the new business and explain how such a legal relationship is established. **(12 marks)**

(b) Outline for the three parties whether a private limited company would be more a suitable legal structure for the new business. **(8 marks)**

(Total = 20 marks)

PART F CHOICE OF BUSINESS MEDIUM

The formation of the company and its consequences

Company formation

Topic list	Syllabus reference
1 Promoters and company formation	3.2
2 Pre-incorporation expenses and contracts	3.2
3 Registration procedures	3.2
4 Statutory books and records	3.2
5 Confirmation statements	3.2
6 Legal personality	3.2
7 Ignoring separate personality	3.2

Introduction

Having studied what companies are, together with the differences between companies, sole traders and partnerships in the previous chapter, we shall now look at the formalities needed to form a company.

The first three sections of this chapter concentrate on the **procedural aspects of company formation**. Important topics in these sections include the **formalities** that a company must observe in order to be formed, and the liability of **promoters for pre-incorporation contracts**.

The next two sections consider the concept of the **public accountability** of **limited companies**. Later on in your coverage of the syllabus you will meet references to a company's obligation to publicise certain decisions, so it is important to understand at this stage how and why this should be done.

Finally, this chapter outlines the doctrine of **separate legal personality** that we briefly saw in the previous chapter. Here we discuss its implications and the exceptions to it (known as lifting the **veil of incorporation**).

The **Companies Act 2006**, (TSO, 2006) and the **Small Business, Enterprise and Employment Act 2015**, (TSO, 2015) apply to this and all chapters unless otherwise stated.

1 Promoters and company formation

> **FAST FORWARD**
>
> A promoter **forms** a company. They must act with **reasonable skill** and **care**, and if shares are to be allotted they are the agent of the company, with an agent's fiduciary duties.

A company cannot form itself. The person who forms it is called a '**promoter**'. A promoter is an example of an **agent**, that is someone who acts on behalf of another person (the **principal**).

Key term

> A **promoter** is one who undertakes to form a company with reference to a given project and to set it going and who takes the necessary steps to accomplish that purpose: *Twycross v Grant 1877*.

In addition to the person who takes the procedural steps to get a company incorporated, the term 'promoter' includes anyone who makes **business preparations** for the company. **However** a person who acts **merely** in a **professional capacity** in company formation, such as a solicitor or an accountant, **is not** on that account a **promoter**.

1.1 Duties of promoters

Promoters have the general duty to exercise **reasonable skill and care**.

If the promoter is to be the owner of the company there is no conflict of interest and it does not matter if the promoter obtains some advantage from this position, for example, by selling their existing business to the company for 100% of its shares.

If, however, **some or all the shares** of the company when formed **are to be allotted to other people**, the promoter is as **agent** of the company. This means they have the customary **duties** of an agent and the following fiduciary duties towards the principal.

(a) A promoter must account for any **benefits obtained** through acting as a promoter.
(b) Promoters must not put themselves in a position where their own **interests conflict** with those of the company.
(c) A promoter must provide **full information** on their transactions and account for all monies arising from them. The promoter must therefore make **proper disclosure** of any personal advantage to **existing** and **prospective** company **members** or to an **independent board of directors**.

A promoter may make a **profit** as a result of their position.

(a) A **legitimate** profit is made by a promoter who acquires interest in property **before promoting** a company and then makes a profit when they sell the property to the promoted company, provided they disclose it.
(b) A **wrongful** profit is made by a promoter who enters into and makes a profit personally in a contract as a promoter. They are in breach of fiduciary duty.

A promoter of a public company makes their disclosure of legitimate profit through listing particulars or a prospectus. If they make proper disclosure of a legitimate profit, they may retain it.

1.1.1 Remedy for breach of promoter's fiduciary duty

If the promoter does not make a proper disclosure of legitimate profits or if they make wrongful profits the primary remedy of the company is to **rescind** the **contract** and **recover its money**.

However sometimes it is too late to rescind because the property can no longer be returned or the company prefers to keep it. In such a case the company can **only recover** from the promoter their **wrongful profit**, unless some special circumstances dictate otherwise.

Where shares are sold under a **prospectus offer**, promoters have a statutory liability to compensate any person who acquires securities to which the prospectus relates and suffered loss as a result of any untrue or misleading statement, or omission.

Statutory and listing regulations together with rigorous investigation by merchant banks have greatly lessened the problem of the dishonest promoter.

As you would expect, various expenses are incurred when forming a company. In the next section we shall see who has liability for these costs and whether so-called 'pre-incorporation contracts' have any legal effect.

2 Pre-incorporation expenses and contracts

> **FAST FORWARD**
>
> A promoter has **no automatic right** to be reimbursed **pre-incorporation expenses** by the company, though this can be expressly agreed.

2.1 Pre-incorporation expenses

A promoter usually incurs **expenses** in preparations, such as drafting legal documents, made before the company is formed. They have **no automatic right to recover these 'pre-incorporation expenses'** from the company. However they can generally arrange that the first directors, of whom they may be one, **agree** that the company shall pay the bills or refund to them their expenditure. They could also include a special article in the company's constitution containing an indemnity for the promoter.

2.2 Pre-incorporation contracts

> **FAST FORWARD**
>
> Pre-incorporation contracts **cannot** be ratified by the company. A new contract on the same terms must be expressly created.

Key term

> A **pre-incorporation contract** is a contract purported to be made by a company or its agent at a time before the company has been formed.

In agency law a principal may ratify a contract made by an agent retrospectively. However, a company can **never ratify** a contract made on its behalf **before it was incorporated**. It did not exist when the pre-incorporation contract was made so one of the conditions for ratification fails.

A company may enter into a **new contract** on **similar terms** after it has been incorporated (**novation**). However there must be **sufficient evidence** that the company has made a new contract. Mere recognition of the pre-incorporation contract by performing it or accepting benefits under it is not the same as making a new contract.

2.3 Liability of promoters for pre-incorporation contracts

The company's **agent** is **liable** on a contract to which they are deemed to be a party. The agent may also be entitled to enforce the contract against the other party and so they could transfer the right to **enforce** the contract to the company. Liability is determined by s 51(1) of the Companies Act 2006.

'A contract that purports to be made by or on behalf of a company at a time when the company has not been formed has effect, subject to any agreement to the contrary, as one made with the person purporting to act for the company or as agent for it, and he is personally liable on the contract accordingly.'

2.4 Other ways of avoiding liability as a promoter for pre-incorporation contracts

There are various other ways for promoters to avoid liability for a pre-incorporation contract.

(a) The contract remains as a **draft** (so not binding) until the company is formed. The promoters are the directors, and the company has the power to enter the contract. Once the company is formed, the directors take office and the company enters into the contract.

(b) If the contract has to be finalised before incorporation it should contain a clause that the personal liability of promoters is to cease if the company, when formed, enters a **new contract** on identical terms. This is known as **novation**.

(c) A common way to avoid the problem concerning pre-incorporation contracts is to buy a company **'off the shelf'**. Even if a person contracts on behalf of the new company before it is bought the company should be able to ratify the contract since it existed 'on the shelf' at the time the contract was made.

> **Exam focus point**
>
> A favourite question in law exams is the status of a pre-incorporation contract.

Question — Promoter

Farouk is the promoter of Enterprise Ltd. Before the company is incorporated, he enters into a contract purportedly on its behalf. After the certificate of incorporation is issued, the contract is breached. Who is liable?

Answer

Farouk is liable as promoters are liable for pre-incorporation contracts: s 51(1).

3 Registration procedures

> **FAST FORWARD**
>
> A company is **formed** and registered under the Companies Act 2006 when it is issued with a **certificate of incorporation** by the Registrar, after submission to the Registrar of a number of documents and a fee.

Most companies are registered under the Companies Act 2006 (TSO, 2006). The **Small Business, Enterprise and Employment Act 2015** (TSO, 2015) improved registration procedures and improved the transparency and simplified filing requirements for corporations. We shall come to these aspects throughout your study of company law.

A company is formed under the Companies Act 2006 by one or more persons subscribing to a memorandum of association who comply with the requirements regarding registration.

A company may not be formed for an unlawful purpose.

3.1 Documents to be delivered to the Registrar

To obtain registration of a company limited by shares, an application for registration, various documents and a fee must be sent to the Registrar (usually electronically).

3.1.1 Application for registration: Form IN01

S 9 requires an **application for registration** to be made on Form IN01 and submitted to the Registrar with the other documents described in the table below.

The application must contain:

- The company's proposed name (prior to completing form IN01, a check should be made of the register of names at Companies House, to ensure that there is no company already registered with the proposed name).
- The **location** of its **registered office** (England and Wales, Wales, Scotland or Northern Ireland).

- That the **liability of members** is to be **limited** by shares or **guarantee**.
- Whether the company is to be **private** or **public**.
- A statement of the **intended address** of the **registered office**.

Documents to be delivered	Description
Memorandum of association	This is a **prescribed form** signed by the subscribers. The memorandum states that the subscribers wish to form a company and they agree to become members of it. If the company has share capital each subscriber agrees to subscribe for at least one share.
Articles of association (only required if the company does not adopt model articles)	Articles of association contain the rules that govern how the company is to be run. They are signed by the same subscriber(s), dated and witnessed. **Model articles** are provided by statute and are adopted by a new company if: • No other articles are registered, or • If the articles supplied do not exclude or modify the model articles.
Statement of proposed officers	The statement gives the particulars of the proposed **director(s)** and **company secretary** if applicable. The persons named as directors must consent to act in this capacity. When the company is incorporated they are deemed to be appointed.
Statement of compliance	The statement that the **requirements** of the **Companies Act** in respect of registration have been **complied** with.
Statement of capital and initial shareholdings (only required for companies limited by shares)	A statement of capital and initial shareholdings must be delivered by all companies with **share capital**. Alternatively, a statement of guarantee is required by companies limited by guarantee.
Registration fee	A registration fee is also payable on registration.

Exam focus point

Questions on incorporation could require you to identify the documents which should be sent to the Registrar.

3.2 Certificate of incorporation

The Registrar considers whether the documents are formally in order. If satisfied, the company is given a **'registered number'**. A **certificate of incorporation is** issued and notice of it is publicised.

A company is registered by the inclusion of the company in the register, and the issue of a **certificate of incorporation** by the Registrar. The certificate:

- Identifies the company by its **name** and **registered number**.
- States that it is **limited** (if appropriate) and whether it is a **private** or **public** company.
- States whether the **registered office** is in England and Wales, Wales, Scotland or Northern Ireland.
- States the **date of incorporation**.
- Is **signed** by the **Registrar**, or authenticated by the Registrar's official seal.

Key term

A **certificate of incorporation** is a certificate issued by the Registrar which denotes the date of incorporation, 'the subscribers, together with any persons who from time to time become members, become a body corporate capable of exercising all the functions of an incorporated company'.

The certificate of incorporation is conclusive evidence that:

- All the **requirements** of the **Companies Act** have been **followed.**
- The company is a **company authorised** to be **registered** and has been **duly registered.**

If the certificate states that the company is a **public company**, the certificate is conclusive evidence of this.

If irregularities in formation procedure or an error in the certificate itself are later discovered, the certificate is nonetheless **valid** and **conclusive**: *Jubilee Cotton Mills Ltd v Lewes 1924*.

Upon incorporation persons named as **directors** and **secretary** in the statement of proposed officers automatically become such officers.

3.3 Companies 'off the shelf'

FAST FORWARD — Buying a company 'off the shelf' avoids the administrative burden of registering a company.

Despite the **Small Business, Enterprise and Employment Act 2015** introducing changes to streamline company administration, the registration of a new company can be a lengthy business and it is often easiest for people wishing to operate as a company to purchase an **'off-the-shelf' company**.

This is possible by contacting enterprises specialising in registering a stock of companies, ready for sale when a person comes along who needs the advantages of incorporation.

Normally the persons associated with the company formation enterprise are registered as the company's subscribers, and its first secretary and director. When the company is purchased, the **shares** are **transferred** to the **buyer**, and the Registrar is notified of the director's and the secretary's resignation.

The principal **advantages** for the purchaser of purchasing an off the shelf company are as follows.

(a) The **following documents** will **not need** to be **filed** with the Registrar by the purchaser:

  (i) Memorandum and articles (unless the articles are not model articles)
  (ii) Application for registration
  (iii) Statement of proposed officers
  (iv) Statement of compliance
  (v) Statement of capital and initial shareholdings
  (vi) Fee

  This is because the specialist has already registered the company. It will therefore be a quicker, and very possibly cheaper, way of incorporating a business.

(b) There will be **no risk** of **potential liability** arising from pre-incorporation contracts. The company can trade without needing to worry about waiting for the Registrar's certificate of incorporation.

The **disadvantages** relate to the changes that will be required to the off-the-shelf company to make it compatible with the members' needs.

(a) The off-the-shelf company is likely to have **model articles**. The directors may wish to amend these.
(b) The directors may want to **change** the **name** of the company.
(c) The **subscriber shares** will need to be **transferred**, and the transfer recorded in the register of members. Stamp duty will be payable.

Question — Documents required on formation of a company

What are the documents which must be delivered to the Registrar for registration of a company?

Answer

The memorandum of association (and articles if not in model form), application for registration, a statement of proposed officers, a statement of intended registered office address, a statement of compliance, a statement of capital and initial shareholdings, and a fee.

3.4 Re-registration procedures

FAST FORWARD

A **private company** with share capital may be able to re-register as a **public company** if the share capital requirement is met. A public company may re-register as a private one.

Note. For a private company to re-register as a public company it must fulfil the share capital requirement of a public company: Its allotted share capital must be at least £50,000 of which a quarter must be paid up, plus the whole of any premium.

	Re-registering as a public company	**Re-registering as a private company**
Resolution	The **shareholders must agree** to the company going public. • Convene a general meeting. • Pass a **special resolution** (75% majority) since this decision affects the company's constitution.	The **shareholders must agree** to the company going private. • Convene a general meeting. • Pass a **special resolution** (75% majority of those present and voting) since this decision affects the company's constitution.
Application	The **company must** then **apply** to the Registrar to go public. • Send application to the Registrar. • Send additional information to the Registrar, comprising: – Copy of the special resolution. – Copy of proposed new public company articles. – Statement of the company's proposed name on re-registration. – Statement of proposed company secretary. – Balance sheet and related auditors' statement which states that at the balance sheet date the company's net assets are not less than its called-up share capital and undistributable reserves. – Statement of compliance. – Valuation report regarding allotment of shares for non-cash consideration since the balance sheet date.	The **company must** then **apply** to the Registrar to go private. • Send the application to the Registrar. • Send additional information to the Registrar, comprising: – Copy of the special resolution. – Copy of altered new private company articles. – Statement of Compliance. – Statement of the company's proposed name on re-registration.
Approval	The Registrar must accept the statement of compliance as sufficient evidence that the company is entitled to be re-registered as public. A certificate of incorporation on re-registration is issued.	The Registrar issues a certificate of incorporation on re-registration.
Compulsory re-registration	If the **share capital** of a public company **falls below £50,000**, it must re-register as a private company.	There is **no such compulsion** for a private company.

3.5 Commencement of business rules

> **FAST FORWARD**
>
> To **trade** or **borrow**, a public company needs a **trading certificate**. Private companies may commence business on **registration**.

3.5.1 Public companies

A **public company** incorporated as such may not do business or exercise any borrowing powers unless it has obtained a **trading certificate** from the Registrar: s 761. This is obtained by sending an application to the Registrar. A private company which is re-registered as a public company is not subject to this rule.

The application:

- States the nominal value of the allotted share capital is not less than £50,000 (s 763).
- States the particulars of preliminary expenses and payments or benefits to promoters.
- Must be accompanied by a statement of compliance.

If a public company does business or borrows before obtaining a certificate the other party is protected since the **transaction is valid**. However the company and any officer in default have committed an offence **punishable** by a **fine**. They may also have to indemnify the third party.

Under s 122 of the Insolvency Act 1986 (HMSO, 1986) a court may **wind up** a public company which does not obtain a trading certificate within **one year** of incorporation.

3.5.2 Private company

A **private company** may do business and exercise its borrowing powers from the date of its incorporation. After registration the following procedures are important.

(a) A **first meeting** of the directors should be held at which the chairman, secretary and sometimes the auditors are appointed, shares are allotted to raise capital, authority is given to open a bank account and other commercial arrangements are made.

(b) A **return of allotments** should be made to the Registrar.

(c) The company may give notice to the Registrar of the **accounting reference date** on which its annual accounts will be made up. If no such notice is given within the prescribed period, companies are deemed to have an accounting reference date of the **last day of the month** in which the **anniversary of incorporation** falls.

Now we have seen the formalities that must be followed to form a company, we shall turn our attention to some of the other administrative requirements that must be followed after a company comes into existence.

4 Statutory books and records

4.1 The requirement for public accountability

> **FAST FORWARD**
>
> The price of limited liability is greater **public accountability** via the Companies Registry, registers, the *London Gazette* and company letterheads.

Under the Companies Act 2006 (TSO, 2006) the privileges of trading through a separate corporate body are matched by the duty to provide information which is available to the public about the company.

Basic sources of information on UK companies
The Registrar keeps a file at **Companies House** which holds all documents delivered by the company for filing. Any member of the public, for example someone who intends to do business with the company, may inspect the file (usually electronically).

11: COMPANY FORMATION

Basic sources of information on UK companies
The **registers and other documents** which the company is required to hold at its registered office (or in some cases at a different address).
The *London Gazette*, a specialist publication in which the company itself or the Registrar is required to publish certain notices or publicise the receipt of certain documents.
The **company's letterheads** and other forms which must give particulars of the company's place of registration, its identifying number and the address of its office.

4.2 The Registrar of Companies

The Registrar of Companies ('the Registrar') and the Registrar's department within the Government is usually called Companies House (in full it is 'the Companies Registration Office').

For **English** and **Welsh** companies the Registrar is located at the Companies House in **Cardiff**; for **Scottish** companies the Registrar is in **Edinburgh**.

The company is identified by its **name** and **company registration number** which must be stated on every document sent to Companies House for filing.

On first incorporation the company's file includes a copy of its **certificate of incorporation** and the **original documents** presented to secure its incorporation.

Once a company has been in existence for some time the file is likely to include the following.

- Certificate of incorporation
- Public company trading certificate
- Each year's annual accounts and return
- Copies of special and some ordinary resolutions
- A copy of the altered articles of association if relevant
- Notices of various events such as a change of directors or secretary
- If a company issues a prospectus, a signed copy with all annexed documents

4.3 Statutory books

> **FAST FORWARD**
>
> A company must keep **registers** of certain aspects of its constitution, including the registers of members and directors.

Various people are entitled to have access to **registers** and copies of records that the company must keep. To enable the documents to be found easily the company must keep them at its **registered office** or a **single alternative inspection location** (SAIL) which is registered with Companies House. All documents may be kept at either location or a combination of the two. Companies are not permitted to have more than one single alternative inspection location. Private companies are permitted to file their registers of members, directors and secretaries, PSC and directors' residential addresses at **Companies House** instead of a registered office or SAIL.

Register/copies of records
Register of **members**
Register of **people with significant control (PSC)**
Register of **directors (and secretaries)**
Register of **directors' residential addresses**
Records of **directors' service contracts and indemnities**
Records of **resolutions and meetings** of the company
Register of **debentureholders**
Register of disclosed **interests** in shares (public company **only**)

4.4 Register of members

Every company must keep a register of members. It must contain:

(a) The **name** and **address** of **each member**.

(b) **The shareholder class** (if more than one) to which they belong unless this is indicated in the particulars of their shareholding.

(c) If the company has a share capital, the **number of shares** held by each member. In addition:

   (i) If the shares have **distinguishing numbers**, the member's shares must be identified in the register by those numbers.

   (ii) If the company has more than one class of share the member's shares must be **distinguished** by their **class**, such as preference, ordinary, or non-voting shares.

(d) The date on which each member **became** and eventually the date on which they **ceased** to be a member.

The company may choose where it keeps the register of members available for inspection from:

- The registered office
- Another office of the company
- The office of a professional registrar

Any member of the company can inspect the register of members of a company without charge. A member of the public must pay but has the right of inspection.

A company with more than 50 members must keep a separate index of those members, unless the register itself functions as an index.

4.5 Register of people with significant control (PSC)

All private and public companies are required to keep a **register of people with significant control**. This register contains information on individuals who own or control over 25% of a company's shares or voting rights, or who exercise control over the company and its management in other ways (for example through the ability to appoint or remove directors).

The information which is required to be collected includes the individual's **name, date of birth, nationality** and **service address** and **details of their interest in the company**. This information will be checked and updated each year when the company submits its confirmation statement and is available for public inspection. It an **offence** not to comply with the requirement to file this register.

4.6 Register of directors

The register of directors must contain the following details in respect of a director who is an individual (that is, not a company).

- **Present** and **former** forenames and surnames
- A **service address** (may be the company's registered address rather than the director's home address)
- **Residency** and **nationality**
- **Business occupation** (if any)
- Date of birth

The register does not include shadow directors. It must be open to inspection by a member (free of charge), or by any other person (for a fee).

Note. The company must keep a separate **register** of **directors' residential addresses** but this is not available to members of the general public.

4.7 Records of directors' service contracts

The company should keep **copies** or written memoranda of all **service contracts** for its directors, including contracts for services which are not performed in the capacity of director. Members are entitled to view these copies for free, or request a copy on payment of a set fee.

Key term

> Under s 227 a director's **service contract**, means a contract under which:
>
> (a) A director of the company undertakes personally to perform services (as director or otherwise) for a company, or for a subsidiary of the company, or
>
> (b) Services (as director or otherwise) that a director of the company undertakes personally to perform are made available by a third party to the company, or to a subsidiary of the company.

4.8 Register of debenture holders

Companies with debentures issued nearly always keep a **register of debenture holders**, but there is no statutory compulsion to do so.

5 Confirmation statements

FAST FORWARD

> Every twelve months a company must send a **confirmation statement** to the Registrar.

Every company must send a **confirmation statement** to the Registrar. The statement can be sent at any time, but no more than twelve months may elapse between statement submissions.

The purpose of the **confirmation statement** is to keep the Registrar informed about certain changes to the company. Much of this information would have been submitted when the company is formed.

Confirmation statements are used to **confirm** that there have been **no changes** to the information held by the Registrar during the previous twelve months, if none have been made. If changes have been made, it records just the changes have occurred.

Examples of information requiring confirmation are:

- The address of the **registered office** of the company
- The address (if different) at which the **register of members** or **debenture holders** is kept
- The type of company and its principal **business activities**
- The total number of **issued shares,** their **aggregate nominal value** and the amounts paid and unpaid on each share
- For each **class of share**, the **rights** of those shares, the **total number** of shares in that class and their **total nominal value**
- Particulars of **members** of the company
- Changes to the **Register of people with significant control**
- Particulars of those who have **ceased** to be members since the last return
- The number of shares of each **class** held by members at the return date, and transferred by members since incorporation or the last return date
- The particulars of **directors,** and **secretary (if applicable)**

Now we have seen some of the administrative consequences of incorporation, we shall return to a subject that we briefly looked at in the previous chapter – **separate legal personality**. When we looked at it last time, we saw that a consequence of this was that the liability of members was limited. In the next couple of sections we shall look in more detail of what this means and explore the circumstances where this 'veil of incorporation' can be lifted and liability imposed on those seeking its protection.

PART G THE FORMATION OF THE COMPANY AND ITS CONSEQUENCES

6 Legal personality

FAST FORWARD

As we saw in the previous chapter, companies have their own legal personality. This means that they are legally separate from the people who own it. The case of *Salomon v Salomon & Co Ltd 1897* clearly demonstrates the **separate legal personality** of companies and is of great significance to any study of company law.

Salomon v Salomon & Co Ltd 1897

The facts: The claimant, S, had carried on business for 30 years. He decided to form a limited company to purchase the business so he and six members of his family each subscribed for one share.

The company then purchased the business from S for £38,782, the purchase price being payable to the claimant by way of the issue of 20,000 £1 shares, the issue of debentures, £10,000 of debentures and £8,782 in cash thereby making him a secured creditor.

The company did not prosper and was wound up a year later, at which point its liabilities exceeded its assets. The liquidator, representing unsecured trade creditors of the company, claimed that the company's business was in effect still the claimant's (he owned 20,001 of 20,007 shares). Therefore he should bear liability for its debts and that payment of the secured debt to him should be postponed until the company's trade creditors were paid.

Decision: The House of Lords held that the business was owned by, and its debts were liabilities of, the company. The claimant was under no liability to the company or its creditors, his debentures were validly issued and the security created by them over the company's assets was effective. This was because the company was a legal entity separate and distinct from S.

The principle of separate legal personality was confirmed in the following case.

Lee v Lee's Air Farming Ltd 1960

The facts: Mr Lee, who owned the majority of the shares of an aerial crop-spraying business, and was the sole working director of the company, was killed while piloting the aircraft.

Decision: Although he was the majority shareholder and sole working director of the company, he and the company were separate legal persons. Therefore he could also be an employee with rights against it when killed in an accident in the course of his employment.

The following is a more **recent case** on separate legal personality which confirms the previous case law is still valid.

MacDonald v Costello 2011

The facts: Mr and Mrs Costello entered into an agreement with MacDonald (a firm of builders) to develop land which they owned. For tax purposes, the Costellos used a special purpose vehicle (Oakwood Residential Limited) to finance the work and the contract was between Oakwood and MacDonald. Oakwood had been used in previous dealings between the parties. Oakwood failed to pay some invoices when there was disagreement about the work which had been done. MacDonald was awarded a payment order against Oakwood and an award in restitution against the Costellos personally for unjust enrichment. The Costellos appealed the award for unjust enrichment.

Decision: Although the Costellos had been enriched by the work done by MacDonald, it was decided that the award against them should not be upheld. They were not party to the contract and, as shareholders of Oakwood, they were protected by the 'veil of incorporation'.

6.1 Veil of incorporation

FAST FORWARD

Incorporation '**veils**' members from outsiders' view but this veil may be lifted in **some circumstances**, so creditors and others can seek redress directly from members. The veil may be lifted: by statute to enforce the law; to prevent the evasion of obligations; and in certain situations where companies trade as a group.

Because a company has separate legal personality from the people who own or run it (the members/shareholders/directors), people can look at a company and not know who or what owns or runs it. The fact that members are 'hidden' in this way is sometimes referred to as the '**veil of incorporation'**. Literally, the members are 'veiled' from view.

6.2 Liability of the company for tort and crime

As a company has a separate legal identity, it may also have liabilities in **tort** and **crime**. Criminal liability of companies in particular is a topical area but, is outside the scope of your syllabus. An example of how a company can have a liability in tort, is through being **vicariously liable** for the actions of its employees, as we saw in Chapter 5.

7 Ignoring separate personality

FAST FORWARD

It is sometimes necessary by law to look at who the owners of a company are. This is referred to as '**lifting the veil**'.

Separate personality can be ignored to:

- **Identify** the **company** with its **members** and/or directors.
- Treat a **group of companies** as a **single commercial entity** (if a company is owned by another company).

The more important of these two reasons is the first one, although the second reason can sometimes be more complex. The main instances for lifting the veil are given below.

7.1 Lifting the veil by statute to enforce the law

Lifting of the veil is permitted under a number of statutes to enforce the law.

7.1.1 Liability for trading without trading certificate

A public company must obtain a trading certificate from the Registrar before it may commence to trade. Failure to do so leads to **personal liability** of the directors for any loss or damage suffered by a third party resulting from a transaction made in contravention of the trading certificate requirement. They are also liable for a fine.

7.1.2 Fraudulent and wrongful trading

When a company ceases to trade because of insolvency or some other reason, and is 'wound up', it may appear that its business has been carried on with **intent** to **defraud creditors** or others. In this case the court may decide that the persons (usually the directors) who were knowingly parties to the **fraudulent trading** shall be **personally responsible** under civil law for debts and other liabilities of the company: s 213 Insolvency Act 1986 (HMSO, 1986).

Fraudulent trading is also a criminal offence; under s 993 of the Companies Act 2006 any person guilty of the offence, even if the company has not been or is not being wound up, is liable for a fine or imprisonment for up to 10 years.

If a company in insolvency proceedings is found to have traded when there is no reasonable prospect of avoiding insolvent winding up, its directors may be liable under civil law for **wrongful trading**. Again a court may order such directors to make a contribution to the company's assets: s 214 Insolvency Act 1986.

7.1.3 Disqualified directors

Directors who participate in the management of a company in contravention of an order under the Company Directors Disqualification Act 1986 (HMSO, 1986) will be **jointly** or **severally liable** along with the company for the company's debts.

7.1.4 Abuse of company names

In the past there were a number of instances where directors of companies which went into **insolvent liquidation** formed another company with an identical or similar name, as a so-called 'phoenix' company. This new company bought the original company's business and assets from its liquidator.

The Insolvency Act 1986 (s 217) makes it a criminal offence and the directors personally liable where they are a director of a company that goes into insolvent liquidation and they become involved with the directing, managing or promoting of a business which has an **identical name** to the original company, or a **name similar** enough to suggest a connection. The directors are also likely to be disqualified from acting as a director.

> **Exam focus point**
>
> It is very important to know the statutory reasons for lifting the veil.

7.2 Lifting the veil to prevent evasion of obligations

A company may be identified with those who control it, for instance to determine its residence for tax purposes. The courts may also ignore the distinction between a company and its members and managers if the latter use that distinction to **evade** their **existing legal obligations**.

> *Gilford Motor Co Ltd v Home 1933*
>
> *The facts:* The defendant had been employed by the claimant company under a contract which forbade him to solicit its customers after leaving its service. After the termination of his employment he formed a company of which his wife and an employee were the sole directors and shareholders. However he managed the company and through it evaded the covenant that prevented him from soliciting customers of his former employer.
>
> *Decision:* An injunction requiring observance of the covenant would be made both against the defendant and the company which he had formed as a 'a mere cloak or sham'.

7.2.1 Public interest

In time of war a company is not permitted to trade with '**enemy aliens**'. The courts may draw aside the veil if, despite a company being registered in the UK, it is suspected that it is controlled by aliens.

The question of nationality may also arise in peacetime, where it is convenient for a foreign entity to have a British **facade** on its operations.

> *Re F G Films Ltd 1953*
>
> *The facts:* An English company was formed by an American company to 'make' a film which would obtain certain marketing and other advantages from being called a British film. Staff and finance were American and there were neither premises nor employees in England. The film was produced in India.
>
> *Decision:* The British company was the American company's agent and so the film did not qualify as British. Effectively, the corporate entity of the British company was swept away and it was exposed as a 'sham' company.

7.2.2 Evasion of liabilities

The veil of may also be lifted where directors **ignore** the separate legal personality of two companies and transfer assets from one to the other in disregard of their duties in order to avoid an existing liability.

Re H and Others 1996

The facts: The court was asked to rule that various companies within a group, together with the minority shareholders, should be treated as one entity in order to restrain assets prior to trial.

Decision: The order was granted. The court thought there was evidence that the companies had been used for the fraudulent evasion of excise duty.

7.2.3 Evasion of taxation

The court may lift the veil of incorporation where it is being used to **conceal** the nationality of the company.

Unit Construction Co Ltd v Bullock 1960

The facts: Three companies, wholly owned by a UK company, were registered in Kenya. Although the companies' constitutions required board meetings to be held in Kenya, all three were in fact managed entirely by the holding company.

Decision: The companies were resident in the UK and liable to UK tax. The Kenyan connection was a sham, the question being not where they ought to have been managed, but where they were actually managed.

7.2.4 Quasi-partnership

An application to wind up a company on the 'just and equitable' ground under the Insolvency Act 1986 may involve the court lifting the veil to reveal the company as a **quasi-partnership.** This may happen where the company only has a few members, all of whom are actively involved in its affairs. Typically the individuals have operated contentedly as a company for years but then fall out, and one or more of them seeks to remove the others.

The courts are willing in such cases to treat the central relationship between the directors as being that of partners, and rule that it would be unfair therefore to allow the company to continue with only some of its original members. This is illustrated by the case of *Ebrahimi v Westbourne Galleries Ltd 1973.*

Question
Quasi-partnership

Sandy and Patrice have carried on business together for twenty years, most recently through a limited company in which each holds 500 shares. They share the profits equally in the form of directors' remuneration. Patrice's son Craig joins the business, buying 100 shares from each of Sandy and Patrice. Disputes arise and Patrice and Craig use their voting majority to remove Sandy from the board. Advise Sandy.

Answer

Sandy cannot prevent her removal from her directorship. However, a court may find that, on the basis of the past relationship, it is unjust and inequitable to determine the case solely on legal rights. It could, on equitable principles, order liquidation of the company.

The veil of the company may be lifted to reveal a quasi-partnership.

7.3 Lifting the veil in group situations

The principle of the veil of incorporation extends to the holding (parent) company/subsidiary relationship. Although holding companies and subsidiaries are part of a group under company law, they retain their **separate legal personalities**.

In *Adams v Cape Industries plc 1990*, three reasons were put forward for identifying the companies as one, and lifting the veil of incorporation. They are:

- The subsidiary is acting as **agent** for the holding company.
- The group is to be treated as a **single economic entity** because of statutory provision.
- The **corporate structure** is being used as a **facade** (or sham) to conceal the truth.

Adams v Cape Industries plc 1990

The facts: Cape, an English company, headed a group which included many wholly owned subsidiaries. Some of these mined asbestos in South Africa, and others marketed the asbestos in various countries including the USA.

Several hundred claimants had been awarded damages by a Texas court for personal injuries suffered as a result of exposure to asbestos dust. The defendants in Texas included one of Cape's subsidiaries, NAAC. The courts also considered the position of AMC, another subsidiary, and CPC, a company linked to Cape Industries.

Decision: The judgement would not be enforced against the English holding company, either on the basis that Cape had been 'present' in the US through its local subsidiaries or because it had carried on business in the US through the agency of NAAC. Slade LJ commented in giving the judgement that English law 'for better or worse recognises the creation of subsidiary companies ... which would fall to be treated as separate legal entities, with all the rights and liabilities which would normally be attached to separate legal entities'.

Whether desirable or not, English law allowed a group structure to be used so that legal liability fell on an individual member of a group rather than the group as a whole.

Exam focus point

Lifting the veil in group situations is easily forgotten. Ensure you know the *Cape Industries* case and the three reasons for lifting the veil in groups which it sets out.

7.4 The corporate veil and tortious liability

The *Adams v Cape Industries* case above established the principle that a parent company is a separate legal entity from its subsidiaries, and that the veil of incorporation therefore cannot be lifted to impose a liability incurred by a subsidiary on it. However, a more recent case involving the same company has established the principle that such a company can still be liable in tort, even though it is a separate legal entity.

Chandler v Cape Industries 2012

The facts: Chandler was employed by a subsidiary of Cape Industries in the late 1950s and early 1960s. In 2007 he discovered that he had developed asbestosis due to his work. The subsidiary no longer existed so he sought damages from Cape instead.

In this case it was noted that Cape employed a group medical advisor who had responsibility for the health and safety of all employees within the group. It also employed a scientific officer, who was involved in seeking ways of suppressing asbestos dust.

Decision: On appeal, the court found that a parent company can owe a duty of care for the health and safety of the employees of a subsidiary where:

- The parent and subsidiary are essentially in the same business
- The parent had or should have had superior knowledge in respect of health and safety within the industry
- The parent knew or ought to have known that the subsidiary's system of work was unsafe
- The parent knew or ought to have known that the subsidiary or employees would rely on its superior knowledge of health and safety within the industry

In the similar case of *Thompson v Renwick Group 2014*, the claimant **did not** establish that a duty of care was owed to them. This was due to a lack of proximity between the parent company and the employees of the subsidiary. A duty was owed in the *Cape* case because it employed a medical advisor and scientific officer to look after the employees of the **whole group**. In the case of *Thompson*, by contrast, the group company hired a director responsible for the health of employees, but they were employed by and had responsibility to the **subsidiary only**.

Following the *Chandler* and *Thompson* cases there are (at the time of writing) several cases going through the Supreme Court which may further **limit the ability of claimants** to establish that a **duty of care** was owed to them. It appears that parent companies may only owe a duty of care if they had a **high level of control** over the subsidiary. This means that in future, the four part test in *Chandler* may become more limited, and could possibly be developed further.

7.5 Summary of situations in which the veil can be lifted

The instances in which the veil will be lifted are as follows.

Lifting the veil by statute to enforce the law	• Liability for trading without a trading certificate • Fraudulent and wrongful trading • Disqualified directors • Abuse of company names
Evasion of obligations	• Evasion of legal obligations • Public interest • Evasion of liabilities • Evasion of taxation • Quasi-partnership
Group situations	• Subsidiary acting as agent for the holding company • The group is to be treated as a single economic entity • The corporate structure is being used as a sham

7.6 Lifting the veil and limited liability

The above examples of lifting the veil include examples of where, if they have broken the law, **directors** can be made **personally liable** for a company's debts. This is very rare.

If those directors are also members, then limited liability **does not apply**. This is the only time that limited liability is overridden and that the **member** becomes **personally liable** for the company's debts **due to their actions as a director**.

Chapter Roundup

- A promoter **forms** a company. They must act with **reasonable skill** and **care**, and if shares are allotted they are the agent of the company, with an agent's fiduciary duties.

- A promoter has **no automatic right** to be reimbursed pre-incorporation expenses by the company, though this can be expressly agreed.

- Pre-incorporation contracts **cannot** be ratified by the company. A new contract on the same terms must be expressly created.

- A company is **formed and registered** under the Companies Act 2006 when it is issued with a **certificate of incorporation** by the Registrar, after submission to the Registrar of a number of documents and a fee.

- Buying a company **'off the shelf'** avoids the administrative burden of registering a company.

- A **private company** with share capital may be able to re-register as a **public company** if the share capital requirement is met. A public company may re-register as a private one.

- To **trade** or **borrow**, a public company needs a **trading certificate**. Private companies may commence business on **registration**.

- The price of limited liability is greater **public accountability** is via the Companies Registry, registers, the *London Gazette* and company letterheads.

- A company must keep **registers** of certain aspects of its constitution, including the registers of members and directors.

- Every twelve months a company must send a **confirmation statement** to the Registrar.

- As we saw in the previous chapter, companies have their own legal personality. This means that they are legally separate from the people who own it. The case of *Salomon v Salomon & Co Ltd 1897* clearly demonstrates the **separate legal personality** of companies and is of great significance to any study of company law.

- Incorporation **'veils'** members from outsiders' view but this veil may be lifted in **some circumstances**, so creditors and others can seek redress directly from members. The veil may be lifted: by statute to enforce the law; to prevent the evasion of obligations; and in certain situations where companies trade as a group.

- It is sometimes necessary by law to look at who the owners of a company are. This is referred to as **'lifting the veil'**.

Quick Quiz

1. A company can confirm a pre-incorporation contract by performing it or obtaining benefits from it.

   True ☐

   False ☐

2. If a public company does business or borrows before obtaining a trading certificate from the Registrar, the transaction is:

   A   Invalid, and the third party cannot recover any loss
   B   Invalid, but the third party may recover any loss from the directors
   C   Valid, and the directors are punishable by a fine
   D   Valid, but the third party can sue the directors for further damages

3. A company must keep a register of directors. What details must be revealed?

   A   Full name
   B   Service address
   C   Nationality
   D   Date of birth
   E   Business occupation

4. An accountant or solicitor acting in their professional capacity during the registration of a company may be deemed a promoter.

   True ☐

   False ☐

5. If a certificate of incorporation is dated 6 March, but is not signed and issued until 8 March, when is the company deemed to have come into existence?

6. What was the name of the case that originally demonstrated the principle of separate legal personality?

7. Put the examples given below in the correct category box.

   - Wrong use of company name
   - Single economic entity
   - Corporate structure a sham
   - Disqualified directors
   - Fraudulent and wrongful trading
   - Legal obligations
   - Quasi-partnership
   - Public interest

WHEN THE VEIL OF INCORPORATION IS LIFTED		
To enforce law	**To enforce obligations**	**To expose groups**

Answers to Quick Quiz

1. False. The company must make a new contract on similar terms.
2. C. The directors are punished for allowing the company to trade before it is allowed to.
3. All of them.
4. False. A person acting in a professional capacity will not be deemed a promoter.
5. 6 March. The date on the certificate is conclusive.
6. *Salomon v Salomon Ltd 1897*.
7.

WHEN THE VEIL OF INCORPORATION IS LIFTED		
To enforce law	**To enforce obligations**	**To expose groups**
Wrong use of company name	Legal obligations	Single economic entity
Disqualified directors	Quasi-partnership	Corporate structure a sham
Fraudulent and wrongful trading	Public interest	

End of chapter question

Registering a company

Identify the key documents required to register a company under the Companies Act 2006 and analyse the legal effects of each of the documents. **(20 marks)**

Capitalisation of the company

Share capital

Topic list	Syllabus reference
1 Members	3.3
2 The nature of shares and capital	3.3
3 Types of share and class rights	3.3
4 Allotment of shares	3.3
5 Transfer of shares	3.3
6 Take-over procedures	3.3

Introduction

So far in our study of company law we have seen what a company is, the various types of company, and how companies are formed. We have also seen the concept of separate legal personality which protects **members** from the debts of the company.

This chapter follows on from this by explaining what a **member** is, and how they invest in the company by the purchase of **shares**. We shall look at the nature of share capital and the different types of capital that are important for company law purposes.

The rest of the chapter discusses procedural matters relating to the **issue** and **transfer** of shares. You will see that there are built-in safeguards to protect members' rights, **pre-emption rights** and the necessity for directors to be authorised to **allot** shares. There are also safeguards that ensure that a company receives **sufficient consideration** for its shares.

The **Companies Act 2006**, (TSO, 2006) and the **Small Business, Enterprise and Employment Act 2015**, (TSO, 2015) apply to this and all chapters unless otherwise stated.

PART H   CAPITALISATION OF THE COMPANY

1 Members

FAST FORWARD

A member of a company is a person who has **agreed to become a member**, and whose name has been **entered** in the **register of members**. This may occur by: subscription to the memorandum; applying for shares; presentation to the company of a transfer of shares to the prospective member applying as personal representative of a deceased member or as a trustee of a bankrupt.

1.1 Becoming a member

Key term

A **member** of a company is a person who has agreed to be a member and whose name has been entered in the register of members.

Entry in the register is **essential**. Mere delivery to the company of a transfer does not make the transferor a member until the transfer is entered in the register.

1.2 Subscriber shares

Subscribers to the memorandum are deemed to have agreed to become members of the company. As soon as the company is formed their names should be entered in the register of members.

Other persons may acquire shares and become members:

- By **applying** and being allotted shares.
- By presenting to the company for registration a **transfer** of shares to them.
- By applying as **personal representative** or **trustee** of a
    - Deceased member
    - Bankrupt member

1.3 Ceasing to be a member

FAST FORWARD

There are **eight** ways in which a member ceases to be so.

A member ceases to be a member in any of the following circumstances.

- They **transfer** all their shares to another person and the transfer is registered.
- The member **dies**.
- The **shares** of a bankrupt member are **registered** in the name of their trustee.
- A **member who is a minor repudiates their shares**.
- The **trustee** of a **bankrupt member disclaims their** shares.
- The **company forfeits** or **accepts** the **surrender of shares**.
- The **company** sells them in exercise of a lien.
- The **company is dissolved** and **ceases to exist**.

1.4 The number of members

FAST FORWARD

Public and **private companies** must have a minimum of **one** member (s 7). There is **no maximum number**.

(a) The **register of members** must contain a statement that there is **only one member** and give their address.

(b) **Quorum**. The Companies Act 2006 (TSO, 2006) **automatically permits** a **quorum of one** for general meetings.

2 The nature of shares and capital

> **FAST FORWARD**
>
> A **share** is a transferable form of property, carrying rights and obligations, by which the interest of a member of a company limited by shares is measured.

2.1 Shares

> **Key term**
>
> A **share** is 'the interest of a shareholder in the company measured by a sum of money, for the purpose of a liability in the first place, and of interest in the second, but also consisting of a series of mutual covenants entered into by all the shareholders *inter se*': *Borland's Trustee v Steel Bros & Co Ltd 1901*.

The key points in this definition are:

- The share must be **paid for** ('liability'). The nominal value of the share fixes this liability, it is the base price of the share eg a £1 ordinary share.
- It gives a **proportionate entitlement** to dividends, votes and any return of capital ('interest').
- It is a form of **bargain** ('mutual covenants') between shareholders which underlies such principles as majority control and minority protection.

> **Key term**
>
> A share's **nominal value** is its face value. So a £1 ordinary share for instance, has a nominal value of £1. No share can be issued at a value below its nominal value.

A share is a form of personal property, carrying rights and obligations. It is by its nature **transferable**.

A member who holds one or more shares is a **shareholder**. However some companies (such as most companies limited by guarantee) do not have a share capital. So they have members who are not also shareholders.

Information about any special rights attached to shares is obtainable from one of the following documents which are on the file at Companies House:

- The **articles** which are the normal context in which share rights are defined.
- A **resolution** or agreement incidental to the creation of a new class of shares (copies must be delivered to the Registrar).
- A **statement of capital** given to the Registrar within one month of **allotment**, together with the return of allotment.

2.2 Types of capital

> **FAST FORWARD**
>
> The term **'capital'** is used in several senses in company legislation, to mean issued, allotted or called up share capital or loan capital.

2.2.1 Authorised share capital

Companies incorporated under previous company legislation had to specify a maximum authorised share capital that it could issue, although this could be increased by ordinary resolution of the members. Under the Companies Act 2006 (TSO, 2006), the concept of authorised share capital was removed, so companies registered under this Act will not have to consider it. Furthermore, companies incorporated under earlier legislation are permitted by the 2006 Act to treat any limit on authorised capital as a provision in the company's articles of association which can therefore be altered or removed entirely, by ordinary rather than special resolution.

PART H CAPITALISATION OF THE COMPANY

2.2.2 Issued and allotted share capital

Key terms

Issued and **allotted share capital** is the type, class, number and amount of the shares issued and allotted to specific shareholders, including shares taken on formation by the subscribers to the memorandum.

A company need not issue all its share capital at once. If it retains a part, this is **unissued share capital**.

Issued share capital can be **increased** through the allotment of shares (s 617).

Rights issues and the issue of **bonus shares** (see later) will also increase the amount of a company's capital.

2.2.3 Called up and paid up share capital

Key terms

Called up share capital is the amount which the company has required shareholders to pay now or in the future on the shares issued.

Paid up share capital is the amount which shareholders have actually paid on the shares issued and called up.

For example, a company has issued and allotted 70 £1 (nominal value) shares, has received 25p per share on application and has called on members for a second 25p. Therefore its issued and allotted share capital is £70 and its **called up** share capital is £35 (50p per share). When the members pay the call, the '**paid up**' share capital is then £35 also. Capital not yet called is '**uncalled capital**'. Called capital which is not yet paid is termed '**partly paid**'; the company therefore has an outstanding claim against its shareholders and this debt is transferred to the new shareholder if the share is transferred.

As we saw earlier, on allotment **public companies** must receive at least **one quarter** of the nominal value of the shares paid up, plus the **whole of any premium**.

2.2.4 Loan capital

Key term

Loan capital comprises debentures and other long-term loans to a business.

Loan capital, in contrast with the above, is the term used to describe **borrowed money** obtained usually by the issue of debentures. **It is nothing to do with shares**.

2.3 Market value of shares

Shares of a public company are freely transferable (providing the appropriate procedures are followed) and therefore may be subsequently sold by some or all of the shareholders. The sale price will not necessarily be the nominal value, rather it will reflect the prospects of the company and therefore may be greater or less than the nominal value.

Having looked at what a member is as well as the nature of shares and capital, we will now consider the various types of share that members can acquire and the rights that members of each class of share enjoy.

3 Types of share and class rights

FAST FORWARD

If the constitution of a company states no differences between shares, it is assumed that they are all **ordinary** shares with parallel rights and obligations. There may, however, be other types, notably **preference shares** and **redeemable shares**, which have different **class rights**.

3.1 Ordinary shares (equity)

If no differences between shares are expressed then all shares are equity shares with the **same rights**, known as ordinary shares.

Key terms

> **Equity** is the residual interest in the assets of the company after deducting all its liabilities. It comprises issued share capital excluding any part that does not carry any right to participate beyond a specified amount in a distribution.
>
> **Equity share capital** is a company's issued share capital less capital which carries preferential rights.
>
> **Ordinary shares** are shares which entitle the holders to the remaining divisible profits (and, in a liquidation, the assets) after prior interests, eg creditors and prior charge capital, have been satisfied.

3.2 Preference shares

FAST FORWARD

> The most common right of preference shareholders is a **prior right** to receive a fixed dividend. This right is not a right to **compel payment** of a dividend, but it is **cumulative** unless otherwise stated. Usually, preference shareholders **cannot participate** in a dividend over and above their fixed dividend and **cease to be entitled to arrears of undeclared dividends** when the company goes into liquidation.

Key term

> **Preference shares** are shares carrying one or more rights such as a fixed rate of dividend or preferential claim to any company profits available for distribution.

A preference share may and generally will carry a **prior right** to receive an annual dividend of fixed amount, say a dividend of 6% of the share's nominal value.

Ordinary and preference shares are deemed to have identical rights. However, a company's articles or resolutions may create differences between them.

As regards the priority dividend entitlement, four points should be noted.

(a) **The right is merely to receive a dividend at the specified rate before any other dividend may be paid or declared.** It is **not** a right to compel the company to pay the dividend, *(Bond v Barrow Haematite Steel Co 1902)*. The company can decline to pay the dividend if it decides to transfer available profits to reserves instead of using the profits to pay the preference dividend.

(b) **The right to receive a preference dividend is deemed to be cumulative unless the contrary is stated.** If, therefore, a 6% dividend is not paid in Year 1, the priority entitlement is normally carried forward to Year 2, increasing the priority right for that year to 12% – and so on.

When arrears of cumulative dividend are paid, the holders of the shares at **the time when the dividend is declared** are entitled to the whole of it even though they did not hold the shares in the year to which the arrears relate.

An intention that preference shares should not carry forward an entitlement to arrears is usually expressed by the word **'non-cumulative'**.

(c) **If a company which has arrears of unpaid cumulative preference dividends goes into liquidation, the preference shareholders cease to be entitled to the arrears unless:**

  (i) A **dividend** has been **declared** though **not yet paid** when liquidation commences.
  (ii) The **articles** (or other terms of issue) **expressly provide** that in a liquidation arrears are to be paid in priority to return of capital to members.

(d) **Holders of preference shares have no entitlement to participate in any additional dividend over and above their specified rate.** If, for example, a 6% dividend is paid on 6% preference shares, the entire balance of available profit may then be distributed to the holders of ordinary shares.

This rule also may be expressly overridden by the terms of issue. For example, the articles may provide that the preference shares are to receive a priority 6% dividend and are also to participate equally in any dividends payable after the ordinary shares have received a 6% dividend. Preference shares with these rights are called **participating preference shares**.

In all other respects preference shares carry the **same** rights as ordinary shares **unless otherwise stated**. If they do rank equally they carry the same rights, no more and no less, to return of capital, distribution of surplus assets and voting.

In practice, it is unusual to issue preference shares on this basis. More usually, it is expressly provided that:

(a) The preference shares are to carry a **right** to **return of capital,** to be paid in priority to the ordinary shareholders.

(b) They are **not to carry a right to vote, or voting is permitted only in specified circumstances**, for example failure to pay the preference dividend, variation of their rights or a resolution to wind up.

When preference shares carry a **priority right** to **return** of **capital** the result is that:

(a) The amount paid up on the preference shares, say £1 on each £1 share, is to be repaid in liquidation before anything is repaid to ordinary shareholders.

(b) Unless otherwise stated, the holders of the preference shares are **not** entitled to share in surplus assets when the share capital has been repaid. Instead this will all go to the ordinary shareholders.

3.2.1 Advantages and disadvantages of preference shares

The advantages of preference shares are **greater security of income** and (if they carry priority in repayment of capital) **greater security of capital**. However, in a period of persistent inflation, the benefit of entitlement to fixed income and to capital fixed in money terms is an illusion.

A number of other drawbacks and pitfalls, such as loss of arrears, poor rights on winding up and enforced payment, have been indicated above. Preference shares may be said to fall between the two stools of risk and reward (as seen in ordinary shares) and security (debentures).

Question — Types of share

Give brief definitions of the following types of share.

(a) Equity share
(b) Ordinary share
(c) Preference share

Answer

(a) An equity share is a share which gives the holder the right to participate in the company's surplus profit and capital. In a winding up the holder is entitled to a repayment of the nominal value plus a share of surplus assets. The term equity share embraces ordinary shares, but also includes preference shares when the terms of issue include either the right to an additional dividend or the right to surplus assets in a winding up.

(b) An ordinary share is the more common type of equity share, as discussed in (a) above. The dividend is payable only when preference dividends, including arrears, have been paid.

(c) Preference shares carry a prior right to receive an annual dividend of a fixed amount, usually as a percentage of the share's nominal value. There are no other implied differences between preference and ordinary shares, although there may be express differences between them. For example, preference shares may carry a priority right to return of capital. Generally preference shares do not carry voting rights in the company other than those relating to their own class. Unless otherwise stated, dividends allocated to preference shares are assumed to be cumulative. This means that, if the company does not make sufficient profits to pay a dividend in one year, the arrears are carried forward to future years.

3.3 Redeemable shares

Redeemable shares are shares issued on terms that they may be bought back by a company either at a future specific date or at the shareholder's or company's option. We shall look at these in detail in a later chapter.

3.4 Treasury shares

Treasury shares are created when a **private** or **public limited company** legitimately **purchases its own shares** out of **cash** or **distributable profit.** The purchased shares are then held by the company 'in treasury' which means the company can re-issue them without the usual formalities. They can only be sold for cash and the company cannot exercise the **voting rights** which attach to them.

This type of share is a relatively **new innovation** which allows a company to purchase its own shares when previously it would have been unable to so because of the **rules on capital maintenance.**

The rights attached to different classes of share are not set in stone. By the agreement of members of the class of share concerned, the rights can be varied as we shall see below.

3.5 Class rights

Key term

> **Class rights** are rights which are attached to particular types of shares by the company's constitution.

A company may at its option attach special rights to different shares regarding:

- Dividends
- Return of capital
- Voting
- The right to appoint or remove a director

Any share which has different rights from others is grouped with the other shares carrying identical rights to form a **class**.

The most common types of share capital with different rights are **preference shares** and **ordinary shares**. There may also be ordinary shares with voting rights and ordinary shares without voting rights.

3.6 Variation of class rights

FAST FORWARD

> The holders of **issued** shares have **vested rights** which can only be varied by using a strict procedure. The standard procedure is by **special resolution** passed by at least **three quarters** of the votes cast at a **separate class meeting** or by written consent.

Key term

> A **variation of class rights** is an alteration in the position of shareholders with regard to those rights or duties which they have by virtue of their shares.

The holders of issued shares have **vested rights** which can only be varied by the company with the consent of all the holders or with such consent of a majority as is specified (usually) in the articles.

The standard procedure for variation of class rights requires that a **special resolution** shall be passed by a **75% majority** cast either at a **separate meeting** of the class, or by **written consent**: s 630. If any other requirements are imposed by the company's articles then these must also be followed.

3.6.1 When variation rules apply

FAST FORWARD

It is **not** a variation of class rights to issue shares to new members, to subdivide shares of another class, to return capital to preference shareholders, or to create a new class of preference shareholders.

It is only necessary to follow the variation of class rights procedure **if what is proposed amounts to a variation of class rights**. There are many types of transaction that do not actually constitute a variation of class rights.

3.6.2 Examples: Not a variation of class rights

(a) **To issue shares of the same class to allottees who are not already members of the class** (unless the defined class rights prohibit this).

> *White v Bristol Aeroplane Co Ltd 1953*
>
> *The facts:* The company made a bonus issue of new ordinary and preference shares to the existing ordinary shareholders who alone were entitled under the articles to participate in bonus issues. The existing preference shareholders objected. They stated that reducing their proportion of the class of preference shares (by issuing the bonus of preference shares) was a variation of class rights to which they had not consented.
>
> *Decision:* This was not a variation of class rights since the existing preference shareholders had the same number of shares (and votes at a class meeting) as before.

(b) **To subdivide shares of another class with the incidental effect of increasing the voting strength of that other class.**

> *Greenhalgh v Arderne Cinemas Ltd 1950*
>
> *The facts:* The company had two classes of ordinary shares, 50p shares and 10p shares. Every share carried one vote. A resolution was passed to subdivide each 50p share into five 10p shares, thus multiplying the votes of that class by five.
>
> *Decision:* The rights of the original 10p shares had not been varied since they still had one vote per share as before.

(c) **To return capital to the holders of preference shares**: *House of Fraser plc v ACGE Investments Ltd 1987*.

(d) **To create and issue a new class of preference shares with priority over an existing class of ordinary shares**: *Re John Smith's Tadcaster Brewery Co Ltd 1953*.

The cases cited in the preceding paragraph illustrate the principle that without a **'literal variation'** of class rights there is no alteration of rights to which the safeguards of proper procedure and appeal to the court apply. The fact that the **value** of existing rights may be affected will not concern the court if the rights are unchanged.

Exam focus point

Knowledge of what does **not** constitute a variation of class rights is vital in this area.

3.6.3 Special situations

To deal with unusual special situations which in the past caused some difficulty, the following rules apply.

(a) If the class rights are set **by the articles and** they **provide** a **variation procedure**, that procedure must be followed for any variation even if it is less onerous than the statutory procedure.

(b) If class **rights** are **defined otherwise than by the articles** and there is **no variation procedure**, consent of a **three quarters majority** of the class is both necessary and sufficient.

3.6.4 Minority appeals to the court for unfair prejudice

> **FAST FORWARD**
>
> A **dissenting minority** holding 15% or more of the issued shares may apply to the court within 21 days of class consent to have the variation cancelled as 'unfairly prejudicial'.

Under the Companies Act 2006 (TSO, 2006), whenever class rights are varied under a procedure contained in the constitution, a minority of holders of shares of the class may apply to the court to have the variation cancelled. The objectors together must:

- Hold **not less** than **15%** of the **issued shares** of the class in question.
- **Not** themselves have **consented** to or voted in favour of the variation.
- **Apply** to the court within **21 days** of the consent being given by the class: s 633.

The court can either approve the variation as made or cancel it as 'unfairly prejudicial'. It cannot, however, modify the terms of the variation.

To establish that a variation is 'unfairly prejudicial' to the class, the minority must show that the majority was seeking **some advantage** to themselves as **members** of a **different class** instead of considering the interests of the class in which they were then voting.

Question — Variation of class rights

Fill in the blanks in the statements below.

If there has been a variation of class rights, a minority of holders of shares of the class (who have not consented or voted in favour of the variation) may apply to the court to have the variation cancelled. The objectors must hold not less than ……………….. of the issued shares of that class, and apply to the court within ……………….. days of the giving of consent by that class.

Answer

If there has been a variation of class rights, a minority of holders of shares of the class (who have not consented or voted in favour of the variation) may apply to the court to have the variation cancelled. The objectors must hold not less than **15%** of the issued shares of that class, and apply to the court within **21 days** of the giving of consent by that class.

3.7 Statement of capital

We have already seen that a return known as a **statement of capital** is required to be made to the **Registrar** in certain circumstances.

The statement of capital must give the following details in respect of the **share capital** of the company and be **up to date** as at the statement date.

(a) The **total number of shares** of the company.
(b) The **aggregate nominal value of the shares**.
(c) For **each class** of share:
 (i) The **prescribed particulars** of any rights attached.
 (ii) The **total number of shares** in the class.
 (iii) The **aggregate nominal value** of shares in the class.
(d) The **aggregate amount unpaid** on the **total number of shares**

(e) **Information that identifies the subscribers to the memorandum of association**.

(f) In respect of **each subscriber**, the **number**, **nominal value** and **class of shares** taken by them on formation and the **amount** to be **paid up**.

The statement of capital must include details of initial shareholdings when it is submitted on registration of the company.

Whilst the number of shares is initially set when the company is formed, as we shall see in the next section, further issues of shares can be made and allotted to members during the lifetime of the company. However, there are a number of rules concerning the allotment of new shares which must be followed.

4 Allotment of shares

> **FAST FORWARD**
>
> Directors exercise the **delegated power** to allot shares, either by virtue of the articles or a resolution in general meeting.

4.1 Definition

Key term

> **Allotment of shares** is the issue and allocation to a person of a certain number of shares under a contract of allotment. Once the shares are allotted and the holder is entered in the register of members, the holder becomes a member of the company. The member is issued with a share certificate.

The allotment of shares is a **form of contract**. The intending shareholder applies to the company for shares, and the company accepts the offer.

The terms 'allotment' and 'issue' have slightly different meanings.

(a) A share is **allotted** when the person to whom it is allotted acquires an unconditional right to be entered in the register of members as the holder of that share. That stage is reached when the board of directors (to whom the power to allot shares is usually given) considers the application and formally resolves to allot the shares.

However, if the directors imposed a condition, for instance that the shares should be allotted only on receipt of the subscription money, the allotment would only take effect when payment was made.

(b) The **issue** of shares is not a defined term but is usually taken to be a later stage at which the allottee **receives** a **letter of allotment** or share certificate issued by the company.

4.2 Private company allotment of shares

The allotment of shares of a private company is a simple and immediate matter. As private companies cannot sell securities to the public the following procedure should be followed.

- An **application** to buy shares must be made to the directors directly. While a private company may not, as a general rule, offer its shares to the public it may, by private arrangement, issue shares to anyone it chooses.

- Shares are **allotted** and **issued**.

- The names of the allottees are entered in the **register of members** soon after, and as a direct consequence of the allotment of shares to them; they then become members (the allotment must be recorded in the register of members within two months).

- A **return of allotment of shares** must be sent within one month to the Registrar on Form SH01 containing prescribed particulars and a statement of capital.

4.3 Public company allotment of shares

The difference in procedure for **allotment of shares in a public company** only arises at the first stage. There are various methods for a public company to sell shares to the public.

- **Public offer**: members of the public subscribe for shares directly to the company. This is often associated with a public company's initial listing on a recognised investment exchange, when it offers a substantial number of new shares for sale (an initial public offering or IPO).
- **Offer for sale**: an offer to members of the public to apply for shares based on information contained in a prospectus.
- **Placing**: a method of raising share capital where shares are offered in a small number of large 'blocks', to persons or institutions who have previously agreed to purchase the shares at a predetermined price.

In order to encourage the public to buy shares in a public company, it may issue a **prospectus** which is a public advertisement for shares, and is thus an invitation to potential investors to make an offer for the shares. A company listed on the London Stock Exchange must issue a prospectus under the **Prospectus Rules** and the **Listing Rules** set down by the UK Listing Authority (part of the Financial Conduct Authority).

4.3.1 Allotment procedure

Public companies listed on the London Stock Exchange usually follow a two-stage procedure.

- They first issue a **renounceable allotment letter** which the original allottee may, for a limited period (up to six weeks), transfer to another person by signing a **form of renunciation** (included in the letter) and delivering it to the transferee. The original allottee, or the ultimate renouncee, sends in the allotment letter with a completed **application for registration** of the shares in their name.
- On receipt of an application for registration the company enters the name of the applicant in the register of members and delivers a **return of allotments** to the Registrar made up to show who is then on the register. The applicant **becomes a member by entry on the register** and receives a share certificate from the company.

Public companies face the further restriction that no allotment can be made unless:

- The shares offered are **subscribed for in full** (in which case money must be returned to applicants at the expiry of 40 days after the first issue of the prospectus), or
- The offer states that even if the capital is not subscribed in full, the amount of the capital subscribed for may be allotted in any event, or in the event of the conditions specified in the offer being satisfied.

4.4 Directors' powers to allot shares

Directors of **private companies** with **one class of share** have the **authority** to allot shares **unless restricted** by the articles: s 550.

Directors of **public companies** or **private companies with more than one class of share may only allot shares if they are authorised to do so by ordinary resolution of the members, or if authority is contained in the articles: s 551.** Authority cannot be given for a period of more than five years.

4.5 Pre-emption rights: s 561

FAST FORWARD

If the directors propose to allot 'equity securities' wholly for cash, there is a general requirement to offer these shares to **holders** of **similar shares** in proportion to their holdings.

Key term

Pre-emption rights are the rights of existing ordinary shareholders to be offered new shares issued by the company *pro rata* to their existing holding of that class of shares.

If a company proposes to allot ordinary shares wholly for cash, it has a **statutory obligation** to offer those shares first to holders of similar shares in **proportion to their holdings** and on the same or more favourable terms as the main allotment. This is known as a **rights issue**.

4.6 Rights issues

Key term

A **rights issue** is a right given to a shareholder to subscribe for further shares in the company, usually *pro rata* to their existing holding in the company's shares.

A rights issue must be made **in writing** (hard copy or electronic) in the same manner as a notice of a general meeting is sent to members. It must specify a period of **not less than 21 days** during which the offer may be accepted but may not be withdrawn. If not accepted or renounced in favour of another person within that period the offer is deemed to be declined.

Equity securities which have been offered to members in this way but are **not accepted** may then be allotted on the same (or less favourable) terms to non-members.

If equity securities are allotted in breach of these rules the members to whom the offer should have been made may within the ensuing two years recover **compensation** for their loss from those in default. The allotment will generally be valid.

4.6.1 Exclusion of pre-emption rights: s 567

A **private** company may by its articles permanently exclude these rules so that there is no statutory right of first refusal.

4.6.2 Disapplication of pre-emption rights: s 570

Any company may, by special resolution, resolve that the statutory right of first refusal shall not apply: s 570. Such a resolution to 'disapply' the right must be sent to the Registrar and may either:

(a) Be combined with the grant to directors of authority to allot shares, or

(b) Simply permit an offer of shares to be made for cash to a non-member (without first offering the shares to members) on a particular occasion.

In case (b) the directors, in inviting members to 'disapply' the right of first refusal, must issue a circular. This sets out their reasons, the price at which the shares are to be offered direct to a non-member and their justification of that price.

4.7 Bonus issues

Key term

A **bonus issue** is the capitalisation of the reserves of a company by the issue of additional shares to existing shareholders, in proportion to their holdings. Such shares are normally fully paid-up with no cash called for from the shareholders.

A bonus issue is more correctly but less often called a '**capitalisation issue**' (also called a 'scrip' issue). The articles of a company usually give it power to apply its reserves to paying up unissued shares wholly or in part and then to allot these shares as a bonus issue to members.

Question — Share issues

Fill in the blanks in the statements below.

A .... issue is an allotment of additional shares to existing members in exchange for consideration payable by the members.

A .... issue is an allotment of additional shares to existing members where the consideration is paid by using the company's reserves.

Answer

A **rights** issue is an allotment of additional shares to existing members in exchange for consideration payable by the members.

A **bonus** issue is an allotment of additional shares to existing members where the consideration is effectively paid by using the company's reserves.

Once shares have been issued and allotted they continue to exist until they are cancelled. If a member wishes to dispose of any shares that they own, this must be done through the transfer of shares which is the subject of the next section.

5 Transfer of shares

> **FAST FORWARD**
>
> Once shares have been allotted they may be **transferred** by the allottee to a purchaser.

Under the Companies Act 2006 (TSO, 2006), shares are generally freely transferable in accordance with and subject to and restrictions contained in the company's articles (s 544).

5.1 Unlisted shares

Once the member-transferor and the transferee have reached an agreement, the transferor holds the shares as trustee for the transferee until the company registers the transfer but remains a member of the company with the right to vote as they choose. Once the transferee pays for the shares the transferor must vote as directed by the transferee. Once the transferee's name is entered on the register of members, the transferor ceases to be a member and the transferee acquires all the member's rights.

The transferor executes a paper stock transfer form in the favour of the transferee and gives it to them with the share certificate. Both are sent to the company for registration. Once the company receives a proper instrument of transfer, it must either register the transfer and prepare a share certificate (certification) or give notice of refusal to the proposed transferee, with reasons for the refusal, **within two months.** Model articles contain no restrictions on the right to transfer fully paid shares but directors may refuse to register the transfer. Alterations to the articles could be made to specify for instance that directors could **refuse to register a transfer** to anyone except an existing shareholder, or to a family member. Where notice of refusal is given the transferee's beneficial interest is not affected (that is, they are still entitled to any dividend or the return of capital on winding up), but they cannot exercise all members' rights, including voting rights, until the transfer is registered and their name is entered on the register of members. They are also entitled to such information as they may reasonably require as to the reasons of refusal (but they are not entitled to minutes of directors' meetings). Where the company fails to comply with these provisions, it and its officers are guilty of an offence punishable by a fine.

There is no requirement for certification where shares are transmitted by operation of the law, for example where a bankrupt member's trustee in bankruptcy or a deceased member's personal representative become entitled to the member's shares.

Stamp duty of 0.5% is payable on purchases of shares over £1,000 using a stock transfer form.

5.2 Listed shares

Securities may be transferred paperlessly without a written instrument (stock transfer form), and this is the current situation where the shares are listed and traded on a recognised stock exchange.

A number of firms connected with all sections of the equities market operate the CREST system owned by Euroclear, a private company. CREST is a paperless electronic system which enables shareholders to hold and transfer their securities without the need for written instruments of transfer. Under the system a member appoints a custodian broker to hold their shares under a customer agreement, which provides for the broker to deal with the shares only in accordance with the shareholder's directions. Any transfer of shares is normally completed in three days.

Stamp Duty Reserve Tax at 0.5% is charged on paperless purchases of shares through a stockbroker.

Regulations under the Act may provide that companies may be **required**, rather than just permitted, to adopt such a paperless holding and transfer of shares (s 785). Such regulations might impose such a requirement in relation to particular types of company or security or provide for the company to pass an ordinary resolution to that effect.

You should be aware that there are very detailed rules for the disclosure of substantial interests in the relevant share capital (essentially voting shares) of public companies. For example, in the case of companies listed either on the Main Market or Alternative Investment Market (AIM), issuers are obliged to publish their total share capital and voting rights at the end of each calendar month in which a change has occurred. A shareholder must notify the issuer (by completing a notification form) when their percentage of voting rights reaches 3% of the total voting rights of the company, and each 1% thereafter. It follows that this threshold may be reached even where a shareholder does not actually deal in the shares. They are therefore obliged to make the notification within two trading days of when they became or should have become aware of the notifiable change. These provisions are set out in the Disclosure and Transparency Rules.

The rules that we have just seen cover the general transfer of shares between members in fairly small amounts. However, where a company or individual wishes to take-over control of another company by acquiring all or substantially all of its shares, then specific take-over procedures must be followed. These are the subject of the next section.

6 Take-over procedures

> **FAST FORWARD**
>
> A take-over occurs when a bidder seeks to buy a company by acquiring all, or substantially all, its issued shares from its shareholders. If a very large proportion of the company – **90%** or more – is acquired then the acquirer may compulsorily acquire the remainder (**'squeeze-out'**). There are also provisions for the minority shareholders to demand to be bought out even if the acquirer does not really want to buy their shares (**'sell-out'**).

A **take-over** of a company (the **target company**) occurs when control (ownership) of the target is taken over by another company or individual (the **offeror** or **bidder**) by buying the shares from their current owners.

6.1 Types of take-over

Take-overs are usually classed as either friendly or hostile:

- A **friendly take-over** (which is usually the situation in a private or unlisted public company, since the directors usually know the wishes of their shareholders quite well) occurs when the offeror:
    - Approaches the target's board with the terms of an offer the offeror wishes to make to the holders of all the target's shares that are not already owned by the offeror.
    - The target's board approves of the offer as being in the best interests of the shareholders and recommends it to the shareholders.
- A **hostile take-over** occurs when an offeror:
    - Approaches the target's board with the terms of an offer to the holders of all the target's shares not already owned by the acquirer.
    - The board rejects the offer as not being in the interests of shareholders.
    - The offeror announces its firm intention to make an offer, then goes ahead and makes the offer to shareholders.

6.2 Take-over regulations

The law on take-overs is contained in the Companies Act and, in relation to listed companies, the City Code on Take-overs and Mergers, known simply as the Take-over Code, published by the Take-over Panel. The aims of the regulations are principally to ensure that:

- Shareholders are treated fairly.
- Shareholders are not denied an opportunity to decide on the true merits of a take-over, so there are rules on what information companies must and cannot release publicly in relation to the bid.
- Shareholders of the same class are afforded equivalent treatment by an offeror.
- There is an orderly framework within which take-overs are conducted, for example there are timetables for certain aspects of the bid.

Under the Companies Act 2006 (TSO, 2006), a **take-over offer** is an offer to acquire either **all the allotted shares** in the target or, where there is more than one class of shares, all the shares of one or more classes, other than shares that at the date of the offer are already held by the offeror. The **terms of the offer must be the same** in relation to all the shares to which the offer relates or, where the shares to which the offer relates include shares of different classes, in relation to all the shares of each class: s 974.

6.2.1 'Squeeze out' notices

A key aspect of the rules on take-overs is that if a **large majority of shareholders (90% or more** by nominal value and voting rights) like the terms of the offer and agree to sell their shares before the offer lapses, the offeror can then choose **to buy out the minority shareholders** by giving them a **'squeeze-out' notice** within a maximum of three months after the take-over offer lapsed: s 979. Any shares in the target that were already owned by the offeror at the date of the take-over offer are excluded when calculating the 90% threshold.

The squeeze-out notice **requires the shareholder to sell** their shares to the offeror on the terms of the take-over offer, and also **requires the offeror to buy them**: s 981.

If a shareholder believes the offer in the squeeze-out notice (ie the take-over offer terms) to be **unfair**, they may challenge the notice by application to the court within six weeks of being given the notice: s 986. The court may order that the offeror is not entitled and bound to acquire the shares to which the notice relates, or that the terms on which the shares can be acquired are to be determined by the court. As the offeror by definition has already managed to persuade 90% of the shareholders that the offer is fair, it can be difficult to argue this case, especially as the test for fairness relates to the shareholders as a whole rather than an individual shareholder in the target company. An application may be successful however if, for example:

- Insufficient information was given to shareholders about the offer: *Fiske Nominees Ltd v Dwyka Diamond Ltd 2002*, or
- There was a common interest between the offeror and the shareholders who accepted the offer: *Re Bugle Press Ltd 1961*.

6.2.2 'Sell-out' provisions

Even if the take-over offer is accepted by a large number of shareholders there may still be a minority who did not accept at the time of the offer and so retain their shares. The offeror, which becomes the acquirer of those shares, may be happy to live with there being minority shareholders in the company and so may choose not to issue a squeeze-out notice for compulsory acquisition, even if it reached the 90% mark. However a **minority shareholder may compel the acquirer to buy their shares** in the target under the **'sell-out' provisions** of s 983, but only if:

- The offeror has acquired 90% of the shares (by value and voting rights) in the target before the period within which the offer can be accepted, and
- The shareholder writes to the acquirer requiring their shares to be purchased on the same terms as the original take-over offer or on such other terms as may be agreed: s 985.

Even if the acquirer is happy to live with minority shareholders, once it reaches the 90% threshold it must within one month give the minority shareholders **notice of their right to sell out** to the acquirer: s 984. Failure to give this notice is a criminal offence.

Note that, unlike for squeeze-out notices, any shares in the target that are already owned by the offeror at the date of the take-over offer are included when calculating the 90% threshold for sell-out.

6.3 Paying for the acquisition

To pay for the target company's shares, the acquiring organisation usually has two choices; either to pay in cash, or to exchange the shares it is acquiring for new shares in itself (a share exchange).

6.3.1 Acquisitions by cash

Under this arrangement, the organisation simply pays the seller of the shares an **agreed amount of cash per share** that they are acquiring. Once agreement has been reached, the share transfer continues like any other transfer of shares that we have already seen. The key advantage for purchasing the shares through cash is that the organisation will **own the target company outright** and therefore its shareholders will **keep all of the rewards** that might accrue following the take-over. However, it also means that the organisation will **shoulder all the risk** that the take-over may not be profitable. It also requires the organisation to have **sufficient cash reserves** to fund the acquisition and may require it taking on more debt to finance it.

6.3.2 Acquisitions by share exchange

A **share exchange** involves the acquiring company offering a **certain number of shares** in its company for every share that the shareholder owns in the target company. The number of shares offered will be subject to an agreement. Since the target shareholder will still own shares (and therefore rights to future dividends) the actual value of the shares offered may be different than if they were offered cash.

The main advantage for the acquiring company of a share exchange is that it can make an acquisition **without having large amounts of cash available**. However, it does mean that shareholders in the company pursuing the take-over will have their **ownership diluted** due to the new shareholders joining the company. It also means that they will have to **share any future rewards** with them (however, the **risk of failure is also shared**).

Chapter Roundup

- A member of a company is a person who has **agreed to become a member**, and whose name has been **entered** in the **register of members**. This may occur by: subscription to the memorandum; applying for shares; the presentation to the company of a transfer of shares to the prospective member; applying as personal representative of a deceased member or a trustee of a bankrupt.

- There are **eight** ways in which a member ceases to be so.

- **Public** and **private companies** must have a minimum of **one** member (s 7). There is **no maximum** number.

- A **share** is a transferable form of property, carrying rights and obligations, by which the interest of a member of a company limited by shares is measured.

- The term **'capital'** is used in several senses in company legislation, to mean issued, allotted or called up share capital or loan capital.

- If the constitution of a company states no differences between shares, it is assumed that they are all **ordinary** shares with parallel rights and obligations. There may, however, be other types, notably **preference shares** and **redeemable shares**, which have different **class rights**.

- The most common right of preference shareholders is a **prior right** to receive a fixed dividend. This right is not a right to **compel payment** of a dividend, but it is **cumulative** unless otherwise stated. Usually, preference shareholders **cannot participate** in a dividend over and above their fixed dividend and **cease to be entitled to arrears of undeclared dividends** when the company goes into liquidation.

- The holders of **issued** shares have **vested rights** which can only be varied by using a strict procedure. The standard procedure is by **special resolution** passed by at least **three quarters** of the votes cast at a **separate class meeting** or by written consent.

- It is **not** a variation of class rights to issue shares to new members, to subdivide shares of another class, to return capital to preference shareholders, or to create a new class of preference shareholders.

- A **dissenting minority** holding 15% or more of the issued shares may apply to the court within 21 days of class consent to have the variation cancelled as 'unfairly prejudicial'.

- Directors exercise the **delegated power** to allot shares, either by virtue of the articles or a resolution in general meeting.

- If the directors propose to allot 'equity securities' wholly for cash, there is a general requirement to offer these shares to **holders** of **similar shares** in proportion to their holdings.

- Once shares have been allotted they may be **transferred** by the allottee to a purchaser.

- A take-over occurs when a bidder seeks to buy a company by acquiring all, or substantially all, its issued shares from its shareholders. If a very large proportion of the company – **90%** or more – is acquired then the acquirer may compulsorily acquire the remainder (**'squeeze-out'**). There are also provisions for the minority shareholders to demand to be bought out even if the acquirer does not really want to buy their shares (**'sell-out'**).

PART H CAPITALISATION OF THE COMPANY

Quick Quiz

1 If a company fails to pay preference shareholders their dividend, they can bring a court action to compel the company to pay it.

   True ☐

   False ☐

2 Which two of the following are implied rights of preference shareholders?

   A   The right to receive a dividend is cumulative.
   B   If the company goes into liquidation, preference shareholders are entitled to claim all arrears of dividend from the liquidator.
   C   As well as rights to their preference dividends, preference shareholders can share equally in dividends payable to ordinary shareholders.
   D   Preference shareholders have equal voting rights to ordinary shareholders.

3 If a company issues new ordinary shares for cash, the general rule is that:

   A   The shares must first be offered to existing members in the case of a public but not a private company.
   B   The shares must first be offered to existing members whether the company is public or private.
   C   The shares must first be offered to existing members in the case of a private but not a public company.
   D   The shares need not be issued to existing members.

4 What is the minimum number of members that a plc must have?
   A   One
   B   Two
   C   Three
   D   Four

5 Match the definitions to the correct type of capital.

   A   Issued share capital
   B   Called up share capital
   C   Paid up share capital

   (i)   The amount which the company has required shareholders to pay on shares issued.
   (ii)   The type, class, number and amount of the shares held by the shareholders.
   (iii) The amount which shareholders have actually paid on the shares issued and called up.

Answers to Quick Quiz

1. False. The company may decide not to pay any dividend, or may be unable to because it does not have any distributable profits. What the preference shareholders have is a right to receive their dividends before other dividends are paid or declared.

2. A and D are implied rights; the others have to be stated explicitly.

3. B. The shares must be first offered to existing members whether the company is public or private.

4. A. All companies must have a minimum of one member (s 7).

5.   A (ii)
     B (i)
     C (iii)

End of chapter question

Allotment and types of shares

Keysure Limited (Keysure) is a local alarm and security company specialising in the security of commercial premises. Keysure was incorporated in 2010 with Model Articles (unamended) and ordinary shares of £1 each. Keysure is currently in need of a capital injection and one of the directors has asked his brother Tony, whether he would be interested in purchasing £20,000 of Keysure shares.

Required

(a) Advise Tony as to the benefits for him, if he were to become a shareholder of Keysure, in Keysure having a separate legal personality and the circumstances in which such benefits may be lost.

(9 marks)

(b) Discuss the procedural steps Keysure must take in order to allot the shares to Tony, including any documentation and filing required. **(8 marks)**

(c) Tony holds preference shares in another company. Discuss the difference between ordinary and preference shares. **(3 marks)**

(Total = 20 marks)

PART H CAPITALISATION OF THE COMPANY

Borrowing and loan capital

Topic list	Syllabus reference
1 Borrowing	3.3
2 Loan capital and debentures	3.3
3 Charges	3.3
4 Registration of charges	3.3
5 Debenture holders' remedies	3.3

Introduction

In this chapter we shall look at the second type of capital businesses may have – **debt capital**. Unlike members who own shares in a company, lenders have very few rights connected with running the company because they do not own it. Instead, they have a contractual arrangement whereby they supply funds usually in return for the payment of interest.

This chapter covers how loan capital providers can protect themselves, specifically through taking out **fixed or floating charges**.

You need to understand the differences between fixed and floating charges, and also how they can protect loan creditors, for example by giving chargeholders the ability to appoint a **receiver**.

The **Companies Act 2006**, (TSO, 2006) and the **Small Business, Enterprise and Employment Act 2015**, (TSO, 2015) apply to this and all chapters unless otherwise stated.

PART H CAPITALISATION OF THE COMPANY

1 Borrowing

> **FAST FORWARD**
>
> Companies have an **implied power** to borrow for purposes incidental to their trade or business.

All companies registered under the Companies Act 2006 (TSO, 2006) have an **implied power to borrow** for purposes **incidental to their trade or business**. A company formed under earlier Acts will have an implied power to borrow if its object is to carry on a trade or business.

In delegating the company's power to borrow to the directors it is usual, and essential in the case of a company whose shares are quoted on the Stock Exchange, to impose a **maximum limit** on the **borrowing** arranged by directors.

A contract to repay borrowed money may in principle be unenforceable if either:

- It is money borrowed for an *ultra vires* (or restricted) purpose, and this is known to the lender.
- The directors **exceed their borrowing powers** or have no powers to borrow.

However:

- In both cases the lender will probably be **able** to **enforce** the contract.
- If the contract is within the capacity of the company but beyond the delegated powers of the directors the company may **ratify** the **loan contract**.

Case law has determined that if a company has power to borrow, it also has power to **create charges** over the company's assets as **security** for the loan. *Re Patent File Co 1870.*

1.1 Personal guarantees

Some lenders may require directors and/or members to agree to repay a loan out of their personal wealth should the company default on the debt. This is known as requesting a **personal guarantee**, which is a promise by a person (the directors or shareholders) to assume a debt obligation in the event of non-payment by the borrower (the company). Personal guarantees are a means of protecting the lender by preventing the shareholders/members from hiding behind the protection of limited liability. It is commonly used where the lender is very powerful (such as a bank) and the borrower has no other source of funds available to it (such as a new or small company).

The main implication for directors or shareholders when giving personal guarantees to their company's creditors is that their liability will not be limited in respect to the amounts owing to the creditors. By giving a personal guarantee their personal assets will be used to repay the creditors should the company default on the loan, that is they cannot rely on the limited liability status of the company for any protection.

2 Loan capital and debentures

2.1 Loan capital

> **FAST FORWARD**
>
> **Loan capital** comprises all the longer term borrowing of a company. It is distinguished from share capital by the fact that, at some point, borrowing must be repaid. Share capital on the other hand is only returned to shareholders when the company is wound up.

A company's **loan capital** comprises all amounts which it borrows for the long-term, such as:

(a) Permanent overdrafts at the bank.
(b) Unsecured loans, from a bank or other party.
(c) Loans secured on assets, from a bank or other party.

Companies often issue long-term loans as capital in the form of **debentures**.

2.2 Debentures

FAST FORWARD

A **debenture** is a document stating the terms on which a company has borrowed money. There are three main types.

- A **single debenture**.
- **Debentures issued as a series** and usually registered.
- **Debenture stock** subscribed to by a large number of lenders. Only this form requires a **debenture trust deed**, although the others may often incorporate one.

Key term

A **debenture** is the written acknowledgement of a debt by a company, normally containing provisions as to payment of interest and the terms of repayment of principal. A debenture may be secured on some or all of the assets of the company or its subsidiaries.

A debenture may create a **charge** over the company's assets as security for the loan. However a document relating to an unsecured loan is also a debenture in company law.

2.3 Types of debenture

A debenture is usually a formal legal document, often in printed form. Broadly, there are three main types.

(a) **A single debenture**

If, for example, a company obtains a secured loan or overdraft facility from its bank, the latter is likely to insist that the company signs the bank's standard form of debenture creating the charge and giving the bank various safeguards and powers.

(b) **Debentures issued as a series and usually registered**

Different lenders may provide different amounts on different dates. Although each transaction is a separate loan, the intention is that the lenders should rank equally *(pari passu)* in their right to repayment and in any security given to them. Each lender therefore receives a debenture in identical form in respect of their loan.

The debentures are transferable securities.

(c) **The issue of debenture stock subscribed to by a large number of lenders**

Only a public company may use this method to offer its debentures to the public and any such offer is a prospectus; if it seeks a listing on The Stock Exchange then the rules on listing particulars must be followed.

Each lender has a right to be **repaid** their **capital** at the **due time** (unless they are perpetual) and to receive **interest** on it until **repayment**. This form of borrowing is treated as a single loan 'stock' in which each debenture stockholder has a specified fraction (in money terms) which they or some previous holder contributed when the stock was issued. Debenture stock is transferable in multiples of, say, £1 or £10.

A company must maintain a **register of all debenture holders** and register an allotment within two months.

One advantage of debenture stock over debentures issued as single and indivisible loan transactions is that the holder of debenture stock can sell part of their holding, say £1,000 (nominal), out of a larger amount.

Debenture stock must be created using a **debenture trust deed** though single and series debenture's may also use a debenture trust deed.

2.4 Debenture trust deed

Major elements of a debenture trust deed for debenture stock
The appointment usually of a trustee for prospective debenture stockholders. The trustee is usually a bank, insurance company or other institution but may be an individual.
The nominal amount of the debenture stock is defined, which is the maximum amount which may be raised then or later. The date or period of repayment is specified, as is the rate of interest and half-yearly interest payment dates.
If the debenture stock is secured **the deed creates a charge or charges** over the assets of the company.
The trustee is authorised to **enforce the security** in case of default and, in particular, to appoint a receiver with suitable powers of management.
The company enters into **various covenants**, for instance to keep its assets fully insured or to limit its total borrowings; breach is a default by the company.
There may be elaborate provisions for **transfer of stock** and **meetings** of debenture stockholders.

Advantages of a debenture trust deed for debenture stock
The **trustee** with appropriate powers can **intervene promptly** in case of default.
Security for the debenture stock in the form of charges over property can be **given to a single trustee**.
The **company** can **contact a representative of the debenture holders** with whom it can negotiate.
By calling a **meeting of debenture holders**, the trustee can consult them and obtain a decision binding on them all.
The **debenture holders** will be able to **enjoy the benefit of a legal mortgage** over the company's land.

2.5 Register of debenture holders

The Companies Act 2006 (TSO, 2006) does not specifically require a register of debenture holders be maintained. However, a company is normally required to maintain a register by the debenture or debenture trust deed when debentures are issued as a series or when debenture stock is issued.

When there is a register of debenture holders, the following regulations apply.

(a) The company is required by law to keep the **register** at its registered office, or at an **address** notified to the registrar: s 743.

(b) The register must be open to **inspection** by **any person** unless the constitution or trust deed provide otherwise. Any person may obtain a copy of the register or part of it for a fee. A holder of debentures issued under a trust deed may require the company (on payment) to supply them with a copy of the deed: s 749.

Under s 745 a company has **five working days** to respond to an inspection request or seek exemption to do so from the court.

(c) The register should be **properly kept** in accordance with the requirements of the Companies Act.

2.6 Rights of debenture holders

The position of debenture holders is best described by comparison with that of shareholders. At first sight the two appear to have a great deal in common.

- Both **own transferable company securities** which are usually long-term investments in the company.
- The **issue procedure** is much the same. An offer of either shares or debentures to the public is a prospectus as defined by the Act.
- The **procedure** for **transfer** of registered shares and debentures is the same.

13: BORROWING AND LOAN CAPITAL

But there are significant differences.

Differences	Shareholder	Debenture holder
Role	Is a proprietor or owner of the company	Is a creditor of the company
Voting rights	May vote at general meetings	May not vote
Cost of investment	Shares may not be issued at a discount to nominal value	Debentures may be offered at a discount to nominal value
Return	Dividends are only paid • Out of distributable profits • When directors declare them	Interest must be paid when it is due
Tax	Dividends are paid out of post-tax distributable profits	Interest is deducted from profits before tax is calculated
Redemption	Statutory restrictions on redeeming shares	No restriction on redeeming debentures
Liquidation	Shareholders are the last people to be paid in a winding up	Debentures must be paid back before shareholders are paid

From the investor's standpoint debenture stock is often **preferable to preference shares**. Although both yield a fixed income, debenture stock offers greater security.

2.6.1 Advantages and disadvantages of debentures (for the company)

Advantages	Disadvantages
Easily traded	May have to pay high interest rates to make them attractive
Terms clear and specific	Interest payments mandatory
Assets subject to a floating charge may be traded	Interest payments may upset shareholders if dividends fall
Popular due to guaranteed income	Debenture holder's remedies of liquidators or receivers may be disastrous for the company
Interest tax-deductible	Crystallisation of a floating charge can cause trading difficulties for a company
No restrictions on issue or purchase by a company	

3 Charges

FAST FORWARD

A charge over the assets of a company gives a creditor a **prior claim** over other creditors to payment of their debt out of these assets.

Charges may be either **fixed**, which attach to the relevant asset on creation, or **floating**, which attach on 'crystallisation'. For this reason it is not possible to identify the assets to which a **floating** charge relates (until **crystallisation**).

Because providers of loan capital do not own a share in the company, they can be in a weak position if the company fails and its debts cannot be repaid. To protect against this, they can make it a term of the loan that they take out a **legal charge** over a company asset or assets. For example, if the company borrows to purchase a new office, then the lender may require a charge over the office that it can use if the company cannot repay its debt. The lender can take over ownership of the office, sell it, and recover some or all of its investment.

3.1 Definition

Key term

A **charge** is an encumbrance upon real or personal property granting the holder certain rights over that property. They are often used as security for a debt owed to the charge holder. The most common form of charge is by way of legal mortgage, used to secure the indebtedness of borrowers in house purchase transactions. In the case of companies, charges over assets are most frequently granted to persons who provide loan capital to the business.

A charge **secured** over a company's assets gives to the creditor (called the 'chargee') a prior claim (over other creditors) to payment of their debt out of those assets. Charges are of two kinds, fixed and floating.

3.2 Fixed charges

Key term

A **fixed charge** is a form of protection given to secured creditors relating to specific assets of a company. The charge grants the holder the right of enforcement against the identified asset (in the event of default in repayment or some other matter) so that the creditor may realise the asset to meet the debt owed. Fixed charges rank first in order of priority in corporate insolvency.

Fixed (or specific) charges attach to the relevant asset as soon as the charge is created. By its nature a fixed charge is best suited to assets which the company is likely to retain for a long period. A mortgage is an example of a fixed charge.

If the company disposes of the charged asset it will either **repay the secured debt** out of the proceeds of sale so that the charge is discharged at the time of sale, or **pass the asset over to** the purchaser still subject to the charge.

3.3 Floating charges

Key term

A **floating charge** has been defined, in *Re Yorkshire Woolcombers Association Ltd 1903*, as:

(a) A charge on a class of assets of a company, present and future ...
(b) Which class is, in the ordinary course of the company's business, changing from time to time and ...
(c) Until the holders enforce the charge the company may carry on business and deal with the assets charged.

Floating charges do not attach to the relevant assets until the charge crystallises.

A floating charge is **not restricted** to assets such as **receivables** or **inventory**. A floating charge over 'the undertaking and assets' of a company (the most common type) applies to future as well as to current assets.

3.4 Identification of charges as fixed or floating

It is not always immediately apparent whether a charge is fixed or floating. Chargees often do not wish to identify a charge as being as it may get paid later than preferential debts in insolvency proceedings.

A charge contract may declare the charge as fixed, or fixed and floating, whether it is or not. **The label attached** by parties in this way is **not a conclusive statement of the charge's legal nature**.

The general rule is that a **charge over assets will not be registered as fixed if it envisages that the company will still be able to deal with the charged assets without reference to the chargee**.

> *R in Right of British Columbia v Federal Business Development Bank 1988*
>
> *The facts:* In this Canadian case the Bank had a charge over the company's entire property expressed as 'a fixed and specific mortgage and charge'. Another term allowed the company to continue making sales from stock in the ordinary course of business until notified in writing by the bank to stop doing so.
>
> *Decision:* The charge was created as a floating, not a fixed, charge.

However, the courts have found **exceptions** to the general rule concerning permission to deal.

(a) In *Re GE Tunbridge Ltd 1995* it was held that as the three criteria stated in the *Yorkshire Woolcombers* case applied. The charge over certain fixed assets was a floating charge even though the company was required to obtain the chargee's permission before dealing with the assets.

(b) In *Re Cimex Ltd 1994* the court decided that the charge in dispute was a fixed charge. The assets did not in the ordinary course of business change from time to time. This was despite the company being able to deal with the assets without the chargee's permission.

3.4.1 Charges over receivables

Charges expressed to be fixed which cover **present and future receivables** (book debts) have historically been particularly tricky. Again the general rule applies. If the company is allowed to deal with money collected from customers without notifying the chargee, the courts have decided that the charge is floating. If the money collected must be paid in to a blocked account or to the chargee, say in reduction of an overdraft, the courts have determined that the charge is fixed over the proceeds: *Siebe Gorman & Co Ltd v Barclays Bank Ltd 1979*.

Following the decision by the House of Lords in *Re Spectrum Plus Ltd 2005* it will be unusual for fixed charges to be created over book debts, and such a charge will only be possible with very careful drafting.

3.5 Creating a floating charge

A **floating charge** is **often created by express words**. However no special form of words is essential. If a **company** gives to a chargee rights over its assets while **retaining freedom to deal with them in the ordinary course of business** until the charge crystallises, that will be a charge which 'floats'. The particular assets subject to a floating charge cannot be identified until the charge attaches by crystallisation.

3.6 Crystallisation of a floating charge

FAST FORWARD

Floating charges **crystallise** or harden (convert into a fixed charge) on the happening of certain relevant events.

Key term

Crystallisation of a floating charge occurs when it is converted into a fixed charge: that is, a fixed charge on the assets owned by the company at the time of crystallisation.

Events causing crystallisation
The **liquidation** of the company
Cessation of the company's **business**
Active intervention by the chargee, generally by way of appointing a receiver
If the **charge contract so provides**, when notice is given by the chargee that the charge is converted into a fixed charge (on whatever assets of the relevant class are owned by the company at the time of the giving of notice)
The **crystallisation** of **another floating charge** if it causes the company to cease business

Floating charge contracts sometimes make provision for 'automatic crystallisation'. This is where the charge is to crystallise when a **specified event** – such as a breach of some term by the company – occurs, regardless of whether:

- The chargee learns of the event.
- The chargee wants to enforce the charge as a result of the event.

Such clauses have been accepted by the courts if they state that, on the event happening, the floating charge is converted to a fixed one. Clauses which provide only that a company is to cease to deal with charged assets on the occurrence of a particular event have been rejected.

3.7 Comparison of fixed and floating charges

FAST FORWARD
Floating charges rank **behind** a number of other creditors on liquidation, in particular preferential creditors such as employees.

A **fixed charge** is normally the more satisfactory form of security since it **confers immediate rights** over identified assets. A **floating charge** has some advantage in being applicable to **current assets which may be easier to realise** than long term assets subject to a fixed charge. If for example a company becomes insolvent it may be easier to sell its inventory than its empty factory.

The principal disadvantages of floating charges

The **holder** of a floating charge **cannot be certain** until the charge crystallises which assets will form their security.

Even when a floating charge has crystallised over an identified pool of assets the **chargeholders** may find themselves **postponed** to the claim of **other creditors** as follows.

(a) A **judgement creditor or landlord** who has seized goods and sold them may retain the proceeds if received before the appointment of the debenture holder's receiver or administrator: s 183 IA.

(b) **Preferential debts** such as wages may be paid out of ring-fenced assets subject to a floating charge unless there are other uncharged assets available for this purpose: ss 40 and 175 IA.

(c) The **holder** of a **fixed charge** over the same assets will usually have priority over a floating charge on those assets even if that charge was created before the fixed charge (see below).

(d) A creditor may have sold goods and delivered them to the company on condition that they are to retain legal ownership until they have been paid (a **Romalpa** or retention of title clause).

A **floating charge** may become **invalid automatically** if the company creates the charge to secure an existing debt and goes into liquidation within a year thereafter (s 245 IA). The period is only six months with a fixed charge.

3.8 Priority of charges

FAST FORWARD
If more than one charge exists over the **same class of property** then legal rules must be applied to see which takes priority in the event the company goes into liquidation.

Different charges over the **same** property may be given to different creditors. It will be necessary in such cases to determine which party's claim has **priority**.

Illustration

If charges are created over the same property to secure a debt of £5,000 to X and £7,000 to Y and the property is sold yielding only £10,000, either X or Y is paid in full and the other receives only the balance remaining out of £10,000 realised from the security.

Priority of charges

Fixed charges rank according to the **order of their creation**. If two successive fixed charges over the same factory are created on 1 January and 1 February the earlier takes priority over the later one.

A **floating charge created before a fixed charge** will only take priority if, when the latter was created, the **fixed chargee** had **notice** of a clause in the floating charge that prevents a later prior charge.

A **fixed charge created before** a **floating charge** has **priority**.

Two floating charges take priority according to the **time of creation**.

If a floating charge is existing and a fixed charge over the same property is created later the fixed charge has priority. This is unless the fixed chargeholder knew of the floating charge. The **fixed** charge ranks **first** since it attached to the property at the time of **creation** but the **floating** charge attaches at the time of **crystallisation**. Once a floating charge has crystallised it becomes a fixed charge and a fixed charge created subsequently ranks after it.

A floating chargeholder may seek to protect themselves against losing their priority by including in the terms of their floating charge a prohibition against the company creating a fixed charge over the same property (sometimes called a **'negative pledge clause'**).

If the company **breaks that prohibition** the creditor to whom the fixed charge is given nonetheless obtains priority, unless at the time when their charge is created they have **actual** knowledge of the prohibition.

If a company sells a charged asset to a **third party** the following rules apply.

- A chargee with a fixed charge still has recourse to the property in the hands of the third party – the **charge** is **automatically** transferred with the property.

- Property only remains charged by a floating charge if the **third party** had **notice** of it when they acquired the property.

Exam focus point

You should be aware of what fixed and floating charges are and what the implications are of the differences between them.

Question — Registering charges

A floating charge is created on 1 January 20X1. A fixed charge over the same property is created on 1 April 20X1. Assuming both are registered within the prescribed time limits, which ranks first?

Answer

The fixed charge attaches to the asset on creation; the floating charge only attaches on crystallisation, and the effect of crystallisation is not retrospective. Therefore the fixed charge ranks first.

As we shall see in the next section, creating a charge is not enough in itself to protect a lender. It must also be registered to be valid. If a charge is not registered correctly then it may not have priority over other charges, or worse still may not be valid at all.

4 Registration of charges

FAST FORWARD

To be valid and enforceable, a charge needs to be **registered** by the Registrar within **21 days** of its creation.

Most charges created by a company **may be registered** with the Registrar within **21 days,** beginning with the day after the date of creation of the charge.

Excluded charges which may NOT be registered are:

- A charge in favour of a landlord on a cash deposit given as a security in connection with the lease of land.

- A charge created by a member of Lloyd's to secure the company's obligations in connection with its underwriting business at Lloyd's.

- A charge that any other Act specifically excludes from registration.

4.1 The registration process

Under the Companies Act 2006 (TSO, 2006), application for the charge **to be registered** may be made by the company or **by any other person** interested in the charge: s 859A.

To apply to register a charge a **statement of particulars relating to the charge must be delivered to the Registrar**. The statement of particulars sets out (s 859D):

- The registered name and number of the company.
- The date when the charge was created.
- Further particulars depending on whether or not there is an instrument creating or evidencing the charge.

Creation of a charge is usually effected by **execution of a instrument,** usually as a **deed**. Where the charge is created or evidenced by an instrument, the Registrar will only register the charge if a **certified copy of the instrument** is delivered along with the statement of particulars.

The Registrar allocates a unique reference code to the charge and places a note in the register recording that reference code. The certified copy of any instrument is also included in the register. The Registrar then issues a **certificate** which is **conclusive evidence** that the **charge had been duly registered**.

The 21 day period for registration runs from the day after the **creation** of the **charge**, or the acquisition of property charged, and not from the making of the loan for which the charge is security.

4.2 Failure to deliver particulars

The duty to deliver particulars falls upon the **company** creating the charge and, if no one delivers particulars within 21 days or any extension period, the **company and its officers are liable to a fine**: s 860.

Non-delivery in the original or any extended time period results in the **charge** being **void** against an administrator, liquidator or any creditor of a company: s 859H.

Non-delivery of the relevant documents relating to a charge means that the sum secured by it is **payable immediately**: s 859H.

4.3 Late delivery of particulars

A **court order** is required for registration of particulars after the 21 day deadline: s 859F.

A court will only allow an order for a charge to be registered late if the failure to deliver the documents was accidental or due to inadvertence or to some other sufficient cause, or it does not prejudice the creditors or shareholders of the company, or it is otherwise just and equitable to grant an extension. Therefore a correctly registered fixed charge has priority over a fixed charge created earlier but registered after it, if that charge is registered late. s 873.

4.4 Rectification of register

A mis-statement or omission in registered particulars on the register can be rectified by the Registrar on receipt of an order of the court, which itself must be registered: s 859M. The court will only make the order if the error or omission was accidental or due to inadvertence or to some other sufficient cause, or if it does not prejudice creditors or shareholders, or if it is just and equitable to do so.

4.5 Register of charges

As you already know, every company is under an obligation to keep a copy of instruments creating charges, and a register of charges, at its registered office or any other location permitted by regulations, so that they may be inspected. The Registrar must be notified of the place where the documents are available for inspection: s 859Q.

Question — Registering more charges

A company creates a charge over a property in favour of Mizuho on 1 May 20X7. It creates a further charge of the same type in favour of Jun over the same property on 13 May 20X7. The company has Jun's charge registered on 25 May 20X7, and Mizuho's charge on 29 May 20X7.

Whose charge ranks first, and why?

Answer

Mizuho's charge would have taken precedence because it was created first, had it been registered within the allowed period of 21 days, up to 22 May. However it was not registered until 29 May, and Jun's charge was legitimately registered in the period between 22 and 29 May when Mizuho's charge was void. The court would probably have allowed late registration of Mizuho's charge but not at the expense of Jun's rights per s 873.

Providing a charge is correctly created and registered then it will offer the owner protection in the event of the borrower defaulting on the loan. In the next section we shall see the various remedies available to debenture holders if the company cannot repay its debt.

5 Debenture holders' remedies

5.1 Rights of unsecured debenture holders

FAST FORWARD A debenture holder **without security** has the same rights as any other creditor.

Any debenture holder is a creditor of the company with the normal remedies of an unsecured creditor. They could:

- **Sue** the company for debt and seize its property if their judgement for debt is unsatisfied.
- Present a petition to the court for the **compulsory liquidation** of the company.
- Apply to the court for an **administration order**, that is, a temporary reprieve to try and rescue a company.

5.2 Rights of secured debenture holders

FAST FORWARD A **secured** debenture holder may enforce the security if the company defaults on payment of interest or repayment of capital. They may take possession of the asset subject to the charge and sell it or apply to the court for its transfer to their ownership by a foreclosure order. They may also appoint a receiver or administrator of it. A floating charge holder may place the company into administration.

A **secured** debenture holder (or the trustee of a debenture trust deed) may enforce the security. They may:

- Take **possession of the asset** subject to the charge if they have a fixed charge (if they have a floating charge they may only take possession if the contract allows).
- **Sell it** (provided the debenture is executed as a deed).
- Apply to the court for its **transfer** to their ownership by foreclosure order (rarely used and only available to a legal chargee).
- Appoint a **receiver** of it, provided an administration order is not in effect, or – in the case of floating chargeholders only – appoint an administrator without needing to apply to the court.

PART H CAPITALISATION OF THE COMPANY

Question — Debenture holder remedies

List the steps that a fixed debenture holder can take to enforce their security.

Answer

Take possession of the asset subject to the charge
Sell it
Apply to the court for a transfer to their ownership
Appoint a receiver of it

Exam focus point

The last part of a question on charges may well ask what debenture holders can do if a company defaults.

Chapter Roundup

- Companies have an **implied power** to borrow for purposes incidental to their trade or business.

- **Loan capital** comprises all the longer term borrowing of a company. It is distinguished from share capital by the fact that, at some point, borrowing must be repaid. Share capital on the other hand is only returned to shareholders when the company is wound up.

- A **debenture** is a document stating the terms on which a company has borrowed money. There are three main types.

    - A **single debenture**.
    - **Debentures issued as a series** and usually registered.
    - **Debenture stock** subscribed to by a large number of lenders. Only this form requires a **debenture trust deed**, although the others may often incorporate one.

- A charge over the assets of a company gives a creditor a **prior claim** over other creditors to payment of their debt out of these assets.

- Charges may be either **fixed**, which attach to the relevant asset on creation, or **floating**, which attach on 'crystallisation'. For this reason it is not possible to identify the assets to which a **floating** charge relates (until **crystallisation**).

- Floating charges **crystallise** or harden (convert into a fixed charge) on the happening of certain relevant events.

- Floating charges rank **behind** a number of other creditors on insolvency, in particular preferential creditors such as employees.

- If more than one charge exists over the **same class of property** then legal rules must be applied to see which takes priority in the event the company goes into liquidation.

- To be valid and enforceable, a charge needs to be **registered** by the Registrar within **21 days** of its creation.

- A debenture holder **without security** has the same rights as any other creditor.

- A **secured** debenture holder may enforce the security if the company defaults on payment of interest or repayment of capital. They may take possession of the asset subject to the charge and sell it or apply to the court for its transfer to their ownership by a foreclosure order. They may also appoint a receiver or administrator of it. A floating charge holder may place the company into administration.

PART H   CAPITALISATION OF THE COMPANY

Quick Quiz

1   Which of the following are correct statements about the relationship between a company's ordinary shares and its debentures?

    A   Debentures do not confer voting rights, whilst ordinary shares do.
    B   The company's duty is to pay interest on debentures, and to pay dividends on ordinary shares.
    C   Interest paid on debentures is deducted from pre-tax profits, dividends are paid from net profits.
    D   A debenture holder takes priority over a member in liquidation.

2   A fixed charge

    A   Cannot be an informal mortgage
    B   Can be a legal mortgage
    C   Can only attach to land, shares or book debts
    D   Cannot attach to land

3   What are the elements of the definition of a floating charge?

4   Company law requires a company to maintain a register of charges, but not a register of debenture holders.

    True   ☐

    False   ☐

5   In which of the following situations will crystallisation of a floating charge occur?

    A   Liquidation of the company
    B   Disposal by the company of the charged asset
    C   Cessation of the company's business
    D   After the giving of notice by the chargee if the contract so provides

6   Certain types of charges need to be registered within 28 days of creation.

    True   ☐

    False   ☐

Answers to Quick Quiz

1. A, C and D are correct. Whilst the company has a contractual duty to pay interest on debentures, there is no duty on it to pay dividends on shares. B is therefore incorrect.

2. B. A mortgage is an example of a fixed charge. It can extend to, for instance, plant and machinery as well as land.

3. The charge is:
   (a) A charge on a class of assets, present and future
   (b) Which class is in the ordinary course of the company's business changing from time to time
   (c) Until the holders enforce the charge, the company may carry on business and deal with the assets charged

4. True. A register of charges must be kept, a register of debenture holders is not required to be kept by the Act (though if it is kept, Companies Act rules must be followed).

5. A, C and D are true. As the charge does not attach to the asset until crystallisation, B is untrue.

6. False. Certain charges such as charges securing a debenture issue and floating charges need to be registered within 21 days, not 28 days.

End of chapter question

Charges and guarantees

Ecowood Floors Limited (Ecowood) supplies and fits wooden floors sourced from sustainably managed forests. The directors and majority shareholders of Ecowood are two brothers, Michael and Thomas Daniels. Michael is very wealthy; Thomas is married to Isobel with two small children and much less wealthy than Michael. Ecowood would like to expand into supplying floors to commercial properties, predominantly boutique hotels and designer shops. Ecowood needs some additional finance to achieve this expansion and has approached City Bank plc (City Bank) who have agreed to lend Ecowood £80,000. City Bank has requested personal guarantees from the directors of Ecowood, as well as either a fixed or floating charge over Ecowood's assets.

Required

(a) Explain to the directors of Ecowood the implications of them granting personal guarantees in relation to City Bank's proposed loan to Ecowood. **(6 marks)**

(b) Advise Ecowood on the legal effect of granting either a fixed charge or a floating charge over Ecowood's assets and any procedures which must be complied with in relation to either such charge.

(10 marks)

(c) Assume now that it has been decided that Michael, rather than City Bank, will lend the money to Ecowood. What procedures would Ecowood need to follow to put the loan in place? **(4 marks)**

(Total = 20 marks)

PART H CAPITALISATION OF THE COMPANY

Capital maintenance and dividends

Topic list	Syllabus reference
1 Capital maintenance	3.3
2 Reduction of share capital	3.3
3 Redemption and purchase by a company of its own shares	3.3
4 Financial assistance for the purchase of shares	3.3
5 Issuing shares at a premium or at a discount	3.3
6 Distributing dividends	3.3

Introduction

This is the third and final chapter in our study of the capital of a company. We have already seen **share capital** and **debt capital**. This chapter links the two sources of capital – members and lenders.

Share capital that a company obtains from its **members** is sometimes called **'the creditors' buffer'**. No one can prevent an unsuccessful company from losing its capital by trading at a loss. However, whatever capital the company does have must be held for payment to the **lenders** for the company's debts. It may not be returned to members except under procedures which safeguard the interest of creditors. That is the price which members of a limited company are required to pay for the protection of limited liability.

This principle has been developed in a number of detailed applications.

- Capital may only be distributed to members under the formal procedure of a **reduction** of **share capital** or a **winding up** of the company.
- A **premium** obtained on the allotment of shares and profits used to redeem or purchase shares of the company are statutory reserves subject to the basic rules on capital.
- **Dividends** may only be paid out of distributable profits.

The **Companies Act 2006**, (TSO, 2006) and the **Small Business, Enterprise and Employment Act 2015**, (TSO, 2015) apply to this and all chapters unless otherwise stated.

PART H   CAPITALISATION OF THE COMPANY

1 Capital maintenance

FAST FORWARD

The rules which dictate how a company is to manage and maintain its capital exist to maintain the delicate balance between the **members' enjoyment of limited liability** and the **creditors' requirements that the company shall remain able to pay its debts**.

Key term

Capital maintenance is a fundamental principle of company law, that limited companies should not be allowed to make payments out of capital to the detriment of company creditors. Therefore the Companies Act contains many examples of control upon capital payments. These include provisions restricting dividend payments, and capital reduction schemes.

Exam focus point

The rules affecting the possible threats to capital are complicated in certain areas. However, provided you know the rules, questions on capital maintenance tend to be straightforward.

2 Reduction of share capital

FAST FORWARD

Reduction of capital can be achieved by: **extinguishing/reducing liability on partly-paid shares**; **cancelling paid-up share capital**; or **paying off part of paid-up share capital**. Court confirmation is required for public companies. The court considers the interests of creditors and different classes of shareholder. There must be power in the articles and a special resolution.

Having seen the principle of capital maintenance above, we shall now apply it. In this instance we consider the situation where a company wishes to reduce the amount of its share capital.

2.1 Why reduce share capital?

A company may wish to reduce its capital for one or more of the following reasons.

- The company has suffered a **loss** in the **value** of its **assets** and it reduces its capital to reflect that fact.
- The company wishes to **extinguish** the **interests** of some members entirely.
- The capital reduction is part of a **complicated arrangement** of capital which may involve, for instance, replacing share capital with loan capital.

2.2 Reducing unissued and issued share capital

Under the Companies Act 2006 (TSO, 2006), a limited company is permitted without restriction to cancel **unissued shares** as that change does not alter its financial position.

If a limited company with a share capital wishes to **reduce** its **issued share capital** it may do so if:

- It has **power** to do so in its articles. (If it does not have power in the articles, these may be amended by a **special resolution**.)
- It passes a **special resolution**. (If the articles have been amended, this is another special resolution.)
- It obtains **confirmation** of the reduction **from the court**.

There are three basic methods of reducing share capital specified in s 641 of the Act.

Method	What happens	Effects
Extinguish or reduce liability on partly paid shares.	Eg Company has nominal value £1 shares 75p paid up. Either (a) reduce nominal value to 75p; or (b) reduce nominal value to a figure between 75p and £1.	Company gives up claim for amount not paid up (nothing is **returned** to shareholders).
Pay off part of paid-up share capital out of surplus assets.	Eg Company reduces nominal value of fully paid shares from £1 to 70p and repays this amount to shareholders.	Assets of company are reduced by 30p in £.
Cancel paid-up share capital which has been lost or which is no longer represented by available assets.	Eg Company has £1 nominal fully paid shares but net assets only worth 50p per share. Difference is a debit balance on reserves. Company reduces nominal value to 50p, and applies amount to write off debit balance.	Company can resume dividend payments out of future profits without having to make good past losses.

2.3 Solvency statement

A private company need not apply to the court if it supports its special resolution with a solvency statement: s 643.

Key term

> A **solvency statement** is a declaration by the directors, provided 15 days in advance of the meeting where the special resolution is to be voted on. It states there is no ground to suspect the company is currently unable or will be unlikely to be able to pay its debts for the next 12 months. All possible liabilities must be taken into account and the statement should be in the prescribed form, naming all the directors.

It is an **offence** for directors to deliver to the Registrar a solvency statement without having **reasonable grounds** for the opinions expressed in it.

2.4 Role of the court in reduction of share capital

When the court receives an application for reduction of capital its **first concern** is the effect of the reduction on the company's ability to pay its debts, that is, that the creditors are protected.

If the reduction is by extinguishing liability or paying off part of paid-up share capital, the court requires that **creditors** shall be **invited** by advertisement to state their objections (if any) to the reduction. Where paid-up share capital is cancelled, the court **may** require an invitation to creditors.

Normally the company persuades the court to dispense with advertising for creditors' objections (which can be commercially damaging to the company).

Two possible approaches are:

- To **pay off** all **creditors** before application is made to the court; or, if that is not practicable.
- To produce to the court a **guarantee**, say from the company's bank, that its existing debts will be paid in full.

The **second** concern of the court, where there is more than one class of share, is whether the reduction is fair in its effect on different classes of shareholder.

If the reduction is, **in the circumstances**, a **variation of class rights** (for example removal of the right to an interest in the surplus on a winding-up) the **consent** of the class must be obtained under the variation of class rights procedure.

Within each class of share it is usual to make a uniform reduction of every share by the same amount per share, though this is **not** obligatory.

The court may also be concerned that the **reduction should not confuse or mislead people who may deal with the company in future**. It may insist that the company add 'and reduced' to its name or publish explanations of the reduction.

2.4.1 Confirmation by the court

If the court is satisfied that the reduction is in order, it confirms the reduction by making an order to that effect. A **copy of the court order** and a **statement of capital**, approved by the court, to show the altered share capital is delivered to the Registrar who issues a certificate of registration.

| Question | Reduction of share capital |

What are the main methods for a public company to reduce its share capital? What procedures must it follow?

Answer

If a public company wishes to reduce its **issued** share capital it may do so provided that:

(a) It has power to do so in its articles.
(b) It passes a special resolution.
(c) It obtains confirmation of the reduction from the court: s 641.

Requirement (a) is simply a matter of procedure. Articles usually contain the necessary power. If not, the company in general meeting would first pass a special resolution to alter the articles appropriately. They would then proceed to pass a special resolution to reduce the capital.

There are three basic methods of reducing share capital under s 641:

(a) Extinguish or reduce liability on partly-paid shares.
(b) Cancel paid-up share capital which has been lost or which is no longer represented by available assets.
(c) Pay off part of the paid-up share capital out of surplus assets.

Although these are the methods specified in s 641, they are not the only possibilities.

If method (a) or (b) is used (or is part of a more complex scheme to reduce capital) creditors must be invited to object, and their consent must be granted. An alternative is that they are paid off, which will allow the court to confirm the reduction.

It should be remembered that public companies are subject to a minimum capital requirement, currently of £50,000. This means that any public company wishing to reduce its capital below this figure will only be allowed to do so by the court if it re-registers as a private company, which is not subject to the minimum capital requirement. This situation is relatively rare.

3 Redemption and purchase by a company of its own shares

FAST FORWARD Specific rules govern the ability of private and public companies to **redeem** or **purchase** their own shares.

In this section we shall apply the principle of capital maintenance to a scenario where a company wishes to purchase or redeem its own shares.

3.1 The basic rule

Under s 658 of the Companies Act 2006 (TSO, 2006), **a company cannot acquire its own shares** by purchase, subscription or other method. To do so is an **offence**, and the purported acquisition is **void**.

The prohibition is subject to exceptions in s 659. A company may:

- Purchase its own shares in compliance with a **court order.**
- Issue and redeem **redeemable** shares.
- **Purchase** (buyback) its **own shares** under certain specified procedures.
- Forfeit, or **accept** the **surrender** of, its shares.

3.2 Redeemable shares

Both ordinary and preference shares may be issued on terms which allow the company to redeem them. The expression 'redeemable shares' means only shares which are redeemable from the time of issue, so shares not issued as redeemable cannot later be made so.

Key term

> **Redeemable shares** are shares which are issued on terms which may require them to be bought back by the issuer at some future date, either at the discretion of the issuer or of the holder.

The conditions for the issue and redemption of redeemable shares are set out in ss 684 and 687. The rules for private and public companies differ slightly so you should read them carefully.

The articles of a public company must give **authority** for the issue of redeemable shares. If the articles do not they must be altered before the shares are issued (public companies only). In private companies the directors have authority to allot redeemable shares unless restricted by the articles.
Redeemable shares may only be issued if, at the time of issue, the company also has **issued shares** which are **not redeemable**. A company's capital may not consist entirely of redeemable shares.
Redeemable shares may only be redeemed if they are **fully paid.**
The terms of redemption must provide for **payment on redemption** or on a later date.
The shares may be redeemed out of: • **Distributable profits** • The **proceeds of a new issue** of shares • **Capital** (if it is a **private** company)
Any **premium payable on redemption** must generally be provided out of **distributable profits**.
The company may redeem shares on such **terms** and in such manner as may be provide by the company's **articles** or company **resolution** subject only to the specific provisions set out in the Act.

When shares are redeemed they are cancelled and may not be reissued.

(a) The amount of the company's **issued** share capital is **reduced** by the nominal amount of the shares.

(b) Any new shares issued to raise money to redeem shares are treated as a **replacement** for them to the extent that the nominal value of the new shares does not exceed the nominal value of the shares redeemed.

(c) If shares are redeemed wholly out of profits an amount equal to the nominal value of shares redeemed must be transferred to a **capital redemption reserve** which is to be treated as if it were share capital, except that it may be applied in paying up issued shares as a bonus issue: s 733.

3.3 Purchase of own shares

Any company limited by shares may purchase or 'buyback' its own fully paid shares **out of distributable profits or the proceeds of an issue of new shares** under the redemption of shares rules: s 692(2).

PART H CAPITALISATION OF THE COMPANY

A private company may in addition purchase its own fully paid shares:

- Out of capital using a 'permissible capital payment' or
- With cash (if authorised to do so by its articles, which require a special resolution to be altered) at nominal value up to a 'de minimis' amount in a financial year not exceeding the lower of £15,000 or 5% of its share capital: s 692(1). The Act states that the company does not have to identify this cash amount as distributable profits, meaning that this is a payment out of capital to which the more extensive 'permissible capital payment' rules do not apply. Separate authority by ordinary resolution is required for the specific purchase (or multiple purchases) in question.

A company cannot, however, purchase ordinary shares if, as a result, only redeemable shares are left.

An **unlimited** company can reduce its share capital or purchase its own shares without statutory restriction.

There are two methods of carrying out the purchase: off-market or market purchase. Either can be used for any type of share, but only public companies can use the market method, as private companies will not have shares available on a public market.

- **Market purchase** is purchase by a public company under the normal market arrangements of a recognised investment exchange.
- **Off-market purchase** is any other purchase, usually by private treaty. This will apply to shares of private companies, but it can also apply to public companies.

Market purchase of own shares (s 701)	

Authority	The purchase must be authorised in advance by ordinary resolution specifying:
	• Maximum number of shares to be acquired.
	• Maximum and minimum prices to be paid
	   – By global sum, or
	   – By price formula.
	• A date (< five years after resolution) on which authority expires.

Filing	A return must be sent to the Registrar within 28 days.
Changes	The authority may be varied, revoked or renewed by ordinary resolution.
Off-market purchase of own shares (s 694)	
Authority	A contract for the purchase of shares must be approved in advance by ordinary resolution.
Inspection	A copy of the proposed contract must be available for inspection by members • At the registered office • For 15 days before the meeting for approval • At the meeting It must disclose the names of the sellers. If the resolution is a written one, a copy of the contract must be sent to all eligible members.
Voting	The members who intend to sell the shares should not vote. If they do vote and the resolution would not have been carried without their vote, it is invalid. They may cast votes attached to other shares which they are not selling.
Public company	A public company may only be given authority for a limited period (max five years).
Changes	The authority may be varied, revoked or renewed by ordinary resolution.

Question — Purchase of shares

A limited company may without restriction purchase its own shares providing the purchase is out of profits or an issue of new shares.

True or false?

Answer

False. Such an action is prevented if the purchase would leave only redeemable shares.

3.4 Payment for shares out of capital – private companies only

A private limited company which has a share capital may redeem or purchase its shares 'out of capital' by a '**permissible capital payment**' to which elaborate rules apply: s 709. These rules are designed to ensure that the company does not make itself insolvent by making a large return of capital to shareholders.

The conditions for a permissible capital payment are as follows.

(a) There must be **no restrictions** in the **articles** for redemption or purchase of shares out of capital.

(b) Capital may only be used to '**top up**' distributable profits and the proceeds of any issue of new shares in cases where those resources, fully used, do not suffice to make up the required amount.

| Cost of redemption or purchase | = | Available distributable profits | + | Proceeds of fresh issue | + | Permissible capital payment |

(c) A **capital redemption reserve** must be created where the amount of the permissible capital payment is less than the nominal amount of the shares redeemed or purchased: s 734.

If the payment is greater than the nominal amount then the capital redemption reserve, share premium account, share capital or revaluation reserve of the company may be reduced by the excess.

(d) A **statutory declaration of the directors** must be made and supported by a **report of the auditors** to the effect that after the payment is made the company will be able to pay its debts and to carry on its business for at least a year to come: s 714.

(e) Shareholders must approve the payment by passing a **special resolution s 716**. In this decision any vendor of shares may **not** use the votes attached to the shares which they are to sell to the company: s 717.

(f) A member who did not vote for the resolution and a creditor (for any amount) may within five weeks **apply to the court to cancel the resolution**, which may not be implemented until the five weeks have elapsed: s 721.

(g) A **notice** must be placed in the *London Gazette* and in an appropriate national newspaper, **or** every creditor must be informed: s 719.

If the company goes into insolvent liquidation within a year of making a payment out of capital the person who received the payment and the directors who authorised it may have to make it good to the company.

Note that different, less onerous rules apply where the payment out of capital relates to the purchase of own shares for the purposes of or pursuant to an **employees' share scheme**: s 720A. These rules require a special resolution supported by a solvency statement and statement of capital.

3.5 Subsidiary not to be a member of its holding company

The restrictions on acquisition by a company of its own shares are extended by a general prohibition against a subsidiary being a member of its holding company: s 136.

4 Financial assistance for the purchase of shares

FAST FORWARD

A **public** company may not give **financial assistance** to a third party to purchase shares in the company. A private company can do so.

This section extends the application of the capital maintenance principle that we saw in the previous section to the situation where the company offers some kind of financial assistance to enable another party to buy its shares.

4.1 The rule against financial assistance

The general rules under the Companies Act 2006 (TSO, 2006), apply to all **public companies only**.

(a) A company is prohibited from giving any financial assistance for the purpose of the acquisition of shares either of the company or of its holding company or to discharge liabilities incurred in making the acquisition: s 678.

(b) 'Financial assistance' is elaborately defined to mean:

- A loan or gift
- A guarantee indemnity or security
- A realise from debt or a waiver
- 'Any other financial assistance given by a company which reduces to a material extent, its net assets': s 677.

Key term

Financial assistance is the provision of benefit by a company to a person to put that person in funds so that they may purchase shares in the company.

A public company may give a person financial assistance if its principal purpose in doing so is not to reduce or discourage the person's liability, or if it is an incidental part of a larger purpose of the company, **and** if it is done in good faith: s 678(4). Two main tests have to be applied to any suspect transaction.

What was its **purpose**? It is not objectionable if its **principal purpose** was **not** to give financial assistance for the purchase of the shares nor if it was an incidental part of some **larger purpose** of the company.

What was the state of mind of the directors in approving the transaction? Did they act in **good faith** in what they deemed to be the interests of the company and not of a third party?

4.2 Group companies

Under the Act:

- A **private subsidiary** may give assistance to purchase its own shares and that of its parent (if it also is a private company).
- A **public subsidiary** may not give assistance to purchase its own shares or that of its parent (even if the parent is a private company).

4.3 Other exceptions from the financial assistance rules

Three other specific exceptions are also made. By s 682 a company is not prohibited from entering into any of the following transactions provided it is either a private company, or it is a public company and either its net assets are not reduced by giving the assistance, or it gives the assistance out of distributable profit.

(a) Making a loan if **lending is part of its ordinary business**, and the loan is made in the ordinary course of its business; this exception is restricted to money-lending companies.

(b) Providing money in good faith and in the best interests of the company for the purpose of an **employees' share scheme** or for other share transactions by *bona fide* employees or connected persons.

(c) **Making loans** or providing assistance to persons (other than directors) employed in good faith by the company with a view to those **persons acquiring fully paid shares** in the company or its holding company to be held by them as beneficial owners.

Exam focus point

Do not confuse a company purchasing its own shares with a company providing financial assistance for **someone else** to purchase its shares.

Question

Financial assistance

Which of the following transactions for assistance to purchase a company's own shares are allowable under the Companies Act 2006?

Select all that apply.

A   A private subsidiary can give assistance to a private parent.
B   A public subsidiary can give assistance to a private parent.
C   A private subsidiary can give assistance to a third party.
D   A public company can give assistance to a third party company.

Answer

A and C. Public companies may never give assistance in these circumstances. Private companies can.

5 Issuing shares at a premium or at a discount

FAST FORWARD

In issuing shares, a company must fix a **price** which is **equal** to or **more than** the **nominal value of the shares**. It may not allot shares at a discount to the nominal value.

Companies may wish to issue shares at a higher or lower price than their nominal value. Issuing shares at a higher price is known as issuing at a premium and at a lower price is known as issuing at a discount. We will now consider how the principle of capital maintenance is applied to these situations.

Under the Companies Act 2006 (TSO, 2006), every share has a **nominal value** and **may not be allotted at a discount** to that: s 580.

In allotting shares every company is required to obtain in money or money's worth, consideration of a value at least equal to the nominal value of the shares plus the whole of any premium. To issue shares '**at par**' is to obtain equal value, say, £1 for a £1 share.

> *Ooregum Gold Mining Co of India v Roper, 1892*
>
> *The facts:* Shares in the company, although nominally £1, were trading, at a market price 12.5p. In an honest attempt to refinance the company, new £1 preference shares were issued and credited with 75p already paid, so the purchasers of the shares were actually paying twice the market value of the ordinary shares. When, however, the company subsequently went into insolvent liquidation the holders of the new shares were required to pay a further 75p.

If shares are allotted at a discount to their nominal value, the allottee, if they agree to the issue, must nonetheless pay the **full nominal value** with **interest** at the appropriate rate. Any subsequent holder of such a share who knew of the underpayment must make good the shortfall: s 588.

Consideration for shares	
Partly-paid shares	The no-discount rule only requires that, in allotting its shares, a company shall not fix a price which is less than the nominal value of the shares. It may leave part of that price to be paid at some later time. Thus £1 shares may be issued partly-paid – 75p on allotment and 25p when called for or by instalment. The unpaid capital passes with the shares. If transferred, they are a debt payable by the holder at the time when payment is demanded.
Underwriting fees	A company may pay underwriting or other commission in respect of an issue of shares if so permitted by its Articles. This means that, if shares are issued at par the net amount received will be below par value. This is not a contravention of s 580 (prohibiting allotment of shares at a discount).
Bonus issue	The allotment of shares as a 'bonus issue' is for full consideration since reserves, which are shareholders' funds, are converted into fixed capital and are used to pay for the shares.
Money's worth	The price for the shares may be paid in **money** or **'money's worth'**, including goodwill and know-how: s 582. It need not be paid in cash and the company may agree to accept a **'non-cash' consideration** of sufficient value. For instance, a company may issue shares in payment of the price agreed in the purchase of a property.

5.1 Private companies

FAST FORWARD

> **Private** companies may issue shares for **inadequate consideration** provided the directors are behaving reasonably and honestly.

A private company may allot shares for **inadequate consideration** by acceptance of goods or services at an over-value. This loophole has been allowed to exist because in some cases it is very much a matter of opinion whether an asset is or is not of a stated value.

The **courts** therefore have **refused** to overrule directors in their valuation of an asset acquired for shares if it appears **reasonable** and **honest**: *Re Wragg 1897*. However a blatant and unjustified overvaluation will be declared **invalid**.

5.2 Public companies

FAST FORWARD

> There are **stringent rules** on consideration for shares in public companies.

More stringent rules apply to public companies.

(a) The company must, at the time of allotment, receive **at least one quarter of the nominal value** of the shares and the **whole** of any premium: s 586.

(b) Any **non-cash consideration** accepted must be **independently valued** (see below).

(c) **Non-cash consideration** may **not** be accepted as payment for shares if an undertaking contained in such consideration is to be, or may be, **performed more than five years after the allotment**. This relates to, say, a property or business in return for shares. To enforce the five year rule the law requires that:

   (i) At the time of the allotment the **allottee** must **undertake** to **perform** their side of the agreement within a specified period which must not exceed five years. If no such undertaking is given the **allottee** becomes **immediately liable** to pay cash for their shares as soon as they are allotted.

   (ii) If the **allottee later fails** to **perform** their undertaking to transfer property at the due time they become liable to pay **cash** for their shares when they default.

(d) An **undertaking to do work or perform services is not to be accepted as consideration**. A public company may, however, allot shares to discharge a debt in respect of services already rendered.

   If a public company does accept future services as consideration the holder must pay the company their **nominal value** plus any **premium** treated as paid-up, and **interest** at 5% on any such amount.

(e) Within **two years of receiving its trading certificate**, a public company **may not receive a transfer of non-cash assets from a subscriber** to the memorandum. This is unless its value is less than 10% of the issued nominal share capital and it has been independently valued and agreed by an ordinary resolution.

5.2.1 Valuation of non-cash assets

When a public company allots shares for a non-cash consideration the company must usually obtain a **report on its value** from an independent valuer.

The valuation report must be made to the company within the six months before the allotment. On receiving the report the company must send a copy to the proposed allottee and later to the Registrar.

The independent valuation rule does not apply to an allotment of shares made in the course of a take-over bid.

5.3 Allotment of shares at a premium

FAST FORWARD

> If shares are issued at a premium, the **excess** must be credited to a **share premium** account.

Key term

> **Share premium** is the excess received, either in cash or other consideration, over the nominal value of the shares issued.

An established company may be able to obtain consideration for new shares in excess of their nominal value. The excess, called 'share premium', must be credited to a **share premium account**: s 610.

Exam focus point

> The prohibition on offer of shares at a discount on **nominal** value is often confused with a company issuing shares at a price below **market** value (which is not, provided there is no discount below nominal value, prohibited).

If a company obtains non-cash consideration for its shares which exceeds the nominal value of the shares the excess should also be credited to the **share premium account.**

5.3.1 Example: Using a share premium account

If a company allots its £1 (nominal) shares for £1.50 in cash, £1 per share is credited to the share capital account, and 50p to the share premium account.

Illustration

We will use the above example to illustrate the effects of the transaction on the balance sheet. The company has issued 100 shares.

	Before share issue £	After share issue £
Cash	100	250
Share capital	100	200
Share premium	–	50
	100	250

The general rule is that reduction of the share premium account is subject to the **same** restrictions as reduction of share capital. You should learn the fact that **a company cannot distribute any part of its share premium account as dividend**.

5.4 Uses of the share premium account

> **FAST FORWARD**
> Use of the share premium account is limited. It is most often used for **bonus issues**.

According to s 610, the **permitted uses of share premium** are to pay:

- **Fully paid shares under a bonus issue** since this operation merely converts one form of fixed capital (share premium) into another (share capital).
- **Issue expenses** and **commission** in respect of a **new share issue**.

Additionally, under s 687, the share premium account may be used to finance any premium due when **redeemable shares** are redeemed.

Question — Increasing a company's share capital

Explain the rule concerning issuing shares at a discount to their nominal value.

Answer

Shares may not be issued at a discount to their nominal value: s 580. However shares may be issued 'partly paid' with, for example, 75p of a £1 share paid up. The 25p balance remains a liability that the shareholder must pay when demanded.

6 Distributing dividends

> **FAST FORWARD**
> Various rules have been created to ensure that dividends are only paid out of **available profits**.

Key term

A **dividend** is an amount payable to shareholders from profits or other distributable reserves.

Dividends are a means that companies use to distribute capital back to members. They are the return that members receive on their investment, much like interest paid to lenders on loan capital. In this final section, we shall see how the principle of capital maintenance is applied to their payment.

6.1 Power to declare dividends

Under the Companies Act 2006 (TSO, 2006), a company may only pay dividends out of **profits available for the purpose.**

The power to declare a dividend is given by the articles which often include the following rules.

Rules related to the power to declare a dividend
The **company** in **general meeting** may declare dividends.
No dividend may exceed the **amount recommended** by the directors who have an implied power in their discretion to set aside profits as reserves.
The directors may declare such **interim dividends** as they consider justified.
Dividends are normally declared payable on the **paid up amount** of **share capital**. For example a £1 share which is fully paid will carry entitlement to twice as much dividend as a £1 share 50p paid.
A dividend may be paid **otherwise than in cash**.
Dividends may be paid by **cheque** or **warrant** sent through the post to the shareholder at their registered address. If shares are held jointly, payment of dividend is made to the first-named joint holder on the register.

Listed companies generally pay two dividends a year; an **interim dividend** based on interim profit figures, and a **final dividend** based on the annual accounts and approved at the AGM.

A **dividend becomes a debt** when it is **declared** and **due for payment**. A shareholder is not entitled to a dividend unless it is declared in accordance with the procedure prescribed by the articles and the declared date for payment has arrived.

This is so even if the member holds **preference shares** carrying a priority entitlement to receive a specified amount of dividend on a specified date in the year. The directors may decide to withhold profits and cannot be compelled to recommend a dividend.

If the articles refer to 'payment' of dividends this means **payment in cash**. A power to pay dividends **in specie** (otherwise than in cash) is not implied but may be expressly created. **Scrip dividends** are dividends paid by the issue of additional shares.

Any provision of the articles for the declaration and payment of dividends is subject to the overriding rule that **no dividend may be paid except out of profits distributable by law**.

6.2 Distributable profits

FAST FORWARD

Distributable profits may be defined as 'accumulated realised profits ... less accumulated realised losses'. **'Accumulated'** means that any losses of previous years must be included in reckoning the current distributable surplus. **'Realised'** profits are determined in accordance with generally accepted accounting principles.

Key term

Profits available for distribution are accumulated realised profits (which have not been distributed or capitalised) less accumulated realised losses (which have not been previously written off in a reduction or reorganisation of capital).

The word **'accumulated'** requires that any **losses** of **previous years** must be included in reckoning the current distributable surplus.

A profit or loss is deemed to be **realised** if it is treated as realised in accordance with generally accepted accounting principles. Hence, financial reporting and accounting standards in issue, plus generally accepted accounting principles (GAAP), should be taken into account when determining realised profits and losses.

Depreciation must be treated as a **realised loss**, and debited against profit, in determining the amount of distributable profit remaining.

However, a **revalued asset** will have deprecation charged on its historical cost and the increase in the value in the asset. The Companies Act allows the depreciation provision on the valuation increase to be treated also as a realised profit.

Effectively there is a cancelling out, and at the end **only depreciation that relates to historical cost will affect dividends**.

Illustration

Suppose that an asset purchased for £20,000 has a 10 year life. Provision is made for depreciation on a straight line basis. This means an annual depreciation charge of £2,000 (£20,000/10 years) must be deducted in reckoning the company's realised profit less realised loss.

After five years the asset's written down value is £10,000 (£20,000 less £2,000 × 5 years). Suppose that the asset is then revalued to £50,000. The increase in the value of the asset (£40,000) is credited to the revaluation reserve.

The consequences of this revaluation are that the annual depreciation charge is raised to £10,000 (£50,000/5 remaining years of the asset's life) and £8,000 (£40,000/5 years) is transferred from the revaluation reserve to realised profit each year for the remaining life of the asset.

The net effect is that each year realised profits are still reduced by £2,000 (£10,000 − 8,000) in respect of depreciation.

If, on a general revaluation of all fixed assets, it appears that there is a diminution in value of any one or more assets, then any related provision(s) need **not** be treated as a realised loss.

The Act states that if a company shows **development expenditure** as an asset in its accounts it must usually be treated as a realised loss in the year it occurs. However it can be carried forward in special circumstances (generally taken to mean in accordance with accounting standards).

6.3 Dividends of public companies

FAST FORWARD

A public company may only make a distribution if its **net assets** are, at the time, **not less than the aggregate of its called-up share capital and undistributable reserves**. It may only pay a dividend which will leave its net assets at not less than that aggregate amount.

A public company may only make a distribution if its **net assets** are, at the time, **not less than the aggregate of its called-up share capital and undistributable reserves**. The dividend which it may pay is limited to such amount as will leave its net assets at not less than that aggregate amount: s 831.

Undistributable reserves in s 831 are defined as:

(a) **Share premium account**.
(b) **Capital redemption reserve**.
(c) Any **surplus** of **accumulated unrealised profits** over **accumulated unrealised losses** (known as a revaluation reserve). However a deficit of accumulated unrealised profits compared with accumulated unrealised losses must be treated as a realised loss.
(d) Any **reserve** which the company is **prohibited** from **distributing** by **statute** or by its constitution or any law.

Illustration

Suppose that a public company has an issued share capital (fully paid) of £800,000 and £200,000 on share premium account (which is an undistributable reserve). If its assets less liabilities are less than £1 million it may not pay a dividend. If however its net assets are say £1,250,000 it may pay a dividend but only of such amount as will leave net assets of £1 million or more, so its maximum permissible dividend is £250,000.

The dividend rules apply to every form of distribution of assets except the following:

- The **issue of bonus shares** whether fully or partly paid
- The **redemption** or **purchase** of the company's **shares** out of **capital** or **profits**
- A **reduction** of **share capital**
- A **distribution** of **assets** to members in a **winding up**

Exam focus point

You must appreciate how the rules relating to public companies in this area are more stringent than the rules for private companies.

Question — Distribution of profit

What are the main rules affecting a company's ability to distribute its profits as dividends?

Answer

Dividends may only be paid by a company out of profits available for the purpose. There is a detailed code of statutory rules which determines what are distributable profits. The profits which may be distributed as dividend are accumulated realised profits, so far as not previously utilised by distribution or capitalisation, less accumulated realised losses, so far as not previously written off in a reduction or reorganisation of capital duly made.

The above rules on distributable profits apply to all companies, private or public. A public company is subject to an additional rule which may diminish but cannot increase its distributable profit as determined under the above rules.

A public company may only make a distribution if its net assets are, at the time, not less than the aggregate of its called-up share capital and undistributable reserves. The dividend which it may pay is limited to such amount as will leave its net assets at not less than that aggregate amount.

6.4 Relevant accounts

FAST FORWARD

The profits available for distribution are generally determined from the **last annual accounts** to be prepared.

Whether a company has profits from which to pay a dividend is determined by reference to its **'relevant accounts'**, which are generally the last annual accounts to be prepared: s 836.

If the auditor has qualified their report on the accounts they must also state in writing whether, in their opinion, the subject matter of their qualification is **material** in determining whether the dividend may be paid. This statement must have been circulated to the members (for a private company) or considered at a general meeting (for a public company).

A company may produce **interim accounts** if the latest annual accounts do not disclose a sufficient distributable profit to cover the proposed dividend. It may also produce **initial accounts** if it proposes to pay a dividend during its first accounting reference period or before its first accounts are laid before the company in general meeting. These accounts may be unaudited, but they must suffice to permit a proper judgement to be made of amounts of any of the relevant items.

If a **public** company has to produce initial or interim accounts, which is unusual, they must be full accounts such as the company is required to produce as final accounts at the end of the year. They need not be audited. However the auditors must, in the case of initial accounts, satisfy themselves that the accounts have been 'properly prepared' to comply with the Act. A copy of any such accounts of a public company (with any auditors' statement) must be delivered to the Registrar for filing.

6.5 Infringement of dividend rules

FAST FORWARD

> In certain situations the **directors** and **members** may be liable to make good to the company the amount of an **unlawful dividend**.

If a dividend is paid otherwise than out of distributable profits the company, the **directors and** the **shareholders** may be involved in making good the unlawful distribution.

The directors are held **responsible** since they either recommend to members in general meeting that a dividend should be declared or they declare interim dividends.

(a) **The directors are liable if they declare a dividend which they know is paid out of capital**.

(b) **The directors are liable if, without preparing any accounts, they declare or recommend a dividend which proves to be paid out of capital**. It is their duty to satisfy themselves that profits are available.

(c) **The directors are liable if they make some mistake of law or interpretation of the constitution which leads them to recommend or declare an unlawful dividend**. However in such cases the directors may well be entitled to relief as their acts were performed 'honestly and reasonably'.

The directors may however **honestly** rely on proper accounts which disclose an apparent distributable profit out of which the dividend can properly be paid. They are not liable if it later appears that the assumptions or estimates used in preparing the accounts, although reasonable at the time, were in fact unsound.

The position of members is as follows.

- A member may obtain an **injunction** to restrain a company from paying an unlawful dividend.
- Members voting in general meeting **cannot authorise** the payment of an unlawful dividend nor release the directors from their liability to pay it back.
- The company can **recover from members** an **unlawful dividend** if the **members knew** or had **reasonable grounds** to believe that it was unlawful, s 847.
- If the directors have to make good to the company an unlawful dividend they may claim **indemnity from members** who at the time of receipt knew of the irregularity.
- Members knowingly receiving an unlawful dividend may **not bring an action** against the directors.

If an unlawful dividend is paid by **reason of error** in the **accounts** the company may be unable to claim against either the directors or the members. The company might then have a claim against its **auditors** if the undiscovered mistake was due to negligence on their part.

> *He London & General Bank (No 2) 1895*
>
> *The facts:* The auditor had drawn the attention of the directors to the fact that certain loans to associated companies were likely to prove irrecoverable. The directors refused to make any provision for these potential losses. They persuaded the auditor to confine his comments in his audit report to the uninformative statement that the value of assets shown in the balance sheet 'is dependent on realisation'. A dividend was paid in reliance on the apparent profits shown in the accounts. The company went into liquidation and the liquidator claimed from the auditor compensation for loss of capital due to his failure to report clearly to members what he well knew affecting the reliability of the accounts.
>
> *Decision:* The auditor has a duty to report what he knows of the true financial position: otherwise his audit is 'an idle farce'. He had failed in this duty and was liable.

Chapter Roundup

- The rules which dictate how a company is to manage and maintain its capital exist to maintain the delicate balance between the **members' enjoyment of limited liability** and the **creditors' requirements that the company shall remain able to pay its debts**.
- Reduction of capital can be achieved by: **extinguishing/reducing liability on partly-paid shares; cancelling paid-up share capital;** or **paying off part of paid up share capital**. Court confirmation is required for public companies. The court considers the interests of creditors and different classes of shareholder. There must be power in the articles and a special resolution.
- Specific rules govern the ability of private and public companies to **redeem** or **purchase** their shares.
- A **public** company may not give **financial assistance** to a third party to purchase shares in the company. A private company can do so.
- In issuing shares, a company must fix a **price** which is **equal** to or **more than** the **nominal value of the shares**. It may not allot shares at a discount to the nominal value.
- **Private** companies may issue shares for **inadequate consideration** provided the directors are behaving reasonably and honestly.
- There are **stringent rules** on consideration for shares in public companies.
- If shares are issued at a premium, the **excess** must be credited to a **share premium** account.
- Use of the share premium account is limited. It is most often used for **bonus issues**.
- Various rules have been created to ensure that dividends are only paid out of **available profits**.
- Distributable profits may be defined as 'accumulated realised profits ... less accumulated realised losses'. **'Accumulated'** means that any losses of previous years must be included in reckoning the current distributable surplus. **'Realised'** profits are determined in accordance with generally accepted accounting principles.
- A public company may only make a distribution if its **net assets** are, at the time, **not less than the aggregate of its called-up share capital and undistributable reserves**. It may only pay a dividend which will leave its net assets at not less than that aggregate amount.
- The profits available for distribution are generally determined from the **last annual accounts** to be prepared.
- In certain situations the **directors** and **members** may be liable to make good to the company the amount of an **unlawful dividend**.

PART H CAPITALISATION OF THE COMPANY

Quick Quiz

1 Where application is made to the court for confirmation of a reduction in capital, the court may require that creditors should be invited by advertisement to state their objections. In which of the following ways can the need to advertise be avoided?

   A   Paying off all creditors before application to the court.
   B   Producing a document signed by the directors stating the company's ability to pay its debts.
   C   Producing a guarantee from the company's bank that its existing debts will be paid in full.
   D   Renouncement by existing shareholders of their limited liability in relation to existing debts.

2 A share premium account can be used for bonus issues of shares or issue costs for new share issues.

   True ☐

   False ☐

3 **Fill in the blanks** in the statements below.

   Distributable profits may be defined as (1) .... profits less (2) .... losses.

4 If a company makes an unlawful dividend, who may be involved in making good the distribution?

   A   The company
   B   The directors
   C   The shareholders

5 Give four examples of undistributable reserves.

6 What normally are a company's relevant accounts in the context of payments of dividends?

Answers to Quick Quiz

1. A and C. The only guarantee that the courts will accept is from the company's bank.
2. True. Both are acceptable uses for the share premium account.
3. (1) accumulated realised (2) accumulated realised
4. All three may be liable.
5.
   1. Share premium account
   2. Capital redemption reserve
   3. A surplus of accumulated unrealised profits over accumulated unrealised losses (revaluation reserve)
   4. Any reserve which the company is prohibited from distributing by statute or by its constitution or any law
6. The relevant accounts are the last accounts to have been prepared and laid in general meeting.

End of chapter question

Maintenance of share capital

Discuss the rules in the Companies Act 2006 relating to the maintenance of share capital.   **(20 marks)**

PART H CAPITALISATION OF THE COMPANY

The administration and control of the company

Meetings and resolutions

Topic list	Syllabus reference
1 The importance of meetings to members	3.4
2 Types of company meetings	3.4
3 Types of resolution	3.4
4 Procedure for calling a general meeting	3.4
5 Proceedings at meetings	3.4
6 Class meetings	3.4
7 Single member private companies	3.4

Introduction

So far in our study of company law, we have seen what companies are and how they are financed. This chapter is the first of three which examine how companies are **controlled** and **managed**.

We shall consider the **procedures** by which companies are controlled by the shareholders, namely general meetings and resolutions. These afford members a measure of protection of their investment in the company. There are many transactions which, under the Act, cannot be entered into without a **resolution** of the company.

Moreover, a general meeting at which the annual accounts and the auditor's and directors' reports will be laid must normally be held by public companies annually. This affords the members an opportunity of questioning the directors on their **stewardship**.

We shall see throughout this chapter that **meetings are vital for members** because they are the main vehicle for getting their views heard, having an input into the running of the company and for controlling directors. For these reasons, they have the **power to requisition a meeting** of the company providing certain criteria are met. They have the **power to requisition resolutions** to be voted on as well.

The **Companies Act 2006**, (TSO, 2006) and the **Small Business, Enterprise and Employment Act 2015**, (TSO, 2015) apply to this and all chapters unless otherwise stated.

PART I   THE ADMINISTRATION AND CONTROL OF THE COMPANY

1 The importance of meetings to members

FAST FORWARD

Although the management of a company is in the hands of the directors, the **decisions which affect the existence of the company**, its structure and scope are **reserved to the members** in general meeting.

It is important to realise that company meetings are not just an exercise in bureaucracy, or for ticking a corporate governance box. They are the main vehicle for the **members** of the company to **express their views** on how the company is being run and to **hold the directors to account** where they are not happy with their management. Meetings also allow members **resolve differences** between themselves. Some key purposes of meetings are as follows.

1.1 Making important company decisions

The main purpose of meetings is to make important decisions in regards the running of the company. Decisions are taken at meetings through **resolutions**. A resolution is simply a statement that is voted on my members. They are usually listed in the agenda for the meeting so members have an opportunity to consider how they will vote beforehand. An example of a resolution might be "Resolution 1: To re-appoint XYZ LLP as company auditor".

It is important to note that the decisions taken at meetings are not in connection with the day-to-day running of the business because that role is delegated to the directors. Instead, company meetings are used to make the **most important decisions** (such as changing the company's name, approving the financial statements or removing auditors) that require the consent of the members.

Under the Companies Act 2006 (TSO, 2006), the decision of a general meeting is only valid and binding if the meeting is **properly convened** by notice and if the **business** of the meeting is **fairly** and **properly conducted**. Most of the rules on company meetings are concerned with the issue of notices and the casting of votes at meetings to carry resolutions of specified types.

1.2 Controlling directors

The members in general meeting can **exercise control over the directors**, though only to a limited extent. The ability to control directors is a key reason why it is important for members to have the ability to **requisition company meetings** (see below) even if the directors do not wish to convene one themselves.

The main power members have over directors is the ability to remove them from office by passing an **ordinary resolution**, s.168. They also have the power to appoint new directors through the same procedure.

Members also have a degree of control over the actions of directors because their approval is required if the directors wish to:

- **Exceed their delegated power** or to use it for other than its given purpose.
- **Allot shares** (unless private company with one class of shares).
- **Make a substantial contract** of sale or purchase with a director.
- Grant a director a **long-service agreement**.

1.3 Power of members to requisition a meeting

We shall later that meetings are usually called by the directors of a company. However, it is important to realise that members, of both private and public companies, have the ability to **requisition a meeting**. This means that rather than the members calling the meeting themselves, they can (under the Companies Act 2006) require the directors to convene a general meeting: s 303. If members requisition a meeting, it is common for them to also **requisition a resolution** or **resolutions,** to be voted on as well (see below).

15: MEETINGS AND RESOLUTIONS

Rules for members requisitioning a general meeting (s 303)	
Shareholding	• The requisitioning members must hold at least **5%** of the **paid up share capital** holding **voting rights**.
Requisition	• They must deposit a **signed requisition** at the registered office or make the request in electronic form. • This must state the 'objects of the meeting': the **resolutions proposed** (s 303(4)).
Date	• A notice conveying the meeting must be sent out within **21 days** of the requisition. • It must be held within **28 days** of the notice calling to a meeting being sent out. • If the directors have not called the meeting within 21 days of the requisition, the **members may convene** the meeting for a date within three months of the deposit of the requisition.
Quorum	• If **no quorum** is present, the meeting is **adjourned**.

1.4 Power of members to requisition a resolution

The directors normally have the **right to decide** what resolutions will be voted on at a company meeting. However, apart from the right to requisition a general meeting, members can also take the initiative to requisition certain resolutions be considered at any general meeting, or at the company's annual general meeting (AGM).

Rules for members requisitioning a resolution at the AGM	
Qualifying holding s 338	• The members must represent 5% of the voting rights, or • Be at least 100 members holding shares with an average paid up of £100, per member.
Request s 338	• Must be in hard copy or electronic form, identify the resolution and be delivered at least six weeks in advance of an AGM or other general meeting.
Statement s 314	• Members may request a statement (<1,000 words) be circulated to all members by delivering a **requisition**. Members with a qualifying holding may request a statement regarding their own resolution or any resolution proposed at the meeting. • The company must send the statement with the notice of the meeting or as soon as practicable after.

In either instance, the **requisitionists** must bear the incidental costs unless the company resolves otherwise.

We shall see later how **members of a private company may also requisition a written resolution** of the company rather than having to requisition a general meeting and then a resolution for that meeting.

Having seen how resolutions are used to control a company, we shall now look at the two types of company meeting at which they are voted on.

Exam focus point

The right of members to have resolutions included on the agenda of AGM or other meetings is asked frequently in law assessments. It is an **important consideration if some of the members disagree with the directors**.

2 Types of company meeting

FAST FORWARD

There are two kinds of general meeting of members of a company:
- Annual general meeting (AGM)
- General meetings at other times

2.1 Annual general meeting (AGM)

The **AGM** plays a major role in the life of a public company although often the business carried out seems fairly routine. It is a statutorily protected way for members to have a regular assessment and discussion of their company and its management.

Under the Companies Act 2006 (TSO, 2006), **private companies** are **not required** to have an **AGM** each year and therefore their business is usually conducted through **written resolutions**. However, members holding sufficient shares or votes can requisition a general meeting or written resolution.

Rules for directors calling an AGM	
Timing s 336	• Public companies must hold an AGM within **six months** of their year end.
Notice s 337	• Must be in **writing** and in **accordance** with the **articles**. • May be in **hard** or **electronic form** and may also by means of a **website** (s 308). • At least **21 days' notice** should be given; a longer period may be specified in the articles. • Shorter notice is only **valid** if all members agree. • The notice must specify the **time**, **date** and **place** of the meeting and that the meeting is an AGM. • Where notice is given on a **website** it must be available from the **date of notification** until the **conclusion of the meeting** (s 309).

The business of an annual general meeting usually includes:

- Considering the accounts
- Receiving the directors' report, the directors' remuneration report and the auditors' report
- Dividends
- Electing directors
- Appointing auditors

2.2 General meetings at other times

Apart from **members requisitioning** a general meeting, or the **directors invoking their power** in the **articles** to call a general meeting whenever they see fit, a general meeting must be held in the following circumstances.

2.2.1 Court order

The court, on the application of a director or a member entitled to vote, may order that a meeting shall be held and may give instructions for that purpose including fixing a quorum of one: s 306.

This is a method of last resort to resolve a deadlock such as the refusal of one member out of two to attend (and provide a quorum) at a general meeting.

2.2.2 Auditor requisition

An auditor who gives a statement of circumstances for their resignation or other loss of office in their written notice may also requisition a meeting to receive and consider their explanation: s 518.

2.2.3 Loss of capital by public company

The directors of a public company must convene a general meeting if the net assets fall to half or less of the amount of its called-up share capital: s 656.

In the next section we shall consider the two types of resolution that are used to make corporate decisions.

3 Types of resolution

FAST FORWARD

A meeting can pass two types of resolution. **Ordinary resolutions** are carried by a simple majority (more than 50%) of votes cast and require 14 days' notice to be given to members. **Special resolutions** require a 75% majority of votes cast and also 14 days' notice to members.

Under the Companies Act 2006 (TSO, 2006), a meeting reaches a decision by passing a resolution (either by a show of hands or a poll). There are **two major kinds** of resolution, and an additional one for **private** companies.

Types of resolution	
Ordinary (s 282)	For most business. Requires simple (50%+) majority of the votes cast by those entitled to vote. 14 days' notice.
Special (s 283)	For major changes. Requires 75% majority of the votes cast by those entitled to vote. 14 days' notice.
Written (for private companies)	Can be used for all general meeting resolutions except for removing a director or auditor before their term of office expires. Either a simple (50%+) or 75% majority of total voting rights of eligible members is required depending on the business being passed.

3.1 Differences between ordinary and special resolutions

Apart from the required size of the majority, the main differences between the types of resolution are as follows.

(a) The **text** of **special resolutions** must be **set out** in **full** in the notice convening the meeting, and it must be described as a special resolution. This is not necessary for an ordinary resolution if it is routine business.

(b) A **signed copy** of every **special resolution** must be **delivered** to the **Registrar** for filing. Although **some ordinary resolutions**, particularly those relating to share capital, have to be **delivered** for filing, many do not.

3.2 Special resolutions

A special resolution is required for **major changes** in the company such as the following.

- A change of name
- Restriction of the objects or other alteration of the articles
- Reduction of share capital
- Winding up the company
- Presenting a petition by the company for an order for a compulsory winding up

Question

Notice period

The period of notice for a general meeting (not an AGM) at which a special resolution is proposed is:

A 14 days
B 21 days
C 28 days
D 42 days

Answer

A   A general meeting at which a special resolution is proposed requires 14 days' notice.

3.3 Written resolutions

FAST FORWARD: A private company can pass any decision needed by a **written resolution**, except for removing a director or auditor before their term of office has expired.

As we saw earlier, a private company is **not** required to hold an **AGM**. Therefore the Act provides a mechanism for directors and members to conduct business solely by **written resolution**.

3.3.1 Written resolutions proposed by directors

Copies of the resolution proposed by directors must be sent to **each member** eligible to vote by hard copy, electronically or by a website. Alternatively, the same copy may be sent to each member in turn.

The resolution should be accompanied by a statement informing the member:

- How to **signify their agreement** to the resolution.
- The **date** the resolution must be passed by.

3.3.2 Written resolutions proposed by members

Members holding 5% (or lower if authorised by the articles) of the **voting rights** may request a written resolution providing it:

- **Would be effective** (not prevented by the articles or law).
- Is **not defamatory, frivolous** or **vexatious**.

A **statement** containing no more than **1,000 words** on the subject of the resolution may accompany it.

Copies of the resolution, and statements containing information on the subject matter, how to agree to it and the date of the resolution must be sent to each member within **21 days** of the request for resolution.

Expenses for circulating the resolution **should be met by the members** who requested it unless the company resolves otherwise.

The company may **appeal to the court** not to circulate the 1,000 word statement by the members if the rights provided to the members are being abused by them.

3.3.3 Agreement

The members may indicate their agreement to the resolution in **hard copy** or **electronically**. If no **period for agreement** is specified by the articles, then the default period is **28 days** from the date the resolution was circulated. Agreement after this period is ineffective. Once agreed, a member **may not revoke** their decision.

Either a **simple** (50%+) or **75% majority** is required to pass a written resolution depending on the nature of the business being decided.

Three further points should be noted concerning written resolutions.

(a) Written resolutions can be used **notwithstanding any provisions** in the company's **articles**.

(b) A written resolution **cannot** be **used to remove a director or auditor** from office, since such persons have a right to **speak** at a **meeting**.

(c) **Copies of written resolutions** should be **sent to auditors** at or before the time they are sent to shareholders. Auditors do not have the right to object to written resolutions. If the auditors are not sent a copy, the resolution remains valid; however the directors and secretary will be liable to a fine. The purpose of this provision is to ensure auditors are kept informed about what is happening in the company.

Question

Resolutions

Briefly explain the main features of the following types of resolution which may be passed at a general meeting of a company:

(a) An ordinary resolution
(b) A special resolution

Answer

(a) Ordinary resolutions require a simple majority of votes cast (ie over 50%). 14 days' notice is sufficient. Ordinary resolutions of a routine nature need not be set out in full in the notice of an annual general meeting, and most ordinary resolutions need not be filed with the Registrar.

(b) Special resolutions require a 75% majority of votes cast and also require 14 days' notice of the intention to propose such a resolution. The full text of the resolution should be set out in the notice.

Having seen the types of resolution and meeting that can be used to make decisions, we shall now turn our attention to the formalities involved in calling a meeting. Meetings do not just happen on their own. They must be properly convened in accordance with the Companies Act or any decisions made will not be valid.

4 Procedure for calling a general meeting

FAST FORWARD

A meeting cannot make valid and binding decisions until it has been properly convened. Notice of general meetings must be given at least **14 days** in advance of the meeting. The notice should contain **adequate information** about the meeting.

Meetings must be called by a **competent person** or authority.

Under the Companies Act 2006 (TSO, 2006), a meeting cannot make valid and binding decisions until it has been properly convened according to the company's articles, though there are also statutory rules.

(a) The meeting must generally be **called by** the **board of directors** or other competent person or authority.

(b) The notice must be issued to members in advance of the meeting so as to give them **14 days'** 'clear notice' of the meeting. The members may agree to waive or increase this requirement (see below).

(c) The **notice** must be sent to every member (or other person) entitled to receive the notice.

(d) The notice must include any information **reasonably necessary** to enable shareholders to know in advance what is to be done.

(e) As we saw earlier members may require the directors to call a meeting if:

(i) They hold at least **5% of the voting rights**.

(ii) They provide a **statement of the general business** to be conducted and the text of any proposed resolution.

The directors must within **21 days call a meeting** to be held no later than **28 days from the date of the notice** they send calling the meeting.

An example of a rule in the articles as opposed to statute states that 21 days' notice must be given of a general meeting called for the purpose of considering the board's appointment of a director, or at which a special resolution is being considered.

In most cases the notice need **not** be sent to a member whose only shares do not give them a right to attend and vote (as is often the position of **preference shareholders**).

4.1 Electronic communication

Notice may be given by means of a **website** and in **electronic form** (s 308). Section 333 extends this by deeming that where a company gives an **electronic address** in a notice calling a meeting, any information or document relating to the meeting may be sent to that address.

4.2 Timing of notices

> **FAST FORWARD** — **Clear notice** must be given to members. **Notice** must be **sent to all members** entitled to receive it.

Members may – and in small private companies often do – waive the required notice. For **short notice** to be effective:

(a) **All members** of a public company must consent in respect of an **AGM**.

(b) In **any other case**, a **majority of members** in a private company who hold at least **90%** of the **issued shares** or voting rights must consent. 95% is required by a public company: s 307.

The following specific rules by way of exception should be remembered.

- When **special notice** of a resolution is given to the company in the two circumstances mentioned below, it must be given **28 days** in advance as prescribed.

- In a **creditors' voluntary winding up** there must be at least **seven days' notice** of the **creditors' meeting** (to protect the interests of creditors). The members may shorten the period of notice down to seven days but that is all: s 98 Insolvency Act.

The **clear days rule** in s 360 provides that the day of the meeting and the day the notice was given are **excluded** from the required notice period.

4.3 Special notice of a resolution

> **FAST FORWARD** — **Special notice of 28 days** of intention to propose certain resolutions (removal of directors/auditors) must be given.

Key term

> **Special notice** is notice of 28 days which must be given to a company of the intention to put certain types of resolution at a company meeting.

Special notice must be given **to the company** of the intention to propose a resolution for any of the following purposes.

- To **remove** an **auditor** or to **appoint** an **auditor other** than the **auditor** who was **appointed** at the **previous year's meeting**.

- To **remove a director from office** or to appoint a substitute in their place after removal.

A member may request a resolution to be passed at a particular meeting. In this case, the **member must give special notice** of their intention **to the company** at **least 28 days** before the date of the meeting. If, however, the company calls the meeting for a date less than 28 days after receiving the special notice that notice is deemed to have been **properly given**.

On receiving special notice a **public company may be obliged** to **include the resolution** in the **AGM notice** which it issues.

If the company gives notice to members of the resolution it does so by a **21 day notice** to them that special notice has been received and what it contains. If it is not practicable to include the matter in the notice of meeting, the company may give notice to members by newspaper advertisement or any other means permitted by the articles.

Where special notice is received of intention to propose a resolution for the removal of a director or to change the auditor, the company must send a copy to the **director** or **auditor**. This is to allow them to exercise their statutory right to defend themself by issuing a memorandum and/or addressing the meeting in person.

The essential point is that a **special notice is given to the company**; it is **not a notice from the company to members** although it will be followed (usually) by such notice.

4.4 Content of notices

FAST FORWARD

The **notice** convening the meeting must give certain details. The **date**, **time** and **place** of the meeting, and identification of AGM and special resolutions. Sufficient information about the business to be discussed at the meeting should be provided to enable shareholders to know what is to be done.

The notice of a general meeting must contain adequate information on the following points.

(a) The **date**, **time** and **place** of the meeting must be given.
(b) An **AGM** or a **special resolution** must be described as such.
(c) Information must be given of the business of the meeting **sufficient** to enable members (in deciding whether to attend or to appoint proxies) to **understand what will be done** at the meeting.

4.4.1 Routine business

In issuing the notice of an AGM it is standard practice merely to list the **items of ordinary or routine business** to be transacted, such as the following.

- Declaration of dividends (if any)
- Election of directors
- Appointment of auditors and fixing of their remuneration

The articles usually include a requirement that members shall be informed of any intention to **propose** the **election** of a director, other than an existing director who retires by rotation and merely stands for re-election.

Question — Removal of a director

How can members remove a director from office? What is the significance of special notice in this context?

Answer

A company may by ordinary resolution remove any director from office, notwithstanding any provision to the contrary in the articles or in a contract such as a director's service agreement.

However, this procedure requires that special notice shall be given to the company at least 28 days before the meeting of the intention to propose such a resolution. Moreover, the directors are not required to include the resolution in the notice of the meeting unless the person who intends to propose it has a sufficient shareholding.

If a company receives special notice it must send a copy to the director concerned who has the right to have written representations of reasonable length circulated to members. They may also speak before the resolution is put to the vote at the meeting.

Question — General meeting

When is a public company compelled to call a general meeting?

Answer

Members of a company who hold not less than 5% of the company's paid up share capital carrying voting rights, or members representing 5% of the voting rights, may requisition the holding of a general meeting. The directors are then required within 21 days to issue a notice convening the meeting to transact the business specified in the requisition. This must be within 28 days.

An auditor who resigns giving reasons for their resignation may requisition a general meeting so that they may explain to members the circumstances of their resignation.

If the net assets of a public company are reduced to less than half in value of its called-up share capital, the directors must convene a general meeting to consider what, if any, steps should be taken.

The court has statutory power in certain circumstances to direct that a meeting shall be held.

Once a meeting has be properly convened, it must proceed in accordance with the Companies Act. As with calling a meeting, any decision taken at a meeting which did not proceed correctly may be invalidated.

5 Proceedings at meetings

5.1 How a meeting proceeds

FAST FORWARD — Company meetings need to be properly run if they are to be **effective** and within the **law**.

Under the Companies Act 2006 (TSO, 2006), a meeting can only reach binding decisions if:

- It has been properly **convened** by notice.
- A **quorum is present**.
- A **chair presides**.
- The **business** is **properly transacted** and **resolutions** are **put to the vote**.

There is no obligation to allow a member to be present if their shares do not carry the right to attend and vote. However **full general meetings** and **class meetings** can be held when shareholders not entitled to vote are present.

Each **item of business** comprised in the notice should be taken separately, discussed and **put to the vote**.

Members may propose **amendments** to any resolutions proposed. The chair should reject any amendment which is outside the limits set by the notice convening the meeting.

If the relevant business is an **ordinary resolution** it may be possible to amend the resolution's wording so as to **reduce its effect** to something less (provided that the change does not entirely alter its character). For example, an ordinary resolution authorising the directors to borrow £100,000 might be amended to substitute a limit of £50,000 (but not to increase it to £150,000 as £100,000 would have been stated in the notice).

5.2 The chair

FAST FORWARD — The meeting should usually be chaired by the **chair** of the board of directors. They do not necessarily have a casting vote.

The articles usually provide that the **chair** of the board of directors **is to preside** at general meetings; in their absence another director chosen by the directors shall preside instead. In the last resort a member chosen by the members present can preside.

The chair derives their authority from the articles and they have **no casting vote unless** the **articles give them one**. Their duties are to **maintain order** and to **deal** with the **agenda** in a methodical way so that the business of the meeting may be properly transacted.

The chair:

- **May dissolve** or **adjourn** the **meeting** if it has become disorderly or if the members present agree.
- Must **adjourn** if the meeting **instructs** them to do so.

5.3 Quorum and proxies

FAST FORWARD

The **quorum** for meetings may be two or more (except for single member private companies). **Proxies** can attend, speak and vote on behalf of members.

Key term

A **quorum** is the minimum number of persons required to be present at a particular type of (company) meeting. In the case of shareholders' meetings, the figure is usually two, in person or by proxy, but the articles may make other provisions.

There is a legal principle that a 'meeting means a coming together of more than one person'. Hence it follows that as a matter of law **one person generally cannot be a meeting**.

The rule that at least two persons must be present to constitute a 'meeting' does not require that both persons must be members. Every member has a **statutory right to appoint a proxy** to attend as their representative.

In theory, **ultimate control** over a company's business lies with the **members** in a **general meeting**. One would obviously conclude that a meeting involved more than one person, and indeed there is authority to that effect in *Sharp v Dawes 1876*. In this case a meeting between a lone member and the company secretary was held not to be validly constituted. It is possible, however, for a meeting of only one person to take place and we shall consider this shortly.

Attention!

In single member private companies there is an inconsistency in the model articles in regards to quorum. Article 7(2) provides that where a company has one director and the company's articles do not require it to have more than one director then the sole director may take decisions "without regard to any of the provisions of the articles relating to directors' decision-making". This is in conflict with Article 11(2) which provides that the quorum cannot be less than two and that unless otherwise fixed, the default quorum is two directors.

This issue has been raised in two cases and the recommendation now is for single member private companies with default model articles to amend the articles to change their quorum to one.

5.3.1 Proxies

Key term

A **proxy** is a person appointed by a shareholder to vote on behalf of that shareholder at company meetings.

Any member of a company which has a share capital, provided they are entitled to attend and vote at a general or class meeting of the company, has a statutory right (s 324) to appoint an **agent**, called a **'proxy'**, to attend and vote for them.

Rules for appointing proxies	
Basic rule	• Any **member** may appoint a proxy. • The proxy **does not** have to be a member. • Proxies **may speak** at the meeting. • A member may **appoint more than one proxy** provided each proxy is appointed in respect of a different class of share held by the member.

Rules for appointing proxies	
Voting	• Proxies **may vote** on **poll** and on a **show of hands**. • Proxies may **demand a poll** at a meeting. • Most companies provide **two-way proxy cards** that the member can use to instruct a proxy how to vote, either for or against a resolution.
Notice	• Every notice of a meeting must **state** the member's right to a proxy. • **Notice** of a proxy appointment should be given to the company at least 48 hours before the meeting (excluding weekends and bank holidays).

Hence one member and another member's proxy may together provide the quorum (if it is fixed, as is usual, at 'two members present in person or by proxy'). However one member who is also the proxy appointed by another member cannot by themselves be a meeting, since a **minimum of two individuals** present is required.

There may, however, be a meeting attended by one person only, if:

(a) It is a **class meeting** and all the **shares** of that class are **held** by **one member.**

(b) The **court**, in exercising a power to order a general meeting to be held, **fixes** the **quorum** at one. This means that in a two-member company, a meeting can be held with one person if the other deliberately absents themself to frustrate business.

(c) The company is a **single member private company**.

The articles usually fix a **quorum** for general meetings which may be as low as two (the minimum for a meeting) but may be more – though this is unusual.

If the articles do fix a quorum of two or more persons present, the meeting lacks a quorum (it is said to be an 'inquorate' meeting) if either:

- The **required number** is **not present** within a **stipulated time** (usually half an hour) of the appointed time for commencing a meeting.
- The **meeting begins** with a **quorum** but the **number present dwindles** to less than the quorum – unless the articles provide for this possibility.

The articles usually provide for automatic and compulsory **adjournment of an inquorate meeting**.

The articles can provide that a meeting which begins with a quorum may continue despite a reduction in numbers present to less than the quorum level. However, there must still be **two or more persons present**.

5.4 Voting and polls

FAST FORWARD Voting at general meetings may be on a **show of hands** or a **poll**.

The **rights of members** to **vote** and the **number of votes** to which they are entitled in respect of their shares are fixed by the **articles**.

One vote per share is normal but some shares, for instance preference shares, may carry no voting rights in normal circumstances. To shorten the proceedings at meetings the procedure is as follows.

5.4.1 Voting on a show of hands

Key term A **show of hands** is a method of voting for or against a resolution by raising hands. Under this method each member has one vote irrespective of the number of shares held, in contrast to a poll vote.

On putting a resolution to the vote the chair calls for a show of hands. One vote may be given by each member present in person, including proxies.

Unless a poll is then demanded, the chair's declaration of the result is **conclusive**. However, it is still possible to challenge the chair's declaration on the grounds that it was fraudulent or manifestly wrong.

5.4.2 Voting on a poll

Key term

A **poll** is a method of voting at company meetings which allows a member to use as many votes as their shareholding grants them.

If a **real test of voting strength** is required a poll may be demanded. The result of the previous show of hands is then disregarded. On a poll every member and also proxies representing absent members may cast the full number of votes to which they are entitled. A poll need not be held at the time but may be postponed so that arrangements to hold it can be made.

A poll may be **demanded** by:

- Not **less than five members** having the right to vote on the resolution.
- Member(s) **representing** not less than **10%** of the **total voting rights**.
- Member(s) **holding shares** which **represent** not less than **10%** of the **paid-up capital**.

Any provision in the articles is **void** if it seeks to prevent such members demanding a poll or to exclude the right to demand a poll on any question other than the election of a chair by the meeting or an adjournment: s 321.

When a poll is held it is usual to appoint **'scrutineers'** and to ask members and proxies to sign voting cards or lists. The votes cast are checked against the register of members and the chair declares the result.

Members of a quoted company may require the directors to obtain an **independent report** in respect of a poll taken, or to be taken, at a general meeting if:

- They represent at least 5% of the voting rights, or
- Are at least 100 in number holding at least £100 of paid up capital: s 342.

5.4.3 Result of a vote

In voting, either by show of hands or on a poll, the **number of votes cast determines the result**. Votes which are not cast, whether the member who does not use them is present or absent, are simply disregarded. Hence the majority vote may be much less than half (or three quarters) of the total votes which could be cast.

Results of quoted company polls of must be made available on a **website**. The following information should be made available as soon as **reasonably practicable**, and should remain on the website for at least **two years**.

- Meeting date
- Text of the resolution or description of the poll's subject matter
- Number of votes for and against the resolution

5.5 Minutes of company meetings

FAST FORWARD

Minutes must be kept of all **general, directors'** and **management meetings**, and members can inspect those of general meetings.

Key term

Minutes are a record of the proceedings of meetings. Company law requires minutes to be kept of all company meetings including general, directors' and managers' meetings.

Every company is **required to keep minutes** which are a formal written record of the proceedings of its general meetings for ten years: s 355. These minutes are usually kept in **book form**. If a loose-leaf book is used to facilitate typing there should be safeguards against falsification, such as sequential prenumbering.

The chair **normally signs** the minutes. If they does so, the signed minutes are admissible evidence of the proceedings, though evidence may be given to contradict or supplement the minutes or to show that no meeting at all took place.

Members of the company have the **right to inspect** minutes of general meetings. The minutes of general meetings must be held at the **registered office** or the **single alternative inspection location (SAIL)** and be available for inspection by members, who are also entitled to demand copies.

5.6 The assent principle

A unanimous decision of the members is often treated as a substitute for a formal decision in general meeting properly convened and held, and is equally binding.

We saw in our study of share capital that meetings of different classes of share may be called, for example to approve a variation of class rights. In this next section we shall consider some rules that concern them.

6 Class meetings

> **FAST FORWARD**
>
> **Class meetings** are held where the interests of different groups of shareholders may be affected in different ways.

6.1 Types of class meeting

Under the Companies Act 2006 (TSO, 2006), class meetings are of two kinds.

(a) If the company has more than one class of share, for example if it has 'preference' and 'ordinary' shares, it may be necessary to call a meeting of the holders of one class of shares, to approve a proposed **variation** of the **rights** attached to their shares.

(b) Under a **compromise** or **arrangements with creditors** (s 895), the holders of shares of the same class may nonetheless be divided into **separate** classes if the scheme proposed will affect each group differently.

When separate meetings of a class of members are held, the same procedural rules as for general meetings apply (but there is a different rule on quorum).

6.2 Quorum for a class meeting

The standard general meeting rules, on issuing notices and on voting, apply to a class meeting.

However, the **quorum** for a class meeting is fixed at two persons who hold, or represent by proxy, at least **one third** in nominal value of the issued shares of the class (unless the class only consists of a single member).

If no quorum is present, the meeting is **adjourned** (under the standard adjournment procedure for general meetings). When the meeting resumes, the quorum is **one** person (who must still hold at least one third of the shares).

Having considered the rules on meetings that involve more than one individual, in the section below we shall see how the Companies Act treats companies that have a single member.

7 Single member private companies

> **FAST FORWARD**
>
> There are **special rules** for **private companies** with only **one shareholder**.

Under the Companies Act 2006 (TSO, 2006), if the sole member takes any decision that could have been taken in general meeting, that member shall (unless it is a written resolution) provide the company with a **written record** of it. This allows the sole member to conduct members' business informally without notice or minutes.

Filing requirements still apply, for example, in the case of alteration of articles.

Written resolutions **cannot** be used to remove a director or auditor from office as these resolutions require special notice.

Chapter Roundup

- Although the management of a company is in the hands of the directors, the **decisions which affect the existence of the company**, its structure and scope are **reserved to the members** in general meeting.
- There are two kinds of general meeting of members of a company:
  - **Annual general meeting (AGM)**
  - **General meetings at other times**
- A meeting can pass two types of resolution. **Ordinary resolutions** are carried by a simple majority (more than 50%) of votes cast and require 14 days' notice to be given to members. **Special resolution**s require a 75% majority of votes cast and also 14 days' notice to members.
- A private company can pass any decision needed by a **written resolution**, except for removing a director or auditor before their term of office has expired.
- A meeting cannot make valid and binding decisions until it has been properly convened. Notice of general meetings must be given **14 days'** in advance of the meeting. The notice should contain adequate information about the meeting.
- Meetings must be called by a **competent person** or authority.
- **Clear notice** must be given to members. **Notice** must be **sent to all members** entitled to receive it.
- **Special notice of 28 days** of intention to propose resolutions for removal of directors/auditors must be given.
- The **notice** convening the meeting must give certain details. The **date**, **time** and **place** of the meeting, and identification of AGM and special resolutions. Sufficient information about the business to be discussed at the meeting should be provided to enable shareholders to know what is to be done.
- Company meetings need to be properly run if they are to be **effective** and within the **law**.
- The meeting should usually be chaired by the **chair** of the board of directors. They do not necessarily have a casting vote.
- The **quorum** for meetings may be two or more (except for single member private companies). **Proxies** can attend, speak and vote on behalf of members.
- Voting at general meetings may be on a **show of hands** or a **poll**.
- **Minutes** must be kept of all **general, directors'** and **management meetings**, and members can inspect those of general meetings.
- **Class meetings** are held where the interests of different groups of shareholders may be affected in different ways.
- There are **special rules** for **private companies** with only **one shareholder**.

Quick Quiz

1. Which of the following decisions can only be taken by the members in general meeting?

    A   Alteration of articles
    B   Change of name
    C   Reduction of capital
    D   Appointment of a managing director

2. Before a private company can hold a general meeting on short notice, members holding a certain percentage of the company's shares must agree. Which one of the following percentages is correct?

51%	90%
75%	95%

3. A plc must hold its AGM within six months of its year end.

    True ☐

    False ☐

4. Minutes of company meetings must be kept for

    A   One year
    B   Five years
    C   Ten years
    D   Fifteen years

5. A member of a public company may only appoint one proxy, but the proxy has a statutory right to speak at the meeting.

    True ☐

    False ☐

Answers to Quick Quiz

1. A, B and C. The board can appoint someone to be managing director, so D is incorrect.
2. 90%.
3. True. A plc must hold its AGM within six months of its year end.
4. C. Under s 355, minutes must be kept for ten years.
5. False. Public company members can appoint more than one proxy. They have a statutory right to speak.

End of chapter question

Resolutions

Discuss the different types of resolution which members of a private company can pass and explain the procedure for passing each of these types of resolution. **(20 marks)**

PART I THE ADMINISTRATION AND CONTROL OF THE COMPANY

Company directors and other company officers

Topic list	Syllabus reference
1 The role of directors	3.4
2 Appointment of directors	3.4
3 Remuneration of directors	3.4
4 Vacation of office	3.4
5 Disqualification of directors	3.4
6 Powers of directors	3.4
7 Agency law and the authority of directors	3.4
8 Duties of directors	3.4
9 The company secretary	3.4

Introduction

In this second chapter on how companies are controlled, we turn our attention to those people charged with running the business on a day-to-day basis – the **directors** and **company secretary**.

We shall firstly study the **appointment** and **removal**, and the **powers, authority and duties, of the directors**.

The important principle to grasp is that the **extent of directors' powers is defined by the articles**.

If **shareholders** do not approve of the directors' acts they must either **remove them** under s 168 or **alter the articles** to regulate their future conduct. However, they **cannot** simply **take over** the functions of the directors.

In essence, the directors act as **agents of the company**. This ties in with the **agency** part of your law studies that we saw previously. The different types of authority a director can have are important in this area.

We also consider the **duties** of directors under statute and **remedies for the breach of such duties**.

Statute also imposes some duties on directors, specifically concerning openness when transacting with the company.

Finally, we look at the duties and powers of the **company secretary**.

The **Companies Act 2006**, (TSO, 2006) and the **Small Business, Enterprise and Employment Act 2015**, (TSO, 2015) apply to this and all chapters unless otherwise stated.

PART I   THE ADMINISTRATION AND CONTROL OF THE COMPANY

1 The role of directors

> **FAST FORWARD**
>
> Any person who occupies the position of director is treated as such, the test being one of **function**.

Key term

> A **director** is a person who is responsible for the overall direction of the company's affairs. In company law, director means any person occupying the position of director, by whatever name called.

We begin our study of directors by considering what a director is and the role they have in the business.

Any person who occupies the position of director is treated as such. The test is one of **function**. The directors' function is to take part in **making decisions** by **attending meetings** of the board of directors. Anyone who does that is a director whatever they may be called.

A person who is given the title of director, such as 'sales director' or 'director of research', to give them status in the company structure is not a director in company law. This is unless by virtue of their appointment they are a **member** of the **board** of **directors**, or they carry out functions that would be properly discharged only by a director.

1.1 De jure and de facto directors

Most directors are **expressly appointed** by a company and are known as **de jure** directors. A **de facto** director is **anyone** who is **held out by a company** as a director, **performs the functions** of a director and is **treated by the board** as a director although they have **never been validly appointed**.

1.2 Shadow directors

A person might seek to **avoid the legal responsibilities of being a director** by avoiding appointment as such but using their power, say as a major shareholder, to manipulate the acknowledged board of directors. In other words they seek the **power** and **influence** that come with the position of director, but **without the legal obligations** it entails.

The **Small Business Enterprise and Employment Act 2015** (TSO, 2015) includes measures aimed at increasing transparency around who controls UK companies, and as a consequence, statutory rules relating to directors are extended to **shadow directors**. Shadow directors are directors for legal purposes if the board of directors are accustomed to act in **accordance with their directions** and **instructions**. This rule does **not** apply to **professional advisers** merely acting in that capacity.

1.2.1 Shadow directors and de facto directors

Shadow directors differ from de facto directors because the **public** (and the **authorities**) are **rarely aware of their existence**. Whereas a **de facto director performs the everyday tasks that a director would** (dealing with suppliers and customers and being present at general meetings), the shadow director exerts their influence away from the day-to-day running of the business.

1.3 Alternate directors

A director may, if the articles permit, appoint an **alternate director** to attend and vote for them at board meetings which they are unable to attend. Such an alternate may be another director, in which case they have the vote of the absentee as well as their own. More usually they are an outsider. Company articles could make specific provisions for this situation.

1.4 Executive directors

Key term

> An **executive director** is a director who performs a specific role in a company under a **service contract** which requires a regular, possibly daily, involvement in management.

A director may also be an **employee** of their company. Since the company is also their **employer** there is a potential conflict of interest which, in principle, a director is required to avoid.

To allow an individual to be **both a director and employee** the articles usually make express provision for it, but prohibit the director from voting at a board meeting on the terms of their own employment.

Directors who have additional management duties as employees may be distinguished by **special titles**, such as 'Finance Director'. However **any such title does not affect their personal legal position**. They have two distinct positions as:

- A member of the board of directors; and
- A manager with management responsibilities as an **employee**.

1.5 Non-executive directors

Key term

> A **non-executive director** does not have a function to perform in a company's management but is involved in its governance.

In **listed companies**, good corporate governance suggests that boards of directors are more likely to be fully effective if they comprise both **executive directors** and strong, independent **non-executive directors**. The main tasks of the NEDs are as follows:

- **Contribute** an **independent view** to the board's deliberations.
- **Help the board provide** the company with **effective leadership**.
- **Ensure** the **continuing effectiveness** of the **executive directors** and management.
- **Ensure high standards** of **financial probity** on the part of the company.

Non-executive and shadow directors are subject to the same duties as executive directors.

1.6 The Chief Executive Officer (Managing Director)

Key term

> A **Chief Executive Officer** (also commonly known as a **Managing Director**) is one of the directors of the company appointed to carry out overall day-to-day management operations.

Boards of directors usually appoint one director to be **Chief Executive Officer** (this position is also commonly known as **Managing Director**). A Chief Executive Officer (CEO) or Managing Director (MD) has a special position and has wider apparent powers than any director who is not appointed to that position.

1.7 Number of directors

Every company must have at least **one director**; for a **public company the minimum is two**. There is no statutory maximum in the UK, but the articles usually impose a limit. At least one director must be a natural person, not a body corporate.

1.8 The board of directors

Companies are run by the directors collectively, in a **board of directors**.

Key term

> The **board of directors** is the elected representative of the shareholders acting collectively in the management of a company's affairs.

One of the basic principles of company law is that the **powers** which are delegated to the directors under the articles are given to them as a **collective body**. The **board meeting** is the **proper place for the exercise of the powers**, unless they have been validly passed on, or 'sub-delegated', to committees or individual directors. In the event of deadlock at a board meeting, the Chair of the meeting has the casting vote.

1.9 The Chair

According to the **UK Corporate Governance Code**, a company's Chair is responsible for leading the board and ensuring its effectiveness. This is a very distinct role from that of the CEO/MD, who is responsible for leading the company's operations. In addition, the company Chair has a key role in relation to chairing company meetings, as we have also seen.

Having seen what a director is, we shall now look at how they are appointed into the role.

2 Appointment of directors

> **FAST FORWARD**
>
> The method of appointing directors, along with their rotation and co-option is **controlled** by the **articles**.

2.1 Appointment of first directors

The **application for registration** delivered to the Registrar to form a company includes particulars of the first directors, with their consents. On the formation of the company those persons become the first directors.

2.2 Appointment of subsequent directors

Under the Companies Act 2006 (TSO, 2006), once a company has been formed further directors can be appointed, either to **replace** existing directors or as **additional** directors.

Appointment of further directors is carried out **as the articles provide**. Most company articles allow for the appointment of directors:

- By **ordinary resolution** of the shareholders; and
- By a **decision** of the directors.

However the articles do not have to follow these provisions and may impose **different methods** on the company. For example, the Companies Act 2006 allows private companies to dispense with AGMs, so the board of a private company can appoint a director indefinitely.

When the appointment of directors is proposed at a general meeting of a public company a **separate** resolution should be proposed for the election of **each director**. However the rule may be waived if a resolution to that effect is first carried without any vote being given against it.

2.3 Publicity

In addition to giving notice of the first directors, every company must within **14 days** give **notice** to the **Registrar** of any change among its directors. This includes any changes to the register of directors' residential addresses.

2.4 Age limit

The **minimum age** limit for a director is **16** and, unless the articles provide otherwise, there is no upper limit.

Having seen how directors are appointed, we shall now think about how they are rewarded for performing the role. As we shall see, they are treated differently to ordinary employees.

3 Remuneration of directors

> **FAST FORWARD**
>
> Directors are entitled to **fees** and **expenses** as directors as per the articles, and **emoluments** (and compensation for loss of office) as per their service contracts (which can be inspected by members). Some details are published in the directors' remuneration report along with accounts.

3.1 Directors' service contracts

Details of directors' remuneration is usually contained within their **service contract**. This is a contract where the director agrees to personally perform services for the company. **Written service contracts** set out their entitlement to emoluments and expenses. Under the Companies Act 2006 (TSO, 2006), where service contracts **guarantee employment** for longer than **two years** then an **ordinary resolution** must be passed by the members of the company that the contract is with: s 188.

3.2 Directors' expenses

Most articles state that directors are entitled to **reimbursement** of **reasonable expenses** incurred while carrying out their duties or functions as directors.

3.3 Compensation for loss of office

Any director may receive **non-contractual** compensation for loss of office paid to them voluntarily. Any such compensation is lawful **only if** approved by members of the company in general meeting after proper disclosure has been made to all members, whether voting or not: s 217.

This only applies to uncovenanted payments; approval is not required where the company is contractually bound to make the payment.

Compensation paid to directors for loss of office is distinguished from any payments made to directors **as employees**, for example to settle claims arising from the premature termination of the service agreements. These are contractual payments which do not require approval in general meeting.

3.4 Directors' remuneration report

Quoted companies are required to include a **directors' remuneration report** as part of their annual report, part of which is subject to audit: s 420. Failure to produce the report is an offence. The report must cover:

- The details of each **individual directors' remuneration package**.
- The company's **remuneration policy**.
- The **role** of the **board** and **remuneration committee** in deciding the **remuneration** of **directors**.

Under s 421(3), it is the duty of the directors (including those who were a director in the preceding five years) to provide any information about themselves that is necessary to produce this report.

Quoted companies are required to allow a vote by members on the directors' remuneration report. The vote is purely advisory and does not mean the remuneration should change if the resolution is not passed. A negative vote would be a strong signal to the directors that the members are unhappy with remuneration levels.

Items not subject to audit

- Consideration by the directors (remuneration committee) of matters relating to directors' remuneration
- Statement of company's policy on directors' remuneration
- Performance graph (share performance)
- Directors' service contracts (dates, unexpired length, compensation payable for early termination)

Items subject to audit

- Salary/fees payable to each director
- Bonuses paid/to be paid
- Expenses
- Compensation for loss of office paid
- Any benefits received
- Share options and long term incentive schemes – performance criteria and conditions
- Pensions
- Excess retirement benefits
- Compensation to past directors
- Sums paid to third parties in respect of a director's services

3.5 Inspection of directors' service agreements

A company must make available for inspection by members a copy or particulars of **contracts of employment** between the company or a subsidiary with a director of the company. Such contracts must cover all services that a director may provide, including services outside the role of a director, and those made by a third party in respect of services that a director is contracted to perform.

Contracts must be **retained** for **one year** after expiry and must be available either at the **registered office**, or any other location permitted by the Secretary of State.

Prescribed particulars of **directors' emoluments** must be given in the accounts and also particulars of any **compensation for loss of office** and directors' **pensions**.

Directors do not remain in position for ever, at some point they will leave their position. In the next section we shall look at the various ways in which directors may leave office.

4 Vacation of office

> **FAST FORWARD**
>
> A director may vacate office as director due to: **resignation**; **not going** for **re-election**; **death**; **dissolution** of the company; **removal**; **disqualification**.

A director may leave office in the following ways.

- **Resignation**
- Not **offering themselves for re-election** when their term of office ends
- **Death**
- **Dissolution of the company**
- Being **removed** from office
- Being **disqualified**

A form should be filed with the Registrar whenever and however a director vacates office.

4.1 Retirement and re-election of directors

The Model articles for public companies provide the following rules for the **retirement and re-election** of all directors ('rotation') at AGMs.

(a) At the **first AGM** of the company **all directors shall retire**.
(b) At every subsequent AGM any **directors appointed by the other directors** since the **last AGM** shall retire.
(c) Directors who were **not appointed** or **re-elected at one of the preceding two AGMs** shall retire.

Directors who are **retired by rotation** are eligible to offer themselves for **re-election**. This mandatory retirement of directors provides another **control over their performance**. Rather than having to go through the process of seeking a resolution to remove a director, members have the opportunity every three years to dispose of an underperforming director by **simply not electing** them.

4.2 Removal of directors

In addition to provisions in the articles for removal of directors, under the Companies Act 2006 (TSO, 2006), a director may be removed from office by **ordinary** resolution at a meeting of which **special notice** to the company has been given by the person proposing it: s 168.

On receipt of the special notice the company must send a copy to the director who may require that a **memorandum of reasonable length** shall be issued to members. They also have the **right to address the meeting** at which the resolution is considered.

The articles and the service contract of the director **cannot override the statutory power**. However, the articles can **permit dismissal without the statutory formalities** being observed, for example dismissal by a resolution of the board of directors.

The power to remove a director is **limited** in its effect in four ways.

Restrictions on power to remove directors	
Shareholding qualification to call a meeting	In order to propose a resolution to remove a director, the shareholder(s) involved must call a general meeting. To do this they must hold 5% of the paid up share capital: s 303.
Shareholding to request a resolution	Where a meeting is already convened, 100 members holding an average £100 of share capital each may request a resolution to remove a director: s 338.
Weighted voting rights	A director who is also a member may have weighted voting rights given to them under the constitution for such an eventuality, so that they can automatically defeat any motion to remove them as a director: *Bushell v Faith 1970*.
Class right agreement	It is possible to draft a shareholder agreement stating that a member holding each class of share must be present at a general meeting to constitute quorum. If so, a member holding shares of a certain class could prevent a director being removed by not attending the meeting.

Exam focus point

The courts have stressed that the s 168 power of members to remove directors is an important right, but you should remember the ways in which members' intentions might be frustrated.

The dismissal of a director may also entail payment of a **substantial sum** to settle their claim for breach of contract if they have a service contract. Under s 168(5), no resolution may deprive a removed director of any compensation or damages related to their termination to which they are entitled to.

Southern Foundries (1926) Ltd v Shirlaw 1940

The facts: In 1933 S entered into a written agreement to serve the company as Managing Director for ten years. In 1936 F Co gained control of the company and used their votes to alter its articles to confer on F Co power to remove any director from office. In 1937 F Co exercised the power by removing S from his directorship and thereby terminated his appointment as Managing Director (which he could only hold so long as he was a director).

Decision: The alteration of the articles was not a breach of the service agreement but the exercise of the power was a breach of the service agreement for which the company was liable.

Question — Resolution for removal of director

A company has three members who are also directors. Each holds 100 shares. Normally the shares carry one vote each, but the articles state that on a resolution for a director's removal, the director to be removed should have three votes per share. On a resolution for the removal of Jeremy, a director, Jeremy casts 300 votes against the resolution and the other members cast 200 votes for the resolution. Has Jeremy validly defeated the resolution?

Answer

Yes. This was confirmed in a case called *Bushell v Faith 1970*.

As well as being removed from office, we shall see in the next section that a director can be disqualified from acting as director through the company's articles or the Company Directors Disqualification Act 1986. As we shall see, if a director is disqualified by the Act, then they are not permitted to act as a director for any company for a period of time. If they are disqualified by company articles, then they are only prevented from acting as a director for the company concerned.

5 Disqualification of directors

FAST FORWARD

Directors may be required to vacate office because they have been disqualified on grounds dictated by the articles. Directors **may** be disqualified from a wider range of company involvements under the Company Directors Disqualification Act 1986 (CDDA).

A person cannot be appointed as a director or continue in office if they are or become **disqualified** under the articles or statutory rules (such as the Company Directors Disqualification Act 1986 (HMSO, 1986) and the Small Business Enterprise and Employment Act 2015 (TSO, 2015)).

5.1 Disqualification under model articles

Model articles under the Companies Act 2006 (TSO, 2006), include a number of grounds for disqualification. These include where:

- A person **ceases to be a director** by virtue of any **provision of the Companies Act 2006**, or is prohibited from being a director by law;
- A **bankruptcy order** is made against that person;
- A composition is made with that **person's creditors** generally in satisfaction of that person's debts;
- A **registered medical practitioner**, who is treating that person, gives a written opinion to the company stating that that person has become physically or mentally incapable of acting as a director and may remain so for more than three months;
- Notification is received by the company from the director that the **director is resigning from office**, and such resignation has taken effect in accordance with its terms.

Unless the court approves it, an **undischarged bankrupt** cannot act as a director nor be concerned directly or indirectly in the management of a company. If they do continue to act, they become personally liable for the company's relevant debts.

In addition to the main grounds of disqualification, the articles may provide that **a director shall automatically vacate office** if they are **absent** from **board meetings** (without obtaining the leave of the board) for a **specified period** (say six months). The effect of this disqualification depends on the words used.

- If the articles refer merely to 'absence' this includes involuntary absence due to illness.
- The words 'if they shall absent themself' restrict the disqualification to periods of voluntary absence.

The **specified period** is reckoned to begin from the **last meeting** which the absent director did attend. The normal procedure is that a director who foresees a period of absence, applies for leave of absence at the last board meeting which they attend; the leave granted is duly minuted. They are not then absent 'without leave' during the period.

If they fail to obtain leave but later offer a reasonable explanation the other directors may let the matter drop by simply not resolving that they shall vacate office. The general intention of the rule is to **impose a sanction against slackness**; a director has a duty to attend board meetings when they are able to do so.

5.2 Disqualification under statute

The **Company Directors Disqualification Act 1986** (HMSO, 1986) (CDDA 1986) provides that a **court may** formally **disqualify a person from being a director** or in any way directly or indirectly being concerned or taking part in the promotion, formation or management of a company: s 1. To avoid the need for court proceedings, a director may give a disqualification undertaking, which has the same effect as a disqualification order.

The terms of the disqualification order are very wide, and include acting as a consultant to a company. The Act, despite its title, is not limited to the disqualification of people who have been directors. **Any person** may be disqualified if they fall within the appropriate grounds.

In addition to the grounds of disqualification described above, the articles may provide that **a director shall automatically vacate office** if they are **absent** from **board meetings** (without obtaining the leave of the board) for a **specified period** (three months is usual). The effect of this disqualification depends on the words used.

- If the articles refer merely to 'absence' this includes involuntary absence due to illness.
- The words 'if they shall absent himself' restrict the disqualification to periods of voluntary absence.

The period of **three months** is reckoned to begin from the **last meeting** which the absent director did attend. The normal procedure is that a director who foresees a period of absence, applies for leave of absence at the last board meeting which they attend; the leave granted is duly minuted. They are not then absent 'without leave' during the period.

If they fail to obtain leave but later offer a reasonable explanation the other directors may let the matter drop by simply not resolving that they shall vacate office. The general intention of the rule is to **impose a sanction against slackness**; a director has a duty to attend board meetings when they are able to do so.

The Registrar keeps a **register of disqualification orders and undertakings** at Companies House.

Question — Vacation of office

The articles of Robert Ltd provide that if a director should 'absent themselves' for a period exceeding three months from board meetings, the director shall automatically vacate office.

Mila, a director, obtains a twelve month leave of absence to go abroad. Whilst abroad, she contracts a rare illness; on her return she is rushed to hospital and remains there for nine months. On the day of her release, there is a board meeting which she does not attend, and she resolves not to attend board meetings again. After a further two months she has a relapse and dies a fortnight later.

At what point does she cease to be a director?

A After three months of her holiday
B After three months of hospitalisation
C At the point where she decides not to attend board meetings again
D When she dies

Answer

D The board can grant leave of absence, and 'absenting themselves' does not include forced hospitalisation. The period of three months **begins** on her release from hospital, and has not been completed when she dies.

5.3 Grounds for disqualification of directors

FAST FORWARD

Directors may be **disqualified** from acting as directors or being involved in the management of companies in a number of circumstances. They must be disqualified if the company is insolvent, or the director is found to be unfit to be concerned with management of a company, especially in relation to breach of competition law.

Under the CDDA 1986 the court **may** make a disqualification order on any of the following grounds.

(a) **Where a person is convicted of an indictable offence (either in the UK or overseas) in connection with the promotion, formation, management or liquidation of a company or with the receivership or management of a company's property (s 2).**

An indictable offence is an offence which may be tried at a crown court; it is therefore a serious offence. It need not actually have been tried on indictment but if it was the maximum period for which the court can disqualify is 15 years, compared with only five years if the offence was dealt with summarily (at the Magistrates' court).

(b) **Where it appears that a person has been persistently in default in relation to provisions of company legislation (s 3).**

This legislation requires any return, account or other document to be filed with, delivered or sent or notice of any matter to be given to the Registrar. Three defaults in five years are conclusive evidence of persistent default.

The maximum period of disqualification under this section is five years.

(c) **Where it appears that a person has been guilty of fraud or fraudulent trading.** This means carrying on business with intent to defraud creditors or for any fraudulent purpose whether or not the company has been, or is in the course of being, wound up.

The person does not actually have to have been convicted of fraudulent trading. The legislation also applies to anyone who has otherwise been guilty, of any fraud in relation to the company or of any breach of their duty as an officer (s 4).

The maximum period of disqualification under this section is 15 years.

(d) **Where a person has three or more indictable or summary convictions for breaches of companies legislation in relation to returns and accounts in the previous five years (s 5).**

(e) **Where the Secretary of State, acting on a report made by the inspectors or from information or documents obtained under the Companies Act, applies to the court for an order believing it to be expedient in the public interest.**

If the court is satisfied that the person's conduct in relation to the company makes that person unfit to be concerned in the management of a company, then it may make a disqualification order (s 8). Again the maximum is 15 years.

(f) **Where a director of an insolvent company has participated in wrongful trading (s 10).** Maximum – 15 years.

The court **must** make an order where it is satisfied that the following apply:

(a) A person has been a director of a company which has at any time become **insolvent** (whether while they were a director or subsequently).

(b) Their conduct as a director of that company makes them **unfit** to be **concerned** in the **management** of a company, particularly as a result of a breach of competition law (in which case a **competition disqualification order** will be made: s 9A). The courts may also take into account their conduct as a director of other companies, whether or not these other companies are insolvent. Directors can be disqualified under this section even if they take no active part in the running of the business.

When determining **unfitness**, the following factors should be taken into account (the company concerned may be based in the UK or overseas):

- The extent to which the person was responsible for the company breaking the law
- The extent to which the person was responsible for causing the company to become insolvent
- The nature and extent of the loss or damage caused by the person's conduct

In such cases the **minimum** period of disqualification is two years.

Illustration

Offences for which directors have been disqualified include the following.

(a) **Insider dealing**: *R v Goodman 1993*
(b) **Failure to keep proper accounting records**: *Re Firedart Ltd, Official Receiver v Fairall 1994*
(c) **Failure to read the company's accounts**: *Re Continental Assurance Co of London plc 1996*
(d) **Loans** to another company for the purposes of purchasing its own shares with **no grounds for believing the money would be repaid**: *Re Continental Assurance Co of London plc 1996*
(e) **Loans** to associated companies on **uncommercial terms** to the detriment of creditors: *Re Greymoat Ltd 1997*

5.4 Disqualification periods

In *Re Sevenoaks Stationers (Retail) Ltd 1991* the Court of Appeal laid down certain 'disqualification brackets'. The appropriate period of disqualification which should be imposed was a **minimum of two to five years** if the conduct was not very serious, **six to ten years** if the conduct was serious but did not merit the maximum penalty, and **over ten years** only in particularly serious cases.

Disqualification as a director need not mean disqualification from all involvement in management: (*Re Griffiths 1997*), and it may mean that the director can continue to act as an **unpaid director** (*Re Barings plc 1998*), but only if the court gives leave to act.

5.4.1 Mitigation of disqualification

Examples of circumstances which have led the court to imposing a lower period of disqualification include the following.

- **Lack of dishonesty**: *Re Burnham Marketing Services Ltd 1993*
- **Loss of director's own money** in the company: *Re GSAR Realisations Ltd 1993*
- **Absence of personal gain**, for example excessive remuneration: *Re GSAR Realisations Ltd 1993*
- **Efforts to mitigate** the situation: *Re Burnham Marketing Services Ltd 1993*
- **Likelihood of re-offending**: *Re Grayan Building Services Ltd 1995*
- **Proceedings hanging over director** for a long time: *Re Aldermanbury Trust 1993*

5.5 Procedures for disqualification

Company administrators, receivers and liquidators all have a statutory duty to report directors to the Government where they believe the conditions for a disqualification order have been satisfied.

The Secretary of State then decides whether to apply to the court for an order, but if they do decide to apply they must do so within two years of the date on which the company became insolvent.

5.6 Acting as a director whilst disqualified

Acting as a director whilst disqualified is a **serious offence** and where it is committed, **directors are personally liable for the debts of the company**.

Question — Disqualification

In what circumstances can a court make a disqualification order against a director of a company?

Answer

The provisions for disqualification of directors are contained in the Company Directors Disqualification Act 1986. A court may, by order, disqualify a person from being a director, liquidator, administrator, receiver or manager of a company, and from being concerned in the promotion or management of any company.

The order may be made in any one of the following circumstances.

(a) The director concerned is convicted of an indictable offence in connection with a company.

(b) The director concerned has been persistently in default in relation to company law requirements requiring the delivery to the Registrar of annual accounts, the annual return and other documents. A previous decision of a court on three previous occasions in five years that the person concerned has been in default in compliance with these requirements is conclusive evidence of 'persistent' default.

(c) The director concerned has been guilty of fraudulent trading.

(d) The Secretary of State applies for disqualification in the public interest. This would arise from an investigation by Government inspectors or documents obtained under the Companies Act.

(e) The director has been found to be in breach of certain aspects of competition law.

(f) The director has participated in wrongful trading in insolvency.

In general, disqualification may be ordered for up to 15 years. But the maximum is 5 years in case (b) above or when the order is made by a magistrates' court. A person subject to disqualification may apply to the court for remission of the order.

Bankruptcy

An undischarged bankrupt may not, without leave of the court, act as a director of a company or be concerned in the management or promotion of a company.

Here the disqualification is the automatic result of the bankruptcy order made against them by the court.

So far in this chapter we have seen how directors are appointed and removed from office. In the next three sections we shall look at what powers directors have to make business decisions and how agency law grants them authority to act. We shall also see how having these powers and authority means that directors also owe the company certain common law and statutory duties.

6 Powers of directors

> **FAST FORWARD**
> The **powers** of the directors are **defined** by the **articles**.

The powers of the directors are **defined by the articles**. The directors are usually authorised 'to manage the company's business' and 'to exercise all the powers of the company for any purpose connected with the company's business'.

Therefore they may take **any decision which is within the capacity** of the company **unless** either **the Act** or **the articles** themselves **require** that the **decision shall be taken by the members in general meeting**.

6.1 Restrictions on directors' powers

> **FAST FORWARD**
> Directors' powers may be restricted by statute or by the articles. The directors have a duty to exercise their powers in what they honestly believe to be the **best interests** of the company and for the **purposes** for which the powers are given.

6.1.1 Statutory restrictions

Under the Companies Act 2006 (TSO, 2006), many transactions, such as an alteration of the articles or a reduction of capital, must by law be effected by passing a **special resolution**. If the directors propose such changes they must secure the passing of the appropriate resolution by shareholders in a general meeting.

6.1.2 Restrictions imposed by articles

As an example, the articles often set a maximum amount which the directors may borrow. If the directors wish to exceed that limit, they should **seek authority** from a **general meeting**.

When the directors clearly have the necessary power, their decision may be challenged if they exercise the power in the wrong way.

They must exercise their powers:

- In what they **honestly believe to be the interests of the company:** *Re Smith v Fawcett Ltd 1942*
- For a **proper purpose**, being the purpose for which the power is given: *Bamford v Bamford 1969*.

We shall come back to these points when we consider directors' duties.

6.1.3 Members' control of directors

There is a **division of power** between the board of directors who manage the business and the members who as owners take the major policy decisions at general meetings. How, then, do the owners seek to 'control' the people in charge of their property?

- The members **appoint** the directors and may **remove** them from office under s 168, or by other means.
- The members can, by **altering the articles** (special resolution needed), re-allocate powers between the board and the general meeting.
- Articles may allow the members to pass a **special resolution ordering** the **directors to act** (or **refrain from acting**) in a **particular way**. Such special resolutions cannot invalidate anything the directors have already done.

Directors are not agents of the members. They cannot be instructed by the members in general meeting as to how they should exercise their powers. **The directors' powers are derived from the company as a whole** and are to be exercised by the directors as they think best in the **interests of the company**.

6.1.4 Control by the law

Certain powers must be exercised **'for the proper purpose'** and all powers must be exercised *bona fide* for **the benefit of the company**. Failure by the directors to comply with these rules will result in the **court setting aside their powers** unless the shareholders **ratify** the directors' actions by **ordinary resolution** (50% majority).

7 Agency law and the authority of directors

FAST FORWARD

> **Directors** will have **actual authority** granted to them, but they may also have **apparent authority** in the eyes of third parties depending on the position they hold.

We have seen previously that **company directors** act as **agents** for their company and make contracts on the company's behalf with third parties. It is important that directors are aware of what **authority** they have to bind the company into contracts.

7.1 Agency law and directors

The directors are **agents of the company, not the members**. Where they have **actual or usual** authority they can **bind the company**. In addition a director may have **apparent authority** by virtue of **holding out**.

Holding out is a basic rule of the law of agency. It means that if the principal (the company) holds out a person as its authorised agent they are estopped from denying that they are its **authorised agent**. They are bound by a contract entered into by them on the company's behalf.

There are **four conditions** which must be satisfied in claiming under the principle of **holding out**. The claimant must show that:

(a) A **representation** was made to them that the **agent had** the **authority** to enter on behalf of the company into the contract of the kind sought to be enforced.

(b) Such **representation** was **made by a person** who had **'actual' authority** to **manage** the **business** of the company.

The board of directors would certainly have actual authority to manage the company. Some commentators have also argued that the CEO has actual or apparent authority to make representations about the extent of the actual authority of other company agents. (However, a third party cannot rely on the representations a CEO makes about their own actual authority.)

(c) They were **induced** by the **representation** to enter into the contract; they had in fact relied on it.

(d) There must be **nothing** in the **articles** which would prevent the company from giving valid authority to its agent to enter into the contract.

Key term

> **Apparent authority** is the authority which an agent appears to have to a third party. A contract made within the scope of such authority will bind the principal even though the agent was not following their instructions.

7.1.1 The Chief Executive Officer (CEO)

In their dealings with outsiders the CEO has **apparent authority** as agent of the company to **make business contracts**. No other director, even if they work full time, has that **apparent** authority as a director, though if they are employed as a manager they may have apparent authority at a slightly lower level.

The CEO or MD's **actual authority** is whatever the board gives them.

Although appointment as CEO has special status, it may be **terminated** just like that of any other director (or employee); they then revert to the position of an ordinary director. Alternatively the company in general meeting may **remove them from their office of director** and they immediately cease to be CEO since being a director is a necessary qualification for holding the post.

> *Freeman & Lockyer v Buckhurst Park Properties (Mangal) Ltd 1964*
>
> *The facts:* A company carried on a business as property developers. The articles contained a power to appoint a Managing Director (CEO) but this was never done. One of the directors of the company, to the knowledge but without the express authority of the remainder of the board, acted as if he were Managing Director. He found a purchaser for an estate and also engaged a firm of architects to make a planning application. The company later refused to pay the architect's fees on the grounds that the director had no actual or apparent authority.
>
> *Decision:* The company was liable since by its acquiescence it had represented that the director was a Managing Director with the authority to enter into contracts that were normal commercial arrangements, and which the board itself would have been able to enter.

Exam focus point

Situations where the facts are similar to the *Freeman & Lockyer* case often occur in law exams so be prepared to spot them.

7.1.2 Other directors

The position of any other individual director (not a CEO) who is also an employee is that:

(a) They **do not have the apparent authority to make general contracts** which attaches to the position of CEO, but they have **whatever apparent authority attaches** to their **management position**.

(b) **Removal** from the office of director may be a **breach** of their **service contract** if that agreement stipulates that they are to have the status of director as part of the conditions of employment.

If the board of directors **permits a director** to behave as if they were a duly appointed CEO when in fact they are not, the company may be bound by their actions.

7.2 Director authority and third parties

In most cases, directors will only enter into contracts that they have authority to. However, the question arises of what happens if a director enters their company into a contract where they do not have authority? The approach taken by the Companies Act 2006 is to protect and give **security** to commercial transactions for **third parties**.

There are two important sections of the Companies Act 2006:

Section 39 provides as follows:

'the validity of an act done by a company shall not be called into question on the ground of lack of capacity by reason of anything in the company's constitution.'

Section 40 provides as follows:

'in favour of a person dealing with a company in good faith, the power of the directors to bind the company, or authorise others to do so, shall be deemed to be free of any limitation under the company's constitution.'

There are a number of **points to note** about s 40.

(a) The section applies in favour of the **person dealing with the company**; it does not apply to the members.

(b) In contrast with s 39, **good faith** is required on the part of the third party. The company has, however, to prove lack of good faith in the third party and this may turn out to be quite difficult.

(c) The **third party** is not required to **enquire** whether or not there are any **restrictions** placed on the power of directors. They are free to assume the directors have any power they profess to have.

(d) The section covers not only acts beyond the capacity of the company, but acts beyond **'any limitation under the company's constitution'**.

Whilst sections 39 and 40 deal with the company's transactions with **third parties**, the **members** may take action against the directors for permitting such acts. However, the main problem for **members** is that they are most likely to be **aware** of these acts only **after** they have occurred. Therefore they are not normally in a position to prevent it, although in theory they could seek an **injunction** if they found out about the potential unauthorised act before it took place.

Question — Directors' powers

Under the articles of association of Recycle Ltd the directors of the company need the consent of the general meeting by ordinary resolution to borrow sums of money in excess of £50,000. The other articles are all standard model articles.

Milana has been appointed CEO of the company and she holds 1% of the issued shares of the company. Early in May 20X5 Milana entered into two transactions for the benefit of Recycle Ltd. First, she arranged to borrow £100,000 from Conifer Bank Ltd, secured by a floating charge on the company's assets. She had not sought the approval of the members as required by the articles. Secondly, she placed a contract worth £10,000 with Saw Ltd to buy some agricultural machinery.

Advise the directors of Recycle Ltd whether they are bound by the agreements with Conifer Bank Ltd and Saw Ltd.

Answer

The enforceability of the loan agreement and floating charge by Conifer Bank Ltd against Recycle Ltd is determined by reference to s 40. The transaction is beyond the authority of the CEO. Milana failed to obtain an ordinary resolution of the company as required by its articles of association.

S 40 provides that, in favour of a person dealing in good faith with a company, the power of the board of directors to bind the company or (importantly in this case) to authorise others to do so, shall be deemed to be free of any limitation under the company's constitution.

There is no suggestion that Conifer Bank Ltd has not acted in good faith and it will be presumed that it has in fact acted in good faith unless the contrary is proved by the company.

The articles allow the board to appoint a CEO. In that position, Milana has apparent authority as agent of the company to make business contracts including the type of transaction entered into with Saw Ltd.

Under the Act, the restriction placed on her actual authority (by the article requiring an ordinary resolution) shall be deemed not to exist in favour of the third party, Conifer Bank Ltd. The power of the board to authorise Milana to bind the company is deemed to be free of any constitutional limitation.

In conclusion, Recycle Ltd will be bound to the contracts with both Conifer Bank Ltd and Saw Ltd.

8 Duties of directors

FAST FORWARD — The Companies Act 2006 sets out the **seven principal duties** of **directors**.

The Companies Act 2006 (TSO, 2006) sets out the **principal duties** that directors owe to their company. Many of these duties developed over time through the operation of **common law** and **equity,** or are **fiduciary duties** which have now been codified to make the law clearer and more accessible.

Attention! When deciding whether a duty has been broken, the courts will consider the Companies Act primarily. All case law explained in this section applied before the 2006 Act and is included here to help you understand the types of situation that arise and how the law will be interpreted and applied by the courts in the future.

Key term **Fiduciary duty** is a duty imposed upon certain persons because of the position of trust and confidence in which they stand in relation to another. The duty is more onerous than generally arises under a contractual or tort relationship. It requires full disclosure of information held by the fiduciary, a strict duty to account for any profits received as a result of the relationship, and a duty to avoid conflict of interest.

Broadly speaking directors must be **honest** and **not allow their personal interests to conflict with their duties as directors**. The directors are said to hold a **fiduciary position** since they make contracts as **agents** of the company and have control of its property.

The duties included in the Companies Act 2006 effectively form a **code of conduct** for directors. They do not tell them what to do but rather create a framework that sets out how they are expected to **behave** generally. This code is important as it addresses situations where:

- A director may put their **own interests** ahead of the company's, and
- A director may be **negligent** and liable to an action under tort.

8.1 To who are the duties owed?

Section 170 makes it clear that directors owe their duties to the company, **not** the members. This means that the **only company itself can take action against a director** who breaches them. However, it is possible for a member to bring a derivative claim against the director on behalf of the company.

The effect of the **duties are cumulative**, in other words, a director owes **every duty** to the company that could apply in any given situation. The Act provides guidance for this. Where a director is offered a bribe for instance they will be breaking the duty not to accept a benefit from a third party and they will also not be promoting the company for the benefit of the members.

When deciding whether or not a director has breached a duty, the court should consider their actions in the context of **each individual duty** in turn.

8.2 By who are the duties owed?

Every person who is **classed as a director** under the Act owes the duties that are outlined below. Certain aspects of the duties regarding conflicts of interest and accepting benefits from third parties also apply to **past directors**. This is to prevent directors from exploiting a situation for their own benefit by simply resigning. The courts are directed to apply duties to **shadow directors** where they are capable of applying.

Directors must at all times continue to **act in accordance with all other laws**; no authorisation is given by the duties for a director to breach any other law or regulation.

8.3 The duties and the articles

The articles may provide more onerous regulations than the Act, but they may not reduce the level of duty expected unless it is in the following circumstances:

- If a director has **acted in accordance with the articles** they cannot be in breach of the duty to exercise independent judgement.
- Some **conflicts of interest by independent directors** are permissible by the articles.
- Directors will not be in breach of duty concerning **conflicts of interest** if they follow any **provisions in the articles for dealing with them** as long as the provisions are lawful.
- The company may **authorise anything** that would otherwise be a breach of duty.

8.4 The duties of directors

FAST FORWARD

The **statutory duties** owed by directors are to:

- Act within their powers
- Promote the success of the company
- Exercise independent judgement
- Exercise reasonable skill, care and diligence
- Avoid conflicts of interest
- Not to accept benefits from third parties
- Declare an interest in a proposed transaction or arrangement

We shall now consider the duties placed on directors by the Act. Where cases are mentioned it is to **demonstrate** the previous common law or equitable principle that courts will follow when interpreting and applying the Act.

8.4.1 Duty to act within powers (s 171)

The directors owe a duty to act in accordance with the company's constitution, and only to exercise powers for the purposes for what they were conferred. They have a **fiduciary duty to the**

company to exercise their powers bona fide in what they honestly consider to be the interests of the company:

Re Smith v Fawcett Ltd 1942. This honest belief is effective even if, in fact, the interests of the company were not served.

This duty is owed **to the company** and **not generally to individual shareholders**. The directors will not generally be liable to the members if, for instance, they purchase shares without disclosing information affecting the share price: *Percival v Wright 1902.*

In exercising the powers given to them by the articles the directors have a fiduciary duty not only to act *bona fide* **but also only to use their powers for a proper purpose**: *Bamford v Bamford 1969.*

The powers are restricted to the **purposes** for **which they were given**. If the directors infringe this rule by exercising their powers for a collateral purpose the transaction will be invalid **unless** the **company** in **general meeting authorises it, or subsequently ratifies it**.

Most of the directors' powers are found in the **articles,** so this duty means that the directors must not act outside their power or the capacity of the company (in other words *ultra vires*).

If the irregular use of directors' powers is in the **allotment of shares** the votes attached to the new shares may not be used in reaching a decision in general meeting to sanction it.

Howard Smith Ltd v Ampol Petroleum Ltd 1974

The facts: Shareholders who held 55% of the issued shares intended to reject a takeover bid for the company. The directors honestly believed that it was in the company's interest that the bid should succeed. The directors therefore allotted new shares to the prospective bidder so that the shareholders opposed to the bid would then have less than 50% of the enlarged capital and the bid would succeed.

Decision: The allotment was invalid. 'It must be unconstitutional for directors to use their fiduciary powers over the shares in the company purely for the purpose of destroying an existing majority or creating a new majority which did not previously exist'.

Any **shareholder** may **apply to the court** to declare that a transaction in breach of s 171 should be set aside. However the practice of the courts is generally to **remit the issue** to the **members in general meeting** to see if the members wish to confirm the transaction. If the majority approve what has been done (or have authorised it in advance) that decision is treated as a proper case of **majority control** to which the minority must normally submit.

Hogg v Cramphorn 1966

The facts: The directors of a company issued shares to trustees of a pension fund for employees to prevent a takeover bid which they honestly thought would be bad for the company. The shares were paid for with money belonging to the company provided from an employees' benevolent and pension fund account. The shares carried 10 votes each and as a result the trustees and directors together had control of the company. The directors had power to issue shares but not to attach more than one vote to each. A minority shareholder brought the action on behalf of all the other shareholders.

Decision: If the directors act honestly in the best interests of the company, the company in general meeting can ratify the use of their powers for an improper purpose, so the allotment of the shares would be valid. But only one vote could be attached to each of the shares because that is what the articles provided.

Bamford v Bamford 1969

The facts: The directors of Bamford Ltd allotted 500,000 unissued shares to a third party to thwart a takeover bid. A month after the allotment a general meeting was called and an ordinary resolution was passed ratifying the allotment. The holders of the newly-issued shares did not vote. The claimants (minority shareholders) alleged that the allotment was not made for a proper purpose.

Decision: The ratification was valid and the allotment was good. There had been a breach of fiduciary duty but the act had been validated by an ordinary resolution passed in general meeting.

These cases can be distinguished from the *Howard* Smith case (where the allotment was invalid) in that in the *Howard Smith* case the original majority would not have sanctioned the use of directors' powers. In the *Bamford* case the decision could have been sanctioned by a vote which excluded the new shareholders.

Ratification is not effective when it attempts to validate a transaction when

- It constitutes **fraud on a minority**.
- It involves **misappropriation of assets**.
- The transaction **prejudices creditors' interests** at a time when the company is insolvent.

Under s 239, any resolution which proposes to ratify the acts of a director which are negligent in default or in breach of duty or trust regarding the company must exclude the director or any members connected with them from the vote.

Most of the cases discussed above concern the **duty of directors** to exercise their power to allot shares. This is only one of the powers given to directors that are subject to this **fiduciary duty**.

Others include:

- Power to borrow
- Power to give security
- Power to refuse to register a transfer of shares
- Power to call general meetings
- Power to circulate information to shareholders

8.4.2 Duty to promote the success of the company (s 172)

An overriding theme of the Companies Act 2006 is the principle that the **purpose of the legal framework** surrounding companies should be **to help companies do business**. Their main purpose is to create wealth for the shareholders.

This theme is evident in the **duty of directors to promote the success of a company**. During the development of the Act, the independent Company Law Review recommended that company law should consider the interests of those who companies are run for. It decided that the new Act should embrace the principle of **'enlightened shareholder value'**.

In essence, this principle means that the law should encourage **longtermism** and **regard for all stakeholders** by directors and that **stakeholder interests** should be **pursued** in an **enlightened** and **inclusive** way.

To achieve this, a duty of directors to act in a way, which, in **good faith**, promotes the success of the company for the benefit of the members as a whole, was created.

The requirements of this duty are difficult to define and possibly problematic to apply, so the Act provides directors with a **non-exhaustive list** of issues to keep in mind. The list identifies areas of **particular importance** and **modern-day expectations** of **responsible business behaviour**. When exercising this duty directors should consider:

- The **consequences of decisions** in the long term.
- The **interests of** their **employees**.
- The need to **develop good relationships** with **customers** and **suppliers**.
- The **impact of the company** on the **local community** and the **environment**.
- The desirability of **maintaining high standards of business conduct** and a **good reputation**.
- The need to **act fairly as between all members** of the company.

In terms of **sustainability**, directors' duties are expanding into compliance with Environmental, Social and Governance (ESG) principles. For example, directors must take into account the interests of the company's employees, of the community and of the environment in which it operates when taking business decisions.

The **Companies Act does not define** what should be regarded as the **success of a company**. This is down to a director's judgement in good faith. This is important as it ensures that business decisions are for the directors rather than the courts.

No guidance is given for what the **correct course of action** would be where the various s 172 **duties are in conflict**.

PART I THE ADMINISTRATION AND CONTROL OF THE COMPANY

For example a decision to shut down a factory may be in the long-term best interests of the company, and perhaps the environment, but it is certainly not in the interests of the employees affected, nor the local community in which they live which benefits from the business' investment in the area. Conflicts such as this are inevitable and could potentially leave directors open to breach of duty claims by a wide range of stakeholders if they do not deal with them carefully.

Company strategic reports provide important information to shareholders and can help them to assess how the directors have performed their duty, under section 172.

Such reports reflect the directors view of the company and provide context for the related financial statements. Their contents are derived from the Companies Act 2006, and include a description of the business' strategy, objectives and business model. In addition, they also include an explanation of the main trends and factors affecting the entity, principal risks and uncertainties and an analysis of the development and performance of the business.

Other elements that are associated with the section 172 duty include disclosures about the environment, employees, social, community, human rights, and anti-corruption and anti-bribery matters when material. There is also a requirement to include disclosures on gender diversity.

The Companies (Strategic Report) (Climate-related Financial disclosure) Regulations 2022 (TSO, 2022)

These regulations require companies with over 500 employees, which are also listed, admitted to the AIM market, or have an annual turnover of over £500 million, to make "climate-related financial disclosures" in the Non-Financial and Sustainability Information Statement part of their strategic report. These disclosures include:

(a) A description of the company's governance arrangements in relation to assessing and managing climate-related risks and opportunities;

(b) A description of how the company identifies, assesses, and manages climate-related risks and opportunities;

(c) A description of how processes for identifying, assessing, and managing climate-related risks are integrated into the company's overall risk management process;

(d) A description of:

  (i) the principal climate-related risks and opportunities arising in connection with the company's operations; and

  (ii) the time periods by reference to which those risks and opportunities are assessed;

(e) A description of the actual and potential impacts of the principal climate-related risks and opportunities on the company's business model and strategy;

(f) An analysis of the resilience of the company's business model and strategy, taking into consideration different climate-related scenarios;

(g) A description of the targets used by the company to manage climate-related risks and to realise climate-related opportunities and of performance against those targets; and

(h) A description of the key performance indicators used to assess progress against targets used to manage climate-related risks and realise climate-related opportunities and of the calculations on which those key performance indicators are based."

If the directors of a company reasonably believe that, having regard to the nature of the company's business, and the manner in which it is carried on, the whole or a part of a climate-related financial disclosure is not necessary for an understanding of the company's business, then the directors may omit the whole or some of the relevant part of that climate-related financial disclosure. Where the directors do omit all or part of a disclosure they must provide a clear and reasoned explanation of the directors' reasonable belief why the disclosure can be omitted.

The UK has endorsed the **Task Force on Climate-related Financial Disclosure (TCFD) framework** for compliance and these regulations are consistent with this framework.

> **Additional Reading**
>
> It is recommended that you read the TCFD framework which is available from the website below:
>
> https://www.gov.uk/government/publications/tcfd-aligned-disclosure-application-guidance/task-force-on-climate-related-financial-disclosure-tcfd-aligned-disclosure-application-guidance

8.4.3 Duty to exercise independent judgement (s 173)

This is a simple duty that states directors must **exercise independent judgement. This means they should** remain independent and open-minded when exercising their discretion. They should **not delegate** their powers of decision-making or be **swayed by the influence of others**. It is sometimes said the directors must not 'fetter their discretion'. However unless a decision is expressly reserved to directors, a director can delegate their functions to any person they think fit.

The Companies Act 2006 does recognise that a director's **future discretion** may legitimately be restricted on account of a contract entered into between the company and a third party. The duty to exercise independent judgement is not infringed therefore by acting in accordance with any agreement by the company that restricts the exercise of discretion by directors, or by acting in a way authorised by the company's constitution.

8.4.4 Duty to exercise reasonable skill, care and diligence (s 174)

Directors have a **duty of care** to show **reasonable skill, care and diligence**.

Section 174 provides that a director 'owes a duty to his company to exercise the same standard of 'care, skill and diligence that would be exercised by a reasonably diligent person with:

(a) The general knowledge, skill and experience that may reasonably be expected of a person carrying out the functions carried out by the director in relation to the company; and

(b) The general knowledge, skill and experience that the director has.

There is therefore a **reasonableness test** consisting of two parts:

(a) An **objective test**

   Did the director act in a manner reasonably expected of a person performing the same role?

   A director, when carrying out their functions, must show such **care** as could **reasonably** be expected from a **competent person** in that role. If a 'reasonable' director could be expected to act in a certain way, it is no defence for a director to claim, for example, lack of expertise.

(b) A **subjective test**

   Did the director act in accordance with the skill, knowledge and experience that they actually have?

   In the case of *Re City Equitable Fire and Insurance Co Ltd 1925* it was held that a director is expected to show the **degree of skill** which may **reasonably be expected** from a person of their knowledge and experience. The standard set is personal to the person in each case. An accountant who is a director of a mining company is not required to have the expertise of a mining engineer, but they should show the expertise of an accountant.

The duty to be competent extends to **non-executive directors**, who may be liable if they fail in their duty.

> *Dorchester Finance Co Ltd v Stebbing 1977*
>
> *The facts:* Of all the company's three directors S, P and H, only S worked full-time. P and H signed blank cheques at S's request who used them to make loans which became irrecoverable. The company sued all three; P and H, who were experienced accountants, claimed that as non-executive directors they had no liability.
>
> *Decision:* All three were liable, P's and H's acts in signing blank cheques being negligent and not showing the necessary objective or subjective skill and care.

In other words, the **standard of care** is an objective 'competent' standard, plus a higher 'personal' standard of application. If the director actually had particular expertise that leads to a higher standard of competence being reasonably expected.

The company may recover damages from its directors for loss caused by their negligence. However something more than imprudence or want of care must be shown. It must be shown to be a case of **gross negligence**. This was defined in *Overend Gurney & Co v Gibb 1872* as conduct such that 'no men with any degree of prudence, acting on their own behalf, would have entered into such a transaction as they entered into'.

Therefore, in the absence of fraud it was difficult to control careless directors effectively. The statutory provisions on disqualification of directors of insolvent companies and on liability for wrongful trading therefore both set out how to judge a director's competence, and provide more effective enforcement (discussed below).

The company by decision of its members in general meeting decides whether to sue the directors for their negligence. Even if it is a case in which they could be liable **the court has discretion under s 1157 to relieve directors of liability** if it appears to the court that:

- The directors acted **honestly** and **reasonably**.
- They **ought**, having regard to the circumstances of the case, **fairly to be excused**.

> *Re D' Jan of London Ltd 1993*
>
> *The facts:* D, a director of the company, signed an insurance proposal form without reading it. The form was filled in by D's broker. An answer given to one of the questions on the form was incorrect and the insurance company rightly repudiated liability for a fire at the company's premises in which stock worth some £174,000 was lost. The company became insolvent and the liquidator brought this action under s 212 of the Insolvency Act 1986 alleging D was negligent.
>
> *Decision:* In failing to read the form D was negligent. However, he had acted honestly and reasonably and ought therefore to be partly relieved from liability by the Court under s 727 of the Companies Act 1985, (now s 1157 under the Companies Act 2006).

In the absence of **fraud**, **bad faith** or **ultra vires** the members may vote unanimously to forgive the director's negligence, even if it is those negligent directors who control the voting and exercise such forgiveness: *Multinational Gas & Petrochemical Co v Multinational Gas and Petrochemical Services Ltd 1983*. Where there is no fraud on the minority, a majority decision is sufficient: *Pavlides v Jensen 1956*.

8.4.5 Duty to avoid conflicts of interest (s 175)

Directors have a **duty to avoid circumstances** where their **personal interests conflict**, or may possibly conflict, **with the company's interests**. It may occur when a director makes personal use of information, property or opportunities belonging to the company, whether or not the company was able to take advantage of them at the time.

Therefore directors must be careful not to breach this duty when they **enter into a contract** with their company or if they **make a profit in the course of being a director**.

This duty does not apply to a conflict of interest in relation to a transaction or arrangement with the company, provided the director declared an interest.

As **agents**, directors have a **duty to avoid a conflict of interest**. In particular:

- The directors must **retain their freedom of action** and **not fetter their discretion** by agreeing to vote as some other person may direct.
- The directors owe a fiduciary duty to **avoid a conflict of duty and personal interest.**
- The directors **must not obtain any personal advantage** from their position as directors **without the consent of the company** for whatever gain or profit they have obtained.

The following cases are important in the area of conflict of interest.

Regal (Hastings) Ltd v Gulliver 1942

The facts: The company owned a cinema. It had the opportunity of acquiring two more cinemas through a subsidiary to be formed with an issued capital of £5,000. However the company could not proceed with this scheme since it only had £2,000 available for investment in the subsidiary.

The directors and their friends therefore subscribed £3,000 for shares of the new company to make up the required £5,000. The Chair acquired his shares not for themselves but as nominee of other persons. The company's solicitor also subscribed for shares. The share capital of the two companies (which then owned three cinemas) was sold at a price which yielded a profit of £2.80 per share of the new company in which the directors had invested. The new controlling shareholder of the company caused it to sue the directors to recover the profit which they had made.

Decision:

(a) The directors were **accountable** to the company for their profit since they had obtained it from an opportunity which came to them as directors.

(b) It was **immaterial** that the **company** had **lost nothing** since it had been unable to make the investment itself.

(c) The directors might have kept their profit if the company had **agreed** by resolution passed in general meeting that they should do so. The directors might have used their votes to approve their action since it was not fraudulent (there was no misappropriation of the company's property).

(d) The Chair was not accountable for the profit on his shares since he did not obtain it for himself. The solicitor was not accountable for his profit since he was **not a director** and so was not subject to the rule of accountability as a director for personal profits obtained in that capacity.

Industrial Development Consultants Ltd v Cooley 1972

The facts: C was Managing Director of the company which provided consultancy services to gas companies. A gas company was unlikely to award a particular contract to the company but C realised that, acting personally, he might be able to obtain it. He told the board of his company that he was ill and persuaded them to release him from his service agreement. On ceasing to be a director of the company C obtained the contract on his own behalf. The company sued him to recover the profits of the contract.

Decision: C was accountable to his old company for his profit.

Directors will not be liable for a breach of this duty if:

- The **members** of the company **authorised** their actions.
- The **situation cannot reasonably be regarded** as likely to give rise to a conflict of interest.
- The **actions have been authorised by the other directors**. This only applies if they are genuinely independent from the transaction and:
    - If the company is private – the articles do not restrict such authorisation, or
    - If it is public – the articles expressly permit it.
- The company explicitly rejected the opportunity they took up: *Peso Silver Mines v Cropper*.

8.4.6 Duty not to accept benefits from third parties (s 176)

This duty **prohibits the acceptance of benefits** (including bribes) from third parties conferred by reason of them being director, or doing, (or omitting to do) something as a director. Where a director accepts a benefit that may also create or potentially create a conflict of interest, they will also be in breach of their s 175 duty (see above).

Unlike s 175, an act which would potentially be in breach of this duty **cannot be authorised** by the **directors**, but **members do have the right to authorise it**.

Directors will not be in breach of this duty if the acceptance of the benefit **cannot reasonably** be regarded as likely to give rise to a conflict of interest.

8.4.7 Duty to declare interest in proposed transaction or arrangement (s 177)

Directors are required to disclose to the other directors the nature and extent of any interest, direct or indirect, that they have in relation to a **proposed transaction** or **arrangement** with the **company**. Even if the director is not a party to the transaction, the duty may apply if they are aware, or ought reasonably to be aware, of the interest. For example, the interest of another person in a contract with the company may require disclosure under this duty if that other person's interest is a direct or indirect interest on the part of the director. Directors are required to disclose their interest in any transaction **before** the company enters into the transaction.

Disclosure can be made by:

- Written notice
- General notice
- Verbally at a board meeting

Disclosure to the **members** is **not** sufficient to discharge the duty. Directors must declare the **nature** and **extent** of their interest to the **other directors** as well. If the declaration becomes **void** or **inaccurate**, a **further declaration** should be made. No declaration of interest is required if the director's interest in the transaction **cannot reasonably** be regarded as likely to give rise to a conflict of interest.

8.5 Consequences of breach of duty

Breach of duty comes under the **civil law** rather than criminal law and, as mentioned earlier, the company itself must take up the action. This usually means the other directors starting proceedings.

Consequences for breach include:

- **Damages** payable to the company where it has suffered loss.
- **Restoration** of company property.
- **Repayment of any profits** made by the director.
- **Rescission of contract** (where the director did not disclose an interest).

8.6 Declaration of an interest in an existing transaction or arrangement (s 182)

Directors have a statutory obligation to declare any direct or indirect interest in an existing transaction entered into by the company. This obligation is almost identical to the duty to disclose an interest in a **proposed** transaction or arrangement under s 177 (see above). However, this section is relevant to transactions or arrangements that have **already occurred**.

A declaration under s 182 is **not** required if:

- It has **already been disclosed** as a proposed transaction under s 177.
- The director is **not aware** of either
  - **The interest** they have in the transaction, or
  - In **the transaction** itself.
- The director's interest in the transaction **cannot reasonably** be regarded as likely to give rise to a conflict of interest.
- The **other directors are aware** (or reasonably should be aware) of the situation.
- It concerns the **director's service contract** and it has been considered by a board meeting or special board committee.

Where a declaration is required it should be made as soon as **reasonably practicable** either:

- By written notice
- By general notice
- Verbally at a board meeting

If the declaration becomes **void** or **inaccurate**, a **further declaration** should be made.

8.7 Long-service contracts, substantial property transactions, loans and other dealings between the company and its directors

The table below summarises other statutory controls over dealings between directors and their companies included in the Companies Act 2006.

CA06 Ref	Control
188	**Long service contracts:** directors' service contracts lasting more than two years must be approved by the members.
190	**Substantial property transactions:** directors or any person connected to them (see below) may not acquire a 'substantial' non-cash asset from the company without approval of the members. An asset's value is substantial if it is more than £5,000, or more than 10% of the company's asset value. All sales of assets with a value exceeding £100,000 must be approved.
197	Any **loans over £10,000 given to directors**, or **guarantees** provided as security for loans provided to directors, must be approved by members by ordinary resolution at a meeting or by written resolution. Persons connected to public company directors are also covered. Members should have been given information as to the nature of the transaction, the amount and purpose of the loan and the extent of the company's liability: s 197(4). This information must be in a memorandum circulated at the same time as a written resolution. If the general meeting procedure is used, the memorandum must be made available to members at the company's registered office for at least 15 days prior to the meeting, as well as at the meeting itself.
198	Expands section 197 to prevent unapproved **quasi-loans** to directors and connected persons (public companies only).
201	Expands section 197 to prevent unapproved **credit transactions** by the company for the benefit of a director (public companies only).
217	**Non-contractual payments to directors for loss of office** must be approved by the members.

Loans etc made without shareholder approval are voidable at the instance of the company and the director would be liable to account for any gain made as a result of the transaction, or indemnify the company for any loss: s 213.

Transactions under s 197, s 198 and s 201 do not require shareholder approval if they are to meet expenditure in the company's business where the total value does not exceed £50,000: s 204.

8.7.1 Connected persons

For the purpose of s 190 (substantial property transactions), s 197 (loans by public companies) and s 198 (quasi-loans by public companies) a person is connected with a director if:

- They are a member of the director's **family** (spouse, civil partner, long-term partner, child, step-child, parent – not grandparent or grandchild, sister, brother, aunt or uncle, or nephew or niece).
- They are a **body corporate** with which the director is connected (the director has an interest in 20% or more of the equity capital or voting rights).
- They act as a **trustee** of a trust which includes the director or a connected person as a beneficiary, or which requires the person to act for the director's or a connected person's benefit.
- They are a **partner** of the director or a connected person.
- They are a **firm** that is a legal person in which the director or a connected person is a partner: s 252.

8.8 Examples of remedies against directors

Remedies against directors for breach of duties include accounting to the company for a **personal gain**, **indemnifying the company**, and **rescission of contracts** made with the company.

The type of remedy varies with the breach of duty.

(a) The director may have to **account for a personal gain**: *Regal (Hastings) Ltd v Gulliver 1942.*

(b) They may have to **indemnify the company** against loss caused by their negligence such as an unlawful transaction which they approved.

(c) If they contract with the company in a conflict of interest the **contract may be rescinded by the company**. However under common law rules the company cannot both affirm the contract and recover the director's profit: *Burland v Earle 1902.*

(d) The court may declare that a transaction is *ultra vires* or unlawful: *Re Lee Behrens & Co 1932.*

A company may, either by its **articles** or by **passing a resolution** in general meeting, **authorise or ratify** the conduct of directors in breach of duty. There are some limits on the power of members in general meeting to **sanction a breach of duty** by directors or to release them from their strict obligations.

(a) If the directors **defraud** the company and vote in general meeting to approve their own fraud, their votes are invalid (*Cook v Deeks 1916*).

(b) If the directors **allot shares** to alter the balance of votes in a general meeting the votes attached to those shares may not be cast to support a resolution approving the issue (see *Bamford's* case above).

8.9 Directors' liability for acts of other directors

A director is **not liable** for acts of fellow directors. However if they become aware of serious breaches of duty by other directors, they may have a duty to inform members of them or to take control of assets of the company without having proper delegated authority to do so.

In such cases the director is **liable for their own negligence** in what they allow to happen and not directly for the misconduct of the other directors.

8.10 Directors' personal liability

As a general rule a director has no personal liability for the debts of the company. But there are certain exceptions.

- Personal liability **may arise** by **lifting the veil** of incorporation.

- A **limited company** may by its articles or by **special resolution** provide that its directors shall have unlimited liability for its debts.

- A director may be **liable** to the **company's creditors** in certain circumstances.

Can a director be held personally liable for **negligent advice** given by their company? The case below shows that they can, but only when they assume responsibility in a personal capacity for advice given, rather than simply giving advice in their capacity as a director.

Williams and Another v Natural Life Health Foods Ltd 1998

The facts: The director was sued personally by claimants who claimed they were misled by the company's brochure. The director helped prepare the brochure, and the brochure described him as the source of the company's expertise. The claimants did not however deal with the director but with other employees.

Decision: The House of Lords overruled the Court of Appeal, and ruled that the director was not personally liable. In order to have been liable, there would have had to have been evidence that the director had assumed personal responsibility. Merely acting as a director and advertising his earlier experience did not amount to assumption of personal liability.

8.11 Fraudulent and wrongful trading

In cases of **fraudulent or wrongful trading** liquidators can apply to the court for an order that those responsible (usually the directors) are liable to repay all or some specified part of the **company's debts**. The liquidator should also report the facts to the Director of Public Prosecutions so that the DPP may **institute criminal proceedings**.

We have now completed our study of the key company officer – directors. In the next section we shall turn our attention to another company officer – the company secretary.

8.12 Directors' responsibility to comply with legislation related to ESG

Directors have a **responsibility** to ensure their company complies with all relevant legislation. In recent times, the focus has been on sustainability and **Environment, Social and Governance issues**.

The tables below summarise some of the key legislation in the ESG areas.

Environmental legislation	Description
Government Environment Act 2021	Gives the government powers to set targets in relation to environmental factors such as air and water quality.
Company reporting Companies Act 2006 (Strategic Report and Directors' Report) Regulations 2013 The Companies (Strategic Report) (Climate-related Financial disclosure) Regulations 2022	The Companies Act 2006 (Strategic Report and Directors' Report) Regulations 2013 requires a report on environmental matters by quoted companies as part of the Strategic Report section of their Annual Report. The Companies (Strategic Report) (Climate-related Financial disclosure) Regulations 2022 was covered in Section 8.4.2 above.
Directors Companies Act 2006 s172	The Companies Act 2006 s172 was covered in Section 8.4.2 above

Social legislation	Description
General The Equality Act 2010	Protects people against discrimination at work based on nine protected characteristics including age disability, gender reassignment, marriage and civil partnership, pregnancy and maternity, race, religion or belief, sex, and sexual orientation. The Act also prohibits discrimination in the healthcare and education sector.
Employment law The Employment Rights Act 1996 National Minimum Wage Act 1998	The Employment Rights Act 1996 established rights for employees to request flexible working and family-friendly practices. The National Minimum Wage Act 1998 established a minimum hourly rate of pay for employees depending on their age. This is known as the National Living Wage.
Working practices and reporting Modern Slavery Act 2015	Requires large organisations to make an annual statement regarding modern slavery (such as servitude and forced labour) and the risks of it occurring in their supply chain.

Social legislation	Description
Criminal law Bribery Act 2010 Money Laundering Regulations 2017	These Acts attempt to prevent criminals from profiting from their illegal activities. The Bribery Act makes it a criminal offence to make or accept bribes when performing services or trying to obtain services. The Money Laundering Regulations sets rules for organisations (especially accountants and those working in finance) to follow which help identify potential money laundering (attempts to make illegally obtained money look like it originates from a legitimate source). Procedures are established for suspicious activity to be reported and it is an offence not to report suspicions of money laundering. 'Tipping off' someone that they are under investigation for money laundering is also an offence.

Governance legislation	Description
Business controls and procedures Data Protection Act 2018	The Data Protection Act 2018 controls how organisations may collect, process and use data collected about individuals.

9 The company secretary

Every public company must have a **company secretary**, who is one of the officers of a company and may be a director. Private companies are not required to have a secretary.

Under the Companies Act 2006 (TSO, 2006), every public company must have a **company secretary**, who is one of the officers of a company and may be a director: s 271. Private companies are not required to have a secretary: s 270. In this case the roles normally done by the company secretary may be done by one of the directors, or an approved person. The Secretary of State may require a public company to appoint a secretary where it has failed to do so.

9.1 Appointment of a company secretary

To be appointed as a company secretary to a plc, the directors must ensure that the candidate should be qualified (s 273) by virtue of:

- **Employment** as a plc's secretary for **three out of the five years** preceding appointment.
- **Membership** of one of a list of **qualifying bodies**: the ACCA, CIMA, ICAEW, ICAS, ICAI or CIPFA.
- **Qualification** as a **solicitor**, **barrister** or **advocate** within the UK.
- **Employment** in a position or **membership** of a professional body that, in the opinion of the directors, **appears to qualify that person** to act as company secretary.

They should also have the **'necessary knowledge and experience'** as deemed by the directors.

A **sole director** of a private company can also be the company secretary because having a company secretary for a private company is optional. A company is permitted to have **two** or more joint secretaries. A **corporation** can fulfil the role of company secretary. A register of secretaries must be kept. Under the **UK Corporate Governance Code**, the appointment of the company secretary is a matter for the board as a whole.

9.2 Duties of a company secretary

The specific **duties** of each company secretary are **determined by the directors** of the company. As a company officer, the company secretary is responsible for ensuring that the company complies with its statutory obligations. In particular, this means:

- **Establishing** and **maintaining** the company's **statutory registers**
- **Filing accurate returns** with the Registrar on time
- **Organising** and **minuting** company and **board meetings**
- **Ensuring** that **accounting** records meet **statutory requirements**
- **Ensuring** that **annual accounts** are **prepared** and **filed** in accordance with **statutory requirements**
- **Monitoring statutory requirements** of the company
- **Signing company documents** as may be required by law

Under the UK Corporate Governance Code, the company secretary must:

- **Ensure good information flows** within the board and its committees
- **Facilitate induction of board members** and assist with professional development
- **Advise** the Chair and the **board** on all **governance issues**

9.3 Powers and authority of a company secretary

The powers of the company secretary have historically been very limited. However, the common law increasingly recognises that they may be able to act as agents to exercise apparent or **ostensible authority**, therefore, they may enter the company into contracts connected with the administrative side of the company.

Panorama Developments (Guildford) Ltd v Fidelis Furnishing Fabrics Ltd 1971

The facts: B, the secretary of a company, ordered cars from a car hire firm, representing that they were required to meet the company's customers at London Airport. Instead he used the cars for his own purposes. The bill was not paid, so the car hire firm claimed payment from B's company.

Decision: B's company was liable, for he had apparent authority to make contracts such as the present one, which were concerned with the administrative side of its business. The decision recognises the general nature of a company secretary's duties.

PART I THE ADMINISTRATION AND CONTROL OF THE COMPANY

Chapter Roundup

- Any person who occupies the position of director is treated as such, the test being one of **function**.
- The method of appointing directors, along with their rotation and co-option is **controlled** by the **articles**.
- Directors are entitled to **fees** and **expenses** as directors as per the articles, and **emoluments** (and compensation for loss of office) as per their service contracts (which can be inspected by members). Some details are published in the directors' remuneration report along with the accounts.
- A director may vacate office as director due to: **resignation**; **not going** for **re-election**; **death**; **dissolution** of the company; **removal**; **disqualification**.
- Directors may be required to vacate office because they have been disqualified on grounds dictated by the articles. Directors **may** be disqualified by court order or via a voluntary disqualification undertaking from a wider range of company involvements under the Company Directors Disqualification Act 1986 (CDDA).
- Directors may be **disqualified** from acting as directors or being involved in the management of companies in a number of circumstances. They must be disqualified if the company is insolvent, or the director is found to be unfit to be concerned with management of a company, especially in relation to breach of competition law.
- The **powers** of the directors are **defined** by the **articles**.
- Directors' powers may be restricted by statute or by the articles. The directors have a duty to exercise their powers in what they honestly believe to be the **best interests** of the company and for the **purposes** for which the powers are given.
- **Directors** will have **actual authority** granted to them, but they may also have **apparent authority** in the eyes of third parties depending on the position they hold
- The Companies Act 2006 sets out the **seven principal duties** of **directors**.
- The **statutory duties** owed by directors are to:
    - Act within their powers
    - Promote the success of the company
    - Exercise independent judgement
    - Exercise reasonable skill, care and diligence
    - Avoid conflicts of interest
    - Not accept benefits from third parties
    - Declare an interest in a proposed transaction or arrangement
- Every public company must have a **company secretary**, who is one of the officers of a company and may be a director. Private companies are not required to have a secretary.

Quick Quiz

1. A person who is held out by a company as a director and performs the duties of a director without actually being validly appointed is a

    A Shadow director
    B De facto director
    C Non-executive director
    D Executive director

2. **Fill in the blanks** in the statements below.

    Under model articles directors are authorised to (1) ………………….. the (2) ………………….. of the company, and (3) ………………….. the (4) ………………….. of the company.

3. Under which of the following grounds may a director be disqualified if they are guilty, and under which must a director be disqualified?

    A Conviction of an indictable offence in connection with a company.

    B Persistent default with the provisions of company legislation.

    C Wrongful trading.

    D Director of an insolvent company whose conduct makes them unfit to be concerned in the management of the company.

4. What is the extent of a CEO's actual authority?

5. What are the two principal ways by which members can control the activities of directors?

6. A public company must have two directors, a private company only needs one.

    True ☐

    False ☐

7. The directors of a company are in breach of the rule requiring them to act for a proper purpose. A general meeting can

    A Do nothing that will authorise the transaction.
    B Authorise the transaction by ordinary resolution.
    C Authorise the transaction by special resolution only.
    D Relieve the directors of any liability under the transaction by special resolution only.

8. Describe the subjective test that directors must pass in order to meet their duty of care.

9. A private company with a sole director is not legally required to have a company secretary, but if it does, the sole director can also be the company secretary.

    True ☐

    False ☐

Answers to Quick Quiz

1. B. The description is of a de facto director.
2. (1) manage (2) business (3) exercise all (4) powers
3. A to C are grounds under which a director may be disqualified; D is grounds under which a director must be disqualified.
4. The actual authority is whatever the board gives them.
5. Appointing and removing directors in general meeting

    Reallocating powers by altering the articles
6. True. Private companies only need one director.
7. B. This was the decision in *Bamford v Bamford 1969*.
8. A director is expected to show the degree of skill, knowledge and expertise that they actually have in order to meet the subjective test.
9. True. Sole directors of private companies can be company secretaries. Private companies are not legally required to have a company secretary.

End of chapter question

Director dealings

Discuss how the Companies Act 2006 regulates dealings between directors and their companies, with particular reference to long-term service contracts, substantial property transactions and loans.

(20 marks)

Majority control and minority protection

Topic list	Syllabus reference
1 Majority control: the rule in *Foss v Harbottle*	3.4
2 Minority protection: fraud on the company	3.4
3 Minority protection: s 994	3.4
4 Derivative claims	3.4
5 'Just and equitable' winding up	3.4
6 Other statutory rights of minorities	3.4

Introduction

In this third chapter covering how companies are managed and controlled, we look at a key principle concerning company decisions – **majority control**. Every member of a company is bound by the articles to the company and to their fellow members. By implication, a member agrees to be bound by the decisions of the **majority** as expressed at a general meeting. This principle of majority rule was established in the UK in the case of *Foss v Harbottle*.

Companies often have many shareholders and it is unlikely that all members will be happy with decisions that are made. The general principle (which is supported by the two types of resolution) is the **will of the majority** prevails.

However, while **directors** must exercise their power *bona fide* for the benefit of the company and for a proper purpose, shareholders are under no such obligation. Clearly shareholders may exercise their votes in their own interests and not those of the company. There must, therefore, be some restraint on the power of those able to command a majority vote. Minorities are therefore protected by **common law** and **statute**, and the various rules are all covered in this chapter.

The **Companies Act 2006**, (TSO, 2006) and the **Small Business, Enterprise and Employment Act 2015**, (TSO, 2015) apply to this and all chapters unless otherwise stated.

PART I THE ADMINISTRATION AND CONTROL OF THE COMPANY

1 Majority control: the rule in *Foss v Harbottle*

FAST FORWARD

The majority ultimately control the company, though the minority may need to be protected. It is the company which should bring actions to recover goods etc, not the shareholders individually.

Attention!

Foss v Harbottle confirmed the rule that the **majority shareholders control the company** and therefore established the **need** for minority protection. It did not establish a right to minority protection.

A key principle of company law is that **members** voting in general meeting have **ultimate control of a company**, and therefore its directors.

A problem arises if a person or number of people who are directors dominate the general meeting (that is, they hold more than 75% of the shares) and **behave unfairly** to minority shareholders or improperly to the company who are powerless to do anything about it. This is illustrated by the following case.

Foss v Harbottle 1843

The facts: A shareholder (Foss) sued the directors of the company alleging that the directors had defrauded the company by selling land to it at an inflated price. The company was by this time in a state of disorganisation and efforts to call the directors to account at a general meeting had failed.

Decision: The action must be dismissed.

- The company as a personal separate from its members is the only proper plaintiff in an action to protect its rights or property (see the Fischer case below).
- The company in general meeting must decide whether to bring such legal proceedings.

A shareholder in a company may be entitled to recover damages for the diminution of the value of their shareholding, where such diminution was the result of loss inflicted on the company by the actions of the controlling majority. If the company successfully sues the wrongdoers then the company's losses are made good and the shares should not lose value. If a shareholder suffers losses which are simply a reflection of the company's losses (eg dividends not paid because of the losses), they cannot recover losses from the wrongdoers: *Johnson v Gore Wood 2002*.

In laying down the general principles of procedure the court did nonetheless recognise that 'the **claims of justice**' must prevail over '**technical rules**'.

The protection of a minority in various situations is provided by making **exceptions to the rule in *Foss v Harbottle***.

Question Foss v Harbottle

Foss v Harbottle established the rights of minority shareholders to obtain relief from oppressive acts by the majority.

True ☐

False ☐

Answer

False. *Foss v Harbottle* emphasised the principle of majority rule. (It was thus evident that the minority needed protection.)

Having established the principle of majority control, for the rest of this chapter we shall look at the various protections available to minorities. The first protection we shall consider is where the majority have committed a fraud against the company.

2 Minority protection: fraud on the company

FAST FORWARD

A minority can bring proceedings to prevent a **fraud** on the company or minority shareholders. Fraud can mean misappropriation of property or discrimination against a minority.

There is an exception to the rule (in *Foss v Harbottle*) over fraud by a controlling majority. It aims to **protect the company** (by a member's action) **since the company cannot protect itself**. It must be shown that:

- What was taken **belonged to the company**.
- It **passed to those against** who the claim is made.
- Those who **appropriated the company's property are in control** of the company.

A member may bring an action to **enforce the company's rights** (a derivative action). Any remedy awarded goes to the company.

2.1 Majority control and minority protection

Diverting profitable contracts away from the company is to deprive it of its 'property'.

Cook v Deeks 1916

The facts: The directors who were also controlling shareholders negotiated a contract in the name of the company. They took the contract for themselves and passed a resolution in general meeting declaring that the company had no interest in the contract. A minority shareholder sued them as trustees for the company of the benefit of the contract.

Decision: The contract 'belong in equity to the company' and the directors could not, by passing a resolution in general meeting, bind the company to approving this action of defrauding it.

2.2 Passing of property to controlling shareholders

Passing property to **controlling shareholders** (though **not** to **third parties**) may well be equivalent to fraud even though no dishonesty is shown.

Daniels v Daniels 1978

The facts: The company was controlled by its two directors, husband and wife. It bought land for £4,250 (probate value) from the estate of a deceased person and alter resold it at the same price to the lady director. She re-sold it for £120,000. A minority shareholder sued the directors but did not allege fraud. Objection was raised that a member could not sue the directors on the company's behalf for negligence (Pavlides' case above) but only for fraud.

Decision: The circumstances required investigation and a member might sue the directors and controlling shareholders for negligence if one of them secured a benefit form the company by reason of it.

In particular those directors who are also managers of the company's business are able to **control the flow of information** to the full board and to a general meeting. If the information is inaccurate or incomplete it may result in a wrong decision by the independent majority.

2.3 Discrimination against minority

The courts have taken **fraud** to mean not just misappropriation of company property but **discrimination against** the minority in some cases.

> *Clemens v Clemens Bros Ltd 1976*
>
> *The facts:* A and B (who were aunt and niece) held 55% and 45% respectively of the shares with voting rights. A proposed to vote in favour of ordinary resolutions to increase the authorised share capital and to approve the allotment of new shares to or for the benefit of employees of the company. No more shares would be allotted to A or B but the effect of the scheme would be to reduce B's shareholding from 45% to 24.5% with the object of depriving B of her power to block a special resolution to alter the articles as A desired. B sought a declaration that A could not use her votes in this way.
>
> *Decision:* A should be restrained from using her votes to deprive B of her 'negative control' (her ability to block an alteration of the articles to which B objected).

As well as protecting the company against fraud by the majority, the law also provides statutory protection for minorities against unfairly prejudicial conduct by the majority.

3 Minority protection: s 994

FAST FORWARD

> S 994 offers a statutory remedy to a minority if **unfairly prejudicial conduct** has occurred. Unfairly prejudicial conduct generally involves **discrimination against a minority** or **exclusion of a director** from a **quasi-partnership company**, and includes removal of the company's auditor from office on grounds of divergence of opinions on accounting treatments or audit procedures, or on any other improper grounds.

Statute law also gives protection to minority shareholders.

Any member may apply to the court for relief under s 994 Companies Act 2006 (TSO, 2006) on the grounds that the company's affairs are being or have been conducted in a manner which is **unfairly prejudicial** to the interests of the members **generally or of some part** of the members. Application may also be made in respect of a single prejudicial act omission.

3.1 Definition of unfairly prejudicial conduct

Unfair prejudice to some of the members includes **removal of the company's auditor** from office on grounds of divergence of opinions on accounting treatments or audit procedures, or on any other improper grounds: s 994(1A).

There is **no** other statutory definition of what constitutes unfairly prejudicial conduct. Applications against unfairly prejudicial conduct often arise from:

(a) **Exclusion of a director** from participation in the management of a quasi-partnership company when they could legitimately have expected to be involved in management. A **'quasi-partnership' company** is a small, generally private and often family-owned company where essentially the relationship between the directors and members is equivalent to partners in a partnership.

(b) **Discrimination against minority shareholders**.

Whatever the reason for the application, the complaint must be based on prejudice to the **member as a member** and not as an employee, nor as an unpaid creditor. The complaint must relate to **breach of the terms by which it has been agreed the company should be run**, and not to private acts of shareholders.

Courts will have regard to the **expectations** of members when considering whether conduct is unfairly prejudicial, particularly in quasi-partnership cases where the 'partner' expects to be involved in management. It is therefore unfairly prejudicial for the members to ignore that expectation and expel them.

Re Bird Precision Bellows 1986

The facts: A minority with 26% of the shares suspected the MD of this 'quasi-partnership' company of concealing bribes paid to secure contracts. When the DTI refused to investigate the minority was removed from the board. They claimed unfair prejudice under s 994.

Decision: The claim was allowed as it was a 'quasi-partnership'.

3.2 Limits to unfair prejudice claims

The courts have established **limits** to claims under s 994.

(a) There has to have been an **actual act** by the company, for example a breach in the terms on which it was agreed the company would be run. A minority shareholder will not be able to obtain relief just because they have lost trust or confidence in the way the company is being run.

(b) The court will take into account the **contents** of the company's **constitution** in deciding whether the minority had legitimate expectations: *Re Tottenham Hotspur plc 1994*. It is unlikely that 'expectations' can override the terms of the memorandum and articles whether company is a plc.

(c) In **public companies**, shareholders are unlikely to have a reasonable expectation of being involved in management.

The courts may also take the **petitioner's conduct into account** when deciding whether certain actions are unfairly prejudicial.

Re R A Noble & Sons (Clothing) Ltd 1983

The facts: B had provided the capital but left the management in the hands of N, the other director, on the understanding that N would consult B on major company matters. N did not do so and B confined themselves to enquiries to N on social occasions; he accepted N's vague assurances that all was well. The petition followed from a breakdown of the relationship.

Decision: B's exclusion from discussion of company management questions was largely the result of his own lack of interest. The petition was dismissed.

Re London School of Electronics 1985

The facts: The other shareholders had removed the petitioner from his directorship after he had alleged that they were diverting business form the company to themselves. He then setup a rival business and took part of the company's connections with him.

Decision: He had a right to relief even though he did not have 'clean hands'. The majority had to buy out the minority without any discount for the fact that his were minority shareholders and therefore of less value.

Unfairly prejudicial conduct need not be **illegal**, nor need it be intention nor discriminatory. It is the effect of the conduct that is considered.

The courts will not generally intervene in cases of disputes about **management** (even bad management).

Re A Company 1983

The facts: The petitioners' grievance was the directors' refusal to put forward a scheme of reconstruction or a proposal to purchase their shares (by the company). The directors were preoccupied with plans for diversification of the business.

Decision: The directors' duty was to manage the company to its advantage as they saw it. It was not a case of 'unfair prejudice'.

In *Re Five Minute Car Wash Service Ltd 1966*, the complaint was of incompetent management causing loss but tolerated by the controlling shareholder. The petition failed.

3.3 Examples: Unfairly prejudicial contract

- **Exclusion** and **removal** from the **board**. When the company was one in which the director had legitimate expectations of being involved in management: *Re Bird Prediction Bellows Ltd 1986*.
- **Improper allotment** of shares.

> *Re DR Chemicals Ltd 1989*
>
> *The facts:* The majority shareholder allotted further shares to themselves to increase their holding.
>
> *Decision:* The allotment was a blatant case of unfair prejudicial conduct (and also, incidentally, a breach of the Companies Act pre-emption rules).

- **Failure** to **call a meeting**: *Re McGuinness and Another 1988*
- **Making an inaccurate statement to shareholders.**

> *Re A Company 1986*
>
> *The facts:* The petitioners complained that the directors had misled them in recommending acceptance of a bid by another company which the directors owned.
>
> *Decision:* The directors' conduct was unfairly prejudicial since it affected members' rights to sell their shares at the best price.

- A managing director using **assets** for his own **personal benefit** and the personal benefit of his family and friends: *Re Elgindata Ltd 1991*.
- **Diversion of a company's business** to a director-controlled company: *Re Cumana 1986*.
- Making a **rights issue** which minority shareholders could not take up: *Re Cumana 1986*.
- Payment of **excessive directors' bonuses** and **pension contributions**: *Re Cumara 1986*.
- **Continued mismanagement** caused serious financial damage to the company and the minority's interests: *Re Macro (Ipswich) Ltd 1994*.

3.4 Examples: Not unfairly prejudicial conduct

- **Late presentation** of **accounts**: *Re Ringtower Holdings plc 1989*
- **Failure** by a parent company **to pay** the **debts** of a **subsidiary**: *Nicholas v Soundcraft Electronics Ltd 1993*
- **Non-compliance** with **Stock Exchange rules** and the UK Corporate Governance Code: *Re Astec (BSR) plc 1998*

The limits on the application of s 994 remain under debate and are determined on a case by case basis. It has been argued for example that a s 994 action could be used as a check on excessive board remuneration packages. *Re Cumana 1986* laid down the principle that excessive directors' remuneration can be conduct that is unfairly prejudicial to numbers' interests.

> *Maidment v Attwood and Others 2012*
>
> A shareholder petitioned for relief from unfair prejudice under s 994 on the grounds that the company's sole director paid themselves excessive remuneration in the years prior to the company going into insolvency
>
> *Decision:* The director had breached their duties by fixing their remuneration by reference to their own interests, contrary to their duty as a director, which subsequently amounted to unfairly prejudicial conduct under s 994 CA 2006.

In *O'Neill v Phillips 1999* it was stressed that the relationship between shareholders is primarily governed by the **constitution**, so if this has been complied with, or any breach is only minor, the courts will not rush to find unfair prejudice. It is only where there is an equitable consideration of unfairness that the constitution **does not represent the understandings** on which the members are associated that an act which actually complies with the document may be found to be **unfairly prejudicial**.

3.5 Court order where there is unfair prejudice

FAST FORWARD

Courts may take whatever orders they deem fit, most often **purchase of a dissenting minority's shares**.

When a petition is successful the court may make **whatever order** it deems fit.

- An order regulating the **future conduct** of the company's affairs, for example that a controlling shareholder shall conform to the decisions taken at board meetings.

- An authorisation to any person to bring **legal proceedings** on behalf of the company; the company is then responsible for the legal costs.

- An order requiring the company to **refrain** from doing or continuing an act complained of.

- An order for the wrongdoer to account to the company for its losses.

- Provision for the **purchase of shares** of the **minority**.

- **Inclusion in the articles** of provisions which may only be altered or removed thereafter by leave of the court.

Where the issue is a **minority objecting to a take-over**, a common relief is an order that either the controlling shareholder or the company shall **purchase the petitioner's shares at a fair price**. This ends a relationship which has probably broken down beyond repair.

- The shares should be valued on the basis of their **worth before** the controlling shareholders' conduct had diminished it.

- The **court** may determine what is **fair**; in particular no allowance need be made because the shares to be brought are only a minority holding and do not give control.

- When the articles provide a method for valuing shares this should be used unless it would be unfair to the petitioners.

Question
S 994

James is the majority shareholder in Elan Ltd, holding 52% of the issued shares. The other shareholders are Chris, Dhian, Juno and Manrika, each of whom holds 12% of the shares. The minority shareholders feel that James has been abusing his position as majority shareholder and have lost confidence in him. They approach you for general advice.

Advise them on the nature of the action available under s 994 Companies Act 2006 on the basis of unfair prejudice to the minority.

Answer

Under s 994, any member may now apply to the court for relief on the grounds that the company's affairs are being or have been conducted in a manner which is unfairly prejudicial to the interests of the members generally or some part of the members or in respect of a particular act or omission which has been or will be prejudicial. Applications are commonly made in cases of discrimination against a minority or exclusion of a director in a quasi-partnership company.

The prejudice complained of must affect the complainant-member in his capacity as member and not as an employee or unpaid creditor. The member need not prove bad faith or even an intention to discriminate.

The court will take into account the surrounding circumstances including the parties' conduct and may make such orders as it deems fit. It might regulate the company's future affairs in some way, order the purchase of the minority's shares by the majority or by the company itself (*SCWS v Meyer 1958*), authorise some person to bring proceedings on the company's behalf, order the company to refrain from doing the act complained of or include in the company's constitution provision which could then only be altered by the court.

Loss of confidence in itself will rarely be found to be unfair prejudice.

Exam focus point

A shareholder who is unhappy about the conduct of the company's affairs will often try to obtain a remedy under s 994, so remember to include it in any answer on this area.

Although s994 is a key source of protection for minorities, there are some other sources of protection too. The first is a derivative claim, which we shall look at in the next section.

4 Derivative claims

FAST FORWARD

Under English common law members may, under certain circumstances, bring an action on behalf of a company that they are a member of. This is known as a **derivative claim**

As we saw when considering the law governing directors under section 170 of the Act, directors owe their **general duties** to the company as a whole rather than to an individual member and therefore the company is the only proper claimant which can enforce them.

The purpose of derivative claims is to enforce liability for breach of duty by one of the directors. After all, if the company itself is the only proper claimant and the directors claim for negligence, default, breach of trust or breach of duty against a director or other person, even if the director has not benefitted personally.

Sections 260 to 269 of the Companies Act 2006 (TSO, 2006) provide a **statutory basis** for deciding whether or not a member has a right to bring a **derivative claim**. They do not replace the rule in *Foss v Harbottle*, but instead set out new rules that allow a derivative claim for negligence, default, breach of trust or breach of duty against a director or other person, even if the director has not benefitted personally. The sections introduce a two-stage procedure for derivative claims.

(a) The applicant presents a *prima facie* case for their claim and the court considers the issues on the basis of the evidence filed by the applicant only. At this stage courts can dismiss applications if the applicant cannot establish a *prima facie* case.

(b) If a *prima facie* case is established then the court shall consider a range of other matters before giving permission for a substantive claim.

Under a substantive claim, the claimant brings an action on behalf of the company to **enforce the company's rights** or to recover its property. Any **benefits** received from the claim will **accrue to the company** and not to the member. The claimant would usually combine the derivative action with a **representative action** (on behalf of the other members who are not defendants) and a **personal claim** for damages.

Another source of protection for minorities is to seek a **'just and equitable' winding up** under insolvency rules. As we shall see in the next section, this is a very drastic step and can only be requested in limited circumstances.

5 'Just and equitable' winding up

FAST FORWARD

A dissatisfied member may get the court to wind the company up on the just and equitable ground.

A member who is dissatisfied with the directors or controlling shareholders over the management of the company may petition the court for the company to be wound up (liquidated) on the **just and equitable ground**. For such a petition to be successful, the member must show that no other remedy is available. It

is not enough for a member to be **dissatisfied** to make it just and equitable that the company should be wound up, since winding up what may be an otherwise healthy company is a **drastic step**.

5.1 Examples: When companies have been wound up

(a) **The substratum of the company has gone** – the only main object(s) of the company (its underlying basis or substratum) cannot be or can no longer be achieved.

> *Re German Date Coffee Co 1882*
>
> *The facts:* The objects clause specified very pointedly that the sole object was to manufacture coffee from dates under a German patent. The German government refused to grand a patent. The company manufactured coffee under a Swedish patent for sale in Germany. A contributory petitioned for compulsory winding up.
>
> *Decision:* The company existed only to 'work a particular patent' and as it could not do so it should be wound up.

(b) The **company was formed for an illegal** or **fraudulent purpose** or there is a **complete deadlock** in the **management** of its affairs.

> *Re Yenidje Tobacco Co Ltd 1916*
>
> *The facts:* Two sole traders merged their businesses in a company of which they were the only directors and shareholders. They quarrelled bitterly and one sued the other for fraud. Meanwhile they refused to speak to each other and conducted board meetings by passing notes through the hands of the secretary. The defendant in the fraud action petitioned for compulsory winding up.
>
> *Decision:* 'In substance these two people are really partners' and by analogy with the law of partnership (which permits dissolution if the partners are really unable to work together) it was just and equitable to order liquidation.

(c) The **understandings between members or directors** which were the basis of the association have been **unfairly breached** by lawful action.

> *Ebrahimi v Westbourne Galleries Ltd 1973*
>
> *The facts:* E and N carried on business together for 25 years, originally as partners and for the last 10 years through a company in which each originally had 500 shares. E and N were the first directors and shared the profits as directors' remuneration; no dividends were paid. When N's son joined the business he became a third director and E and N each transferred 100 shares to N's son. Eventually there were disputes; N and his son used their voting control in general meeting (600 votes against 400) to remove E from his directorship under the power of removal given by the Companies Act (removal by ordinary resolution).
>
> *Decision:* The company should be wound up. N and his son were within their legal rights in removing E from his directorship, but the past relationship made it 'unjust or inequitable' to insist on legal rights and the court could intervene on equitable principles to order liquidation.

> *Re A Company 1983*
>
> *The facts:* The facts were similar in essentials to those in Ebrahimi's case but the majority offered and the petitioner agreed that they would settle the dispute by a sale of his shares to the majority. This settlement broke down however because they could not agree on the price. The petitioner then petitioned on the just and equitable ground.
>
> *Decision:* An order for liquidation on this ground may only be made 'in the absence of any other remedy'. As the parties had agreed in principle that there was an alternative to liquidation the petition must be dismissed.

(d) The **directors deliberately withheld information** so that the **shareholders have no confidence** in the company's management.

Question: Just and equitable winding up

Give four examples of instances where the court has ordered a company to be wound up on the just and equitable grounds.

Answer

Four examples are:

The substratum of the company has gone.

The company was formed for an illegal or fraudulent purpose, or there is complete deadlock in its affairs.

The understandings between members or directors which were the basis of association have been unfairly breached.

The directors deliberately withhold information so that the shareholders have no confidence in the company's management.

6 Other statutory rights of minorities

We have noted a number of rights for minority shareholders as we have worked through this company law Workbook. Here is a summary.

Minority rights	
Subject	**Required**
Variation of class rights	Holders of 15%+ of class of shares can apply to court for cancellation
Company meeting	Can be requisitioned by holders of 5% of company's voting capital
Notice of members' resolution	Must be given by company on requisition of members holding 5%+ of voting rights/100 or more members holding shares in the company on which an average sum of £100+ per member has been paid up
Full notice of special resolution	Must be given if members with 5%+ of voting capital insist
Conversion of public company to private	50+ members or members holding 5%+ of issued share capital can apply to court for cancellation
Purchase of own shares out of capital by private company	Holders of 10%+ of shares/any class of shares can apply to court to prohibit the transaction
Financial assistance by private company	Any member can apply to court to prohibit the transaction
Poll	Can be demanded by at least 5 members/members holding 10%+ of voting rights or have 10%+ of total of all paid up shares
Off-market purchase of own shares	Poll can be demanded by individual members
Full notice of AGM	Can be demanded by individual members
Registration of limited company as unlimited	Can be prevented by individual members
Government investigation into affairs/ownership of company	Can be requested by 200+ members/members holding 10%+ of issued shares
Public company investigation into membership of company	Can be demanded by holders of 10%+ of company's voting capital

Chapter Roundup

- The majority ultimately control the company, though the minority may need to be protected. It is the company which should bring actions to recover goods etc, not shareholders individually.
- A minority can bring proceedings to prevent a **fraud** on the company or minority shareholders. Fraud can mean misappropriation of property or discrimination against a minority.
- S 994 offers a statutory remedy to a minority if **unfairly prejudicial conduct** has occurred. Unfairly prejudicial conduct generally involves **discrimination against a minority** or **exclusion of a director** from a **quasi-partnership company** and includes removal of the company's auditor from office on grounds of divergence of opinions on accounting treatments or audit procedures, or on any other improper grounds.
- Courts may make whatever orders they deem fit, most often **purchase of a dissenting minority's shares**.
- Under English common law members may, under certain circumstances, bring an action on behalf of a company that they are a member of. This is known as a derivative claim
- A dissatisfied member may get the court to wind the company up on the just and equitable ground.

Quick Quiz

1. The three conditions to succeed in a claim for a fraud on the company are:

    (1) ....

    (2) ....

    (3) ....

2. Give four examples of remedies a court may provide for unfairly prejudicial conduct.

3. **Fill in the blanks** in the statements below.

    S 994 gives relief on the grounds that the company's affairs are being or have been conducted in a manner that is (1) .... to the interests of (2) .... or (3) ....

4. Which of the following are statutory rights of individual members?

    A   To demand full notice of an AGM

    B   To prevent re-registration of a limited company as unlimited

    C   To apply for a cancellation of a variation of class rights

    D   To demand a poll on a resolution for an off market purchase of own shares

    E   To require the Government to investigate a company's ownership

    F   To insist on full notice for a special resolution

5. **Fill in the blanks** in the statements below.

    Petitions under s 994 often arise from exclusion of a director from participation in the management of a (1) .... company, or (2) .... against a minority.

Answers to Quick Quiz

1. (1) What was taken belonged to the company
   (2) It passed to those against whom the claim is made
   (3) Those who appropriated the company's property are in control of the company

2. An order regulating the future conduct of the company's affairs
   Authorising the company to bring legal proceedings
   Ordering the company to refrain from actions
   Providing for the purchase of shares of the minority

3. (1) unfairly prejudicial (2) members generally (3) some part of the members

4. A, B and D represent individual rights. C requires application by holders of at least 15% of the shares of the class. E requires 200 members or the holders of at least 10% of issued shares. F requires members holding at least 5% of voting shares.

5. (1) quasi-partnership (2) discrimination

End of chapter question

Minority shareholders

Brakes Catering Limited (Brakes) is a catering company which provides national and international event catering. Harry Jackson and his wife Julia founded the company over 15 years ago but no longer hold positions on the board or significant shareholdings. The current directors are Martin Toller, Umara Khan and Kieran Dyer, each of whom owns 30% of the shares in Brakes. The remaining 10% is owned by a number of small shareholders, including Harry and Julia who own 5% and 2% respectively. Over the last 12 months, Harry and Julia have become increasingly frustrated with how the company is being run and do not believe that Martin, Umara and Kieran are acting in the best interests of the company and its shareholders.

Required

Discuss and analyse the statutory rules which would provide assistance to Harry and Julia as minority shareholders in this company. **(20 marks)**

Accounts and audit

Topic list	Syllabus reference
1 Accounting records and annual accounts	3.4
2 The company auditor	3.4

Introduction

In previous chapters on company law we have seen what companies are, how they are managed and by whom. In this chapter we look at some of the **consequences** of choosing to run a business as a company rather than as a sole trader or partnership.

In particular, we shall look at the statutory requirements for companies to

- Keep accounting records
- Prepare accounts and file them with the Registrar
- Appoint auditors (unless exempt)

We shall also cover the vital role of the auditor. As well as appointment, resignation and removal of auditors we look at eligibility and ineligibility for office, the auditor's independence and their duties and rights.

Finally, this chapter summarises the position regarding auditors' liability which ties in to your previous study of the tort of negligence.

The **Companies Act 2006**, (TSO, 2006) and the **Small Business, Enterprise and Employment Act 2015**, (TSO, 2015) apply to this and all chapters unless otherwise stated.

PART I THE ADMINISTRATION AND CONTROL OF THE COMPANY

1 Accounting records and annual accounts

1.1 Accounting records

FAST FORWARD

> Companies must keep **sufficient accounting records** to explain the company's transactions and its financial position, in other words so that accurate financial statements can be prepared.

Under the Companies Act 2006 (TSO, 2006), a company is required to keep accounting records sufficient to **show and explain** the company's transactions. At any time, it should be possible:

- To **disclose** with reasonable accuracy the **company's financial position** at intervals of not more than six months.
- For the directors to ensure that any accounts required to be prepared **comply** with the **Act** and **International Accounting Standards.**

Certain specific records are required by the Act.

(a) Daily entries of **sums paid** and **received**, with details of the source and nature of the transactions.

(b) A **record** of assets and **liabilities**.

(c) **Statements of stock** held by the company at the end of each financial year.

(d) **Statements of stocktaking** to back up the records in (c).

(e) **Statements of goods bought and sold** (except retail sales), together with details of buyers and sellers sufficient to identify them.

The requirements (c) to (e) above apply only to businesses involved in dealing in goods.

Accounting records must be kept for **three** years (in the case of a **private** company), and **six** years in that of a **public** one.

Accounting records should be kept at the company's **registered office** or at some other place thought fit by the directors. Accounting records should be open to **inspection** by the **company's officers**. Shareholders have **no statutory rights** to inspect the records, although they may be granted the right by the articles.

Failure in respect of these duties is an offence by the officers in default.

Question Minimum accounting records

What are the minimum specific accounting records required by the Companies Act for a company that does NOT deal in goods?

Answer

The minimum accounting records for companies that do not deal in goods are:

- Daily entries of sums paid and received, with details of the source and nature of the transactions.
- A record of assets and liabilities

1.2 Annual accounts

FAST FORWARD

> A registered company must prepare **annual accounts** showing a true and fair view, lay them and various reports before members, and file them with the Registrar following directors' approval.

For each **accounting reference period** (usually 12 months) of the company the directors must prepare accounts for the members, and deliver or file them with the Registrar of Companies. Where they are prepared in Companies Act format they must include a **balance sheet** and **profit and loss account** which, for the accounting reference period up to the **accounting reference date,** give a **true and fair view** of the individual company's and the group's

- Assets
- Liabilities
- Financial position
- Profit or loss

The accounts can either be in **Companies Act format** or prepared in accordance with **International Accounting Standards**. Where international accounting standards are followed a note to this effect must be included in the notes to the accounts. After a financial year in which the directors of a company prepare IAS accounts for the company, the directors may change to preparing Companies Act accounts for a reason other than a relevant change of circumstance provided they have not changed to Companies Act individual accounts in the period of five years preceding the first day of that financial year: s 395(4A).

The accounts can be prepared for a different period than 12 months if the company changes its accounting reference date. There is no restriction on how often a company can change the date if it means the accounting reference period is 12 months or less, but it cannot be extended beyond 12 months more than once in five years except in limited circumstances.

1.2.1 Approving, laying and filing accounts

The company's board of directors must **approve** the **annual accounts** and they must be signed by a director on behalf of the board. When directors approve annual accounts that do not comply with the Act or IAS they are **guilty** of an **offence**.

A public company is required to **lay its accounts**, and the **directors' report**, before **members** in **general meeting**. A quoted company must also lay the **directors' remuneration report** before the general meeting.

A company must **file** its annual accounts and its report with the **Registrar** within a maximum period reckoned from the accounting reference date, to which the accounts are made up. The standard permitted interval between the end of the accounting reference period and the filing of accounts is **six months** for a **public** and **nine months** for a **private company.**

1.2.2 Auditing accounts

The accounts must be **audited** (unless the company is exempt). The **auditors' report** must be attached to the copies issued to members, filed with the Registrar or published. Exemptions apply to **small and dormant companies,** though members may require an audit. The accounts must also be accompanied by a **directors' report** giving information on a number of prescribed matters. These include (where an audit was necessary) a statement that there is no relevant information of which the auditors are unaware, and another statement from the directors that they exercised due skill and care in the period. Quoted companies must submit the **directors' remuneration report**.

1.2.3 Abridged accounts

Most private companies are permitted to file **abridged accounts with the Registrar.** This right to prepare abbreviated accounts for Companies House does NOT affect the company's obligations to prepare full accounts for its members.

An entity is classed as 'micro' if it meets at least two of the following conditions:

- Annual turnover must be not more than £632,000
- The balance sheet total must be not more than £316,000
- The average number of employees must be not more than 10.

A private company is classed as 'small' if it meets at least two of the following conditions:

- Annual turnover must be not more than £10.2 million
- The balance sheet total must be not more than £5.1 million
- The average number of employees must be not more than 50.

A private company is classed as 'medium-sized' if it meets at least two of the following conditions:

- Annual turnover must be not more than £36 million
- The balance sheet total must be not more than £18 million
- The average number of employees must be not more than 250.

Public companies and certain types of organisation, such as banks, cannot benefit from the micro-entity and small and medium-sized company disclosure exemptions.

A **micro-entity** has to option to take advantage of certain accounting exemptions. These include using **simple profit and loss accounts** and **balance sheets** and only providing a minimum of accounting information (referred to in the regulations as **minimum accounting terms**). No notes to the accounts are required and the entity can apply the small company rules (see below) in relation to other aspects such as the directors' report.

A **small company** can either choose to file a copy of the full accounts which it prepared for its members, or to file **an abridged balance sheet but no directors' report or profit and loss account**: s 444. They must be filed with a special auditor's report unless the company is also exempt from audit (see 1.3 below).

A **medium-sized company** must deliver its annual accounts and directors' report to the Registrar, plus a copy of the auditor's report (unless the company is exempt from audit). The accounts must include **a balance sheet plus a profit and loss account in which certain items are combined**, that is a different form of abridged accounts to small companies: s 445. Again, a special auditor's report is required: s 449.

Attention!

> As already covered in Chapter 10, the turnover and balance sheet thresholds for micro, small and medium size companies have been proposed to increase from October 2024. At the time of publication, this has not yet been confirmed.
>
> The proposed new thresholds are:
>
> Micro-companies: Turnover <£1million, balance sheet <£500,000
> Small companies: Turnover <£15m, balance sheet <£7.5million
> Medium companies: Turnover <£54million, balance sheet <£27million
>
> The thresholds for average number of employees are proposed to remain the same.
>
> The same set of proposals also set out changes to the reporting requirements (including filing abridged accounts) of the different types of company.
>
> These new thresholds will also impact the requirements for audit exemption (see Section 1.3)
>
> Unless you are notified otherwise, you should treat the current thresholds and reporting requirements as still valid.

1.2.4 Recipients of annual accounts

Each **member** and **debentureholder** is entitled to be sent a copy of the **annual accounts**, together with the directors' and auditor's reports. In the case of public companies, they should be sent at least 21 days before the meeting at which they shall be laid. In the case of private companies, they should be sent at the same time as the documents are filed, if not earlier.

Anyone else entitled to **receive** notice of a general meeting, including the company's auditor, should **also be sent** a copy. At any other time, any member or debentureholder is entitled to a copy free of charge within **seven days** of requesting it.

All companies may prepare a **summary financial statement** to be circulated to members instead of the full accounts, subject to various requirements as to form and content being met. However, members have the right to receive full accounts should they wish to.

Quoted companies must make their annual accounts and reports available on a website which is maintained on the company's behalf and which identifies it. The documents must be made available as soon as reasonably practicable and access should not be conditional on the payment of a fee or subject to other restrictions.

Where the company or its directors **fail to comply** with the Act, they may be subject to a **fine**.

1.2.5 Late filing of accounts with Companies House

Late filing of accounts will result in a fine being due.

1.3 Exemption from audit

> **FAST FORWARD**
>
> Certain companies are **exempt from audit** provided that certain conditions are fulfilled.

These conditions are as follows:

(a) A small private company is totally exempt from the annual audit requirement in a financial year if its turnover for that year is **not more** than **£10.2 million**, and its **balance sheet total** is **not more than £5.1 million: s 477**.

(b) The exemptions do not apply to **public companies**, **banking** or **insurance companies** or those subject to a **statute-based regulatory regime**.

(c) **Members** holding **10%** or more of the capital of any company can veto the exemption: s 476.

(d) **Dormant companies** also qualify for exemption from an audit.

Question — Audit exemption

Blandings plc has turnover of £5 million for the current year and its balance sheet total is £3 million. Can the company be exempt from audit?

Answer

No, because it is a public company.

So, as we have just seen, certain companies are required to have their financial statements audited. Whilst we do not need to concern ourselves with the audit itself in this syllabus, we shall look at the rules concerning the appointment of auditors, their duties and rights and how they are removed from office.

2 The company auditor

> **FAST FORWARD**
>
> Every company (apart from certain small companies) must appoint appropriately qualified **auditors**. An audit is a check on the stewardship of the directors.

Under the Companies Act 2006 (TSO, 2006), **every company** (except a dormant private company and certain small and subsidiary companies) must **appoint auditors** for each financial year: s 475.

2.1 Appointment of auditors

The **first auditors** may be appointed by the directors, to hold office until the **first general meeting** at which their appointment is considered.

Subsequent auditors may not take office until the previous auditor has ceased to hold office. They will hold office until the end of the next financial period (private companies) or the next accounts meeting (public companies) unless re-appointed.

Appointment of auditors	
Members	• Usually appoint auditor in general meeting by ordinary resolution. • Auditors hold office from 28 days after the meeting in which the accounts are laid until the end of the corresponding period the next year. This is the case even if the auditors are appointed at the meeting where the accounts are laid. • May appoint in general meeting to fill a casual vacancy.
Directors	• Appoint the first ever auditors. They hold office until the end of the first meeting at which the accounts are considered. • May appoint to fill a casual vacancy.
Secretary of State	• May appoint auditors if members fail to do so. • Company must notify Secretary of State within 28 days of the general meeting where the accounts were laid.

2.2 Eligibility as auditor

FAST FORWARD Membership of a **Recognised Supervisory Body** is the main prerequisite for eligibility as an auditor.

Membership of a **Recognised Supervisory Body** is the main prerequisite for eligibility as an auditor. An audit firm may be either a body corporate, a partnership or a sole practitioner.

The Act requires an auditor to hold an **'appropriate qualification'**. A person holds an 'appropriate qualification' if they:

- Have satisfied **existing criteria** for appointment as an auditor.
- Hold a **recognised qualification** obtained in the UK.
- Hold an **approved overseas qualification**.

2.3 Ineligibility as auditor

FAST FORWARD Under the Companies Act 2006, a person may be ineligible on the grounds of **'lack of independence'**.

A person is ineligible for appointment as a company auditor if they are:

- An **officer** or **employee** of the company being audited
- A **partner** or **employee** of such a person
- A **partnership** in which such a person is a partner
- **Ineligible** by virtue of the above for appointment as auditor of any parent or subsidiary undertaking where there exists a **connection** of any description as may be specified in regulations laid down by Secretary of State.

2.4 Effect of lack of independence or ineligibility

No person may act as auditor if they become ineligible or lack independence. If during their term of office an auditor loses their independence or eligibility they must **resign** with immediate effect, and **notify** their client of their resignation, giving the reason.

A person continuing to act as auditor despite losing their independence or becoming ineligible is **liable to a fine**. However it is a defence if they can prove they were not aware that they lost independence or became ineligible.

The legislation does **not** disqualify the following from being an auditor of a limited company:

- A shareholder of the company
- A debtor or creditor of the company
- A close relative of an officer or employee of the company

However, the **regulations** of the **accountancy bodies** applying to their own members are **stricter than statute in this respect**.

2.5 Re-appointing auditors of a private company

FAST FORWARD

As private companies are not required to hold annual general meetings, auditors of **private companies** are normally deemed **automatically re-appointed** each year.

The rules on appointment make reference to a **meeting** where the accounts are laid. This is not always relevant for private companies as under the Act they are not required to hold an AGM or lay the accounts before the members at a meeting. Therefore **auditors of private companies are deemed automatically re-appointed** unless one of the following circumstances applies.

- The auditor was **appointed by the directors** (most likely when the first auditor was appointed).
- The **articles require formal re-appointment**.
- **Members holding 5% of the voting rights** serve notice that the auditor should not be reappointed s 488.
- A **resolution** (written or otherwise) has been passed that prevents reappointment.
- The **directors have resolved that auditors should not be appointed** for the forthcoming year as the company is likely to be exempt from audit.

In the first case – where auditors have been appointed by the directors - there will have to be a members' meeting at an early stage so that they can be appointed by the members.

2.6 Auditors' remuneration

Whoever appoints the auditors has power to **fix their remuneration** for the period of their appointment. It is usual when the auditors are appointed by the general meeting to leave it to the directors to fix their remuneration (by agreement at a later stage). The auditors' remuneration must be **disclosed** in a **note to the accounts**.

2.7 Duties of auditors

The **statutory duty** of auditors is to report to the members whether the accounts give a **true and fair view** and have been properly prepared in accordance with the Companies Act.

They must also:

- **State** whether or not the **directors' report** is **consistent** with the **accounts**.
- For **quoted companies**, **report** to the members on the **auditable** part of the **directors' remuneration report** including whether or not it has been properly prepared in accordance with the Act: s 497.
- For listed companies, state in their report whether, in their opinion, the information given in the **corporate governance statement** about internal control and risk management systems in relation to financial reporting processes, and about share capital structures, is consistent with those accounts: s 497A.
- Be **signed** by the **auditor**, stating their **name**, and **date**. Where the auditor is a firm, the **senior auditor** must sign in their **own name** for, and on behalf, of the auditor.

If the directors of the company have prepared accounts in accordance with the **small companies regime**, or have taken advantage of small companies exemption in preparing the directors' report, and in the auditor's opinion they were not entitled to do so, the auditor shall state that fact in their report: s 497(5).

To fulfil their statutory duties, the auditors **must carry out such investigations as are necessary** to form an opinion as to whether:

(a) **Proper accounting records** have been kept and proper returns adequate for the audit have been received from branches.

(b) The **accounts** are in **agreement** with the **accounting records**.

(c) The **information** in the **directors' remuneration report** is consistent with the **accounts**.

The auditors' report must be **read** before any general meeting at which the accounts are considered and must be open to inspection by members. Auditors have to make disclosure of other services rendered to the company and the remuneration received.

Where an auditor **knowingly** or **recklessly** causes their report to be **materially misleading**, **false** or **deceptive**, they commit a criminal offence and may be liable to a **fine**: s 507.

2.8 Rights of auditors

> **FAST FORWARD**
>
> The Companies Act provides **statutory rights** for auditors to enable them to carry out their duties.

The **principal rights** of auditors, excepting those dealing with resignation or removal, are set out in the table below, and the following are notes on more detailed points.

Access to records	A right of access at all times to the books, accounts and vouchers of the company: s 499 (1)
Information and explanations	A right to require from the company's officers, employees or any other relevant person, such information and explanations as they think necessary for the performance of their duties as auditors: s 499 (1)
Attendance at/notices of general meetings	A right to attend any general meetings of the company and to receive all notices of and communications relating to such meetings which any member of the company is entitled to receive: s 502 (2)
Right to speak at general meetings	A right to be heard at general meetings which they attend on any part of the business that concerns them as auditors: s 502 (2)
Rights in relation to written resolutions	A right to receive a copy of any written resolution proposed: s 502 (1)

If auditors have **not received** all the information and explanations they consider necessary, they should state this fact in their audit report. The Act makes it an **offence** for a company's officer knowingly or recklessly to make a statement in any form to an auditor which:

- Conveys or purports to convey any information or explanation required by the auditor and
- Is materially misleading, false or deceptive.

The **penalty** is a maximum of two years' imprisonment, a fine or both.

2.9 Termination of auditors' appointment

> **FAST FORWARD**
>
> Auditors may leave office in the following ways: **resignation**; **removal from office** by an ordinary resolution with special notice passed before the end of their term; **failing** to **offer themselves** for re-election; and **not being re-elected** at the general meeting at which their term expires.

Departure of auditors from office can occur in the following ways.

(a) Auditors may **resign** their appointment by giving notice in writing to the company delivered to the registered office.

(b) Auditors may **decline reappointment**.

(c) Auditors may be **removed** from office before the expiry of their appointment by the passing of an ordinary resolution in general meeting. Special notice is required and members and auditors must be notified. **Private companies cannot remove an auditor by written resolution;** a meeting must be held.

(d) Auditors **do not have to be reappointed** when their term of office expires, although in most cases they are. Special notice must be given of any resolution to appoint auditors who were not appointed on the last occasion of the resolution, and the members and auditor must be notified.

Where a private company resolves to **appoint** a replacement auditor by **written resolution**, copies of the resolution must be sent to the proposed and outgoing auditor. The outgoing auditor may circulate a **statement of reasonable length** to the members if they notify the company within 14 days of receiving the copy of the written resolution.

2.10 Procedure for resignation of auditors

FAST FORWARD

However auditors leave office they must either: state there are **no circumstances** which should be brought to **members' and creditors' attention**; or list **those circumstances**. Auditors who are resigning can also: **circulate a statement** about their resignation to members; **requisition a general meeting'**, **or speak** at a general meeting.

Procedures for resignation of auditors	
Statement of circumstances	Auditors must deposit a statement at the registered office with their resignation stating: • For quoted companies – the circumstances around their departure. • For non-quoted public companies and all private companies – there are no circumstances that the auditor believes should be brought to the attention of the members or creditors. • If there are such circumstances the statement should describe them. • Statements should also be submitted to the appropriate audit authority.
Company action	• The company must send notice of the resignation to the Registrar. Failure to do so is an offence: s 521. • The company must **send** a copy of the statement of circumstances to **every person entitled to receive a copy of the accounts.**
Auditors' rights	If the auditors have deposited a statement of circumstances, they may: • Circulate a statement of reasonable length to the members. • Requisition a general meeting to explain their reasons: s 518. • Attend and speak at any meeting where appointment of successors is to be discussed.

If the auditors decline to seek reappointment at an AGM, they must nevertheless fulfil the requirements of a **statement of the circumstances** just as if they had resigned during the year.

The reason for this provision is to prevent auditors who are unhappy with the company's affairs keeping their suspicions secret. The statement must be deposited not less than **14 days** before the time allowed for next appointing auditors. It is an offence on the part of the auditor to fail to deposit the statement of circumstances: s 518.

2.11 Removal of auditors from office

Procedures for removal from office	
Auditor representations	If a resolution is proposed either to: • Remove the auditors before their term of office expires; or • Change the auditors when their term of office is complete the auditors have the right to make representations of reasonable length to the company.
Company action	The company must:

	• Notify members in the notice of the meeting of the representations. • Send a copy of the representations in the notice. • If it is not sent out, the auditors can require it is read at the meeting.
Attendance at meeting	Auditors removed before expiry of their office may: • Attend the meeting at which their office would have expired. • Attend any meeting at which the appointment of their successors is discussed.
Statement of circumstances	If auditors are removed at a general meeting they must: • Make a statement of circumstances for members and creditors as above.

Exam focus point

Remember that:

(a) A statement of circumstances/no circumstances must be deposited **however** the auditors leave office.

(b) The auditors have **additional rights** depending on how they leave office.

In the exam you **must** read any question on this area carefully to ensure you answer it correctly.

In your previous study of the tort of **negligence** you saw how professionals, such as accountants and auditors might be liable to pay damages if they provide negligent advice or services. We shall now consider the nature of an auditor's liability and what they can do to minimise it.

2.12 Auditors' liability

2.12.1 Nature of auditors' liability

FAST FORWARD

Auditors may be liable for **negligence** to anyone to whom they owe a **duty of care**.

The Companies Act allows companies and their auditors to make agreements which limit the auditors' **liability** to a **'fair and reasonable amount'**.

The development (by means of case-law) of the liability of auditors for negligence is covered elsewhere in the syllabus. The current position, in summary, is that auditors may be liable for negligence to anyone to whom they owe a **duty of care** – namely:

- The company
- The members as a whole
- Anyone who they know, at the time of signing the audit report, is likely to rely on that report; to be liable they also must be aware of the reasons for that reliance.

2.12.2 Liability limitation agreements

Under the Companies Act 2006 (TSO, 2006), s 532 any **agreement** between an auditor and a company that seeks to **indemnify the auditor** for their own negligence, default, or breach of duty or trust is **void**. However, under s 534, an agreement can be made which **limits the auditor's liability** to the company. Such **liability limitation agreements** (LLAs) can only stand for **one financial year** and must therefore be replaced annually.

Liability can only be **limited** to what is **fair and reasonable** having regard to the auditor's responsibilities, their contractual obligations and the professional standards expected of them. Such agreements must be approved by the members and **publicly disclosed** in the **accounts** or **directors' report**. The Financial Reporting Council (FRC) has issued guidance on these agreements.

Perhaps not surprisingly, companies are not rushing to sign up to liability limitation agreements, and they may never become widespread.

Question — Auditor duty of care

To whom do auditors owe a duty of care?

Answer

Auditors owe a duty of care to:

- The company
- The members as a whole
- Anyone who they know, at the time of signing the audit report, is likely to rely on that report; to be liable they also must be aware of the reasons for that reliance

Chapter Roundup

- Companies must keep **sufficient accounting records** to explain the company's transactions and its financial position, in other words so that accurate financial statements can be prepared.

- A registered company must prepare **annual accounts** showing a true and fair view, lay them and various reports before members, and file them with the Registrar following directors' approval.

- Certain companies are **exempt from audit** provided that certain conditions are fulfilled.

- Every company (apart from certain small companies) must appoint appropriately qualified **auditors**. An audit is a check on the stewardship of the directors.

- Membership of a **Recognised Supervisory Body** is the main prerequisite for eligibility as an auditor.

- Under the Companies Act 2006 a person may be ineligible for office as auditor on the grounds of **'lack of independence'**.

- As private companies are not required to hold AGMs, auditors of **private companies** are normally deemed **automatically re-appointed** each year.

- The Companies Act provides **statutory rights** for auditors to enable them to carry out their duties.

- Auditors may leave office in the following ways: **resignation**; **removal from office** by an ordinary resolution with special notice passed before the end of their term; **failing** to **offer themselves** for **re-election**; and **not being re-elected** at the general meeting at which their term expires.

- However auditors leave office they must either: state there are **no circumstances** which should be brought to **members' and creditors' attention**; or provide a **statement of circumstances**. Auditors who are resigning can also: **circulate a statement** about their resignation to members; **requisition a general meeting**; or **speak** at a general meeting.

- Auditors may be liable for **negligence** to anyone to whom they owe a **duty of care**.

- The Companies Act allows companies and their auditors to make liability limitation agreements which limit the auditors' **liability** to a **'fair and reasonable amount'**.

Quick Quiz

1. What is the maximum period after a company's year-end within which its accounts must be filed?

   Private company...............

   Public company...............

2. When may directors appoint auditors, and for how long may auditors so appointed hold office?

3. State two reasons a person would be ineligible to be an auditor under Companies Act 2006.

   (1) ....

   (2) ....

4. When an auditor resigns, to whom must they supply a statement of circumstances?

5. If a company does not need an audit, its accounts are not required to give a true and fair view.

   True ☐

   False ☐

Answers to Quick Quiz

1. Public companies six months; private companies nine months.
2. The first auditors may be appointed by the directors, to hold office until the first general meeting at which their appointment is considered. Directors may also appoint auditors to fill a casual vacancy.
3. Any of:
   (1) Is an officer/employee of the company being audited
   (2) A partner or employee of a person in (1)
   (3) A partnership in which (1) is a partner
   (4) Ineligible by (1), (2) and (3) to be auditor of any of the entity's subsidiaries
4. To the company at its registered office, and to the appropriate audit authority.
5. False. All companies' statutory accounts are required to give a true and fair view.

End of chapter question

Auditors

Omar Rashid is the newly appointed company secretary of Shopmart Limited, a company which operates a large chain of supermarkets. It has been brought to his attention that the company's current auditors have become ineligible and new auditors need to be appointed.

Required

Advise Omar on the requirements for eligibility as auditor, the ways in which auditors can be appointed and the duties and rights of the new auditors.

Your answer does not need to consider exemptions available to small and medium sized companies.

(20 marks)

Criminal law

Topic list	Syllabus reference
1 Financial crime	3.4
2 Insider dealing	3.4
3 Market abuse	3.4
4 Money laundering	3.4
5 Bribery	3.4
6 Criminal activity relating to companies	3.4

Introduction

Running or being involved in the **management** of a company may present directors, managers and other employees with an opportunity to take advantage of situations for **financial** or other types of **personal gain**. The legal system has made a number of actions a criminal offence and that is the subject of this chapter.

As we saw in Chapter 1, criminal law is the law governing the behaviour of people within society and towards the state. In a criminal case, the state prosecutes the accused and, if they are found guilty, a penalty can be imposed. In this chapter, we shall look specifically at some **financial crimes** and the **measures** that have been put into place to combat them.

Insider dealing is a statutory offence relating to the trading of shares or other securities. It has proved difficult to convict people of the crime of insider dealing, hence the introduction of the civil wrong of **market abuse**.

Money laundering is a serious criminal offence that is often related to other types of organised crime and is highly topical. Money laundering is the process of 'legalising' funds raised through crime. Money laundering crosses national boundaries and it can be difficult to enforce the related laws. Accountants in particular are key to efforts to prosecute money launderers

Finally we shall look at **bribery offences** and offences in relation to **companies**, especially **insolvent companies**.

PART I THE ADMINISTRATION AND CONTROL OF THE COMPANY

1 Financial crime

FAST FORWARD

Crime is **conduct prohibited by the law**. Financial crime can be international in nature, and there is a need for international cooperation to prevent it.

We shall begin our study of financial crime by considering what a crime is. It is simply **conduct prohibited by the law**.

Law tends to be organised on a **national basis**. However, some crime, particularly money laundering, is perpetrated **across national borders**. Indeed the international element of the crime contributes to its success.

Particularly with regard to money laundering, international bodies are having to **co-operate** with one another in order to control financial crimes which spreads across national boundaries.

1.1 Example: international financial crime

Suppose money laundering is a crime in Country A but not in Country B. Money laundering can be effected legally in Country B and the proceeds returned to Country A. Hence Country A cannot prosecute for the crime of money laundering, which has not been committed within its national boundaries.

2 Insider dealing

FAST FORWARD

Insider dealing is the criminal offence of **dealing** in securities while in **possession** of **inside information** as an insider, the securities being price affected by the information.

The first financial crime we shall look at is **insider dealing**. The **Criminal Justice Act 1993** (HMSO 1993) (CJA) contains the rules on **insider dealing**. It was regarded and treated as a crime since a few people are enriched at the expense of the reputation of the stock market and the interests of all involved in it.

2.1 What is insider dealing?

Key term

Insider dealing is dealing in securities while in possession of inside information as an insider, the securities being **price-affected** by the information.

To prove insider dealing, the prosecution must prove that the possessor of inside information (under s 52 CJA):

- **Dealt** in **price-affected securities** on a regulated market, or
- **Encouraged another** to **deal** in them on a regulated market, or
- **Disclosed** the **information** other than in the proper performance of their employment, office or profession.

2.1.1 Dealing

Dealing is **acquiring or disposing** of or **agreeing** to **acquire** or **dispose** of relevant securities whether **directly** or **through an agent** or nominee or a person acting according to direction: s 55 CJA.

2.1.2 Encouraging another to deal

An offence is also committed if an individual, having information as an insider, **encourages another person** to deal in price-affected securities in relation to that information. They must **know** or have reasonable cause to believe that **dealing** would **take place**.

It is irrelevant whether:

- The person encouraged realises that the securities are **price-affected** securities.
- The **inside information is given** to that person. For example, a simple recommendation to the effect that 'I cannot tell you why but now would be a good time to buy shares in Bloggs plc' would infringe the law.
- **Any dealing takes place**, the offence being committed at the time of encouragement.

2.2 Securities covered by the Act

Securities include shares, debt securities and warranties: s 54 CJA.

2.3 Inside information

Key term

> **Inside information** is **'price sensitive information'** relating to a **particular issuer** of **securities** that are price-affected and not to securities generally: s 56 CJA.

Inside information must, if made public, be likely to have a **significant effect on price** and it must be **specific or precise**. Specific would, for example, mean information that a takeover bid would be made for a specific company; precise information would be details of how much would be offered for shares.

2.4 Insiders

Under s 57 a person has information as a **primary insider** if it is (**and** they **know** it is) inside information, and if they have it (**and know** they have) from an inside source:

- Through being a **director**, **employee** or **shareholder** of an issuer of securities.
- Through access because of **employment**, **office** or **profession**.

If the direct or indirect source is a person within these two previous categories then the person who has inside information from this source is a **secondary insider**.

2.5 General defences

Under s 53, the individual has a defence regarding dealing and encouraging others to deal if they prove that:

- They did **not expect** there to be a **profit** or avoidance of loss.
- They had **reasonable grounds** to **believe** that the information had been **disclosed widely** enough to ensure that those taking part in the dealing would be prejudiced by having the information.
- They would have **done** what they did **even** if they did not have the **information**, for example, where securities are sold to pay a pressing debt.

Defences to disclosure of information by an individual are that:

- They **did not expect** any person to deal.
- Although dealing was expected, **profit** or **avoidance of loss** was **not expected**.

2.6 'Made public'

This term is not exhaustively defined by the statute, leaving final determination to the Court. Information **is** made public if:

- It is **published** under the rules of the regulated market, such as the Stock Exchange.
- It is in **public records**, for example, notices in the *London Gazette*.
- It can **readily be acquired** by those likely to deal.
- It is **derived** from **public information**.

Information **may** be treated as made public even though:

- It can **only** be **acquired** by **exercising diligence** or expertise (thus helping analysts to avoid liability).
- It is **communicated only** to a **section** of the **public** (thus protecting the 'brokers' lunch' where a company informs only selected City sources of important information).
- It can be **acquired** only by **observation**.
- It is **communicated** only on a **payment of a fee** or is published outside the UK.

2.7 Penalties

Maximum penalties given by the statute are **seven years' imprisonment** and/or an **unlimited fine**. Contracts remain valid and enforceable at civil law.

2.8 Territorial scope

The offender or any professional intermediary must be **in the UK** at the time of the offence or the market must be a UK regulated market.

2.9 Problems with the laws on insider dealing

> **FAST FORWARD**
>
> The law on insider dealing has had some **limitations**, and new offences, such as market abuse, have been brought in to reduce security related crime.

The courts may have problems deciding whether information is **specific** or **precise**.

The statute states that information shall be treated as relating to an issuer of securities not only when it is **about the company** but also where it may **affect the business prospects** of the company.

The requirement that price-sensitive information has a **significant effect on price** limits the application of the legislation to fundamental matters. These include an impending takeover, or profit or dividend levels which would be out of line with market expectations.

As a result, the concept of **'market abuse'** was introduced. This was partly in response to the perceived ineffectiveness of the insider dealing provisions in the Criminal Justice Act 1993. We shall look at market abuse in the next section.

Exam focus point

> Future exam questions may be set on insider dealing and market abuse. If this is the case, remember that while insider dealing is primarily a criminal offence, market abuse also covers insider dealing and market manipulation as civil matters. Furthermore, there are criminal market abuse offences concerning making misleading statements and creating misleading impressions.

3 Market abuse

> **FAST FORWARD**
>
> **Market abuse** relates to behaviour which amounts to abuse of a person's position regarding the stock market.

Key term

> **Market abuse** is behaviour which satisfies one or more of the prescribed conditions likely to be regarded as a failure on the part of the person or persons concerned to **observe the standard of behaviour reasonably expected of a person in their position in relation to the market**.

The offence of **market abuse** under the Financial Services and Markets Act 2000 (TSO, 2000) complements legislation covering insider dealing, by providing a civil law alternative. The FCA has issued a

Market Abuse Regulation, which applies to any person dealing in certain investments on recognised exchanges and which does not require proof of intent to abuse a market.

3.1 Types of market abuse

Market abuse is often connected with activities such as **recklessly making a statement** or **forecast** that is **misleading, false or deceptive**, or engaging in a **misleading course of conduct** for the purpose of inducing another person to exercise, or refrain from exercising, rights in relation to investments.

The following are other examples of behaviour that would constitute **market abuse**.

3.1.1 Misuse of information

This is any behaviour by an individual that is based on information that is **not publicly available**, but if it was, it would **influence an investor's decision**. For example, a person who buys shares in a company that they know is a takeover target of their employer, before a general disclosure of the proposed takeover is made.

3.1.2 Manipulating transactions

This behaviour involves **interfering with the normal process of share prices** moving up and down in accordance with supply and demand for the shares. For example, an individual who trades, or places orders to trade, who creates a misleading impression of the supply or demand of securities and that has the effect of raising the price of the investment to an abnormal or artificial level.

3.1.3 Manipulating devices

This behaviour is the same as manipulating transactions except that the trading is followed by the **creation of false statements** so that other investors make incorrect trading decisions. For example, an individual buys a large number of shares to artificially raise the share price and then makes false statements to the market that encourage other investors to buy the shares, driving the price up further.

3.1.4 Market distortion

This is any behaviour that **interferes with the normal process of market prices** moving up and down in accordance with supply and demand, such as a Chief Executive Officer who increases the activities of their business in order to make the company appear busier than it actually is. This improves the image and prospects of the business and suggests that a share price increase is imminent, encouraging investors to buy shares.

3.1.5 Dissemination of information

This behaviour involves the creation of **false or misleading information** about supply and demand, or prices and values of investments, and then leaking it into the public domain. For example, a person who posts an inaccurate story about a company's future plans on an internet bulletin board.

Remarks made by the judge when sentencing in *R v Bailey 2005* suggested that **directors will be held personally responsible for public announcements** in order to ensure the integrity of the market is preserved and the public protected.

3.2 Penalties for market abuse

The FCA has statutory civil powers to impose unlimited fines for the offence of **market abuse**. It also has **statutory** powers to require information, and requires anyone to co-operate with investigations into market abuse.

PART I   THE ADMINISTRATION AND CONTROL OF THE COMPANY

> **Question** — Market abuse
>
> Explain whether market abuse is tried under criminal or civil law and what the maximum penalty is for committing it.
>
> **Answer**
>
> Market abuse is tried under civil law. The FCA has civil power to hand out unlimited fines for those who commit it.

Having looked at two crimes that can be committed in the financial markets, we shall now look at **money laundering**. In this offence, the proceeds of criminal activity is processed to make it look like it came from a legitimate source.

4 Money laundering

4.1 What is money laundering?

FAST FORWARD

Money laundering is the attempt to **make money from criminal activity appear legitimate**, by disguising its original source.

Key term

Money laundering is the term given to attempts to make the proceeds of crime appear respectable.

It covers any activity by which the apparent source and ownership of money representing the proceeds of income are changed so that the money appears to have been obtained legitimately.

Money laundering is a **crime** that is **against the interests of the state**, and it is associated with drug and people trafficking in particular, and with organised crime in general.

Money laundering legislation has been influenced on a number of different Acts of Parliament:

- Drug Trafficking Offences Act 1986
- Criminal Justice Act 1993
- Terrorism Act 2000
- Anti-terrorism Crime and Security Act 2001
- Proceeds of Crime Act 2002
- Money Laundering Regulations 2017

4.2 Categories of criminal offence

FAST FORWARD

In the UK, there are various offences relating to **money laundering**, including tipping off a money launderer (or suspected money launderer) and failing to report reasonable suspicions.

There are **three categories of criminal offences** in the Proceeds of Crime Act 2002 (TSO, 2002).

- **Laundering**: acquisition, possession or use of the proceeds of criminal conduct, or assisting another to retain the proceeds of criminal conduct and concealing, disguising, converting, transferring or removing criminal property. This relates to its nature, source, location, disposition, movement or ownership of the property. Money laundering includes possession of the proceeds of one's own crime, and facilitating any handling or possession of criminal property, which may take any form, including in money or money's worth, securities, tangible property and intangible property. There is no *de minimis* limit, so an offence may be committed in respect only of £1.

- **Failure to report** by an individual: failure to disclose knowledge or suspicion of money laundering ('suspicion' is more than mere speculation, but falls short of proof or knowledge).
- **Tipping off**: disclosing information to any person if disclosure may prejudice an investigation into drug trafficking, drug money laundering, terrorist-related activities, or laundering the proceeds of criminal conduct.

For the purposes of laundering, '**criminal property**' is defined by the CJA as a property which the alleged offender knows (or suspects) constitutes or represents being related to any criminal conduct.

This is any conduct that constitutes or would constitute an offence in the UK. In relation to **laundering**, a person may have a **defence** if they make disclosure to the authorities:

- As soon as possible after the transaction
- Before the transaction takes place

Alternatively, they may have a defence if they can show there was a **reasonable excuse** for not making a disclosure.

In relation to **failure to report**, the person who suspects money laundering must disclose this to a **nominated officer** (known as a **Money Laundering Reporting Officer**) within their organisation, or alternatively directly to the **National Crime Agency** (NCA) in the form of a Suspicious Activity Report (SAR). The NCA has responsibility in the UK for collecting and disseminating information related to money laundering and related activities. The nominated officer in an organisation acts as a filter and notifies NCA too.

In relation to **tipping off**, this covers the situation when a person making a disclosure to the NCA also tells the person at the centre of their suspicions about the disclosure. There is a **defence** to the effect that the person did not know that tipping off would prejudice an investigation.

4.3 Penalties

The law sets out the following penalties in relation to money laundering:

(a) 14 years' imprisonment and/or a fine, for **knowingly assisting** in the **laundering** of criminal funds

(b) Five years' imprisonment and/or a fine, for **failure to report knowledge** or the **suspicion** of money laundering

(c) Two years' imprisonment and/or a fine for **tipping off** a suspected launderer.

The **money laundering process** usually involves three phases:

- **Placement** – this is the initial disposal of the proceeds of the initial illegal activity into apparently legitimate business activity or property
- **Layering** – this involves the transfer of monies from business to business, or place to place, to conceal the original source
- **Integration** – having been layered, the money has the appearance of legitimate funds

For accountants, the most worrying aspect of the law on money laundering relates to the offence of '**failing to disclose**'. It is relatively straightforward to identify actual 'knowledge' of money laundering, and therefore of the need to disclose it, but the term 'suspicion' of money laundering is not defined. The nearest there is to a definition is that suspicion is more than mere speculation but falls short of proof or knowledge. It is a question of judgement.

4.4 Anti-money laundering supervision

The **Office for Professional Body Anti-Money Laundering Supervision** was established as a regulator by the UK Government to strengthen the UK's anti-money laundering regime (FCA, 2024). The organisation is responsible for the oversight of professional bodies in relation to the money laundering regulations, and aims to improve the consistency of professional body supervision in the accountancy and legal sectors. However, it does not directly supervise legal and accountancy firms.

Question
Money laundering

Explain how an accountant could commit a money laundering offence even if they do not actually launder any money.

Answer

A person (such as an accountant) who suspects money laundering is taking place must disclose this to a nominated officer within their organisation, or alternatively directly to the National Crime Agency (NCA) in the form of a Suspicious Activity Report (SAR). If they fail to do this then they will be committing the offence of failure to report.

An accountant might also commit the offence of tipping off. This is where a person makes a money laundering disclosure, but also tells the person at the centre of their suspicions about the disclosure.

This means that accountants must disclose any suspicions of money laundering to the NCA and must not tell the person they are suspicious of that they are doing so.

4.5 The Money Laundering Regulations 2017

The **Money Laundering Regulations 2017** (TSO, 2017) require **organisations** to **establish internal systems** and **procedures** which are designed to deter criminals from using the organisation to launder money or finance terrorism. Such systems also assist in detecting the crime and prosecuting the perpetrators.

These regulations apply to all **'relevant persons'**, a term which covers a wide range of organisations, including banking and investment businesses, accountants and auditors, tax advisers, lawyers, estate agents and casinos. They set out a prescriptive approach in the form of a firm-wide written risk assessment that includes a number of factors that must be taken into account.

As each organisation is different, **systems** should be designed which are **appropriate and tailored to each business**. Businesses are required to regularly review and update their policies, controls and procedures and maintain written records of them.

These include:

(a) **Risk management practices**

The business should take a 'whole firm' approach to assessing the money laundering risks it faces. The business should assess the risk of clients being involved in money laundering or terrorist financing. The risk management approach adopted will depend on the size of the business and the nature of its activities. The overall objective for any business is to properly identify and assess the risk of money laundering, or terrorist financing, and to document the assessment.

In making the assessment, any information provided by the organisation's supervisory body (an organisation responsible for overseeing the sector the business operates in) should be considered. Risk factors relating to customers, geographic areas the business operates in, its products and services, its transactions and its delivery channels should also be considered.

(b) **Internal controls**

Businesses are required to have a number of internal controls in place. These include:

- Appointing an officer responsible for compliance (known as a Money Laundering Compliance Principal (MLCP)) who must sit on the board of directors.
- Appointing a nominated officer (the Money Laundering Reporting Officer (MLRO)) to receive internal reports of suspected money laundering and, where appropriate, to report them to the NCA.

- Screening relevant employees by assessing the skills, knowledge, conduct and integrity of those responsible for identifying, mitigating, preventing or detecting money laundering and terrorist financing.
- Appointing an individual to ensure that relevant employees are made aware of the law in relation to money laundering and the associated requirements of data protection legislation. The individual must also ensure that relevant employees are given regular training to help them recognise and deal with transactions and situations related to money laundering. They must also maintain a written record of such training.
- Establishing an independent audit function whose role is to assess the adequacy and effectiveness of anti-money laundering policies, controls and procedures.

(c) **Customer due diligence**

Businesses are required to perform customer due diligence before establishing the business relationship. They must also identify instances where factors relevant to the risk assessment change.

Customer due diligence work includes, for example, identifying and independently verifying customers, business organisations and their agents and monitoring the business relationship or transaction according to the level of risk of money laundering. There are two levels of due diligence: **simplified** and **enhanced**.

Simplified due diligence is permitted where the risk assessment indicates that the business relationship or transaction presents a low risk of money laundering or terrorist financing. For example where an organisation is in the public sector, an individual resides in a geographical area of lower risk or is an organisation that is regulated or supervised (such as a bank). Customer due diligence should still be performed, but at a level that reflects the low-level of risk.

Enhanced due diligence measures are required to be applied in a number of circumstances. Such circumstances include where a transaction is unusually large or complex, a transaction is part of an unusual pattern or has no apparent economic or legal purpose, the business relationship involves a person established in a 'high risk third country', if the individual is, or if a family member is a 'politically exposed person' or is a known associate of one, and any other situation that presents a higher risk of money laundering or terrorist financing.

Examples of **enhanced due diligence measures** include:

- Understanding the background and purpose of transactions.
- Increased monitoring of the business relationship or transaction to determine whether there is any reason to be suspicious about them.
- Obtaining additional independent, reliable verification of information provided by the customer.
- Taking additional measures to obtain satisfaction that customer transactions are consistent with the purpose and nature of their business relationship.
- Placing transactions under greater scrutiny and increased monitoring of the business relationship.

(d) **Reliance and record-keeping procedures**

Businesses should have policies, controls and procedures in place to prevent activities related to money laundering and terrorist financing. A written record of these procedures, as well as employee training on them (see below), must be maintained. Such procedures may include, for example, retaining copies of customer identity details such as passports. These procedures are important in proving compliance with the regulations. Copies of documents used to satisfy customer due diligence requirements must be kept for 5 years.

(e) **Monitoring and management of compliance**

Businesses should continuously monitor and manage compliance with the policies, controls and procedures that they have in place. Employees should receive appropriate training concerning the law relating to money laundering and the business's policies and procedures in dealing with it. Employee training records should also be monitored to ensure compliance and that the employees are up-to-date as requirements develop over time.

Should a business fail to implement these measures a criminal offence, punishable with a maximum sentence of **two years' imprisonment and/or an unlimited fine**, is committed irrespective of whether money laundering has taken place.

4.6 The role of the Financial Conduct Authority

In addition to the Money Laundering Regulations 2017, there are other rules which apply to **investment firms** (that is firms which sell financial services or shares).

The **FCA** and the **Joint Money Laundering Steering Group (JMLSG)** provide similar guidance, and therefore parallel but separate rules. Investment firms are required to have:

(a) **Control systems** in place to monitor possible money laundering activities.

(b) A **Money Laundering Reporting Officer (MLRO)** who is responsible for the oversight of the anti-money laundering activities.

(c) **Internal reporting procedures**. Staff must be able to identify suspicious transactions, understand reporting procedures, and be able to notify the MLRO of any person who they suspect of engaging in money laundering.

(d) **Adequate records** such as:

  (i) A copy of the evidence of identity obtained

  (ii) A record of where a copy of the identity evidence can be obtained

  (iii) Procedures for internal and external reporting

  (iv) Evidence of an applicant's identity must be retained for five years from the end of the firm's relationship with the client, or

  (v) Money laundering training given to all staff who handle transactions (or who manage others who are responsible for handling transactions) that may involve money laundering.

Although investment firms may be particularly at risk of being involved with clients who are seeking to launder money, **methods used** for laundering such dirty money **can be extremely complex**. They may involve **trusts, companies** (both offshore and onshore) and could involve the use of relatively complex bank instruments.

Therefore **all companies**, their **managers** and their **advisers need to be aware** of the issue of money laundering and not fall foul of the regulations.

There is a **legal requirement** for organisations to take the following actions.

- To set up procedures and establish accountabilities for senior individuals to take action to prevent money laundering.
- To educate staff and employees about the potential problems of money laundering.
- To obtain satisfactory evidence of identity where a transaction is for more than £10,000.
- To report suspicious circumstances (according to the established procedures).
- Not to alert persons who are or might be investigated for money laundering.
- To keep records of all transactions for five years.

Exam focus point | You must be clear on how this guidance seeks to prevent or minimise money laundering.

5 Bribery

FAST FORWARD

Bribery is a serious offence which often relates to the **offering** and **receiving** of **gifts** or **hospitality**.

The final key criminal offence we shall look at is that of **bribery**. This offence is controlled by the **Bribery Act 2010** (TSO, 2010) which came into effect in July 2011. The Act brought together, and was intended to simplify, the previous law on bribery and corruption which was contained in both common law and statute.

5.1 Bribery offences

The **Bribery Act** created **four main offences,** the first three of which are committed by **individuals** while the fourth is a **corporate** offence. The offences are:

- Bribing another person
- Being bribed
- Bribing a foreign public official
- Corporate failure to prevent bribery

5.1.1 Bribing another person

This offence is committed where a person **offers, promises or gives financial** or **other advantages** to another person with the intention of inducing that person to **perform improperly** a **relevant function** or **activity**, or to **reward** them for such **improper performance**.

It does not matter whether or not the person being bribed is the **same person** as the one who would **usually perform** the function or whether the offer is made **directly** or via a **third party**. This offence can also be committed where **acceptance of an advantage** itself **constitutes improper performance** of a function or activity.

5.1.2 Being bribed

This offence is committed where a person requests or accepts a financial or other advantage improperly, or as a reward for improper performance of a relevant function or activity, or intending that improper performance should result. It does not matter whether the advantage is received directly or through a third party. The offence also applies if a person receives a benefit on behalf of another person.

5.1.3 Relevant function or activity

Both of the above offences make reference to a '**relevant function or activity**' and it is important to be aware of what this means. In terms of the Act, a relevant function or activity includes any function of **a public nature** or any **activity connected with business** or **carried out in the course of employment**. It applies to individuals who perform that function or activity from a **position of trust** or are otherwise expected to perform it in **good faith** or **impartially**.

It is irrelevant whether the **function** or **activity** has a **connection with the UK** – for example, if it is performed outside the UK. 'Improper' performance means performance which does not meet the **standard** that a **reasonable person** in the UK would expect.

5.1.4 Bribing a foreign public official

This offence is similar to that of **bribing another person**, but is committed where the bribe is offered to a **foreign public official** (FPO). It is committed where a person offers financial or other advantages to an **FPO** or a **third party** with the intention of influencing the FPO in that capacity and to obtain or retain business or an advantage in the conduct of business, where that official is not permitted or required by the written law applicable to them to be so influenced.

An **FPO** is any individual who holds a **legislative, administrative** or **judicial position** of any kind outside the UK, or who exercises a **public function** outside the UK, or who is an **official** or **agent** of a **public international organisation**.

5.1.5 Defences and penalties for individual offences

It is a **defence** for an individual charged with a bribery offence if they can prove that their **conduct was necessary for the proper exercise of any function of an intelligence service or the proper exercise of any function of the armed forces when engaged on active service**.

The maximum **penalty** for bribery under the Act is **10 years' imprisonment** and/or an **unlimited fine**.

5.1.6 Corporate failure to prevent bribery

The offence of corporate failure to prevent bribery is **committed by an organisation** that **fails to prevent** a **bribery offence** being committed by a **person who performs services** for it in any capacity — such as an agent, employee or subsidiary. Under the Act, an **organisation** includes **companies** and **partnerships** based in the UK or doing business in the UK.

5.1.7 Defence and penalties for corporate offences

An organisation has a **defence** to this offence if it can prove that it had in place '**adequate procedures**' designed to prevent persons associated with it from committing bribery.

'**Adequate procedures**' are not defined by the Act, but the Secretary of State's non-prescriptive published guidance on adequate procedures is based around six principles:

(a) **Proportionate procedures** – organisations should have procedures in place aimed at preventing bribery. The scale and complexity of the procedures should be proportionate to the size of the organisation. The procedures expected of a small organisation will differ from that of a large one.

(b) **Top-level commitment** – an organisation's senior management should be committed to preventing bribery and should foster a culture in the organisation that sees bribery as unacceptable.

(c) **Risk assessment** – organisations should assess the nature and extent of their exposure to bribery from both inside and outside the organisation. Some industries and some overseas markets are seen as, by their nature, more susceptible to bribery and therefore risk assessments in these areas should be even more stringent.

(d) **Due diligence** – organisations should perform due diligence procedures in respect of those who perform services for the organisation or on its behalf, to mitigate the risk of bribery.

(e) **Communication** – anti-bribery policies and procedures should be embedded in the fabric of the organisation and communicated both internally and externally. This is likely to include relevant training if proportionate to the risk.

(f) **Monitoring and review** – the anti-bribery policies and procedures should be regularly monitored and reviewed. Amendments and improvements must be made as appropriate. This is because the risks an organisation faces will change so adaptation is necessary.

Whether an organisation had **adequate procedures is a matter for the courts** who will look at the particular circumstances an organisation is faced with. However, the onus is on the organisation to prove that its procedures were adequate.

Reasonable and **proportionate hospitality** is **not prohibited,** although what is reasonable and proportionate will be determined in future cases.

The **maximum penalty** that may be imposed on a guilty organisation is an **unlimited fine**. However, it is likely that its **business will suffer** too as a consequence of **loss of reputation** and **compensation payable** for civil claims against the directors for failure to maintain adequate procedures.

Having studied four key financial crimes, in the last section below we shall bring together a number of other offences which might be committed in the course of running a business.

6 Criminal activity relating to companies

> **FAST FORWARD**
>
> With regard to the **operation and management of companies**, a company as a legal person may be prosecuted for many different types of crime. However, this is nearly always in conjunction with the directors and/or managers of the company.

We have already seen a number of potential crimes in relation to the operation and management of companies, and the way in which these can be investigated. Companies have been prosecuted for manslaughter (unsuccessfully), fraud, and breaches of numerous laws for which fines are stated as being punishment, such as health and safety laws.

Prosecutions are often brought against directors of **insolvent** companies for **fraudulent trading** and **wrongful trading**.

6.1 Criminal offences in relation to winding up

> **FAST FORWARD**
>
> **Criminal offences** in relation to **winding up** include: making a declaration of solvency without reasonable grounds; fraudulent trading; wrongful trading.

We shall study company insolvency and winding up in a later chapter so you may wish to refer back here once you have studied them in more detail. The following section summarises the criminal offences that could be committed in an insolvency situation. It is important to understand that the law seeks to **protect creditors** who may be disadvantaged by the company being liquidated. **Directors** can be found guilty of various criminal offences if they try to **deceive** creditors, and, in some cases, even if they do not attempt to deceive creditors, but the effect is the same as if they had.

6.2 Declaration of solvency

A winding up can only be a members' voluntary winding up if the company is solvent. If the company is not solvent, the creditors are far more involved in the winding up process. In order to carry out a members' voluntary winding up, the directors have to file a **declaration of solvency**.

It is a **criminal offence** punishable by fine or imprisonment for a director to make a **declaration of solvency without** having **reasonable grounds** for it. If the company proves to be insolvent, they will have to justify their previous decision, or be punished.

6.3 Fraudulent trading

This **criminal offence** occurs under the **Companies Act 2006** (TSO, 2006) where the business of a company in liquidation or administration has been carried on with **intent to defraud creditors** or for any fraudulent purpose. Offenders are liable to imprisonment for up to 10 years or a fine (s 993).

There is also a **civil offence** of the same name under s 213 of the Insolvency Act 1986. Under this offence courts may declare that **any persons** who were knowingly parties to carrying on the business in this fashion shall be liable for the debts of the company.

Various rules have been established to determine **what is fraudulent trading**:

(a) Only persons who **take the decision** to carry on the company's business in this way or play some active part are liable.

(b) **'Carrying on business'** can include a single transaction and also the mere payment of debts as distinct from making trading contracts.

(c) It relates not only to **defrauding creditors**, but also to carrying on a business for the purpose of any kind of fraud: *R v Kemp 1988*.

If the liquidator considers that there has been fraudulent trading they should apply to the court for an order that those responsible are liable to make good to the company all or some specified part of the **company's debts**.

6.4 Wrongful trading

The problem which faced the creditors of an insolvent company before the introduction of **'wrongful trading'** was that it was exceptionally difficult to prove the necessary fraud. Therefore a further civil liability for 'wrongful trading' was introduced, which means that the **director will have to make such contribution to the company's assets as the court sees fit**.

Directors will be liable if the liquidator or administrator proves the following.

(a) The director(s) of the insolvent company **knew**, or **should have known**, that there was **no reasonable prospect** that the **company** could **have avoided insolvency**. This means that directors cannot claim they lacked knowledge if their lack of knowledge was a result of failing to comply with Companies Act requirements, for example preparation of accounts: *Re Produce Marketing Consortium 1989* (see below).

(b) The director(s) did not take **sufficient steps** to minimise the potential loss to the creditors.

Directors will be deemed to know that the company could not avoid insolvency if that would have been the conclusion of a **reasonably diligent person** with the **general knowledge, skill and experience** that might reasonably be expected of a person carrying out that particular director's duties. If the director has greater than usual skill then they will be judged with reference to their own capacity.

6.5 Other offences in relation to winding up

We have already seen that it is a criminal offence for directors to make a **false declaration of solvency** during a liquidation – further offences include the following.

6.5.1 Acting as a director whilst disqualified

S 15 **Company Directors Disqualification Act 1986** (HMSO, 1986) makes a person who **acts as a director whilst disqualified** personally liable for the company's debts. Directors of insolvent companies may be disqualified under the Act if the court deems they are unfit to be involved in the management of a company.

6.5.2 Phoenix companies

Phoenix companies are created by directors of insolvent companies as a **method of continuing their business**. Very often they have similar names as (or similar enough to suggest an association with) the insolvent company. S 216 Insolvency Act 1986 (HMSO, 1986) makes it a **criminal offence** where a director **creates such a company within five years of the original company being liquidated**. The person is liable for a fine or imprisonment. S 217 makes a person who creates such a company personally liable for its debts.

6.5.3 Fraud and deception

S 206 Insolvency Act 1986 makes it a criminal offence to **conceal** or **fraudulently remove company assets** or **debt** – including falsifying records. It is also an offence to **dispose of property** that was **acquired on credit** that has **not been paid** for.

6.5.4 Defrauding creditors

Once a winding up commences, s 207 Insolvency Act 1986 makes it an offence to make a **gift** of, or **transfer company property**, unless it can be proved there was no intent to defraud creditors.

6.5.5 Misconduct during a liquidation

A company officer may be liable for a number of offences due to their misconduct. These include:

- Not identifying company property to the liquidator.
- Not delivering requested books and papers to the liquidator.
- Not informing the liquidator if identified debts do not turn out to be debts.

6.5.6 Falsification of company books

The destruction, mutilation, alteration or falsification of company books is an offence under s 209 Insolvency Act 1986.

6.5.7 Omissions

It is an offence under s 210 Insolvency Act 1986 to omit material information when making statements concerning a company's affairs.

6.6 Examples: Offences in relation to winding up

The standard expected of a listed company director would be **higher** than for the director of a small owner-managed private company.

Halls v David and Another 1989

The facts: The directors sought to obtain relief from liability for wrongful trading by the application of what is now s 1157 Companies Act 2006. This stated that in proceedings for negligence, default, breach of duty or breach of trust against a director, if it appears that he has acted honestly and reasonably the court may relieve him wholly or partly from liability on such terms as it sees fit.

Decision: S 1157 Companies Act 2006 is not available to excuse a director from liability under s 214.

Re Produce Marketing Consortium Ltd 1989

The facts: Two months after the case above, the same liquidator sought an order against the same directors this time, that they should contribute to the company assets (which were in the hands of the liquidator) since they had been found liable for wrongful trading.

Decision: The directors were jointly and severally liable for the sum of £75,000 plus interest, along with the costs of the case. The judge stated that the fact that wrongful trading was not based on fraud was not a reason for giving a nominal or low figure of contribution. The figure should, however, be assessed in the light of all the circumstances of the case.

This case was significant for creditors, since the assets available for distribution in a winding up will (potentially) be much increased by a **large directors' contribution**. It serves as a warning to directors to take professional advice sooner rather than later. The prospect of making a personal contribution may prove much more expensive than winding-up at the appropriate stage.

6.7 Companies Act 2006 offences

The Companies Act 2006 (TSO, 2006) includes provision for a **large number of offences** in relation to the **management** and **operation** of a company.

6.7.1 Company records

Company records and **registers**, such as the register of members and record of resolutions **must be kept adequately for future reference**. Officers in default are liable to a fine (s 1135 Companies Act 2006). **Falsification** of **information**, **hiding falsification**, or **failing to prevent falsification** are also offences and the wrongdoer is liable to a fine (s 1138 Companies Act 2006).

6.7.2 Accounting records

Where a company fails to **keep adequate accounting records**, every officer who defaults is subject to a fine (s 387 Companies Act 2006). However, they have a **defence** if they **acted honestly** and the **circumstances** surrounding the company's business makes the default **excusable**.

6.7.3 Trading disclosures

Companies are required to disclose **certain information** (such as its name) in **specific locations**. If these disclosures are not made then defaulting officers are criminally liable for a fine and may also be liable for losses under the civil law.

6.7.4 Filing accounts

If a company fails to **file its accounts within the time limit following its year end** then any defaulting officer is liable to a fine (s 451 Companies Act 2006). However they will have a **defence** if they took **reasonable steps** to **ensure the requirements** were **complied with**.

6.7.5 False information

Under s 463 Companies Act 2006, officers are liable for making **false disclosures** in relation to the **directors' report**, **directors' remuneration report** and **summary financial statements** based on those reports. An officer is also liable under s 501 Companies Act 2006 for **providing false** or **misleading information to an auditor**. Punishment is either imprisonment or a fine.

6.8 The Fraud Act 2006

The **Fraud Act 2006** (TSO, 2006), to which directors and secretaries are subject, created a **single offence of fraud**, which a person can commit in three different ways by:

- **False representation**: dishonestly making a false representation of fact or law, intending thereby to make a gain for themselves or another, or to cause another party loss, or to expose that party to the risk of making loss.

- **Failure to disclose information when there is a legal duty to do so**: dishonestly failing to disclose to another person information which they are under a legal duty to disclose, thereby intending to make a gain for themselves or another, or to cause another party loss or expose that party to the risk of making loss.

- **Abuse of position**: occupying a position in which they are expected to safeguard, or not to act against, the financial interest of another person, and dishonestly abusing that position, thereby intending to make a gain for themselves or another, or to cause another party loss or expose that party to the risk of suffering loss.

6.9 The Criminal Finances Act 2017

The **Criminal Finances Act 2017** (TSO 2017) potentially makes 'relevant bodies' criminally liable if 'associated persons' are involved in tax evasion.

A **relevant body** is defined by the Act as a company or partnership whether formed in the UK or elsewhere.

An **associated person** is anyone acting in the capacity of an employee, an agent, or any other person who performs services on behalf of the relevant body.

6.9.1 The offence

Under the Act, an **offence will be committed** by a relevant body if the following three stages occur:

- There is criminal tax evasion by a taxpayer or business under existing UK or foreign tax evasion law.
- An associated person of the relevant body facilitated the tax evasion under existing aiding and abetting law.
- The relevant body failed to prevent the associated person from committing the aiding and abetting offence.

6.9.2 Defence

Under the Act, a relevant body has a defence if it can demonstrate that it **had reasonable prevention procedures in place**, or in the circumstances it was unreasonable or unrealistic to have such procedures in place.

It applies even if the business was not involved in the act or had no knowledge of it. The maximum penalty under the Act is a conviction and unlimited fine.

Question — Criminal Finances Act 2017

Janice is employed as an accountant and tax advisor by Jones & Co LLP to provide all aspects of tax advice to clients. One of the firm's clients, Lucas Ltd, contacted Janice for help to minimise its tax bill for the current tax year. To keep the client happy, Janice suggested that they provide her with copies of fake purchase invoices so that she can include them in their accounts to reduce their profit for the year and therefore reduce their tax bill.

Explain whether Jones & Co LLP has any liability under the Criminal Finances Act 2017.

Answer

Lucas Ltd has committed a tax evasion offence by providing fake purchase invoices in an attempt to reduce its tax bill. Janice has aided and abetted Lucas Ltd's tax evasion by suggesting how it can evade tax and by using the fake invoices to reduce the business's profit.

Therefore the first two stages of an offence under the Criminal Finances Act 2017 have been committed. Jones & Co LLP will be liable under the Act unless it can demonstrate that it had reasonable prevention procedures in place, or in the circumstances it was unreasonable or unrealistic to have such procedures in place.

Chapter Roundup

- Crime is **conduct prohibited by the law**. Financial crime can be international in nature, and there is a need for international cooperation to prevent it.
- Insider dealing is the statutory offence of **dealing** in securities while in **possession** of **inside information** as an insider, the securities being price affected by the information.
- The law on insider dealing has had some **limitations**, and the **market abuse offences** were brought in to reduce security-related crime.
- **Market abuse** relates to behaviour which amounts to abuse of a person's position regarding the stock market.
- Money laundering is the attempts to **make money from criminal activity appear legitimate** by disguising its original source.
- In the UK, there are various offences relating to **money laundering**, including **tipping off** a money launderer (or suspected money launderer) and **failing to report** reasonable suspicions.
- **Bribery** is a serious offence which often relates to the **offering** and **receiving** of **gifts** or **hospitality**.
- With regard to the **operation and management of companies**, a company as a legal person may be prosecuted for many different types of crime. However, this is nearly always in conjunction with the directors and/or managers of the company.
- **Criminal offences** in relation to **winding up** include: making a declaration of solvency without reasonable grounds; fraudulent trading; wrongful trading.

Quick Quiz

1. Insider dealing is a criminal offence

   True ☐

   False ☐

2. Fill in the blanks

   Inside information is '(1) .... ' relating to a (2) .... of **securities** that are price-affected and not to securities generally.

3. Define money laundering.

4. Which of the following is not a UK offence relating to money laundering?

   A Concealing the proceeds of criminal activity
   B Tipping off
   C Dealing in price affected securities
   D Failing to report suspicion of money laundering

5. What is placement?

6. Lionel is a share trader who trades very large volumes of shares on the stock market. He has found that he can create the impression in the market that demand is increasing for certain shares. By doing this, the price of the shares increases to an artificially high level.

   Has Lionel committed a market abuse offence?

Answers to Quick Quiz

1. True. Insider dealing is a criminal offence.
2. (1) price sensitive information (2) particular issuer
3. Money laundering is the term given to attempts to make the proceeds of crime appear respectable.

   It covers any activity by which the apparent source and ownership of money representing the proceeds of income are changed so that the money appears to have been obtained legitimately.
4. C. This could be insider dealing, if the person dealing was an insider and was using inside information.
5. Placement is the disposal of the initial proceeds of the illegal activity.
6. Yes – Lionel has been manipulating transactions. This behaviour involves interfering with the normal process of share prices moving up and down in accordance with supply and demand for the shares.

End of chapter question

Insider dealing

Henry Bradfield is the chief executive officer of Yensert plc, an oil exploration company listed on the London Stock Exchange. Henry was working from home and discussing on the telephone the fact that the company had just discovered a new drilling area which could be extremely profitable for the company. The family's nanny, Isabel Drake, overheard the conversation. Isabel is also a business and economics graduate student working towards her masters at the local university. The next day, without Henry's knowledge, she bought £3,000 worth of Yensert plc shares with the money set aside to pay next term's fees, hoping that their value would increase and that she would make a profit once the information became public.

Required

Advise as to the potential consequences under the Criminal Justice Act 1993 arising from the events set out above for:

(a) Isabel Drake **(14 marks)**
(b) Henry Bradfield **(6 marks)**

(Total = 20 marks)

PART I THE ADMINISTRATION AND CONTROL OF THE COMPANY

Company rescue and action short of winding up

Company rescue and other actions

Topic list	Syllabus reference
1 Administration	4.1
2 Receivership and administrative receivership	4.1
3 Company voluntary arrangements	4.1

Introduction

We are now nearing the end of your study of business law. In this and in the final chapter we look at what happens when a company is in financial difficulty.

A **company in difficulty** or **in crisis** (an **insolvent** company) fundamentally has a choice from two alternatives:

(1) To carry on with the business, using statutory methods to help remedy the situation

(2) To stop

A company which is heading towards insolvency can often be **saved**, using a variety of **legal protections** from creditors until the problem is sorted out and therefore alternative (1) is the focus of this chapter.

However, this option does not always mean carrying on as if everything is normal. It can mean **seeking help** from the court or a qualified insolvency practitioner to put a plan together to save the company and get it out of its bad financial position.

Unfortunately, many companies cannot be saved, and the members and directors are forced to take alternative (2), **to stop** operating the business through the company. This is the focus of the next chapter.

We shall begin this chapter by looking at **administration** as a way of protecting a business while it seeks to overcome its financial problems. We shall then consider the role of **receivers** before considering **voluntary arrangements** that companies can make with their creditors to avoid insolvency occurring.

1 Administration

Statutory references in this chapter are to the Insolvency Act 1986 (HMSO, 1986) (as amended) unless stated otherwise.

Administration is a method of **'saving' a company from liquidation**, under the Enterprise Act 2002 (TSO, 2002). Liquidation will be covered in detail in the next Chapter, however; broadly speaking, it is the final destruction of a company that cannot be saved. When it is liquidated, a company is brought to an end and is formally dissolved.

On account of the destructiveness of a company liquidation, administration has come into being as a way of protecting the company (and those interested in it) so that its fortunes can be turned around.

1.1 What is administration?

FAST FORWARD

An **administrator** is appointed primarily to try to rescue the company as a going concern. A company may go into administration to carry out an established plan to save the company.

Key term

Administration puts an **insolvency practitioner** in **control** of the company with a defined programme for **rescuing the company** from insolvency as a going concern.

Its purpose is to **insulate** the company **from its creditors while it seeks**:

- To save itself as a going concern, or failing that
- To achieve a better result for creditors than an immediate winding up would secure, or failing that
- To realise property so as to make a distribution to creditors

Administration orders and liquidations are **mutually exclusive**. Once an administration order has been passed by the court, it is **no longer possible to petition the court** for a **winding up** order against the company. Similarly, however, once an order for winding up has been made, an administration order cannot be granted (except when appointed by a floating chargeholder).

Administration can be initiated **with** or **without a court order**.

1.2 Appointment without a court order

FAST FORWARD

Some parties – **secured creditors with a floating charge** and **directors** and the **members** by resolution – can appoint an administrator without a court order.

It is possible to appoint an administrator **without reference to the court**. There are three sets of people who might be able to do this:

- Floating chargeholders
- Directors
- Company

1.2.1 Floating chargeholders

Floating chargeholders have the right to appoint an administrator without reference to the court even if there is no actual or impending insolvency. They may also **appoint an administrator even if the company is in compulsory liquidation**. This enables steps to be taken to save the company before its financial situation becomes irreversible.

In order to qualify for this right, the **floating charge must entitle the holder to appoint an administrator**. This would be in the terms of the charge. It must also be over all, or substantially all, the company's property.

Point to note

> In practice, such a floating chargeholder with a charge over all or substantially all the company's property is likely to be a **bank**.

However, the **floating chargeholder may only appoint an administrator** if:

- They have given **two days** written notice to the holder of any prior floating charge where that person has the right to appoint an administrator.
- Their floating charge is **enforceable**.

After any relevant two day notice period the floating chargeholder will file the following **documents** at court:

- A **notice of appointment** in the prescribed form identifying the administrator
- A **statement by the administrator** that they **consent to the appointment**
- A **statement by the administrator** that, in their **opinion**, the **purpose of the administration** is likely to be **achieved**
- A **statutory declaration** that they **qualify** to make the appointment

Once these documents have been filed, the **appointment is valid**. The appointer must notify the administrator and other people prescribed by regulations of the appointment as soon as is reasonably practicable.

1.2.2 Company and directors

The process by which a company commences appointing an administrator will depend upon its **constitution**. A company or its directors may appoint an administrator if:

- The company has not done so in the last 12 months or been subject to a **moratorium** as a result of a voluntary arrangement with its creditors in the last 12 months
- The company is, or is likely to be, **unable to pay its debts**
- **No petition for winding up** nor any **administration order** in respect of the company has been presented to the court and is outstanding
- The company is **not in liquidation**
- **No administrator** or **receiver** is already in office

The company or its directors must give notice to any floating chargeholders entitled to appoint an administrator. This means that the **floating chargeholders may** appoint their own administrator within this time period, and so **block the company's choice of administrator**.

1.3 Appointment with a court order

Various parties can apply for **administration** through the court.

There are **four sets of parties** that may **apply to the court** for an administration order:

- The **company** (that is, a majority of the members by 50% resolution)
- The **directors** of the company
- One or more **creditors** of the company
- The **Justice and Chief Executive of the Magistrates' Court** following non-payment of a fine imposed on the company

Exam focus point

> **Individual** members **cannot** apply to the court for an administration order.

The court will grant the **administration order** if it is satisfied that:

- The company is, or is likely to be, **unable to pay its debts**, and
- The administration order is reasonably likely to **achieve the purpose of administration**

The application will name the person whom the applicants want to be the **administrator**. Unless certain interested parties object, this person is appointed as administrator.

Question — Administration

Which parties can appoint an administrator without reference to the court?

Answer

The parties who can appoint and administrator without reference to the court are:

- Floating chargeholders
- Directors
- Company

1.4 The effects of appointing an administrator

The **effects** of administration depend on whether it is effected by the **court** or by a **floating chargeholder**, to some degree.

Effects of an administrator appointment
A **moratorium** over the company's debts commences (that is, no creditor can enforce their debt during the administration period without the court's permission). This is the advantageous aspect of being in administration.
The court must give its permission for: • **Security** over company property to be **enforced** • Goods held under hire purchase to be **repossessed** • A landlord to conduct **forfeiture** by peaceable entry • Commencement/continuation of any **legal process** against the company
The **powers of management** are subjugated to the authority of the administrator and managers can only act with their consent.
All outstanding **petitions for winding-up** of the company are **dismissed.**
Any **administrative receiver** in place must **vacate office**. No appointments to this position can be made.

1.5 Duties of the administrator

The administrator has **fiduciary duties** to the company as its agent, plus some legal duties.

The administrator is an **agent of the company** and the **creditors as a whole**. They therefore owe fiduciary duties to them and has the following legal duties.

Legal duties of the administrator
As soon as **reasonably practicable** after appointment they must:
• **Send notice** of appointment to the company.
• **Publish notice** of appointment.
• Obtain a list of **company creditors** and sent notice of appointment to each.
• Within seven days of appointment, send notice of appointment to **Registrar**.
• Require certain relevant people to provide a **statement of affairs** of the company.
• Ensure that every **business document** of the company **bears the identity** of the administrator and a statement that the affairs, business and property of the company are being managed by them.
• Consider the **statements of affairs** submitted to them and set out their **proposals** for achieving the aim of administration. The proposals must be **sent to the Registrar** and the company's **creditors,** and be made available to **every member of the company** as soon as is reasonably practicable, and **within eight weeks**.
• Whilst preparing their proposals, the administrator must **manage the affairs** of the company.

The **statement of affairs** must be provided by the people from whom it is requested within 11 days of it being requested. It is in a prescribed form, and contains:

- Details of the **company's property**
- The company's **debts** and **liabilities**
- The **names** and **addresses** of the **company's creditors**
- Details of any **security** held by any **creditor**

Failing to provide a statement of affairs, or providing a statement in which the writer has no reasonable belief of truth, is a **criminal offence** punishable by fine.

1.6 Administrator's proposals

FAST FORWARD

The administrator must either **propose a rescue plan**, or state that the **company cannot be rescued**.

Having considered all information the administrator must within **8 weeks** (subject to possible extension) either:

- Set out their **proposals for achieving the aim of the administration**; or
- Set out why it is not **reasonable and practicable** that the company be rescued. In this case they will also set out why the creditors as a whole would benefit from winding up.

The **proposal** must **be sent to all members** and **creditors** they are aware of. It must not:

- Affect the right of a **secured creditor** to enforce their security
- Result in a non-preferential debt being paid in priority to a preferential debt
- Result in one preferential creditor being paid a smaller proportion of their debt than another

1.6.1 Creditors' meeting

The administrator must call a **meeting of creditors** within **10 weeks** of their appointment to approve the proposals. Such a meeting can be a physical meeting or a virtual meeting. Electronic voting or other forms of correspondence can be used to come to a decision. Any procedure that enables all creditors to participate in the making of the decision equally can be used.

The creditors may either accept or reject the proposals. Once proposals have been agreed, the administrator cannot make any substantial amendment without first gaining the creditors' consent.

1.6.2 Deemed consent procedure

Creditor consent for the proposals is usually obtained at the creditors' meeting. However, the deemed consent procedure can also be used. Under this method, the directors write to the creditors with their proposal. If less than 10% of the creditors in value object, the proposal is deemed to be approved.

1.7 Administrator's powers

> **FAST FORWARD** The administrator takes on the **powers** of the directors.

The **powers of the administrator** are summed up as follows:

> 'The administrator of a company may do **anything necessarily expedient** for the management of the affairs, business and property of the company.'

Administrators have **the same powers as those granted to directors** and the following **specific powers** to:

- Remove or appoint a **director**
- Call a **meeting of members or creditors**
- **Apply to court for directions** regarding the carrying out of their functions
- Make payments to **secured or preferential creditors**
- With the permission of the court, **make payments to unsecured creditors**

The administrator usually requires the permission of the court to make payments to unsecured creditors. However, this is not the case if the administrator feels that paying the unsecured creditor will assist the **achievement of the administration**. For example, paying a major supplier to enable trading to continue. Any creditor or member of the company may **apply to the court** if they feel that the administrator has acted or will act in a way that has harmed or will harm their interest.

1.8 End of administration

> **FAST FORWARD** Administration can last up to **12 months**.

The **administration period ends** when:

- The administration has been successful
- Twelve months have elapsed from the date of the appointment of administrator
- The administrator or a creditor applies to the court to end the appointment
- An improper motive of the applicant for applying for the administration is discovered

The administrator automatically vacates office after **12 months of their appointment**. This time period can be extended by court order or by consent from the appropriate creditors. Alternatively, the administrator may **apply to the court** when they think:

- The purpose of administration cannot be achieved
- The company should not have entered into administration
- The administration has been successful (if appointed by the court)

They must also apply to the court if required to by the **creditors' meeting**. Where the administrator was appointed by a chargeholder or the company/its directors, and they feel that the purposes of administration have been achieved, they must file a **notice** with the court and the Registrar.

1.9 Advantages of administration

> **FAST FORWARD** Administration has many advantages for the **company**, the **members** and the **creditors**.

Advantages of administration	
To the company	The company does not necessarily cease to exist at the end of the process, whereas liquidation will always result in the company being wound up.
	It provides a temporary breathing space from creditors to formulate rescue plans.
	It prevents any creditor applying for compulsory liquidation.
	It provides for past transactions to be challenged.
To the members	They will continue to have shares in the company which has not been wound up. If the administration is successful, regenerating the business should enhance share value and will restore any income from the business.
To the creditors	Creditors should obtain a return in relation to their past debts from an administration.
	Unsecured creditors will benefit from asset realisations.
	Any creditor may apply to the court for an administration order, while only certain creditors may apply for other forms of relief from debt. For example, the use of receivers or an application for winding up.
	Floating chargeholders may appoint an administrator without reference to the court.
	It may also be in the interests of the creditors to have a continued business relationship with the company once the business has been turned around.

Having seen how administration can be used to protect a business we shall now briefly study the role of receivers. These are essentially managers brough in to control certain company assets on behalf of a lender.

2 Receivership and administrative receivership

FAST FORWARD

A **receiver** may be appointed by a charge holder to take charge of the asset to which the charge related in order to realise it.

Rather confusingly, the term 'receiver' may denote two types of office, one of which was virtually abolished by changes made to the Insolvency Act 1986 by the Enterprise Act 2002, whilst the other remains.

2.1 Administrative receiver

An **administrative receiver** is appointed by the holder of a floating charge created before 15 September 2003 when the charge crystallises on some or all of the company's assets. An administrative receiver is essentially a manager with control over the whole, or substantial part, of the company's property and extensive powers over its business. The restriction on appointment of administrative receivers to holders of older charges only means that administration and company voluntary arrangements are much more likely to be adopted in the case of company insolvency, as an alternative to liquidation.

2.2 Fixed charge receiver

The term **fixed charge receiver** may also indicate **'non-administrative receiver'** or 'LPA receiver' (so-called because such receivers were traditionally appointed under the Law of Property Act 1925). A receiver may be appointed by the holder of a fixed charge over land in the event of the borrower's default. Their role is to collect rent and/or sell the property. The appointment of a receiver may provide a relatively quick and inexpensive remedy for a lender and may be attractive where a straightforward exercise of their power of sale is not appropriate.

Although the appointment of a receiver is often followed by liquidation, it is quite possible for the company to remain solvent and to continue in business once the receiver has performed their duties and vacated office.

2.3 Relationship between administration and receiverships

Companies that are in **administrative receivership** can only have an administrator appointed by the court and only in certain circumstances. If such an organisation does have an administrator appointed, the administrative receiver is automatically dismissed. Any future appointment of an administrative receiver is prevented.

Having a **non-administrative receiver** does not prevent the appointment of an administrator. However, the administrator is entitled to require the current receiver to vacate their office. Once an administrator is appointed, any fixed chargeholders are prevented from enforcing their security, except with the consent of the administrator or the court.

Question — Receivership

By what name is a non-administrative receiver also be known?

Answer

Non-administrative receivers are also known as LPA receivers or fixed charge receivers.

Administration and receivership may not be appropriate for all companies. Instead, some companies may seek to make voluntary arrangements with creditors. These arrangements consist of alternative strategies for satisfying debts when the business can no longer afford repayments. It is important to remember that such arrangements may not always be acceptable to all creditors and in some circumstances a creditor may actually prefer the alternative, which is usually winding up of the business.

3 Company voluntary arrangements

FAST FORWARD

A **company voluntary arrangement** is an agreement with creditors as to how and when the company will pay its debts.

A **company voluntary arrangement** (CVA) is a formal insolvency procedure that allows a company with debt problems or a company which is actually insolvent to reach a voluntary agreement (known as a **composition in satisfaction of its debt** or a **scheme of arrangement of its affairs**) with its business creditors as to how all, or part, of its corporate debts will be paid back over an agreed period of time. It is an **alternative to administration** as a method of trying to save a business from liquidation. However, it can also be used as part of the administration or liquidation process if either of those have already commenced.

Key term

A **company voluntary arrangement** (CVA) is a form of agreement or 'composition' with creditors.

A CVA must be implemented by a **nominated insolvency practitioner** who will draft a detailed proposal for the company's creditors. If the company is already in administration or liquidation, the nominated insolvency practitioner is likely to be the administrator or liquidator.

Once proposals for the CVA have been drafted, there must be a **meeting of creditors** to see if it is accepted. To be accepted, at least 75% by debt value of the creditors must vote for the proposal.

As with administration, creditors' meetings can be virtual and consent may be obtained electronically or using other approved methods. The deemed consent procedure may also be used.

Once accepted, all the company's creditors are bound to the proposal's terms whether or not they voted in favour, or indeed at all. Creditors may take no further legal actions as long as the CVA's terms are adhered to by the company. Existing legal actions such as a winding up order ceases once a CVA is accepted.

The CVA process is as follows:

- A CVA is proposed by an **administrator**, a **liquidator** or, if there is no administration order or insolvency proceeding, the **directors**, and court approval is sought.

- The court may decide the company is eligible for a **moratorium** from other proceedings for debts, which will normally last for a period of 28 days and will be managed by a nominee, who may or may not be a registered insolvency practitioner. At the end of a moratorium a company may (or may not) proceed to a corporate voluntary arrangement.

- Where the proposal is made by the directors then either immediately, or following a moratorium, a **nominee** is appointed to supervise the implementation of the proposal, reporting to the court within 28 days on whether, in their opinion, meetings of the company and of its creditors should be called.

- Where there is a **liquidator or administrator** in post they become the nominee and proceed straight to summoning meetings (see below).

- The **company and creditors meetings** summoned by the nominee decide whether to approve the proposal either with or without modifications. The arrangement is then binding on all creditors who had notice of the meeting and were entitled to vote. The nominee of the proposal or a replacement then becomes the **supervisor** of the arrangement.

- At least once every 12 months the supervisor must send a **report** on the progress and prospects for the full implementation of the voluntary arrangement to all interested parties including the Registrar.

- When the arrangement is **suspended or revoked** the Registrar must be notified.

- When the arrangement is **completed**, that is the debts are settled in line with the agreement, or when it is terminated the supervisor must notify the Registrar within 28 days.

During the CVA, payments to creditors are made by a **single monthly amount paid** to the insolvency practitioner. The **insolvency practitioner's fees** are deducted from these payments before they are passed on to the creditors as agreed.

3.1 Other voluntary arrangements

Rather than undertake a formal insolvency procedure, a company which is still solvent and can continue to trade, but which is facing liquidity problems in paying its creditors on time, may seek other forms of voluntary arrangements with creditors:

3.1.1 Increased interest

One option that is available to a business concerns the **interest** it is paying on the debts that it owes. The business could offer to start paying interest at an agreed rate where the debt is currently interest-free. Or where interest is currently being paid, it could offer a higher rate of interest to the creditor. In return, the creditor agrees to give the business more time to pay back the debt. The creditor will have to decide whether or not the extra interest it would receive on the debt is sufficient to balance the risk of the debtor defaulting on the debt. The creditor will also think about whether or not they would reclaim more of their debt if the debtor was to apply for administration or liquidation instead.

3.1.2 Charge over company assets

Businesses that own **substantial assets** could offer creditors (such as banks) security over some of its assets in return for a delay in payment. This would mean granting the creditor a **fixed charge** over a particular asset, or a **floating charge** over a class of assets such as inventory or receivables. Once registered, such a charge would allow the creditor, on the occurrence of certain events (such as the non-payment of a particular debt within an agreed time), to appoint a receiver of the asset(s) in order to realise (sell) it and take payment from the proceeds.

From the creditor's point of view, **charges take some of the risk out of the debt** and may make them more amenable when asking for an extension to the debt. However, from the debtor's point of view, the creditor may wish to choose which assets they want a charge over and are more likely to require a fixed charge due to the higher security they provide. They may also ask for a **higher value** in terms of security than the debt is currently worth. This means the debtor may be risking important business assets to service a debt, which puts them at greater risk of failure if the terms of the charge are not met and the asset is subsequently sold.

Question

CVAs

Which parties can apply for a CVA?

Answer

A CVA can be applied for by:

- All directors of the company together;
- The company's administrators; or
- The appointed company liquidator.

Chapter Roundup

- An **administrator** is appointed primarily to try to rescue the company as a going concern. A company may go into administration to carry out an established plan to save the company.
- Some parties – **secured creditors with a floating charge** and **directors** and the **members** by resolution – can appoint an administrator without a court order.
- Various parties can apply for **administration** through the court.
- The **effects** of administration depend on whether it is effected by the **court** or by a **floating chargeholder**, to some degree.
- The administrator has **fiduciary duties** to the company as its agent, plus some legal duties.
- The administrator must either **propose a rescue plan**, or state that the **company cannot be rescued**.
- The administrator takes on the **powers** of the directors.
- Administration can last up to **12 months**.
- Administration has many advantages for the **company**, the **members** and the **creditors**.
- A **receiver** may be appointed by a chargeholder to take charge of the asset to which the charge related in order to realise it.
- A **company voluntary arrangement** is an agreement with creditors as to how and when the company will pay its debts.

PART J   COMPANY RESCUE AND ACTION SHORT OF WINDING UP

Quick Quiz

1   Which parties can apply for administration through the court?

2   Complete the following definition, using the words given below.

   An (1) ………………….. is an arrangement which puts an (2)…………………
   (3)………………………. in control of the business to attempt to save it.

   | • insolvency | • practitioner | • administration |

3   Name two advantages of administration.

   (1) ....
   (2) ....

4   Which of the following parties can appoint an administrative receiver?

   A   A member of the company
   B   A Director of the company
   C   A floating chargeholder
   D   A fixed charge holder

5   For a CVA to be approved, what percentage of creditors by debt value must vote in favour of it?

   A   25%
   B   50%
   C   75%
   D   90%

Answers to Quick Quiz

1. There are four sets of parties that may apply to the court for an administration order:
   - The company (that is, a majority of the members by 50% resolution)
   - The directors of the company
   - One or more creditors of the company
   - The Justice and Chief Executive of the Magistrates' Court following non-payment of a fine imposed on the company

2. Administration, insolvency, practitioner

3. (1) It does not necessarily result in the dissolution of the company
   (2) It prevents creditors applying for compulsory liquidation

   Subsidiary advantages are

   (3) All creditors can apply for an administration order
   (4) The administrator may challenge past transactions of the company

4. C. An administrative receiver is appointed by the holder of a floating charge (if the charge was created before 15 September 2003).

5. C. To be accepted, at least 75% by debt value of the creditors must vote for the proposal.

End of chapter question

Administration

Discuss in what circumstances an administrator may be appointed and explain the role of an administrator. **(20 marks)**

PART J COMPANY RESCUE AND ACTION SHORT OF WINDING UP

Winding up of the company

Company winding up

Topic list	Syllabus reference
1 What is liquidation?	4.2
2 Voluntary liquidation	4.2
3 Compulsory liquidation	4.2
4 Powers and other roles of the liquidator	4.2
5 Order of payments on liquidation	4.2
6 Differences between compulsory and voluntary liquidation	4.2
7 Other insolvency rules	4.2
8 Revision: insolvency situations	4.2

Introduction

As we saw in the previous chapter, a **company in difficulty** or **in crisis** (an **insolvent** company) has a choice from two alternatives:

(1) To carry on with the business, using statutory methods to help remedy the situation; or

(2) To stop.

We have already looked at alternative 1, so now, in the final chapter of your study of business law, we shall consider alternative 2. This option is the last resort and is used when companies **cannot be saved** and is known as **liquidation**. However, liquidation is also used when a decision is taken to close an otherwise healthy business.

Liquidation is also sometimes called 'winding up', but both terms are used to describe the process **when a company is formally dissolved** and **ceases to exist**.

Various methods of achieving liquidation are covered in the first three sections of this chapter and the differences between them are summarised in section 6. We shall conclude the chapter by looking at some other provision of Insolvency and Companies Act rules.

The **Insolvency Act 1986**, (HMSO, 1986) applies to this chapter unless otherwise stated.

PART K   WINDING UP OF THE COMPANY

1 What is liquidation?

FAST FORWARD

> Liquidation is the dissolution or 'winding up' of a company.

Key terms

> **Liquidation** means that the company must be dissolved and its affairs 'wound up', or brought to an end. It is often referred to as **winding up**.
>
> The assets are realised, debts are paid out of the proceeds, and any surplus amounts are returned to members. Liquidation leads on to **dissolution** of the company.

1.1 Who decides to liquidate?

FAST FORWARD

> There are three different methods of **liquidation: compulsory, members' voluntary** and **creditors' voluntary**. Compulsory liquidation and creditors' voluntary liquidation are proceedings for insolvent companies which cannot pay their debts, and members' voluntary liquidation is for solvent companies.

The parties most likely to be involved in the decision to liquidate are:

- The directors
- The creditors
- The members

The **directors** are best placed to know the financial position and difficulty that the company is in. The **creditors** may become aware that the company is in financial difficulty when their invoices do not get paid on a timely basis, or at all.

The **members** are likely to be the last people to know that the company is in financial difficulty, as they rely on the directors to tell them. In public companies, there is a rule that the directors must call a general meeting of members if the net assets of the company fall to half or less of the amount of its called-up share capital. There is no such rule for private companies.

As we shall see, there are three methods of winding up. They depend on **who has instigated the proceedings**. Directors cannot formally instigate proceedings for winding up, they can only make recommendations to the members.

However, if the **members refuse** to put the company in liquidation and the directors feel that to continue to trade will prejudice creditors, they could resign their posts to avoid committing **fraudulent** or **wrongful trading**.

In any case, if the company was in such serious financial difficulty for this to be an issue, it is likely that a **creditor** would have commenced proceedings against it.

1.1.1 Creditors

If a creditor has grounds they may **apply to the court** for the **compulsory winding up** of the company.

Creditors may also be closely involved in a **creditors' voluntary winding up**, if the company is **insolvent** when the **members** decide to wind the company up.

1.1.2 Members

The members may decide to wind the company up (probably on the advice of the directors). If they do so, the company is **voluntarily wound up**. This can lead to two different types of members' winding up:

- Members' voluntary winding up (if the company is solvent)
- Creditors' voluntary winding up (if the company is insolvent)

1.2 Role of the liquidator

FAST FORWARD

A **liquidator** must be an authorised, qualified insolvency practitioner.

Once the decision to liquidate has been taken, the company goes under the **control of a liquidator** who must be a **qualified** and **authorised insolvency practitioner**.

We shall shortly look at the procedures that the liquidator carries out, however, the liquidator also has a statutory duty to **report** to the Secretary of State where they feel that any **director** of the insolvent company is **unfit** to be involved in the management of a company. This may lead to disqualification of directors.

1.2.1 Qualified insolvency practitioners

Only **individuals** (not firms or companies) can act as a **qualified insolvency practitioner**. To qualify, an individual must:

- Be **licensed** by one of the **Recognised Professional Bodies** (ACCA, ICAEW, CAI, ICAS, IPA)
- **Pass two examinations** from the **Joint Insolvency Examination Board** (one on corporate insolvency and one on personal insolvency)
- Meet the **minimum criteria for experience** (600 hours over 3 years)
- Be approved as a **fit and proper person** by the Insolvency Licensing Committee;
- Be granted an **insolvency licence**;
- Have **professional indemnity insurance** (PII);
- Comply with the **Insolvency Licensing Regulations** and **Guidance Notes**;
- Agree to be **monitored by in accordance with minimum standards** agreed with the Insolvency Service; and
- Pay the appropriate **fee**.

Individuals may obtain a **partial licence** by passing **one of the JIEB examinations** that enables them work in the area of insolvency covered by the exam that they passed.

1.3 Common features of liquidations

FAST FORWARD

Once **insolvency procedures** have commenced, share trading must cease, the company documents must state that the company is in liquidation and the directors' power to manage ceases.

Regardless of what method of liquidation is used, similar **legal problems** may arise in each of them. In addition, the following factors are true at the start of any liquidation:

- **No share dealings** or **changes in members** are allowed.
- All company documents (eg invoices, letters, emails) and the website must **state the company is in liquidation**.
- The **directors' power to manage ceases**.

Question — Liquidation

Fill in the missing words.

Liquidation means that a company must be .... and its affairs ....

> **Answer**
>
> Liquidation means that a company must be **dissolved** and its affairs **wound up**.

Having seen what liquidation is, the next two sections cover what happens in a voluntary and compulsory liquidation.

2 Voluntary liquidation

FAST FORWARD
> A **winding up** is **voluntary** where the decision to wind up is taken by the company's members, although if the company is insolvent, the creditors will be heavily involved in the proceedings.

There are two types of voluntary liquidation under the Insolvency Act 1986 (HMSO, 1986):

- A **members' voluntary winding up**, where the company is **solvent** and the members merely decide to 'kill it off'.
- A **creditors' voluntary winding up**, where the company is **insolvent** and the members resolve to wind up in consultation with creditors.

The effect of the voluntary winding up being a creditors' one is that the **creditors** may **influence** the conduct of the liquidation because their input on the choice of liquidator is required.

In both kinds of voluntary winding up, the **court has the power to appoint a liquidator** (if for some reason there is none acting) or to remove one liquidator and appoint another: s 108.

2.1 Members' voluntary liquidation

FAST FORWARD
> In order to be a members' winding up, the directors must make a **declaration of solvency**. It is a criminal offence to make a declaration of solvency without reasonable grounds.

Type of resolution to be passed	
Ordinary	This is **rare, but** if the **articles** specify liquidation at a certain point, only an ordinary resolution is required.
Special	A company may resolve to be **wound up** by special resolution.

The winding up **commences** on the passing of the resolution. A signed copy of the resolution must be delivered to the Registrar within 15 days. A **liquidator** is usually appointed by the same resolution (or a second resolution passed at the same time).

2.1.1 Declaration of solvency

A voluntary winding up is a members' voluntary winding up **only** if the directors make and deliver to the Registrar a **declaration of solvency:** s 89.

This is a **statutory declaration** that the directors have made full enquiry into the affairs of the company and are of the opinion that it will be able to pay its debts, within a specified period not exceeding 12 months.

(a) The declaration is made by all the directors or, if there are more than two directors, by a **majority** of them.

(b) The declaration includes a **statement of the company's assets and liabilities** as at the latest practicable date before the declaration is made.

(c) The declaration must be:
  (i) Made not more than five weeks before the resolution to wind up is passed, and
  (ii) Delivered to the Registrar within 15 days after the meeting.

If the liquidator later concludes that the company will be unable to pay its debts they must call a meeting of creditors and lay before them a **statement of assets and liabilities**: s 95.

> **Exam focus point**
>
> It is a **criminal offence** punishable by fine or imprisonment for a director to make a declaration of solvency without having **reasonable grounds** for it. If the company proves to be insolvent they will have to justify their previous declaration or be punished.

In a members' voluntary winding up the **creditors play no part** since the assumption is that their debts will be paid in full. However, a members' voluntary liquidation may become a creditors' voluntary liquidation where the liquidation process is not progressing to the satisfaction of the company's creditors.

2.2 Creditors' voluntary liquidation

> **FAST FORWARD**
>
> When there is no declaration of solvency there is a **creditors' voluntary winding** up.

If no declaration of solvency is made and delivered to the Registrar the liquidation proceeds as a creditors' voluntary winding up **even if** in the end the company pays its debts in full.

The **meeting of members** is held first and its business is as follows:

- To resolve to wind up, and
- To nominate a liquidator.

Creditor approval is required for the **nomination of the liquidator**. This is achieved through the **deemed consent procedure** or by one of a number of alternative consent methods (such as correspondence, electronic voting, virtual meetings, physical meetings, or any other procedure that enables all creditors entitled to participate in the making of the decision to participate equally).

Under the **deemed consent procedure**, the directors write to the creditors with their proposal. If less than 10% of the creditors in value object, the proposal is deemed to be approved.

If the creditors nominate a different person to be liquidator, **their choice prevails** over the nomination by the members.

Of course, the creditors may decide **not to appoint a liquidator** at all. They cannot be compelled to appoint a liquidator, and if they do fail to appoint one it will be the members' nominee who will take office.

In the past, the presence of the members' nominee as liquidator has been exploited for the purpose known as **'centrebinding'**.

> *Re Centrebind Ltd 1966*
>
> *The facts:* The directors convened a general meeting, without making a statutory declaration of solvency, but failed to call a creditors' meeting for the same or the next day. The penalty for this was merely a small default fine. The liquidator chosen by the members had disposed of the assets before the creditors could appoint a liquidator. The creditors' liquidator challenged the sale of the assets (at a low price) as invalid.
>
> *Decision:* The first liquidator had been in office when he made the sale and so it was a valid exercise of the normal power of sale.

In a 'centrebinding' transaction the assets are sold by an **obliging liquidator** to a new company formed by the members of the insolvent company. The purpose is to defeat the claims of the creditors at minimum cost and enable the same people to continue in business until the next insolvency supervenes.

The Government has sought to limit the abuses during the period between the members' and creditors' meetings. The **powers of the members' nominee as liquidator are now restricted** to:

- Taking control of the company's property,
- Disposing of perishable or other goods which might diminish in value if not disposed of immediately, and
- Doing all other things necessary for the protection of the company's assets.

If the members' liquidator wishes to perform any act other than those listed above, they will have to **apply to the court for leave**.

Question — Voluntary liquidation

What are the key differences between a creditors' voluntary liquidation and a members' voluntary liquidation?

Answer

Creditors' voluntary liquidation	Members' voluntary liquidation
Company is insolvent	Company is solvent
Creditors approve members' nominee for liquidator	Members appoint liquidator

3 Compulsory liquidation

FAST FORWARD

> A creditor may apply to the court to wind up the company, primarily if the company is **unable to pay its debts**. There are statutory tests to prove that a company is unable to pay its debts.

Under the Insolvency Act 1986 (HMSO, 1986) a **creditor** may apply to the court for a compulsory winding up. There are seven statutory reasons they can give, which can all be found in s 122.

We shall consider the two most important here.

	Statutory reasons for compulsory liquidation
s 122(1)(f)	Company is unable to pay its debts
s 122(1)(g)	It is just and equitable to wind up the company

The **Government** may petition for the compulsory winding up of a company:

- If a public company has not obtained a, **trading certificate** within one year of incorporation.
- Following a report by Government inspectors that it is in the **public interest** and **just and equitable** for the company to be wound up.

3.1 Company unable to pay its debts

A creditor who petitions on the grounds of the company's insolvency must show that the company is unable to pay its debts. There are three permitted ways to do that: s 123.

(a) A **creditor owed more than £750 serves** the company at its registered office a **written demand** for payment and the **company neglects** either to **pay the debt** or to offer reasonable security for it within **21 days**.

If the company denies it owes the amount demanded on apparently reasonable grounds, the court will dismiss the petition and leave the creditor to take legal proceedings for debt.

(b) A creditor obtains **judgement** against the company for debt, and attempts to enforce the judgement. However, they are **unable to obtain payment** because no assets of the company have been found and seized.

(c) A creditor satisfies the court that, taking into account the contingent and prospective liabilities of the company, it is **unable to pay its debts**. The creditor may be able to show this in one of two ways:

(i) By proof that the company is not able to pay its debts as they fall due – the **commercial insolvency test**

(ii) By proof that the company's assets are less than its liabilities – the **balance sheet test**

This is a residual category. Any suitable evidence of actual or prospective insolvency may be produced.

3.2 The just and equitable ground

> **FAST FORWARD** A **dissatisfied member** may get the court to wind the company up on the **just and equitable ground**.

We saw in Chapter 17 that a member who is dissatisfied with the directors or controlling shareholders over the management of the company may petition the court for the company to be wound up on the **just and equitable ground**. We shall now review the main points of this ground here.

3.2.1 Examples: When companies have been wound up

(a) **The substratum of the company has gone – the only or main object(s) of the company (its underlying basis or substratum) cannot be or can no longer be achieved.**

Re German Date Coffee Co 1882

(b) **The company was formed for an illegal or fraudulent purpose or there is a complete deadlock in the management of its affairs.**

Re Yenidje Tobacco Co Ltd 1916

(c) **The understandings between members or directors which were the basis of the association have been unfairly breached by lawful action.**

Ebrahimi v Westbourne Galleries Ltd 1973 and Re A company 1983

(d) **The directors deliberately withheld information so that the shareholders have no confidence in the company's management.**

3.3 Other circumstances for compulsory liquidation

Under s 122, there are **five other circumstances** where compulsory liquidation may be commenced. These are:

- The **company passed a special resolution** that it should be wound up by the court
- The company registered as a **public limited company** more than a year previously but has not yet been issued with a **trading certificate**
- The company is an **'old' public company**
- The company has **not begun trading within a year** of its incorporation or **has suspended its trading** for a whole year
- A **moratorium for a voluntary arrangement** for the company has passed and no voluntary arrangement is in place

3.4 Proceedings for compulsory liquidation

When a petition is presented to the **court** a copy is delivered to the **company** in case it objects. It is advertised so that other creditors may intervene if they wish.

The petition **may** be presented by a member. If the petition is presented by **a member** they **must show** that:

(a) The company is **solvent** or alternatively refuses to supply information of its financial position, and

(b) They have been a **registered shareholder** for at least 6 of the 18 months up to the date of their petition. However this rule is not applied if the petitioner acquired their shares by allotment direct from the company or by inheritance from a deceased member or if the petition is based on the number of members having fallen below two.

Attention!

> The court will not order compulsory liquidation on a member's petition if they have nothing to gain from it. If the company is insolvent they would receive nothing since the creditors will take all the assets.

Once the court has been petitioned, a **provisional liquidator** may be appointed by the **court**. The **Official Receiver** is usually appointed, and their powers are conferred by the court. These usually extend to taking control of the company's property and applying for a special manager to be appointed.

Key term

> The **Official Receiver** is an officer of the court. They are appointed as liquidator of any company ordered to be wound up by the court, although an insolvency practitioner may replace them.

3.5 Effects of an order for compulsory liquidation

The effects of an **order** for compulsory liquidation are:

(a) The **Official Receiver** (an official of the Government whose duties relate mainly to bankruptcy of individuals) **becomes liquidator**: s 136.

(b) The liquidation is **deemed to have commenced at the time** (possibly several months earlier) **when the petition was first presented**.

(c) Any **disposition** of the **company's property** and any transfer of its shares subsequent to the commencement of liquidation is **void** unless the court orders otherwise: s 127.

(d) Any **legal proceedings** in progress against the company are halted (and none may thereafter begin) unless the court gives leave. Any seizure of the company's assets after commencement of liquidation is void: ss 130 and 128.

(e) The **employees** of the company are **automatically dismissed**. The liquidator assumes the powers of management previously held by the directors.

(f) Any **floating charge crystallises**.

The assets of the company may remain the company's legal property but **under the liquidator's control** unless the court by order **vests** the assets in the liquidator. The business of the company may continue but it is the liquidator's duty to continue it with a view only to realisation, for instance by sale as a going concern.

Within 21 days of the making of the order for winding up a **statement of affairs** must be delivered to the liquidator verified by one or more company officers (and possibly by other persons). The statement shows the assets and liabilities of the company and includes a list of creditors with particulars of any security: s 131.

The liquidator may require that any **officers or employees** concerned in the recent management of the company shall join in submitting the statement of affairs.

Question — Compulsory liquidation order

What are the six effects of a compulsory liquidation order?

Answer

- Official Receiver appointed as liquidator
- Liquidation deemed to have commenced at time when petition first presented
- Disposition of company property since commencement of liquidation deemed void
- Legal proceedings against the company are halted
- Employees are dismissed
- Any floating charge crystallises

We have seen how a business may be subject to voluntary and compulsory liquidation. In either case, a liquidator takes over the business and acts in a similar way to a director, although their main role is to end the company's life. In the next section we shall look at the powers of a liquidator and the roles that they perform.

4 Powers and other roles of the liquidator

FAST FORWARD

However a liquidation commenced, the **powers of the liquidator** are the same. The **official receiver** has a number of **additional roles** that are not required as part of a voluntary liquidation.

When a **liquidator** has been appointed, the **powers of the directors cease**. The **liquidator assumes all of the powers** that the directors previously enjoyed in order to achieve the objectives of the liquidation. However, one or more directors may be permitted to continue if that is desired by the liquidator, the company or the creditors.

If, while the **liquidation is in progress**, the liquidator decides to call meetings of contributories or creditors they may arrange to do so under powers vested in the court.

An **Official Receiver** may also apply to the Registrar for an **early dissolution** of the company if its realisable assets will not cover their expenses and further investigation is not required: s 202

The **objectives of the liquidator** and the **powers** they have to achieve them are as follows:

Objective	Power
Settle the list of contributories (ie, members who have a liability to contribute in the event of a winding up)	Order any members to pay up any unpaid share capital that they owe
Collect and realise the company's assets	Take custody of company assets (such as buildings, equipment and inventory)
Discharge the company's debts	Sell they company's assets for whatever price they deem appropriate
Settle the debts of the company in the prescribed order (see below)	Repay any amounts owing to fixed charge holders from the sale of charged assets. Make distributions to other creditors in accordance with the priority of order of payments
Redistribute any surplus to the contributories	according to the entitlement rights attached to their shares

4.1 Other roles of the liquidator

Once the **liquidation is complete**, the **liquidator** must act as follows:

(a) In a **voluntary winding up,** they must prepare an account showing how the winding up has been dealt with and lay it before a meeting of the members and/or creditors. Within the following week they should then file details with the Registrar who will enter the details on the company's file and the company will be deemed to be dissolved three months thereafter.

(b) In a **compulsory winding up**, the liquidator must go back to the court which then makes an order dissolving the company. They then file the order and the Registrar records on the company file that the company is dissolved as from the date of the order.

4.2 Additional roles the Official Receiver

The Official Receiver has a number of additional roles. In particular they **must investigate** (s 132)

- The **causes of the failure** of the company, and
- Generally the **promotion, formation, business dealings** and **affairs** of the company.

The Official Receiver **may report** to the court on the results.

(a) The Official Receiver may require the **public examination** in open court of those believed to be implicated (a much-feared sanction).

(b) The Official Receiver may apply to the court for public examination where half the **creditors** or three-quarters of the **shareholders** (in value in either case) so request. Failure to attend, or reasonable suspicion that the examinees will abscond, may lead to arrest and detention in custody for contempt of court.

5 Order of payments on liquidation

FAST FORWARD

In a **compulsory liquidation** (and often in a voluntary one) the liquidator **distributes the assets** that remain after any fixed charge-holder has satisfied its secured debt following appointment of a receiver, as follows.

	Order	Explanation
1	Costs	These include the costs of selling the assets, the liquidator's remuneration and all costs incidental to the liquidation procedure.
2	Preferential debts	• Employees' wages (subject to a statutory maximum) • Accrued holiday pay • Contributions to an occupational pension fund • Money borrowed by the company to enable it to pay wages
3	Secondary preferential creditors	HMRC is the secondary preferential creditor. Any taxes collected by the company (such as income tax and VAT) is paid to HMRC.
4	Debts secured by floating charges	Subject to the ring-fenced 'prescribed part' (see below).
5	Debts owed to unsecured ordinary creditors	A proportion of assets (known as the 'prescribed part') is 'ring-fenced' for unsecured creditors. This proportion (which is subject to a statutory maximum) is calculated as 50% of the first £10,000 of realisations of debts secured by floating charge and 20% of the floating charge realisations thereafter (subject to a prescribed maximum).
6	Deferred debts	For example dividends declared but not paid and interest accrued on debts since liquidation
7	Members	Any surplus (unlikely in compulsory and creditors' voluntary liquidations since the company is solvent if it has a surplus) is distributed to members according to their rights under the articles or the terms of issue of their shares.

It is important to remember that secured **creditors with fixed charges may appoint a receiver** to sell a charged asset, passing any surplus on to the liquidator.

Floating charge-holders with charges created before 15 September 2003 can appoint **administrative receivers** to manage and sell the charged asset. However those with charges created on/after that date may only appoint an **administrator**.

In the event of a **shortfall** secured creditors become unsecured creditors for the balance. However, a floating charge-holder who faces a shortfall on their secured debt (which is therefore treated as unsecured) cannot share in the ring-fenced part available to unsecured creditors.

6 Differences between compulsory and voluntary liquidation

The differences between compulsory and voluntary liquidation are associated with **timing**, the **role** of the **Official Receiver, stay of legal proceedings** and the **dismissal of employees**.

Exam questions may test your knowledge of the **differences** between compulsory and voluntary liquidations. In the table below we shall briefly summarise them.

	Differences
Control	Under a members' voluntary liquidation the members control the liquidation process. Under a creditors' voluntary liquidation the creditors control the process. The court controls the process under a compulsory liquidation.
Timing	A voluntary winding up commences on the day when the **resolution to wind up is passed**. It is not retrospective. A compulsory winding up, once agreed to by the court, commences on the day the **petition was presented**.
Liquidator	The **Official Receiver** plays **no role** in a **voluntary winding up**. The members or creditors select and appoint the liquidator and they are not an officer of the court.
Legal proceedings	In a **voluntary winding up** there is **no automatic stay of legal proceedings** against the company, nor are previous dispositions or seizure of its assets void. However the liquidator has a general right to apply to the court to make any order which the court can make in a compulsory liquidation. They would do so, for instance, to prevent any creditor obtaining an unfair advantage over the other creditors.
Management and staff	In any **liquidation the liquidator replaces the directors** in the management of the company (unless they decides to retain them). However, the employees are **not automatically dismissed by commencement of voluntary liquidation**. Insolvent liquidation may amount to repudiation of their employment contracts (provisions of the statutory employment protection code apply).

7 Other insolvency rules

The **Insolvency Act 1986** and **Companies Act 2006** include a number of important rules that apply in insolvency situations.

Insolvency situations often create unique problems and challenges that need to be overcome. In this section we shall look at a number of rules that apply in certain circumstances.

7.1 Avoidance of floating charges

Under the **Insolvency Act** 1986 (HMSO, 1986) s 245, liquidation automatically renders void any floating charge created within the period of 12 months (or in the case where the charge was created in favour of a 'connected person', two years) subject to the following exceptions.

(a) The charge is **valid** if the company was **solvent** at the time when the charge was created, unless as a result of the transaction under which the charge was created the company became unable to pay its debts. This exception does not apply where the charge was created in favour of a '**connected person**'. Note that a company is not solvent unless it can pay its **debts in full** as they fall **due**.

(b) If the company was not solvent at the time the charge was created, the floating charge is still valid to the extent of **money paid** or **goods and services** received by the company at the same time or after the charge is created, or discharge or reduction of the company's liability.

Only the charge (as security), not the debt, becomes void: s 247.

7.2 Transactions at an undervalue, preferences and connected persons

When a company goes into liquidation the **court may avoid transactions** at an **undervalue** and **preferences**.

7.2.1 Transactions at an undervalue

A transaction '**at an undervalue**' is a gift or a transaction in the two years previous to liquidation (or administration), by which the company gives consideration of greater value than its receives, for instance a sale at less than full market price: s 238.

However, such a **transition does not become void** if the company enters into it:

- In **good faith**.
- For the **purpose of carrying on its business**.
- **Believing on reasonable grounds** that it will benefit the company.

7.2.2 Preference

A company '**gives preference**' to a creditor or guarantor of its debts if it does anything by which this position will be benefited if the company goes into insolvent liquidation and the company does this with the intention of producing that result: s 239.

If at the time of the undervalue or preference the company was unable to pay its debts, or became so by reasons of the transaction, and the company later goes into liquidation or administration, the liquidator or the administrator can apply to the court for an order to restore the position to what it would have been if no such transaction had taken place.

7.2.3 Applicable time periods

The **relevant period** which brings the avoidance powers into operation in relation to a transaction are as follows.

- **Undervalues two years** before the commencement of liquidation.
- **Preferences**
  - With a person **unconnected** with the company **six months** before the commencement of liquation.
  - With a person **connected** with the company **two years** prior to commencement.

Unless the person in whose favour the undervalue or preference operates is connected with the company, the company must be **insolvent** at the time of entering into the disputed transaction, or must have become so in consequence of it, if it is to be disputed by the court.

If the court is satisfied that a preference has been given it can (under s 241):

- **Order return** of **property** or of the proceeds of its sale
- **Discharge any security** given
- **Order payment** in respect of benefit to the liquidator
- **Renew guarantee obligations** discharged by the preference
- **Charge property**

7.2.4 Connected persons

The term **'connected persons'** appears in the law both in the context of preferences and transactions at an undervalue and also in relation to floating charges.

A person is 'connected' with the company if they are:

- A **director** or **shadow director** of the company.
- An **associate** of a director, shadow director or the company itself.

These provisions are summarised below.

Transaction with		Transactions at an undervalue	Preference
Unconnected person	Time period before commencement	2 years	6 months
	Company insolvent at that time?	Yes	Yes
Connected person	Time period before commencement	2 years	2 years
	Company insolvent at that time?	Yes	No

7.2.5 Transactions defrauding creditors

If the transaction at an undervalue was **intended to defraud creditors**, that is the transaction was undertaken with the intention of putting assets beyond the reach of creditors, there is **no statutory time limit**.

Sands v Clitheroe 2006

The facts: Mr Clitheroe, a practising solicitor, gifted his interest in his home to his wife in 1988. At the time he was solvent and a partner in a fairly secure practice, but he effected the transfer specifically in order to protect the family home in the event of the financial collapse of the partnership. He was made bankrupt 15 years later and the trustee in bankruptcy sought an order that the transaction should be overturned and the half-share treated as Mr Clitheroe's assets when the bankruptcy order was made.

Decision: As the intent of the transaction had been to put assets beyond creditors' reach, even though the debtor was not engaging in 'risky business' and none of the bankruptcy debts existed at the time, the transaction fell within s 423, for which there is no time limit. Notably, s 423 applies equally to companies as to individuals.

7.3 Other offences in connection with winding up

In Chapter 19 we looked at a number of offences that can be committed by directors in an insolvency situation. We shall briefly review them here.

Offence	Description
Fraudulent trading	A **criminal offence** under the **Companies Act 2006** (TSO, 2006). Occurs where the business of a company in liquidation or administration has been carried on with **intent to defraud creditors** or for any fraudulent purpose.
	There is also a **civil offence** of the same name under s 213 of the Insolvency Act 1986. Under this offence courts may declare that **any persons** who were knowingly parties to carrying on the business in this fashion shall be liable for the debts of the company.
Wrongful trading	Directors may have a **civil liability** for 'wrongful trading' if the liquidator or administrator proves the following.
	The directors **knew**, or **should have known**, that there was **no reasonable prospect** that the **company** could **have avoided insolvency**.
	The director(s) did not take **sufficient steps** to minimise the potential loss to the creditors.

Offence	Description
False declaration of solvency	It is a criminal offence for a director in a **voluntary liquida**tion to make a **declaration of solvency without having reasonable grounds** for it. If the company proves to be insolvent, they will have to justify their previous decision, or be punished.
Fraud and deception	S 206 Insolvency Act 1986 makes it a criminal offence to **conceal or fraudulently remove company assets or debt** – including falsifying records. It is also an offence to **dispose of property** that was acquired on credit that has not been paid for.
Defrauding creditors	S 207 Insolvency Act 1986 makes it an offence to make a **gift** of, or **transfer company property** once a liquidation has commenced, unless it can be proved there was no intent to defraud creditors.
Misconduct during a liquidation	A company officer may be liable for a number of offences due to their misconduct. These include: • Not **identifying company property** to the liquidator. • Not **delivering requested books** and **papers** to the liquidator. • Not **informing the liquidator** if identified debts do not turn out to be debts.
Falsification of company books	**Destroying, mutilating, altering** or **falsifying company books** is an offence under s 209 Insolvency Act 1986.
Omissions	It is an offence under s 210 Insolvency Act 1986 to **omit material information** when making statements concerning a company's affairs.

8 Revision: insolvency situations

As we have discussed, various situations could arise when a company gets into financial difficulties.

Exam focus point

It is vital that you do not confuse the various implications for a company of getting into financial difficulties. This can be a difficult area to keep clear in your head, particularly given that many of the terms and the personnel involved sound very similar to each other.

Given the possibility of confusion arising in this area, the following scenarios are given for you to work through using the Insolvency Act 1986 (HMSO, 1986) and the Enterprise Act 2002 (TSO, 2002), to ensure that you understand the implications for the company in each situation.

8.1 Company defaults on secured debt

When the company defaults on secured debt, the creditor can usually take one of four steps under the terms of their security:

- Take **possession of the asset** subject to the charge if they have a fixed charge (if they have a floating charge they may only take possession if the contract allows).
- **Sell it** (provided the debenture is executed as a deed).
- Apply to the court for its **transfer** to their ownership by foreclosure order (rarely used).
- Appoint a **receiver** of it, provided an administration order is not in effect, or — in the case of floating chargeholders only — appoint an administrator without needing to apply to the court.

The most common result is that a receiver, or an administrator, is appointed. The next two scenarios will outline this in relation to both fixed and floating charges.

Fixed charge

X Ltd has a mortgage with ABC Bank which is secured by a fixed charge over the building to which it relates. X Ltd fails to keep up its payments to ABC Bank. Under the terms of its security, ABC Bank appoints a receiver of the building, who sells the building and realises the debt.

Once the bank had realised its debt, the receiver would leave and the business would be left to continue (as best it could without its premises). In such a situation, liquidation might follow this act of the receiver if the business could no longer operate (see Illustration below on the petition for compulsory liquidation).

Floating charge

Y Ltd has a loan from EFG Bank which is secured by a fixed and floating charge over all the company's assets. Y Ltd defaults on the loan. EFG Bank demands in writing that the repayment be made. Y Ltd continues to default on the loan. Under the terms of its security, EFG Bank appoints a receiver to take control of the company's assets.

The receiver's purpose is to realise the debt for the bank. He may achieve this by selling the business as a going concern or by breaking up the business and realising individual assets.

Unsecured creditors may apply for a petition for a compulsory winding up (see Illustration below) during the course of a receivership. The two can run simultaneously.

If the terms of the floating charge so provided, EFG Bank could instead have appointed an administrator of the company, without referring to the court

8.2 Company defaults on unsecured debt

An unsecured creditor has the following rights against a company who has defaulted on a debt:

- Sue the company for the debt/seize the asset if their judgement is not satisfied.
- Petition the court for the compulsory liquidation of the company.
- Petition the court for an administration order.

It is important to note that a secured creditor also has these remedies open to them. However, a secured creditor has more to gain from appointing a receiver or administrator as discussed above than commencing liquidation proceedings.

Petition for compulsory liquidation

A has sold goods worth £29,567 to B on credit. B Ltd has exceeded the credit terms extended and A has presented B Ltd with a written demand to their registered office, which B Ltd has not responded to after a month. B Ltd have sold on the goods which they purchased from A and do not dispute the value of the invoice.

A can apply to the court for the compulsory winding up of the company because the company has not paid its debts.

The court appoints the Official Receiver to be the provisional liquidator until it gives an order for compulsory liquidation.

Illustration

Petition for administration order

A has sold goods worth £29,567 to B Ltd on credit. B Ltd has exceeded the credit terms extended. A has discovered that the management of B Ltd is experiencing difficulties, but believes that the business is sound and that the debt could be paid if the business was managed properly. A is also aware that B Ltd has a loan from the bank which is secured by a floating charge.

A suspects that if the bank exercises its right to bring in a receiver, the business will be wound up and the unsecured debts might not be paid. It therefore applies to the court of an administration order so that debt collection will be frozen while an action plan is undertaken to ensure that debts can be paid. However, if the terms of the floating charge allow the bank to appoint an administrator, this can be done by the bank without reference to the court so the bank's choice of administrator would prevail.

An unsecured creditor would benefit from an administration order over a compulsory liquidation as once an administration order has been granted, secured creditors are barred from appointing receivers to realise their debts without the court's permission.

Remember that 'in receivership' and in liquidation, the priority of claims is as follows:

- Costs of selling assets
- Receiver's expenses
- Preferential debts
- Debts secured under a floating charge
- (By implication) any other unsecured debt (with rights over a 'ring-fenced' element)

The administration order can represent a good alternative to liquidation to the unsecured creditor.

8.3 Actions of members

The only way that a company can be wound up is if its members determine that this should be so. In this case, a voluntary winding up would take place.

Exam focus point

The following are issues which as a minimum you must learn and remember:

- Distinction between liquidator/receiver/Official Receiver/administrator.
- A company can have a receiver and be in liquidation at the same time.
- Once an administration **order** has been made, no receiver can be appointed or liquidation proceedings started (although they can until the court grants the petition).
- A secured creditor will usually enforce their security and appoint a receiver, where possible, or an administrator.
- A voluntary liquidation is always instigated by the members.

You should consider the advantages of administration as opposed to liquidation from the point of view of all the parties involved.

Advantages of administration	
To the company	It does not necessarily cease to exist at the end of the process. Liquidation will always result in the company being wound up. It also provides temporary relief from creditors to allow breathing space to formulate rescue plans.
To the members	They will continue to have shares in the company which has not been wound up. If the administration is successful, regenerating the business should enhance share value and will restore any income from the business (dividends or any salary for owner-managed business).

Advantages of administration	
To the creditors	Creditors should obtain a return in relation to their past debts from an administration. Unsecured creditors will benefit from the 'prescribed part' of asset realisations. Any creditor may apply to the court for an administration order, while only certain creditors may apply for other forms of relief from debt, for example, the use of receivers or an application for winding up. Floating chargeholders may appoint an administrator without reference to the court if the terms of the charge so provides. It may also be in the interests of the creditors to have a continued business relationship with the company once the business has been turned around.

Chapter Roundup

- **Liquidation** is the **dissolution** or '**winding up**' of a company.
- There are three different methods of **liquidation: compulsory, members' voluntary** and **creditors' voluntary**. Compulsory liquidation and creditors' voluntary liquidation are proceedings for insolvent companies, and members' voluntary liquidation is for solvent companies.
- A **liquidator** must be an authorised, qualified insolvency practitioner.
- Once **insolvency procedures** have commenced, share trading must cease, the company documents must state that the company is in liquidation and the directors' power to manage ceases.
- A **winding** up is **voluntary** where the decision to wind up is taken by the company members in general meeting, although if the company is insolvent, the creditors will be heavily involved in the proceedings.
- In order to be a members' winding up, the directors must make a **declaration of solvency**. It is a criminal offence to make a declaration of solvency without reasonable grounds.
- When there is no declaration of solvency there is a **creditors' voluntary winding** up.
- A creditor may apply to the court to wind up the company, primarily if the company is **unable to pay its debts**. There are statutory tests to prove that a company is unable to pay its debts.
- A **dissatisfied member** may get the court to wind the company up on the **just and equitable ground**.
- However a liquidation commenced, the **powers of the liquidator** are the same. The **official receiver** has a number of **additional roles** that are not required as part of a voluntary liquidation
- In a **compulsory liquidation** (and often in a voluntary one) the liquidator **distributes the assets** that remain after any fixed charge-holder has satisfied its secured debt following appointment of a receiver, as follows.
- The differences between compulsory and voluntary liquidation are associated with **timing**, the **role** of the **Official Receiver**, **stay of legal proceedings** and the **dismissal of employees**.
- The **Insolvency Act 1986** and **Companies Act 2006** include a number of important rules that apply in insolvency situations.

Quick Quiz

1. Name three common effects of liquidations.

    (1) ....

    (2) ....

    (3) ....

2. What are the two most important grounds for **compulsory liquidation**?

    (1) ....

    (2) ....

3. A members' voluntary winding up is where the members decide to dissolve a healthy company.

    True ☐

    False ☐

4. Briefly state who 'connected persons' are.

5. List two courses of action that a creditor can take when a debtor defaults on a secured loan?

    (1) ....

    (2) ....

Answers to Quick Quiz

1. (1) No further changes in membership permitted
   (2) All documents must state prominently that company is in liquidation
   (3) Directors' power to manage ceases

2. (1) Company is unable to pay its debts
   (2) It is just and equitable to wind up the company

3. True. Members can decide to wind up a healthy company.

4. A person is 'connected' with the company if they are a director or shadow director of the company or an associate of a director, shadow director or the company itself.

5. (1) Take possession of the asset subject to the charge if they have a fixed charge (if they have a floating charge they may only take possession if the contract allows).
   (2) Sell the asset (provided the debenture is executed as a deed).

   Other courses of action include:

   - Apply to the court for the asset's transfer to their ownership by foreclosure order (rarely used).
   - Appoint a receiver of the asset, provided an administration order is not in effect, or — in the case of floating chargeholders only — appoint an administrator without needing to apply to the court.

End of chapter question

Insolvency

Explain the meaning of compulsory and voluntary liquidation and the main differences between them.

(20 marks)

Answers to end of chapter questions

… ANSWERS TO END OF CHAPTER QUESTIONS

Chapter 1: Introductory question: Legal system and courts

(a) (i) **Criminal law**

A **crime** is conduct prohibited by the law. In a **criminal case** the State is the prosecutor because it is the community as a whole which suffers as a result of the law being broken. Persons guilty of crime may be punished by **fines** payable to the State, **imprisonment**, or a **community-based** punishment. Criminal cases are usually referred to as *R v Jones*. The prosecution is brought in the name of the Crown against the alleged wrongdoer, the **accused**. In a criminal trial, the **burden of proof** to convict the accused rests with the **prosecution**, which must prove its case **beyond reasonable doubt**.

(ii) **Civil law**

Civil law exists to **regulate disputes** over the **rights** and **obligations** of persons dealing with each other, and seeks to compensate injured parties. It is a form of **private law** and covers areas such as tort, contract and employment law. In civil proceedings, the case must be proved on the **balance of probability,** the object is to convince the court that it is more probable than not that a person's assertions are true. There is no concept of **punishment**, and **compensation** is paid to the wronged person. Both parties may choose to **settle** the dispute **out of court** should they wish.

Terminology in civil cases is different from that in criminal cases. The **claimant** sues the **defendant**. A civil case would therefore be referred to as, for example, *Smith v Megacorp plc*.

It is not an act or event which creates the distinction between criminal and civil law, but the **legal consequences**. A single event might give rise to both criminal and civil proceedings.

(b) **Jurisdiction of criminal courts**

All criminal cases begin in **Magistrates' Courts** where the case is introduced into the system. Where the decision in a **criminal case** is appealed against, a court further up the hierarchy will hear it. **Appeals** from Magistrates' Courts are either to the **Crown Court** or the **King's Bench Division** (KBD) of the **High Court**.

Appeals against **conviction** or **sentence** from the **Crown Court** are heard at the **Court of Appeal** and this may in turn be appealed to the **Supreme Court**.

Jurisdiction of civil courts

County Courts deal with almost every kind of civil case that is **small** or which is deemed to be a simple case. **Complicated** or high value cases are heard at the **High Court**.

The **King's Bench Division** hears cases of **contract** and **tort**. The **Family Division** hears cases involving **children** and **matrimonial** issues such as divorce. The **Chancery Division** hears cases concerning **trusts, bankruptcy** and **corporate** matters.

Appeals are to the **Civil Division** of the **Court of Appeal** As with criminal cases, a further appeal to the **Supreme Court** may be permitted.

Chapter 2: Offer or invitation to treat?

(a) An offer must be definite and unequivocal and exhibit a clear intention to be bound. Ordinarily, advertisements constitute a mere invitation to treat (an opportunity for negotiation), rather than an offer that can form the basis of contractual relations. For example, advertising bramblefinch hens for sale in a magazine was held not to constitute an offer to sell (*Partridge v Crittenden* 1968). The terms of sale are not sufficiently certain as demand might outstrip the offeror's supply, and in such circumstances the law will not impose contractual liability.

However, in this case the subject matter of the contract and the terms of sale are both sufficiently certain to form the basis of a contract. New Build Ltd pledges in its advertisement to sell its entire stock to the highest bidder. The advertisement is thereby a tender for the sale of goods. As the terms on which the goods are sold are clear from the terms of the tender, it amounts to the offer of a unilateral contract, which arises where the offeror agrees to be bound if the offeree performs a specified action (in this case, the offer takes the form of a promise to supply goods in return for the promise of money).

(b) If a contract is to be formed, acceptance must be communicated to the offeror. In the unilateral contract situation created by New Build Ltd's tender, Workman Ltd accepts the offer by fulfilling the conditions stipulated by the tender (within the time limit imposed). The problem in this case is that New Build Ltd does not receive the acceptance from Workman Ltd until after the expiry of its offer. The rules governing timing of acceptance are therefore key to determining whether an agreement is formed.

There is as yet no authority on the time when a contract is formed when an acceptance is submitted by email. Under the postal rule, as established in *Adams v Lindsell* 1818, when communication of acceptance is effected by letter (or telegram), the acceptance is effective as soon as the letter is posted. If this rule does apply to email communications, the contract is formed (and the offer cannot be revoked without legal consequences) as soon as Workman Ltd sends the email.

(c) In *Entores v Miles Far East Corporation* 1955 it was held that where an instantaneous method of communication is used, the contract is only complete when the acceptance is received by the offeror. However, in this case there was some judicial opinion to the effect that where acceptance is effected by telex (or any form of delayed communication not covered by the postal rule), and through the fault of the offeror the acceptance is not received, then the agreement will be accepted as being formed. This position was confirmed in *Re Brinkibon Investments* [1983], where Lord Wilberforce stated whilst no universal rule could cover all such scenarios, they would be judged by reference to the intention of the parties, sound business practice and a judgment of where the risks should lie.

Given that New Build Ltd did not specify a particular means of communication and its employees should have checked its email during normal office hours, it is likely that an agreement will be found to be in existence even if the postal rule is not taken into consideration.

Chapter 3: Frustration of contract

(a) The general rule is that a party which fails to perform its obligations under a contract is liable for damages. However, where an unforeseen event occurs which radically alters the situation envisaged by the contracting parties (depriving the contract of a purpose or radically changing the nature of the obligation) then the contract may be automatically discharged under the doctrine of frustration. The event must not be the fault of one of the parties. A contract will not be frustrated simply because something occurs after a contract is agreed which makes it more difficult or expensive for one of the parties to carry out their obligations.

Examples of the types of event which may cause a contract to be frustrated are destruction of the subject matter upon which the contract was based (*Taylor v Caldwell* 1863), a change in the law rendering it illegal to perform the contract (*Avery v Bowden* 1855) and the non-occurrence of the event on which the contract was based (*Krell v Henry* 1903). The difficulty with frustration is that the law may impose the burden of a loss arising from circumstances on one party, when neither is to blame. Under the Law Reform (Frustrated Contracts) Act 1943 a frustrated contract is not rendered void *ab initio* (which could result in unfairness where one of the parties had already carried out some of its obligations under the contract). It remains possible to convey some benefit under a frustrated contract, and such benefits must be reimbursed.

(b) Whether or not a court would hold that the contract has been frustrated firstly depends upon whether the Victory Parade amounts to the foundation of the contract. Two cases following the postponement of the coronation of Edward VII illustrate this issue. In *Krell v Henry* 1903 it was held that a contract to rent a room to view the parade was frustrated and Henry was not required to pay rent for the room. By contrast, in *Herne Bay Steamboat Co v Hutton* 1903 a contract for the hire of a boat to see the naval review that accompanied the coronation was held not to be frustrated; the King's review was not the foundation of the contract and it was still possible to sail around the fleet.

In this case it is clear that the contract for the open-top bus is contingent on there being a parade for it to take part in. As in *Krell v Henry* 1903, the bus was not hired for any other purpose. However, whether the Council had to cancel the parade remains questionable. The members of the team who were not injured could have still participated in the parade (meaning that the accident might not have frustrated the entire purpose of the contract).

If the contract is held not to be frustrated then Fun Fairs Ltd is entitled to the sum of £5,000. If it has been frustrated then the position of the parties is governed by the Law Reform (Frustrated Contracts) Act 1943. Under this Act, Fun Fairs Ltd will be entitled to recover from a sum equal to the value of any benefit conferred upon the Council by virtue of the delivery of the open-top bus. The court is required to award a sum that is just in the circumstances (most importantly, the circumstance of the parade being cancelled). Thus, the sum awarded may be less than £5,000. However, if the Council can show that it derives no value from the bus, then it will not have to make a payment to Fun Fairs Ltd.

Chapter 4: Misrepresentation

(a) Pre-contractual statements of fact which do not enter the contract are classified as representations, and may still have legal consequences if they constitute actionable *misrepresentations*. A misrepresentation may either be express (by statement) or implied (by conduct). A misrepresentation is a false statement of fact made by one of the parties, provided that it constitutes one of the factors which induced another party to enter a contract.

The general rule is that silence does not amount to a misrepresentation. However, this does not mean that Bella's failure to correct a mistaken impression created by her comments is not actionable. Where a statement, accurate when made, becomes false prior to the conclusion of the contract, failure to correct the other party's subsequent misapprehension may amount to misrepresentation (as in *With v O'Flanagan* 1936, where the turnover of a business dropped substantially between a representation and its purchase).

Whilst T.V. Diners Ltd could have checked the veracity of Bella's statement before the conclusion of the agreement, this does not negate Bella's liability. Rather, the firm's failure to do so provides evidence that they relied on Bella's statement in making the offer for Ramshackle Restaurant. The statement must have been one of the factors which influenced the other party in their decision to enter into the contract. However, the false representation need not be the only inducement which operated on the other party in order to be actionable.

(b) Where it is established that a party has been induced to enter into a contract by a false statement of fact, that contract is not rendered void *ab initio*. Nevertheless, that party is able to seek the rescission of the contract and, depending on the type of misrepresentation, it may also be able to seek damages.

Rescission is an equitable remedy which sets aside the contact, putting the parties back in the position they would have been if the contract had not been formed. It is available regardless of the type of misrepresentation. However, it will not be available where one of the 'bars' to rescission has occurred. These include where the misrepresentee, after discovering that it has entered a contract on the basis of a misrepresentation, acts in a manner which affirms the contract. Although T.V. Diners Ltd has only delayed two weeks after the misrepresentation became known (rescission must be sought within a reasonable time), the firm's statement to Bella that it wants to retain ownership of the restaurant is likely to be sufficient to forfeit the option to rescind.

Damages are available, at common law, for fraudulent misrepresentation under the tort of deceit. The Misrepresentation Act 1967 created a statutory right to damages for a misrepresentee (unless the misrepresentor can show that it had reasonable grounds for believing the veracity of its statement, rendering the misrepresentation innocent). In the instant case, as Bella concealed the changed situation from T.V. Diners Ltd, it is likely that her misrepresentation will be considered at least negligent (under s.2(1) of the 1967 Act). In such circumstances, Bella will be liable to damages sufficient to leave T.V. Diners Ltd in the position it would have been in had the tort never occurred (including recompense for losses and expenses incurred subsequent to the contract).

Chapter 5: Negligence

(a) In order for Peter to bring a successful action in the tort of negligence he must, as the claimant, establish all of the positive elements of the tort against the appropriate defendant. Here the most obvious defendant would be his fellow employee who unsafely stacked the compact discs (CDs). However, Peter is more likely to bring an action against Power House Ltd as the company is likely vicariously liable for the tort of an employee carrying out company stacking policy (the company clearly condoned such unsafe stacking as it was a 'common occurrence' in the warehouse). The company is more likely to be insured and able to pay any damages awarded.

In a negligence action the claimant is required to prove the following three elements (settled in the case of *Caparo v Dickman* 1990):

- That the defendant owed the claimant a duty of care
- That the defendant breached that duty of care and
- That, as a result of this breach, the claimant suffered damage

If Peter is able to discharge his burden of proof (on the balance of probabilities) in respect of these elements then he will succeed in his action.

A generalised duty of care was first established in *Donoghue v Stevenson* 1932. Lord Atkin stated in that case that there was a legal duty to take reasonable care not to cause foreseeable injury to one's neighbour (ie those who will foreseeably be affected by one's act or omission). In this instance it seems relatively clear that Power House Ltd owed Peter a duty of care. It was reasonably foreseeable that one of its employees would need to retrieve a CD from the poorly stacked pile and also that that they might suffer injury as a result of that pile falling.

The law measures the defendant's conduct in discharging his duty of care against a standard. That standard is the objective one of 'the reasonable man'. Peter can argue, entirely sensibly, that 'the reasonable man' would not have left this stack of CDs in their unstable state and that it therefore constitutes a breach of the employer's duty of care.

Peter must also prove that the accident and the injury that he suffered injury occurred as a result of Power House Ltd's breach of duty. On the facts this looks straightforward: 'but for' Power House Ltd's unstable stacking of the CDs he would not have fallen. It cannot be said that the injured leg is too remote a consequence of Power House Ltd leaving the unstable stack of CDs (it is foreseeable that personal injuries would result due to the falling stack).

Therefore, it seems likely that Peter can make a successful claim against Power House Ltd.

(b) If Peter's negligence claim is successful then he will be entitled to seek damages to compensate him for the negative impact of that negligence. This will include damages in respect of Peter's pain and suffering, his loss of amenity as a result of the injury (the difficulty in moving around whilst suffering the broken leg) and for consequential economic loss of earnings.

The only defence which may be available to Power House Ltd is contributory negligence. This is not a complete defence, but would allow Power House Ltd to argue that Peter's positioning of the ladder and overreaching was in itself negligent and should be taken into account. Peter's contribution to his own injuries (in his misuse of the ladder) is important, not any contribution to the cause of the accident (if he had been causally responsible for the fall his claim would have failed).

If the defence was made out then Peter's damages would be reduced to reflect his own negligence. Even if Peter's positioning of the ladder had increased his injuries by over 50 per cent the claim for negligence could still succeed, although with a proportionate reduction of damages.

Chapter 6: Agency

(a) Agency is the name given to a fiduciary relationship by which one person (Larry – the agent) is authorised to act as the representative of another (Doug – the principal). Where there is an intention to enter a contract creating binding agency relations the principal, expressly or impliedly, consents that the agent should act on their behalf so as to change their legal relationship with third parties. For example, Larry's role includes entering into contracts with third parties on behalf of Doug. An agency relationship can be created by a verbal agreement as in this case.

It is also unimportant that there is no evidence that Doug has arranged to pay Larry for his services, as agents are entitled to reasonable remuneration for carrying out their role as agent.

The principal will be bound by transactions made, on the principal's behalf, by their agent with third parties, so long as the agent acted within the scope of the authority delegated to them by the principal. The scope of an agent's authority is, therefore, important when assessing whether a principal is liable to third parties for the acts of their agent.

(b) These two scenarios reveal a contrast between the actual authority given by principal to agent and the apparent authority which the principal has led third parties to believe the agent possesses.

The scope of an agent's actual authority can be defined by the terms of the agreement. In this case there is an express agreement that Doug (as principal) grants Larry (as agent) the ability to negotiate contracts with existing suppliers (such as Bill). However, as the terms of an agency agreement need not be in writing, there is scope for dispute as to the scope of the agent's express actual authority. In addition, the agent will have implied actual authority to do anything which is incidental to acting under the express agreement, or (in the absence of express authority) to do whatever an agent of the relevant type would usually have authority to do. Thus the managing director of a company has 'usual authority' to act for a company and enter it into legal relations with third parties in respect of commercial matters connected with managing the company (*Hely-Hutchinson v Brayhead Ltd* 1968). Likewise, Larry likely has implied actual authority to agree the exclusive supplier clause as part of his express power to negotiate renewal contracts. This means that Doug will be bound by the contract with Bill.

By contrast, an agent's *apparent* or *ostensible* authority may exceed the scope of their actual authority where third parties believe that the agent has the authority to act in a particular manner (raising the question of whether the principal ought to be bound by the agent's acts). Ostensible authority is that authority which another believes that the agent has, based upon representations made by the principal. In the present case, when Doug told Fred that Larry, as an agent, would have the power to negotiate a contract this could give rise to ostensible authority.

Ostensible and actual authority are therefore quite independent of each other (*Freeman & Lockyer v Buckhurst Park Properties* 1964). Here Larry has no actual authority to enter into contract with Fred (as he would be a new supplier), but Doug will be estopped from withdrawing from contractual relations with Fred because of his representations to Fred that Larry did have such authority.

Chapter 7: Partnerships

A general partnership is governed by the Partnership Act 1890. This act in section 1(1) defines a partnership as 'the relation which subsists between persons carrying on a business with a view of profit'. It is a structure for two or more persons to be in a business together. So it will be suitable for Ben, Will and Diane. Each of them would be self-employed and would take a share of the profits. Usually, each partner participates in the decision-making and each partner will be personally responsible for any debts or liabilities of the business. Ben and Diane will not be personally liable for Will's own debt, but if Will was to make financial decisions (which he can since there is equal power) that ran the business into debt they would all have to share in repaying this money. There are no specific requirements for the formation of a partnership. The partnership is a contractual agreement between the partners, and may be express or implied (just as with any other contract). The partnership commences when the partners begin their business activity (not when the agreement is made see Khan v Miah).

Some of the advantages of setting up a partnership are that partnership can be formed quickly and easily without any great legal formalities. This might be preferable to Ben, Will and Diane, as it seems as though they have little business experience. A partnership is also inexpensive to set up and costs less to run than a company. The partnership can also be easily dissolved.

The most significant disadvantage of setting up a general partnership is the unlimited liability of the partners for all debts and obligations of the partnership. This means that Ben, Will and Diane will be personally liable for the debts of the business if it fails. This is a very big disadvantage for Ben because not only does he want to invest a large sum of money in the business, but he will have substantial personal assets too. If the business fails then Ben will suffer most. The creditors can target Ben's personal assets because each partner will be jointly and severally liable for the debts of the partnership. This means that Ben could end up paying all the debts of the partnership if Will and Diane have no personal money to contribute. The partners also have mutual liability for their business actions and decisions. Therefore Will can incur liabilities within the ordinary course of business that can bind Ben and Diane. It may also be difficult to raise finance from outsiders. The death or bankruptcy of a partner can end the partnership. This may be of concern for Ben and Diane if they are worried that Will could be made bankrupt from his own personal debt.

If Ben, Will and Diane were to set up a general partnership whilst it *can* be implied by conduct, or come into being through an oral agreement, most partnerships are established by a written document known as a 'deed'. This will set out the terms of the partnership. As a general rule, the partners can agree whatever terms they wish as between themselves in respect of their rights and duties. In regard to the general partnership, if any terms are missing, or there is no written agreement, there are rules in the Partnership Act 1890 which apply by default (eg s.24 presumption that profits will be divided equally between partners).

So, a written partnership can be advantageous in providing clear, easily ascertained terms that will govern the relationship between the parties. It can also be advantageous if the parties want to change any of the terms that the Partnership Act 1890 implies in the absence of such an agreement. That may be important to Ben (and Diane), who may for example wish to limit Will's ability to make financial decisions. They can also avoid the dissolution of the partnership should Will become bankrupt. Ben might also include provisions for him to receive a greater share of the profit if he invests the most money (for example the share of profit could be equal to the percentage of investment). The main disadvantage in having an express partnership agreement is simply the cost of paying a lawyer to prepare such an agreement.

Chapter 8: Employers' duties

Terms

The terms to be included will be found in a number of sources.

Express terms need not be set out in writing but before, or on the day employment commences, employers must give employees certain written particulars of their employment covering such things as salary, hours of work, sick pay, holidays, notice, disciplinary procedures and so on: s 1 Employment Rights Act 1996. This will not be necessary if, as is usual, the written particulars refer the employee to some other written notice of the terms, usually included in an employee handbook, wall notices and other documents.

An employee is also entitled periodically to receive a **pay statement** itemising gross pay and deductions.

Some terms are inserted **by operation of law**. Case law has led to certain terms being implied into contracts such as the employee's duty to account for all money and property received during employment (*Boston Deep Sea Fishing & Ice Co v Ansell 1888*) and the employer's duty to provide work to a person specifically employed to do that work: *Collier v Sunday Referee Publishing Co 1940*.

A more important source is the extensive **legislation** on employment which imposes a number of requirements on the parties as to the terms of employment. An employee has rights to engage in union duties and activities and is protected from discrimination (for example on the grounds of race or sex). The 1996 Act gives important rights as to dismissal and redundancy and to minimum periods of notice. Statute also allows time off from main duties to find work if an employee is about to be made redundant.

Duties

The **implied duties** owed by an employer to their employee will be governed both by common law and statute, subject to any express agreement between the parties to the contrary, assuming that such agreement is not contrary either to law or public policy.

Safety

Common law implies several terms into the contract of employment, all of which are fundamental to the relationship. First, the employer has a duty to take reasonable care for the **safety** of the worker.

Thus, they must provide competent staff, safe premises and equipment and a safe system of work. This term is also governed by statute and the employer must comply with those regulations too.

Remuneration

In the unlikely circumstances of there being no agreement as to remuneration, the rate of **remuneration must be reasonable**. However, statute largely governs the method and rate of payment.

Work

In certain circumstances, the common law will imply a duty to **provide work**. Employees protected include those paid on a piecework or commission basis and those whose earning power and reputation is founded on active occupation; such workers would include actors and journalists: *Collier v Sunday Referee Publishing Co Ltd 1940*.

Reimbursement

If an employee properly incurs **expenses** in the performance of their duties, the employer has a common law duty to **reimburse** them. The employee must also be indemnified against liability for any unlawful act, provided that they have no knowledge that the act is unlawful.

There are many terms implied by **statute** into the employer/employee relationship. It would be impractical to attempt to deal with more than a selection of these terms.

Discrimination

The **Equality Act 2010** provides a range of **anti-discriminatory provisions**. These generally prevent an employer from discriminating, harassing or victimising an individual on the basis of 'protected characteristics', for example their age, sex, disability or race.

Time-off

The employer must in certain circumstances allow their employee **time off work**. This would include time to attend for ante-natal and other maternity care and to perform duties for local government or as a Magistrate. In some cases the employee will be paid for the time spent away from work.

Termination

Finally, there are statutory provisions regulating the **termination of employment**; that is, redundancy and unfair dismissal. These provisions are too complex to be discussed in the context of this question, but, basically, they protect the worker in circumstances where the employment is terminated through no fault of their own.

Chapter 9: Unfair dismissal

(a) The right not to be unfairly dismissed is provided to employees with more than two years of continuous employment. If this right has been infringed, Derek can seek a remedy from an Employment Tribunal. As Derek is 34 years old, the limitations imposed by s 109 ERA 1996 do not apply, and as he has been working for the company for four years, he will satisfy the continuous employment requirement imposed by s 94(1) ERA.

Derek must establish that he was an employee of Multi Media Ltd (as opposed to merely a worker or independent contractor, both classes which do not enjoy legal protection from dismissal). Under the economic reality test set out in *Ready Mixed Concrete* 1968, Derek will be classed as an employee if he provides work and skills in return for a wage and is under the control of the company paying for the work. Other factors such as provision of equipment and payment of tax are also important. On these facts, there is no evidence to suggest that Derek is in business on his own account (he has a position within the company and has been there for four years) and, depending on the terms on which he is engaged, he would appear to be an employee.

Derek must also establish that he was dismissed, and in this case the facts disclose a termination by Multi Media Ltd (the phone call from Derek's manager).

(b) Once a dismissal has been established, the burden of proof shifts to the employer to establish that the employee was dismissed for one of the 'fair reasons' set out in s 98 ERA. Multi Media Ltd must bring evidence either that Derek is unqualified or incapable of performing his role, or that he committed an act of misconduct, or he was made redundant or that his employment contravened statute (the four detailed 'fair' reasons for dismissal). There is also a catch-all provision; the s 98 requirement is satisfied where an employer can show some substantial reason for dismissing Derek.

In Derek's case, his actions appear to fit most clearly within the category of misconduct. An employee can be fairly dismissed where their conduct (either inside or outside work) is sufficiently bad. The fact that Derek was entertaining clients might be sufficient to bring these events inside the work context. Even if not, conduct outside of the employment context can still form the basis of a summary dismissal where it is sufficiently serious in nature to affect the employer's business (*Gardiner v Newport County Council Borough* 1974).

Multi Media Ltd would need to satisfy the tribunal not only that Derek was dismissed for one of the above reasons but also that it acted reasonably. In other words, it is not enough that Derek is dismissed for a potentially valid reason, under s 98(4) ERA Multi Media Ltd must show that dismissing the employee was a reasonable response.

(c) Employment law requires Multi Media Ltd to maintain fair dismissal procedures. Under s 98A(1) ERA 1996, a proper procedure involving a written statement of why the employer is acting to dismiss the employee, a meeting to discuss the matter and an appeal procedure is ordinarily required before the employee is dismissed. However, in Derek's case, his gross misconduct allows Multi Media Ltd to employ a modified procedure, which permits the summary dismissal of an employee to be followed up with a written statement of reasons. There is no need for a meeting to discuss the dismissal.

In the absence of these procedures, a dismissal will be automatically unfair. There is no evidence that Multi Media Ltd have made any effort to follow either process in Derek's case. The phone call that Derek receives is insufficient to meet even the modified requirements (although it would have been if followed up in writing).

Chapter 10: Partnerships and companies

(a) John and Sarah currently have a partnership. The fact that they have not drawn up a formal partnership agreement has not prevented a partnership arising because the only requirement for a partnership to exist is that contained in s1 of the Partnership Act 1890: persons carrying on a business in common with a view to profit. Clearly, John and Sarah's business satisfies this definition of a partnership.

There are advantages to a partnership. As already noted, such a firm requires no formalities to set up. In addition, unlike a company, there are no requirements imposed to report matters (as there are in the Companies Act) so that their accounts would remain private. However, a partnership is probably not the most appropriate form for John, Joe and Sarah's new business because of Joe's stipulation that he wishes to have no part in its management. Under s24 Partnership Act, the norm is established that in a partnership every partner should take part in the management of the business.

This requirement could be avoided by drawing up a partnership agreement excluding Joe from the task of management. However, Joe may not be content with the limitations which the Act imposes upon 'sleeping partners', notably that John and Sarah will bind Joe by their decisions (see s5 Partnership Act) and, in particular, the fact that if the new business suffers losses or founders completely, he will be jointly and severally liable for its debts (see s24(1) Partnership Act).

(b) The key advantage of a company over a partnership is that a company, but not a partnership, has an existence separate from its members. This means that the debts of a company are not the debts of its members. Joe, in particular, should welcome the fact that his exposure to loss would be limited to the value of his shares in the company rather than, in the case of a partnership, an unlimited liability extending over his other assets.

Setting up a private company would permit the three parties to adopt roles appropriate to their factual circumstances. Thus, as John and Sarah wish to continue the day-to-day management of the company, the role of managing directors would suit such an intention. They would be salaried in return for such services to the company. All three, in addition, would draw a dividend on their shares so that Joe (along with John and Sarah) could benefit from any profit over and above the operating costs (including John and Sarah's salary) of the company. Since their initial contributions are £100,000 each (due to the £200,000 value of the existing partnership being held equally between John and Sarah) they should share equally in the profit.

Chapter 11: Registering a company

A company is formed and registered under the Companies Act 2006 when it is issued with a certificate of incorporation by the Registrar, after submission to the Registrar of a number of documents and a fee.

Memorandum of Association

This is a simple document signed by the subscribers. The memorandum states that the subscribers wish to form a company and they agree to become members of it. Before the Companies Act 2006, the memorandum was an extremely important document containing information concerning the relationship between the company and the outside world – for example its aims and purpose (its objects). The position changed with the Companies Act 2006 and most of the information contained in the old memorandum is now found in the articles of association. The essence of the memorandum has been retained, although it is now a very simple historical document which states that the subscribers (the initial shareholders):

- Wish to form a company under the Companies Act 2006; and
- Agree to become members of the company and take at least one share each if the company is to have share capital.

Articles of Association

The articles contain detailed rules and regulations setting out how the company is to be managed and administered. The Companies Act states that the registered articles should be contained in a single document which is divided into consecutively numbered paragraphs. Articles should contains rules on a number of areas including:

- Appointment and dismissal of directors;
- Powers, responsibilities and liabilities of directors;
- Board meetings;
- General meetings;
- Members' rights;
- Dividends;
- Decision making by directors and shareholders;
- Issue and transfer of shares;
- Documents and records;
- Company secretary.

Rather than a company having to draft their own articles and to allow companies to be set up quickly and easily, the Companies Act 2006 allows the provision of Model (or standard) articles that apply to companies by default unless excluded or amended.

Statement of proposed officers

This statement gives the particulars of the proposed directors and company secretary (if applicable). The persons named as directors must consent to act in this capacity. When the company is incorporated they are deemed to be appointed.

Statement of compliance

This is a statement that the requirements of the Companies Act 2006 in respect of registration have been complied with.

Statement of capital and initial shareholdings

A statement of capital and initial shareholdings must be delivered by all companies with share capital.

Form IN01

This document is submitted with those listed above and is the application for registration. It contains:

- The company's proposed name;
- The location of its registered office;
- The liability of its members;
- Whether the company is private or public;
- The intended address of the registered office.

Chapter 12: Allotment and types of shares

(a) A company is both an association of members and a person separate from its members. This means that a company is treated in law as having the capacity to enter into legal relationships, has perpetual succession and survives the death of its members. The leading case on this is *Salomon v A. Salomon & Co Ltd* [1897] AC 22 which shows that the concept of separate legal personality gives rise to limited liability. A company acquires separate legal personality on incorporation by registering and complying with the requirements of the Companies Act 2006. Once registered a company is defined as a 'body corporate' s 16(2). For Tony this means that as a shareholder of Keysure he would only be liable for the amount unpaid (if any) on any shares he purchases. He would not be liable for the debts of the company if it should subsequently go into any form of insolvency.

There have been a number of cases where the separate legal identity of the company has been ignored which could mean that the benefit of limited liability for Tony would be lost. This is referred to as lifting or piercing the veil of incorporation. For example, in *Gilford Motor Co Ltd v Horne* [1933] Ch 935, Horne attempted to evade a covenant not to compete with the claimant by getting his wife to set up a company which carried on business in competition with the claimant. It was held that both the company and Horne were restrained from enticing away the claimant's customers.

There are also a number of statutory provisions which allow the corporate veil to be pierced. The Insolvency Act 1986 imposes personal liability on directors who are found guilty of wrongful trading (s 214) or fraudulent trading (s 213). Directors in these circumstances will be ordered to contribute to the assets of the company.

(b) S 550 Companies Act 2006 applies as Keysure is a private limited company with only one class of shares. This means that the directors have the authority to allot shares to Tony without seeking authorisation from the company's shareholders.

However, s 561 pre-emption rights will apply as the shares are being allotted for cash consideration. The impact of this provision is that when the directors issue the new shares they must first be offered to existing shareholders pro rata to their existing shareholding. This would mean that the shares Keysure is planning to issue must first be offered to the existing shareholders. This does not appear to be what the shareholders want, they want Tony to become a member of the company.

Pre-emption rights can be excluded in a company's articles (s 567), however this is not the case here as Keysure has Model Articles. Pre-emption rights can also be disapplied by special resolution (s 570). A special resolution could be passed by a 75% majority of shareholders at a general meeting or by way of written resolution.

A return of allotment of shares must be sent within one month to the Registrar of Companies on Form SH01 along with any special resolution disapplying the statutory pre-emption rights.

(c) Ordinary shares are the most common type of share in a company. They give their holders a proportionate share in any dividends and a right to the remaining divisible profits (and in liquidation, the assets) after prior interests eg creditors and prior charged capital, have been satisfied. They also give their holders the right to vote at company meetings. Preference shares is a term often used to embrace shares with a number of different rights (different to ordinary shares). The common characteristic of preference shares is that they will rank ahead of ordinary shares as to dividend payments but often do not give their holders the right to vote.

Chapter 13: Charges and guarantees

(a) As Ecowood is a limited company, the liability of the directors in relation to the loan from City Bank is, in theory, limited. However, if the directors give personal guarantees in respect of the loan, they are required to pay if the company defaults on the loan. This means that the directors' personal assets (houses, cars, savings etc) would be at risk.

If the guarantee is given by both directors for the full amount on a joint and several basis City Bank will be able to choose which of the directors to go against to recover the amount in default under the loan. Given the assets of the two directors are quite different, it seems likely that City Bank would pursue Michael, as he is 'asset rich'. Michael would however be able to claim against his brother to recover his 'share' of the amount he is required to pay to the bank. The guarantee could however be structured such that each of the directors are liable for a defined proportion of the loan eg £40,000 each.

(b) If Ecowood grants a charge over the company's assets in favour of City Bank it gives City Bank a prior claim over other creditors to repayment of its £80,000 loan out of the company's assets.

A fixed charge attaches to specific assets as soon as the charge is created. The fixed charge is likely to attach to assets which Ecowood will retain for a long period; for example, it may attach to Ecowood's premises. If Ecowood disposes of the charged assets, it will repay the loan out of the proceeds of sale so that the charge is discharged.

A floating charge is a charge on a class of assets which, in the ordinary course of business, is changing from time to time. The floating charge may attach to Ecowood's stock as the exact stock and stock levels will fluctuate over the period of the loan. Until crystallisation of a floating charge occurs, Ecowood can carry on business and deal with the assets which are charged. When it crystallises, it is converted into a fixed charge on the assets owned by the company at the time of crystallisation.

To be valid and enforceable, a charge must be registered within 21 days of creation by the Registrar of Companies. Ecowood would be responsible for registering the charge but City Bank may also register it, as it is interested in the charge. The Registrar should be sent a copy of the instrument by which the charge is created and a statement of particulars. The Registrar issues a certificate which is evidence that the charge has been registered.

(c) The company will convene a board meeting and record the transaction in board minutes, recording that the company is authorised to take the loan and the reasons for it. The company will draw up a loan agreement setting out the dates and amounts of the loan, the proposed repayments, rate of interest etc. As this is a loan from a director, there is a need to consider an s 177 Companies Act 2006 declaration of interest. There is perhaps no need to expressly declare interest as the board should already be aware of the interest.

Chapter 14: Maintenance of share capital

Capital maintenance is a fundamental principle of company law. What this means is that capital contributed to a limited liability company must not be returned to shareholders. Limited liability companies should not be allowed to make payments out of capital to the detriment of company creditors. The Companies Act contains many rules which dictate how a company is to manage and maintain its capital to balance members' enjoyment of limited liability and creditors' requirements that the company shall remain able to pay its debts.

The above principle requires that shares must be paid for, or agreed to be paid for, in full. S 580 prohibits the issue of shares at a discount to their nominal value and makes the allottee liable for the difference between the issue price and the nominal value (s 580(2)).

As far as dividends are concerned, the capital maintenance principle requires that a company may only pay dividends to its shareholders out of distributable profits (s 830(1)). Capital cannot be used to fund dividend payments.

Companies are prohibited from buying their own shares, as this would effectively be a return of capital to the selling shareholder. However, under s 690, buy-back is permitted in certain circumstances. The relevant shares must be fully paid and, in the case of an off-market purchase, shareholders' approval by ordinary resolution is required prior to the transaction (s 694). The general rule is that the purchase price must be paid out of distributable profits, however private companies may purchase shares out of capital provided special resolution approval has been given (s 709 and s 713). There must be nothing in the company's articles prohibiting the use of capital in this way and the directors must make a statement of solvency, supported by an auditor's report. S 710 requires that capital can only be used to buy back shares to the extent that distributable profits and the proceeds of any fresh issue of shares made to fund the purchase have been used but fall short. Under s 734, the company's accounts are required to reflect a buyback of shares using capital.

The Companies Act 2006 has removed the prohibition against a company giving financial assistance for the purchase of its own shares in the case of a private company. A public company is prohibited from giving financial assistance for the purchase of its own shares, which includes using its assets as security for a loan used to buy its shares s 678(1) and s 677(1)(b). Financial assistance is permitted where the assistance is given in good faith in the interests of the company, and the principal purpose of the assistance is not the acquisition of shares or, if the assistance is for that purpose, it forms an incidental part of some larger purpose of the company, s 678(2).

In some circumstances, a company may wish to reduce its share capital, for example to write off losses or to return excess capital to shareholders. Such reductions of capital can only be effected if authorised by a special resolution and supported by a solvency statement (private limited company) or authorised by the court (public limited company). The option of using a statement of solvency is not available to a public company.

Chapter 15: Resolutions

Members of a private company can pass ordinary resolutions and special resolutions.

Ordinary resolutions are passed by a simple majority (more than 50%) of the votes cast by those entitled to vote. An ordinary resolution is the decision making tool for most business within a company (s282 CA 06). Examples of where an ordinary resolution would be required include a vote to:

- Remove a company director (s168 CA 06)
- Approve a directors' long term service contract (s188 CA 06)
- Approve the sale to or purchase from a director of a substantial asset (s190 CA 06) etc.

14 days' notice is required.

Special resolutions are passed by at least 75% of the votes cast by those entitled to vote. A special resolution is required for major changes in a company (s283 CA 06). Examples of where a special resolution would be required include a vote to:

- Change a company's name (s77 CA 06)
- Restrict the company's objects or alter the company's articles (s21 CA 06)
- Disapply pre-emption rights (s569 CA 06)
- Reduce the company's share capital (s641 CA 06)
- Purchase of the company's own shares from capital (s716 CA 06) etc.

14 days' notice is required.

CA 06 indicates where a special resolution is required. If CA 06 does not specify the type of resolution needed, stating only that "a resolution of the company is required", then no more than an ordinary resolution is legally needed. However, unless CA 06 prevents it from doing so, a company would be free to include provision in its articles insisting on a special resolution, if it prefers a greater number of members to be in favour before that particular matter is passed.

Apart from the size of the majority, the main differences between the types of resolution are:

- The text of a special resolution must be set out in full in the notice convening the meeting, and it must be described as a special resolution. This is not necessary for an ordinary resolution if it is routine business.
- A signed copy of every special resolution must be delivered to the Registrar for filing. Although some ordinary resolutions, particularly those relating to share capital have to be delivered for filing, many do not.

Both ordinary and special resolutions can be passed:

- On a show of hands at a general meeting – members representing the requisite majority of members who are entitled to vote, do so in person or by proxy (s282(3), 283(4) CA 06)
- On a poll at a general meeting – members representing the requisite majority of the total voting rights of members who are entitled to vote, do so in person or by proxy (s282(4), 283(5) CA 06)
- By way of written resolution (without the need for a physical meeting) – members representing the requisite majority of the total voting rights of all eligible members (s282(2), 283(2) CA 06).

Written resolutions may be proposed by directors (s291 CA 06) or by members holding 5% of the voting rights (s292 CA 06). They are subject to strict rules to ensure that all members are notified of the business to be transacted and how and when they may vote. The written resolution must be sent to all shareholders together with a statement informing them how to signify acceptance and the date (known as the "lapse date") by which the resolution will fail if it is not approved by the requisite majority. In the absence of anything to the contrary in a company's articles (there is nothing in the Model Articles) the lapse date will be 28 days from the circulation date (s297 CA 06). The directors should also ensure that, where necessary, required documentation (eg copies of service agreements for s188 CA 06) accompany the written resolutions and are made available at the company's registered office. Shareholders do not all have to sign the same resolution and any number of counterparts can be issued.

Chapter 16: Director dealings

Under s177 CA 06, directors are required to disclose to the other directors the nature and extent of any interest, direct or indirect, that they have in relation to a proposed transaction or arrangement with the company. Even if the director is not a party to the transaction, the duty may apply if they are aware, or ought reasonably to be aware, of the interest. For example, the interest of another person in a contract with the company may require disclosure under this duty if that other person's interest is a direct or indirect interest on the part of the director.

Directors are required to disclose such an interest before the company enters into the transaction. Disclosure can be made by written notice, general notice or verbally at a board meeting. Disclosure to members is not sufficient, it must be to other directors as well and the declaration must set out the nature and extent of their interest. If the declaration becomes void or inaccurate, a further declaration should be made.

Under s177(6) CA 06, no declaration of interest is required if the director's interest cannot reasonably be regarded as likely to give rise to a conflict of interest, or to the extent that the other directors either already are, or ought reasonably to be aware of it.

Under Model Article 14, if a director is interested in a transaction they may not count as participating in the decision-making process of the board for quorum or voting purposes. This provision may be excluded.

Long term service contracts

The terms of a service contract will normally be for the director and the company, acting through the board, to decide (Model Article 19). However, in certain circumstances, s188 CA 06 must first be complied with.

This provides that where the guaranteed term of a director's employment is, or may be, longer than two years, the company may not agree to such a provision unless it has been approved by an ordinary resolution of the members. This is so that a service contract provision which could result in an ex-director receiving a very substantial payment if they are dismissed, can be first scrutinised by the company's members.

Furthermore, the resolution itself must not be passed unless a memorandum setting out the proposed contract has been on display at the company's registered office for at least 15 days prior to the members' meeting or is attached to a written resolution sent to the eligible members.

Substantial property transactions

The authorisation of most contracts merely requires director consent. However, under s190 CA 06, when a director or a person connected with a director is either selling an asset to or acquiring an asset from the company, consideration needs to be given as to whether that asset is deemed to be "a substantial non-cash asset". Where it is, the contract will need to be approved by the members by ordinary resolution before the directors can successfully conclude matters. Approval from the members can either be sought before the contract is entered into or the contract can be made conditional upon such consent.

The rules to determine what is a substantial non-cash asset are set out in s191 CA 06:

- An asset worth less than £5,000 is never substantial
- An asset worth in excess of £100,000 is always substantial
- An asset worth between £5,000 and £100,000 will be substantial if it exceeds 10% of the company's asset value.

Loans

Usually, whether a company is to lend money or not will be a decision for its directors under their delegated powers (Model Article 3). However, where the proposed loan is to a director of the company, s197 CA 06 makes such lending subject to the prior consent of the company's members by ordinary resolution unless the loan is for:

- Expenditure on company business (s204 CA 06)
- The cost of the directors defending themselves against legal proceedings in connection with the company (s205 CA 06)
- The cost of the directors defending themselves against investigation by any regulatory authority regarding matters relating to the company (s206 CA 06)
- £10,000 or less (s207 CA 06).

In this context, a "loan" to a director would also include indirect "lending" by the company such as it agreeing to guarantee the director's own personal borrowing from another lender eg a bank.

Chapter 17: Minority shareholders

Foss v Harbottle (1843) confirmed the rule that the majority shareholders control a company and consequently established a need for minority protection.

Since a company cannot protect itself, a member may bring an action to enforce the company's rights (a derivative action). The Companies Act 2006 introduced a statutory process for deciding whether or not a member has a right to bring a derivative action on behalf of the company (ss 260-264 Companies Act). This does not replace *Foss v Harbottle* but sets out additional rules (but it does abolish a 'fraud' requirement). Permission of the court is required to continue a derivative claim and any remedy awarded goes to the company (as the claim is brought in its name) – thus damages do not flow to the claimants directly. Further information is required from Harry and Julia as to how the company is being run to determine whether they could bring a derivative action but they need to be aware of the significant drawbacks in doing so.

Statutory protection for minority shareholders is also found in s 994 Companies Act 2006. A member may petition the court on the grounds that the affairs of the company are being conducted in a manner unfairly prejudicial to the interests of the members generally, or some part of the members. A petition may be made in respect of past, present or proposed future conduct. Examples include:

- Exclusion from management;
- Improper allotment of shares;
- Failure to call meetings;
- Making inaccurate statements to shareholders;
- Management using assets for personal benefit;
- Failure to pay dividends for prolonged period;
- Payment of excessive directors' bonuses or pension contributions; and
- Continued mismanagement causing financial damage.

Discussions with Harry and Julia are required to establish whether any of these grounds exist. If they make a successful application the court may make a variety of orders including regulating the company and authorising proceedings to be brought on its behalf. More commonly, courts tend to order that the shares of the minority are bought by the majority, or by the company, but this does not appear to be what Harry and Julia want.

In addition, a minority shareholder may use s 122(1)(g) Insolvency Act 1986 to petition that a company be wound up because it is 'just and equitable' to do so. Harry and Julia do not appear to want this outcome.

Chapter 18: Auditors

No person may act as auditor if they become ineligible. They must resign with immediate effect and notify Shopmart Limited of their resignation, giving the reason (s 516 Companies Act 2006).

Membership of a Recognised Supervisory Body is the main prerequisite for eligibility as an auditor. An audit firm may be either a body corporate, a partnership or a sole practitioner. The auditor must hold an 'appropriate qualification'. A person holds an appropriate qualification if they:

- Have satisfied existing criteria for appointment as an auditor
- Hold a recognised qualification obtained in the UK
- Hold an approved overseas qualification.

The replacement auditors cannot take office until the previous auditor has ceased to hold office. Auditors can be appointed in different ways:

- By members – usually in general meeting by ordinary resolution. This may be done to fill a casual vacancy as has occurred with Shopmart Limited.

- By directors – usually in board meeting by majority. This may also be done to fill a casual vacancy. This would be the most straightforward option for Shopmart Ltd.

- By Secretary of State – only necessary if members fail to make an appointment – unlikely on the facts.

The statutory duty of auditors is to report to the members whether the accounts give a true and fair view and have been properly prepared in accordance with the Companies Act. In order to carry out the statutory duties, s 498 Companies Act 2006 requires the auditors to carry out such investigation as necessary to form an opinion as to whether:

- Proper accounting records have been kept and proper returns adequate for the audit have been received from branches.

- The accounts are in agreement with the accounting records.

- The information in the directors' remuneration report is consistent with the accounts.

The auditor's report must be read before any general meeting at which the accounts are considered and must be open to inspection by members. Auditors' remuneration must be disclosed in a note to the accounts. Auditors also have to make disclosure of other services rendered to the company and the remuneration received.

S 499 and 502 Companies Act 2006 set out the principal statutory rights for auditors to enable them to carry out their duties. These are:

- A right of access to records.

- A right to require from officers or employees information and explanations as necessary.

- A right to attend any general meeting and receive all notices and communications relating to such meetings.

- A right to speak at general meetings.

- A right to receive a copy of any written resolution proposed.

Chapter 19: Insider dealing

(a) Under s 57 Criminal Justice Act 1993, Isabel has information as an insider if she has inside information from an inside source and she knows both of these things.

Under s 56 Criminal Justice Act 1993, Isabel has inside information as it:

- Relates particularly to Yensert plc

- Is specific or precise – it relates to the discovery of a new drilling area

- Does not appear to have been made public – only just discovered

- Is price sensitive/likely to have a significant effect on price – it would result in an increase in Yensert's share price

Isabel has this information from an inside source as she obtained it from Henry who is a director and the CEO of Yensert plc (s 57 Criminal Justice Act 1993). As a nanny to the family and business and economics graduate she will have known that she had inside information from an inside source.

Isabel has dealt in price-affected securities, by acquiring Yensert plc's shares, on a regulated market, the London Stock Exchange (s 52 and s 55 Criminal Justice Act 1993).

The defences under s 53 Criminal Justice Act 1993 which could be relevant to this dealing offence are unlikely to apply:

- She did not expect there to be a profit – contrary to facts.
- She had reasonable grounds to believe the information had been disclosed widely – contrary to facts.
- She would have done what she did even if she did not have the information – £3,000 was intended for university fees.

She is likely to be guilty of dealing s 52 Criminal Justice Act 1993. The sanctions include up to seven years in prison and/or an unlimited fine.

(b) Henry is unlikely to be guilty of an offence. Certainly, he has neither 'dealt', nor 'encouraged' under s 52 Criminal Justice Act 1993. He might be liable under s 52 if he had 'disclosed' inside information as a result of his phone call. However, this seems unlikely. Henry would likely be able to argue, successfully, either that he disclosed the information in the proper performance of his office s 52(2)(b) or that he did not expect Isabel to deal in the company's securities s 53(3)(a).

Chapter 20: Administration

Administration is a corporate rescue procedure and an administrator is appointed to try to rescue a company as a going concern. The purpose of administration is to insulate the company from its creditors while it seeks:

- To save itself as a going concern, or failing that;
- To achieve a better result for creditors than an immediate winding up would secure, or failing that;
- To realise property so as to make a distribution to creditors.

Administration orders and liquidations are mutually exclusive. Once an administration order has been passed by the court, it is no longer possible to petition the court for a winding up order against the company. Similarly, once an order for winding up has been made, an administration order cannot be granted (except when appointed by a floating chargeholder).

Administration can be initiated with or without a court order. There are three sets of people who can appoint an administrator without reference to the court:

- Floating chargeholders
- Directors
- The company

In addition, various parties can apply for administration through the court:

- The company
- Directors
- One or more creditors of the company
- The Justice and Chief Executive of the Magistrates' Court following non-payment of a fine imposed on the company

The court will grant the administration order if it is satisfied that the company is, or is likely to be, unable to pay its debts, and the administration order is reasonably likely to achieve the purpose of administration. Individual members cannot apply to the court for an administration order.

The effects of an administrator appointment is that a moratorium over the company's debts commences ie no creditor can enforce their debt during the administration period without the court's permission and all outstanding petitions for winding-up of the company are dismissed.

The administrator is an agent of the company and the creditors as a whole. They owe fiduciary duties to them and has a number of legal duties relating to notification to the company and creditors etc. They also require a statement of affairs to be submitted to them. This sets out the company's property, debts and liabilities, details of creditors and any security they hold. They must consider the statement of affairs and within eight weeks, set out their proposals for achieving the aims of the administration. The proposals must be sent to the Registrar and the creditors and be made available to all members of the company. While preparing the proposals the administrator manages the affairs of the company and managers can only act with the consent of the administrator.

The administrator must either propose a rescue plan or state that the company cannot be rescued. They must call a meeting of creditors within 10 weeks of their appointment to either accept or reject the proposals.

The administration period ends when the administration has been successful or 12 months has elapsed from appointment of the administrator. This time period can be extended by court order or consent from appropriate creditors. Alternatively, the administrator may apply to the court if the purpose of the administration cannot be achieved or the company should not have entered into administration.

Chapter 21: Insolvency

When a company cannot meet its **financial liabilities** it is likely to enter a process of liquidation. This process sees the company's **assets** realised and arrangements made to settle its **liabilities** where possible. Liquidation can be compulsory or voluntary.

Compulsory liquidation

Under this method, the company is **forced into liquidation** by one or more of its creditors.

Under s122 of the **Insolvency Act 1986** creditors may apply to the court for the compulsory liquidation of a customer for seven reasons. The two most important reasons are:

- The company **cannot** pay its debts
- It is **just and equitable** to wind up the company (members may also apply)

Voluntary liquidation

Voluntary liquidation is a **decision taken by the members** to wind up the company. There are two methods that can be used.

- **Members' voluntary winding up** – where the company is solvent but the members decide to close the business down.
- **Creditors' voluntary winding up** – where the company is insolvent and the members decide to wind the company up in conjunction with the creditors.

Differences between compulsory and voluntary liquidation

Timing

A compulsory winding up commences (once granted by the court) on the day the court is presented with the petition. Voluntary liquidation commences on the day the resolution to wind up the company is passed.

Liquidator

The official receiver administers a compulsory winding up, the members and creditors chose and appoint a liquidator under the voluntary process. Unlike the official receiver, this liquidator is not an officer of the court.

Legal action

Unlike compulsory liquidation, under the voluntary process the company receives no automatic stay of legal proceedings. However the liquidator can apply to the court for any order that it would grant under compulsory liquidation.

Employment

Employees are not automatically dismissed under voluntary liquidation. In circumstances of compulsory or 'insolvent' liquidation, employment contracts are effectively repudiated as the company can no longer pay its staff.

Practice question bank

Offer and acceptance

(a) Explain the difference between an offer and an invitation to treat. **(6 marks)**

(b) On Monday, Carl receives a letter from Rick, in which Rick states that he will sell his antique vase to Carl, for £300. Carl immediately writes to Rick. He tells Rick that he is accepting his offer, provided the price is reduced by 10%. Rick reads the letter on Tuesday. However, by then Rick has discovered that the vase is actually worth £500, and he decides he is not going to sell it after all. He does not, however, bother to tell Carl this. By Thursday, Carl has become concerned that he has not heard from Rick, and therefore writes to him saying that he is now prepared to buy the vase for Rick's original price of £300. He adds that if he has not heard from Rick by Saturday lunchtime, he will assume that Rick is happy with this, and he will call at Rick's house on Sunday to collect the vase. Rick receives Carl's letter on Friday, but throws it away without replying to Carl. Carl calls at Rick's house on Sunday to collect the vase, but Rick refuses to sell it to him.

Required

Advise Carl whether Rick must sell him the vase and, if so, at what price. **(14 marks)**

(Total = 20 marks)

Frustration

Explain:

(a) What is meant by frustration of a contract? **(3 marks)**
(b) In what circumstances a contract will and will not be held to be frustrated. **(10 marks)**
(c) What is the effect of a contract being held to be frustrated? **(7 marks)**

(Total = 20 marks)

Misrepresentation

Julian wants to sell a piece of land he inherited from his father. The land is in a very desirable area of London. In order to make it more saleable, and generate more profit, he applies to the local council for planning permission to build a block of 10 flats on the land. The permission is however refused by the council. The council explains that only a small number of two storey houses, which must be in keeping with the other traditional buildings in the area, can be built on the land.

A week after Julian receives this news Xiu, a property developer, approaches him about purchasing the land. She tells him she wants to build a number of high rise blocks of modern flats on the land. Julian encourages Xiu to purchase the land stating that it would be 'perfect for blocks of modern flats'. He does not disclose to Xui his failed attempt at obtaining planning permission. On the strength of Julian's statement Xui purchases the land for £1 million. After Xui submits her own application for planning permission she learns that she cannot build the modern blocks of flats and that Julian had recently submitted similar plans.

Required

Explain misrepresentation to Xui and advise whether there are any remedies available to her.

(20 marks)

Vicarious liability

FoodMart Plc runs a large supermarket. One day, a customer spilled a carton of milk on the floor. It was part of the job description of Brian, an employee of FoodMart, to clean up all spillages. However, Brian was busy serving another customer. He asked his friend, Abraham, to clean up the spillage instead. Abraham was working in the store updating its computer facilities. Abraham had received no training from FoodMart on how to clean up spillages. He used the wrong type of cleaning product, which made the floor very slippery, and he also failed to place a warning sign next to the newly cleaned and wet floor warning of the risk of slipping.

Shortly afterwards, Simran, who was shopping for groceries in the supermarket slipped on the floor and was seriously injured.

Required

Assume that Abraham was negligent. Explain to Simran whether Abraham, or FoodMart, or both, would be liable for the injuries she has suffered. **(20 marks)**

Agency

(a) Explain the principles of agency. **(5 marks)**

(b) Compare and contrast the following concepts:

  (i) Express and implied authority **(6 marks)**
  (ii) Actual and apparent authority **(9 marks)**

(Total = 20 marks)

Employer and employee duties

Explain the common law duties imposed on employers and employees. **(20 marks)**

Termination of employment

Ted has been dismissed by his employer The Kitchen Company Ltd. He explains that he was not given any notice, and believes that he has not done anything wrong. He is not sure if his contract was for a fixed term or not.

Required

Advise Ted:

(a) Of the situations in which his employer could have lawfully terminated his contract. **(16 marks)**

(b) Of the remedies available to Ted if the termination is not in accordance with one of these lawful grounds. **(2 marks)**

(c) In what circumstances Ted might be able to bring a successful claim for unfair dismissal, and what relief could the court give in such a case. **(2 marks)**

(Total = 20 marks)

Social security

(a) With regard to the UK's social security system, explain:

    (i) The purpose of the social security system. **(2 marks)**

    (ii) How the social security system is funded. **(6 marks)**

    (iii) The factors that determine who is eligible for benefits. **(2 marks)**

(b) Briefly explain any FIVE benefits that are available under the UK social security system.

(10 marks)

(Total = 20 marks)

Companies and partnerships

Clare has been running her own business, as a sole proprietor, for ten years in the field of recruitment. Jack has also been running, as a sole proprietor, a similar business to Clare's. Clare and Jack wish to merge their businesses. Clare wishes to know whether she and Jack should form a private limited company or an unlimited partnership to carry forward their joint enterprise.

Required

Explain to Clare the advantages and disadvantages of these two forms of business organisation.

(20 marks)

Separate legal personality

Discuss the concept of separate legal personality in company law and the circumstances in which it can be lost. **(20 marks)**

Company name, pre-incorporation contracts and accounts

Jack Slater and Graham Dickson are builders who would like to form a private company limited by shares called Redbrick Limited (Redbrick). Jack is aware of another company within the local area called Redybrick Limited which operates a similar business to the construction business that will be undertaken by Redbrick Limited.

Required

(a) Discuss any legal risks that Jack and Graham are taking in incorporating a company with the name Redbrick Limited and consider any alternative course of action they could take to avoid these risks whilst still using this name. **(8 marks)**

(b) Just before incorporation, Jack signed a contract 'for and on behalf of Redbrick Limited' to secure storage premises for the new company. Discuss where liability lies in relation to this contract.

(5 marks)

(c) Following incorporation, explain to Jack and Graham what Redbrick's obligations will be in relation to the production and filing of accounts and whether Redbrick will need to appoint an auditor.

(7 marks)

(Total = 20 marks)

PRACTICE QUESTION BANK

Issue and transfer of shares

KidsTime Limited (KidsTime) is a company which operates a chain of children's day nurseries. It has four directors, who all own shares in the company, and a further seven shareholders. KidsTime was incorporated in January 2010 and has Model Articles (unamended).

The directors now want to issue new ordinary shares in the company to themselves, but not to any of the other shareholders in the company. One of the directors, Helena Fiennes, also wants to sell some of her shares to her son David, who is not currently a shareholder in KidsTime.

Required

(a) Discuss the procedure that the directors of KidsTime must follow to issue new ordinary shares to themselves.

Note to candidates: You need not consider any fiduciary duties relevant to this transaction.

(9 marks)

(b) Discuss the procedure that must be followed in order to transfer some of Helena's shares to David.

(6 marks)

(c) How would your answer to (b) differ if KidsTime's articles contained the following clause:

Any shares which a member wishes to transfer must first be offered to the existing members of the company in proportion to their existing shareholding, who have 21 days in which to accept or reject the offer. Any shares not accepted may be freely transferred. **(5 marks)**

(Total = 20 marks)

Takeovers and minority shareholdings

HeavenlyCocoa plc (HeavenlyCocoa) is a large chocolate manufacturing company which wants to acquire Choc Deluxe plc (Choc Deluxe), a company which produces luxury organic chocolates. HeavenlyCocoa has approached the board of directors of Choc Deluxe with an offer of £2.39 per share, which is four pence above the price at which Choc Deluxe shares are trading. Despite the fact that the board of Choc Deluxe did not recommend the offer, HeavenlyCocoa went ahead and made the offer to Choc Deluxe shareholders. By the end of the period in which HeavenlyCocoa's offer could be accepted, 90% of the shareholders of Choc Deluxe had accepted the offer. However, Brian, a close friend of the directors, who owns 10% of Choc Deluxe's shares, did not accept the offer.

Required

(a) Discuss whether the transaction would be classified as a friendly takeover or a hostile takeover and the difference between the two. **(8 marks)**

(b) Will HeavenlyCocoa now be able to compel Brian to sell his shares to HeavenlyCocoa and, if so, on what terms? **(6 marks)**

(c) Will Brian be able to compel HeavenlyCocoa to purchase his shares and, if so, on what terms?

(6 marks)

(Total = 20 marks)

Shareholder v debenture holder rights

Sartorial Limited (Sartorial) manufactures and distributes children's clothing to wholesalers and retailers. The company is very successful but would like to expand into online retail and requires a financial investment to do so. They have approached an investor, Kate Simms, who seems very keen. The directors of Sartorial have suggested that Kate either buys £25,000 worth of shares in the company, or loans the company £25,000 at an interest rate and with security over assets to be agreed.

Required

Discuss how Kate's rights would differ if she became a shareholder of the company compared to if she became a debenture holder. **(20 marks)**

Dividends and financial information

Xavier and Roberto each own 25% of the share capital of Leyland Limited. The remainder of the shares are owned by Paula (40%) and John (10%) who are the only directors of the company. The company has been trading for three years and has made a reasonable profit over the last twelve months.

The relationship between Xavier, Roberto, Paula and John has always been good. However Xavier and Roberto feel that they only have informal discussions with the other two about how the company is doing and feel that John and Paula are of the opinion that they can run the company without ever taking Xavier or Roberto's views or opinions on matters.

Required

(a) Discuss the rules relating to the ability of a private limited company to declare a dividend including the implications for the directors of the company if the rules are breached. **(12 marks)**

(b) Xavier and Roberto have not received any financial information about the company for 24 months. Discuss the obligations of the directors to produce financial information about the company and to provide information to Roberto and Xavier. **(8 marks)**

(Total = 20 marks)

Director appointment

Amy, Charles, Omar and Sarah are the directors of Dream Landscaping Limited (Dream Landscaping). Amy and Charles would like to bring an additional director onto the board of the company, to advise on Dream Landscaping's growth strategy and generally to improve financial performance. Omar and Sarah are opposed to the proposal.

Dream Landscaping has Model Articles (unamended). Omar and Sarah each hold 23% of the company's issued share capital and Amy and Charles hold 12% each. Omar is the chair of the company.

Required

Advise Amy and Charles whether, and if so how, they can appoint a new director against the wishes of Omar and Sarah. **(20 marks)**

Transactions with directors

Thomas Potts has been a shareholder in Similian Limited (Similian), an industrial chain manufacturer, for a number of years. He owns eight per cent of the shares in Similian but is not a director. Thomas has recently discovered that some of the directors of Similian, specifically Charles, Zainab and Stephanie, have engaged in various transactions with Similian. Thomas is very concerned about the activity of these directors and wants to bring their actions to the attention of the other shareholders in Similian. The transactions which are of concern to Thomas are:

(a) Last month, a company set up by Charles, of which he is the sole shareholder and director, was awarded a contract that Charles had previously been attempting to secure for Similian.

(b) In the last year, Zainab has received a number of loans from Similian totalling £30,000.

(c) Six months ago, Stephanie bought industrial vehicles and computer equipment from Similian for £150,000. The property was valued in Similian's company books at £200,000.

Required

Discuss what action, if any, Similian can take in respect of the transactions set out above and whether Thomas can requisition a meeting of Similian's shareholders to discuss these transactions. **(20 marks)**

Debentures, auditors and voting

Forresters Limited is a newly incorporated company. The company has adopted the Model Articles for private companies limited by shares without amendment. The board of directors require some advice as to the administrative requirements in respect of the company.

In addition the company has borrowed £150,000 from London Bank PLC to help with start-up costs and for working capital. The bank requires the loan to be secured by an all monies debenture containing both fixed and floating charges.

Required

(a) Discuss any registration requirements in respect of the debenture. **(5 marks)**

(b) Discuss the procedure for the company to appoint auditors. **(4 marks)**

(c) Discuss the role of auditors in a private company limited by shares. **(5 marks)**

(d) Explain the procedure to demand a poll at a shareholders' meeting, and analyse the effect on voting where a poll is demanded. **(6 marks)**

(Total = 20 marks)

Criminal offences

Fair Law Solicitors is a medium-sized law firm. A year ago, the firm started acting for Kite Properties Ltd (KPL). KPL specialises in purchasing high value properties and selling them on at a profit. The directors of the company advised Fair Law that the company's funding comes from profits and bank loans and KPL's bank statements support this.

Six months ago, the directors told their client partner at Fair Law that they were having some difficulties with the company's bank account. They asked if the company could use Fair Law's client account as a temporary measure. By this stage, KPL was one of Fair Law's most lucrative clients, so the partner agreed. Over the following six months, the partner allowed KPL to make in excess of one hundred high value deposits and withdrawals on the client account. None of the transactions related to any legal matter in which KPL was involved.

The partner is aware that Fair Law's Head of Finance has recently become suspicious that KPL's activities may involve money laundering. Not wanting to jeopardise the relationship with KPL, the partner has alerted KPL and withdrawn access to the client account.

Required

Advise Fair Law as to what, if any, offences may have been committed by KPL, the partner or Fair Law.

(20 marks)

Administration and winding up

Boomcycle Ltd invested heavily in the development and marketing of a new motorbike. Boomcycle took out a large overdraft with one of its creditors, Big Bank plc, in order to fund some of the motorbike's development. The overdraft was secured by a fixed and floating charge over all the assets of Boomcycle.

When the motorbike was released for sale it sold well in the UK. However Boomcycle makes the majority of its profits by exporting its motorbikes to China and the USA. Unfortunately, due to a change in exporting taxes, sales in those countries were very poor, and Boomcycle's profits were drastically reduced.

Boomcycle is now suffering serious cash-flow problems. Big Bank is demanding immediate repayment of its overdraft, which Boomcycle will struggle to do. The directors of Boomcycle are considering whether they should carry on trading and risk being subject to a compulsory winding up of the company, or whether they should immediately put the company into voluntary winding up.

Required

(a) Explain to the directors of Boomcycle the advantages and the disadvantages of putting the company into a *voluntary* winding up immediately, rather than continuing to trade and risk a *compulsory* winding up of the company. **(10 marks)**

(b) Advise whether, as a floating chargeholder, Big Bank can appoint an administrator. **(10 marks)**

(Total = 20 marks)

Compulsory liquidation

Discuss the circumstances in which compulsory liquidation of a company is likely to occur. Consider the procedure to effect the liquidation and the outcomes of such liquidation. **(20 marks)**

Practice answer bank

Offer and acceptance

(a) An offer is a definite promise to be bound on specific terms and can be defined as: an express or implied statement of the terms on which the maker is prepared to be contractually bound if it is accepted unconditionally. An offer may be made to one person, to a class of persons or to the world at large, and only the person, or one of the persons to whom it is made, may accept it. An offer must be distinguished from a statement which merely supplies information, a statement of intention and from an invitation to treat.

An invitation to treat is not an offer, because it is not a promise to be bound by specific terms. This is because an invitation to treat arises when a party initiates negotiations. An invitation to treat can be defined as: an indication that a person is prepared to receive offers with a view to entering into a binding contract, for example, an advertisement of goods for sale or a company prospectus inviting offers for shares. Other examples of invitations to treat are auction sales, exhibitions of goods for sale and invitations for tenders. They must be distinguished from an offer which requires only an acceptance to conclude the contract.

(b) The first essential element in the formation of a binding contract for sale is an agreement. A binding contract is usually evidenced by an offer and an acceptance. In order to determine whether Rick must sell Carl his vase, an offer and an acceptance must therefore be established. As we know, an offer is a definite promise to be bound on specific terms, and must be distinguished from the mere supply of information and from an invitation to treat. Rick's initial letter, stating that he will sell his old antique vase to Carl for £300, is not a mere supply of information nor an invitation to treat. It is an express statement of the terms on which he is prepared to be contractually bound if his offer is accepted. He will sell the vase to Carl for £300.00. Rick has therefore made an offer to Carl.

The next step is therefore to consider whether there has been an acceptance of Rick's offer. If Carl has accepted Rick's offer the contract will come into effect, and they will both be bound by it. As such, Rick will not be able to withdraw from the agreement and will therefore have to sell Carl the vase for £300. In order for an acceptance to be effective, it must be communicated to the offeror. Acceptance may be communicated by express words, by action or inferred from conduct. Carl has certainly communicated to Rick by letter that he would like to buy the vase. However, an acceptance must be an unqualified agreement to all the terms of the offer in order for the acceptance to result in a binding agreement. So has Carl accepted all the terms of Rick's offer?

The answer is no, Carl did not accept the offer on the terms that were presented by Rick. In Carl's initial letter, Carl instead added in a further term, which was the reduction of the price of the vase by 10%. As such there has been no acceptance of Rick's original offer of £300. By introducing new terms, Carl has effectively terminated Rick's offer by presenting a counter offer. He has therefore only given 'a purported acceptance' by requesting a reduction of the price by 10%. A counter offer is seen as a final rejection of the original offer. Carl therefore can no longer accept Rick's original offer, and as such, his second letter in which he changes his mind and agrees to buy the vase at the original price will not count as an acceptance. This is because the original offer no longer exists. This principle was observed in Butler Machine Tool Co v Ex-cell-O Corp (England) 1979, when the Claimant offered to sell tools to the defendant. The Claimant's quotation included details of their standard terms. The defendant 'purported to accept' the offer, but enclosed their own standard terms within their 'acceptance'. The Claimant acknowledged acceptance by returning a tear-off slip from the order form. It was held that the defendant's order was really a counter-offer. The Claimant had however accepted this by returning the tear-off slip, and had therefore agreed to be bound by the original terms. In this scenario, however, Rick has not said or acted in a way which would amount to an acceptance of Carl's counter-offer.

On Thursday Carl's second letter constitutes a new offer by him to purchase the vase for £300. Does Rick accept this? It seems he clearly does not, since he never communicates with Carl.

However, could his silence amount to an acceptance? As we know from *Felthouse v. Bindley 1862*, silence does not amount to an acceptance. There must be some act on the part of the offeree to indicate their acceptance. Carl's letter which he sends to Rick agreeing to the original price will also constitute another new offer. Rick is therefore free to reject both of Carl's offers to buy the vase. Though Rick is also still free to accept on the terms of the original offer (to sell for £300) if he wishes to, as the offeror. This however is unlikely. Rick could also make a new offer to Carl to sell the vase to him for the new price of £500. Rick however does not have to sell Carl the vase for any price.

Frustration

(a) A contract is an agreement between parties which is enforceable at law. Once the components of a contract (offer, acceptance, intention to create legal relations and consideration) are in place the parties are legally bound to carry out their obligations under the contract until the contract is discharged. A contract may be discharged in a number of ways (performance, agreement, breach and frustration).

A contract is said to be frustrated when, although possible to perform the contract at the time it was created, it subsequently becomes impossible through the happening of a supervening event which was not the fault of the parties to the contract.

(b) The doctrine of frustration is applied sparingly by the courts. A contract will **not** be frustrated simply because something occurs after the making of the contract which makes it more difficult or expensive for one of the parties to carry out their obligations. Thus where closure of the Suez canal resulted in much more expensive shipping costs the court held that the contract was not frustrated in *Tsakiroglou v Noblee Thorl*.

Similarly a contact will not be frustrated where one party has warranted to do something which it is later discovered they cannot do.

Where a party, by their own choice, induces impossibility the contract, also, will not be frustrated.

By way of contrast, a contract has been held to be frustrated in a number of categories of circumstances in which, as noted above, the contract became impossible to perform without fault by the parties.

Where the subject matter of the contract is destroyed or seriously damaged, as in *Taylor v Caldwell* in which the rental of a hall became impossible when the hall was destroyed by fire.

A number of reported cases deal with the non-occurrence of an event upon which the contract was based. Two cases, concerning the postponement of the coronation of Edward VII, illustrate the distinction drawn by the courts. In *Krell v Henry* the court held that the occurrence of the coronation was the basis for the contract to rent a room and that the contract was frustrated. In *Herne Bay Steam Boat Co v Hutton* it was held that the contract was not frustrated because part of the basis of the contract (a cruise around the fleet) was capable of performance.

A further circumstance in which a contract has been held to be frustrated include where an extensive delay would render performance impracticable or essentially different to that contemplated by the parties (*Metropolitan Water Board v Dick Kerr & Co Ltd*).

Finally, where a contract is for personal services and unforeseen circumstances such as illness or death prevent the contract being performed the contract will be frustrated.

(c) As noted above, the effect of a contract being held to be frustrated is that the contract is discharged at the time the frustrating event occurs. It is important to note that the contract is not rendered void *ab initio*. At common law this could result in unfairness to one of the parties who had already carried out some of their obligations under the contract. This possibility of an unfair result was addressed by Parliament in the Law Reform (Frustrated Contracts) Act 1943. However, it should be noted that the Act does not apply to certain types of contracts such as shipping and insurance contracts and contracts which contain a provision dealing with the possibility of frustration (see s.2).

Under s.1(2) of the Act any moneys paid out under the contract are recoverable and any sums still to be paid cease to be payable. If a party has incurred expenses under the contract a court may permit that party to retain or recover from the money paid or owing to him under the contract, the cost of those expenses.

Under s.1(3), if one of the parties to the contract has already received a 'valuable benefit' under the contract, then they are required to pay the other party the value of the benefit.

Misrepresentation

A misrepresentation is a statement of fact, given before the contract is made, which is untrue and is made by one party to the other in order to induce the latter to enter into an agreement. A contract entered into following a misrepresentation is voidable by the person to whom the misrepresentation was made.

In order to establish whether there are any remedies available to Xui, it must first be shown that Julian made a misrepresentation. A misrepresentation is (1) a representation of fact which is untrue; (2) made by one party to the other before the contract is made; (3) which is an inducement to the party, who is misled, to enter into the contract. Each of these factors will now be considered.

In order to analyse whether a statement may be a misrepresentation it is first necessary to conclude that the statement was a statement of fact. A statement of opinion or mere sales talk is not a statement of fact (see Bisset v Wilkinson 1927). When Julian makes his statement to Xui that the land would be 'perfect for blocks of modern flats' this is not just a mere opinion or sales talk because he *knows* that planning permission for a similar project (which he submitted) has been rejected by the council (see Smith v Land and House Property Corporation 1884).

The statement was made to Xui prior to her entering into a contract with Julian for the sale of the land and she relied on his statement in deciding whether to purchase the land. Xui was unaware of the truth that she could not build blocks of modern flats on the land (see Horsfall v Thomas 1862).

Julian has therefore made a misrepresentation to Xui. This type of misrepresentation is fraudulent as Julian made the statement with the knowledge that what he was saying was untrue (see Derry v Peek 1889). Under the Misrepresentation Act 1967 the remedies for fraudulent and negligent misrepresentation are the same, which are damages for Xui.

The contract between Julian and Xui will also be voidable (not void). The contract therefore remains valid unless Xui wishes to set it aside. Xui may therefore decide to affirm the contract or to rescind it. If Xui wishes to rescind the contract she must do so reasonably promptly and must communicate her decision to Julian (see Car & Universal Finance Co Ltd v Caldwell 1965). Since the misrepresentation was fraudulent Xui can claim damages in addition to, or instead of, rescinding the contract. If Julian ignores the cancellation of the contract (if Xui rescinds the agreement) and does not return the £1 million she can commence legal action to recover the money.

Vicarious liability

This question involves the law of torts. Torts are wrongful acts against an individual, a company or their property that give rise to a civil liability against the person who committed them. There are a number of torts including negligence, trespass, defamation and nuisance. This question is concerned with the personal injury of Simran, which arose from the negligence of Abraham.

As the tortfeaser, Abraham will be liable for any wrong. However an employer can be liable for the torts committed by his employees in the course of their employment under the principle of vicarious liability. Therefore FoodMart could also be vicariously liable for Abraham's actions. Nevertheless, even if FoodMart is vicariously liable for the injuries caused by Abraham, Abraham will himself also remain liable: the vicarious liability of the employer does not remove the personal liability of the actual tortfeasor (Abraham).

The courts have been known in the past to apply the vicarious liability principle widely. Thus, even where an employee was acting illegally or with gross negligence the employer has been found vicariously liable. It is also worth stressing that the vicarious liability of the employer does not depend on finding that the employer was itself negligent (for example, in failing to supervise appropriately its employee). In order to establish vicarious liability however, there must firstly be an employee/employer relationship and, secondly, a close connection between the employee's tort and his employment. Whether these two conditions are satisfied must be decided on the facts of each individual case (eg *Dubai Aluminium v Salaam; Attorney General v Hartwell*).

So, the first point to establish is whether Abraham was indeed an employee of FoodMart (as opposed, say, to being an independent contractor). The distinction here is between a person under a contract *of* service (employee) and a person under a contract *for* services (independent contractor). In practice this distinction depends on many factors. For instance Abraham could be agency staff (ie he is contracted by an agency firm, and works temporarily for FoodMart). The courts will therefore apply a series of tests. In applying these tests the courts will primarily look at the reality of the situation and also the agreement between the parties. The tests include, the tests of control (where the courts will consider whether the employer has control over the way in which the employee performs his duties), integration into the employer's organisation (here the courts consider whether the employee is so skilled that he cannot be controlled in the performance of his duties, this lack of control indicates that an employee is not integrated into the employer's organisation and therefore not an employee), and economic reality (and here the court considers whether the employee was working on his own account). Some of the other relevant factors which are considered when deciding whether a person is an employee, is whether the employee uses his own equipment, does the employer have the power to select or appoint its employees, payment of a salary would also indicate that Abraham is an employee, and whether Abraham works for a number of different people. We do not know from the information given what the true relationship is between Abraham and FoodMart.

Secondly, even if Abraham is an employee of FoodMart, the tort must have been committed by the employee in the course of his employment and not as a result of doing something which falls outside that employment (when he is 'on a frolic of his own'). The question of which acts fall within the relevant employment is one on which there has been considerable litigation. The courts have drawn a distinction between an employee's act which was a wrongful method of carrying out something he was authorised to do, and one which he was not authorised to perform. Thus, a school warden's abuse of children under his care led to the vicarious liability of the school in *Lister v Hesley Hall*. The employers had entrusted the employee with their position and therefore they should be held responsible for the employees' abuse of it. An example, by contrast, is where a bus conductor drives a bus, the employer will not liable because the conductor is not authorised to drive the bus. Whether Abraham was in fact acting within the course of his employment will be determined by whether or not he was authorised by his employer to clean up spillages or whether it was within his 'field of duties'. If he was not authorised to do so, it is likely that FoodMart will not be vicariously liable. If he was authorised to clean up spillages, for example if it was included in

his job description or he cleaned up spillages in the past for the employer, or it fell within his field of duties then it would fall within an authorised action.

In conclusion, Simran may make a claim against Abraham or against FoodMart if they can be shown to be vicariously liable. In order to do this it must be confirmed whether Abraham is an employee of FoodMart and whether he was authorised to clean up spillages. If FoodMart can be held vicariously liable then it would be more advantageous for Simran to claim against them rather than Abraham, due to the assumption that FoodMart would have 'deeper pockets' or insurance to cover the cost of damages.

Agency

(a) Agency is the name given to a fiduciary relationship by which one person (the agent) is authorised to act as the representative of another (the principal). The principal, expressly or impliedly, consents that the agent should act on their behalf so as to effect their relationship with third parties. The principal will therefore be bound by transactions made, on the principal's behalf, by their agent with third parties, so long as the agent acted within the scope of the authority delegated by the principal to the agent. The scope of an agent's authority is, therefore, important when assessing whether a principal is liable to third parties for the acts of their agent.

(b) (i) **Express and implied authority**

An agent has express authority when the principal expressly appoints him to act for the principal. We can contrast this position with implied authority where there is no express agreement but instead the authority of the agent arises from the circumstances.

No formality is generally required to expressly appoint an agent; the agreement may be oral or in writing. One exception to this rule is that a power of attorney (by which the agent is authorised to execute deeds on behalf of the principal) must be created by deed. Where the agreement is express the scope of the agent's authority will depend upon the construction of the words of the agreement.

As noted above implied authority arises from the particular circumstances of the relevant parties. Thus a managing director of a company has implied authority to act upon the company's behalf. Similarly, the factual circumstance of a man and woman cohabiting has been held to give rise to implied authority for the woman to pledge the man's credit for necessary domestic expenses.

(ii) **Actual and apparent authority**

The contrast here is between the reality of the authority given by principal to agent and the authority which the principal has led third parties to believe the agent to have. Thus an agent's apparent authority may be different in scope to the agent's actual authority; third parties may believe that the agent's authority is greater than their actual authority so giving rise to issues of whether the principal ought to be bound by the agent's acts.

As stated above, where the agreement between principal and agent is express the scope of the agent's actual authority is defined by the terms of the agreement. In addition, the agent will have implied actual authority to do anything which is incidental to acting under the express agreement. Thus, a legal representative with authority to conduct litigation may have implied actual authority to settle the action.

Where there is no express agreement an agent will have implied actual authority to do whatever an agent of the relevant type would usually have authority to do. Thus the managing director of a company has 'usual authority' to act for a company and enter it into legal relations with third parties in respect of commercial matters connected with managing the company.

By contrast, apparent (or ostensible) authority is that authority which it appears to others the agent has, based upon representations made by the principal. Apparent and actual authority are quite independent of each other (per Diplock LJ in *Freeman & Lockyer v Buckhurst Park Properties*). The representation of authority by the principal to the third party may be express but more often it is implied by conduct. Thus, for example, where a third party has been used to dealing with an agent and, unknown to that third party, the agent has ceased to act for the principal the principal may, nevertheless, be bound by acts of the agent (see eg *Summers v Solomon*).

Employer and employee duties

Although a contract of employment need not be in writing, the employer must provide the employee with particulars of the main terms of the contract in writing as required by the Employment Rights Act 1996. Such express terms are agreed upon by the employer and employee on entering into the contract of employment. However, in the absence of stated terms the law will impose duties on both employer and employee. Such implied terms have to be read subject to any express terms to the contrary. Although where the implied term is necessary to give efficacy to the contract, the implied term will take precedence over the express term.

Duties of the employer:

(i) **To provide work**

The employer normally will be expected to provide work for the employee and where the employee is skilled and needs practice to maintain those skills, there may be an obligation to provide a reasonable amount of work. No breach of this implied duty will occur so long as the employee continues to be paid even though there may be no work available.

(ii) **To pay wages**

Normally the rate of pay is expressly stated in the contract of employment. However, in the absence of an express provision, the law will impose the duty to pay a reasonable remuneration for the work done. Following from (i) above, an employer must pay employees their wages even if there is no work available, although an express term to the contrary may be included in the contract of employment. Where workers, in the pursuit of an industrial dispute, offer only part performance by working to rule or adopting a 'go-slow' policy, the employer can refuse to accept such part performance and can refuse to make any payment for work done.

(iii) **To indemnify the employee**

Where the employee in the course of their employment incurs any legal liability or necessary expenses on behalf of the employer, the employee is entitled to be indemnified or reimbursed.

(iv) **Mutual respect**

The employment relationship is assumed to be based on mutuality of respect, trust and confidence and the employer must not act in a way calculated to damage such mutuality. As will be seen this is a reciprocal relationship, but it is clear that employers cannot treat their employees in an abusive manner (Isle of Wight Tourist Board v Coombes (1976)) and must be prepared to address any grievances they might have (WA Goold (Pearmak) Ltd v McConnell & Another (1995)).

(v) **To provide a safe system of work**

At common law the employer is required to take reasonable care for the health and safety of their employees. Failure to comply will render the employer liable for an action in negligence. The duty extends to the provision of competent fellow employees, safe plant and equipment, a safe place of work and a safe system of work. If the employer has taken all reasonable steps to comply with the duty of care then they will not be liable for any injury sustained (Latimer v AEC Ltd (1953)).

There are a number of implied duties imposed on employees, which may all be understood as deriving from their relationship of trust and confidence with their employer and the consequential duty of loyalty and faithful service that derives from that relationship. The specific duties may be cited as:

(i) **to act faithfully**

This is the fundamental duty and it covers such aspects of confidentially, ie not passing on information derived from one's employment to outsiders and not competing with the employer either directly or indirectly.

The courts are reluctant to accept that what workers do in their spare time should be of any concern to their employer. However, sometimes an employer's interests may be harmed by an employee's spare-time work if this involved direct competition with the employer's business (Hivac Ltd v Park Royal Scientific Instruments Ltd (1946)).

An employee may not do anything while still employed, which is in breach of the duty to act faithfully. However, it is perfectly lawful for ex-employees to canvass customers of their former employer after leaving service. Moreover, they are entitled to make use of any knowledge and skills acquired while in the former employer's business, apart from such information which can be classified as a trade secret. In this sense the implied duty of confidentiality for ex-employees is narrower than in the case of an existing employee (Faccenda Chicken Ltd v Fowler (1986)).

(ii) **to obey reasonable orders**

Employees must obey any reasonable and lawful instruction given to them by their employer. Whether any instruction fulfils these criteria is a matter of fact in each instance. The classic case in this area is Pepper v Webb (1969) in which a gardener not only indicated that they were not willing to follow an instruction but actually swore at their employer. In a subsequent action it was held that as the order was both lawful and reasonable the gardener had breached their implied duty.

(iii) **to use skill and care**

Should an employee not exercise the level of skill and care that may reasonably be expected, then they will not only be liable to dismissal, but they may also lose the protection of the employer's duty to indemnify them for losses (see part (a) above), and be made personally liable for claims for compensation. The classic case in this instance is Lister v Romford Ice and Cold Storage Ltd (1957) in which an employee lorry driver, rather than their employer, was held liable to compensate a fellow worker, due to their gross negligence in driving their lorry, which was held to breach their implied duty of skill and care.

(iv) **not to take bribes or make a secret profit**

This duty almost goes without saying, as an example of the general duty of good faith, but it covers the situation where an employee has received money or gifts from customers or clients. In this instance the classic case is Boston Deep Sea Fishing Ice Co v Ansell (1888) in which a managing director of a company was held to have been properly dismissed for having taken money as commission from the company's suppliers for orders they placed with them.

Termination of employment

(a) The relationship between Ted and his employer was a contractual one. The starting point is therefore the common law of contract, however, a great deal of statute law has been enacted which regulates the employment relationship.

There are a number of ways in which Ted's contract of employment may have been lawfully terminated. If Ted's contract of employment was for a fixed term then his contract may have simply expired. This is a general contractual principle because once a contract has been performed it will expire. Provided that the full term of the contract of employment has run, there will be no breach by The Kitchen Company Ltd.

A second general contractual principle is that a contract may be terminated by frustration. This applies to contracts of employment. If the contract had become impossible to perform without fault on either side, then the contract is terminated by operation of law. For example, if an employee were to suffer a long term illness which prevented them from carrying out their duties their employment might be terminated under this heading. Also under the heading of general contractual principles is termination by agreement. If there was genuine agreement between Ted and his employer to terminate the contract of employment then the contract will have come to an end without breach. The courts will, however, be astute to the possibility that the employee did not, freely and with full knowledge, agree. This however does not seem to be the case, as Ted does not understand why he has been dismissed. There may however have been a breach under general contractual principles, if Ted has breached a fundamental term of his contract. Clearly if Ted was in breach of such a term then the termination was indeed lawful.

In addition to the above principles drawn from general contract law there are two methods of termination which are peculiar to employment law. First, a contract of employment can be terminated by either party giving the appropriate notice of termination. The notice period will often be provided for in the contract but, as noted above, minimal notice periods are now provided by statute. As we know however Ted was not given any notice and his employer may therefore be in breach of contract if they have not otherwise legally ended his employment. Finally, the employer may lawfully dismiss an employee, without notice, if the employee has committed a serious breach of contract, such as dishonesty.

If Ted is not in a fixed term contract, has not been in breach of his employment contract or has not fallen under any of the other circumstances in which The Kitchen Company Ltd may legally terminate his contract there are remedies potentially available to Ted. As noted above, employment law has at its base contract law but with considerable statutory intervention. This picture is carried over to the remedies position. Ted may be entitled to a contractual claim (called wrongful dismissal) and/or a claim for unfair dismissal under the Employment Rights Act 1996.

(b) Ted may have a claim for wrongful dismissal if his employer has terminated his contract of employment other than by one of the lawful methods outlined above (eg by giving proper notice). If Ted is not in serious breach of his contract and his employer failed to give the required notice period then he may succeed in a claim for wrongful dismissal. An action for wrongful dismissal is brought in either the High Court or County Court and the remedy is damages. The quantum of such damages is usually the net wages which he would have earned during the normal notice period. Unlike for claims for unfair dismissal there is no upper limit on the level of damages which may be awarded. A wrongful dismissal claim may be brought at any time up to 6 years after the breach (the general contract limitation period applies).

(c) In order to qualify to bring proceedings for unfair dismissal Ted must have had two years' continuous employment with The Kitchen Company prior to the termination of his employment. We do not know how long Ted has been with The Kitchen Company. We do not know whether Ted was recently dismissed. Finding out when he was dismissed will be important because a claim for unfair dismissal needs to be commenced, normally within three months (Employment Rights Act 1996 s.111). It is up to Ted to establish that he was dismissed but then the burden will fall upon The Kitchen Company to establish that Ted was dismissed for one or more of the statutory potential 'fair reasons' under s.98 ERA 1996. A tribunal will then decide whether Ted has been unfairly dismissed and may order that he be reinstated (on the same terms) or re-engaged (under a

new contract of employment). If these remedies are inappropriate the tribunal is required to make a monetary award.

Social security

(a) (i) The overall purpose of the UK's **social security system** is to provide **monetary assistance** to those who do not have an adequate income to live on, for example due to illness, disability or loss of employment. In the UK the state also supports those who work, but who have low levels of income, for example if they work part-time or irregular hours. Support is also given to **parents of children** to help with the costs of raising them. The **social** aspect of the name is because the assistance is provided by society; **security** refers to the sense of protection that the system offers.

(ii) The UK government funds the costs of the social security system from **national insurance contributions** and **general taxation**.

National insurance contributions

When an individual reaches 16 years of age, they are issued with a **national insurance number**. On starting work they must provide this number to their employer who uses it to make payments out of the employee's salary to their **national insurance record.** Employers are also required to make their own contributions for their employees as well. If an individual is self-employed then they supply their national insurance number when they submit their tax return.

Over time, each individual builds up **'contributions'** on their national insurance record and it is these contributions that makes them eligible for some of the benefits under the system. For example, to be entitled to the full state pension, an individual must have 35 full years of national insurance contributions. However, the state recognises that sometimes individuals are not able to make contributions (for example if they are out of work or raising children) and therefore the state will **'credit'** their national insurance record when they claim certain benefits to ensure that they do not lose out.

Employees and **employers** pay what is known as **class 1** national insurance contributions. They can also make **class 3 voluntary contributions** to their national insurance record at any time (for example to fill gaps in their contributions). The **self employed** make **class 4 contributions** once their profit exceeds a certain amount. They can also choose to make **voluntary class 2 contributions** if they wish if their profit is less than this amount. The different classes are just the way the system groups the types of payment made.

General taxation

Certain benefits are also payable regardless of whether or not an individual has made national insurance contributions. They are made because the UK believes that it is important to **support those on low incomes** or have **illnesses and disabilities**, as well as those **raising children** to help support the child. The objective is to ensure that all have a basic level of income to enable them to live and support their families.

These benefits are funded through the UK's **taxation system**. Taxes are payable for many things, such as on an individual's income from work or self-employment, profits made by companies and where profits are made on the sale of assets or on a person's estate when they die. All of these taxes are collected by government who then decides how best to use the money raised, including making benefit payments.

(iii) Eligibility for benefits is either through an individual having made **sufficient national insurance contributions** or if an individual's **personal circumstances** meets certain criteria (such as having a low income, having a disability or being responsible for children).

Individuals can receive more than one benefit depending on their situation. However, the **total amount of benefit** that can be paid is **capped** (currently at £25,320 per year for couples or single parents with children in London and £22,020 for those outside of London. The cap is lower for individuals without children).

(b) The following **benefits** are available under the **UK's social security system**.

> **Note:** You were only required to explain any five of the benefits, although more are listed here for study purposes. You would also be awarded credit if you discussed Universal Credit as a single benefit that replaces six of the other benefits (jobseeker's allowance (income-based), employment and support allowance (income based), income support, working tax credit, child tax credit and housing benefit).

Job seeker's allowance (JSA)

A payment to individuals who are capable of work and are actively seeking it. Individuals can work up to 16 hours per week and still be entitled to claim it.

There are two types of JSA, income-based and contributions-based. Income-based is means tested and takes into account of any income or capital an individual and their partner have. Contribution-based ignores capital and income for 6 months but eligibility depends on national insurance contributions made.

Employment and support allowance (ESA)

This benefit works in a similar way to JSA and also is income and contribution based. However, it is paid to those who have a limited capacity for work due to illness or disability.

Income support (IS)

A means-tested payment made to carers and pregnant or a lone parents of a child under 5 years old.

Housing benefit (HB)

A means-tested payment made to help pay rental costs for those on low incomes.

Child tax credit (CTC)

A payment made to those on low incomes to help support bringing up a child. Eligibility depends on issues such as the number of children, their ages and whether any have a disability.

Working tax credit (WTC)

Personal independence payment (PIP)

A non-means tested benefit paid to those between 16 and 64 who have additional care needs due to illness or disability. It consists of two parts, a daily living component and a mobility component.

Disability living allowance (DLA)

A non-means tested payment made for children under 16 who have additional care needs. It consists of a personal care component and a mobility component.

Attendance allowance (AA)

A non-means tested benefit paid to those over 64 who have a physical or mental disability who require assistance or supervision in regards their personal care.

Carer's allowance (CA)

A payment made to those who provide 35 hours or more care per week to a person who has an illness or disability. To claim this benefit, the person being cared for must be themselves in receipt of AA, PIP or DLA.

Maternity allowance (MA)

A payment to pregnant women who are not entitled to statutory sick pay.

Bereavement allowance (BA)

A payment to an individual whose husband, wife or civil partner has died.

State pension (SP)

A payment to individuals who are over the state pension age. Depending on when the pensioner was born, they will be paid either the basic state pension and/or an additional state pension. A new state pension scheme that replaces these has also been established.

Pension credit (PC)

A means-tested benefit paid to pensioners who are on a low income and tops up their income to a minimum level.

Companies and partnerships

Clare and Jack may choose either a private limited company or a partnership to carry forward their joint business. Both forms of business organisation would be suitable for their new enterprise in general terms. However, the two different methods of organising their new business have different advantages and disadvantages. The fundamental difference between the two lies in the fact that if they chose to create a company they would create a separate legal personality whereas a partnership would create a legal framework between them but no separate legal entity.

Partnership

The first point to note is that partnership would be the default position if Clare and Jack started working together. Partnership is defined in s.1 of the Partnership Act 1890 (PA) as 'the relation which subsists between persons carrying on a business in common with a view to profit'. Therefore a partnership would arise without any formal agreement between Clare and Jack; it would be implied by their conduct. However, if they do decide that a partnership suits them best then it would be advisable to draw up an agreement regulating their respective positions.

Once a partnership is in existence Clare and Jack would be in the position of agents towards each other and their firm. The acts and agreements of each would bind the other and the firm (s.5 PA).

Private Limited Company

There are formalities which must be observed in relation both to the creation of a company and as to its subsequent trading. Companies Act 2006 (CA 2006) governs private limited companies. Modal Articles for Private Companies Limited by Shares Sch.1 provides default articles for companies. S. 4 defines a private company and part 2 of the CA 2006 provides details of company formation. A company is required to have a written constitution and be registered with the Registrar of Companies. A company must submit annual accounts to the Registrar and these accounts are available for public inspection. The key advantage of the company arises from the concept of separate legal personality and the 'corporate veil' which lies between the company and its shareholders (in this case Clare and Jack). This means that the personality liability of shareholders is limited to their initial contributions to the company.

Advantages and disadvantages

(i) There is less formality and expense in creating a partnership than a company;

(ii) Similarly it is easier to dissolve a partnership than a company. Thus, if Clare and Jack found that they did not get on as well as anticipated they could extricate themselves more easily if they had formed a partnership.

(iii) Their affairs would be kept private as a partnership but as a company they would be required to publish annual accounts.

(iv) If the business expands then it might be sensible to form a company at that later stage; they lose no flexibility by opting for a partnership at this stage.

(v) The company option would provide them with protection from debts should the company founder. As partners they would be jointly and severally liable for all the debts of the business.

Conclusion

On balance it seems likely that the best option for Clare and Jack is to form a partnership rather than a company. It is anticipated that the ease of formation and, possibly, dissolution will appeal. Since both businesses have been successful up to now the advantage of limited liability may be less of an attraction than if, for example, they were setting up a potentially more risky, absolutely new, venture. Should their business venture grow and become more complex they should then consider whether incorporation would be appropriate at that stage.

Separate legal personality

The concept of the separate legal personality of a company following its incorporation is illustrated in cases such as *Salomon v A. Salomon & Co Ltd [1897]* AC 22 and gives rise to limited liability. Limited liability means that a shareholder in a company has limited liability for the debts of that company – liability is limited to the amount unpaid, if any, on members' shares. So, for example, if an individual shareholder has paid in full for their shares, and the company subsequently goes into insolvent liquidation, that shareholder has no liability for the company's unpaid debts and cannot be required to contribute to the assets of the company to pay off those debts. The concept of separate legal personality was confirmed in *Lee v Lee's Air Farming Ltd [1961]* AC 12 and more recently in *MacDonald v Costello [2011]* EWCA Civ 930.

There are circumstances in which the separate legal identity of the company can be lost, often referred to as situations where the veil of incorporation is lifted by the courts. This could result in the benefits of limited liability being lost.

Lifting the veil by statute to enforce the law:

There are provisions in the Companies Act 2006 which result in the benefits of limited liability being lost. For example, in circumstances where a public company does business without a trading certificate, the directors are liable to indemnify a third party for any loss or damage suffered as a result (s 767 Companies Act 2006). There are also Insolvency Act 1986 provisions that have the effect of removing limited liability for directors of a company in liquidation, where those directors are found liable for fraudulent or wrongful trading (ss 213–214 Insolvency Act 1986). Liability can result in directors being required to contribute to the assets of the company.

Lifting the veil to prevent evasion of obligations:

The courts may ignore the distinction between a company and its members and managers if the members use that distinction to evade their pre-existing legal obligations. Examples include to prevent the transfer of assets from one company to another in order to avoid a liability, as in *Re H and Others [1996]* 2 All ER

391 CA and to conceal the nationality of a company and avoid taxation, as in *Unit Construction Co Ltd v Bullock [1960]* AC 455.

Lifting the veil in group situations:

The principle of the veil of incorporation extends to the parent company/subsidiary relationship. Although parent companies and their pre-existing subsidiaries are part of a group under company law, they retain their separate legal personalities.

In *Adam v Cape Industries plc [1990]* Ch 433, three reasons were put forward for identifying companies as one and lifting the veil of incorporation:

- The subsidiary is acting as an agent for the parent company;
- The group is to be treated as a single economic entity because of statutory provision;
- The corporate structure is being used as a facade to conceal the truth.

Company name, pre-incorporation contracts and accounts

(a) It may be possible to incorporate Redbrick Limited, provided that there is no company with this name already on the register at Companies House.

However, the risk is that Redybrick might bring a passing off action against Redbrick, alleging that the similarity between the companies' names is causing confusion in the minds of the public, particularly as the two companies operate a similar business in the same geographical area. An injunction could be granted preventing Redbrick from using this name.

Alternatively, a complaint could be made to Companies House, alleging that the names are too similar, which may result in Redbrick being directed to change its name (s 67(1) Companies Act 2006). In addition, Redybrick may appeal to the Company Names Tribunal, alleging that Redbrick's name is too similar to its own and asking that a decision be made by the Company Names Adjudicator to require Redbrick to change its name.

To avoid these risks, Jack and Graham could decide to incorporate the company with a different name. Another option would be to conduct their business using a name different to that of their registered name Redbrick; ie, use a business or trade name. If they decide to do this, they must state the company's registered name on all documents used by the company, such as letters, invoices and receipts and it must be displayed at the company's business premises. Use of a different business name may not be enough to prevent a passing off action or an appeal to the Adjudicator by Redybrick Limited.

(b) The contract will constitute a pre-incorporation contract, as Jack has entered into the contract prior to the date of the certificate of incorporation, thus prior to the company's legal existence.

The company will not be bound by such a contract. Jack will be personally liable under s 51 Companies Act 2006. This is subject to any agreement to the contrary, but the words 'signed for and on behalf of Redbrick Limited' would not amount to such an agreement.

If all parties agree, following incorporation, there could be a novation of the contract with Jack replaced as a party by Redbrick.

(c) For each accounting reference period, the directors of Redbrick must prepare accounts for its members and file them with the Registrar of Companies. They must include a balance sheet and a profit and loss account, to give a true and fair view of the company's assets, liabilities, financial position and profit or loss for the accounting reference period up to the accounting reference date (s 396 Companies Act 2006). The board of directors must approve the annual accounts and they must be signed by a director on behalf of the board.

A company is permitted to file abbreviated accounts with the Registrar of Companies if it is classed as 'small' by satisfying two of the following conditions:

- Annual turnover must be not more than £10.2 million
- The balance sheet total must be not more that £5.1 million
- The average number of employees must be not more than 50

Filing must be within nine months of the end of the accounting period.

A small company will also be exempt from the requirement to appoint an auditor and produce an audit report.

We do not have the requisite information to determine whether Redbrick is a 'small' company for these purposes.

Issue and transfer of shares

(a) S 550 Companies Act 2006 allows directors to allot shares without authority from the company's shareholders (where there is only one class of share in issue and no relevant restriction in the company's articles of association). This section applies to a company incorporated on or after 1 October 2009, which is the case here. The Model Articles for private companies limited by shares do not contain restrictions on a director's authority to allot; therefore, the directors of KidsTime may allot themselves new shares without authority from the members.

However, the statutory rights of pre-emption found in s 561 Companies Act 2006 require these new shares to be offered first to KidsTime's existing shareholders in the same proportion as they currently own shares in the company. The Model Articles do not disapply the statutory rights of pre-emption; therefore, these rights will either have to be waived by the existing members or disapplied in relation to this transaction by the members passing a special resolution in general meeting s 569 Companies Act 2006. The meeting needs to be held on 14 days' notice (s 307 Companies Act 2006).

Form SH01 recording the allotment of the new shares must be sent to the Registrar of Companies, together with a copy of the special resolution disapplying the statutory pre-emption rights. New share certificates must be issued within two months (s 769 Companies Act 2006).

(b) The company currently has Model Articles which do not contain any restrictions on the transfer of shares except for Model Article 26, which gives the directors discretion to refuse to register a transfer of shares.

To begin the transfer process, Helena must execute a stock transfer form in respect of the shares she wishes to sell to David and send this, together with the relevant share certificates, to David, who must pay stamp duty of 0.5% on the stock transfer form. The stamped form can then be sent to the company together with the share certificates. The transfer must be put to the board of KidsTime for its formal approval. The board then has two months to decide whether to approve the transfer. If the board does not take a decision refusing to register the transfer within the two-month period, the board then loses the right to do so. If the transfer is approved, David must be sent a new share certificate within two months of the date upon which the stock transfer form was lodged with the company's 776 Companies Act 2006.

(c) This clause gives existing shareholders rights of pre-emption on the transfer of any shares in the company, similar to the statutory rights of pre-emption found in s 561 Companies Act 1986, which apply on the allotment of shares. The above process will therefore change because Helena must offer her shares to existing members of the company, who have a period of 21 days in which to decide whether to buy their proportion of the offer, before Helena can transfer her shares to David. If Helena attempted to transfer her shares to David without offering those shares first to the other members of the company, then action would be taken against Helena for breaching the articles of association. Such action could be brought either by KidsTime or by other members.

Takeovers and minority shareholdings

(a) A takeover of a company (the target) occurs when control (ownership) of the target is taken over by another company (the offeror or bidder) by buying shares from their current owners. Takeovers are usually classed as either friendly (recommended) or hostile.

Friendly takeover – this is a situation where a target company's management and board of directors agree to an acquisition by another company. In a friendly takeover, a public offer is made by the offeror, and the target board will publicly approve the terms, which may yet be subject to shareholder or regulatory approval. In most cases, if the board approves an offer from an offeror, on the basis that it is in the best interests of shareholders, the shareholders will vote to pass it as well. The key determinant in whether the buyout will occur is if the price per share being offered. The offeror will offer a premium to the current market price, but the size of this premium (given the company's growth prospects) will determine the overall support for the buyout within the target.

Hostile takeover – this is where the target does not approve of the acquisition and fights against it. The offeror approaches the target's board with the terms of an offer but the board rejects it as not being in the best interests of shareholders. Regardless of this, the offeror announces its intention to make an offer, then goes ahead and makes the offer to shareholders.

The facts here indicate that this will be a hostile takeover, perhaps because the four pence premium is not considered to be enough for the board to recommend the offer as in the best interests of shareholders.

(b) A key aspect of the rules on takeovers is that if a large majority of shareholders (90% or more by nominal value and voting rights) like the terms of the offer and agree to sell their shares before the offer lapses, the offeror can then choose to buy-out the minority shareholders (here the remaining shares in Choc Deluxe).

They do this by giving them a "squeeze-out" notice within a maximum of three months after the takeover offer has lapsed (s979 CA 06). Any shares in the target that were already owned by the offeror at the date of the takeover are excluded when calculating the 90% threshold.

The squeeze-out notice requires the minority shareholders to sell their shares to the offeror on the terms of the takeover offer and also requires the offeror to buy them (s981 CA 06). So if HeavenlyCocoa wants to acquire the remaining shares in Choc Deluxe it can.

(c) HeavenlyCocoa may choose to live with there being a minority of shareholders, who did not accept the offer, still holding shares in the company, and therefore choose not issue a squeeze-out notice for compulsory acquisition. Even if HeavenlyCocoa is happy to live with the minority shareholders, once it reaches the 90% threshold it must within one month give the minority shareholders notice of their right to sell under s983 CA 06.

And those minority shareholders (Brian, in our question) may compel HeavenlyCocoa to buy their shares under the "sell-out" provisions of s983 but only if:

- The offeror has acquired 90% of the shares in the target before the period within which the offer can be accepted, and
- The shareholder (Brian) writes to the acquirer requiring their shares to be purchased on the same terms as the original takeover offer or on such other terms as may be agreed (s985 CA 06).

Unlike for squeeze-out notices, any shares in the target already owned by the offeror at the date of the takeover are included when calculating the 90% threshold for sell-out.

Shareholder v debenture holder rights

As a shareholder, Kate would be a member of the company. As a debenture holder she would be a creditor but not a member of the company.

A company's relationship with its shareholders is governed by its articles which operate as a contract between them and between the shareholders and each other and also governed by the Companies Act.

The relationship between a company and its debenture holders is regulated by the terms of the trust deed or other formal document and different provisions of the Companies Act. We have not been given any detailed terms of the debenture other than it is for £25,000 and the interest rate and security over assets are to be agreed.

There are a number of practical differences between a shareholder and a debenture holder:

- Voting – As a member of the company, a shareholder has the right to attend and vote at meetings. A debenture holder has no such automatic right, although they may have votes if the articles and deed allow although this is not very common.

- Income – A shareholder, even if he holds preference shares on which fixed dividends are due on specific days, can only receive dividends out of distributable profits. In addition, they cannot force the company to pay dividends *Bond v Barrow Haematite Steel Co* [1902] 1 Ch 353. By contrast, interest at the agreed rate must be paid on debentures even if that interest has to be paid out of capital.

- Rights on securities – The Companies Act confers pre-emption rights on shareholders, entitling them to first call on any new shares which are to be issued. Debenture holders have no right of objection to further loans and debentures being taken out, unless the trust deed sets out restrictions. However, there is no statutory restriction on debenture holders having debentures redeemed or purchased by the company. By contrast, there are detailed rules regulating redemption or purchase of a company's own shares.

- Rights if aggrieved – Shareholders have the right to complain to the court if the company is breaching the articles or acting in a manner unfairly prejudicial to the shareholders' interests. Shareholders can, by simple majority, remove directors from the board. We do not know how many shares Kate will have and whether other shareholders would vote in the same way as her. Debenture holders may have rights under the trust deed if the company breaches the agreement. These include the right to appoint a receiver or the right to enforce charges and sell the property under the charge to realise their debts. Their consent may also be required before the company deals with certain of its assets when the debenture holders have secured their loan by means of a fixed charge over those assets.

- Rights on liquidation – In liquidation debenture holders must be repaid in full before anything is distributed to shareholders.

Dividends and financial information

(a) A dividend is a payment to the shareholders of a company representing a share of the profit that the company has made and a return on the shareholders' investments in the company.

Shareholders do not have an automatic right to a dividend; there is a process by which it is declared to be lawful.

A dividend may only be paid out of profits which are available for this purpose (defined in s 830 Co Act 2006 – basically with reference to the year-end accounts accumulated realised profits so far as not previously utilised by distribution less accumulated realised losses).

The process that must be followed is that the directors will consider what dividend if any ought to be declared and will make a recommendation of that amount. A general meeting will then be held where the question of declaring a dividend will be considered. To approve the dividend an ordinary resolution is required. The shareholders may in general meeting reject the recommendations of the directors with regard to the dividend or declare a dividend that is smaller than that recommended. They may not declare a dividend in excess of the amount recommended by the directors.

Once declared the dividend will be paid to the members.

Directors may during the course of an accounting period pay interim dividends to members, these do not need to be formally declared by ordinary resolution however the basic rule that they can only be paid out of distributable profits applies.

There are consequences for both shareholders and directors of unlawful dividends (ie one paid otherwise than out of distributable profits of the company). Directors will normally be personally liable. If directors honestly rely on properly prepared accounts which show a distributable profit, the directors will not be liable if it turns out that the assumptions or estimates used in preparing the accounts although reasonable at the time were in fact unsound.

Directors will be liable if:

- They declare a dividend which they know is paid out of capital;
- Without preparing accounts they declare a dividend which consequently turns out to be paid out of capital; or
- They make some mistake of law or interpretation of the constitution which leads them to recommend or declare an unlawful dividend, the directors may get some relief if they acted honestly and reasonably.

Shareholders will be liable if the member knew or had reasonable grounds to believe the dividend was unlawful.

A member may apply for an injunction to prevent a company paying an unlawful dividend. Members are not entitled to authorise the payment of an unlawful dividend or release the directors from liability for such. If a member knowingly receives an unlawful dividend it may not bring an action against the directors.

(b) The company has a duty to keep adequate accounting records that show the financial position of the company reasonably accurately s 386. The directors must produce a balance sheet that gives a true and fair view of the company's financial state at the end of the financial year and a profit and loss account that gives a true and fair view of the profit (or loss) for the financial year in question.

The directors must also prepare a directors' report reviewing the development of the company over the financial year and stating the amount (if any) of the dividend to be declared.

The Companies Act 2006 requires the accounts to be audited, the auditor must prepare a report to the shareholders confirming that the accounts give a true and fair view of the company's position and performance (to the standards laid out in the Companies Act 2006) and must confirm whether or not the directors' report is consistent with the accounts. Certain companies are exempt from the audit requirements, the conditions to be satisfied are: if in a financial year the company's turnover doesn't exceed £6.5 million and its balance sheet is not more than £3.26 million.

Once the accounts have been 'audited' the directors must approve them and they must be signed on behalf of the board.

Xavier and Roberto are entitled to receive copies of the accounts, the directors' report and the auditors' report (or summaries if Roberto and Xavier have agreed to accept shortened reports). The accounts and directors' and auditors' reports must also be sent to the Registrar of Companies within 9 months after the end of the relevant financial period.

The directors of Leyland Limited may be guilty of a criminal offence if they fail to send information as set out above to Roberto and Xavier.

Director appointment

A new director can be appointed at a general meeting, where the members appoint by ordinary resolution (MA 17(1)(a)), or at a board meeting, where the board can appoint by board resolution (MA 17(1)(b)). There is no maximum number of directors under the Model Articles.

The most straightforward way of making the appointment would be at a board meeting by board resolution. The difficulty in this case is that two of the company's four directors are opposed to the new appointment. Decision making by directors must be by majority in number (MA 7(1)). However as Omar is the chairman and the chairman gets a casting vote (MA 13) it would not be possible to make the appointment by way of board resolution.

If Amy and Charles wish to try to persuade the company's other shareholders (30% of the company's shares are held by non-directors) to agree to the appointment of a new Finance Director they will have to requisition a general meeting following the procedure under s 303 Companies Act 2006.

Amy and Charles each hold 12% of the shares, so separately or together they have sufficient shares to validly requisition a general meeting under s 303 Companies Act 2006 (5% is needed).

Following their requisition, the board is obliged to call a general meeting within 21 days (s 304(1)(a) Companies Act 2006) of receiving the requisition and hold the meeting within 28 days (s 304(1)(b) Companies Act 2006) of the notice calling it. In the notice of the general meeting, the time, date and place of the meeting is stated in addition to the general nature of the business to be dealt with at the meeting (s 311 Companies Act 2006). On this basis, information that would appear in the register of directors if the new director were to be appointed would be circulated to members.

Amy and Charles need sufficient support from the other shareholders to pass the required ordinary resolution. They hold 24% of the shares between them, therefore they need shareholders holding more than 26% to vote with them to pass the resolution.

If the new director is appointed Form 288(a) recording the appointment must be completed and returned to Companies House. The company's register of directors must also be amended.

Transactions with directors

Generally, must consider fiduciary duties. The Companies Act 2006 includes a statutory statement of the duties that a director owes to a company (ss 170-177). Although these duties take effect in place of the rules developed at common law, s 170(4) makes it clear that the statutory duties shall be interpreted in the same way as the corresponding common law rules. The case law that has developed regarding directors' duties is therefore still relevant in interpreting the provisions in the Companies Act 2006.

(a) The fiduciary duties owed by a director to the company involve a director acting in the best interests of the company and not for personal reasons benefiting him or herself. The rule extends to cover a personal profit arising as a result of a corporate opportunity coming to a director by reason of their office. If a director diverts a corporate opportunity to themselves away from the company this is regarded as a breach of fiduciary duty, *Cook v Deeks* [1916] 1 AC 554. This approach is taken even where the company itself would not have been awarded the contract as in *Industrial Developments Consultants Ltd v Cooley* [1972] 1 WLR 443. Charles appears to have actively diverted a corporate opportunity away from Similian to a company in which he is the sole shareholder and director. He may be required to account for profits made as a result. The director's duties under the Companies Act 2006 directly relevant to the above situation are to avoid conflict of interest (s 175) and to declare at board meetings interests in existing and proposed transactions and arrangements with the company (s 177).

(b) The general rule set out in s 197 Companies Act 2006 is that loans to directors of over £10,000 are prohibited, unless approved by an ordinary resolution of the members of the company. A memorandum must be made available to the members of the company setting out the nature of the transaction, the amount of the loan and the purpose for which it is required. This memorandum must be sent with a written resolution if the approval is to be given by written resolution or to be available before and at a general meeting where the resolution is to be proposed. Transactions in contravention of these provisions are voidable at the instance of the company and the director is liable to account for any gain made as a result of the transaction or indemnify the company for any loss. It appears that this will be the case for Zainab in relation to her loans from Similian. Zainab cannot rely on the exception under s 207 as it is possible that the individual loans were less that £10,000 but aggregated they are more than £10,000.

(c) The purchase of industrial vehicles and computer equipment from Similian by Stephanie should have been approved by the shareholders passing an ordinary resolution (simple majority of those present at a general meeting voting in favour), or the transaction should have been made conditional on this approval being obtained. The purchase is viewed as a substantial property transaction, provided the property is of the requisite value, and therefore requires approval under s 190 Companies Act 2006. Failure to obtain such approval makes the transaction voidable at the option of the company. The directors who approved the transaction, would also be liable to indemnify the company for any loss it has suffered and account to the company for any gain made as a result of the transaction (s 195). The requisite value is defined as exceeding £100,000 or 10% of the company's asset value. The property here was sold for £150,000 and would therefore fall within these provisions. Stephanie should also have declared her interest in the transaction as required by s 177.

Thomas has sufficient shares in Similian to requisition a general meeting, s 303. Thomas needs to deposit a signed requisition at Similian's registered office. The directors of Similian must call the meeting within 21 days of receiving the requisition and hold the meeting within 28 days of the notice calling it.

Debentures, auditors and voting

(a) To be valid and enforceable all charges created by companies must be registered at Companies House within 21 days of their creation. The instrument creating the charge together with the requisite particulars of charge (form MG01) and the registration fee must be sent to the Registrar. If a charge is not validly registered it will be void against a liquidator, administrator and any creditor of the company. Every officer of a company in default of the registration requirements would also be liable to a fine (s 860(4)).

(b) Every company must appoint appropriately qualified auditors for each financial year. As Forresters is a newly incorporated company, the directors can appoint the first auditors to hold office until the first general meeting of the company at which their appointment can be considered by the shareholders.

To be appropriately qualified, auditors must be a member of a Recognised Supervisory Body. The following may not act as auditors:

- Any officer or employee of the company
- A partner or employee of such a person
- A partnership in which any of the above is a partner
- Any other person excluded by law

(c) Auditors are under a duty to review the balance sheet and profit and loss account of the company for the relevant financial year and prepare a report for the shareholders stating that the accounts give a true and fair view and have been properly prepared in accordance with the Companies Act (2006). The auditors' report must also consider and state whether or not the directors' report is consistent with the accounts.

In order to be able to prepare their report the auditors must review the accounts and carry out such investigations as are necessary to be able to form the required opinions and make the required statements. Auditors are entitled to have access to the books and accounts of the company at any time, a right to require information from the company's officers, employees and any other relevant persons. Auditors must receive copies of all written resolutions and can attend and speak at all general meetings of the company.

(d) Every holder of a voting share is entitled to attend a general meeting and vote on any resolutions considered. Voting under the Model Articles can take place by way of a show of hands or by demanding a poll. The difference in the outcome can be considerable. On a show of hands each shareholder is entitled to one vote. On a poll each shareholder is entitled to so many votes as the constitution provides (usually one vote per share).

A poll can be demanded at the meeting or in advance of the meeting. It can be demanded after the vote on a show of hands as long as the result has not yet been declared. A poll can be demanded by the chairman of the meeting, two or more shareholders having the right to vote at the meeting or one or more shareholders holding at least one tenth of the total voting rights.

Criminal offences

The offence which must be considered is money laundering. Money laundering is generally defined as the process by which the proceeds of crime, and the true ownership of those proceeds, are changed so that the proceeds appear to come from a legitimate source.

Law and regulations relevant to money laundering are found in the Proceeds of Crime Act 2002 and the Money Laundering Regulations 2007.

There are three acknowledged phases to money laundering:

- Placement – the initial disposal of the proceeds of the illegal activity into an apparently legitimate business activity or property. This would be putting the proceeds of some illegal activity, although it is not certain from the facts that there is such activity, into KPL which appears to be a legitimate property business.

- Layering – this is the transfer of monies from one business to another or one place to another to conceal the original source. This would be the transfer of funds from KPL to Fair Law's client account and the subsequent deposits and withdrawals.

- Integration – once it has been layered, the money appears to be legitimate funds.

There are three categories of criminal offence under the Proceeds of Crime Act:

- Laundering – this is the acquisition, possession or use of the proceeds of crime or assisting another to retain the proceeds of crime by concealing, disguising, converting, transferring or removing the criminal property.

- Failure to report – this is in respect of an individual relevant person failing to disclose knowledge or suspicion of money laundering.

- Tipping off – this is disclosing information to any person which may prejudice an investigation.

More information is needed in relation to the original source of KPL's funds to determine whether the offence of money laundering has been committed by KPL, although the activity does have many of the hallmarks of money laundering. If this is the case, it seems likely that the partner will have committed the offence of failing to report and tipping off.

The penalties are a maximum sentence of 15 years' imprisonment and/or a fine for knowingly assisting in the laundering of criminal funds, for failure to report, five years' imprisonment and/or a fine and for tipping off, two years imprisonment and/or a fine.

The Money Laundering Regulations apply to a wide range of organisations including accountants and auditors and solicitors. As each organisation is different, systems have to be designed appropriate to each organisation to ensure there are:

- Internal reporting procedures
- Due diligence in relation to clients
- Record-keeping
- Employee training.

The facts suggest that Fair Law may have failed to implement these measures.

This is a criminal offence punishable with a maximum sentence of two years' imprisonment and/or a fine, irrespective of whether money laundering has taken place (further investigations are needed to determine whether the initial proceeds are as a result of illegal activity). Civil penalties may also be imposed.

Administration and winding up

(a) We might advise the directors that there are two types of winding up: a voluntary winding up, commenced by a resolution of the company's own shareholders (usually by 'special resolution', passed by 75%), and a compulsory winding up. The latter is usually commenced by a creditor of the company, and so is in a sense 'forced on' the company.

Is there any advantage to the directors in choosing a voluntary winding up? To answer this, we need to differentiate further between the two types of voluntary winding up: a members', and a creditors', voluntary winding up. Both are commenced by a resolution of members. However, in the case of a members' voluntary winding up, the directors make a 'declaration of solvency' – saying the company will be able to pay all its debts within 12 months (s108 Insolvency Act 1986). If the directors do not make such a declaration, then the winding up will be a creditors' voluntary winding up.

Certainly, there are big advantages in having a *members'* voluntary winding up. In such a winding up, the members of the company have most control over the winding up process. They choose the liquidator, and the liquidator acts for their benefit. They control the actions of the liquidator. Creditors have little influence over what assets of the company are sold, at what price, and to whom. However, the directors' must be willing to make the declaration of solvency. And we could advise them that they must have reasonable grounds for making such a declaration, and that they would commit a criminal offence if they made the declaration without reasonable grounds. If the company is wound up and all its debts are not paid, then there's a presumption the director did not have reasonable grounds. Here, we are told the company is already in financial difficulties, and the directors clearly know this. So, there are certainly risks here for the directors in trying to make the declaration and have a members' voluntary winding up.

The directors could still choose to wind up the company voluntary, immediately, but not make the declaration, so the winding up would then be a *creditors'* voluntary winding up. Is there any advantage in that, compared to waiting for a *compulsory* winding up? In fact, the procedures applying to a creditors' voluntary winding up are very similar to a compulsory winding up. Ultimately, the creditors can, if they want, control a creditors' voluntary winding up, just as they can control a compulsory winding up. In both cases, the creditors have the final say over who the liquidator will be. In both cases, a liquidation committee can be appointed to oversee the process of the winding up, and in both cases the creditors have ultimate control over the membership of that committee.

However one important consideration for the directors in deciding whether to choose voluntary liquidation is that under a compulsory winding up employees are immediately dismissed. This would mean that if an order for compulsory liquidation was made, not only would the directors employment with the company immediately end, but so too would the employment of other individuals. If the directors chose a voluntary winding up of the company they, and other employees, would have more notice and therefore more time to find new employment.

The disadvantage of initiating a voluntary winding up immediately is that the company might be able to trade its way out of its present difficulties. If it were able to trade in this way, it might be able to avoid any creditor successfully presenting a petition for the compulsory winding up of the company.

(b) Big Bank as a floating chargeholder may wish to appoint an administrator. Big Bank will have a right to do this without reference to the court, and even if there is no actual or impending insolvency. Big Bank could also appoint an administrator even if Boomcycle is in compulsory liquidation (which may be petitioned by another creditor). In order for Big Bank to do this, the floating charge must entitle them to appoint an administrator (this would be in the terms of the charge). The floating charge must also be over all, or substantially all, of Boomcycle's property. As Big Bank's charge is over all of Boomcycle's assets then they will qualify for the right to appoint an administrator. However, they may only appoint an administrator if they have given Boomcycle two days written notice of the right to appoint an administrator and that their floating charge is enforceable.

After the relevant two day notice period Big Bank will have to file a number of documents with the court. These documents are: a notice of appointment, a statement by the administrator, that they consent to the appointment, and a second statement confirming that in their opinion the purpose of administration can be achieved. A statutory declaration must also be filed which states that the administrator has the qualifications to be appointed. Once these documents have been filed the appointment is valid. The appointer must then notify the administrator and other people prescribed by regulations of the appointment as soon as reasonably practicable. An administrator is appointed primarily to rescue the company as a going concern. They have a fiduciary duty and are an agent of the company and the creditors as a whole. They send notices, publish notices, obtain a list of company creditors, notice to registrar, receive a statement of affairs and consider these and manage the affairs of the company.

Compulsory liquidation

Compulsory liquidation of a company is likely to occur when the company is insolvent and involves applying to the court to wind it up. The most common reasons for compulsory liquidation are:

- The company is unable to pay its debts (s 122(1)(f) Insolvency Act 1986)
- It is just and equitable to wind up the company (s 122(1)(g) Insolvency Act 1986).

A creditor may apply to the court for compulsory winding up of a company on the basis that the company is unable to pay its debts. There are three permitted ways to show that a company is unable to pay its debts (s 123 Insolvency Act 1986):

- A creditor who is owed more than £750 serves the company with a written demand for payment and the company does not pay within 21 days;

- A creditor obtains judgment against the company for a debt and attempts to enforce judgment but no payment is obtained; or
- A creditor satisfies the court that the company is unable to pay its debts by proving either that the company cannot pay its debts as they fall due (commercial insolvency test) or that the company's assets are less than its liabilities (balance sheet test).

A member who is dissatisfied with the directors or controlling shareholders in relation to the management of the company may petition the court for the company to be wound up on the just and equitable ground. For such petition to be successful, the member must not be unreasonably refusing to pursue some other remedy. Examples of circumstances when companies have been wound up on the just and equitable ground include when:

- The only or main object(s) of the company can no longer be achieved;
- The company was formed for an illegal or fraudulent purpose;
- There is complete deadlock in the management of the company's affairs; and
- The understandings between members or directors which were the basis of the company have been unfairly breached by lawful action.

When a petition to bring proceedings for compulsory liquidation is presented to the court, a copy is also delivered to the company in case it wishes to object. It is also advertised so that other creditors may intervene if they wish. The court appoints the Official Receiver who takes control of the company's property and acts as liquidator (s 136 Insolvency Act 1986), with a view to realising value in the company's assets for the benefit of creditors. The Official Receiver may hold a meeting of members and creditors to appoint their own nominee as replacement liquidator. If different persons are nominated, the creditors' nominee takes precedence. The liquidation is deemed to have commenced at the time when the petition was first presented.

Having realised the company's assets, the liquidator distributes them in a prescribed order as follows:

(a) Costs
(b) Preferential debts
(c) Secondary preferential debts
(d) Debts secured by floating charges
(e) Debts owed to unsecured ordinary creditors
(f) Deferred debts
(g) Members

Creditors with fixed and floating charges may appoint a receiver to sell the charged asset. Any surplus is passed on to the liquidator and, in the event of a shortfall, those with the benefit of the charge become unsecured creditors for the balance.

PRACTICE ANSWER BANK

Exam question bank

November 2021

1 Camille

Camille is a small business owner. She approaches React Accountancy to prepare her company's accounts for the end of year.

Required

Advise Camille on each of the following alternative scenarios:

(a) Before instructing the firm, Camille asks for a quote from one of React's accountants. She is told that React can prepare her accounts 'for around £1,000.00.' Advise Camille whether the statement 'around £1,000.00' is an offer to form a contract? **(10 marks)**

(b) React offers to prepare Camille's accounts for £1,200.00. Camille thinks this price is too high and sends an email to React saying she will pay £900.00. React does not respond to her email. Camille approaches another firm of accountants. When this firm offers to complete her accounts for £1,400.00, Camille regrets having sent the email to React.

Can Camille still accept React's original offer to complete her accounts for £1,200.00? **(10 marks)**

(Total 20 marks)

2 Percy Ltd

Percy Ltd makes and sells ceramic pottery. Dhian delivers Percy Ltd's pottery orders that have been sold online. To make the deliveries, Dhian uses his own van, but must wear a uniform supplied by Percy Ltd. He must make the deliveries according to a schedule supplied by Percy Ltd, and following some 'delivery rules' drawn up by Percy Ltd. Dhian makes deliveries for Percy Ltd for three days each week, and on those days he is not allowed to undertake work for anyone else. Dhian is also not permitted to use another driver to make the deliveries for him. Dhian has been delivering Percy Ltd's pottery for five years.

In early February 2021, Dhian is delivering an order of pottery to a customer of Percy Ltd. On his way to the customer, Dhian takes a ten mile deviation to visit his friend. Whilst doing so, he skids on a patch of ice on the road, and crashes into Vicki, a pedestrian. Vicki is badly injured in the accident.

Required

Advise Vicki whether she can bring a claim for vicarious liability against Percy Ltd. **(20 marks)**

3 Mizuho and Jun

Mizuho and Jun are friends and chartered accountants. They currently work at two different accountancy firms as employees. Mizuho and Jun want to work for themselves and set up their own accountancy firm. They both have ten years' experience working as accountants but have little experience in running a business. They each have savings of £15,000 that they want to invest in the business, which they hope to grow over the next few years.

Required

Advise Mizuho and Jun of the different forms of business they can use and which form you think would be the most suitable, and why. **(Total 20 marks)**

4 Sakura

Sakura is a director at Daisy's Café Ltd ('the company'). The company runs a café, which was opened in 2018. The café had been thriving until early 2020 but then, due to the global pandemic, it was required to stop trading on a number of occasions in 2020 and early 2021. The company began to suffer financially and was in danger of becoming insolvent.

In order to try and save the company, Sakura made it take out a large loan from Anybank plc in April 2021. The company created a floating charge in favour of Anybank plc. The loan was used to start up an online delivery service. The company also purchased large amounts of stock from suppliers on credit.

Unfortunately, the company is still struggling financially, as a result of the earlier closures of the café. It has failed to make the latest repayment due under its loan from Anybank, and many of its suppliers are pressing the company for payment. Some are now threatening to start winding up proceedings against the company. Sakura fears the company may be wound up, but her accountants have advised her that it may be possible to avoid this by obtaining an 'administration order' instead.

Required

Advise Sakura:

(a) On the procedure for appointing an administrator for Daisy's Café Ltd, and the consequences of such an appointment; and **(14 marks)**

(b) Whether the directors of Daisy's Café Ltd can be held personally liable in respect of the debts of the company if it is wound up. **(6 marks)**

Make reference to the Insolvency Act 1986 and any other relevant legislation in your answer.

(Total 20 marks)

5 Cheri, Kyle and Lucy

Cheri, Kyle and Lucy are shareholders of an accountancy company, Watts and Lacey Ltd ('the company'). Cheri and Kyle each have 250 shares with one vote per share and are directors of the company. Lucy is not a director but has 500 shares, also with one vote per share. The company was incorporated in April 2011 and has unamended Model Articles.

Recently, Lucy's relationship with Cheri and Kyle has deteriorated. Cheri and Kyle told Lucy, at their last board meeting, that they decided the company will issue 500 new ordinary shares. They told Lucy the reason for this share issue is to fund the development of a new website for the company, which will attract new clients and increase the profits of the business.

Whilst Lucy agrees it would be beneficial to develop a new website, she disagrees with the proposal to issue new shares to pay for this. Lucy cannot afford to invest any more money in the company and thinks Cheri and Kyle will buy all the new shares themselves. Lucy thinks there are lots of other ways the company could raise the money for the website development. She thinks that the real reason Cheri and Kyle are choosing to issue the shares is to become the majority shareholders in the company.

Required

Advise Cheri and Kyle:

(a) Whether, as directors, they can issue the new ordinary shares without the approval of Lucy, and whether they can buy all the new shares themselves; and **(10 marks)**

(b) Whether they will breach their directors' duties if they are, as Lucy believes, issuing the new shares as a means of becoming the majority owners of the company; and **(5 marks)**

(c) What other methods the company could use to pay for the new website. **(5 marks)**

(Total 20 marks)

May 2022

1 Camille and React Accountancy

On 13 November 2021 Camille contracted with React Accountancy to prepare her end of year company accounts. They agree that the accounts will be completed by 1 March 2022. In January 2022, React telephones Camille to tell her it has taken on too much work from other clients and it will no longer be able to complete her accounts by 1 March 2022. React has told Camille that it will send her an invoice for the work completed to date.

Required

Advise Camille whether React has breached the contract and if so what type of breach has occurred, and advise Camille if she must pay React's invoice. **(20 marks)**

2 Red Shell plc

Red Shell plc (RS) is a construction company with many large and lucrative contracts. It was listed on the London Stock Exchange in 2005. In 2018 concerns were raised by investors over the slow growth of RS and the large amount of debt it had accumulated. Despite this RS's directors continued to pay dividends to the company's shareholders and approve large pay packages and bonuses for themselves.

In late 2021, a number of RS's projects failed, which had serious financial consequences for the company. Paul, one of RS's directors, told the company's shareholders that they had accepted too many projects that turned out to be unprofitable and that the directors had not properly assessed the risk of the company's strategy.

In April 2022 RS's share price fell further incurring a huge loss for its shareholders. It also became impossible for the company to meet its debt repayment obligations. The directors therefore decided to meet to discuss voluntary liquidation.

Required

(a) Advise RS's directors whether they can commence voluntary liquidation and the procedure for doing so. **(6 marks)**

(b) The directors of RS are now concerned about their failure to properly assess the risks of their decisions, and their approval of large bonuses when there was concern about the financial stability of the company. Advise RS's directors whether this behaviour may have breached any of their duties in the Companies Act 2006 (and if so, which ones). **(10 marks)**

(c) Advise the directors of RS whether they are at risk of being disqualified under the Company Directors Disqualification Act 1986. **(4 marks)**

(Total 20 marks)

3 Anthony

Anthony is out running errands and is walking on a path next to a busy road, when he is suddenly struck by a van which is driven by Christian. Due to Christian's negligence, Anthony is seriously injured. At the time of the accident, Christian was working for The Flower Shop Ltd, for whom he was supposed to be delivering flowers. However, Christian was not going to deliver flowers but instead was on his way to pick up more stock for The Flower Shop Ltd. He had been asked by his colleague and friend Susie, whose job it was to order and pick up stock, to pick up the stock on her behalf.

Christian has been working for the Flower Shop Ltd for two years. He also has a second part-time job with another company delivering food. Christian is not required to wear a uniform for the Flower Shop Ltd and drives his own van. The Flower Shop Ltd pays Christian a monthly wage of £900.

Required

Advise Anthony against whom he could bring a claim in this situation. **(20 marks)**

4 Manrika and Felix

Manrika and Felix are friends and experienced accountants. In 2018 they decided to start a new business together as partners in a general partnership. They invited Cheng, a colleague, to join the firm as a partner. Cheng is less experienced than Manrika and Felix, but has a number of valuable clients and contacts that were beneficial to the new business venture. They all agreed that they should create a partnership deed and Cheng agreed to limit her authority, including limiting her financial power in the firm. Cheng therefore cannot borrow money, nor make purchases over £1000, without permission from Manrika and Felix.

In early 2020 the business celebrated its 2nd anniversary. It had a number of loyal clients and two employees, Stephen and Bebe, who are administrative assistants. Cheng believed that whilst the firm had been successful it should start to put further efforts in to growing its client base. She decided to take out a loan with the firm's bank for £5,000 for the purpose of advertising and purchased new promotional materials with the business's logo for £2,000.

The impact of the global pandemic in 2020, however, caused the firm to suffer significant losses. In assessing the firm's financial position Manrika and Felix discovered that Cheng has taken out the loan from the bank and spent £2,000 on materials without consulting them. They also decided that they would have to dismiss one of their employees.

Required

(a) Advise Manrika and Felix whether the partnership is required to pay for the loan repayments for £5,000 and the materials purchased for £2,000. They specifically want to know if there is recourse for the loan because their bank knew that Cheng did not have the authority to borrow money on behalf of the firm. **(10 marks)**

(b) Advise Manrika, Felix and Cheng on redundancy procedure, including which of their employees is most suitable for redundancy (Stephen or Bebe). Stephen started working for the firm before Bebe did, but he has been late on a number of occasions and Felix is concerned about the quality of his work. Bebe has shown aptitude for the work and is liked by all the partners. **(10 marks)**

(Total 20 marks)

5 Elliott Accountancy Limited

Elliott Accountancy Limited (EA) is a company which operates a chain of accountancy firms. It has four directors, who all own shares in the company, and a further seven shareholders. EA was incorporated in January 2015 and has adopted the Model Articles, with the addition of the following regulation:

> 'Any shares which a member wishes to transfer must first be offered to the existing members of the company in proportion to their existing shareholding, who have 21 days in which to accept or reject the offer. Any shares not accepted may be freely transferred.'

The directors now want to issue new ordinary shares in the company to themselves, but not to any of the other shareholders in the company. One of the directors, Michelle, also wants to sell some of her shares to her niece Ellen, who is not currently a shareholder in EA.

Required

(a) Advise the directors of the procedure they must follow to **issue new ordinary shares** only to themselves (and not to the other shareholders). You do not need to refer to the directors' fiduciary duties in your answer. **(10 marks)**

(b) Advise Michelle as to whether she can **transfer** her shares to Ellen. **(10 marks)**

(Total 20 marks)

November 2022

1 Busola

Busola is a carpenter who builds and sells furniture from his shop. In his shop he has a table which he made a year ago. He decides to offer the table, at a reduced price, to three of his existing customers. He sends each of them a letter, by post, offering the table for £1700. On 4th November, the customers – Nell, Rhys and Maleka – each receive Busola's letter.

On 7th November Nell emails Busola to say she would like to buy the table for £1500.

Rhys telephones Busola, on the same day, but Busola has closed the business for a week's holiday and is not there to answer. Rhys therefore leaves a message on Busola's answering machine to say he will buy the table for £1700.

On 8th November Maleka writes a letter to Busola stating that she would like to buy the table for £1700. She posts the letter on the same day.

When Busola returns from holiday on 11th November, and reopens the shop, he listens to Rhys' message and reads Nell's email. He does not respond to either. Later that day Gemma visits Busola's shop and offers to buy, for £2000, the same table Busola offered to Nell, Rhys and Maleka. Busola accepts Gemma's offer and immediately contacts Nell, Rhys and Maleka by email to say the table is no longer for sale.

On 12th November Busola receives Maleka's letter accepting his initial offer to sell the table for £1700.

Nell, Rhys and Maleka are each insisting that Busola must sell them the table.

Required

Advise Busola to whom, if anyone, he is bound to sell the table, and for what price. **(20 marks)**

2 Squires Limited

Ravneet, Zhiyun, Henry and Patty are shareholders and directors in a successful chartered accountants' company called Squires Limited. All the directors actively participate in the management of the company and each owns 25% of the company's shares. The company was incorporated in 2012 and has model articles (unamended).

Ravneet, Henry and Patty have become unhappy with Zhiyun's commitment to the business, as he has failed to attend any of the last six board meetings and has missed numerous client meetings.

Ravneet suspects that Zhiyun has recently become involved with another rival accountancy firm, Freemans Ltd, as he (Zhiyun) has developed a personal connection with one of Freemans' directors. When Ravneet, Henry and Patty approach Zhiyun about his behaviour he denies involvement with Freemans.

Ravneet, Henry and Patty would like to remove Zhiyun as a director of Squires.

Required

(a) Discuss the procedural requirements for removing Zhiyun as a director. **(7 marks)**

(b) Following his removal as a director, Zhiyun wants to sell his shares in Squires, and Henry has agreed to buy them. Discuss the procedure that must be followed in order to transfer all Zhiyun's shares to Henry. **(6 marks)**

(c) Ravneet, Henry and Patty would also like Zhiyun to be disqualified as a director so that he cannot become a director of Freemans. Discuss the grounds for disqualification and advise whether or not he could be disqualified. **(7 marks)**

(Total 20 marks)

3 Precision Accounting

Precision Accounting (PA) is the auditor for Kings Group plc (KG). KG's most recent audited accounts, prepared by PA, showed a profit of £3 million. Relying on these accounts, Mega Holdings plc (Mega) made a successful takeover bid for KG, paying £10 per share. In fact, the accounts should have shown a loss of £1 million. Mega says that KG is clearly worth far less than the price it paid to acquire it, and Mega now wishes to sue PA for the loss it says it has made through its takeover of KG. Its claim is based on the argument that PA made a negligent misstatement regarding the accounts, and owed a duty of care to KG because PA should have been aware that potential bidders would rely upon the audited accounts when considering a takeover.

Required

(a) Advise Precision Accounting whether Mega has a strong claim for negligent misstatement.

(15 marks)

(b) Discuss how your answer would change if the error regarding KG's profits were contained not in the audited accounts of KG, but instead in a report prepared by PA for KG to show to Mega in connection with its proposed takeover of KG? **(5 marks)**

(Total 20 marks)

4 Reputatio

Latifah and Sam are accountants who would like to form a private company limited by shares. They want the company to be called Reputatio Ltd, because, they understand, 'reputatio' in Latin means 'account'. Latifah is aware of another company within the local area called Reputation Limited which also operates an accountancy business similar to the one that will be undertaken by her and Sam.

Latifah and Sam decide to use Fast Formations Ltd, a company incorporation service, to incorporate their company. Kendal, who works at Fast Formations Ltd, tells Latifah that Reputatio Ltd will be registered on 29th May.

On 5th June, Latifah interviews and hires a receptionist and administrative assistant, Kelly, for the new business. Latifah offers Kelly a starting salary of £18,000 per year. Latifah signs Kelly's employment contract. Above her signature, Latifah writes "for and on behalf of Reputatio Limited."

Required

(a) Discuss any legal risks that Latifah and Sam are taking in incorporating a company with the name Reputatio Limited, and consider any alternative course of action they could take to avoid these risks whilst still using this name. **(10 marks)**

(b) Latifah has now discovered that Reputatio was not incorporated until 18th June. Advise Latifah if she has any personal liability in respect of Kelly's employment contract and what, if anything, can be done to protect Latifah against such liability. **(10 marks)**

(Total 20 marks)

5 Haywood and Taseer Ltd

Haywood and Taseer Ltd ('H&T') is an accountancy firm, which has expanded rapidly over the past two years. H&T invested heavily in opening new offices around the UK and took out a large overdraft with one of its creditors, Big Bank plc, in order to fund some of the expansion. The overdraft was secured by a fixed charge over all the assets of H&T.

Although the new offices are attracting new clients, H&T makes most of its profits from clients in the restaurant industry. Unfortunately, these clients were badly impacted by the Covid pandemic, and the demand for H&T's services has been significantly reduced.

H&T is now suffering serious cash-flow problems. Big Bank is demanding immediate repayment of its overdraft, which H&T will struggle to do. The directors of H&T are considering whether they should carry on trading and risk being subject to a compulsory winding up of H&T, or whether they should immediately put H&T into voluntary winding up. They believe that they could rescue the company if they closed some of the worst performing offices.

Required

(a) Explain to the directors of H&T the advantages and the disadvantages of putting the company into a *voluntary* winding up immediately, rather than continuing to trade and risk a *compulsory* winding up of the company. **(15 marks)**

(b) Advise the directors of H&T whether they risk personal liability if they continue to trade.

(5 marks)
(Total 20 marks)

May 2023

1 Sandra

Sandra is a new business owner. She is looking for an accountancy firm to complete her first end of year taxes. She has not used an accountancy firm before, but her friend, who also owns her own business, told Sandra she should expect to pay around £350 for the service.

Sandra comes across a firm called Fast-Count, after completing a quick search for accountancy firms on the internet. Fast-Count's website says that it offers competitive pricing for its services. Sandra calls Fast-Count and asks for a quote. Abdi, who is a new employee at Fast-Count, speaks to Sandra and quotes £150 for the work, which is to be completed by a partner at the firm. Abdi asks Sandra to complete a new client form by the end of the day to 'action the quote' (with the price to be paid upon completion of the work). Delighted by the price of £150, Sandra completes the form and emails it back to Abdi. Within the email Sandra sends to Abdi, she asks whether the quote includes the filing of the accounts with HMRC on her behalf.

Abdi forwards the new client form and quote to Khalid, who is a partner at Fast-Count. When Khalid reads the information sent by Abdi, he realises that Abdi has mistakenly based the quote only on Khalid's hourly rate, rather than on all the work that will need to be completed. Khalid tries to call Sandra but she does not answer. He then emails her to give a new quote of £500 for the work to be carried out.

Required

Advise Sandra on whether a contract has been formed, and if so for what price. **(20 marks)**

2 Gemma, Neha and Tarik

Gemma, Neha and Tarik started an accountancy firm as a general partnership in 2018. All three were partners but they did not create a formal partnership deed.

In February 2023, Gemma's friend, Stephen, qualified as an accountant. Without speaking to Neha and Tarik, Gemma offered Stephen a job with the firm. Gemma told Stephen that he would be working as an employee of the firm for six months but, if all goes well, he would then be made an equal partner in the firm.

Required

Advise Neha and Tarik in each of the following two alternative scenarios:

(a) Neha and Tarik do not wish Stephen to have any involvement with the firm, whether as an employee or as a partner. They are especially concerned about the rights Stephen would enjoy as an employee of the firm. **(10 marks)**

(b) Neha and Tarik are happy with Stephen working for the firm and agree that he should become a partner, but want to ensure that he will receive a lower profit share, and have less authority to bind the firm, than the three original partners. **(10 marks)**

(Total 20 marks)

3 Arlo Designs Ltd

Arlo Designs Ltd ('Arlo') is a company that specialises in designing and manufacturing hand-built cars. It has seven directors, including Yue and Beatrice.

Yue and Beatrice are approached by Carla, who asks them if Arlo would be interested in buying a stake in Carla's business, which makes hand-built motorcycles. Arlo's board discusses Carla's offer, but all the directors decide to reject it. They reach this decision because they believe that, although the investment would be very profitable, motorcycles are environmentally very harmful and that Arlo 'must do its best to protect the environment and develop a sustainable business'.

After the board meeting, Yue asks Beatrice if it would be all right if he invested in Carla's business for himself. Beatrice tells Yue that she "doesn't care." Yue personally purchases a significant stake in Carla's business. Six months later he has already made a large profit for himself on this investment.

Arlo's shareholders have discovered the foregoing and are very angry about their directors' behaviour.

Required

Advise the shareholders whether Arlo's directors breached any of the duties they owed to Arlo.

(20 marks)

4 Blaze Ltd

Blaze Ltd was set up in 2019. It has four directors and equal shareholders, Kym, Anvi, Jakub and Shelly. The company has unamended model articles.

Anvi now wants to retire as a director and to transfer all of her shares to her daughter, Crystal.

Kym, Jakub and Shelly want to appoint a new director to replace Anvi. They want to find a new director who will be beneficial to the company and provide experience that may currently be missing from the board. In order to attract a new director, they envisage that the company will allot new shares to the person appointed.

Required

Advise:

(a) Anvi whether, and how, she can transfer her shares to her daughter. **(10 marks)**

(b) Kym, Jakub and Shelly on the process for appointing a new director and how they can allot the new shares. **(10 marks)**

(Total 20 marks)

5 BoxBuilt plc

BoxBuilt plc is a public company that sells flat-packed furniture online. Initially, it had a unique business model that ran on a just-in-time method, meaning that it did not need to keep much stock within its warehouses. However, after the UK's exit from the European Union it became much more difficult to operate this model for running the business.

The directors of BoxBuilt therefore decided to hold more stock in the UK. This worked well during the pandemic when business boomed for BoxBuilt. However, over the last year the demand for its furniture has decreased significantly and, with most of its assets now tied up in stock, the business has begun to struggle to repay its debts.

The directors of BoxBuilt are very concerned about the future of the company. They have been told that their best chance of saving the company is to 'put the company into administration'.

Required

(a) Advise the directors on whether an administrator could be appointed for BoxBuilt, and what the effect of such an appointment would be. **(15 marks)**

(b) Advise the directors whether they may be held personally liable if the company is unable to repay all its debts. **(5 marks)**

(Total 20 marks)

November 2023

1 Jenny

On 23 December 2022 Jenny contracted with Murray and Co Accountancy (M&C) to prepare her end of year company accounts. They agreed that the accounts would be completed by 1 March 2023.

On 13 February 2023, M&C telephoned Jenny to tell her they had taken on too much work from other clients and that they would no longer be able to complete her accounts by 1 March 2023. Jenny had to find another firm to complete her end of year accounts.

M&C later sent Jenny an invoice for the work they completed up until 13 February 2023.

Required

(a) Advise Jenny whether M&C breached the contract agreed on 23 December 2022, and if so what type of breach has occurred. **(16 marks)**

(b) Advise Jenny if she must pay M&C's invoice. **(4 marks)**

(Total 20 marks)

2 React Accountancy Ltd

In 2021, React Accountancy Ltd ('RA') borrowed a large sum of money from Big Bank Plc in order to expand its business. The loan was secured over RA's assets, including the office building it owns. Due to the increasing costs of running a business (including the rise in the cost of gas and electricity), the financial situation of RA has worsened, and it has now begun to default in repaying the loan to Big Bank Plc.

Required

(a) Explain to RA's directors the different ways in which RA may be wound up as a result of its financial situation. **(15 marks)**

(b) Explain the different roles of an Administrator and of a Liquidator. **(5 marks)**

(Total 20 marks)

3 James and Katie

James and Katie are accountants and are employed to work in Lisa's accountancy firm. Katie, who started working for Lisa in September 2021, is a diligent and trustworthy employee. James, who has been working for Lisa for over three years, is often late to work and is known to be rude to clients.

In September 2023 Lisa tells Katie that she is going to have to make Katie redundant, due to increasing financial pressures on her business. Katie, upset by this decision, tells Lisa that James consistently breaks staff rules and has been verbally abusive to other members of staff. Upon hearing this Lisa immediately dismisses James and asks him to leave the office. Lisa later tells Katie she is still going to make Katie redundant.

Required

Advise both Katie and James whether each of them could claim for unfair dismissal. **(20 marks)**

4 Hill and Qin

Hill and Qin (HQ) is a successful business that has been providing accountancy services to a broad range of clients for the last three years. The business has been operating as a general partnership. The two partners, Dalia Hill and Jun Qin, work full time in the business and employ a team of five accountants and one administrative member of staff.

Over the last twelve months, HQ has secured a number of large, lucrative contracts, and Dalia and Jun have decided that the expanding business should become a limited liability company called HillQin Limited (HQL). The turnover of the business is in the region of £700,000 and its balance sheet total is approximately £250,000. Current projections suggest that both turnover and balance sheet total will increase by approximately twenty-five per cent over the next twelve months.

Dalia and Jun have decided that the company will be incorporated with Model Articles (unamended) and ordinary shares of £1 each. They will each own one share and be appointed as a director of the company.

Required

(a) Advise Dalia and Jun on the procedure for incorporation and what checks should be made in relation to the company name they wish to use. **(10 marks)**

(b) Advise Dalia and Jun on HQL's obligations for the production and filing of accounts and whether HQL will need to appoint an auditor. **(10 marks)**

(Total 20 marks)

5 Black Gold Plc

Black Gold Plc is a company that specialises in the production of oil and gas. It is a multinational corporation that is listed on the London Stock Exchange.

Margot Robinson, a shareholder of Black Gold, is highly concerned with the challenges that climate change presents both globally and to the future of Black Gold. Over the past five years she has tried to engage with the board of directors of Black Gold in order to encourage a move away from the production of fossil fuels and to reduce carbon emissions.

In 2022 Black Gold published its climate strategy. In early 2023 the directors of Black Gold discussed the progress towards meeting the goals outlined in the strategy at the company's Annual General Meeting. The directors reported that this progress had been slower than previously promised, but that the company had made a record annual profit of £2 billion driven by high energy prices.

Margot was very disappointed with the progress of Black Gold. She feels that the directors have mismanaged the climate risks facing the company, and have failed to adopt and implement policies to meet the goals outlined in the 2022 climate strategy.

Required

Advise Margot whether Black Gold directors have breached any of the duties they owe to Black Gold and, if so, what mechanism she could use, as a shareholder, to bring a claim for the breached duties.

(20 marks)

Exam answer bank

November 2021

1 Camille

This question requires the students to understand and apply the contract law principles of offer and acceptance.

(a) An offer is a proposal or promise by one party (the offeror) to enter into the contract, on a particular set of terms, with the intention of being bound as soon as the party to whom the promise is made (the offeree) signifies their acceptance (on those same terms).

An offer must be clear and communicated to the other party. The communication of an offer may be written, spoken, or by conduct.

In the scenario Camille is given a 'quote' from one of React's chartered accountants to prepare her company's accounts for around '£1,000.00'. Whilst the statement is clear and communicated to Camille it does not meet the requirements of an offer.

This is because React has not given an offer on a particular set of terms that can be accepted. React states that they will prepare her accounts 'for around £1,000.00.' This is not specific and is therefore an 'invitation to treat.'

An offer and an invitation to treat are different. An invitation to treat is not an offer that is capable of being accepted by the other party. It is a 'pre-offer' and an indication that a party is open to negotiation.

It can sometimes be hard to tell the difference between an offer and an invitation to treat, but there are conventional situations e.g. adverts where it is usually clear. Other examples are:

- Displays of goods in shops and shop windows are invitations to treat.
- Advertisements are usually invitations to treat but may be unilateral offers.
- Applications inviting tenders, catalogues, and prospectuses are invitations to treat

The quote given by React's accountant is therefore an invitation to treat not an offer.

(b) In this scenario React has made an offer to Camille: to prepare her accounts for £1,200.00. This is a proposal by React to enter into a contract with Camille, on a particular set of terms.

However, Camille thinks this price is too high and in response asks React to complete the work for £900.00. This is a counter offer.

A counter offer is usually an offer made in reply to an offer, where one party makes an offer and the other party suggests different terms. Here the different term is the price: £1,200.00 vs £900.00.

A counter offer was found in the case of Hyde v Wrench (1840): the defendant offered to sell his farm to the claimant for £1,000. The claimant replied offering to buy the farm for £950. The defendant refused to accept the £950 and the claimant then attempted to buy the farm for £1,000.

The court stated that the offer made by the defendant to sell the farm for £1,000 was no longer open and that the offer, made by the claimant, to pay £950 for the farm was a counter offer, which had the effect of a rejection of the original offer. The defendant was therefore under no legal obligation to sell the farm to the claimant for £1,000.

Camille's counter-offer therefore acts as a rejection and destroys the original offer from React, which means it can no longer be accepted by Camille.

However, as React has not responded to Camille to formally reject her offer she has two options. First, she can approach React to ask if they will accept her offer to complete the work for £900.00. Or, secondly, Camille could offer £1,200.00 for the work (as originally offered by React), creating a new offer, which React is then free to accept or reject.

> **Additional areas where credit might be given, note this is not an exhaustive list:**
> - Explanation that React's silence in the face of Camille's counter-offer does not mean that React has accepted that counter-offer.

2 Percy Ltd

This question requires the students to explain the principles of vicarious liability.

As the tortfeaser, Dhian will be liable for any wrong. However, an employer can be liable for the torts committed by his employees in the course of their employment under the principle of vicarious liability. Therefore, Percy Ltd could be held vicariously liable for Dhian's actions.

The employer will usually have greater resources, and as such is more likely to have 'deep pockets,' and may also have insurance cover. It would thus be more lucrative if Vicki could bring a claim against Percy Ltd rather than Dhian.

Another rationale for being able to bring a claim of this nature is that by bringing a claim against an employer it may also promote prevention of accidents and it is a method of making the employer pay for the true cost of their activity. Thus, even where an employee is acting illegally (*Lloyd v Grace, Smith & Co*) or with gross negligence (*Century Insurance v Northern Ireland Transport Board*) the employer has been found vicariously liable.

In order to establish vicarious liability however, there must firstly be an employee/employer relationship and a close connection between the employee's tort and his employment, and whether this is in fact the case must be decided by the facts of each case (eg *Dubai Aluminium v Salaam; Attorney General v Hartwell*).

In order for vicarious liability to apply it is necessary to establish that there is a relationship of employer and employee between Dhian and Percy Ltd, and more importantly, that the tort was committed in the course of employment.

Firstly, it needs to be established that the tort was committed by an employee and not an independent contractor. The distinction here is between a person under a contract of service (employee) and a person under a contract for services (independent contractor). The courts will usually apply a series of tests. One is the control test, where the courts will consider whether the employer has control over the way in which the employee performs his duties. A second is the integration test, where the court asks whether the worker has been 'integrated' into the employer's organisation so as to become its employee. Relevant elements include whether the employer selected the worker to carry out the task, and whether the worker is so skilled that he cannot be controlled in the performance of his duties. A lack of control indicates that the worker is not integrated into the employer's organisation and therefore not an employee. The third test is the 'economic reality' test. This looks at a number of factors to determine if the worker is really working on his own account.

Applying these tests to Dhian's situation, a number of factors seems relevant. One is the fact that Dhian uses his own vehicle to deliver the pottery. It would also seem that Dhian may work for others besides Percy Ltd. These factors are suggestive of Dhian being an independent contractor. However, Dhian is supplied with a uniform by Percy, which is suggestive of an employment relationship. Moreover, Percy Ltd seems to exert a great deal of control over Dhian. It controls the timing of his deliveries, and the manner he must carry them out (the 'delivery rules'). It also requires Dhian personally to provide the delivery services for them – unlike the case of *Ready Mixed Concrete (South East) v Ministry of Pensions* (1968),

Dhian cannot 'subcontract' the work to others. Finally, when Dhian is working for Percy Ltd he must do so exclusively.

It would also be useful to know how Dhian is paid for the work he does for Percy Ltd. If he is paid a salary for the days he works for them, regardless of the number of deliveries he makes, that will again suggest he is an employee.

The way these payments are treated for taxation purposes would also be relevant. If he is being treated as self-employed for taxation purposes, that would be a factor that weighs in favour of his not being considered an employee for the purposes of tort law. However, the law may come to different conclusions about a worker's status for the purposes of different areas of law. There may be policy reasons for finding that someone is an employee for the purposes of tort law (to allow their employer to be held vicariously liable) that do not apply in relation to say tax law.

In conclusion, it is perhaps uncertain from the information given what the true relationship is between Dhian and Percy Ltd, but many of the factors do suggest he might be treated as an employee

Secondly, if the torfeasor is an employee, the tort must have been committed in the course of the employment and not as a result of doing something which falls outside that employment (when he is 'on a frolic of his own'). The question of which acts fall within the relevant employment is one on which there has been considerable litigation.

The courts have drawn a distinction between an employee's act which was a wrongful method of carrying out something he was authorised to do, and one which he was not authorised to perform. Thus, a school warden's abuse of children under his care led to the vicarious liability of the school in *Lister v Hesley Hall*. Off-duty situations are also covered under the employer's vicarious liability as in *Ministry of Defence v Radcliffe*.

By contrast, where a bus conductor drove a bus the employer was not liable because the conductor was not authorised to drive the bus (*Beard v London General Omnibus Co*). It is highly unlikely that Dhian was authorised to visit friends – particularly those who lived a significant distance from the customer's home. Thus, following the decision in *Beard*, Dhian might be considered to be on a 'frolic of his own' and Percy Ltd may not be held vicariously liable for Dhian's negligence.

In conclusion, Vicki may make a claim against Dhian but it is unlikely that she will be able to hold Percy Ltd vicariously liable for Dhian's actions.

> **Additional areas where credit might be given, note this is not an exhaustive list:**
>
> - Discussion and application of other relevant case law

3 Mizuho and Jun

This question requires the student to evaluate the different forms of business in light of the facts of the problem question (largely discussing the advantages and disadvantages of partnerships and companies) and conclude on the most appropriate structure.

There are a number of different legal structures Mizuho (M) and Jun (J) can use to run an accountancy business in the UK. The most appropriate can be split into two main forms: partnerships and companies.

A partnership is a collective business involving two or more persons. There are various forms of partnership: the general partnership, the limited partnership and the limited liability partnership.

Partners jointly own the business and share profits and losses. A general partnership is unincorporated and the partners therefore individually and collectively face unlimited personal liability for their business. An LLP is an incorporated structure and therefore has a separate legal personality from its members.

There are also two main forms of companies M and J might use: a private or a public company. Both of these structures have separate liability from their members.

The main difference between these forms is that only a public company can offer its shares for sale to the general public. Section 755 of the Companies Act 2006 prohibits private companies from offering their shares – or allowing their shares to be offered – for sale to the public. Only shares in a public company can therefore be listed and traded on a share market such as the London Stock Exchange.

A public company is therefore generally subject to more onerous regulation. In particular, a public company must have issued shares with a nominal value of at least £50,000. A public company must have at least two directors, whereas a private company need only have one.

Whilst a public company would allow M and J to grow their business more rapidly and easily than would a private company, the onerous regulations and initial investment will be too burdensome. As they are inexperienced in running a business and have £30,000 available for initial investment in the business a private company may be more suitable.

Partnership vs Company

Should M and J set up a partnership or a private company? Because of their inexperience in business they may prefer to set up a partnership, which is easy to run and is subjected to even less regulation than is a private company (i.e. to prepare accounts and disclosures). This means they will not need to meet the many legal requirements for running their business as a company.

However, a company has a separate legal personality from its members and therefore their liability for its debts would be limited. This would be beneficial for M and J. However, they could also achieve limited liability by setting up an LLP.

In a company the shareholders would elect directors to manage the company whereas all partners have a right to be involved in the management of the partnership. If M and J were to set up a partnership there would be more guarantee that they would have significant control over the running of the business in the long-term.

Growing the business would be easier if M and J used a company structure as they could issue shares to raise capital. It may be more difficult to grow as a partnership as it would involve inviting new partners – and this would mean sharing in profit and management.

There are also differences in tax: a company pays tax on its profits (directors are taxed through PAYE system) whereas partners extract 'drawings' on a weekly or monthly basis and no tax is deducted, although income tax is payable on their share of the final profit for the year.

> **Additional areas where credit might be given, note this is not an exhaustive list:**
> - Other relevant discussion of the advantages or disadvantages of the different forms of business
> - Concluding on a preferred form of business and strength of supporting evidence

4 Sakura

This question requires the student to discuss liquidation and administration, evaluating when it may be appropriate to save a company as a going concern.

(a) A company should not always be wound up because it is in financial difficulty. This is because it may be saved and therefore treated as a 'going concern.' It may be possible for Daisy's Café to enter into administration rather than being wound up.

An alternative to liquidation – administration – is now found in the Insolvency Act 1986 as a mechanism for trying to save a company and return it to profitability. Administration also has benefits for the members of the company. They will continue to have shares in the company, which has not been wound up. If the administration is successful, regenerating the business should enhance share value and will restore any income from the business.

An administrator may be appointed either by the company itself, or by the court. If the appointment is made by the company, then it must be decided on by either its directors or by its shareholders. Also, the company must either already be, or be likely to become, unable to pay its debts. This condition is probably satisfied by Daisy's Café Ltd, in view of its financial problems.

There are certain situations where the company itself cannot make the appointment. These include where a winding up petition has already been presented. We are not told this has happened yet, but as this is being threatened, Sakura should act quickly. The company will have to give notice of the intention to appoint an administrator to Anybank plc, as a floating charge holder. Anybank might then decide to appoint its own administrator instead.

Alternatively, the appointment might be made by the court. Application to the court for such an appointment can be made by, amongst others, the directors. The court will grant an administration order if both i) the company is unable to pay its debts and ii) making the order will 'achieve the purpose of administration'. There are two main purposes. One is to save the company as a going concern. The other is to achieve a better result for the company's creditors than they would get if the company were wound up. So, if an administrator is to be appointed by the court, Sakura will need to show that one or other of these purposes will be achieved.

The consequences of the appointment include the following. The administrator will assume control and attempt to rescue the company. The powers of the existing managers of the company are now subject to the control of the administrator.

An administration order provides a temporary breathing space from creditors in order for Sakura – and the other directors of Daisy Café - to formulate rescue plans. There will be a moratorium on the enforcement of debts against the company, and proceedings against the company cannot be taken without the consent of the court. It may be a relief for Sakura and Daisy's Café to know that whilst under administration, a winding up order cannot be made against the company.

Administrators are subject to a number of legal duties whilst acting, and also have a number of legal powers. The administration itself normally lasts 12 months, but can last longer. The administrator may sell Daisy's Café's property in order to distribute proceeds to secured or preferential creditors.

(b) Sakura – and other directors – will not usually be held personally liable for the debts of the company, due to limited liability.

However, it is important to advise Sakura that directors of a company who continue to trade when in serious financial difficulty may be at risk of liability for 'wrongful trading'. Under s.214 of the Insolvency Act 1986, a director is guilty of 'wrongful trading' where the director knew or ought to have known that the company had no reasonable prospect of avoiding insolvency and failed to take all steps to minimise the loss to creditors. Usually, this will require directors to cease trading once insolvency becomes inevitable. If administration were to fail and Daisy's Café Ltd is wound up, Sakura (and other directors) could be liable for wrongful trading, for incurring further debts, such as borrowing money or obtaining stock on credit. The directors will be judged by a standard of reasonable competency taking into account any special expertise they have as directors (such as experience and qualifications). If found liable, they can be made to 'make such contribution to the assets of the company as the court thinks fit'.

However, note that the Corporate Insolvency and Governance Act 2020 effectively 'suspended' wrongful trading liability between the dates 1st of March 2020 to 30th of September 2020, and 26 November 2020 to 30 April 2021. Directors cannot be held liable for any worsening in the company's financial situation between those dates.

> **Additional areas where credit might be given, note this is not an exhaustive list:**
> - Further detail on process of administration
> - The restrictions on serving 'statutory demands' or on winding-up companies based on inability to pay debts, introduced by the Corporate Insolvency and Governance Act 2020.

5 Cheri, Kyle and Lucy

This question requires the student to evaluate relevant principles of company law and case law in light of the scenario provided. The question also requires a short discussion of alternative methods to raise finance other than by issuing new share capital.

(a) s.550 Companies Act 2006 allows directors to allot shares without authority from the company's shareholders. s.550 CA applies to a company incorporated on or after 1 October 2009, which is the case here.

Cheri and Kyle will only be able to issue new ordinary shares to themselves (without gaining approval from the shareholders, which would require the agreement of Lucy) if there is only one class of share in issue and no relevant restriction in the company's articles of association.

Considering the facts of the scenario it seems that there is only one class of share in issue at Watts and Lacey. Since Watts and Lacey have unamended Model Articles there should be no restrictions on directors' authority to allot. Therefore, under s.550 CA Cheri and Kyle may allot new shares without the approval of Lucy.

However, the statutory rights of pre-emption found in s561 Companies Act 2006 require these new shares to be offered first to Watts and Lacey's existing shareholders in the same proportion as they currently own shares in the company.

Watts and Lacey's unamended Model Articles will not disapply the statutory rights of pre-emption. The rights can be disapplied in relation to any transaction by the members. However, this can only be done by passing a special resolution in a general meeting (s.569 Companies Act 2006). Cheri and Kyle do not have sufficient votes to pass such a resolution. So, Lucy will be entitled to be offered 50% of the new shares that are issued.

However, whilst Lucy must be *offered* half of the new shares, we are told she cannot afford to buy them. If this is so, then once the period of the offer ends, the company will be free to offer the shares only to Cheri and Kyle. In this way, Cheri and Kyle will be able, effectively, to comply with the pre-emption rules and to buy all the shares themselves if Lucy cannot afford to buy them.

(b) Directors are subject to directors' duties, under sections 171-177 Companies Act 2006. The duty that they might breach here is that found in section 171(b). This requires directors 'to exercise their powers for the purpose for which they are conferred'. This duty applies to the power found in section 550, discussed above.

A number of cases have considered directors exercising the power to allot shares. They include *Hogg v Cramphorn* (1966), *Bamford v Bamford* (1969) and *Howard Smith v Ampol Petroleum* (1974). These cases suggest that the proper purpose for which directors are entitled to issue shares is only to raise capital for the company. However, issuing shares in order to manipulate the ownership of the company (say, to block a takeover) would be an improper purpose.

The court here would need to determine the real reason why Cheri and Kyle were issuing the new shares. If the real reason were to make themselves the majority owners, and Lucy a minority, that would probably be an improper purpose, and a breach of section 171.

(c) Cheri and Kyle could consider alternative methods, other than the issue of new shares, to raise funds for the new website. One of the most common methods is loan capital, which comprises debentures and other long-term loans to a business.

Loan capital is the term used to describe borrowed money obtained usually by the issue of debentures. It is distinguished from share capital by the fact that, at some point, borrowing must be repaid.

A company's loan capital comprises all amounts which it borrows for the long-term, such as: permanent overdrafts at the bank; unsecured loans, from a bank or other party; loans secured on assets, from a bank or other party.

Cheri and Kyle may therefore propose to pay for the new website using loan capital – however this may depend on the company's existing loans. If the company has many existing debts it may be that the issue of new shares is more appropriate.

Additional areas where credit might be given, note this is not an exhaustive list:

- Further relevant detail of the procedure to issue new shares
- Discussion of the consequences of breaching s171
- Further detail on loan capital

May 2022

1 Camille and React Accountancy

This question requires the students to understand the different types of breaches in contract law and apply the principles of quantum meruit.

A contract is breached if one of the parties breaks one or more of the terms of the contract, or indicates in advance that they do not intend to perform the contract. In this scenario React has told Camille that they are no longer able to complete her company accounts for the agreed date of 1 March 2022. This would therefore constitute a breach of the contract by React.

The type of breach here is an anticipatory breach. This has arisen because React, prior to the actual date of performance (1 March 2022), expressly informed Camille that they do not intend to perform some or all of their contractual obligations.

Camille is entitled to treat the contract as at an end at the time React indicated their intention not to complete the contract. As such, she will be able to recover damages for the loss of any benefit that she would have received if the contract had been performed.

This is similar to the case of Hochster v De La Tour where the defendant agreed to employ the claimant to act as a courier starting on 1 June. On 11 May, the defendant wrote to the claimant cancelling the contract by informing him that his services were no longer required. The claimant immediately commenced an action for breach of contract. There was no requirement for a claimant to wait until a contract was actually breached. The claimant could bring a court action as soon as he was aware the contract was going to be breached by the defendant.

Camille, as the innocent party, can sue before or after the date of performance because she is aware React intends to breach the contract. Camille does not have to formally communicate acceptance of an anticipatory breach, i.e. she does not have to expressly inform React that she is going to treat the contract as breached. But React must be aware of Camille's intention to treat the contract as at an end.

Once the contract is breached, Camille must take steps to mitigate her losses. This means that a party cannot recover any losses which she could have avoided by taking reasonable steps.

Camille must therefore seek out another accountancy firm or individual to complete her end of year accounts before the deadline. As Camille is informed by React of the anticipatory breach in January – there is still time to mitigate some of the damage caused by React's breach of contract.

Where a breach is anticipated but has not yet happened (as in this scenario – where the breach will take place on 1 March 2022 if Camille does not communicate the breach to React), Camille has no legal obligation to accept the breach and can treat the contract as continuing until the time of performance has passed. Until a breach of contract is accepted, Camille has no duty to mitigate any loss. This principle can have unfair results (see White and Carter Ltd v McGregor)

But, does Camille have to pay React's invoice for the work they have completed to date? Under the principals of quantum meruit claims may be paid for work completed so far by one party, if total performance of a contract is prevented by the other party. In this scenario Camille has not prevented the performance of the contract – React has told Camille that they can no longer finish the work because they are too busy. Therefore Camille does not have to pay React's invoice and may herself be entitled to damages.

> **Additional areas where credit might be given, note this is not an exhaustive list:**
> - Other relevant discussion of breach of contract (including evaluation of conditions and warranties)
> - Details of possible damages Camille can claim

2 Red Shell plc

This question requires the student to understand the procedure for voluntary liquidation and advise on the potential liability and breaches of duties of the directors, including disqualification.

(a) The directors of RS will need to have the co-operation of the members (i.e the shareholders of RS) in the voluntary winding up of the company. This may take place when the company is solvent or insolvent, where in the latter case creditors may be involved as well.

Members of RS may wish to wind up on a voluntary basis where the directors make a declaration of solvency, provided that, there are reasonable grounds for their doing so. In this scenario it may not be possible for the directors to make such a declaration because it requires the directors to state that the company will be able to pay its debts (in a timeframe not exceeding 12 months). A special resolution (75%) is then necessary to wind up.

If the directors cannot make the declaration of insolvency, then the voluntary winding up will proceed as a creditors' voluntary winding up.

The main difference between the different types of voluntary winding up is in the appointment of a liquidator: during the members' voluntary winding up members appoint, whereas in creditors' voluntary winding up, creditors appoint with responsibility to both members and creditors.

(b) General duties of directors are specified in ss.171-177 of Companies Act 2006. In this scenario, the most relevant duties in this scenario are ss.172 and 174.

Under s.172 the directors have a duty to promote the success of the company. This requires the directors to consider the benefits of the company's member as a whole and to act in good faith in exercising their discretion. The directors of RS should not only consider the interests of the shareholders but a wider range of interests such creditors, suppliers and employees (however, they do not owe this duty directly to any of those groups including the shareholders). Where the company is insolvent, or where insolvency is 'likely', the directors must prioritise the interests of creditors (as section 172(3) recognises).

The directors' duty to promote the success of the company is a subjectively assessed obligation. In assessing breaches of this duty the courts will consider whether the director exercised their discretion bona fide in what they consider, not what the courts may consider, to be in the interests of the company *(Re Smith* and *Fawcett Ltd)*. Under this duty the directors of RS are required to have regard to the likely long-term consequence of their decisions including the proper assessment and risk of accepting projects and the decisions to pay dividends and financial rewards to themselves. However, provided that the directors acted in good faith and in the interests of the company, and are not wilfully blind to the company's interests, they will not be liable for breach of this duty if they make a mistake and/or act unreasonably. Courts are often hesitant to question the 'business decisions' that company directors make – so whilst the directors may have made bad decisions in accepting projects and acted unreasonably in awarding dividends and bonuses the court may not have concluded that they breached their duty under s.172.

s.174 requires directors to exercise reasonable care, skill and diligence. The level by which the director will be judged will be what a reasonably diligent person may be expected to have done, having regard to the director's particular role and experience. In order to determine whether a director has breached this duty the courts will therefore look at the director's actions in both a subjective and objective manner. Subjective considerations will include whether the director has any special skills. A director must also acquire and maintain sufficient knowledge of the company's business in order to enable them to discharge their responsibilities (See Re Barings plc (No 5) [1999] 1 BCLC 433). As with s.172, it will be difficult for the shareholders to demonstrate that a director has breached s.174.

(c) A director can be disqualified under the Company Directors Disqualification Act 1986. However, as with directors' duties, the degree of culpability required for the court to disqualify a director is high. In Re Lo-Line Electric Motors Ltd [1988] the court held that while ordinary commercial mis-judgment is not in itself sufficient to establish unfitness, conduct which displays 'a lack of commercial probity' or conduct which is grossly negligent or displays 'total incompetence' would be sufficient to justify disqualification. This is a high bar to justify given the scenario and may depend on how competent the directors had been in assessing risk. The directors in this scenario, however, may be at risk of mandatory disqualification for unfitness – this is because their conduct in the lead up to the liquidation of RS may make them unfit to be involved in the management of other companies.

> **Additional areas where credit might be given, note this is not an exhaustive list:**
> - Other relevant discussion of voluntary liquidation and its procedure
> - Mention of wrongful or fraudulent trading under the Insolvency Act 1986
> - Relevant discussion of the details of the Company Directors Disqualification Act 1986

3 Anthony

This question requires an explanation of the principles of vicarious liability.

As the tortfeaser, Christian will be liable for any wrong. However, an employer can be also liable for the torts committed by his employees in the course of their employment, under the principle of vicarious liability.

The Flower Shop could therefore be vicariously liable for Christian's actions. The employer will usually have greater resources, and as such is more likely to have 'deep pockets,' and may also have insurance cover. It would thus be more lucrative if Anthony could bring a claim against The Flower Shop rather than Christian.

In order to establish vicarious liability there must be (1) an employee/employer relationship and (2) a close connection between the employee's tort and his employment.

It needs to be first established that Christian was an employee of the Flowershop, and was working for them merely as an 'independent contractor'. The distinction here is between a person under a contract of service (employee) and a person under a contract for services (independent contractor). In practice this distinction depends on many factors.

The courts will apply a series of tests, and in doing so consider the facts of the case and the agreement between the parties. The tests include the tests of control (where the courts will consider whether the employer has control over the way in which the employee performs his duties), integration into the employer's organisation, and economic reality (and here the court considers whether the employee was working on his own account).

Relevant factors in this scenario which the court will also consider when deciding whether a person is an employee, are that Christian uses his own equipment (e.g Christian owns his van which he uses to deliver flowers), the fact that Christian doesn't wear a uniform and also works for another company. However, the payment of a fixed monthly salary would indicate that Christian is an employee of the Flower Shop.

The tort, however, must have also been committed by an employee in the course of his employment and not as a result of doing something which falls outside that employment (when he is 'on a frolic of his own').

The question of which acts fall within the relevant employment is one on which there has been considerable litigation. The courts have drawn a distinction between an employee's act which was a wrongful method of carrying out something he was authorised to do, and one which he was not authorised to perform. Thus, a school warden's abuse of children under his care led to the vicarious liability of the school in *Lister v Hesley Hall*. Off-duty situations are also covered under the employer's vicarious liability as in *Ministry of Defence v Radcliffe*. By contrast, where a bus conductor drove a bus the employer was not liable because the conductor was not authorised to drive the bus (*Beard v London General Omnibus Co*).

Whether Christian was in fact acting within the course of his employment will be determined by whether or not he was authorised by his employer to pick up stock in his van. If he was not authorised to do so The Flower Shop will likely not be vicariously liable following the decision in Beard. If he was authorised to pick up stock, for example if it was included in his job description or he picked up stock in the past for the employer, then it would fall within an authorised action.

In conclusion, Anthony may make a claim against Christian or against The Flower Shop if they can be shown to be vicariously liable. In order to do this it must be confirmed whether Christian is an employee of The Flower Shop and whether he was authorised to pick up stock. If the Flower Shop can be held vicariously liable then it would be more advantageous for Anthony to claim against them rather than Christian, due to the assumption that The Flower Shop would have 'deeper pockets' or insurance to cover the cost of damages.

> **Additional areas where credit might be given, note this is not an exhaustive list:**
> - Reference to relevant case law
> - Further detail or discussion of Christian's status as an employee and whether he was on a 'frolic of his own'

4 Manrika and Felix

This question requires students to understand agency relationships in partnerships and advise on actual and apparent authority. Students are also required to advise on the correct procedure for redundancy.

(a) Partners manage the firm's business collectively and as such the default rule is that all partners have equal powers to make decisions. s.5 Partnership Act 1890 (that regulates 'general partnerships') provides that every partner is an agent of the firm and in effect, there is 'mutual agency.' As such, each partner has the authority to make contracts with third parties (as long as they are in the ordinary course of the firm's business). Each partner can thereby bind the other partners to those contracts.

However, Manrika, Felix and Cheng can make specific arrangements for the day-to-day running of the business, including provisions for authority, within a Partnership Deed. This can overrule the default provisions in the Partnership Act. But, liability for the loan and the purchase of materials can still arise for the firm even though the partners made specific arrangements to limit Cheng's authority.

This is based on different mediums of authority in agency relationships. So, whilst Cheng did not have 'actual authority' to enter into the contract for the loan and purchase of materials she may have had 'apparent authority.'

Actual authority is based on the authority given to Cheng via the Partnership Deed. We know that this was limited and that she needed to seek permission from both Manrika and Felix either to borrow money on behalf of the firm, or to spend over £1000 on purchases. Cheng therefore did not have actual authority to enter in to these contracts.

Apparent authority is based on the external appearance of Cheng's position. The third parties (to which Cheng entered into contracts with) can enforce a contract against the firm as long as Cheng acted within the limits of the authority usually associated with their position (i.e. a partner) and it is reasonable in all the circumstances for the third party to rely on this. The transaction (taking out the loan and purchasing materials) must also be in the usual course of business.

In regards to the promotional materials purchased for advertising: Cheng would have been acting within apparent authority as she is purchasing goods, as a partner, for the business. This contract will bind the firm. The bank however knows that Cheng does not have actual authority to take out a loan. Therefore, this contract will not bind the firm.

As Cheng has entered into two contracts in breach of her actual authority she will be personally liable to Manrika and Felix for any loss the firm suffers. The third party contracted for the promotional materials will be able to enforce the contract against the firm because Cheng acted with apparent authority, however the bank will not be able to enforce the loan against the firm because they knew Cheng's authority was limited.

(b) A dismissal will be treated as a lawful redundancy if the only or main reason an employee is dismissed was because: the employer has ceased, or intends to cease, to carry on the business in which they have been employed; or the requirements of that business for employees to carry on the work have ceased or diminished. The latter is relevant to the scenario here.

A key test for determining whether or not an employee has been made lawfully redundant is to assess whether there has been a reduction of the employers' requirements for the employees to work at the place where the person concerned is employed (see High Table Ltd v Horst and Others 1997). In this case the firm needs to use redundancy because of increasing financial pressures on the business. This may be a legitimate reason for making Stephen or Bebe redundant (ie the need for staff at the firm has diminished).

However, the law requires consultancy and an objective criteria for redundancy (see Williams v Compare Maxam Ltd 1982). The firm should also give as much warning as possible of the impending redundancies

The partners need to have criteria for selection: criteria such as attendance records, efficiency at the job and length of service can all be considered as part of the redundancy procedure.

Bebe is a good employee and Stephen seems to be a better choice for redundancy (given his attendance record and concerns over the quality of his work). However, if the partners cannot prove that an employee's redundancy was carried out using the correct procedure in conformity with good industrial relations practice then Stephen may have a claim for unfair dismissal. The partners should therefore ensure the selection process is fair.

> **Additional areas where credit might be given, note this is not an exhaustive list:**
> - Reference to relevant case law (particularly in relation to authority)
> - Further discussion of relevant redundancy regulations and procedure

5 Elliott Accountancy Limited

This question requires the students to discuss the allotment and transfer of shares.

(a) Directors can issue and allot new shares without authority from the company's shareholders where there is only one class of share in issue and where there is no relevant restriction in the company's articles of association – see s.550 Companies Act 2006.

s.550 applies to EA as a company incorporated on or after 1 October 2009 (EA was incorporated in January 2015).

EXAM ANSWER BANK

Unamended Model Articles for private companies limited by shares do not contain restrictions on director's authority to allot. EA's Model Articles are largely unamended and do not apply restrictions on this authority.

However, the statutory rights of pre-emption found in s561 Companies Act 2006 require these new shares to be offered first to EA's existing shareholders in the same proportion as they currently own shares in the company.

We can assume that EA's Model Articles do not disapply the statutory rights of pre-emption. This is because they are unamended except for one clause (which does not impact this issue). Therefore, these rights will either have to be waived by the existing members or disapplied in relation to this transaction by the members passing a special resolution in general meeting (s569 Companies Act 2006).

(b) Unamended Model Articles do not contain any restrictions on the transfer of shares (except for Model Article 26 which gives the directors discretion to refuse to register a transfer of shares).

However, the clause incorporated into EA's Model Articles gives existing shareholders rights of pre-emption on the transfer of any shares in the company.

This is similar to the statutory rights of pre-emption found in s561 Companies Act 1986, discussed above, which applies to the allotment of shares.

Michelle must therefore offer her shares to existing members of the company, who have a period of 21 days in which to decide whether to buy their proportion of the offer, before she can transfer her shares to Ellen.

If Michelle transfers her shares to Ellen without first offering those shares first to the other members of the company, then action could be taken against Michelle for breaching the articles of association. This action could be brought by either by EA or by the other members.

After offering her shares to existing shareholders, Michelle can then request approval from the board to transfer her shares to Ellen and follow the procedure for the transfer of shares

Additional areas where credit might be given, note this is not an exhaustive list:

- The meeting to dis-apply pre-emption rights needs to be held on 14 days notice s307 Companies Act 2006. However, this can be done by written resolution to avoid the need to hold a meeting
- Further relevant details of the procedure for allotting or transferring shares

November 2022

1 Busola

This question requires the student to apply knowledge of the formation of contract to the scenario, and specifically understand the law surrounding offer and acceptance. Assesses learning outcome 1.1. AIA 8 text Part A, chapter 2.

When Busola (B) wrote the letters he made an offer to sell the chairs to Nell (N), Rhys (R) and Maleka (M). An offer is a definite promise to be bound on specific terms. An offer can be defined as an express or implied statement of the terms on which the maker is prepared to be contractually bound if it is accepted unconditionally.

An offer may be made to one person, to a class of persons or to the world at large, and only the person, or one of the persons to whom it is made, may accept it. An offer must be distinguished from a statement which merely supplies information, a statement of intention (an auction), and from an invitation to treat. In B's letter he offered to sell a table to his customers for £1700. This demonstrates his willingness to be bound to specific terms (i.e. the price) if accepted. Generally in business situations it will be assumed that an offeror is willing to be bound by their offer.

The next step is therefore to consider whether there has been an acceptance of B's offer. If N, R or M have accepted his offer, a contract between B and each accepting party will come into effect, and B will be bound by each such contract. He will not be able to revoke his offer once it has been accepted. In order for an acceptance to be effective it must be communicated to the offeror. Acceptance may be communicated by express words, by action or inferred from conduct.

N emailed B; this is an acceptable form of communication (Entores v Miles Far Eastern Corporation). B reads the email on 11th November before he decides to revoke the offer. However, N's email does not contain an acceptance of the offer.

An acceptance must be an unqualified agreement to all the terms of the offer in order for the acceptance to result in a binding agreement. N did not accept the offer on the terms that were presented by B. She instead added in a further term, which was the reduction of the price of the table to £1500. As such there has been no acceptance of B's original offer of £1700.

By introducing new terms, N has effectively terminated B's offer by presenting a counter-offer. She has therefore only given 'a purported acceptance' by requesting a reduction of the price. A counter-offer is seen as a final rejection of the original offer (in Butler Machine Tool Co v Ex-cell-O Corp (England) 1979).

A counter-offer is effectively the making of a new offer. By making this new offer, N also rejects B's original offer. It is up to B whether or not to accept N's counter-offer. B is therefore not bound to sell the table to N for £1500.

R telephoned the shop and left a message for B on 7th November. His message was a 'mirror image' of B's offer (agreeing to pay £1700) and is therefore an acceptance to be bound on the same terms as B's offer.

At this point however the acceptance hasn't been communicated to B because he is on holiday.
The contract is formed when B returns to the shop on 11th November and listens to the message. It is then too late for B to revoke his offer, as he later tries to do. It does not matter that B has not responded to R's voicemail.

Regarding M, she sent her acceptance of the offer via a letter in the post (and like R, her acceptance was a mirror image of B's original offer). The postal rule states that where the use of the post is within the contemplation of both parties, the acceptance is complete and effective as soon as the letter is posted, even though it may be delayed or lost in the post (see Adams v Lindsell).

As B sent his original offer as a letter, it would be reasonable for M to respond via a letter. Under the postal rule, therefore, M accepted B's offer when she posted her letter on 8th November. Crucially, although B purported to withdraw his offer on 11th November, this would be ineffective, since by then M had accepted B's offer. The contract with M is formed when she posts the letter and as such B is bound to sell the table to M.

To summarise: B is in a binding contract with Maleka, Rhys and Gemma. Since he has only one table, he will inevitably breach his contracts with at least two of these (and be liable accordingly).

> **Additional areas where credit might be given, note this is not an exhaustive list:**
> - Discussion of remedies for the inevitable breaches of contract
> - Discussion of how B might, in practice, deal with the inevitable breaches – aiming to perform the contract most lucrative to him and to breach those contracts where the sanctions for doing so (legal and reputational) are least
> - Citation of relevant case law

2 Squires Limited

This question covers the removal and disqualification of directors and transfer of shares. Assesses learning outcome 3.4. AIA 8 text Part H, chapter 12 and Part I, chapter 16.

(a) There are no procedural requirements for a company to remove a director under the model articles. However, a company can remove a director under s168 of the Companies Act 2006 by ordinary resolution of the members. Special notice of the meeting at which the resolution will be put to the members must be given under s312 Companies Act 2006 (at least 28 days).

On receipt of the special notice, the company must send a copy to Zhiyun and inform him of his right to speak at the meeting and to circulate written representations prior to the meeting. The company will need a simple majority of those present and entitled to vote at the meeting to vote for the removal of Zhiyun in order to pass the resolution. This will be possible if the other shareholders (Ravneet, Henry and Patty – together 75%) vote in favour of the resolution as it is suggested that they will.

It is important to note that it is likely Zhiyun will have a service contract, and if the company removes him as a director before the end of his term, they may breach the service contract. This could result in claims for either wrongful, or unfair, dismissal, and would have financial implications for the company. However, it is also likely that the service contract will set out circumstances for early termination. The contract will need to be reviewed to ascertain whether Zhiyun's conduct satisfies any such provision.

(b) The company currently has model articles which do not contain any restrictions on the transfer of shares except for Model Article 26 which gives the directors discretion to refuse to register a transfer of shares.

To begin the transfer process, Zhiyun must execute a stock transfer form in respect of the shares he has agreed to sell to Henry and send this, together with the relevant share certificates, to Henry, who must pay stamp duty of ½% on the stock transfer form.

The stamped form can then be sent to the company together with the share certificates. The transfer must be put to the board of Squires for its formal approval.

The board then has two months to decide whether to approve the transfer. If the board does not take a decision refusing to register the transfer within the two-month period, the board then loses the right to do so.

If the transfer is approved, Henry must be sent a new share certificate within two months of the date upon which the stock transfer form was lodged with the company, s776 Companies Act 2006.

On the facts, there is no reason why the board would refuse to register the transfer, it is entirely in accordance with their wishes that Zhiyun is no longer involved in the business.

(c) The Company Directors Disqualification Act 1986 sets out the grounds upon which the court may make a disqualification order in relation to a director.

The act was partly introduced to prevent directors of failed companies being able to walk away with no personal liability and start a new company carrying on a similar business.

Therefore, most of the grounds relate to actions and the behaviour of directors during insolvency procedures, and convictions of serious offences.

Ordinary commercial misjudgement is generally insufficient to justify disqualification (although it might do so if the company became insolvent and the director was found to have been incompetent, especially if that incompetence were gross and contributed to the company's insolvency).

The fact that the other directors are dissatisfied with Zhiyun's commitment to the business, as he has failed to attend any of the last six board meetings and has missed numerous client meetings, does not satisfy any of the grounds for disqualification. His relationship with a rival company is also not enough to warrant disqualification (though there may be other legal complaints to pursue).

> **Additional areas where credit might be given, note this is not an exhaustive list:**
> - Discussion in relation to provisions of Model Article 18(a) and (f)
> - Mention of weighted voting rights on removal, or proceedings for unfair prejudice in relation to the removal
> - Citation of relevant case law or sections of pieces of regulations

3 Precision Accounting

This question requires an understanding of the concept of negligent misstatement. Assesses learning outcome 1.2. AIA 8 text Part B, chapter 5.

(a) Professional individuals and organisations have a special relationship with their clients and those who rely on their work. This is because they act in an expert capacity. The law of negligence has been refined in the case of professional advisers to form the tort of negligence which causes financial loss.

The English common law of negligent misstatements builds upon the principles laid down in Donoghue v Stevenson and Anns v Merton London Borough Council (i.e. duty of care). The liability for any negligent statement is however limited in scope to those people who have special relationships (Candler v Crane, Christmas & Co 1951).

It follows that a duty could not be owed to complete strangers. In Hedley Byrne & Co Ltd v Heller and Partners Ltd (1963) the test for a special relationship was developed. This test stated the following; if someone possessed of a special skill undertakes to apply that skill for the assistance of another person who relies on that skill, a duty of care will arise. A duty of care will also arise if, in a sphere in which a person is so placed that others could reasonably rely on his skill, a person takes it on himself to give information or advice to another person who, as he knows or should know, will place reliance on the information or advice.

It would be reasonable to assume that Precision Accounting would have a special skill, and as part of their service as accountants would use that skill in the assistance of others, who would reasonably rely on their skills as accountants to make financial decisions.

Whether Precision Accounting will owe a duty of care to Mega however rests upon whether they knew or should have known that Mega would place a reliance on the audit that they conducted on Kings Group. It is assumed that the accounts they prepared would have been meant solely for their clients, Kings Group. Therefore Mega would be a third party in this scenario.

Lord Denning in Candler however noted that accountants owe a duty of care not only to their own clients, but to all those whom they know will rely on their accounts in the transactions for which those accounts are prepared. In JEB Fasteners Ltd v Marks, Bloom & Co (1982) the court began to take account of third parties when reasonable foresight was present. Reasonable foresight, if established, would be enough to create a duty of care between third parties. Since this decision however the courts have shied away from the foresight test and have gone back to looking at whether the adviser has knowledge of the user and the use to which the statement will be put.

A significant case to the area of negligent misstatement is Caparo Industries plc v Dickman and Others (1990). This case changed the way in which negligent misstatements are assessed and is fundamental to the understanding of professional negligence. The facts of the case are similar to the scenario here and are essential to assessing whether Mega would be successful in their claim.

The court held that auditors in Caparo did not owe a general duty of care to the public at large. The auditor's duty of care does not therefore extend to potential investors nor to existing shareholders wishing to increase their stakes. This duty is only owed to the shareholders as a whole. Potential investors and existing shareholders wishing to purchase additional shares were therefore considered as the public at large, and held no special relationship with the auditors.

As such, Precision Accounting would not owe a duty of care to Mega as a potential investor. Therefore, Mega cannot claim for any loss which arose from Precision Accounting's negligent misstatement regarding Kings Group's finances, even if Mega relied on those statements when making a decision to takeover Kings Group.

(b) A duty of care of accountants is held to be higher when advising on matters such as takeovers than when auditing in general.

As noted above a duty will not be owed when a statement is prepared as part of an audit of the company or when a statement is prepared for general circulation. If Precision Accounting did make an express financial statement to Mega regarding the takeover of Kings Group, which they knew that they would rely upon when making this transaction, then PA would be liable.

The directors and financial advisors of the target company in a contested takeover bid owe a duty of care to a known bidder in respect of express representations made about financial statements prepared for the purpose of contesting the bid on which they know the bidder would rely (see Morgan Crucible Co plc v Hill Samuel Bank Ltd and others 1991). Therefore if the report was prepared by Precision Accounting for showing to Mega, Mega would have a claim for negligent misstatement and financial loss occurring from that particular report.

> **Additional areas where credit might be given, note this is not an exhaustive list:**
> - Discussion of relevant case law
> - Discussion of any contractual liabilities that might arise, in addition to those in tort

4 Reputatio

This question covers the topics of company incorporation, and pre-incorporation contracts. Assesses learning outcome 3.2. AIA 8 text Part, Chapter 11.

(a) It may be possible to incorporate Reputatio Limited, provided that there is no company with this name already on the register at Companies House.

However, the risk is that Reputation might bring a passing off action against Reputatio, alleging that the similarity between the companies' names is causing confusion in the minds of the public, particularly as the two companies operate a similar business in the same geographical area.

An injunction could be granted preventing Reputatio from using this name.

Alternatively, a complaint could be made to Companies House, alleging that the names are too similar, which may result in Reputatio being directed to change its name, s67(1) Companies Act 2006.

In addition, Reputation may apply to the Company Names Tribunal, alleging that Reputatio's name is too similar to its own and asking that a decision be made by the Company Names Adjudicator to require Reputatio to change its name.

To avoid these risks, Latifah and Sam could decide to incorporate the company with a different name.

Another option would be to conduct their business using a name different to that of their registered name, Reputatio ie. use a business or trade name. If they decide to do this, they must state the company's registered name on all documents used by the company, such as letters, invoices and receipts and it must be displayed at the company's business premises. Use of a different business name may not be enough to prevent a passing off action or an appeal to the Adjudicator by Reputation Limited.

(b) The employment contract signed by Latifah will constitute a pre-incorporation contract, as she has entered into the contract prior to the date of the certificate of incorporation and therefore before the company's legal existence.

A contract entered into by anyone purporting to be made by the company, but before the company comes into existence, will not bind the company. Therefore, Reputatio will not be bound by the employment contract with Kelly.

Instead, Latifah will be held personally liable for the contract (including the payment of any salary to Kelly) under s.51 Companies Act 2006. It does not matter that Latifah did not know the company had not been incorporated at the time she entered into the contract.

However, Latifah's personal liability is, according to s.51, 'subject to any agreement to the contrary'. In other words, Latifah will not be personally liable if it were agreed between her and Kelly that Latifah would not be personally liable. Would the words Latifah adds above her signature be treated as evidence of such an agreement? This seems unlikely, based on Phonogram v Lane [1982].

The contract cannot be ratified by Reputatio after incorporation because the company was not in existence at the time the contract was made. The company could agree with Latifah to indemnify Latifah against any liability Latifah might have towards Kelly. However, if Reputatio became insolvent, this indemnity would probably be worthless to Latifah. It would be better for Latifah if all parties (including Kelly) now agreed there could be a novation of the contract, under which Reputatio replaced Latifah as a party.

> **Additional areas where credit might be given, note this is not an exhaustive list:**
> - Restrictions on use of illegal or offensive company names
> - Use and discussion of relevant case law as supporting evidence

5 Haywood and Taseer Ltd

This question requires the understanding of voluntary and compulsory liquidation and the risks associated with continuing to trade when in financial difficulty. Assesses learning outcome 4.1 and 4.2. AIA Law AIA 8 text Part J and K.

(a) There are two types of winding up: a voluntary winding up, commenced by a resolution of the company's own shareholders (usually by 'special resolution', passed by 75%), and a compulsory winding up. The latter is usually commenced by a creditor of the company, and so is in a sense 'forced on' the company.

We can also differentiate two methods of voluntary winding up: a members', and a creditors', voluntary winding up. Both are commenced by a resolution of members.

However, in the case of a members' voluntary winding up, the directors make a 'declaration of solvency' – saying the company will be able to pay all its debts within 12 months (s108 Insolvency Act 1986). If the directors do not make such a declaration, then the winding up will be a creditors' voluntary winding up.

Certainly, there are big advantages in having a **members'** voluntary winding up. In such a winding up, the members of the company have most control over the winding up process. They choose the liquidator, and the liquidator acts for their benefit. They control the actions of the liquidator.

Creditors have little influence over what assets of the company are sold, at what price, and to whom. However, the directors' must be willing to make the declaration of solvency. And we could advise them that they must have reasonable grounds for making such a declaration, and that they would commit a criminal offence if they made the declaration without reasonable grounds.

If the company is wound up and all its debts are not paid, then there's a presumption the directors did not have reasonable grounds. Here, we are told the company is already in financial difficulties, and the directors clearly know this. So, there are certainly risks here for the directors in trying to make the declaration and have a members' voluntary winding up.

The directors could still choose to wind up the company voluntary, immediately, but not make the declaration, so the winding up would then be a *creditors'* voluntary winding up.

In fact, the procedures applying to a creditors' voluntary winding up are very similar to a compulsory winding up. Ultimately, the creditors can, if they want, control a creditors' voluntary winding up, just as they can control a compulsory winding up. In both cases, the creditors have the final say over who the liquidator will be. In both cases, a liquidation committee can be appointed to oversee the process of the winding up, and in both cases the creditors have ultimate control over the membership of that committee.

However, one important consideration for the directors in deciding whether to choose voluntary liquidation is that under a compulsory winding up employees are immediately dismissed.

This would mean that if an order for compulsory liquidation was made, not only would the directors' employment with the company immediately end, but so too would the employment of other individuals. If the directors chose a voluntary winding up of the company they, and other employees, would have more notice and therefore more time to find new employment.

The disadvantage of initiating a voluntary winding up immediately is that the company might be able to trade its way out of its present difficulties. If it were able to trade in this way, it might be able to avoid Huge Bank successfully presenting a petition for the compulsory winding up of the company.

(b) It is important to advise the directors of H&T about continuing to trade when in serious financial difficulty as they may be at risk of liability for 'wrongful trading'.

Under s.214 of the Insolvency Act 1986, a director is guilty of 'wrongful trading' where the director knew or ought to have known that the company had no reasonable prospect of avoiding insolvency and failed to take all steps to minimise the loss to creditors.

Usually, this will require directors to cease trading once insolvency becomes inevitable. If H&T was wound up, the directors could be liable for wrongful trading, for incurring further debts, such as borrowing further money to keep the business afloat.

The directors will be judged by a standard of reasonable competency taking into account any special expertise they have as directors (such as experience and qualifications). If found liable, they can be made to 'make such contribution to the assets of the company as the court thinks fit'.

Additional areas where credit might be given, note this is not an exhaustive list:

- A more detailed discussion of the grounds for a compulsory winding up, in part (a), to see how likely such a winding up is in the case of temporary cash flow problems
- Reference to the Corporate Insolvency and Governance Act 2020 – the dates in the scenario are vague but the pandemic is referred to and therefore this Act could be relevant.

May 2023

1 Sandra

This question requires the student to understand the formation of contracts and the law of mistake. Assesses learning outcome 1. AIA 8 text Part A, chapter 2 and 4.

Abdi is an agent for Khalid and Fast-Count. He quotes £150 to Sandra for the work to be completed. The statement sets out the price in certain terms (ie £150 for the service) and can be deemed to be an offer.

In order for Sandra to accept the offer she has to complete the client form by the end of the day, which she does. Is this a valid acceptance of Abdi's offer? Applying Hyde v Wrench (1840) acceptance has to be the mirror image of the offer.

Within Sandra's email she asks a question about the additional service (the filing of the accounts) – is this a counter offer? The answer is no, as it does not go to the core of the agreement. Sandra's question is just a request for further information. It doesn't seem likely that she would go elsewhere for the accountant services if the quote did not include filing.

The key question is whether Khalid, as the agent, can revoke the offer when he realises Abdi's mistake.

The general principle is that an offer can be revoked at any time before acceptance (Dickinson v Dodd (1876), Routledge v Grant (1828)).

As valid acceptance has been given by Sandra, Khalid cannot now revoke the offer and an agreement is therefore in place for the work to be completed for £150.

Khalid could, however, argue that the contract is void because there has been a mistake as to the terms of the agreement. Unilateral mistake is where one party is mistaken and the other is aware of it.

The facts seem to indicate that Abdi, as a new employee, did not understand the difference between the hourly rate and a comprehensive quote for the work to be carried out. He is mistaken about the correct quote.

But was Sandra aware of the mistake? Sandra as a new business owner did not seem to know how much the end of year accounts service should reasonably cost. There is also nothing in the facts to suggest that Sandra should have known that the quote was incorrect (Hartog v Colin & Shields (1939)).

But should she have reasonably known the cost of the service, as her friend did tell her what she might expect to pay (Centrovincial Estates v Merchant Investors (1983)). Sandra was also delighted with the £150 quoted and therefore may have understood it was a good deal. But, Fast-Count's website did indicate that they had competitive prices.

Generally, parties to a contract are not discharged from their obligations because they are mistaken as to the terms. If a mistake is found by the courts, then there is no contract (rather than a contract at a higher price). If there is no mistake, then there is a contract for the cost of £150.

> **Additional areas where credit might be given, note this is not an exhaustive list:**
> - Discussion of remedies for mistake
> - Citation of other relevant case law

2 Gemma, Neha and Tarik

This question considers the relationship between partners in a general partnership, the partnership agreement (the "deed") and requires the student to understand basic principles relating to agents, as well as the legal rights enjoyed by employees. Assesses learning outcome 1. AIA 8 text, chapters 6–9.

(a) A general partnership is governed by the Partnership Act 1890, which defines a partnership as 'the relation which subsists between persons carrying on a business with a view of profit' (section 1(1)).

Within a general partnership, if any terms are missing (ie who has certain decision making power), or there is no written agreement like in this scenario, there are rules in the Partnership Act 1890 that apply by default (eg s.24 presumption that profits will be divided equally between partners).

Neha and Tarik should be advised about Stephen's legal rights as an employee of the firm. Stephen would have the right to sue for wrongful dismissal, as a matter of common law. He would also have a broad set of rights under the Employment Rights Act 1996. Perhaps of greatest importance, these statutory rights would include the right to claim for unfair dismissal, and possible rights to redundancy payments in the event that Neha and Tarik decided to terminate Stephen's employment with the firm.

Gemma has actual authority by virtue of being a partner. This actual authority includes both any express authority given to her, or the implied authority conferred by s.5 Partnership Act 1890. This implied authority would likely include the authority to appoint Stephen as an employee of the firm. So, the firm (and therefore Neha and Tarik) will be bound by Stephen's employment contract (assuming he accepts Gemma's offer to be an employee).

However, by s.24(7) Partnership Act 1890, 'no person may be introduced as a partner without the consent of all existing partners'. Gemma will not, therefore, have the authority, alone, to decide that Stephen can become a partner.

(b) The Partnership Act 1890 specifies the rules which, in the absence of contrary agreement by partners, deal with the profit shares, and the authority, of partners. However, as a general rule, the partners can agree whatever terms they wish between themselves in respect of their rights and duties.

Under s.24(1), there is a presumption that profits will be split equally between the partner

The partners can (if Neha and Tarik insist) agree to change the 'default rule' in s.24(1) by agreeing some other profit-share instead, which would then exclude the rule in s.24(1). For evidential reasons, it would be best if this alternative agreement were in writing. This could be achieved by all four partners (including Stephen) entering into a formal Partnership deed, setting out the preferred profit share.

The position regarding Stephen's authority is a little more complex. Ordinarily, all partners have the same authority to manage the partnership and to bind the firm (s24(5) and s.24(8) Partnership Act 1890). The partnership deed could, however, specify that Stephen's authority to bind the firm is limited in some way (eg in terms of the value of contracts he has authority to make as agent for the firm). Stephen, as a party to the partnership agreement, would be bound by this term in the partnership contract.

However, Neha and Tarik need to understand that if Stephen, say, entered into a contract beyond his limited authority, the firm (and thus each individual partner) might still be bound by such a contract.

Although Stephen would not have express authority, he might still have implied authority, under s.5 Partnership Act 1890. The firm would not however be bound by such a contract if the other party to the contract actually knew of the limit on Stephen's authority.

Additional areas where credit might be given, note this is not an exhaustive list:

- Relevant discussion relating to the partnership deed, including suggestions on limiting Stephen's power/profit sharing.

- Relevant principles of agents/agency or relationships between partners not otherwise mentioned in regards to Gemma and Stephen, including other conditions for the operation of implied authority under s.5 PA 1890.

3 Arlo Designs Ltd

This question requires students to understand the principles of directors' general duties in the Companies Act 2006, particularly s.175 (conflict of interest), and s.172 (act to promote the success of the company)– and to apply them to the facts of the scenario to consider potential breaches. Assesses learning outcome 2. AIA 8 text, chapter 16 (specifically, topic 8).

The Companies Act 2006 sets out directors' general duties in s.171–s.177. These duties are owed to the company. If a director has breached a duty the shareholders may bring a derivative action in order to enforce the wrong doing.

The most obvious breach of duty by Yue is of the duty found in s.175 - to avoid conflicts of interests.

s.175 – duty to avoid conflicts of interest

Directors have a duty to avoid circumstances where their personal interests conflict or may conflict with the company's interests. This can occur when directors take advantage of opportunities that belong to the company (*Regal Hastings*).

The opportunity does not need to directly fall within the 'existing scope' of the company's own business. For example, in this scenario Arlo sells handmade cars whilst Carla's business involves motorcycles.

In *O'Donnell* v *Shanahan* (2009) a director was liable when he made a personal profit from pursuing an opportunity that he learned about as a director, to acquire certain property. The company had not engaged in property acquisition (its business being restricted to providing advice and assistance to others). The director was nevertheless held liable. So the fact that Arlo and Carla pursue different lines of business does not matter here.

Directors can breach s.175 if they make a profit merely in the course of being a director. Here, Yue has made a profit by investing in Carla's business whilst holding a directorship at Arlo.

Directors must not obtain any personal advantage from their position as directors without consent of the company for whatever gain or profit they obtain.

Yue did ask Beatrice's permission, and she agreed to his investment. Under s175(4), the board can now authorise a director's conflict of interest, preventing a breach of s175. However, for such an authorisation to be effective, it must be given by the board, at a quorate meeting, without counting the votes of the authorised-director. There is no such quorate board meeting here: merely a decision by a single director. So, Beatrice's permission to Yue does not prevent a breach of s175.

If Yue is found to have breached his duty, then he will be required to account for the profits obtained (under s.178).

s.172 Duty to promote the success of the company

The directors, when they decide whether to take up Carla's offer, are all under a duty to promote the success of the company for the benefit of the members'.

This is generally understood as requiring directors to maximise shareholder value. Foregoing a profitable investment seems to breach that duty. In working out what will 'promote the success of the company for the benefit of the members', the directors should have regard to environmental impacts. But, they should do so in order to work out what will actually maximise shareholder value. They should not allow environmental concerns to override the pursuit of shareholder value. If, even taking into account the environmental concerns, the investment in Carla's business would be profitable for Arlo, then this seems to be the decision required by s.172.

However, the duty in s.172 requires directors to act 'in good faith'. It is therefore a 'subjective one'. In assessing breaches of this duty the courts will therefore consider whether the director exercised their discretion bona fide in what they considered, not what the courts may consider, to be in the interests of the company (Re Smith and Fawcett Ltd).

So, if the directors can plausibly argue that they themselves believed that shareholder value would actually be enhanced by rejecting this opportunity (for example, because in the long term, the negative environmental impacts would eventually lose the shareholders money), then they will likely not be held to breach s.172.

Additional areas where credit might be given, note this is not an exhaustive list:

- Other relevant case law relating to s.175 or s.172 of Companies Act
- Relevant discussion of breach of s175 or s172
- Mention of possible relevance of duty of care and skill in s174
- Expansion on enforcement and derivative claims (but this is not to derail the discussion of breach)

4 Blaze Ltd

Students must demonstrate knowledge of the process for the allotment and transfer of shares, and the appointment of new directors. They must also apply these principles to the particular facts of the scenario. Assesses learning outcome 2. AIA 8 text, chapters 12 and chapter 16 (topic 2).

(a) Under the Companies Act 2006 shares are generally freely transferable but can be subject to restrictions contained within the company's articles (s.544).

Anvi will need to check Blaze's constitution because private companies usually do restrict the ability of their shareholders to transfer their shares.

However, we are told that Blaze has unamended model articles. The Model articles (like their predecessor, Table A) contain no restrictions on the right to transfer fully paid shares.

However, the directors may still refuse to register the transfer (article 26), so Anvi should discuss her plans with Kym, Jakub and Shelly to ensure there will be no issues.

If there is any outstanding payment for the shares Anvi should also ensure that she pays these so that the shares are fully paid up.

Once an agreement has been reached between Anvi and Crystal to transfer the shares, Anvi will hold the shares on trust for Crystal until the company registers the transfer.

Once Crystal, as the transferee, has made any agreed payment to Anvi for the shares, and Crystal's name is entered on the register of members, Anvi will cease to be a member and Crystal will acquire all the members rights.

(b) The appointment and process for a new director will depend on the articles of the company. Most companies' articles allow for the appointment of directors by an ordinary resolution of the shareholders and by a decision of the directors (Model article 17, Table A, articles 78 &79).

The company must, within 14 days, give notice to the Registrar of any change among its directors (ie once Anvi has left and a new appointment has been made).

The directors of Blaze can allot shares to the newly appointed director. The allotment of shares is the issue and allocation to a person of a certain number of shares under a contract of allotment. Where the allotment is by a private company, with only one class of share, then the directors have authority to make the allotment (s.550 Companies Act 2006). Those conditions would seem to be satisfied in the case of Blaze.

However, under s.561, new ordinary shares must be offered first to existing shareholders (pro-rata to their existing holdings). This pre-emption right will therefore need to be excluded by the shareholders.

Once shares are allotted and the holder is entered on the register of members the holder becomes a member of the company. The member is then issued with a share certificate.

> **Additional areas where credit might be given, note this is not an exhaustive list:**
> - Process for allotment or transfer of shares not otherwise stated
> - More detailed explanation of how the right of pre-emption could be excluded
> - Any other relevant information regarding appointment of directors

5 BoxBuilt plc

This question requires the understanding of administration and the risks associated with continuing to trade when in financial difficulty. Assesses learning outcome 2. AIA Law AIA 8, chapter 11 and 20.

(a) The process of administration begins with the appointment of an administrator who tries to rescue the company as a "going concern."

The administrator is an insolvency practitioner and is in control of the company with a goal of rescuing the company from insolvency. The administration order will provide breathing space from creditors and delays winding up. A company may survive an administration order but will not do so if it enters into liquidation.

An administrator can be appointed with or without a court order. The company or its directors can therefore appoint an administrator for BoxBuilt without going to court.

The process by which the company or directors will appoint an administrator depends upon BoxBuilt's constitution.

A company will generally be able to appoint an administrator if the company has not done so in the last 12 months and is unlikely to be able to pay its debts. There must also be no petition for winding up and the company must not be in liquidation.

The company(meaning the shareholders, by an ordinary resolution) and the directors can also appoint an administrator by applying for a court order. The court will grant the order if it is satisfied that the company is or is likely to be unable to pay its debts and that the order is reasonably likely to achieve the purpose of administration (i.e. rescue).

Once the administrator has been appointed a moratorium over the company's debts commences. The powers of management are subjugated to the administrator and they will only be able to act with their consent.

The administrator will propose a rescue plan or state if the company cannot be rescued. Administration can last up to 12 months and ends when it has been successful, or the administrator or creditors can apply to the court to end the order within 12 months.

(b) Directors are usually not personally liable for the debts of the company. Usually, the company alone is liable for its debts.

However, under s.214 of the Insolvency Act 1986, a director is guilty of 'wrongful trading' where the director knew or ought to have known that the company had no reasonable prospect of avoiding insolvent liquidation and failed to take all steps to minimise the loss to creditors.

Usually, this will require directors to cease trading once insolvent liquidation becomes inevitable. Putting BoxBuilt into administration does not prevent the directors being found liable for wrongful trading. However, given the protection which administration gives the company (because of the moratorium), the directors might then reasonably believe that insolvent liquidation is no longer inevitable – that the administration protection will allow BoxBuilt to trade its way out of its financial difficulties.

The directors will be judged by a standard of reasonable competency taking into account any special expertise they have as directors (such as experience and qualifications). If found liable, they can be made to 'make such contribution to the assets of the company as the court thinks fit'.

> **Additional areas where credit might be given, note this is not an exhaustive list:**
> - Relevant discussion of the process or impact of administration
> - Mention of the protection from wrongful trading afforded by the Company Insolvency and Governance Act 2020
> - Mention of other grounds on which directors might face liability, including fraudulent trading under s213 IA 1986 and for breach of their general duties to the company under ss171-177 Companies Act 2006

November 2023

1 Jenny

This question requires the students to understand the different types of breaches in contract law and apply the principles of *quantum meruit*.

See Chapter 3 of the AIA Law Text Book, syllabus reference 1.1.

(a) A contract is breached if one of the parties breaks one or more of the terms of the contract, or indicates in advance that they do not intend to perform the contract. In this scenario M&C has told Jenny that they are no longer able to complete her company accounts for the agreed date of 1 March 2023. This would therefore constitute a breach of the contract by M&C.

The type of breach here is an anticipatory breach. This has arisen because M&C, prior to the actual date of performance (1 March 2023), expressly informed Jenny that they did not intend to perform some or all of their contractual obligations.

Jenny is entitled to treat the contract as at an end at the time M&C indicated their intention not to complete the contract. As such, she will be able to recover damages for the loss of any benefit that she would have received if the contract had been performed.

This is similar to the case of Hochster v De La Tour where the defendant agreed to employ the claimant to act as a courier starting on 1 June. On 11 May, the defendant wrote to the claimant cancelling the contract by informing him that his services were no longer required. The claimant was able to immediately commence an action for breach of contract.

Jenny, as the innocent party, can sue before or after the date of performance because she was aware M&C intended to breach the contract. Jenny did not have to formally communicate acceptance of an anticipatory breach, i.e. she did not have to expressly inform M&C, at the time, that she was going to treat the contract as breached. But M&C must have been aware of Jenny's intention to treat the contract as at an end. This may have been the case considering Jenny had to find a new firm (at short notice) to complete her accounts.

Jenny was required to have taken steps to mitigate her losses. This means that a party cannot recover any losses which she could have avoided by taking reasonable steps.

Jenny did this by seeking out another accountancy firm to complete her end of year accounts before the deadline. As Jenny was informed by M&C of the anticipatory breach in February – there was still some time to mitigate some of the damage caused by M&C's breach of contract.

(b) Jenny does not have to pay M&C's invoice for the work they completed. Under the principals of quantum meruit, claims may be paid for work completed so far by one party, if total performance of a contract is prevented by the other party. In this scenario Jenny has not prevented the performance of the contract – M&C told Jenny that they can no longer finish the work because they are too busy. Therefore, Jenny does not have to pay M&C's invoice and may herself be entitled to damages.

> **Additional areas where credit might be given, note this is not an exhaustive list:**
> - Other relevant discussion of breach of contract (including evaluation of conditions and warranties)
> - Details of possible damages Jenny can claim

2 React Accountancy Ltd

This question requires the student to describe the process of liquidation, the different roles of liquidator and administrator, and demonstrate knowledge of the relevant sections of the Insolvency Act 1986.

See Chapters 20 & 21 of the AIA Law Text Book, syllabus reference 3.5 & 3.6.

(a) The 'winding up' of a company is the process of dealing with the assets and liabilities of the company prior to its dissolution. Winding up is also known as 'liquidation'. Directors, creditors or members may be involved in the decision to liquidate React Accountancy Ltd (RA). If Big Bank Plc (BB), as a creditor, has sufficient grounds they may apply to the court for the compulsory winding up of the company.

BB may primarily wish to apply to the court to wind up the company if RA is unable to pay its debts. Ss.122(1)(f) and s.123 of the Insolvency Act 1986 ('IA 1986') are particularly applicable here. This would be a compulsory winding up.

There are certain effects of an order for compulsory winding up. The Official receiver becomes liquidator (s.136 IA 1986); and the liquidation is deemed to have commenced at the time when the petition was first presented (see ss. 127, 128 and 130).

If the members (ie the shareholders of RA) decide to wind up the company, this may be addressed as a voluntary winding up. This may take place when the company is solvent (when it will be a 'members' voluntary winding up') or insolvent (a 'creditors' voluntary winding up'). In the latter case, creditors will have more control over the winding up process.

Members of RA may wish to wind up on a voluntary basis where the directors make a declaration of solvency, provided that there are reasonable grounds for their doing so. A special resolution (75%) of members will then be necessary to wind up. BB may also wish to have a creditors' voluntary liquidation if there is no declaration of solvency.

The main differences between the different parties commencement of 'winding up' is in the appointment of a liquidator: during the members' voluntary winding up members appoint, whereas in creditors' voluntary winding up, creditors appoint with responsibility to both members and creditors.

Additionally, in members' voluntary winding up there is no liquidation committee whereas there may be up to 5 representatives for creditors'; general meeting of members approve liquidators' action whereas in creditors' liquidation committee approves. In both kinds the court has the power to appoint a liquidator if both parties fail to do so (s. 108 Insolvency Act 1986)

The differences between compulsory and voluntary liquidation are control, timing, liquidator, legal proceedings and management and staff.

(b) A liquidator is appointed where a company is wound up (either via voluntary or compulsory methods). A liquidator takes the control of a company once the company goes under liquidation and must be an authorised and qualified insolvency practitioner. The main role is to wind up the company, and report to the Secretary of State where the director is unfit to run the company.

An administrator is appointed primarily to rescue the company as a going concern. An administrator may begin work with or without a court order. He has a fiduciary duty to and is an agent of the company and the creditors as a whole. He sends notice, publishes notice, obtains a list of company creditors, notice to registrar, receives a statement of affairs and considers these and manages the affairs of the company.

> **Additional areas where credit might be given, note this is not an exhaustive list:**
> - Further detail on differences between compulsory and voluntary liquidation
> - Further details of procedure of liquidation
> - Further details of appointment of Administrator

3 James and Katie

This question considers issues relating to unfair dismissal and the procedures for redundancy.

Chapter 9 of the AIA Law Textbook, syllabus reference 2.3.

Both James and Katie may each have a claim for unfair dismissal and could each receive compensation from a tribunal. To establish a claim for unfair dismissal against Lisa, their employer, James and Katie must demonstrate that they have a) been in continuous employment with that employer for a period of *two years*; b) have been *dismissed*; and c) have been *unfairly* dismissed.

James

Firstly, James has been employed by Lisa for over two years – as we know he has worked at her accountancy firm for three years. Therefore the first condition of unfair dismissal is satisfied.

Secondly, it is clear Lisa has indeed dismissed him, during the conversation in the office.

But, is the dismissal unfair? James has been dismissed due to his alleged conduct at work. Lisa may summarily dismiss James without notice if there has been a serious breach of his contract of employment (see Wilson v Racher 1974).

His conduct at work (breaking staff rules, such as coming in late, being rude to clients and allegedly verbally abusive to other staff members) may have amounted to such a breach.

In considering whether there was a breach there is a distinction in common law between gross misconduct and ordinary misconduct. Gross misconduct is action by the employee which can justify summary dismissal on the first occasion. Ordinary misconduct is not usually sufficient grounds for dismissal unless it is persistent.

Although James' conduct at work is unacceptable it may not amount to gross misconduct. The employment tribunal will review the circumstances of a dismissal to decide whether dismissing James was a reasonable response by Lisa to his actions (see Iceland Frozen Foods v Jones 1983). Determining whether Lisa acted reasonably in dismissing James, the tribunal will consider: whether the correct procedure was applied; whether Lisa took all circumstances into consideration; and what would any reasonable employer have done?

The Tribunal places emphasis on the employer giving one or more warnings to the employee before dismissing. This is so the employee has an opportunity to change their conduct or performance. We do not know if a proper disciplinary procedure has been followed by Lisa in the past or whether a previous warning has been given to James, though we have been told James has been known to be rude to clients.

Under the Employment Act 2008 Lisa will be required to follow ACAS's statutory code of Practice on Disciplinary and Grievance Procedures. Lisa will have therefore been expected to investigate the matter to establish the facts of the case; inform James of the problem and hold a meeting between James and herself to discuss the problem.

A decision must then be made regarding appropriate action to be taken. It would not be reasonable for Lisa to dismiss James without first warning him that if his conduct continues, or he repeats his behaviour he is likely to be dismissed (see Newman v T H White Motors 1972).

James' claim for unfair dismissal will therefore hinge on whether Lisa can justify her immediate dismissal. James would have to show that he has not been previously warned about his conduct at work and that Lisa did not properly investigate James' claim that he is verbally abusive to employees (which it is unlikely that she did because Lisa dismissed James after hearing Katie's accusation).

Katie

With regard to Katie, she seems to face two problems. The first is that we cannot be sure she has been continuously employed by Lisa for two years prior to her dismissal. We only know that her employment commenced at some time in September 2021 and that Lisa informs her of her redundancy at some point in September 2023. Therefore she will need to carefully consider the dates of both of these events in order to establish the time frame for unfair dismissal.

Second, her dismissal will not be considered unfair if it was genuinely for reasons of redundancy. Katie's dismissal will be treated as a lawful redundancy if the only or main reason she was dismissed was because: her employer has ceased, or intends to cease, to carry on the business in which she has been employed; or the requirements of that business for employees to carry on the work done by her have ceased or diminished. In Katie's case Lisa has said that she is being made redundant because of 'increasing financial pressures on the business.' This may be a legitimate reason for making Katie redundant (i.e. the need for staff at the accountancy firm has diminished), as in High Table Ltd v Horst and Others 1997.

However the law requires consultancy and an objective criteria for redundancy (see Williams v Compare Maxam Ltd 1982). It is not clear that this process has been carried out by Lisa. Katie is a hard working employee and other staff members seem like they would be a better choice for redundancy. If Lisa cannot prove that Katie's redundancy was carried out using the correct procedure in conformity with good industrial relations practice then she may have a claim for unfair dismissal.

> **Additional areas where credit might be given, note this is not an exhaustive list:**
> - Further discussion or application of relevant case law
> - Further details or discussion of the redundancy procedure or criteria
> - Explanation or details of damages

4 Hill and Qin

This question covers incorporation of a private limited company and the company's accounting obligations. AIA text Chapter 10 & 11, syllabus reference 3.1 & 3.2.

(a) To incorporate HQL, Form IN01 must be completed and submitted to Companies House. This form contains details of the company's name, the situation of its registered office, the type of company it is to be incorporated as, its initial share capital, its first directors, its initial subscribers and a statement of the company's compliance with the provisions of the Companies Act 2006 (the Companies Act).

A copy of the company's memorandum should also be sent to Companies House. If HQL wanted to use a bespoke set of articles or to modify the provisions of the Model Articles, these would also need to be sent to Companies House, but as HQL wants Model Articles (unamended), this is not necessary.

The appropriate fee should accompany the documents.

The Registrar of Companies will issue a Certificate of Incorporation provided the documents are in order. The number which appears on the Certificate of Incorporation is HQL's unique company number and the date on the certificate is the date that HQL legally comes into existence.

Before incorporation, the register of names at Companies House should be checked to make sure that the name, HillQin Limited, is not the same as that of an existing company or that it is not too similar to that of an existing company. If the former is the case, HQL will not be registered (s.66 Companies Act). If the latter is the case, although it will be possible to register HQL, the existing company with the similar name may complain to the Registrar of Companies who may direct HQL to change its name.

(b) For each accounting reference period, the directors of HQL must prepare accounts for its members and file them with the Registrar of Companies. Where they are prepared in Companies Act format, they must include a balance sheet and a profit and loss account, to give a true and fair view of the company's assets, liabilities, financial position and profit or loss for the accounting reference period up to the accounting reference date (s.396 Companies Act). The board of directors must approve the annual accounts and they must be signed by a director on behalf of the board.

A company is permitted to file abbreviated accounts with the Registrar of Companies if it is classed as "small" by satisfying two or more of the following conditions:

- Annual turnover must be not more than £6.5million.
- The balance sheet total must be not more that £3.26million.
- The average number of employees must be not more than 50.

HQL satisfies all three conditions and can therefore choose either to file a copy of the full accounts prepared for its members or to file an abbreviated version. Filing must be within nine months of the end of the accounting period.

As a small company, HQL will also be exempt from the requirement to appoint auditors and produce an audit report.

> **Additional areas where credit might be given, note this is not an exhaustive list:**
> - Discussion of "micro-entities" and whether HQL would qualify

5 Black Gold Plc

This question requires students to understand the principles of directors' general duties in the Companies Act 2006, particularly s.174 (duty of care, skill and diligence), and s.172 (act to promote the success of the company) and to apply them to the facts of the scenario to consider potential breaches. It also requires students to identify the derivative claim as the mechanism by which shareholders enforce these breaches.

Chapter 16 of AIA Law text book, assesses syllabus reference 3.4.

The Companies Act 2006 sets out directors' general duties in ss.171–177. These duties are owed to the company.

The two most relevant duties, which the directors might have breached, are the duties found in s.172 (to promote the success of the company) and s.174 (to act with care, skill and diligence).

s.172 Duty to promote the success of the company

The directors of Black Gold are all under a duty to promote the success of the company for the benefit of the members. This is generally understood as requiring directors to maximise shareholder value, which the directors of Black Gold clearly have done (having announced an annual record profit).

In working out what will 'promote the success of the company for the benefit of the members', the directors should have regard to environmental impacts per s.172(1)(d). But, they should do so in order to work out what will actually maximise shareholder value. They should not allow environmental concerns to override the pursuit of shareholder value.

If, even taking into account Margot's environmental concerns, the current production and sale of fossil fuels has been profitable and a move away from this has to be a considered one, as this seems to be the decision required by s.172.

However, the duty in s.172 requires directors to act 'in good faith', which requires a subjective assessment. The courts will therefore consider whether the director exercised their discretion bona fide in what they considered, not what the courts may consider, to be in the interests of the company *(Re Smith and Fawcett Ltd)*.

So, if the directors can plausibly argue that they themselves believed that shareholder value would be damaged by pursuing environmental concerns too quickly and that the progress made to date is reasonable then they will likely not be held to have breached s.172.

s.174 – to exercise reasonable care, skill and diligence

Margot may also be able to argue that the directors have breached s.174 – the duty to exercise reasonable care, skill and diligence.

This means the care, skill and diligence that would be exercised by a reasonably diligent person with: the general knowledge, skill and experience that may reasonably be expected of a person carrying out the functions of a director in relation to the company, and; the general knowledge, skill and experience that the director has (s.174(2)). This is approached by the courts in both an objective and subjective manner.

As with s.172, demonstrating a breach of this duty is difficult. This is because the courts are reluctant to find directors liable for breaching this duty, and are often cautious about judging directors harshly when making business decisions.

If a director has breached a duty, the shareholders may bring a derivative claim under s.260 of the Companies Act in order to enforce the wrong doing.

A derivative claim is a claim brought by one or more shareholders, but "on behalf of the company." It is used to enforce breaches of directors' duty owed to the company. Margot may use this form of action to pursue potential breach of the directors of Black Gold in relation to its environmental strategies.

However, if Margot did start this type of claim, she would have to get the permission of the court to be permitted to continue this claim. There are a number of factors the court must take into account when deciding whether to give permission. Recent litigation suggests the court might be reluctant to give permission.

> **Additional areas where credit might be given, note this is not an exhaustive list:**
> - Discussion of relevant case law
> - Relevant discussion put forward for other breaches of duty under the Companies Act
> - Further relevant explanation or discussion of s.172, s.174 or derivative claims

Mock exam questions

MOCK EXAM QUESTIONS

Question 1

Printers4U Ltd, a printer dealer, agreed to sell to Terry the only new ultra-light XX printer that it had in stock, at the retail price of £1,500, for delivery on August 1. On that day Terry tendered payment but Printers4U Ltd refused to deliver the printer to her unless she paid the new recommended price of £1,750.

Required

(a) Advise Terry what remedies will be available to her. **(8 marks)**

Also: explain how your answer would differ in each of the following alternative circumstances:

(b) No other ultra-light XX printer is available from any alternative supplier and their production has ceased, but Terry wished to purchase one because she thought its value was likely to increase.
(6 marks)

(c) One other new ultra-light XX printer is available for £1,750 and two second hand ultra-light XX printers are available for £1,600 each. **(6 marks)**

(Total = 20 marks)

Question 2

(a) Explain what is meant by 'vicarious liability' in the law of torts and why the law imposes this liability on employers. **(5 marks)**

(b) Explain in what circumstances an employer will be vicariously liable for injuries caused by those who are working for the employer. **(15 marks)**

(Total = 20 marks)

Question 3

Sprayfinishing Solutions is a successful business providing industrial spray-painting services. The business has been operating as a partnership for the last five years. The two partners, Jed Baker and Tim Gregson, both work full time in the business and employ a team of 25 painters and 5 administrative staff. Over the last 12 months, Sprayfinishing Solutions has secured a number of large contracts and Jed and Tim have decided that the expanding business should become a limited liability company trading as Sprayfinishing Solutions Limited (SSL). The turnover of the business is in the region of £1.5 million and its balance sheet total is approximately £750,000. Current projections suggest that both measures will increase by approximately 20% over the next 12 months.

Jed and Tim have decided that the company will be incorporated with Model Articles (unamended) and ordinary shares of £1 each. They will each own one share and both be appointed as directors of the company.

Required

(a) Advise Jed and Tim as to the procedures that should be followed to incorporate SSL and what checks should be made before doing so. **(10 marks)**

(b) Advise Jed and Tim what SSL's obligations will be in relation to the production and filing of accounts and whether SSL will need to appoint an auditor. **(7 marks)**

(c) Jed and Tim explain that there have been issues in the past where Jed has spent large sums of money on machinery or supplies without consulting Tim. They have agreed that they want to keep a tight rein on finances and that in future they must both agree on any purchases in excess of £20,000. Advise Jed and Tim as to how an individual director's expenditure can be restricted.
(3 marks)

(Total = 20 marks)

Question 4

(a) Gerard Rimes is a shareholder in Vinematters Limited (Vinematters), a fine wine importing company. He is concerned by the limited financial information about the company which he receives. All he recalls receiving in the last twelve months is a summary financial statement.

Required

Advise Gerard on the obligations of Vinematters in relation to the preparation of accounts and the procedures required to approve these accounts. Vinematters is not a small or medium sized company. **(14 marks)**

(b) Gerard is also a minority shareholder in Wineworld plc (Wineworld) and is considering purchasing a controlling interest on the basis of encouraging results and potential further growth shown in Wineworld's latest annual accounts. Gerard waits for the accounts to be approved at Wineworld's AGM and then purchases the shares. Four months later Wineworld is declared insolvent and it is discovered that the accounts approved at the AGM were inaccurate and contained misleading statements.

Required

Advise Gerard as to whether he has a claim against the auditors of Wineworld. **(6 marks)**

(Total = 20 marks)

Question 5

In 2015, Yew Tree Ltd borrowed a large sum of money from Coffee Bank Plc. The loan was secured, in part, by a floating charge over certain assets of Yew Tree. However, Yew Tree's financial situation has recently worsened, due to the economic crisis, and it has begun to default in repaying the loan to Coffee Bank.

Required

(a) Explain whether Yew Tree may be wound up as a result of its financial situation, and if so, by whom. **(12 marks)**

(b) Explain the different roles of administrator and liquidator. **(8 marks)**

(Total = 20 marks)

Mock exam answers

Question 1

(a) A good answer should start with the remedies available to the buyer (ss.51-53). This will depend upon the nature of the breach by the seller and the nature of the goods: Remedies will be (a) *Damages* – this is the normal remedy available to a buyer either where the breach is non-delivery (see s.51) or for breach of warranty (s.53). The measure of damages in each case is the estimated loss directly and naturally resulting in the ordinary course of events from the seller's breach of contract (cf. *Hadley v Baxendale* [1854]), for example, in the case of a breach of warranty the difference between the value of the goods delivered and the value if they had fulfilled the warranty – see s.53(3). (b) *Special damages* – a buyer's right to recover damages for consequential loss under the general law (the second limb of *Hadley v Baxendale*) is preserved by s.54. Thus, where a defect in a pig-feeder caused the death of pigs the buyer was entitled to recover for this loss (*Parsons (Livestock) Ltd v Uttley, Ingham & Co Ltd* [1978]) (c) *Rejection* – where the breach is of a condition of the contract (eg that the goods will correspond to a sample under s.15) the buyer is generally entitled to repudiate the contract and reject the goods although a non-consumer buyer cannot do so where the breach is so slight that it would be unreasonable for them to reject them (s.15A). (d) *Specific performance* – under s.52 a buyer may be awarded specific performance of the contract where the buyer has failed to deliver specific or ascertained goods. This is an equitable remedy and is therefore discretionary. It will be available only where the goods are in some way unique and damages would not be an adequate remedy.

Terry and Printers4U Ltd have created a contract whereby Printers4U has agreed to transfer the property in a specific good (since Printers4U has only one XX printer – see s.61(1)) for the price of £1,500. This is an agreement to sell under the SGA – see s.2(5). S.51(1) provides that where a seller wrongfully refuses to deliver the goods to a buyer the buyer may maintain an action for damages against the seller. In addition, s.52(1) gives the court discretion to order specific performance as a remedy for breach of a contract to deliver specific goods.

(b) It seems that the appropriate remedy may be specific performance rather than damages. However, the courts tend to be reluctant to make an order for the seller to perform their obligation to deliver up the goods. Terry may argue that the printer is unique since no other printer of its description can be bought. Printers4U might argue that although there are no other XX printers available the subject matter of the contract is not unique since other printers in the same category (eg small and light) are available. The fact that Terry appears to be interested in the contract as a profit-making venture would add weight to Printers4U's argument here. If Terry is limited to damages as a remedy the measure of damages is the estimated loss directly and naturally resulting, in the ordinary course of events, from the seller's breach of contract (s.51(2)).

(c) A remedy in damages is appropriate because Terry can buy the same goods elsewhere, albeit at a higher price, so specific performance would not be available. The measure of damages where there is an available market for the goods in question 'is prima facie to be ascertained by the difference between the contract price and the market or current price of the goods at the time or times when they ought to have been delivered' (s.51(3)). Although Terry is under a duty to mitigate her loss this would not require her to buy a second hand printer and so she is entitled to damages in the sum of £250, the difference between the agreed contract price and the market price.

Question 2

(a) This question involves the law of torts. Torts are wrongful acts against an individual, a company or their property that give rise to a civil liability against the person who committed them. There are a number of torts including negligence, trespass, defamation and nuisance. A tortfeasor will be liable for torts committed by her. However, in some cases, another party will be held liable for the tort committed by the tortfeasor. This liability is known as vicarious liability.

An employer can be liable for the torts committed by their employees in the course of their employment under the principle of vicarious liability. It is often not worthwhile to sue the individual employee for damages since they will probably be unable to pay them. The employer will usually have greater resources, and as such is more likely to have 'deep pockets', and may also have insurance cover. This can mean that, by holding an employer vicariously liable, losses can be spread around, or 'distributed' amongst, a larger group who each bear only a small part of the total loss. Another rationale for being able to bring a claim of this nature is that by bringing a claim against an employer it may also promote prevention of accidents and it is a method of making the employer pay for the true cost of their activity.

(b) The courts have been known in the past to apply this principle widely. Thus, even where an employee is acting illegally or with gross negligence, the employer has been found vicariously liable. In order to establish vicarious liability, however, there must firstly be an employee/employer relationship and a close connection between the employee's tort and their employment, and whether this is in fact the case must be decided by the facts of each case (eg *Dubai Aluminium v Salaam; Attorney General v Hartwell*).

In order for vicarious liability to apply, it is necessary to establish two things. Firstly, it needs to be established that the tort was committed by an employee and not an independent contractor. The distinction here is between a person under a contract of service (employee) and a person under a contract for services (independent contractor). In practice this distinction depends on many factors, and it can be very important to know whether an individual is an employee or an independent contractor. The courts will therefore apply a series of tests. In applying these tests the courts will primarily look at the reality of the situation and also the agreement between the parties. The tests include the tests of control (where the courts will consider whether the employer has control over the way in which the employee performs their duties), integration into the employer's organisation (here the courts consider whether the employee is so skilled that they cannot be controlled in the performance of their duties, this lack of control indicates that an employee is not integrated into the employer's organisation and therefore not an employee), and economic reality (and here the court considers whether the employee was working on their own account). Some of the other relevant factors which are considered when deciding whether a person is an employee is whether the worker uses their own equipment, does the employer have the power to select or appoint its employees, payment of a salary would also indicate that the tortfeasor is an employee, and whether Christian the tortfeasor works for a number of different people would be something the court would consider.

Secondly, the tort must have been committed by an employee in the course of their employment and not as a result of doing something which falls outside that employment (when they is 'on a frolic of their own'). The question of which 'acts' fall within the relevant employment is one in which there has been considerable litigation. The courts have drawn a distinction between an employee's act which was a wrongful method of carrying out something they were authorised to do, and one which they were not authorised to perform. Thus, a school warden's abuse of children under his care led to the vicarious liability of the school in *Lister v Hesley Hall*. Off-duty situations are also covered under the employer's vicarious liability as in *Ministry of Defence v Radcliffe*. However, where a bus conductor drives a bus, the employer will not be not liable because the conductor is not authorised to drive the bus.

Question 3

(a) To incorporate Sprayfinishing Solutions Limited (SSL), Form IN01 must be completed and submitted to Companies House. This form contains details of the company's name, the situation of its registered office, the type of company it is to be incorporated as, its initial share capital, its first directors, its initial subscribers and a statement of the company's compliance with the provisions of the Companies Act 2006.

A copy of the company's memorandum should also be sent to Companies House. If SSL wanted to use a bespoke set of articles or to modify the provisions of the Model Articles, these would also need to be sent to Companies House, but as SSL want Model Articles (unamended), this is not necessary.

The appropriate fee should accompany the documents.

The Registrar of Companies will issue a Certificate of Incorporation provided the documents are in order. The number which appears on the Certificate of Incorporation is SSL's unique company number and the date on the certificate is the date that SSL legally comes into existence.

Before incorporation, the register of names at Companies House should be checked to make sure that the name, Sprayfinishing Solutions Limited, is not the same as that of an existing company or that it is not too similar to that of an existing company. If the former is the case, SSL will not be registered (s 66 Companies Act 2006). If the latter is the case, although it will be possible to register SSL, the existing company with the similar name may complain to the Registrar of Companies who may direct SSL to change its name.

(b) For each accounting reference period, the directors of SSL must prepare accounts for its members and file them with the Registrar of Companies. Where they are prepared in Companies Act format, they must include a balance sheet and a profit and loss account, to give a true and fair view of the company's assets, liabilities, financial position and profit or loss for the accounting reference period up to the accounting reference date (s 396 Companies Act 2006). The board of directors must approve the annual accounts and they must be signed by a director on behalf of the board.

A company is permitted to file abbreviated accounts with the Registrar of Companies if it is classed as 'small' by satisfying two of the following conditions:

- Annual turnover must be not more than £10.2million
- The balance sheet total must be not more that £5.1million
- The average number of employees must be not more than 50

SSL satisfies all three conditions and can therefore choose either to file a copy of the full accounts prepared for its members or to file an abbreviated version. Filing must be within nine months of the end of the accounting period.

As a small company, SSL will also be exempt from the requirement to appoint auditors and produce an audit report.

(c) Directors' expenditure can be restricted in the company's articles. This would require SSL to incorporate with a modified version of the Model Articles incorporating an appropriate special article or to amend the articles after incorporation by special resolution (s 21 Companies Act 2006). Alternatively, the directors could pass a resolution at a board meeting to the same effect which would be noted in the company's board minutes.

Question 4

(a) Under the Companies Act 2006 a company has a duty to keep accounting records which are sufficiently adequate to explain the company's transactions and its financial position so that financial statements can be prepared s 386.

The directors are obliged to ensure that annual accounts for the company are prepared showing a true and fair view, the accounts must be laid before the members and then filed with the Registrar of Companies. S 396 provides that the annual accounts must comprise of a balance sheet that gives a 'true and fair view' of the financial position of the company at the end of the financial year and a profit and loss account that gives a 'true and fair view' of the profit or loss for the financial year in question.

In addition to the accounts, the directors must prepare a directors' report to accompany the accounts (s 415) containing details of all directors during the financial year, the principal activities of the company during the year and the amount of any dividend recommended by the directors. The directors must also produce a 'business review' which is an analysis of the company's performance and the risks that it may be facing (s 417). This review gives the shareholders an opportunity to assess how well the directors have fulfilled their duty to promote the success of the company contained in s 172.

Under s 475 the accounts must be audited by auditors appointed annually by the company. The auditors must prepare a report on the accounts confirming the content complies with accounting standards and that the accounts give a true and fair view of the financial state of the company.

The accounts must be approved by the board and signed off. Copies together with a copy of the auditor's report must be sent to all shareholders (s 423). The accounts must be submitted to the Registrar of Companies and copies to shareholders no later than nine months after the end of the accounting period for the company.

The Company can send members a summary financial statement rather than full copies of the reports and accounts (s 426) however a member has the right to request a copy of the full accounts so Gerard can request a copy of the full accounts.

(b) Gerard had no contract with the auditors of Wineworld so he can only sue them in the tort of negligence, not in contract.

Gerard relied upon the accounts laid at the AGM but to sue for economic loss he needs to establish a fiduciary relationship *Hedley Byrne v Heller & Partners* [1964]. The House of Lords decided in *Caparo Industries v Dickman and others* [1991] that the auditors' relationship with individual shareholders was not enough to give rise to a duty of care to shareholders as potential purchasers. It would have done so only if, at the time of signing their report, the auditors were aware of the shareholder's interest.

The auditors were not aware of Gerard's interest since he had not finally decided to make the purchase so he has no claim against the auditors of Wineworld.

Question 5

(a) Liquidation means that the company must be dissolved and its affairs wound up. Directors, creditors or members may be involved in the decision to liquidate. If a creditor has sufficient grounds they may apply to the court for the compulsory winding up of the company. If the members decide to wind up the company, this may be addressed as a voluntary winding up. This may take place when the company is solvent or insolvent where in the latter case creditors may be involved as well. The main differences are that in the appointment of liquidator during the members' voluntary winding up members appoint, whereas in creditors' voluntary winding up creditor approval of the members' nomination for the choice of liquidator is required; in members' voluntary winding up there is no liquidation committee whereas there may be up to five reps in creditors'; general meeting of members approve liquidators' action whereas in creditors' liquidation committee approves. In both kinds the court has the power to appoint a liquidator if both parties fail. s 108 IA 1986.

Members of Yew Tree may wish to wind up on a voluntary basis where the directors may make a declaration of solvency provided that there are reasonable grounds for their doing so. A special resolution (75%) may be necessary to wind up. Coffee Bank may also wish to have a creditors' voluntary liquidation if there is no declaration of solvency.

However, Coffee Bank may primarily wish to apply to the court to wind up the company if Yew Tree is unable to pay its debts. ss122(1)(f) and s123 are particularly applicable.

There are certain effects of an order for compulsory winding up. Official receiver becomes liquidator s136; the liquidation is deemed to have commenced at the time when the petition was first presented; discussion of ss127, 128 and 130; the effect of compulsory liquidation on employees and the floating charge crystallises and becomes a fixed charge.

The differences between compulsory and voluntary liquidation are control, timing, liquidator, legal proceedings and management and staff. These differences need to be discussed.

(b) Coffee Bank may also wish to appoint an administrator as a floating chargeholder. The conditions to appoint an administrator need to be discussed. A liquidator takes the control of a company once the company goes under control and must be an authorised and qualified insolvency practitioner. The main role is to wind up the company, report to the Secretary of State where the director is unfit to run the company.

An administrator is appointed primarily to rescue the company as a going concern. An administrator may begin work with or without a court order. They have a fiduciary duty and is an agent of the company and the creditors as a whole. They send notice, publishes notice, obtains a list of company creditors, notice to registrar, receives a statement of affairs and considers these and manages the affairs of the company.

MOCK EXAM ANSWERS

Bibliography

Bibliography

Bribery Act 2010. (2010). London, TSO.

Civil Aviation Act 1982. (1982). London, HMSO.

Civil Liability (Contribution) Act 1978. (1890). London, HMSO.

Companies (Audit, Investigation and Community Enterprise) Act 2004. (2004). London, TSO.

Companies Act 2006. (2006). London, TSO.

Company Directors Disqualification Act 1986. (1986). London, HMSO.

Constitutional Reform Act 2005. (2005). London, TSO.

Consumer Rights Act 2015. (2015). London, TSO.

Contagious Diseases (Animals) Act 1869. (1869). London, HMSO.

Contracts (Rights of Third Parties) Act 1999. (1999). London, TSO.

Criminal Finances Act 2017. (2017). London, TSO.

Criminal Justice Act 1993. (1993). London, HMSO.

Defamation Act 2013. (2013). London, TSO.

Employment Act 2002. (2002). London, TSO.

Employment Act 2008. (2008), London, TSO.

Employment Relations Act 1999. (1999). London, TSO.

Employment Rights Act 1996. (1996). London, TSO.

Employment Tribunals (Constitution and Rules of Procedure) Regulations 2013. (2013) SI 2013/1237. London, TSO.

Enterprise Act 2002. (2002). London, TSO.

Enterprise and Regulatory Reform Act 2013. (2013). London, TSO.

Equality Act 2010. (2010). London, TSO.

Factories Act 1961. (1961). London, HMSO.

FCA (2024). Office for Professional Body Anti-Money Laundering Supervision (OPBAS). [Online]. Available from: www.fca.org.uk/opbas [Accessed 17 July 2024].

Financial Services and Markets Act 2000. (2000). London, TSO.

Fraud Act 2006. (2006). London, TSO.

Gov.uk (2024). Benefit cap: number of households capped to November 2023 2024. [Online]. Available from: https://www.gov.uk/government/statistics/benefit-cap-number-of-households-capped-to-november-2023/benefit-cap-number-of-households-capped-to-november-2023#:~:text=The%20benefit%20cap%20levels%20were,no%20children)%20in%20Greater%20London [Accessed 17 July 2024].

Gov.uk (2024). Guidance and methodology: Benefit expenditure and caseload tables. [Online]. Available from: https://www.gov.uk/government/publications/benefit-expenditure-and-caseload-tables-information-and-guidance/benefit-expenditure-and-caseload-tables-information-and-guidance [Accessed 17 July 2024].

Health and Safety at Work Act 1974. (1974). London, HMSO.

Human Rights Act 1998. (1998). London, TSO.

Infrastructure Act 2015. (2015). London. TSO.

BIBLIOGRAPHY

Insolvency Act 1986. (1986). London, HMSO.

Law Reform (Frustrated Contracts) Act 1943. (1943). London, HMSO.

Limitation Act 1980. (1980). London, HMSO.

Limited Liability Partnership Act 2000. (2000). London, TSO.

Limited Partnership Act 1907. (1907). London, TSO.

Married Women's Property Act 1882. (1882). London, HMSO.

Misrepresentation Act 1967. (1967). London, HMSO.

Money Laundering Regulations 2017. (2017) SI 2017/692. London, TSO.

National Minimum Wage Act 1998. (1998). London, TSO.

Partnership Act 1890. (1890). London, HMSO.

Proceeds of Crime Act 2002. (2002). London, TSO.

Public Interest Disclosure Act 1998. (1998). London, TSO.

Rehabilitation of Offenders Act 1974. (1974). London, HMSO.

Road Traffic Act 1972. (1972). London, HMSO.

Small Business, Enterprise and Employment Act 2015. (2015). London, TSO.

Theatres Act 1968. (1968). London, HMSO.

Torts (Interference with Goods) Act 1977. (1977). London, HMSO.

Trade Union and Labour Relations (Consolidation) Act 1992. (1992). London, HMSO.

Unfair Contract Terms Act 1977. (1977). London, HMSO.

Unsolicited Goods and Services Act 1971. (1978). London, HMSO.

Working Time Regulations 1998. (1998) SI 1998/1833. London, TSO.

Contains public sector information licensed under the Open Government Licence v3. www.nationalarchives.gov.uk/doc/open-government-licence/version/3/

Index

> Note. **Key Terms** and their page references are given in **bold**

Acceptance, 23
Acceptance of a tender, 25
Acceptance 'subject to contract', 24
Accounting records, 380
Accounting reference date, 244
Acquisitions by cash, 274
Acquisitions by share exchange, 274
Action for the price, 71
Actual authority, 148
Adequacy, 33
Administration, 416
Administrative receiver, 421
Adoption leave and pay, 186
Advertisements, 19
Affirmation after repudiatory breach, 64
Agency, 144
Agency law and directors, 348
Agency relationships, 144
Agency workers, 176
Agent by estoppel, 146
Agent by necessity, 146
Agent liability, 150
Allotment of shares, 268
Allotted share capital, 262
Alternate directors, 336
Annual accounts, 380
Ante-natal care, 186
Anticipatory breach, 63
Apparent authority, 348
Apparent/ostensible authority, 148
Appeal court, 4
Appointment of a company secretary, 362
Appointment of directors, 338
Articles, 241
Assault, 110
Auction sales, 19
Auctioneers, 144
Auditor, 320
Auditor remuneration, 385
Authorised share capital, 261
Authority of directors, 347
Authority of partners, 161
Authority of the agent, 146
Authority of the Chief Executive Officer (CEO), 348
Automatically fair reasons for dismissal, 204
Automatically unfair reasons for dismissal, 204

Basic award, 205
Battery, 111
Being bribed, 403
Bill of exchange, 32
Board of directors, 337
Bonus issue, 270
Borrowing, 280
Breach, 58
Breach of an innominate term, 63
Breach of condition, 63
Breach of contract, 62
Breach of duty of care, 122
Breach of statutory duty, 120
Breach of warranty, 147
Breach of warranty of authority, 150
Bribery, 403
Bribery Act 2010, 403
Bribing a foreign public official, 403
Bribing another person, 403
Brokers, 144

Calculation of redundancy pay, 207
Called up share capital, 262
Capacity, 15
Capital maintenance, 296
Causality, 124
Centrebinding, 435
Certificate of incorporation, 241
Chairman, 326
Charge, 284
Chartered corporations, 223
Chief executive officer, 337
Civil Aviation Act 1982, 109
Civil court structure, 5
Civil law, 3
Civil Liability Act 1978, 161
Class rights, 265
Commencement of business, 244
Commercial agents, 144
Commercial agreements, 37, 38
Common law, 2
Common mistake, 85
Communication of acceptance, 26
Community interest companies (CICs), 223
Companies Act, 241
Company, 221
Company auditor, 383
Company directors, 144
Company Directors Disqualification Act 1986, 342
Company secretary, 362
Company unable to pay its debts, 436

INDEX

Company voluntary arrangement, 422
Company's letterheads and other forms, 245
Compensation for loss of office, 339
Compensatory award, 206
Compulsory liquidation, 436
Condition precedent, 58
Condition subsequent, 58
Conditions, 44
Confirmation statement, 247
Conflict of interest, 360
Connected persons, 443
Consequential economic loss, 134
Consideration, 30
Constructive dismissal, 195, 196
Consumer Credit Act 1974, 15
Content, 15
Continuous employment, 188
Contra proferentem rule, 49
Contract, 14
Contract by deed, 16
Contract for services, 178
Contract law
Contract of employment, 174
Contract of service, 178
Contract terms, 43
Contracts (Rights of Third Parties) Act 1999, 42
Contractual documents, 47
Contributory negligence, 127
Control test, 175
Corporate failure to prevent bribery, 404
Corporate governance statement, 385
Corporate personality, 221
Corporations, 223
Corporations sole, 223
Cost of cure, 68
Counter-offer, 21, 25
County Court, 5
Court of Appeal, 5
Court of first instance, 4
Court order where there is unfair prejudice, 373
'Creditors' buffer, 295
Creditors' voluntary liquidation, 435
Crime, 3, 394
Criminal court structure, 5
Criminal Finances Act 2017, 408
Criminal Justice Act 1993, 394
Criminal law, 3
Cross-offers, 28
Crown Court, 5
Crystallisation, 285

Damages, 65, 84, 109
Damages in tort, 133
Danger to the highway, 114

De facto directors, 336
De jure directors, 336
Dealings between the company and its directors, 359
Debenture, 281
Debenture trust deed, 282
Declaration of solvency, 405, 434
Deemed consent procedure, 420, 423, 435
Defamation Act 2013, 115
Defence of honest opinion, 116
Defence of 'matter of public interest', 117
Defence of truth, 116
Defences to negligence, 127
Deferred debts, 440
Defrauding creditors, 444
Derivative claims, 374
Director, 336
Director authority and third parties, 349
Directors' expenses, 339
Directors' liability for acts of other directors, 360
Directors' personal liability, 360
Directors' remuneration report, 339
Directors' service contracts, 339
Disapplication of pre-emption rights, 270
Discharge of contract, 58
Disciplinary procedure, 201
Discrimination against minority, 369
Disqualification of directors, 342
Disqualification undertaking, 342
Dissemination of information, 397
Distributable profit, 307
Distributing dividends, 306
Diversion of contracts, 369
Dividend, 306
Divisional Court of QBD, 5
Domestic arrangements, 37
Duress, 90
Duties of a company secretary, 363
Duties of auditors, 385
Duties of directors, 350
Duties of partners, 165
Duties of promoters, 238
Duty of care, 121

Economic duress, 90
Economic loss, 134
Ejection, 109
Employee, 174
Employee's duties, 182, 183
Employers' statutory duties, 184
Employment contract, 180
Employment law
Employment tribunals, 197
Enhanced due diligence, 401

INDEX

Enterprise Act 2002, 416
Enterprise and Regulatory Reform Act 2013, 187, 197
Equality Act 2010, 184
Equitable reliefs for mistake, 89
Equitable remedies, 72
Equity, 2
Equity (share), 263
Equity share capital, 263
European Court of Human Rights, 6
European Court of Justice, 6
Exceptions, 41
Exceptions to the right to redundancy payment, 207
Exceptions to the rule of privity of contract, 41
Exclusion clauses, 46
Exclusion of pre-emption rights, 270
Executed consideration, 30
Executive director, 336
Executory consideration, 31
Exhibition of goods for sale, 19
Expectation interest, 67
Express authority, 146
Express term, 43

Factors, 144
Failing to disclose, 399
Failure of a condition, 23
Failure to report, 399
Fair dismissal, 195
False declaration of solvency, 444
False imprisonment, 111
Falsification of company books, 444
Fiduciary duty, 238, 350
Fiduciary position, 350
Financial assistance, 302
Financial assistance for the purchase of shares, 302
Financial crime, 394
Financial Services and Markets Act 2000, 396
Fixed charge, 284
Fixed charge receiver, 421
Flexible working, 186
Floating charge, 284
Form, 15
Form of a contract, 16
Formation of agency, 145
Forming a partnership, 159
Fraud and deception, 444
Fraud on the company, 369
Fraudulent misrepresentation, 82
Fraudulent trading, 405, 406, 443
Freedom of contract, 14
Freezing injunctions, 73

Frustration, 58, 59
Fundamental breach, 49

General meeting, 352
Genuine consent, 15

Health and safety, 187
High Court, 5
Holding out, 148, 348

Ignoring separate personality, 249
Illegal contract, 96
Illegality, 95
Illegitimate pressure, 91
Implied agreement, 145
Implied authority, 147
Implied term, 44, 180
Incapacitation, 63
Independent contractors, 106
Industrial tribunal, 205
Ineligible for appointment, 384
Initial accounts, 309
Injunction, 73, 109, 135
Innocent misrepresentation, 82
Innominate terms, 45
Inside information, 395
Insider dealing, 394
Integration, 399
Integration test, 175
Intention to create legal relations, 37
Interim accounts, 309
Invitation for tenders, 20
Invitation to treat, 17, 19
Issued share capital, 262
Issuing shares at a premium and at a discount, 303
Itemised pay statement, 185

Joint and several liability, 104
Joint money laundering steering group, 402
Just and equitable ground, 437
Just and equitable winding up, 374

Laches, 95
Lack of independence, 384
Lapse of time, 21
Laundering, 398
Law Reform (Frustrated Contracts) Act 1943, 61
Layering, 399
Legal personality, 221, 248
Legality, 15

Letter of intent, 24
Letters of comfort, 39
Liability limited by guarantee, 223
Liability limited by shares, 223
Liability of partners, 161
Libel, 115
Lifting the veil, 249
Limitation Act 1980, 32
Limited companies, 223
Limited liability, 221
Limited liability partnership (LLP), 163
Limited Liability Partnership Act 2000, 163
Limited partnerships, 164
Liquidated damages, 70
Liquidation, 343, **432**
Liquidator, 433
Loan capital, **262**, 280
Loans given to directors, 359
London Gazette, 245
Long service contracts, 359
Loss of capital by public company, 320
LPA receiver, 421

Magistrates' courts, 5
Main purpose rule, 49
Majority control, 368
Managing director, 337
Manifest disadvantage, 94
Manipulating devices, 397
Manipulating transactions, 397
Mareva, 73
Market abuse, 396
Market distortion, 397
Market price rule, 68
Maternity leave and pay, 186
Maternity rights, 186
Measure of damages, 67
Medium-sized companies, 227
Meetings, 318
Member, 260
Members' voluntary liquidation, 434
Micro-entities, 228
Micro-entity, 382
Minimum period of notice, 194
Minority protection, 369, 370
Minors, 15
Minutes, 329
Misconduct during a liquidation, 444
Misrepresentation, 80
Mistake, 84
Mistakes over documents, 88
Misuse of information, 397
Mitigation of loss, 69
Money laundering, 398

Money Laundering Regulations 2017, 399, 400
Money Laundering Reporting Officer, 399
Moratorium, 418
Multinational company, 228
Mutual mistake, **85**, 86
Mutual obligations, 175

National Living Wage, 184
National Minimum Wage Act 1998, 184
Natural events, 126
Negligence, 121
Negligent misrepresentation, 82
Negligent misstatement, 128
Nominal value, 261
Non est factum, 88
Non-administrative receiver, 421
Non-audit role, 131
Non-executive director, **337**, 355
Non-financial loss, 68
Non-operative mistakes, 90
Notice, 323
Novation, 58
Novus actus intervieniens, 125
Nuisance, 108, 111

Obiter dicta, 2
Objectives of the liquidator, 439
Obstruction of the highway, 114
Off the shelf companies, 242
Offences in relation to winding up, 405
Offer, 17
Office for Professional Body Anti-Money Laundering Supervision, 399
Official receiver, 438
Omissions, 444
Onerous terms, 48, 71
Operative mistake, 85
Option contract, 22
Ordinary resolutions, 321
Ordinary shares, 263

Paid up share capital, 262
Parent company, 227
Parental leave, 187
Partners, 144
Partnership, 158
Partnership Act 1890, 160
Passing of property to controlling shareholders, 369
Past consideration, 31
Paternity leave and pay, 186
Penalty clause, 70
Performance, 58

Performance of existing contractual duties, 34
Permissible capital payment, 301
Personal guarantees, 280
Phoenix company, 250
Physical duress, 90
Placement, 399
Poll, 328, **329**
Postal rule, 27
Powers and authority of a company secretary, 363
Powers of directors, 346
Powers of the liquidator, 439
Precedent, 2, 372
Pre-contract negotiations, 43
Pre-emption rights, 269
Preference dividend, 263
Preference shares, 263, 265
Preferences, 442
Preferential debts, 286, 440
Pre-incorporation contract, 239, 240
Prescribed mode of communication, 26
Presumption, 37
Priorities on liquidation, 440
Priority of charges, 286
Private company, 224, 225, 244
Private law, 3
Private nuisance, 112
Privity of contract, 40
Probability of injury, 122
Proceeds of Crime Act 2002, 398
Professional advice special relationship, 128
Profits available for distribution, 307
Promise of additional reward, 35
Promoter, 238, 239
Proxy, 327
Public company, 224, 244
Public law, 3
Public nuisance, 113
Purchase of own shares, 299
Pure economic loss, 134

Qualified insolvency practitioners, 433
Quantum meruit, 72
Quasi-partnership, 251
Quasi-partnership company, 370
Quorum, 327
Quoted companies, 227

Ratification, 353
Reasonableness of employer, 201
Rebuttable, 37
Rectification, 89, 90
Redeemable shares, 265, **299**

Reduction of share capital, 296
Redundancy, 206
Re-engagement, 205
Re-entry, 109
Register of charges, 288
Register of debentureholders, 247, 282
Register of directors, 246
Register of members, 246
Register of people with significant control, 246
Registered companies, 223
Registered number, 241
Registers, 245
Registrar of companies, 241
Registration of charges, 287
Registration procedures, 240
Rehabilitation of Offenders Act 1974, 116
Reinstatement, 205
Rejection, 20
Relatives, 38
Relevant accounts, 309
Reliance interest, 67
Remedies, 65
Remedies for misrepresentation, 83
Remedies for unfair dismissal, 205
Remedies for wrongful dismissal, 199
Remedy for redundancy, 207
Remoteness of damage, 65, 124, 126
Removal of directors, 340
Removal of the auditor from office, 387
Remuneration of directors, 338
Renunciation, 63
Representation, 43
Repudiation, 62
Repudiatory breach, 62
Request for information, 21
Re-registration procedures, 243
Res extincta, 85
Res ipsa loquitur, 124
Res sua, 85
Rescission, 74, **83**, 89, 95
Resignation of auditors, 387
Restitutory award, 72
Revocation of an offer, 22
Rights issue, 270
Rights of auditors, 386
Rights of partners, 165
Romalpa clause, 286
Rotation of directors, 340

Secured debenture holder rights, 289
Self-employed, 174
Sell-out provisions, 273
Separate legal personality, 248, 254
Seriousness of the risk, 123

Service contract, 247
Settlement agreements, 197
Shadow directors, 336
Share, 261
Share premium, 305
Shared parental leave, 186
Show of hands, 328
Signed contracts, 47
Silence, 24
Simple contract, 16
Simplified due diligence, 401
Single alternative inspection location (SAIL), 245
Single member private companies, 330
Slander, 115
Small Business, Enterprise and Employment Act 2015, 197, 240, 336
Small companies, 228
Social, domestic and family arrangements, 37
Social media, 120
Soft law, 4
Sole traders, 220
Solvency statement, 297
Special damage, 116
Special notice, 324
Special resolutions, 321
Specific performance, **72**, 90
Squeeze out notices, 273
Stamp duty, 271
Stamp Duty Reserve Tax, 272
Standard form contracts, 14
Statement, 241
Statement of capital, 267
Statement of intention, 17, 18
Statute, 2
Statutory books and records, 244, 245
Statutory corporations, 223
Statutory duties of directors, 351
Statutory rights of minorities, 376
Statutory shared parental pay, 186
Stock exchange, 225
Strike action, 208
Subscriber shares, 260
Subsidiary companies, 226
Substantial property transactions, 359
Sufficiency, 33
Summary dismissal, **195**, 196
Supply of information, 17, 18
Supreme Court, 5
Supreme Court Act 1981, 73
Sustainability, 353

Take-over procedures, 272
Task Force on Climate-related Financial Disclosure (TCFD) framework, 354
Termination by death, 23
Termination of agency, 149
Termination of auditors' appointment, 386
Termination of employment by breach of contract, 195
Termination of offer, 20
Termination of partnership, 160
Terms, 43
Terms implied by custom, 44
Terms implied by statute, 44
Terms implied by the courts, 44
The 'But for' test, 124
The Chair, 338
The Companies (Strategic Report) (Climate-related Financial disclosure) Regulations 2022, 354
The multiple (economic reality) test, 176
The registrar of companies, 245
The rule in *Foss v Harbottle*, 368
Time off work, 185
Tipping off, 399
Tort, **104**
Tortfeasor, **104**
Tortious liability, 252
Trade Union and Labour Relations (Consolidation) Act 1992, 39
Trading certificate, 244
Transactions at an undervalue, 442
Transactions binding in honour only, 40
Transactions defrauding creditors, 443
Transfer of shares, 271
Transfer of undertakings, 188
Treasury shares, 265
Trespass ab initio, 109
Trespass in airspace, 109
Trespass to goods, **110**
Trespass to land, 108
Trespass to the person, **110**
True and fair view, 385

Undistributable reserves, 308
Undue influence, **92**
Unenforceable contract, **16**
Unfair Contract Terms Act 1977, 46, 49
Unfair dismissal, 182, **195**, 199, 202
Unfairly prejudicial conduct, 370
Unilateral mistake, 29, **85**, 87
Unlimited liability company, **223**
Unpaid parental leave, 187
Unsecured debenture holder rights, 289

Unsigned contracts and notices, 47
Unsolicited Goods and Services Act 1971, 24

Variation of class rights, 265
Varying the terms of an employment contract, 181
Veil of incorporation, 249
Vicarious liability, 104
Void contract, 16
Voidable contract, 16
Volenti non fit injuria, 127
Voluntary liquidation, 434
Voting, 328

Waiver of communication, 26
Waiver of existing rights, 36
Warranties, 44
Workers, 174
Working Time Regulations 1998, 188
Work-life balance, 186
Written particulars, 180
Written partnership agreement, 160
Written resolutions, 322
Wrongful dismissal, 195, 198
Wrongful trading, 344, 406, 443

INDEX